EXPLORER'S GUIDE

YOSEMITE &
THE SOUTHERN
SIERRA NEVADA

EXPLORER'S GUIDE

YOSEMITE & THE SOUTHERN SIERRA NEVADA

THIRD EDITION

DAVID T. PAGE

THE COUNTRYMAN PRESS
A division of W. W. Norton & Company
Independent Publishers Since 1923

WINNER

Best Travel Guidebook (2008),
Outdoor Writers Association

Lowell Thomas Travel
Journalism Award (2009)

Best Guidebook (2010),
Bay Area Travel Writers

Photograph previous page: Bill Becher

Printed in the United States of America

Maps by Erin Greb Cartography, © The Countryman Press

For information about permission to reproduce selections from this book, write to
Permissions, The Countryman Press, 500 Fifth Avenue, New York, NY 10110

For information about special discounts for bulk purchases, please contact
W. W. Norton Special Sales at specialsales@wwnorton.com or 800-233-4830

The Countryman Press
www.countrymanpress.com

A division of W. W. Norton & Company, Inc.
500 Fifth Avenue, New York, NY 10110
www.wwnorton.com

978-1-68268-088-9 (pbk.)

10 9 8 7 6 5 4 3 2 1

For Allison,
Jasper,
and
Beckett

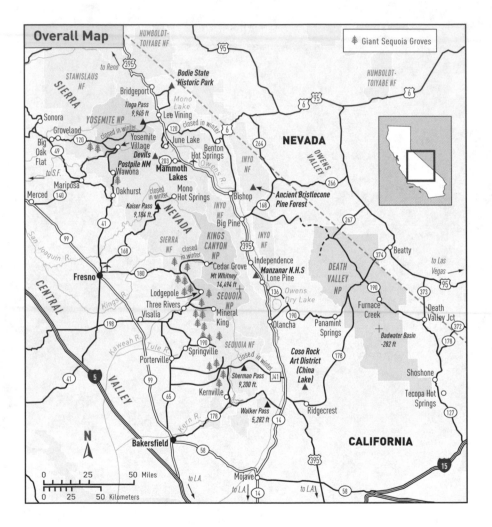

Overall Map

Giant Sequoia Groves

HUMBOLDT-TOIYABE NF

STANISLAUS NF

SIERRA

to Reno 395

Bodie State Historic Park

Bridgeport

Tioga Pass 9,945 ft

YOSEMITE NP

Sonora

Groveland

Big Oak Flat

to S.F.

Yosemite Village

Mono Lake

Lee Vining

closed in winter

June Lake

Devils Postpile NM

Benton Hot Springs

Mammoth Lakes

HUMBOLDT-TOIYABE NF

NEVADA

OWENS VALLEY

INYO NF

Wawona

Oakhurst

Mono Hot Springs

Mariposa

Merced

closed in winter

Kaiser Pass 9,184 ft.

NEVADA

Bishop

INYO NF

Big Pine

Ancient Bristlecone Pine Forest

San Joaquin R.

CENTRAL

Fresno

SIERRA NF

KINGS CANYON NP

closed in winter

Kings R.

Cedar Grove

Mt Whitney 14,494 ft

INYO NF

Independence

Manzanar N.H.S

Lone Pine

Beatty

to Las Vegas

DEATH VALLEY NP

Lodgepole

SEQUOIA NP

Three Rivers

Visalia

Mineral King

Owens Dry Lake

Furnace Creek

Death Valley Jct

Kaweah R.

Tule R.

Springville

SEQUOIA NF

Olancha

Panamint Springs

Badwater Basin -282 ft

Porterville

closed in winter

Coso Rock Art District (China Lake)

Shoshone

VALLEY

Sherman Pass 9,200 ft.

Kernville

Kern R.

Walker Pass 5,282 ft

Ridgecrest

Tecopa Hot Springs

Bakersfield

CALIFORNIA

N

Mojave

to L.A.

to L.A.

to L.A.

0 25 50 Miles

0 25 50 Kilometers

CONTENTS

MAPS

INTRODUCTION

The West of which I speak is but another name for the Wild; and . . . in Wildness is the preservation of the world. Every tree sends its fibres forth in search of the Wild. The cities import it at any price. Men plow and sail for it. From the forest and wilderness come the tonics and barks which brace mankind. Our ancestors were savages. The story of Romulus and Remus being suckled by a wolf is not a meaningless fable. The founders of every state which has risen to eminence, have drawn their nourishment and vigor from a similar wild source. It is because the children of the empire were not suckled by the wolf that they were conquered and displaced by the children of the northern forests who were.
—Henry David Thoreau, *The Atlantic Monthly*, 1862

In the spring of 1868, less than a month before his 30th birthday, a wild-haired itinerant college dropout by the name of John Muir, by his own account "with incredibly little money" and no guidebook, stepped off a Panama steamer at the Port of San Francisco. He'd quit his job at a carriage-parts shop the previous fall and had walked a thousand miles from Indianapolis to the Gulf of Mexico, "holding a generally southward course, like the birds when they are going from summer to winter." He'd spent a few months in Cuba, looking at plants, had had a notion to go to South America—to wander up and then float back down the Amazon—but then crossed the Isthmus at Panama instead, and ended up in California.

The way he tells it, the first thing he did was walk up and ask a fellow for the best way out of town.

"But where do you want to go?" the fellow asked. "To any place that is wild," said Muir.

The fellow pointed the way to the Oakland Ferry.

Muir got himself a pocket map of some kind, booked passage across the bay, took rough bearings from the sun, and then proceeded to wade across the Central Valley through a sea of waist-deep wildflowers—to what he would later describe as "the most divinely beautiful of all the mountain-chains I have ever seen."

Here he would spend the rest of his life—give or take a trip or three around the world. Here he would climb countless peaks, explore innumerable canyons, tally thousands of tree rings. He would write 10 books and hundreds of articles; ride an avalanche; climb to the top of a 100-foot-tall spruce tree in a gale-force windstorm; establish the Sierra Club as a force to be reckoned with; and serve as personal tour guide to Ralph Waldo Emerson and Teddy Roosevelt. "His was a dauntless soul," wrote the president and onetime Rough Rider. At age 73 Muir finally made that trip to Brazil—it was 1911—as part of an epic, 40,000-mile, cross-country, cross-ocean, solo adventure that took him not only up the Amazon to the Andes, but to deep Africa and the headwaters of the Nile.

Muir was not a big fan of guidebooks, especially of the stay-here, eat-this, buy-that variety. "Most people who travel," he wrote, "look only at what they are directed to look at."

WILD MUSTANGS, ADOBE VALLEY, MONO COUNTY JOEL ST. MARIE

And yet he wanted people to see what he had seen: to see that it must be saved—and to save themselves in the process. His unique and enduring guidebook, *The Yosemite*, published upon his return from Africa (two years before his death), is one part fireside chat, one part travelogue, two parts natural history, three parts high-flown panegyric to "the great fresh unblighted, unredeemed wilderness" that had given his life its greatest purpose.

Thanks to Muir, and to the generations of "good wanderers" he inspired, a significant part of this wild country abides—in some ways even wilder than it was a century ago—not merely in Yosemite, but to the south: across the rugged, roadless, granite backlands of the Sierra, from the trickling glacier in the lap of Mount Lyell to the Minarets and Mammoth Mountain; from Kings Canyon to the Whitney Crest; from Giant Forest to the Kern Plateau; and to the east, in the shadow of the range, across the Alabama Hills and Mary Austin's "Land of Little Rain" to Death Valley.

ON THE ROAD TO BALLARAT, PANAMINT BASIN BURKE GRIGGS

It is a place of extremes, of measurements and calculations of the sort that help define the edges of what we know: Here is the largest living thing on the planet. Here is the oldest. Here are the youngest volcanoes in North America. Here is the fastest-rising mountain range, and the longest. Here is the greatest plant and mammal diversity, the biggest snowfall, the tallest single-drop waterfall, the deepest valley. Here, they say, one can experience the greatest number of sunny days per year in the continental United States. Here, within a hundred miles of the lowest, driest, hottest basin (at 282 feet below a rising sea level), one can, in one long push, make his or her way to stand atop the highest peak (14,782 feet higher, also rising). Here, within a few hours' drive of several of the largest, fastest-growing cities in America, lies one of the world's last great wild frontiers, some of the most sparsely populated country in the West, whence one can still strike out on foot—or on horseback, or on skis—into the depths of one of the most extensive wildernesses in the Lower 48.

MINARET VISTA, MONO COUNTY AARON HOROWITZ

Of how the ordinary traveler might get to the edges of this country—where a decent breakfast might be had, or a good glass of wine, or 800-thread-count sheets, or a massage, or a pair of Fred Harvey signature socks—there is precious little, nay nothing, in Muir (except a brief note that most accommodations had by 1912 burned down, and what remained was woefully inadequate). Such was not his concern. "Only by going alone in silence, without baggage," he had once written to his wife, "can one truly get into the heart of the wilderness. All other travel is mere dust and hotels and baggage and chatter."

A CIRRUS PLUME FROM HIGH SIERRA OVER DEATH VALLEY. NOTE THE THICK FOREST BELTS ON THE WESTERN SLOPE, DRY BASIN-AND-RANGE COUNTRY TO THE EAST. MONO LAKE IS AT THE UPPER LEFT. NASA

This book is not a guide to the wilderness, but to the half-devised landscape along its edges. What you will find in these pages, I hope, is dust and hotels and baggage and chatter—that these may in turn, along some road somewhere, provide glimpses of something else, something nourishing. "Even if we never do more than drive to its edge and look in," Wallace Stegner wrote back in the days (not so long ago) when lines were still being drawn around what was wild and what was not, "it can be a means of reassuring ourselves of our sanity as creatures."

The preservation of the world—whatever that means, exactly—has yet to be determined. In the meantime, the wildness from which it may derive awaits your pleasure here in the Southern Sierra Nevada and the great still-wild outback of California.

WHAT'S WHERE IN YOSEMITE & THE SOUTHERN SIERRA NEVADA

You may reach my country and find or not find, according as it lieth in you, much that is set down here. And more. The earth is no wanton to give up all her best to every comer, but keeps a sweet, separate intimacy for each.
　　—Mary Austin, *Land of Little Rain*, 1904

The Southern Sierra is a vast region, held together mostly by its emptiness. By "Southern Sierra" I mean, somewhat arbitrarily, the mostly contiguous series of roadless areas from the northern boundary of Yosemite National Park to the south, some 250 miles along the highest parts of the range, through Kings Canyon and Sequoia to Walker Pass (the Tioga and Sherman Passes being closed in winter). From west to east I include the main gateway towns and last access points on the west side of the range, in the Sierra Foothills, as well as the supply towns and trailheads on "the eastside" (as it's known locally), along and above the Owens River watershed and out the long rain shadow cast by Whitney and its fellows to the Panamint Basin, Death Valley, and the Amargosa.

This book is divided into five regional chapters. Within each are listings for lodging and points of interest, organized as much as possible according to a certain logic of geography—in other words, as you might come upon them along the road, rather than in alphabetical order. For alphabetical reference, use the index at the back of the book. Dining and food purveyors, on the other hand, wherever services are concentrated in one location, are listed alphabetically. An overview of recreational opportunities is provided at the end of each regional section, not as a detailed how-to guide, but as an indication of where to get started and whom to contact for outfitting and specific local beta.

Nuggets: At a site marked with the star symbol (✪), you will find something of significant historic, cultural, culinary, and/or aesthetic value, worth traveling out of one's way for.

✷ General Information

PRICES Prices for lodging are generally based on a per-room, double-occupancy rate at peak season. Peak season in Death Valley (November to April) is the opposite of peak season in Yosemite and Sequoia–Kings Canyon (Memorial Day to Labor Day). Prices are often significantly reduced during off-season. The peak in Mammoth Lakes comes during the two weeks around Christmas and New Year's, and over the Presidents' Day midwinter holiday, when prices are often double what they are during the rest of the year. The price code for lodging in Mammoth is based on an average nonholiday weekend rate. The dining code is based on the cost of a meal for one person, including an entrée and appetizer (or entrée and dessert) and a beverage. Tax and gratuities are not included.

For the latest news, updates, links, and reader feedback, visit www.sierrasurvey.com. Also join us on Facebook at www.facebook.com/sierrasurvey.

✻ Hospitals and Emergency Medical Services

DEATH VALLEY AND THE EASTERN SIERRA

Beatty Medical Clinic: 702 Irving St., Beatty, NV; 775-553-2208.

Death Valley Health Center: CA 127, Shoshone; 760-852-4383.

Northern Inyo County Hospital: 150 Pioneer Lane, Bishop; 760-873-5811; www.nih.org.

Nye County Regional Medical Center: 825 Erie Main St., Tonopah, NV; 775-482-6233; www.nyeregional.org.

Southern Inyo County Hospital: 501 E. Locust St., Lone Pine; 760-876-5501; www.sihd.org.

MAMMOTH LAKES AREA

Mammoth Hospital: 85 Sierra Park Rd., Mammoth Lakes; 760-934-3311; www.mammothhospital.com.

SEQUOIA/KINGS

Kaweah Delta Hospital: 400 W. Mineral King Ave., Visalia; 559-624-2000; www.kaweahdelta.org.

YOSEMITE

Community Medical Center–Oakhurst: 48677 Victoria Lane, Oakhurst; 559-683-2992; www.communitymedical.org/295.htm.

Community Regional Medical Center: 2823 Fresno St., Fresno; 559-459-6000; www.communitymedical.org/crmc.htm.

Sonora Community Hospital: 1000 Greenley Rd., Sonora; 209-532-5000; www.sonora medicalcenter.org.

Yosemite Medical Clinic: 9000 Ahwahnee Drive, behind Yosemite Village; 209-372-4637.

✻ Local Media

DEATH VALLEY AND THE EASTERN SIERRA

Death Valley Guide (www.americanparknetwork.com). Available at visitor centers and park entrance kiosks.

The Inyo Register (www.inyoregister.com). The venerable local, published Tuesday, Thursday, and Saturday; founded by P. A. Chalfant in 1870.

Pahrump Valley Times (www.pahrumpvalleytimes.com). Daily.

Visitor's Guide to Death Valley National Park (www.nps.gov/deva). Best source for park events, activities, news, and current conditions. Published seasonally. Available at visitor centers and park entrance kiosks.

MAMMOTH LAKES AREA

Mammoth Lakes Visitor Guide. Available at the Mammoth Lakes Welcome Center. Published seasonally.

Mammoth Times (www.mammothtimes.com). The weekly 50-center.

The Post (www.nps.gov/depo/photosmultimedia/visitor-newspaper.htm). Published seasonally for Devils Postpile National Monument. Available at entrance station and shuttle kiosk.

The Sheet (www.thesheetnews.com). Ex-royal dishwasher John Domesick Lunch III's weekly, irreverent, informative, and irreplaceable chronicle of local politics and happenings in Mammoth Lakes. Also via the Web, Internet radio, and Twitter.

SEQUOIA/KINGS

The Guide (www.nps.gov/seki/ parknews/newspaper.htm). Best source for park events, activities, news, and current conditions. Published seasonally. Available at visitor centers and park entrance kiosks.

The Kaweah Commonwealth (www .kaweahcommonwealth.com). Weekly for Three Rivers and surrounding communities.

Sequoia & Kings Canyon Guide (www .ohranger.com). Available at visitor centers and park entrance kiosks.

YOSEMITE

Mariposa Gazette (www.mariposagazette .com). Weekly.

Sierra Star (www.sierrastar.com). Published Wednesday and Friday in Oakhurst.

Union Democrat (www.uniondemocrat .com). Daily from Sonora.

Yosemite Guide (www.nps.gov/yose/ planyourvisit/guide.htm). Park events, activities, and news. Published several times per year. Available at visitor centers and park entrance kiosks.

✷ Lost and Found

DEATH VALLEY

Closest visitor center or ranger station.

MAMMOTH LAKES AREA

Lost and Found/Basket Check, Canyon Lodge: 760-934-2571, ext. 3367.

Lost and Found/Basket Check, Main Lodge: 760-934-0667.

Mammoth Lakes Welcome Center: 760-924-5500.

SEQUOIA/KINGS

Closest ranger station or visitor center. Or contact the Property Office at Ash Mountain: 559-565-3181.

YOSEMITE

Yosemite Concession Services: 209-372-4357.

✷ Maps

The best overall PAPER highway maps of California are those published by **Rand McNally** (www.randmcnally.com) and the **American Automobile Association** (news.aaa-calif.com). AAA also publishes indispensable regional guide and recreation maps to Yosemite, Sequoia-Kings Canyon, the Eastern Sierra, and Death Valley.

"Death Valley National Park," AAA Explore! Series.

"Eastern Sierra Guide Map," AAA Explore! Series.

"Sequoia & Kings Canyon National Parks Guide Map," AAA Explore! Series.

"Sierra Nevada-Yosemite Area," AAA Recreation Series.

"Yosemite National Park Guide Map," AAA Explore! Series.

The most thorough and accurate overviews of back roads and campgrounds within each region can be found on the relevant **U.S. Forest Service maps**, available at visitor centers and national

HAILE SELASSIE I, EMPEROR OF ETHIOPIA, AT THE GRIZZLY GIANT, YOSEMITE NATIONAL PARK, JUNE 16, 1954 DOUG HUBBARD, COURTESY NPS, YNP

forest ranger stations or online at www .fs.fed.us/recreation/nationalforeststore.

"Humboldt-Toiyabe National Forest Map."

"Inyo National Forest Map."

"Sierra National Forest Map."

"Stanislaus National Forest Map."

Tom Harrison Maps (1-800-265-9090; www.tomharrisonmaps.com) publishes a series of durable, waterproof, shaded-relief topographic maps covering trails and recreation sites from the Emigrant Wilderness to Death Valley, available online and at most regional bookstores.

"Bishop Pass."

"Death Valley National Park."

"Devils Postpile."

"Half Dome."

"Kearsarge Pass–Rae Lakes Loop."

"Kings Canyon High Country."

"Mammoth High Country."

"Mono Divide High Country."

"Mono Lake."

"Mt. Whitney High Country."

"Mt. Whitney Zone."

"Tuolumne Meadows."

"Yosemite High Country."

"Yosemite National Park."

"Yosemite Valley."

National Geographic Trails Illustrated Maps (www.natgeomaps.com) feature detailed topographic information, clearly marked and named trails, recreational points of interest, and navigational aids, also printed on waterproof, tear-resistant material, and also available online and at most regional bookstores. To create and print your own high-resolution topographic maps from your own computer, on the material of your choice at five different levels of detail, consider purchasing NG's TOPO! California digital map package.

"Death Valley National Park."

"Mammoth Lakes/Mono Divide."

"Merced and Tuolumne Rivers."

"Sequoia/Kings Canyon National Park."

"Shaver Lake/Sierra National Forest."

"Yosemite National Park."

"Yosemite NW—Hetch Hetchy Reservoir."

"Yosemite NE—Tuolumne Meadows & Hoover Wilderness."

"Yosemite SE—Ansel Adams Wilderness."

"Yosemite SW—Yosemite Valley & Wawona."

The most detailed maps for navigating on the ground, and when traveling on foot, are still the traditional U.S. Geological Survey 7.5-minute, 1:24,000-scale quandrangle series, available at most regional visitor centers, specialty bookstores, and sporting goods stores. For map indexes and catalogs or to order maps, contact **USGS Information Services** (303-202-4693 or 1-888-ASK-USGS; ask.usgs.gov).

✳ Road and Auto Service

AAA Emergency Road Service: 1-800-222-4357.

USAA Emergency Road Service: 1-800-531-8555.

DEATH VALLEY

Furnace Creek Chevron: 760-786-2345.

THE EASTERN SIERRA

Dave's Auto Parts: 430 N. Main St., Lone Pine; 760-876-5586.

Miller's Towing & Repair: 1506 S. Main St., Lone Pine; 760-876-4600.

Mr. K Automotive: 175 W. Grove St., Bishop; 760-873-9828; www .mrkautomotive.com.

Perry Motors: 310 S. Main St., Bishop; 760-872-4141; www.perrymotorsinc.com.

MAMMOTH LAKES AREA

The Auto Doc: 159 Commerce Dr., #E8; 760-934-2211.

Napa Auto Parts: 3280 Main St., Mammoth Lakes; 760-934-3375.

Norco/Goodyear Service Center: 3670 Main St.; 760-934-9693.

SEQUOIA/KINGS

Lodgepole Garage: near Lodgepole Visitor Center; 559-565-4070.

Sierra Auto, Truck & Tractor Repair: 340 W. Naranjo Blvd., Woodlake; 559-564-0235.

YOSEMITE

Brand Automotive: 6008 Allred Rd., Midpines; 209-966-5630.

Dan's Auto: 49329 Golden Oak Loop, Oakhurst; 559-683-6006; www.dansauto.com.

Napa Auto Parts: 4907 Joe Howard Rd., Mariposa; 209-966-3697.

Sierra Auto Parts: 4985 CA 140, Mariposa; 209-966-4756.

Yosemite Village Garage: across from Yosemite Village Store; 209-372-8320.

✼ Tourist Information

Big Pine Chamber of Commerce and Visitor Center: 126 S. Main St., Big Pine; 760-938-2114.

Bishop Area Chamber of Commerce and Visitor Center: 690 N. Main St., Bishop; 760-873-8405 or 1-888-395-3952; www.bishopvisitor.com.

Death Valley Chamber of Commerce and Visitor Center: 117 CA 127, Shoshone; 760-852-4524; www.deathvalleychamber.org.

Fresno County Office of Tourism: 2220 Tulare St., Eighth Floor, Fresno; 559-262-4271; www.gofresnocounty.com.

Independence Chamber of Commerce: 440 S. Edwards, #1, Independence; 760-878-0084; www.independence-ca.com.

Inyo County Tourism: www.theothersideofcalifornia.com.

June Lake Chamber of Commerce: P.O. Box 2, June Lake 93529; www.junelakeloop.org.

Lee Vining Chamber of Commerce: CA 395 and Third Street; 760-647-6629; www.leevining.com.

Lone Pine Chamber of Commerce and Inyo County Film Commission: 126 S. Main St., Lone Pine; 760-876-4444 or 1-877-253-8981; www.lonepinechamber.org.

Mammoth Lakes Welcome Center: 2520 Main St. (CA 203), Mammoth Lakes; 760-924-5500 or 1-888-466-2666; www.visitmammoth.com.

Mono County Tourism and Film Commission: P.O. Box 603, Mammoth Lakes, 93546; 1-800-845-7922; www.monocounty.org.

Oakhurst Area Chamber of Commerce: 49074 Civic Circle, Oakhurst; 559-683-7766; www.oakhurstchamber.com.

Sequoia Foothills Chamber of Commerce: 42268 Sierra Dr., Three Rivers; 559-561-3300; www.threerivers.com.

Yosemite Chamber of Commerce: 18583 CA 120, Groveland; 209-962-0429; www.groveland.org.

Yosemite/Mariposa County Tourism Bureau and Visitors Center: 5158 CA 140, Mariposa; 209-966-7081 or 1-866-425-3366; www.homeofyosemite.com.

✼ Visitor Centers and Ranger Stations

DEATH VALLEY NATIONAL PARK

Eastern Sierra Interagency Visitor Center: CA 395 and 136, Lone Pine; 760-876-6222.

Furnace Creek Visitor Center: North of the Ranch at Death Valley; 760-786-3244.

DEVILS POSTPILE NATIONAL MONUMENT

Ranger Station: 760-934-2289.

INYO NATIONAL FOREST

Ancient Bristlecone Pine Forest Visitor Center–Schulman Grove: 10 miles north of CA 168 East, on White Mountain Road; 760-873-2500.

Eastern Sierra Interagency Visitor Center: CA 395 and 136, Lone Pine; 760-876-6222.

Mammoth Ranger Station and Welcome Center: CA 203, Mammoth Lakes; 760-924-5500.

Mono Basin Scenic Area Ranger Station and Visitor Center: CA 395, Lee Vining; 760-647-3044.

Mount Whitney Ranger Station: 640 S. Main St., Lone Pine; 760-876-6200.

White Mountain Ranger Station: 798 N. Main St., Bishop; 760-873-2500.

SEQUOIA NATIONAL FOREST/ NATIONAL MONUMENT

Cannell Meadow Ranger District Office: 105 Whitney Rd., Kernville; 760-376-3781.

Hume Lake Ranger District Office: 35860 E. Kings Canyon Rd., Dunlap; 559-338-2251.

Kern River Ranger District–Kernville Office: 105 Whitney Rd., Kernville; 760-376-3781.

Tule River/Hot Springs Ranger District Office: 32588 CA 190, Springville; 559-539-2607.

SEQUOIA–KINGS CANYON NATIONAL PARK

Cedar Grove Visitor Center: Cedar Grove Village; 559-565-3793.

Foothills/Ash Mountain Visitor Center: 47050 Generals Hwy.; 559-565-3135.

Grant Grove Visitor Center: Grant Grove Village; 559-565-4307.

Lodgepole Visitor Center: Lodgepole Village; 559-565-4436.

Mineral King Ranger Station: Mineral King; 559-565-3768.

Road's End Permit Station: Kings Canyon; no phone.

SIERRA NATIONAL FOREST

Bass Lake Ranger District Office: 57003 Road 225, North Fork; 559-877-2218.

High Sierra Ranger District Office: 29688 Auberry Rd., Prather; 559-855-5355.

High Sierra Ranger Station: Kaiser Pass; 559-877-7173.

STANISLAUS NATIONAL FOREST

Groveland Ranger District Office: 24545 CA 120, Groveland; 209-962-7825.

Mi-Wok Ranger District Office: 24695 CA 108, Mi-Wuk Village; 209-586-3234.

Summit Ranger District Office: 1 Pinecrest Lake Rd., Pinecrest; 209-965-3434.

YOSEMITE NATIONAL PARK

Badger Pass Ranger Station A-Frame: Glacier Point Road; 209-372-0409.

Big Oak Flat Station: CA 120, at the park entrance; 209-379-1899.

Hetch Hetchy Station: Hetch Hetchy Entrance Station; 209-379-1928.

Tuolumne Meadows Visitor Center and Ranger Station: Tuolumne Meadows; 209-372-0263.

Wawona Information Station: Hill's Studio, adjacent to Big Trees (aka Wawona) Hotel; 209-375-9531.

Yosemite Valley Visitor Center and Ranger Station: Yosemite Village; 209-372-0299.

Yosemite Valley Wilderness Center: Yosemite Village, next to Ansel Adams Gallery; 209-372-0740.

✳ Weather and Road Conditions

California Department of Transportation Statewide Road Conditions: 916-445-7623 or 1-800-427-7623; www.dot.ca .gov/cgi-bin/roads.cgi.

Death Valley Conditions: www .nps.gov/deva/planyourvisit/road-conditions.htm or www.maturango.org/ DeathV.html.

"THE SIERRAS" OR "THE SIERRA"?

James Mason Hutchings, one of the earliest pioneers to set up business in the Yosemite Valley and author of its first published guidebook, *Scenes of Wonder and Curiosity in California* (1862), habitually referred to these mountains as the "Sierras," following a long-standing tradition by which most other great and famous ranges—from the Rockies to the Smokies, from the Alps to the Andes to the Himalayas—are referred to in the plural. (California adds another tradition: appropriating original Spanish place names for their obvious romantic value while ignoring their meaning. Thus have we inherited all manner of silly phrasings and redundancies; e.g., the La Brea Tar Pits, or the "the tar pit" tar pits.) Such habits prove hard to break. Joseph Starr King, another early promoter of the range; Joseph LeConte, one of the eminent patriarchs of the Sierra Club (note the singular form); Mary Austin; Teddy Roosevelt; Fred Eaton of the great Los Angeles/Owens Valley land and water grab—all wrote of this collection of granite peaks as "the Sierras." The problem, alas, is that in pronouncing the word "Sierras" (plural), a person is saying "ranges" in Spanish. And there is no disagreement that what we have here, however impressive, is but a single range: the *Sierra Nevada*, the "Snowy Range," or as John Muir suggested, the "Range of Light." If it were multiple ranges, it might have been called *Las Sierras Nevadas.* But it is not and was not. Josiah D. Whitney, chief of the first California Geological Survey, had it right, and Muir, of course, and Ansel Adams. The Park and Forest Services these days generally get it right. And yet to this day, it is not uncommon to overhear someone speaking of his or her latest fabulous weekend adventure in the "Sierras." Alas, so it goes.

A SIERRA WAVE OVER MOUNT TOM JOEL ST. MARIE

Eastern Sierra Avalanche and Snowpack Information: patrol.mammothmountain.com or www.esavalanche.org.

Howard Sheckter's Mammoth Weather Forecast: 760-934-7669; www.mammothweather.com.

Long Valley Volcanic Conditions: lvo.wr.usgs.gov.

Mammoth Ski and Snow Report: 760-934-6166 or 1-888-SNOWRPT; www.mammoth mountain.com.

National Weather Service Reno: www.wrh.noaa.gov/rev.

National Weather Service Hanford: www.wrh.noaa.gov/hnx.

Sequoia-Kings Road Conditions: 559-565-3341, ext. 941.

Wildfire Conditions: inciweb.org.

Yosemite Road Conditions: 209-372-0200; www.nps.gov/yose/planyourvisit/conditions.htm.

NOTES & ACKNOWLEDGMENTS

Anyone pretending to be a guide through wild and fabulous territory should know the territory. I wish I knew it better than I do. I am not Jed Smith. But Jed Smith is not available these days as a guide, and I am. I accept the duty, at least as much for what I may learn as for what I may be able to tell others.
—Wallace Stegner, *Living Dry*, 1987

I came up to Mammoth on a temporary basis with my wife and then-one-year-old son in order to bang out the first edition of this book—and maybe get a little skiing in on the side. We thought we'd probably move on fairly quickly thereafter, for the sake of adventure. Maybe to Argentina. But the winters have been too good, the summers too delightful, the place too beautiful, and the community too solid. So now here we are, more than eleven years later, still living the dream in the High Sierra, with enough exploration ahead of us to last at least a generation or two.

The natural landscapes have not changed significantly since the first edition. Many trees have died, especially on the western slope, due to sustained drought and

LOOKING NORTH OVER TUNGSTEN HILLS AND ROUND VALLEY TO THE WHEELER CREST AND UPPER OWENS CHRISTIAN PONDELLA

historical lack of fire suppression (see page 28), though many experts see this mostly as a natural correction back to the proper order of things—the right number of trees for the carrying capacity of the land and plenty of good habitat for critters. With some help from land and wildlife managers, the Sierra Nevada bighorn sheep have rebounded spectacularly from the brink of extinction, but a tough setback in 2017, due to heavy snows, will likely keep them on the endangered species list for the foreseeable future.

The biggest changes have occurred in the human landscape: A scattering of new restaurants and hotels have appeared, while others have closed; craft breweries and pour-over coffee boutiques have proliferated; DVD-rental stores are gone, cellular telephone service has reached Death Valley, and free Wi-Fi is ubiquitous. The rise of Airbnb, VRBO, and other online vacation rental services has greatly increased the ease and range of accommodations booking for the traveler, while simultaneously reducing affordable housing stock for local employees in gateway towns like Three Rivers and Mammoth Lakes. There's a new publicly-traded concessionaire providing food and accommodations in Yosemite National Park, and with that shift, some startling—perhaps temporary—name changes have taken place within the park (see page 45); the venerable tourist settlement at Furnace Creek has for inscrutable reasons been "re-branded" as The Oasis at Death Valley; and the Aspen Skiing Company has become a primary partner in Mammoth Resorts. In general, the quality of services available to the traveler throughout the region has improved.

The list of people who continue to make this book possible has grown far too long for individual mentions. That said, here's a heartfelt shout-out to the talented photographers who, mostly at the very last minute, were willing to pitch in to help illustrate this and previous editions: Peter Amend, Bill Becher, Jim Bold, Steven Bumgardner, Vern Clevenger, Cat Connor, John DeGrazio, Burke Griggs, Aaron Horowitz, Dan and Janine Patitucci, Rondal Partridge, Christian Pondella, Osceola Refetoff, Sam Roberts, Joel St. Marie, and Laura Alice Watt (individual bios and contact information on page 387).

HISTORY

No range among all the mountain chains which make up the Cordilleras of North America surpasses, if any one equals, the Sierra Nevada, in extent or altitude, and certainly no one on the continent can be compared with it in the general features of interest which characterize it—its scenery, vegetation, mines, the energy and skill with which its resources have been developed and the impetus which this development has given to commerce and civilization.
—Josiah D. Whitney, *The Yosemite Book*, 1868

At just after 2:30 AM on March 26, 1872, anyone who had previously been asleep or otherwise about to doze off anywhere near the Sierra Nevada—from, say, Winnemucca to Oakland, Los Angeles to Sacramento, in a bed, on the ground, or in the back of a freight wagon—was awakened by a rumbling in the earth, as of a train approaching.

Then the quake hit.

Clocks are said to have stopped as far away as San Diego. At the epicenter in the Owens Valley, a crack opened in the earth that was 12 miles long. "Whether the land on the east was lowered or that on the west was raised no scientist ever took the trouble to announce," local historian W. A. Chalfant wrote in 1922, "but a difference of from 4 to 12 feet was made." Another fissure, between Big Pine and the base of the Sierra, measured "from 50 to 200 feet wide and 20 feet deep."

The shaking is said to have lasted for up to 3 minutes, at a magnitude now estimated between 7.4 and 8.3 on the Richter scale (comparable to the Great San Francisco Earthquake of 1906, which killed approximately 300,000 people). The aftershocks, some nearly as violent as the initial jolt, went on all night and into the next day, tapering off only over the course of the next few weeks.

Nearly every structure in the old pueblo of Lone Pine was leveled. Twenty-seven people were killed, mostly crushed by their own adobe-block houses. The original brick courthouse at Independence collapsed. One small lake disappeared; another was created. The course of the Owens River was shifted in such a way that Bend City, site of the first county-constructed bridge across the river, was left standing on the bank of a dry wash. "Not far off," wrote Chalfant, "a horse's hoof protruding from the ground, where a crack had opened and then closed, gave reasonable inference as to where the rest of the animal might be found."

John Muir, working as winter caretaker at Black's Hotel in Yosemite Valley that winter, was one of the many shaken from his bed. "It was a calm moonlight night," he wrote, "and no sound was heard for the first minute or two save a low muffled underground rumbling and a slight rustling of the agitated trees." From behind one such tree he watched with delight as huge blocks of granite, 1,500 feet above him, gave way, shattered into thousands of smaller boulders, sparked and glowed with friction in the air, and crashed to the valley floor. "If all the thunder I ever heard were condensed into one roar," he wrote, "it would not equal this rock roar at the birth of a mountain talus."

For two days the dust hung thick over the Sierra. An uncertain number of Lone Pine's dead—around 14, mostly Mexicans and Indians—were buried in a common grave on the north end of town. Without delay, the county of Inyo issued bonds, raised funds, and built—this time of wood harvested from the Sierra, instead of bricks—a new courthouse. On July 4, 1873, just 15 months after the great quake, the newly finished structure played host to "exercises of the greatest celebration the county had ever had."

✳ Natural History

"The dynamics that have pieced together the whole of California have consisted of tens of thousands of earthquakes as great as that," John McPhee writes in *Assembling California*, "tens of thousands of examples of what people like to singularize as 'the big one' and many millions of earthquakes of lesser magnitude." As much as the earth beneath us is in any given moment the most solid and immoveable thing we know or can imagine, it is, in fact, in constant motion. Every week, the U.S. Geological Survey measures several hundred earthquakes in California alone. Of these, only a handful will be felt by average citizens on the surface. Still, even as you read this, the plates beneath our elaborate system of roads and shopping malls and courthouses are shifting, pushing, and stretching; grinding against each other; building up and releasing pressure; bulging and subsiding and cracking at the seams. Here at the place where the state of California meets the state of Nevada, where at a distance of less than 80 miles the granite atop Mount Whitney has recently been lifted to a height of nearly 15,000 feet above the cracked salt pan at the bottom of Death Valley, the mountain and basin-building that began more than 200 million years ago—the most dramatic of which seems now,

LONE PINE PEAK AND THE EASTERN SCARP OF THE SIERRA NEVADA FROM LONE PINE. IN MARCH 1872, THE RANGE LIFTED AN AVERAGE OF 30 FEET IN LESS THAN THREE DAYS BURKE GRIGGS

according to the latest studies, to have occurred 8 or 9 million years ago (rather than the more recent 3 to 4 million years ago, as was once assumed)—is still very much under way.

The Paiute Indians, who nowadays live in one of the driest places on the planet (the Owens Valley) and make the bulk of their communal income by the operation of a casino and gas station in the town of Bishop, are said to have an old story in which, once upon a time, the world was all water. "At that time," the story goes, according to Chalfant, "the Great Wolf God, the God of Creation, with the assistance of his little brother or son, the coyote, planted the rock seeds in the great water, and from them the rocks and land grew." On the other side of the range, the Yokuts tell a similar tale with a different cast of characters: "Falcon and Crow," they say, according to historian David Beesley, "took some of the earth brought up by Duck from the mud beneath the primeval floodwaters . . . and as they flew they scattered grains of soil and told them to become mountains." Falcon made

EXFOLIATING GRANITE, MARBLE FORK OF THE KAWEAH, SEQUOIA NATIONAL PARK BURKE GRIGGS

the California coastal range, and Crow, who had somehow managed to get more dirt, made the Sierra Nevada.

A version told by contemporary geologists is not wholly at odds with these earlier tales, at least insofar as the primeval abundance of water is concerned. For most of the Triassic Period—from, say, 240 to 200 million years ago, in the days when the first small dinosaurs were just starting to pop up amid the Big Trees, and Pangaea was only just beginning to consider subdividing into Gondwanaland and Laurasia—the western coastline of what we now think of as North America ran right down the middle of Nevada. Out there to the west of Vegas, out beyond the sandy beaches, there was nothing: no California, no Paiutes or Yokuts, no nuclear test sites or proposed waste dumps, no Sierra Nevada, no Yosemite—just open water. The great ancestral Pacific Ocean.

Then came the Pacific plate crashing headlong into the North American. (And here the story diverges from the earlier traditions: it would be another 25 million years, it turns out, before the first protofalcons and crows appeared on Earth; many millions more before wolves and coyotes.) There was some crumpling, of course, and raising of mountains to the east, on the continent, and accretion to the erstwhile seashore of considerable amounts of material—islands and such, ocean floor, crust, a whole mess of material formerly of the Sonomia terrane, of the Pacific plate—material which today makes up the oldest rocks in Death Valley. But the Pacific plate itself, having apparently nowhere else to go, dove eastward beneath the North American plate. Or, to look at it another way, the North American plate plowed westward, right over the top of the Pacific.

The friction created by such a move—geologists call it subduction—caused no small amount of melted rock between the two plates. This stuff—red-hot, highly pressurized magma of the sort one sees in *National Geographic* photo spreads, flowing and splashing from the vents on Kilauea in Hawaii—tried its best to get out into the air. And in some places it did, piling up huge volcanoes—"Stratovolcanoes," writes McPhee, "Kilimanjaros and Fujis" of an ancient California range, a range which in those days more closely resembled the Cascades than the current Sierra. The bulk of the stuff, however, rose beneath the surface in great trapped bubbles that together cooled and crystallized—like (to borrow an image) so many stale marshmallows in a bag. The result: the so-called batholith—150,000 cubic miles of plutonic igneous rock, the famously enormous and complex mass of granite (granodiorite) that today makes up the core, and most of the surface, of the Sierra Nevada.

One hundred thirty million years of steady erosion later, the once-towering volcanic mountains at the edge of the North American continent had been worn down to a series of low, fertile, rolling hills, thickly forested with ancestral cedars, redwood, and giant sequoia. The dinosaurs had begun to die off (coincidentally), and in places the batholith was starting to show through. From high inland plateaus, westward to the coastal plains, wide prehistoric rivers carried gravels laden with gold. Then suddenly the Pacific plate, still shoveling along under the North American but at a considerably diminished pace—having already piled up material enough to form the rest of California all the way to San Francisco—seems to have taken a hit, broadside. Or in any case to have changed direction. This was some 60 million years ago.

At the margin between the two plates, the basic movement changed from subduction to a so-called strike-slip motion. Rather than the one plate sliding beneath or pushing up over top of the other, the two plates now ground against each other side-by-side like clashing, half-stripped gears, the Pacific plate driving generally northward, the North American doing its best to push south. The result was drag, a build-up of pressure, and a sometimes-gradual, sometimes-violent stretching out of the western edge of the North American continent.

Across what we now call the Great Basin, the crust began to pull apart, literally at the seams. Like cracks in an old fan belt, great rifts opened up—rift after rift after rift—and valleys flat as elevator platforms dropped thousands of feet toward the level of the sea. At fault scarps along the rift edges, blocks of the original crust—now ridges made of old bedrock and the metamorphic stuff above it—thrust upward and tilted back like giant ships' hatches opening from below. From east to west into the slow-rising

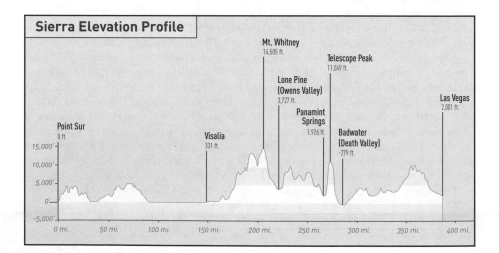

INDIAN BARK HOUSE, YOSEMITE VALLEY, 1887. TABER PHOTO COURTESY NPS, YNP

rubble, the old rivers cut new and ever-deeper V-shaped canyons until they could no longer keep up, until they were cut off by the rising walls and rerouted. On the western slopes of the westernmost ranges, these rivers left only vast deposits of gravel as evidence of their passage—detritus of ancient, gold-rich beds—thereafter to be dredged by glaciers, sifted through by snowmelt creeks, and, finally, in the second half of the nineteenth century, to be called the Mother Lode and hauled off from the top down by assiduous hordes of prospectors and the increasingly industrial mining operations in their wake.

But it would be at least 3.5 million years, maybe more, before anyone was to see the glint of precious metal in the sunlight. In the meantime—so the story goes—the old Pacific plate once again altered its course, this time by 11 degrees to the northeast. The mechanics and timing of it all is still hotly contested. The results are undeniable: "The tectonic effect on North America," writes McPhee, "was something like the deformation that occurs when two automobiles sideswipe."

Volcanic hot spots of the sort that form island archipelagos began to migrate, punching holes through miles of crust and granite, spewing ash, leaking carbon dioxide and superheated water, spilling magma to cool as andesite and basalt and obsidian—from Mono Hot Springs to Mammoth Mountain to Paoha Island in the middle of Mono Lake. Without much recorded ado—other than, say, the recent leveling and rearranging of Lone Pine—the Sierra Nevada, with its colossal heart of granite, crumpled upward nearly halfway to the jet stream. Erosion did its best, meanwhile, to crack apart the rocks, to wear them down even as they lifted. Clouds caught in the crest, gathering ever more snow and rain to feed the rivers along the western flank, while to the east, in the shadow of the new range, from the Owens all the way to the Great Salt Lake, and southeast across the Mojave, once verdant valleys dried up.

❋ Social History

THE FIRST PIONEERS It seems likely they came from the north, with families and dogs and all manner of equipment in tow. Their ancestors had traveled across the old

Bering Land Bridge. (Precisely how many waves of emigration there had already been, or when it had begun, no one is certain. Had they seen the camels headed in the other direction?) Season by season they multiplied, split into groups, separated, explored, learned which plants were poisonous, which salubrious, which could be counted on to intoxicate, which made the color red, which blue. They invented new ways to hunt, found water, made structures to sleep in from local materials, ate, had babies, mourned their dead, drew pictures on the rocks, named local landmarks, made up new languages and recipes (and lost track of the old ones), told stories about where they'd come from and where they were headed, sang, danced, played instruments, followed the herds. Season by season, without much need to consider the possible utility of the wheel, they made their way south.

Then one day, some ten thousand years ago—or maybe it was sixteen thousand years ago, one of these people, traveling alone or with a group of associates, became the first of his friends to gape upward at the Sierra Nevada.

The latest ice age had come and gone. Glaciers had piled up in the crevices between the peaks, had spilled down into the old V-shaped valleys, scooping them out, polishing their granite ribs, driving their crusty innards out onto the basins below in broad, damlike arcs of broken debris—and then had retreated. Where the glaciers had been, there now tumbled clear, perennial streams. There were lakes and waterfalls, rivers impossible to ford in springtime, tall-grass meadows ringed with granite domes, and deep, forested canyons. All up and down the range, and east into the drier country, there were top-notch campsites for winter and summer. There was an abundance of game—deer, elk, antelope, rabbit, squirrel, quail, duck, partridge, turkey, golden and cutthroat trout, and so on—and for the making of spear and arrow points, the best obsidian anyone had ever seen. There were acorns in the foothills for milling into flour; there were sturdy reeds for making arrow shafts and weaving into baskets; there were sweet berries, lettuce, wild grapes, and tobacco. There were hot springs to soak in on a cold night. The bugs, the snakes, and even the grizzly bears were eminently reasonable. And there was firewood to last until the end of time.

It wasn't long, of course, before word got out.

Pretty soon there were people everywhere. There were people camped out above the shores of Mono Lake. There were people all along the Owens River, from June and Mammoth Lakes to Indian Wells, some in permanent villages. There were people living on the shores of an ancient lake in Death Valley, and later, when things dried up, at the springs at Saline and Furnace Creek (The Oasis). There were people at Darwin Falls and in the canyons above Ridgecrest on land now reserved for the testing of weapons by the U.S. Navy. There were people up every fork of the Kern, every fork of the Tule, every fork of the Kaweah.

There were people who passed their winters in bark huts in the foothills, their summers under the stars in Kings Canyon—or at Mono Hot Springs, or in the Valley of Yosemite, or at Hetch Hetchy—people who when the snow melted hiked up over well-worn paths to trade with the sometimes-friendly folks on the other side: acorns for pine nuts; arrow shafts for obsidian; lake perch for Lahontan trout; deerskins for salt.

There were quarrels, raids, and reprisals. There were territorial disputes. There were wars and drought and periods of hunger. People died, were afraid, got sad. But there were great feasts, too, and marriages and dances and games in the woods—games (by the description of A. L. Kroeber) "in which not sticks and luck, but the tensest of wills, the keenest perceptions and the supplest of muscular responses are matched." They built permanent roundhouses for ceremonies. They learned to use fire to clear the woods of brush, to propagate the black oaks across the foothills, to improve foraging for the deer, to make travel easier. Each month brought a return of the full moon. Each

SIERRA TRIBES ARE SAID TO HAVE HAD A HIGHLY EFFICIENT SYSTEM OF RELAYS FOR COMMUNICATION OF NEWS AND IMPORTANT INFORMATION. LATER, INDIAN FIELD DAYS BECAME A POPULAR SPECTACLE FOR TOURISTS TELLES FAMILY ALBUM, COURTESY NPS, YNP

year brought a new crop of acorns, a new crop of pine nuts and blackberries, a fresh run of salmon up the San Joaquin.

ALTA CALIFORNIA When Francisco Vásquez de Coronado wandered into Kansas in the early 1540s, looking for the Seven Cities of Gold, he carried with him a sense of geography derived from a popular sixteenth-century romance that generally held California to be an island "on the right hand of the Indies," abounding with "gold and precious stones" and populated entirely by robust black women. Why Coronado did not endeavor to go there instead of Kansas is mostly a factor of his having been misled by a local guide. There was not a single city of gold upon the Great Plains, of course, nor riches of any sort that Coronado could see. He overlooked the buffalo herds and the farmland, and he missed the petroleum reserves. He ordered his guide garroted on the banks of the muddy Arkansas and turned around for home.

Coronado made it back to Mexico City not much improved for the effort but with a much clearer notion—gleaned from another of his more trustworthy guides—of the "low sandy country" to the west. "That peninsula which was formerly held to be an island," wrote one of the expedition's most thorough chroniclers, "is inhabited by brutish, bestial, naked people who eat their own offal. The men and women couple like animals, the female openly getting down on all fours."

It was another 230 years before the Spanish managed to establish missions at San Diego (1769) and Monterey (1770). The goal, by then, was not so much to find gold, but to muster as many tax-paying, Castilian-speaking, Church-fearing bodies in Alta California as possible—mostly to keep the Russians from acting on any territorial ambitions they may have had in the region—even if the only bodies available at the time were of the native "brutish, bestial, naked" variety.

In October 1775, Lieutenant Colonel Juan de Anza, having already proved the feasibility of crossing overland from Mexico to the new mission at Monterey, undertook

FIRE

Maria Lebrado, granddaughter of Chief Tenaya, was among the last of the Ahwahneechee to be marched out of Yosemite by the Mariposa Batallion. She was 10 years old. Seventy-eight years later, in July 1929, she returned—and was less than pleased to see the way the place had been maintained. "Two young men drove us over the valley she had not seen since her childhood," recorded her companion. "The wide open meadow of her day was covered with trees and shrubs. She shook her head, saying, 'Too dirty; too much bushy.'"

For thousands of years the Sierra tribes had practiced a regimen of annual controlled burning, thereby creating what John Muir would describe as "the inviting openness of the Sierra woods." The Park Service now estimates "that historically an average of 16,000 of Yosemite's 747,000 acres may have burned under natural conditions in the park each year." Beginning in the late 1850s, the valley's new caretakers, James Hutchings and others, planted orchards, cultivated gardens, built fences and hotels, and, for obvious reasons, did their utmost both to keep fires from starting and to keep those that had started naturally (i.e., by lightning) from spreading.

The U.S. Forest Service was established in 1905 by Teddy Roosevelt, with Gifford Pinchot as the first chief forester. "Since 1910," wrote Norman Maclean in *Young Men and Fire*, "much of the history of the Forest Service can be translated into a succession of efforts to get firefighters on fires as soon as possible."

By the early 1960s, decades of diligent and institutional fire suppression had effectively removed fire from the scenario, the result of which, over time, was denser forests and "as much as 75 to 90 percent of meadows . . . lost to tree encroachment." The build-up of debris and underbrush—so-called ladder fuels—also created the potential for larger, more dangerous "crown" fires than had existed in earlier, tidier forests. "Today much of the west slope is a dog-hair thicket of young pines, white fir, incense-cedar, and mature brush—a direct function of overprotection from natural ground fires," Park Service scientist A. Starker Leopold reported in 1963.

In 1968, the Park Service designated 600,000 acres of Sequoia-Kings Canyon a natural fire zone, where wildfires are monitored but generally allowed to run their course. A prescribed

a second such expedition with a group of missionaries and colonists. By the beginning of April they stood, haggard and exhausted, at the crest of Tejon Pass (somewhere above what is now Interstate 5). They looked out across the vast Tulare Lake (formerly the largest freshwater lake west of the Missouri, now mostly fields of cotton, rice, and alfalfa) and saw some very big mountains. "At a distance of about forty leagues," wrote friar Pedro Font, "we saw a great snow-covered range [*una gran sierra nevada*] whose trend appeared to me to be from south-southeast to north-northwest." It was more a vague description than a name, but there it was, written down in a diary and on a map: the future name of a best-selling microbrewed pale ale.

There were in those days anywhere from 30,000 to 250,000 so-called Indians living in the valley of the San Joaquin and in the foothills of the Sierra, beyond the direct influence of the growing Spanish settlements on the coast. The Spaniards did make occasional military forays into the wilds of the interior, at first for purposes of exploration and recruitment, then increasingly to bring back *indios* who had run away from the padres at the missions. ("They [the Indians] have no knowledge of benefits received," lamented one Spanish writer in 1822, "and ingratitude is common amongst them.") Whatever the purpose, it was in the course of such outings that many of the rivers flowing from the western slope of the Sierra received their names: the San Joaquin,

fire program was initiated in Yosemite two years later, and starting in 1972, naturally ignited wildland fires in the higher elevations were allowed to burn. Prescribed burning is now a common sight throughout the parks, in Giant Sequoia National Monument, and in some areas under the management of the Forest Service.

Giant sequoias are especially fire adapted: Their bark is fire-resistant; fire aids in the opening of their cones and the scattering of their seeds, as well as keeping competitive species at bay.

PRESCRIBED BURN, WEST YOSEMITE VALLEY, JUNE 2007

the Calaveras, the Plumas (Feather), the Merced, el Río de los Santos Reyes (Kings). The Spaniards showed little interest in penetrating the range itself, preferring to let it stand as an imagined impenetrable barrier to the French and Americans, still a very dry continent away on the other side.

After the whole of California was ceded to Mexico in 1821, the "unconquered tribes" in the Central Valley began, with greater frequency, to organize expeditions of their own in the other direction, westward to the coast—to, in the words of one contemporary observer, "plunder the farms of the colonists of horses, which they [the natives] eat in preference to beef." These raids were often met with fierce vigilante-style reprisals. "The last expedition which the citizens of this town made to the tulares," complained the governor of Monterey in 1835, "they committed various atrocities against the heathen Indians without distinguishing between the innocent and the guilty. In addition to stealing their ornaments and personal effects, they [the citizens] took away seven small boys to serve them and act as slaves, without informing this government of the occurrences."

THE PATHFINDERS Late in the summer of 1826, at the age of 27, Jedediah Strong Smith set out in a southwesterly direction from the Big Salt Lake in search of a new

CAUGHT IN A SNOW-STORM.

IN THE DAYS BEFORE GORE-TEX FROM *IN THE HEART OF THE SIERRAS* BY J. M. HUTCHINGS (1886)

source of beaver. He took with him fifteen men, a cavalcade of pack horses, a month's supply of dried buffalo meat, traps, guns, powder, lead, and the usual assortment of gifts for the Indians. There were no roads in those days—only game trails, rivers, and the ancient footpaths of the first people. The best map available was "Robinson's *Map of Mexico, Louisiana, & the Missouri Territory &c. (1814),*" the western portion of which represented little more than a challenging compendium of extrapolations and fanciful imaginings.

Smith and his men marched from one thin water source to the next. Across the great deserts they navigated by dead reckoning and intuition, often by the light of the moon. According to Smith's own journal, they chewed "slips of the cabbage pear," dug holes in the sand to sleep in, and not infrequently resorted to eating their mounts. For traveling without passports in Mexican territory (and suspected of spying for the U.S. government), they spent all of December and much of January under house arrest at Mission San Gabriel—within strolling distance of the pueblo of Los Angeles.

The primary condition of their release by the Mexican governor was that they would head back across the deserts from whence they had come. Instead, they cut northeast, crossing the Antelope Valley and over into the San Joaquin by way of Tehachapi. There, in the cottonwoods along the lower stretches of the Kings River, they found what they'd been looking for.

During the first week of May, in an attempt to get 60 horses and 1,500 pounds of beaver back across the range in a snowstorm—without snowshoes—Smith lost five horses and came very close to losing it all. He turned around and left the bulk of his party and all his furs at an encampment in the foothills, to be retrieved, he hoped, the following year. On the 20th, he set out again, this time with two men, seven horses, and two mules. They made the east side in 8 days, to become the first white men ever to cross the High Sierra—in either direction, and in any season. "I found the snow on the top of the mountain from 4 to 8 feet deep," wrote Smith, "but it was so consolidated by the heat of the sun that my horses only sunk from half a foot to 1 foot deep."

Only two horses and a mule were lost in the crossing. The rest starved or otherwise succumbed during the long, dry trudge across the basins and ranges of what would one day be Nevada and Utah. When Smith finally dragged into the rendezvous, alone, the day before Independence Day, 1827—11 months and more than 2,000 miles later— he was riding a horse he'd borrowed that morning from a Snake Indian. His business associates, having long ago given him up for lost, loaded "a small cannon brought up from St. Louis" and fired a salute.

Ten days later he was back on the trail. Two years later, having lost another 25 men in two separate Indian massacres, he again bargained his way out of prison (this time in Monterey), narrowly avoided extradition to Mexico City, forded countless swollen rivers, outran two grizzlies, and trapped and slogged his way through month after month of mud and sheeting rain as far north as the Columbia River, only to have his few remaining beaver pelts judged by the Hudson's Bay Company representative at

Fort Vancouver "of very bad quality the worst indeed I ever saw." After all this, at age 30, he set off once again, eastward, broke as ever, and as ever full of optimism, for the summer rendezvous in Utah.

That it had been done once did not necessarily make it easier for those who followed. The autumn of 1833, for example, saw Joseph R. Walker and more than 70 men trudging across the Sierra from east to west, along the old Mono Trail, surrounded, in the words of expedition chronicler Zenas Leonard, "by snow and rugged peaks—the vigour of every man almost exhausted—nothing to give our poor horses, which were no longer any assistance to us in traveling, but a burthen [sic], for we had to help the most of them along as we would an old and feeble man." Not a few of these faithful beasts were butchered and eaten beside the trail. The discovery of some rather enormous trees, the biggest anyone had ever seen, and likely white man's first distant glimpse of Yosemite (from above) was all of very little consolation. Before they could finally consider themselves through the worst of it, their surviving animals had still to be lowered—one at a time, by ropes—down a sheer rock face to the valley below.

On the way back, Walker pioneered a much easier, if longer, route around the southern end of the range, from the Kern River to the Mojave. A decade later, John C. Frémont and Kit Carson, heeding the advice of no one—except perhaps that they should bring snowshoes—made the next full-scale midwinter run at the range. It was a comparatively mild season, and still it took them more than a month to punch through to the other side. To the snowdrifts and the stew pot they gave up more than half of their 67 horses and mules.

"We had tonight an extraordinary dinner—pea soup, mule, and dog," Frémont wrote in his journal on February 13, 1844.

"I should not mind," wrote the party's mapmaker (and former rider of said unlucky mule), "if we only had salt."

THE ALLURE OF THE SHORTCUT: WAVE I By the mid-1840s, even the fastest-rising mountain range on the planet could not resist the westering impulse of the United States of America. The word was out. "The climate," wrote one of California's first great promoters, Lansford W. Hastings, "is that of perpetual spring, having no excess of heat or cold . . . fuel is never required for any other than culinary purposes." He remarked at great length about the abundance of game, the "innumerable and inexhaustible" fisheries, the way in which herds of domestic animals "require neither feeding nor housing," the year-round growing season, the variety of crops, the incomparable productivity of the land, and so on. "The deep, rich, alluvial soil of the Nile, in Egypt," he wrote, "does not afford a parallel."

All that could be said against the place was that it was not easy to get to, and that it was under the control of the Mexicans. Given the States' annexation of Texas in 1845 and President Polk's subsequent declaration of war against Mexico (May 1846), the latter problem seemed not much of a problem at all, and it was likely to be resolved sooner rather than later. The former problem—that of getting there—could be overcome. All that was required was some decent planning, fair leadership, the proper equipment, a certain amount of innate capability, delusions of grandeur, extraordinary physical fitness, strength of character (or complete lack of scruples), time, money, patience, the very best of luck, and, of course, a modicum of reliable information.

Hastings had made the journey out and back in '43 and '44, had witnessed the prosperity and potential at Johann Sutter's New Helvetia (now Sacramento), had dined and discussed routes with John C. Frémont, and, by the following year, had typed up and published the voluminous *Emigrants' Guide to California and Oregon*. "Perhaps nobody will see him here again," wrote Sutter, "as his life will be in danger about his

WATER AND POWER

On a good year—the sort of year that brings a full 2 inches of precipitation to Death Valley—anywhere from 50 to 80 inches of water will fall on the Sierra Nevada, which is more than what falls on Seattle or Boston by at least one and a half times. Average annual precipitation in the Los Angeles Basin, by contrast, is less than 12 inches—about the same as Tucson, Arizona—while San Francisco, with less than 22, was once upon a time, before it tapped into the Sierra Nevada, as parched as Odessa, Texas. Historically, more than 80 percent of annual precipitation in the Sierra high country comes down between November and April in the form of snow. The most snow ever recorded in a single season was 884 inches (73.7 feet) at Tamarack Station, north of Yosemite, in 1906–7. In 1933, 5 feet of snow is said to have fallen in 24 hours at Giant Forest in Sequoia National Park. For marketing purposes, Mammoth Mountain Ski Area claims an average of 400 inches (33.3 feet) per year, but the numbers vary radically from season to season. A record 45.5 feet fell on Mammoth Mountain during the 1982–83 season, and in 2005–06 the bar was raised to 55.7 feet. 2014–15 was a record on the other end with just 12.5 feet total for the season. The legendary winter of 2016–17 broke six long years of drought with more than 97 inches of seasonal precipitation. In good years, the ski lifts operate all the way until July Fourth.

In the old days, in wet years, spring would come, the snow would melt, the great rivers and valleys would flood—on the west side all the way to the San Francisco Bay; on the east to Mono and Owens Lakes—and by the end of summer everything but the Tule marshes and the highest alpine basins would be dry. And the groundwater recharged. Years of flood were followed by years of drought, which were followed by years of flood. Overall, the past two centuries are thought to have been the wettest in 4,000 years.

By the early 1850s, miners had begun to tap into seasonal runoff by way of flumes and hoses, making jets of water powerful enough to reduce whole mountainsides to washed gravel. Flumes were built to transport cut logs to downstream lumber mills. By the 1860s, farmers were already taking advantage of state and federal subsidies to "reclaim" seasonal swampland in the Central Valley. Dikes were built, as well as levees to control flooding; more improved

THE TUOLUMNE RIVER BELOW THE O'SHAUGHNESSY DAM, HETCH HETCHY, YOSEMITE NATIONAL PARK

OLD FLUME ON THE TULE RIVER ABOVE SPRINGVILLE
BURKE GRIGGS

flumes brought greater volumes of Sierra runoff into canals and irrigation ditches and from there into the fields. Citrus groves were planted in the bottomlands of the San Joaquin, and eventually, down the line, cotton, alfalfa, and rice. In 1898, the Mount Whitney Power and Electric Company began work on a flume to deliver water from the East Fork of the Kaweah to three 440-volt belt-driven generators at its Kaweah Power House No. 1, followed by a series of small dams above Mineral King (to regulate flow through the drier months). Farmers in the San Joaquin converted their old gas or steam-powered well pumps to electric, and as part of the deal they got their homes wired for electric light.

As populations boomed, so too did the demand for water: water to make electricity, to irrigate crops and lawns, to wash cars and dishes and driveways; water for drinking, for swimming and soaking in, for the flushing of toilets, for the making of coffee and concrete and the refining of petroleum.

Enterprising ranchers acquired rights to millions of acre-feet of Sierra runoff on both sides of the range, and then they sold those rights to consolidated utilities like Southern California Edison, or to industrial-sized cotton and rice growers, or to the ever-thirstier cities on the coast. To mitigate periodic cycles of flood and drought, big guns like the Army Corps of Engineers and the Bureau of Reclamation, together with the California Department of Water, the Los Angeles Department of Water and Power, and the San Francisco Public Utilities Commission, over the course of a half-century, built the largest, most complex, and most costly system of water distribution ever conceived.

Today 60 percent of the water used by Californians comes from the Sierra Nevada, most of it from watersheds protected by national parks and wilderness areas. There are dams on every major river and tributary in the range. There are siphons and forebays, pumping stations, storage basins, and pipelines. Eighty-five percent of San Francisco's drinking water travels 165 miles from the Hetch Hetchy reservoir in Yosemite National Park. Forty percent of Los Angeles's supply comes by way of a 223-mile aqueduct from the upper Owens River watershed. The largest single user of electrical energy in California—some of it produced by hydroelectric generators at the foot of the Sierra—is the State Water Project (SWP), which brings water from the Feather River 444 miles by aqueduct across the San Joaquin Valley, then pumps it 2,000 feet up over Tehachapi Pass to Los Angeles and other coastal cities. Meanwhile, one-quarter of the food America eats is grown in the Central Valley of California, almost entirely with water from the Sierra Nevada.

During a fair year, the Sierra makes its quota, sending down about 42 million acre-feet of runoff. And still, after every series of wet years, engineering notwithstanding, comes a series of dry years. On April 1, 1977, during the driest season ever recorded in California—drier even than during the notorious Dust Bowl of the early 1930s—a local snow survey found "only about 10 inches of water on the Mammoth Pass snow pillow." By midsummer there were statewide shortages in hydroelectric power; irrigation pumps in the Central Valley were bringing up air; and the land was subsiding again (it had subsided by as much as 30 feet in some places since 1925). Even the City of Los Angeles began rationing its water. The following year brought one of the Sierra's top 10 wettest winters in recorded history—20 feet in back-to-back storm cycles by mid-January—and all was forgotten. That is, until the next major drought hit in 1987.

SNOW SLIDE ON TIOGA ROAD, JUNE 25, 1942
R. H. ANDERSON, COURTESY NPS, YNP

book, making out California a paradise, even some of the Emigrants in the Valley threatened his life." Aside from all the breathless descriptions of the country, the book also offered some eminently practical information. It was advised, for example, that the traveler leave behind featherbeds and other such cumbersome luxuries, and that he provision himself with, at the very least, "a good gun," an ample supply of powder and lead, "200 pounds of flour, or meal; 150 pounds of bacon; 10 pounds of coffee; 20 pounds of sugar; and 10 pounds of salt." For the conveyance of such stores, Hastings recommended a sturdy wagon, with tires recently reset, and a team of oxen (rather than horses or mules). "Oxen endure the fatigue and heat much better," he wrote, "[and] are not liable to be stolen by the Indians." He neglected to mention how they might taste if it came down to eating them.

Hastings's most important piece of advice, given almost in passing, was that all parties should be sure to put Independence, Missouri, well behind them by the first of May—"after which time they should never start, if it can possibly be avoided." The journey required at least 120 days, give or take a few weeks, and by now the lesson had sunk in: The Sierra Nevada should not be crossed in winter.

The Donners and Reeds had left on time, in April 1846, as had some 2,700 other pioneers. The traffic on the road that year—some sections of the trail could now fairly be called a road—included such notables as Jim Bridger and Joseph R. Walker; a former governor of Missouri; a future founder of the Pony Express; a man who was to become known as the discoverer of Yosemite; Joan Didion's great-great-great-grandparents; a talented mapmaker who may or may not have been the bastard son of Thomas Jefferson; several journalists and best-selling authors-to-be; and, of course, Hastings himself.

Hastings was eager to try out a new shortcut—one he had likely gleaned from his conversations with Frémont. "The most direct route," Hastings proposed in his book, "would be to leave the Oregon route about 200 miles east from Fort Hall; thence bearing west southwest to the Salt Lake; and thence continuing down to the bay of St. Francisco." At Fort Bridger, Wyoming, he met up with a party consisting of some 75 wagons and proceeded to lead them along what would soon become known, rather infamously, as the Hastings Cutoff. It proved to be no shortcut at all.

Hastings and his party encountered no end of unfortunate difficulty and delay, but they nevertheless made it safely to California. The Donner Party, on the other hand, having arrived at Fort Bridger two days after Hastings's departure (because of a broken axle) had a much rougher go of it. Struggling over the Wasatch range, pioneering yet another "shortcut" to the great Salt Lake, they fell another three weeks behind. By the time the motley assemblage of 87 exceedingly unlucky pioneers made the east side of the Sierra, in late October, it was snowing hard. They cut timber, built cabins, slaughtered their starving oxen, boiled the hides for sustenance, and dug in for the winter. It kept snowing.

By mid-December, fifteen starving men had set out to cross the range on snow-shoes. The snowpack was more than 20 feet deep. Only seven made it into Sutter's Fort on January 18, having survived on the flesh of their fallen companions.

Between February and March, three separate rescue parties managed to bring forty more survivors over the mountains. The fourth and last "relief"—a salvage operation motivated at least in part by the possibility of recovering some of the Donners' reputedly considerable stash of gold and jewels—reached the first of the cabins a little past noon on April 17. What they found, according to a well-publicized (though possibly apocryphal) report by one Thomas Fallon of the relief party, was "human bodies terribly mutilated" (including those of George and Tamsen Donner) and all manner of "sights from which we would have fain turned away, and which are too dreadful to put on record." Beside a pan containing what may have been young Landrum Murphy's liver reclined a well-fed but half-deranged Louis Keseburg, the original party's last remaining survivor. "On his person," wrote Fallon, "they discovered a brace of pistols recognized to be those of George Donner, and, while taking them from him, discovered something concealed in his waistcoat which on being opened was found to be $225 in gold."

THE ALLURE OF THE SHORTCUT: WAVE II Many consider gold to have been the first metal used by humans. Banked by Akkadian emperors, described in Egyptian hieroglyphics as early as 2100 BCE, gold—before coffee—was what got conquistadors out of their hammocks in the morning. On the morning of January 24, 1848, less than 300 years after Coronado died bankrupt and disappointed in Mexico City, eight months after a nightmare-hounded Louis Keseburg was hauled into Sutter's Fort, one week before the signing of the Treaty of Guadalupe Hidalgo (by which California and most of the Southwest was ceded to the U.S.), a fellow by the name of James Marshall, a contractor on one of Sutter's sawmills, looked down at a newly eroded bank of Eocene gravels along the American River and saw what he knew "to be nothing else."

In its May 29 issue, the *Californian* reported—despite Sutter's best efforts to keep the whole thing under wraps—that "the whole country from San Francisco to Los Angeles, and from the sea shore to the base of the Sierra Nevadas [sic], resounds with the sordid cry of 'Gold, gold, gold!' while the field is left half-planted, the house half built, and everything neglected but the manufacture of shovels and pickaxes." On August 18, by way of the brig *J.R.S.*, the news reached Valparaiso, Chile. It made the *New York Herald* the following day. "The accounts of abundance of gold are of such an extraordinary character as would scarcely command belief," President Polk wrote in a December 5 message to Congress, "were they not corroborated by the authentic reports of officers in the public service."

By late spring, the overland trail had become a traffic jam of lumbering, ox-drawn wagon trains, thousands of vehicles long, together bearing westward as many as 35,000 "dreamers of the golden dream." Between April and November, 697 ships arrived at the settlement of San Francisco, the non-native population of which had recently been reported at "575 males, 177 females, and 60 children." By the end of 1849, as many as 100,000 so-called Argonauts had made their way to California, by land, by sea, or by some combination, from as far away as Europe, China, and Australia.

One loose confederation of more than a hundred wagons, calling itself the "Sand-walking Company," had set out from Salt Lake City around the first of October. Because

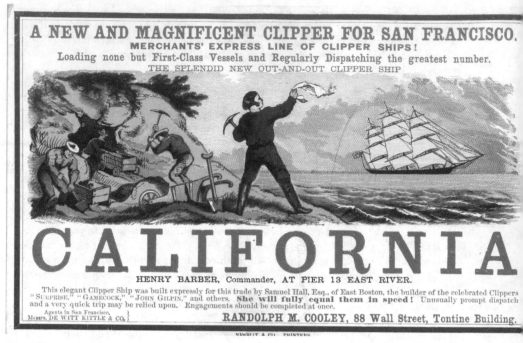

A NEW AND MAGNIFICENT CLIPPER FOR SAN FRANCISCO.
MERCHANTS' EXPRESS LINE OF CLIPPER SHIPS!
Loading none but First-Class Vessels and Regularly Dispatching the greatest number.
THE SPLENDID NEW OUT-AND-OUT CLIPPER SHIP

CALIFORNIA

HENRY BARBER, Commander, AT PIER 13 EAST RIVER.

This elegant Clipper Ship was built expressly for this trade by Samuel Hall, Esq., of East Boston, the builder of the celebrated Clippers "SURPRISE," "GAMECOCK," "JOHN GILPIN," and others. **She will fully equal them in speed!** Unusually prompt dispatch and a very quick trip may be relied upon. Engagements should be completed at once.

Agents in San Francisco,
Messrs. DE WITT KITTLE & CO.

RANDOLPH M. COOLEY, 88 Wall Street, Tontine Building.

THE VOYAGE AROUND CAPE HORN TOOK UPWARDS OF FOUR MONTHS AND COST ABOUT $300. "THE GREATEST OBJECTIONS WHICH CAN BE URGED AGAINST TRAVELING BY THIS ROUTE ARE THE UNPLEASANT, CHEERLESS MONOTONY, AND THE IRKSOME CONFINEMENT INCIDENT TO THIS METHOD OF TRAVELING," WROTE LANSFORD W. HASTINGS COURTESY BANCROFT LIBRARY

it was so late in the season, and because the horrors of the Donner Party were still so fresh in everyone's mind, the plan had been to follow the Old Spanish Trail southwest, via the springs at Las Vegas, to the new Mormon settlement at San Bernardino—thus avoiding the Sierra Nevada entirely. A veteran of the Mormon Battalion by the name of Capt. Jefferson Hunt had agreed, at a rate of $10 to $12 per wagon, to show them the way.

The pace was not what everyone had hoped. On the road and in camp at night there was much discussion and back-and-forth concerning the relative merits and risks of yet another semi-mythical shortcut someone had heard about in Salt Lake City. The Williams Cutoff, as it was called, was said to be a straight shot west across the desert to Walker Pass—some 500 miles shorter than going around by San Bernardino. Five hundred miles! At 10 miles a day, they might be spared nearly 2 months. (Or gain 2 months on all the others.) Captain Hunt was skeptical, but it was the kind of thing that worked on folks' minds. America herself had, after all, been discovered when explorers were trying out a possible shortcut.

Two weeks out, at a camp on Little Salt Lake, the train was overtaken by a smaller party under the direction of a Captain Smith. Smith was bound for the Williams Cutoff. He had with him a map, or a copy of a map, likely drawn from information furnished by Frémont. It seemed pretty convincing. The next morning he and his party were off with Godspeed to the goldfields—never to be heard from again. Three days later, at the place where Smith's tracks diverged from the main trail, there occurred something of a reckoning. "It was really a serious matter," wrote traveler William Lewis Manly. "Team after team turned to the right, while now and then one would keep straight ahead as first intended."

THE CORPS AND THE SIERRA

Franklin Delano Roosevelt was inaugurated President of the U.S. on March 4, 1933. Within five days he called an emergency session of the 73rd Congress and proposed the establishment of a peacetime army consisting of thousands of unemployed men "to relieve the acute condition of widespread distress and unemployment existing in the United States, provide for the restoration of the country's depleted natural resources, and advance an orderly program of useful public works." On April 5, just a month after taking office, with full support from both houses of Congress, Roosevelt declared the Emergency Conservation Work Act, known as the origin of the Civilian Conservation Corps (CCC). The first enrollees were inducted on April 7. The Department of Labor handled enrollment; the Departments of Interior and Agriculture cooperated on planning and organization; and the U.S. Army, with assistance from the Coast Guard, the Navy, the Marines, and the National Park Service, provided leadership and logistical support.

By October 1933, 400 corpsmen (two companies) had arrived in Death Valley. Other companies established camps in locations across the southern Sierra, in Sequoia-Kings and Yosemite National Parks, with ten camps in Yosemite alone. Corpsmen worked for $1 a day through tours of six months. Of $30 per month, $25 was sent home to families. The men graded hundreds of miles of roads and built campgrounds, viewpoints, restrooms, and picnic facilities. They made signs, built and improved trails, developed wells and springs, laid water mains, and strung telephone lines. They wore uniforms and slept in canvas-walled barracks. They removed invasive plants from Sierra meadows, brought historic apple trees back to life, fought fires, carved log benches, and built rock walls. Their handiwork is to this day in evidence throughout the region: in the tight switchbacks on CA 190 into the Panamint Valley; in the stonework along Generals Highway in Sequoia; in the tunnels on the High Sierra Trail, the handrails at Moro Rock, the access stairs to Crystal Cave, and the cables on Half Dome; in the trails and Ski House at Badger Pass; and in the backcountry huts at Ostrander and Pear Lakes.

With a general decline in unemployment, the program's popularity had begun to wane by the beginning of the 1940s. The bombing of Pearl Harbor in December 1941 fixed attention elsewhere, and the remaining corpsmen were among the first to go to war. In the summer of 1942, Congress passed a final appropriation of $8 million for the CCC—to fund its liquidation.

CCC BOYS ERECTING NEW CABLES ON HALF DOME, MAY 1934 R. H. ANDERSON, COURTESY NPS, YNP

THE "PRAIRIE SCHOONER."

IN A PINCH, MULES MADE BETTER EATING THAN OXEN. THEY WERE ALSO FAVORED BY INDIANS FROM *IN THE HEART OF THE SIERRAS* BY J. M. HUTCHINGS (1886)

Hunt considered himself duty bound to lead those few who wanted to continue along the original route. He bade the rest a pleasant journey. Three days later, at the first sign of difficulty—at a place called Poverty Point—the majority turned back to rejoin him (including, it is said, the one person who had made a copy of Smith's map). Twenty-seven wagons pushed on westward. The shortcut parties included, among others, a train of "Hawkeyes from Iowa"; a party of Georgians under the leadership of one Captain Townshend; the Arcane and Bennett families, with seven wagons; a Reverend Brier and his family; a German immigrant by the name of Louis Nusbaumer; and a group of young men from Illinois who had dubbed themselves the Jayhawkers.

The journey for those who had stuck with Hunt—"over barren deserts, volcanic, hill-strewn, sun-parched . . . accompanied by a constant cloud of dust from sands never before disturbed by wheels," as local historian W. A. Chalfant would later describe it—was no easy stroll through the countryside. But their route had been traveled. The great distances between watering holes could at least be anticipated. For the Jayhawkers and their fellow travelers, marching blindly across the lowest, driest desert sinks in North America, it was a character-assaying exercise in thirst, starvation, and pain. A handful of them would die or disappear. Of their 27 vehicles, they would burn or abandon all but one before escaping the desert. Collectively—although the parties generally traveled separately and fended for themselves—they would become known as the Death Valley '49ers.

It was late December before they came together again briefly at the eastern edge of the deepest, driest sink of all, somewhere in the vicinity of today's The Oasis at Death Valley (formerly the Furnace Creek Resort). They were likely the first Americans (and Germans) to see the place. There were no pools, there was no gift shop, there was no golf course. If there was beauty there at all, they were not greatly inclined to its appreciation.

For weeks on end, they had dragged across the dust and scrabble of the Amargosa drainage without finding palatable water, their supplies long dwindled to nothing but flour and coffee, and their oxen, with no feed or forage, getting weaker by the day. There had been skirmishes with Indians, as well as snow (which had saved their lives). It was Christmas Eve when they found a tremendous freshwater spring at Furnace Creek, gushing 2,000 gallons a minute, and some meager forage for the animals. Still, the broad, salt-crusted valley before them looked less promising even than the one they had just escaped. With no idea how many hundreds more miles they might still have to cover, they made camp. "The men killed an ox for our Christmas," wrote Mrs. Brier, "but its flesh was more like poisonous slime than meat. . . . I had one small biscuit, but we had plenty of coffee, and I think it was that which kept us alive."

The Jayhawkers were then but a few miles away, at the dunes near what we now call Stovepipe Wells, burning their wagons to make jerky of the last of their oxen. Chalfant, researching the story in the late 1920s, came upon the diary of a Captain Asa Haines, who had apparently made it out of Death Valley in the company of the Jayhawkers. Of the "terse entries, written in pencil," Chalfant was able to make out the following account:

East 4 mile, laid by; thence south 28 mile, no water, 10 o'clock at night.
Thence west 10 mile, no water.
Thence south 12 mile, no water.
Thence southeast 8 miles, got weak.
Thence due south 20 mile, no water.
Left wagons, packed cattle, six days wandering.
Stayed in canyon three days. Indians stole horses, all but two.
18 miles southwest, no water, one death, Fish from Iowa, starvation. William Ischam died same day in evening.
William G. Robinson and McGowan got through desert but died at foot of mountains. Frank, a Frenchman, wandered off.
Offered Brian Byron $5 for a biscuit but he refused. Old man Townshend left. Bill Rude and Dow Stephens bake flour and offer me food.
Luther Richards found water; snowed same night. One man laid down. Made coffee, went back and he was dead.
Find body of Townshend; scalped.

At a fair spring along what is now the Westside Road, at the base of the Panamint range, the Bennett-Arcane party spent nearly a month camped beneath their wagons, contemplating the end. Meanwhile, John Rogers and William Manly, each with a knap-sack full of ox meat, two spoonfuls of rice, and two of tea, climbed over the range south of Telescope Peak and, following a trail marked by the bones of abandoned horses (and those of the man named Fish, from Iowa), crossed the dry pan of the Panamint Valley. They climbed the Argus Range and, on New Year's Day 1850, found themselves looking out at the shimmering, snow-clad Sierra Nevada.

At sunrise, they found a thin sheet of ice to fill a kettle with, and then contin-ued south along the trail that is now US 395. They overtook what was left of the Jayhawker party at Indian Wells, now home to a mediocre steakhouse and a fine microbrewery. They crossed the Mojave, generally following the route of present-day CA 14, past the gateway to Walker Pass, down Red Rock Canyon and across what is now the sprawling ex-urb of Palmdale and Lancaster. Along the way they found the bones of numerous dead horses and oxen, and saw their first Joshua Trees (which they called "cabbage trees—a brave little tree to live in such a barren country").

DUST STORMS ACROSS BADWATER, FROM DANTE'S VIEW. FOR WEEKS THE '49ERS WANDERED THE EDGE OF THE PAN, LOOKING FOR WATER AND FORAGE BURKE GRIGGS

JOSHUA TREES AND THE SIERRA NEVADA FROM THE MOJAVE DESERT

In Soledad Canyon, by Manly's account, they camped on the banks of a "beautiful little running brook of clear, pure water." They ate roasted quail and a stew of crow and hawk, and thought themselves "on the edge of the promised land." The following day, they sighted a pair of horses in the distance, and later a pack of prairie wolves. Leaving the Santa Clara by way of an old Indian shortcut (in the direction of present-day Saugus), they reached the summit of a spur of hills from which they beheld "a beautiful meadow of a thousand acres, green as a thick carpet of grass could make it, and shaded with oaks equal to those of an old English Park, and a herd of cattle numbering many hundreds, if not thousands." They killed a steer, roasted it, ate it, and made new moccasins from its hide.

Near the end of January 1850, some 15 days and 250 miles from the place where their erstwhile companions were still huddled and starving beneath their wagons, they ran into Darwin French. French, who would later found the town of Darwin, between Owens Lake and Death Valley, was working on the Tejon Ranch at that time. He offered to help them procure supplies for the long march back.

He took them to Mission San Fernando—today found at the center of a triangle formed by the junctions of three major freeways (I-5, I-405, and CA 118). There the Spaniards gave Rogers and Manly a floor to sleep on in the storehouse—a floor Manly described as "not soft." "This was the second house we had slept in since leaving Wisconsin," he wrote, "and it seemed rather pent up to us."

The following day, in exchange for $30 cash, they were furnished with yellow beans, wheat, dried meat, some coarse flour, two packhorses, saddles, and ropes. Later they managed to pick up "a poor little one-eyed mule" and, for Manly's last $15, "a little snow white mare as fat as butter," all of which animals they were eventually forced to abandon on the western flank of the Panamints, above what is now the very quiet town of Ballarat. "One who has never heard the last, despairing, pleading neigh of a horse left to die can form no idea of its almost human appeal," wrote Manly.

They climbed a trail that skirted what later came to be known as Manly Falls—a trail and landscape turned into a memory in the early twenty-first century by the excavation of an open-pit gold mine—and then punched back down the rough scree to the camp they had left nearly a month earlier. They were surprised to find everyone still alive, if a bit deranged.

"Bennett and Arcane embraced us with all their strength," wrote Manly, "and Mrs. Bennett, when she came, fell down on her knees and clung to me like a maniac in the great emotion that came to her, and not a word was spoken. If they had been strong enough, they would have carried us to camp upon their shoulders. As it was, they stopped two or three times and turned as if to speak, but there was too much feeling for words; convulsive weeping would choke the voice."

They were not exactly saved. They had still to abandon the wagons, and all but the most essential gear, to lash the children to the backs of the starving oxen, and to head out once again across 250 miles of some of the roughest desert terrain in the world. But by mid-January 1850, Manly and Rogers had again crested the Panamints heading west, this time with the rest of their ragged party in tow—women, children, and all. "We took off our hats," wrote Manly more than 40 years later, "and then, overlooking the scene of so much trial, suffering and death, spoke the thought uppermost, saying: 'Goodbye, Death Valley!'"

Hence the name.

A HALT IN THE YOSEMITE VALLEY BY ALBERT BIERSTADT GRAVURE, C. 1863, COURTESY NPS, YNP

THE CHANGING OF THE GUARD

*It was one of the last human hunts of civilization, and the basest and
most brutal of them all.*
—Hubert Howe Bancroft, 1890

Jim Savage had come overland from Illinois in 1846. He'd lost a wife and young daughter on the road—whether to privation or Indians, to cholera or some other mishap, is not
recorded. He fought with Frémont against the Mexicans, and, after the war, he drifted
south to what would soon become Mariposa County. He did some prospecting, fell in
with the natives, and started building up a kind of empire.

"Jim was smart as a whip, shrewd," recalled a woman years later who had known
him back in Illinois. "He was vigorous and strong, had blue eyes and a magnificent
physique, was tactful, likable, and interesting." He seems also to have had a remarkable ear for languages. Conversant in French and German, and probably Spanish, too,
it wasn't long before he could manage himself in the dialects of the local Indians.

There were five confederated tribes that then controlled all the territory of the San
Joaquin, from the Tuolumne to the Kern. To their most powerful chiefs—among them
one known as José Juarez, and another, the much-feared José Rey, or "King Joseph," of
the Chowchillas—Savage became something of a friend, an adviser, and a benevolent
dictator. He became a chief himself—of more than one tribe. He took to wearing red
shirts to impress his followers. From the foothills he led successful war parties against
the enemy mountain tribes, especially the so-called Yosemites (alternately understood
to mean "grizzly bears" or "those who kill"). He sealed his position by marrying into a
number of prominent native families.

To the swarms of pioneers, prospectors, and speculators who, by the end of 1848,
much to the chagrin of the natives, had begun to pick and dig and pan their way across
the countryside, killing game and cutting forests as they went, Savage was the subject
of many an evening's storytelling. Some said he had five wives; others said he had more
than twenty. Only when he went to San Francisco, such as the time he rolled a barrelful
of gold dust across a hotel lobby, did he condescend to wear a hat and boots. Otherwise,
they said, he went about in moccasins or bare feet, his thick blond hair hanging to his
shoulders, his beard "halfway to his waist." "His walk and action were so apparently
confirmed in Indian characteristics," wrote one chronicler in 1882, "that the ordinary
observer would intuitively fancy that he was himself a native and to that wild life born
and bred."

There was much speculation as to how Savage was able to exert such powerful
influence over his newfound charges. What is certain is that by the spring of 1849,
he had begun to use that influence to gather a considerable amount of precious metal
for himself. "Never will I forget the impressions of the scene before us," reported
one freshly arrived prospector, having chanced upon the man in Jamestown in May:
"Under a brushwood tent supported by upright poles sat James D. Savage, measuring
and pouring gold dust into the candle boxes by his side. Five hundred or more naked
Indians, with belts of cloth bound around their waists or suspended from their heads,
brought the dust to Savage, and in return for it received a bright piece of cloth or some
beads."

By the end of the year he had freighted a load of supplies from San Francisco and
opened a profitable little trading post on the South Fork of the Merced (near present-day
El Portal), less than 20 miles down-canyon from the yet-to-be-stumbled-upon Yosemite
Valley, thus expanding his market to include the burgeoning population of white prospectors. Historian Carl Russell described Savage's rates of exchange as follows: "An

SIERRA NEVADA BIGHORN SHEEP (*OVIS CANADENSIS SIERRAE*)

"The wild sheep ranks highest among the animal mountaineers," wrote John Muir, reassuring himself that in their rugged habitat, rising to more than 14,000 feet, they were safe from mankind. What he failed to anticipate was the transmission of diseases by domestic sheep and the proliferation of legally protected mountain lions. By 1999, with about 100 adults remaining in five isolated herds, the Sierra Nevada bighorn—not to be confused with its more populous cousin to the east, the desert bighorn (*Ovis canadensis nelsoni*)—was given emergency endangered-species protection and treated to an ambitious multiagency recovery plan. The population has grown steadily ever since, with occasional setbacks during big winters like that of 2016–17.

LISTING: Endangered.

THREATS: Disease borne by domestic sheep, predation by mountain lions, range competition, climate change, avalanches, inbreeding.

HOW MANY LEFT: ~500.

WHERE TO SEE THEM (north to south): Yosemite high country, Lundy Canyon, Lee Vining Canyon, Inyo National Forest (Esha Peak, Wheeler Ridge, Pine Creek), Sequoia-Kings Canyon National Park high country (Mt. Langley). John Wehausen's annual seminar through the Mono Lake Committee offers excellent odds for sighting wild sheep (monolake.org).

ANCIENT BIGHORN GLYPHS, COSO ROCK ART DISTRICT, CHINA LAKE NAVAL AIR WEAPONS STATION BILL BECHER

ounce of gold bought a can of oysters, 5 pounds of flour, or a pound of bacon; a shirt required 5 ounces, and a pair of boots or a hat brought a full pound."

Indians not under Savage's sway—in other words, Indians of the "those who kill" variety—made occasional visits to the post from upriver, boasting, according to early accounts, of a "deep valley in which one Indian is more than 10 white men." In the spring of 1850, they raided the store. "With the Indian miners I had in my employ," Savage later explained, "[I] drove them off, and followed some of them up the Merced

River into a canyon, which I supposed led to their stronghold, as the Indians then with me said it was not a safe place to go into." He retreated, packed up his wares, and established a new post at a safer location near the present-day town of Mariposa (then Agua Fria). Business was good and brisk enough that summer that he opened a branch post to the west of Mormon Bar (along today's CA 49), near the newest diggings on the Fresno River.

For the Indians, on the other hand, conditions deteriorated quickly. "It was found convenient," reported one J. Ross Browne in 1857 (cited by David Beesley in *Crow's Range*), "to take possession of their country without recompense, rob them of their wives and children, kill them in every cowardly and barbarous manner that could be devised, and when that was impracticable, drive them as far as possible out of the way." Whether they had come suddenly "to learn the value of the gold dust they dug from the ground," as another contemporary writer put it, or just felt crowded and annoyed and up against a wall, the Indians began to weigh their options. The law, such as it was, was not on their side: One statute prevented their testifying in court; another, more recent, allowed for their enslavement. Against increasing waves of predation, murder, and trespass, they were afforded about the same legal protection as bears and mountain lions.

At some point in the fall, perhaps through one of his wives, Savage got wind of a plot by the Yosemites to unite all the tribes of California, including their former enemies, thereby driving out the whites for good and keeping their horses and mules for themselves. Savage saw the proverbial writing on the wall. He called a series of councils and endeavored to explain to his fellow chieftains that the warpath was not, in fact, the path to continued wealth and prosperity. "The white men are more numerous than the

THE ATTACK.

HOSTILITIES BETWEEN INDIANS AND WHITE MEN INCREASED AS TIME WENT ON FROM *IN THE HEART OF THE SIERRAS* BY J. M. HUTCHINGS (1886)

242 YEARS IN THE SOUTHERN SIERRA

1775	Pedro Font sees "una gran sierra nevada"
1833	American fur trappers introduce malaria; 20,000 Sierra Indians die
1848	James Marshall discovers gold in Sutter's millrace
1850	California becomes 31st state; population of Los Angeles: 1,610
1855	Thomas Ayres sketches first picture of Yosemite Valley; total number of non-native tourists ever to reach Yosemite: 42
1856	The Lower Hotel, Yosemite's first permanent structure, is built
1859	Charles Leander Weed makes first photograph of Yosemite Valley; gold discovered at Bodie
1862	Abraham Lincoln signs Homestead Act, offering freehold title to 160-acre lots of undeveloped land in the West; smallpox epidemic further reduces native populations in California
1864	Lincoln grants Yosemite Valley and Mariposa Big Tree Grove to State of California to "be held for public use, resort, and recreation . . . inalienable for all time"
1869	Golden Spike driven on Transcontinental Railroad
1870	John Searles discovers borax near Mono Lake
1873	First ascent of Mount Whitney by three fishermen from Lone Pine
1878	Timber and Stone Act allows for purchase of 160-acre lots "unfit for farming"
1882	Construction begins on Tioga Road
1890	Benjamin Harrison creates Sequoia and General Grant National Parks, and declares Yosemite National Park (under state management); Nikola Tesla develops alternating current generators for long-distance transmission of electricity
1891	4th Cavalry Regiment, U.S. Army, arrives in Yosemite
1892	Sierra Club founded; John Muir first president
1893	Harrison establishes 13 million acre Sierra Forest Reserve
1897	Forest Management Act enacted
1900	First motorized vehicle in Yosemite; population of greater Los Angeles: 130,000; California native population reduced by 90 percent

MINE RUINS NEAR CA 6 CAT CONNOR

1905	Theodore Roosevelt creates Forest Service, Gifford Pinchot first chief; Congress withdraws 500 square miles of Yosemite from park status, including Devils Postpile; Los Angeles voters approve bond measure to bring Owens River to Los Angeles
1906	Antiquities Act authorizes President and Congress to declare national monuments; California returns Yosemite to federal government; San Francisco Earthquake
1907	State Legislature lists mountain lion as bountied predator
1908	San Francisco secures water rights to Hetch Hetchy
1909	World's first reinforced-concrete, multiple-arch dam at Hume Lake is constructed
1911	Howard Taft proclaims Devils Postpile a national monument
1913	Woodrow Wilson authorizes damming of Tuolumne at Hetch Hetchy; automobiles admitted to Yosemite Valley; Owens River water arrives in San Fernando Valley
1916	National Park Service created in order to "conserve the scenery and the natural and historic objects and the wildlife therein and to provide for the enjoyment of the same in such manner and by such means as will leave them unimpaired for the enjoyment of future generations"
1926	Sequoia National Park expanded to include Kern Canyon and Mount Whitney
1933	Herbert Hoover proclaims Death Valley a national monument; Franklin Roosevelt creates Civilian Conservation Corps
1934	Taylor Grazing Act allows granting of permits on public land for grazing, fences, reservoirs, and other improvements; Tuolumne River water arrives in San Francisco
1938	Dave McCoy lands a Forest Service permit to run a rope tow up McGee Mountain, sells his Harley for $85 to buy equipment
1940	Roosevelt creates Kings Canyon National Wilderness Park
1941	Water from Mono Basin reaches Los Angeles
1942	Dave McCoy moves his rope tow to Mammoth Mountain
1946	Bureau of Land Management created 1950; Population of Los Angeles: 2 million
1955	Annual visitation to Yosemite reaches 10,000
1963	California becomes most populous state in the Union 1964; Lyndon B. Johnson signs Wilderness Act
1965	Cedar Grove and Tehipite Valley added to Kings Canyon National Park

HORIZON AIR (NOW ALASKA AIR) BEGAN REGULAR COMMERCIAL AIR SERVICE BETWEEN MAMMOTH LAKES AND LAX IN 2009 BRAD PEATROSS, MMSA

1968	Wild and Scenic Rivers Act signed into law; 600,000 acres of Sequoia-Kings Canyon designated "natural fire zone"
1969	National Environmental Policy Act (NEPA) enacted to "encourage productive and enjoyable harmony between man and his environment"; three-week, 25-foot storm cycle buries Mammoth's Main Lodge
1971	Congress passes Wild Free-Roaming Horse and Burro Act; Governor Ronald Reagan signs moratorium on hunting mountain lions
1972	Governor Ronald Reagan, on a 100-animal pack trip out of Red's Meadow, vows to oppose the building of a Trans-Sierra Highway from Mammoth to Fresno
1973	Endangered Species Act enacted
1976	Mining in the Parks Act enacted; Homestead Act repealed
1978	Mineral King added to Sequoia National Park
1980	Yosemite General Management Plan drafted: "The ultimate goal of the National Park Service is to remove all private vehicles from Yosemite Valley"
1983	California Supreme Court rules Mono Basin water diversion a violation of public trust
1984	Yosemite named World Heritage Site; under California Wilderness Act, 89 percent of Yosemite designated wilderness; Town of Mammoth Lakes incorporated
1986	Bighorn sheep reintroduced in Lee Vining Canyon
1990	California Wildlife Protection Act enacted
1994	Desert Protection Act enacted: Death Valley becomes a national park; Saline Valley annexed
1996	4.2 million people visit Yosemite
2000	Bill Clinton designates Giant Sequoia National Monument; population of greater Los Angeles: 16 million
2005	Dave McCoy sells controlling interest in Mammoth Mountain Ski Area to Starwood Capital for $365 million
2008	Forensic testing suggests possible new Manson grave sites at Barker Ranch in Death Valley National Park, but no remains are found; American pika denied endangered species protection; Hans Florine and Yuji Hirayama set new world speed record up 2,900-foot Nose on El Cap in 2 hours, 43 minutes, 33 seconds; regular commercial air service begins between LAX and Mammoth Lakes-Yosemite Airport
2009	Barack Obama signs Omnibus Public Lands Act into law, providing wilderness designation to 85,000 acres in Sequoia-Kings Canyon National Park and tens of thousands more acres in Mono County and in the White Mountains, plus wild and scenic river designation for sections of the Upper Owens River and the Amargosa River
2010	Federal government lifts restrictions on carrying concealed and loaded guns in national parks, though it remains illegal to fire them; more than 33 million viewers watch at least one episode of the Ken Burns television series, *The National Parks: America's Best Idea*
2013	Devil's Hole Pupfish count dips to 35
2015	Yosemite National Park celebrates its 100th anniversary; Dean Potter dies in an attempted (illegal) wingsuit flight from Taft Point to Yosemite Valley; Scotty's Castle suffers major damage in storm that delivers 3 inches of rain and hail in 5 hours
2016	Aramark (ARMK) takes over exclusive 15-year, $2-billion concessionaire contract to provide hospitality services at Yosemite National Park including lodging, food and beverage, retail, recreational and transportation services; historic names Ahwahnee, Curry Village, Yosemite Lodge, Badger Pass, and Wawona changed due to trademark dispute with former concessioner Delaware North
2017	Aspen Skiing Company and KSL purchase Mammoth Resorts

wasps and the ants," he explained, according to Dr. Lafayette Bunnell, who would later accompany Savage into what would then be named the Yosemite Valley. "If the Indians make war on the white men, every tribe will be exterminated; not one will be left."

Savage took his friend José Juarez, various other tribal leaders, and probably a wife or two downriver from Stockton to San Francisco in order to show them the considerable riches, technology, and population of the people they might have wished, in their wildest dreams, to drive out. (And also to put some of his valuables into storage.) With the notorious James D. Savage as their guide, the Indians drank and gambled, shopped and went to shows, witnessed the celebrations attendant on California's newfound statehood, and toured the city. According to Bunnell, the Indians were impressed by these urban tribes, with their "great high hats" and sticks for walking with, "even on a smooth road," and the way they drove poor, ragged gold diggers out of the city with clubs.

"They are not like the tribe that dig gold in the mountains," José explained to his people upon return to the foothills. "They will not help the gold diggers if the Indians make war against them." Savage's station on the Fresno was the first to be sacked, his employees promptly, as Bunnell put it, "filled with arrows." The Mariposa store was next, "plundered and burned," with three men left dead or dying, and Savage's wives carried off upriver "by their own people." A trader by the name of Cassady and four other white men were reported murdered down on the San Joaquin. In Kaweah country, near Visalia, a company of five adventurers, having refused to pay a tribute demanded by some local tribesmen, found themselves suddenly "surrounded by yelling demons." Of the five, three were killed outright, another skinned alive; the last, his arm shattered by an arrow (later amputated), escaped only "by the fleetness of his horse."

On January 6, 1851, Savage guided Sheriff James Burney and a small band of volunteers up the Fresno in pursuit of his old friends, the two Josés. "No dog can follow a trail like he can," one of the volunteers wrote of Savage. "No horse can endure half so much. He sleeps but little, can go days without food, and can run a hundred miles in a day and night over the mountains and then sit and laugh for hours over a campfire as fresh and lively as if he had just been taking a little walk for exercise." In a matter of days, they had surprised several hundred Indians at their *rancheria*, torched the wigwams, and in the ensuing chaos shot King Joseph and 23 of his men dead.

Savage was thereafter appointed head of a rough band of 200 volunteer Indian fighters, assembled by proclamation of the Governor and known as the Mariposa Battalion. "This battalion was a body of hardy resolute pioneers," wrote one of its more prominent members, Dr. Lafayette Bunnell. "Many of them had seen service, and had fought their way against the Indians across the plains; some had served in the war with Mexico and been under military discipline." By mid-March, they had succeeded in convincing the majority of the foothill tribes to sign agreements with the U.S. Indian Commissioners, thus consigning themselves to reservations on the lower Fresno and Kings Rivers.

The so-called Yosemites—a ragtag band of Eastern Monos, Paiutes, and Ahwahneechee with a recalcitrant figure by the name of Tenaya as their chief—remained at large. And so, late in the day on March 19, in rain turning to snow, Savage, with two companies, began a long march over the hill from Mariposa to what is now Wawona. The snow on the ridge was 4 feet deep. At the edge of a meadow where today, in summer, there is a lovely golf course, they surprised and captured an encampment of Savage's former employees and in-laws. By the time the storm let up a few days later, Tenaya and 72 of his tribesmen were under guard and on their way to Fresno. Savage and some of his men pressed on, along a thin trail where the Wawona Road now runs, to see this valley they had heard so much about.

Ralph Waldo Emerson wrote of Yosemite that it was "the only spot that I have ever found that came up to the brag." It was magic hour on March 25, 1851—perfect timing—when the party came into full view of the 3,300-foot-tall granite face now known as El Capitan, or simply El Cap. Bunnell, for one, forgot whatever rancor he had previously been harboring toward the natives. "None but those who have visited this most wonderful valley," he wrote later, "can even imagine the feelings with which I looked upon the view that was there presented . . . and as I looked, a peculiar exalted sensation seemed to fill my whole being, and I found my eyes in tears with emotion."

Around the campfire that night, at the base of Bridalveil Fall, conversation turned to the naming of the valley—"the grandest that had ever yet been looked upon." A number of suggestions were put forward, most having some association with either God or the devil. It was Bunnell, by his own account, who suggested that the place be named Yo-sem-i-ty, "as it was suggestive, euphonious, and certainly American; that by so doing, the name of the tribe of Indians which we met leaving their homes in this valley, perhaps never to return, would be perpetuated."

Tenaya and some of his people, having eluded their escort before reaching the Fresno, did in fact manage, for the time being, to skip back to the valley they knew as Ahwahnee (a word later trademarked by Delaware North Companies, meaning "mouth of the bear" or "gaping mouth" or simply "mouth"). Savage spent the rest of the season working with the commissioners, trying to secure half-decent terms for the defeated tribes. A second expedition, in May, led by one of Savage's captains, resulted in the

TENAYA LAKE AND THE TIOGA ROAD

THE LAST GRIZZLY

When Frémont came down to the lower Merced in 1844, he found the place downright "crowded" with big mammals: elk, deer, wild horses, and bears of one kind or another. "Along the rivers are frequent fresh tracks of the grizzly bear," he wrote, "which are unusually numerous in this country."

The California grizzly, or bruin, is thought to have been a unique subspecies of brown bear (*Ursus arctos horribilis*), perhaps the largest in the Lower 48. One particularly hefty specimen, shot in 1866 near a settlement later called Bear Valley (now Valley Center), is supposed to have stood taller than 8 feet and weighed 2,200 pounds. The Miwok word for "grizzly" is something like *Oo-soó-ma-te*, which for many years was confused with another word, *Yo-se-mi-te*, meaning, perhaps, "those who kill," in reference not to murderous bears but to unfriendly neighbors of the human kind. It was near Yosemite, in the spring of 1854, that James Capen "Grizzly" Adams is supposed to have captured his sidekick, his "firmest friend," Ben Franklin.

There may once have been as many as 15,000 grizzlies in California, ranging across the chaparral from the coastal lowlands to the foothills of the Sierra, up the Tuolumne and the Merced, the Kings and Kaweah, the Tule and the Kern. They ate mostly plants and berries (in vast quantities), but were also not averse to the occasional easy piece of meat. In the mixed conifer belts along the western slope, they shared the range with their smaller cousin, the California black bear (*Ursus americanus*), today the largest carnivore in the Sierra—and the best trained at ripping off car doors to get at coolers.

The symbol on the California flag is a grizzly. The beast grazing in a green-grass meadow in the billboard advertisements for a certain financial institution is a grizzly (probably photographed in Alaska). The mascots of UC Berkeley and UCLA: grizzlies.

The last wild grizzly in California is generally thought to have been shot in Fresno County in 1922 (others say it was Tulare). "But there was no proof to be had," says Susan Snyder, Head of Public Service at Berkeley's Bancroft Library and editor of *Bear in Mind: The California Grizzly* (Heyday, 2003), "and there were so many incongruities in the various versions of the story that it was never verified."

"Frequently seen in herds of 15 or 20 in number," Lansford Hastings wrote in 1845, claiming that at a distance they might easily be confused with buffalo, "their flesh is much admired by the Mexicans as food." The beast could be brought down soon enough, he explained, "with a good rifle [and] about 18 balls to the pound." Spanish and Mexican vaqueros made high sport of roping them, dragging them to market, and pitting them against enraged bulls.

With the rush for gold came a great influx of men with guns—and with a widespread taste for killing bears. George Nidever, "a hunter bold was he," traveling companion of the likes of

---

shooting in the back of Tenaya's youngest son ("while trying to escape," writes Bunnell) and the subsequent recapture of Tenaya himself on the shores of the lake that would thereafter bear his name.

The battalion was decommissioned on July 1.

After much pleading and cajoling and promising to be good, Tenaya was allowed, with some of his people, to return once again to his valley. But the following spring he was up to his old tricks, attacking a group of prospectors, killing two. In June, a detachment of regular infantry, under a Lt. Tredwell Moore, chased the old chief and some of his men across Tuolumne Meadows as far as Bloody Canyon, where, failing to make their quarry, they found instead some "promising" ore deposits.

As might have been expected, there was a vociferous number of white folks in the foothills—squatters, traders, miners—who felt that the federal government, with Savage as consultant, had overstepped its bounds in giving land to the Indians. Pressure

THE CALIFORNIA GRIZZLY FROM *IN THE HEART OF THE SIERRAS* BY J. M. HUTCHINGS (1886)

Frémont and Walker, is said to have killed more than 200 grizzlies before the end of the 1850s. The advent of the repeater rifle by the end of the Civil War put the process into overdrive. The last known grizzly in Yosemite was shot in 1887. Its pelt resides at the University of California Berkeley. One big male grizzly named Monarch, captured at the request of William Randolph Hearst in 1889, died in a concrete pit in San Francisco's Golden Gate Park in 1911. Monarch is said to have been the model for the 1911 version of the state flag. His skin, stuffed and mounted, is displayed today at the California Academy of Sciences. His bones were last seen in a cardboard box at Berkeley's Museum of Vertebrate Zoology.

In 1924, the same year the last wild California gray wolf was supposed to have been captured, up in Lassen County, there were various unconfirmed sightings of a female grizzly and cub in what is now Sequoia National Park. "Even into the 1930s there were sightings," says Snyder, "but nothing proven with a dead bear."

A year-round resident of Fish Camp recently told a tale involving hikers on a disused trail on the south side of Yosemite (off the Jackson Road) and piles of bear scat "so big they had to vault over it." What was scaring off all the little bears? she wondered. This same woman also told of having seen a wolf one winter night not long ago—"the longest, leggiest coyote I ever saw"—beneath the streetlight in front of her house on CA 41. There were no other witnesses.

was put on the legislature to have them removed from the state entirely. Savage had rebuilt his trading post and been made Indian agent, but he found himself generally powerless to defend the treaties he'd helped to negotiate. Encroachments and general depredation continued apace. In one of various unfortunate incidents, as related in W. W. Elliott's *History of Fresno County* (1881), "one Major Harvey, first county judge of Tulare County, either hired or incited a lot of men who rushed into one of the *rancherias* on Kings River and succeeded in killing a number of old squaws."

Savage made his displeasure known. Harvey, in turn, dared Savage to pay him a visit down at the Kings River Agency. Savage found the offer impossible to resist, and on the morning of August 16, 1852, he rode, with witnesses, into the yard in front of Bill Campbell's store. The magistrate, an ex-employee of Savage appointed to the position by Harvey (and by whom Harvey was promptly acquitted), later testified as follows:

After they had got through their breakfast, Savage tied up his hair, rolled up his sleeves, took his six-shooter out of its scabbard and placed it in front of him, under the waistband of his pantaloons. He then walked into Campbell's store and asked Major Harvey if he could not induce him to call him a gentleman. Harvey told him that he had made up his mind and had expressed his opinion in regard to that, and did not think he would alter it. He knocked Harvey down and stamped upon him a little. They were separated by some gentlemen in the house, and Harvey got up. Savage says, "To what conclusion have you come in regard to my gentlemancy?" Harvey replies, "I think you are a damned scoundrel." Savage knocked Harvey down again. They were again separated by gentlemen present. As Harvey straightened himself onto his feet, he presented a six-shooter and shot Major Savage through the heart. Savage fell without saying anything. It was supposed that Harvey shot him twice after he was dead, every ball taking effect in his heart.

"The night he was buried," wrote another of Savage's associates, "the Indians built large fires, around which they danced, singing the while the mournful death chaunt [sic], until the hills around rang with the sound. I have never seen such profound manifestations of grief."

Tenaya spent the rest of the year hiding out on the east side with some of his Mono allies. Late in the summer of 1853—or so the story goes—he stole and ate some of their horses. Or he offended them in a game. Either way, the Monos responded by stoning him to death. Tenaya's body is said to have been burned according to tradition, and his charred remains were carried back to the valley to be mourned over for two weeks by what remained of his people. That fall, with the wily old renegade gone and nothing to fear but the weather (and perhaps the occasional grizzly), a prospector by the name of Leroy Vining led a party over Mono Pass to establish the mining camp that today bears his name.

ketched by Thos. Ayres, June 20, 1855—first ever taken.

GENERAL VIEW OF THE YO SEMITE VALLEY.

THOMAS AYRES'S FIRST SKETCH OF THE YOSEMITE VALLEY, DRAWN IN 1855 FROM *IN THE HEART OF THE SIERRAS* BY J. M. HUTCHINGS (1886)

The summer of 1855 brought an enterprising Englishman by the name of James Mason Hutchings with a pair of Indian guides and the first party of tourists to the Yosemite Valley. Among them was Thomas Ayres, landscape artist, who, from what is now known as Old Inspiration Point, off the Wawona Road, sketched the first picture of the Yosemite Valley. Three other parties made their way into the valley that season, including Galen Clark, who would become the valley's first official custodian; the Mann brothers, who the following year would begin construction on the toll trail now known as the Wawona Road; and yet another writer, a preacher, a painter, and a magazine editor.

"At the close of 1855," wrote Sierra climbing pioneer and historian Francis Farquhar, "the total tourist travel to Yosemite had reached 42. Fifty years later the annual number reached 10,000; a century later one million; and in the year 1961 a million and a half visitors came to Yosemite." The high-water mark came in 1996, with 4.2 million visitors. By 2006, total visitation had declined to just 3,242,644—down nearly 25 percent from a decade earlier.

Some blamed video games and the Internet; others pointed to high gas prices and a $20 entrance fee (it was $5 in 1996). While Park Service officials scratched their heads and enjoyed a brief reprieve from trying to sort out contentious and long-standing issues of traffic and parking, they went for a hike up Half Dome with FOX News to prove the park was still safe and enjoyable. By the time the waterfalls were flowing again in the spring of 2010, more than 33 million viewers worldwide had made it through at least one episode of the Ken Burns television series, *The National Parks: America's Best Idea,* and annual visitation to Yosemite was once again on track to surpass 4 million.

TRANSPORTATION

Good and substantial wagons should always be selected, and however firm and staunch they may appear, they should, invariably, be particularly examined, and repaired, before leaving the States.
—Lansford W. Hastings, *The Emigrants' Guide to Oregon and California*, 1845

When young Samuel Langhorne Clemens set out overland to see the far West in 1861, the route consisted mainly of a "hard, level road," pounded out by more than a decade of heavy wagon trains bound for California. From St. Louis it was six days by steamboat up the Missouri, followed by 20 more alternately inside and on top of a six-horse stage, "swinging and swaying" across the landscape. Every 10 miles the driver stopped to change horses.

Passengers were allowed no more than 25 pounds of baggage each: "no stovepipe hats nor patent-leather boots, nor anything else to make life calm and peaceful." The future Mark Twain and his companions shared the coach with great stacks of mail, "the heft of it for the Injuns," explained the driver, "which is powerful troublesome 'thout they get plenty of truck to read."

Ten years later, lamented Twain, the same journey could have been made in the sumptuous luxury of one of "Pullman's hotels on wheels," downing Krug by the bumper and feasting on garden vegetables and pan-seared antelope steak while out the window the Great American Desert unfurled like an exotic *tableau vivant* at 30 miles an hour. These days, one can still get from St. Louis to Reno by rail, via Chicago, in about 60 hours, give or take 10. But the menu—braised beef, herbed cod fillets, tricolor tortellini, and so on—is not quite what it used to be.

In the spring of 1868, John Muir preferred to go "afoot" from San Francisco to Yosemite.

But he could have spared his boot heels aboard one of the many paddle-wheel steamers that in those days regularly plied the San Joaquin as far upriver as Merced. Muir's onetime employer, J. M. Hutchings, in one of the first and most influential tourist guidebooks to Yosemite, *In the Heart of the Sierras* (1886), described no fewer than seven different routes into the valley, two of which could be reached by steamboat, "all of which can now be traveled by rail and coach to the door of each hotel there."

Alas, the glory days of public transportation in California have long passed. These days, for better or worse, a journey to the southern Sierra Nevada will generally involve loading up an automobile with gear and provisions, and, from the urban center of one's choice, hitting the road. From the northern fringes of Los Angeles one can strike out across the Mojave on good, fast blacktop, and in three or four hours be napping in the shade of a giant sequoia or soaking one's feet in snowmelt at the south fork of the Kern. An easy half-day's drive from the Bay Bridge—across the San Joaquin and the southern end of the Mother Lode country—brings one to the gates of Yosemite. The international airports at Reno and Fresno offer daily flights from as far afield as Shanghai, Sydney, Frankfurt, and Orlando—and the usual fleet of rental vehicles for that last sinuous leg from the tarmac to the woods. Travelers making their way from Sin City can, with a credit card and a driver's license, procure a late-model Ferrari convertible with comprehensive collision insurance and a 3.6-liter V-8; have lunch poolside at Furnace Creek in Death Valley; and in the evening be seated before a campfire in the folds of Mount Whitney, listening to the cooling of the engine.

✳ By Air

The only commercial flights into and out of the High Sierra are by sturdy turboprop Q400 to and from the tiny Mammoth Lakes Yosemite Airport (MMH) (www.visitmammoth.com/fly-mammoth-lakes), right in the very heart of the vast region covered by this book. There are a handful of regular daily flights during the ski season from LAX and SFO, and one daily from LAX in summer. Also try inexpensive seasonal charter flights from Burbank on JetSuiteX. Flying into the upper Owens Valley from over the Southern Sierra is spectacular and wonderfully convenient—you walk right out onto the tarmac in the shadow of Mount Morrison—when the weather's clear and the wind is calm. Otherwise, be prepared

CAMPING AT STONEMAN MEADOW, SPRING 1927 COURTESY NPS, YNP

to glimpse the runway from above and then end up at some other airport hundreds of miles from your point of departure. If you're coming from outside California or Nevada and can't make the schedules work, book a flight to one of the following airports, download a good audiobook, and secure ground transportation. Reno is the easiest and closest dependable airport to the east side of the range, Fresno and Sacramento to the west side. Las Vegas is less than two hours' drive from Death Valley.

Bakersfield-Meadows Field (BFL) (3701 Wings Way; 661-391-1800; www.meadows field.com). Located 93 miles from Sequoia's Ash Mountain Entrance; 60 miles to Kernville. Meadows Field serves a variety of daily domestic flights on United and American. Car rental: **Avis** (661-392-4160), **Budget** (661-399-2367), **Hertz** (661-832-9005), **National** (661-393-2068).

Burbank/Bob Hope (BUR) (2627 N. Hollywood Way; 818-840-8840; www.bob hopeairport.com). The locals' favorite Los Angeles airport, quaint plein-air baggage carousels, easiest in and out, $10/day economy parking, easiest overland access from L.A. to the Sierra and points north. Alaska, American, Delta, JetBlue, SeaPort, Southwest, and United. JetSuiteX flights to Mammoth leave from Hangar 2. Eleven on-site rental car agencies.

Fresno-Yosemite (FAT) (5175 E. Clinton Way; 559-621-4500; www.flyfresno.com). Closest international airport to the Sierra Nevada, with Guadalajara, Mexico being the only international connection: 53 miles to Kings Canyon; 63 miles to Yosemite. Aeromexico, Alaska, Allegiant, American, Continental, Delta, United, Volaris. All major rental car agencies. Bus service to National Parks: **Big Trees Transit** seasonal service to Kings Canyon ($15 round-trip; 800-325-7433; www.bigtreestransit.com); **Yosemite**

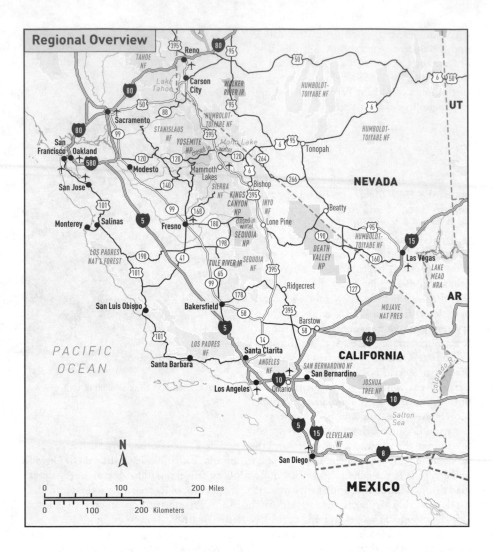

Regional Overview

Area Regional Transportation System (YARTS) daily to Yosemite Valley ($30 round-trip; 209-388-9589, 877-989-2787; www.yarts.com).

Las Vegas/McCarran (LAS) (5757 Wayne Newton Blvd.; 702-261-5211; www.mccarran.com). The eighth busiest airport in North America: more than 28 airlines, more than one hundred domestic and international destinations. Shopping, dining, slot machines, free Wi-Fi. Booming, all-pervasive big-screen infotainment. Easy in and out, plus free long-term parking and ground transportation courtesy of most major casino hotels. For the historic '49er approach to the Sierra, it's 121 speed miles to Furnace Creek (The Oasis); 250 miles to the Whitney Portal; 350 miles to Yosemite (in summer). All major rental car agencies.

Los Angeles (LAX) (1 World Way; 855-463-5252; www.lawa.org). Third busiest in North America; seventh in the world. With 75 million passengers annually, 742 daily nonstop flights, 64 airlines, nine terminals, fewer than 25,000 parking spaces for automobiles (only 145 for airplanes), and chronic construction, the place tends to be quite the circus. Traffic on the tarmac is matched only by that on the freeways. Lines to get

THE GRAND TOUR DE SIERRA: BADWATER TO BRIDALVEIL AND BACK

With a hard-wearing (and/or disposable) private vehicle, at least 3 weeks' free time (to allow for some moments outside the car), plenty of gas money, water, decent tires, a cooler full of cold beverages and picnic supplies, and an extensive archive of soundtrack music, the hardiest of modern travelers, by way of introduction to the place, may wish to undertake an epic, 3,000-mile, figure-eight circumnavigation. From Vegas, for example, one can follow the pioneers' route to Badwater; over the Panamints and Townes Pass to Owens Lake; south to Pearsonville, hubcap capital of the world; west over the Los Angeles Aqueduct to Sherman Pass; down to the Main Fork of the Kern; up over the Great Western Divide Highway to Springville by way of the George Bush Tree; from Three Rivers to the Giant Forest to the depths of Kings Canyon, out by CA 180 to Fresno (with a side trip via the McKinley Grove of Big Trees to Mono Hot Springs and Florence Lake); then north on CA 41 to Wawona, the Yosemite Valley (another side trip to Groveland and Hetch Hetchy); thence over Tioga Pass to Mono Lake, June Lake, Mammoth Lakes, Bishop, Westgard Pass, and the Bristlecone Pine Forest, home of the oldest living things on the planet and hands down the best view of the Sierra Nevada; thence to return to Vegas via Scotty's Castle (check closure updates), Salsberry Pass, and Shoshone. This same route can also be tapped into, with variations, from Los Angeles, San Francisco, or Reno. It cannot be done in winter. But in spring, if timed right (and depending on the season's snowfall), you can catch the last days of the season at the Inn at Death Valley (before May 15), see the Yosemite waterfalls in full glory, and also possibly make the opening of Tioga Pass back to the east side. Consider it a challenge.

OWENS VALLEY SCENIC BYWAY, CA 395 CAT CONNOR

THE FASTEST WAY TO THE INN AT DEATH VALLEY

through security often stretch beyond the terminal doors and along the curb. It's no wonder locals prefer to spend the extra few dollars to fly in and out of Burbank (or Ontario). The best way to escape is by way of at least one daily 50-minute Alaska Airlines (www.alaskaair.com) flight to **Mammoth Yosemite Airport (MMH)**. Otherwise, grab a rental car and head up I-405 north to I-5. It's 220 miles to Lone Pine or Three Rivers. **Escape Campervans** (877-270-8267, 310-672-9909; www.escapecampervans .com) has a location adjacent to the airport.

✪ **Mammoth Yosemite (MMH)** (1200 Airport Rd., Mammoth Lakes; http://www .visitmammoth.com/fly-mammoth-lakes). The latest round of commercial air service into Mammoth Lakes began in the fall of 2008 and has expanded and contracted ever since. At the time of this writing, **Alaska Airlines** (www.alaskair.com) was operating daily 74-seat twin-engine turboprop flights to and from LAX year-round, with expanded service during ski season. JetSuiteX (www.jetsuite.com) offered reasonably-priced seasonal charter flights from Burbank. The terminal is 6 easy miles from downtown Mammoth Lakes, and less than a mile across the sagebrush from the blueribbon trout waters of Hot Creek. Hassle-free security processing, free Wi-Fi, snack vending machines, and jaw-dropping views of Mount Morrison from the waiting room. Overnight airport parking is $8. Free shuttles are available from all major hotels. Car rental: **Enterprise** (760-924-1094) and **Hertz** (760-934-2271); cab service: **Mammoth Taxi** (760-934-8294 or 760-924-TAXI; www.mammoth-taxi.com), **Mammoth Cabs** (760-924-2227, 760-934-2227; www.mammothlakescabs.com).

Oakland (OAK) (1 Airport Dr.; 510-563-3300; www.oaklandairport.com). The friendlier, cheaper alternative to SFO, and on the side of the bay closer to Yosemite—173 road miles from the tarmac to the Ahwahnee. John Muir first walked from here to Yosemite in 1868. Alaska, Allegiant, Azores, Boutique, British Airways, Delta, Hawaiian, Jet-Blue, Norwegian, Southwest, Spirit, Volaris. Easy BART connections to San Francisco. All major car rental agencies and **Jucy RV** (800-650-4180; www.jucyusa.com).

WINTER TRAVEL IN THE SIERRA

It was snowing hard when Stacy Stotko and her daughter Brittany set out from Bishop for their home in Crowley, 35 miles away. It was New Year's Day, 2006. They were trying to find their way to Lower Rock Creek Road, an alternative to US 395, but they became disoriented in the blowing snow. Then they got stuck. Three days later, "January 4 at approximately 7:45 AM," according to the Mono County Sheriff Search and Rescue log, "the vehicle was located by search aircraft in Inyo County in the Pine Creek drainage at about the 7,500-foot level, partially buried in fresh snow." Stacy was in the car—alive. Her daughter, she explained, had set out the previous morning for help. "On January 5 Brittany was located approximately a half-mile from the vehicle and had apparently succumbed to hypothermia. She had left the vehicle wearing light clothing and had waded through 2 to 3 feet of fresh snow."

Lesson: The Sierra Nevada is no place to get caught unprepared. Check road conditions before setting out, and stay abreast of weather forecasts. Carry winter clothing, including hats, gloves, and boots, and carry chains for your tires. Know that there are times—i.e., when a big, wet, winter storm cycle comes crashing in from the North Pacific—when it is most prudent to find someplace warm and stay put.

THE OLD BADGER PASS SKI LODGE, YOSEMITE NATIONAL PARK, MARCH 6, 1969 NORMAN G. MESSINGER, COURTESY NPS, YNP

Ontario (ONT) (2500 E. Airport Dr.; 909-937-2700; www.flyontario.com). L.A.'s newest, fanciest commuter airport. Two hundred miles to Lone Pine; 251 miles to Furnace Creek. Aeromexico, Alaska, American, Delta, Southwest, United, Volaris. All major car rental agencies.

Reno-Tahoe (RNO) (2001 E. Plumb Ln.; 775-328-6400; www.renoairport.com). After Mammoth-Yosemite, Reno is the airport of choice for east-side destinations from Tioga and Tuolumne Meadows to Mammoth Lakes and Bishop. Easy in and out; 140 mostly scenic miles to the shores of Mono Lake. Slow going through the stoplights of Carson

CLIMATE DATA

Average monthly high and low temperatures in Fahrenheit. Average precipitation in inches.

YOSEMITE / SIERRA CLIMATE CHANGE

	YOSEMITE			LODGEPOLE (SEQUOIA)			MAMMOTH LAKES			LONE PINES (OWENS VALLEY)			DEATH VALLEY		
	Precip. (in.)	High	Low	Precip. (in.)	High	Low	Precip. (in.)	High	Low	Precip. (in.)	High	Low	Precip. (in.)	High	Low
January	6.2	49°	26°	9.5	38°	16°	4.9	40°	16°	1.2	54°	27°	0.3	66°	39°
February	6.1	55°	28°	8.6	41°	17°	4.1	40°	16°	1.0	59°	31°	0.5	74°	46°
March	5.2	59°	31°	7.3	44°	21°	2.6	45°	21°	0.4	65°	35°	0.3	81°	54°
April	3.0	65°	35°	3.4	49°	25°	1.4	49°	25°	0.2	72°	42°	0.1	90°	62°
May	1.3	73°	42°	1.4	58°	32°	1.3	60°	33°	0.2	82°	50°	0.1	100°	72°
June	0.7	82°	48°	0.6	68°	39°	0.6	70°	40°	0.1	91°	58°	0.1	109°	81°
July	0.4	90°	54°	0.5	75°	44°	0.5	78°	46°	0.2	97°	63°	0.1	116°	87°
August	0.3	90°	53°	0.3	75°	43°	0.4	77°	45°	0.2	95°	62°	0.1	114°	85°
September	0.9	84°	47°	1.3	69°	38°	0.5	71°	37°	0.3	88°	55°	0.2	106°	75°
October	2.1	74°	39°	2	58°	30°	1.2	61°	28°	0.1	77°	44°	0.1	93°	62
November	5.4	58°	31°	4.6	46°	23°	2.3	48°	21°	0.6	63°	34°	0.2	76°	48°
December	5.6	48°	26°	6.8	38°	16°	4.1	42°	16°	0.9	54°	27°	0.2	65°	38°
Annual	37.2			46.3			23.9			5.4			2.3		

City. Alaska, Allegiant, American, Delta, JetBlue, Southwest, United, Volaris. All major car rental agencies. Bus service to Lone Pine with stops along the Eastern Sierra four times per week via Eastern Sierra Transit Authority (ESTA) (760-872-1901, 800-922-1930; www.estransit.com).

Sacramento (SMF) (6900 Airport Blvd.; 916-929-5411; www.sacramento.aero/smf). SMF serves 33 nonstop destinations in the US and Mexico on ten major carriers 150 miles to Yosemite's Oak Flat Entrance. All major rental car agencies. No direct public transportation to Sierra national parks.

San Jose/Norman Y. Mineta (2077 Airport Blvd.; 408-392-3600; www.flysanjose.com). Silicon Valley's airport; 183 miles to the hotel formerly known as the Ahwahnee. On par with Oakland at about eleven million passengers annually. Named for the former mayor, former U.S. congressman, former transportation secretary under George W. Bush—the only Democrat ever to serve in the Bush cabinet—and the man who, on September 11, 2001, gave the historic order to ground all 4,546 civilian aircraft then in U.S. airspace. Aeromexico, Air Canada, Air China, Alaska, American, ANA, British Airways, Delta, Hainan, Hawaiian, JetBlue, Lufthansa, Southwest, United, Volaris. All major car rental agencies. 210 miles to Grant Grove.

San Francisco (SFO) (US 101; 800-435-9736; www.flysfo.com). In the 1968 movie *Bullitt*, Steve McQueen, playing the title character, chased the "real" Johnny Ross here across the runway, then shot him dead inside the terminal. Today it's the seventh busiest airport in North America, 21st in the world. Traffic is frequently brutal across the Bay Bridge in the direction of the Sierra; opt instead for the southern route across the San Mateo-Hayward Bridge. Forty-nine airlines. All major car rental agencies.

✳ By Rail

In 1927, according to that year's edition of *Rider's California*, the town of Stockton boasted three transcontinental railway terminals, two steamboat lines, and two different motorstage companies serving Yosemite. There were three separate rail spurs from Stockton to Merced (one for each company), whence in 3 hours and 40 minutes the traveler could make the final 78 miles to El Portal aboard the Yosemite Valley Railroad (YVRR). On the east side of the range, the Southern Pacific Railway continued to operate trains on a narrow-gauge spur as far as the depot at Laws, north of Bishop, until April 1960, and standard cars to Lone Pine until 1981. The YVRR bridge at Bagby burned down on August 21, 1945, six days after the surrender of Japan at the end of World War II. The railway was shut down three days later. Today the only functioning train in the Southern Sierra is a reconditioned steam-powered logging outfit called the **Yosemite Mountain Sugar Pine Railroad** (559-683-7273; www.ymsprr.com), which operates along a 4-mile tourist loop near Fish Camp on the south side of Yosemite.

Amtrak (1-800-USA-RAIL; www.amtrak.com). The *California Zephyr* runs on borrowed freight rails from Chicago to Emeryville, California. To access Mono Lake, Mammoth Lakes, and the Owens Valley, disembark at Reno, transfer to ESTA's Reno-Lone Pine service (www.estransit.com), or rent a car (see below). Westbound travelers to Yosemite transfer at Sacramento to Amtrak's **San Joaquin** line. The *San Joaquin* makes several daily runs back and forth between Bakersfield and Sacramento, and also between Bakersfield and Oakland's Jack London Square. Regular **YARTS** bus connections (see below) meet trains at Merced and run as far as the Yosemite Lodge, through Mariposa, Midpines—for those interested in staying at the **Yosemite Bug** (see Chapter 7)—and El Portal. Travel time between Oakland and Merced is 3 to 4 hours, delays notwithstanding. Merced to Yosemite, by bus, is another 3. An Amtrak bus from Hanford

BAGGAGE PLATFORM, YOSEMITE VALLEY RAILROAD, EL PORTAL, C. 1927 COURTESY NPS, YNP

station connects with the **Sequoia Shuttle** (see below), which in summer departs four times daily from Visalia. Private shuttles can also be arranged between the Hanford or Fresno Amtrak stations and Sequoia National Park.

❋ By Bus or Shuttle

Traveling to and/or around the Sierra by bus, especially on the east side, is an undertaking sure to enhance one's appreciation of California's pioneer heritage—and to make one hanker for a good pair of boots, a saddlebag full of hardtack, and a decent mule. Shuttle service within Yosemite and Sequoia National Parks, on the other hand, and within the town of Mammoth Lakes, has improved greatly in the past few years. There is no public transportation in Kings Canyon or Death Valley.

Eastern Sierra Transit Authority (ESTA) (760-872-1901 or 800-922-1930; www .estransit.com). One inter-regional bus makes a round-trip run from Lone Pine to the Reno Airport on Monday, Tuesday, Thursday, and Friday—northbound in the morning, southbound in the afternoon. Another runs southbound from Mammoth Lakes to Lancaster every Monday, Wednesday, and Friday for connections with the Lancaster **Metrolink** station (1-800-371-5465; www.metrolink trains.com). From Lancaster aboard Metrolink, one can make Union Station in downtown Los Angeles in high style for connections to San Diego, Santa Barbara, Flagstaff, Arizona, and beyond. From Union Station to LAX, transfer to the Union Station Flyaway Bus (866-435-9529; www.lawa.org/ flyaway), which runs every 30 minutes. Northbound connections from Union Station up the Owens River can be cobbled together in reverse. Shuttles are also available between Benton and Bishop and between Tecopa and Pahrump, as well as in-town and dial-a-ride services in Mammoth and Bishop.

Greyhound (1-800-231-2222; www.greyhound.com). Experience the last crumbling vestiges of what was once America's most romantic and economical means of running away from home—and then coming back. Daily departures from Los Angeles to Fresno (from $14; 5 to 6 hours), four each day from San Francisco to Merced (from $32; 4 hours). Free Wi-Fi on board. No service to Death Valley or along the east side of the Sierra.

Mammoth Lakes Transportation: ESTA also operates a fleet of free municipal buses and trolleys serving stops all across the town of Mammoth Lakes, from Old Mammoth to the Village, from the Lakes Basin to Main Lodge. Summer trolley service to the Lakes Basin includes bike shuttles. The Mammoth Mountain Bike Park operates a free mountain bike shuttle every half-hour from the Village to the mountain. From Main Lodge in summer, the mandatory shuttle to Reds Meadow, the upper San Joaquin River Valley, and Devils Postpile leaves every 20 to 30 minutes daily (fee). Buses are also available in summer to Whitmore pool.

Sequoia Shuttle (1-877-BUS-HIKE; www.sequoiashuttle.com). Shuttles run up the hill several times a day, seven days a week, from Memorial Day through Labor Day, from points in Visalia, Exeter, and Three Rivers to the Giant Forest Museum in Sequoia National Park ($15 round-trip, includes park entrance fee). Advance reservations are required; check website for schedule and details. From the Giant Forest Museum, free park shuttles run every 15 minutes from 8:00 AM to 6:30 PM to Moro Rock and Crescent Meadow, and to the Sherman Tree and Lodgepole Visitor Center. The purple line runs every 30 minutes between Lodgepole and the Wuksachi Lodge and Dorst Creek Campground. The orange line runs between the General Sherman Tree and Wolverton.

Sequoia Sightseeing Tours (559-561-4189; www.sequoiatours.com). Backcountry denizen Paul Bischoff and his wife, Becky, offer regular full-day van tours, year-round, of the major points of interest along Generals Highway in Sequoia National Park. Pickup and drop-off anywhere in Three Rivers. Private tours and custom hiker/back-packer/skier shuttle service by arrangement, as well as transportation to and from the

STILL AMONG THE MOST DEPENDABLE MEANS OF TRANSPORTATION

KITCHENS ON WHEELS

"Good walkers can go anywhere in these hospitable mountains without artificial ways," wrote Muir, the consummate rambler, who seems regularly to have reached transcendence with but a crust of bread and a ration of tea from his pockets. "But most visitors have to be rolled on wheels with blankets and kitchen arrangements." The advantages are obvious: the well-stocked fridge, the ice maker, the four-burner stove, the sink with running water, the lights, the air conditioner, the screen door, the awning, the Astroturf, the relatively comfortable bed with one's own linens on it. The disadvantages become clearer as the trip wears on: the long, slow, grinding climbs; the long, slow, grinding descents (there is no visit to these ranges that does not involve a gain and subsequent loss of multiple thousands of feet in elevation); the pileup of fellow travelers on one's rear bumper; the pervasive smell of toilet chemicals; the marriage-threatening maneuvers required to get parked and level at the end of a long day. Whatever savings there may be in food and lodging are more than made up for by the cost of fuel. Still, it's a big part of the American Dream, the same old American Dream that got James Reed of the Donner Party to build a two-story wagon for his family—the so-called "pioneer palace car."

YOSEMITE ON THE ROAD IN DEATH VALLEY

Maybe everyone has to try it—once.

CruiseAmerica RV Rental (800-671-8042 www.cruiseamerica.com). Locations in the Bay Area, Fresno, Bakersfield, and Southern California.

El Monte RV (800-337-2214; www.elmonterv.com). Locations in the Bay Area, Sacramento, Southern California, Las Vegas, and Reno. Locations in the Bay Area, Sacramento, Southern California, Las Vegas, and Reno. Locations in the Bay Area, Sacramento, Southern California, Las Vegas, and Reno. Locations in the Bay Area, Sacramento, Southern California, Las Vegas, and Reno.

Escape Campervans (877-270-8267, 310-672-9909; www.escapecampervans.com). Three campervan models, wacky technicolor paintjobs. Locations at LAX, San Francisco, and Las Vegas.

Jucy RV (800-650-4180; www.jucyusa.com). Green and purple minivans outfitted for camping. Locations in Los Angeles, Las Vegas, and at the Oakland Airport.

Outdoorsy (www.outdoorsy.co). Airbnb for RV rentals.

Road Bear RV (866-491-9853; www.roadbearrv.com). Locations in Las Vegas, Los Angeles, and San Francisco.

CAMPING TRAILER DELIVERY AND SETUP

Adventure in Camping (760-935-4890; www.adventureincamping.com). Reserve a campground in the Eastern Sierra and they'll bring the trailer to you.

A GREYHOUND NIGHT COACH ON A TEST RUN TO THE WAWONA TUNNEL IN 1932 COURTESY NPS, YNP

Hanford Amtrak station. Paul is also a backcountry instructor for the **Sequoia Field Institute** (see Chapter 6).

Yosemite Area Regional Transportation System (YARTS) (1-877 98-YARTS; www .yarts.com). Buses serve 100,000 riders annually via four separate routes into Yosemite Valley (with lots of stops along the way) from Merced (including Amtrak Station), Fresno, Sonora/Jamestown, and Mammoth Lakes (summer only). Check website for seasonal closures, routes, schedules, and fares. Some routes are very popular in summer as shuttles for hikers. Cost includes park entry fee. Bikes are allowed in storage compartments as space allows.

Yosemite Shuttle (209-372-0200; www.nps.gov/yose/planyourvisit/bus.htm) runs free hybrid buses every 10 to 20 minutes from 7 AM to 10 PM year-round, covering all major valley and village stops from Camp 4 to the day-use parking lot, Happy Isles, and Mirror Lake Junction. Another route, with buses running every half-hour (only in summer), serves the west valley, El Cap, and the Four Mile Trail. There are fee-based tours from Yosemite Valley to Tuolumne Meadows or Glacier Point in summer only. When the grove is open, a free shuttle has traditionally been available between Wawona and the Mariposa Grove (with shuttle riders guaranteed access to the grove even when the parking lot is full). In winter (December through March), there's a daily free shuttle from valley hotels to the old Badger Pass Ski Area (now called Yosemite Ski and Snowboard Area). Note: Park shuttles are popular and eminently useful tools for hikers interested in point-to-point rather than out-and-back treks, and they make a much better option than driving around and trying to find parking.

✳ By Car

The first summer of the twentieth century brought the first steam-powered "locomobile" chugging into Yosemite beneath the weight of one Oliver Lippincott, a 300-pound photographer from Los Angeles, and his driver/mechanic, Ed Russell. The contraption and much of the fuel it consumed had been shipped to Fresno by Southern Pacific Rail. Lippincott made a series of photographs of himself and his "horseless carriage": beneath the Wawona Tunnel Tree, at Mirror Lake, out on the famous overhanging rock at Glacier Point. "We hung on with tooth and nail while the camera was adjusted," he remarked afterward. "No picture was ever so long in being taken." The following summer, he sold copies of the photographs from a tent in Yosemite Valley. These days, the Sierra Nevada offers the automobile enthusiast some of the craziest, hairiest, best-engineered, most dramatic, and least congested roads in North America. The lazy drive up and back along the Merced River in Yosemite Valley is among the most scenic stretches of parkway in the world—especially in a convertible, in spring or autumn, when the crowds are elsewhere.

How much harm they may have done in the intervening century is, on the one hand, obvious, and on the other a matter of some considerable debate—and the subject of at least one major ongoing legal skirmish between the Park Service and various environmental groups. By 1980, ever-increasing automobile traffic—reportedly about a million vehicles on approximately 30 miles of roadway annually—was, according to the Park Service's General Management Plan, signed and finalized that year, "the single greatest threat to enjoyment of the natural and scenic qualities of Yosemite." The plan was unequivocal: "The ultimate goal of the National Park Service is to remove all private vehicles from Yosemite Valley."

Automobiles were not officially allowed into the park until 1913. John Muir, in his capacity as President of the Sierra Club, had been present at a National Parks conference the previous fall, at which the new machines had become a topic of heated debate. "All signs indicate automobile victory," he reported in a letter to Howard Palmer, Secretary of the American Alpine Club, "and doubtless, under certain precautionary restrictions, these useful, progressive, blunt-nosed mechanical beetles will hereafter be allowed to puff their way into all the parks and mingle their gas-breath with the breath of the pines and waterfalls, and, from the mountaineer's standpoint, with but little harm or good."

PAVE IT AND PAINT IT GREEN, YOSEMITE NATIONAL PARK IN THE MID-1960S © RONDAL PARTRIDGE, WWW .RONDALPARTRIDGE.COM

"The problem at Yosemite is not too many visitors," Interior Secretary Bruce Babbitt said 20 years later, in November 2000, delivering a 20-pound, six-volume, $441.7 million "final" Yosemite Valley plan—a plan that did not, incidentally, involve removing a single vehicle. "The problem is too damn many cars." (On a handful of occasions in the mid-1990s—at all-time peak visitation levels—the park was declared at capacity and the gates closed. "When the theater's full, they don't sell lap-space," Ansel Adams said. Otherwise, the notion of banning cars from the park, despite some successes in that direction at Zion and the Grand Canyon, has proven too ambitious or too

PETS

Dogs are tolerated in the national parks with certain restrictions. They're not allowed off-leash, on trails, off the pavement (except in campsites), in the backcountry, or in any lodging facilities run by Park Service concessionaires. You can't leave them unattended in your vehicle, in your motor home, or tied up at your campsite while you go for a hike, to the visitor center, or to the restroom. Leashes have to be less than 6 feet long. Interactions between dogs and wildlife tend to be less than congenial, so you might consider leaving them at home (see Chapter 8 for local kennel information). Some establishments outside the parks, like the Tenaya Lodge, Château du Sureau, the Westin Monache, or the Buckeye Tree Lodge are more accommodating. Dogs are allowed on and off trails anywhere in the national forests (when duly controlled by voice or leash and picked up after by their owners), including wilderness areas.

LEASHED IN SEQUOIA NATIONAL PARK BURKE GRIGGS

controversial to implement at Yosemite.) Park Service officials are today emphatic that ongoing efforts to reduce traffic congestion in Yosemite do not include reducing the number of cars allowed into the park.

The fact remains, as former Sierra Club president David Brower once pointed out: "Rarely does the number of cars in the valley exceed the capacity of the roads and parking." For the time being—and for the foreseeable future—the car seems likely to be America's conveyance of choice. And so for now visitors are "invited" to station their vehicles at their place of accommodation, or at the day-use parking lot near Yosemite Village, thereafter to seek alternative methods of transport—shuttle bus, beach cruiser, longboard, or on foot—to points around the valley and beyond.

⭐ MOST FORMIDABLE SCENIC MOUNTAIN BYWAYS

O n which to test the fortitude of one's engine, the efficacy of one's cooling system, the condition of one's brake pads, and one's (or one's passengers') general susceptibility to vertigo and/or motion sickness. And for some of the best through-windshield vistas in North America. Each of these roads is passable, except during or after adverse weather conditions, in a four-cylinder, two-wheel drive rental car. Each tends to be even more impressive/hair-raising going down than up.

CA 190 from Father Crowley Point to Panamint Springs, Chapter 3.
Titus Canyon Road from Leadfield to Scotty's Castle Road (one-way only), Chapter 3.
J41 (Sherman Pass) from Kennedy Meadows to the Kern River, Chapters 4 and 6.
CA 168 East (Ancient Bristlecone Scenic Byway) from Big Pine to the Patriarch Grove, Chapter 4.
Whitney Portal Road from Lone Pine to Whitney Portal, Chapter 4.
CA 120 East (Lee Vining Canyon Scenic Byway) from Tioga Pass to Lee Vining, Chapters 5 and 7.
Mineral King Road from CA 198 to Road's End, Chapter 6.
CA 198 (Generals Highway) from the Ash Mountain Entrance to the Giant Forest, Chapter 6.
CA 180 West (Kings Canyon Scenic Byway) from Hume Lake Junction to Road's End, Chapter 6.
CA 168 West (Sierra Heritage Scenic Byway) from Huntington Lake over Kaiser Pass to Mono
    Hot Springs, Chapter 6.
Beasore/Minarets Road (Sierra Vista Scenic Byway) from Bass Lake Road to Clover Meadow
    Station, then looping back to North Fork, Chapter 7.
CA 140 (Yosemite All-Weather Highway) from Midpines to El Portal, Chapter 7.
Big Oak Flat Road from Crane Flat to Valley View, Chapter 7.

THE VIEW FROM WHITNEY PORTAL ROAD CAT CONNOR

✳ Car Rental

A variety of fairly durable late-model vehicles can be hired from major companies at each of the airports listed above. Most offer "unlimited" mileage (always be sure to check the fine print for limitations) and competitive, deep-discounted weekly rates. Specialty vehicles (i.e., convertibles, sports cars, or four-wheel-drive SUVs), children's car seats, ski racks, and snow chains may be arranged with considerable advance notice (up to a month for smaller locations).

Deposits are not generally required on car rental reservations. Significant drop-off and per-mile charges apply for one-way rentals. Most credit card companies offer insurance coverage for rental cars; check yours to see if you can opt out of extra collision insurance charges.

Alamo (888-233-8749; www.alamo.com). BUR, FAT, LAS, LAX, OAK, RNO, SFO, SMF, SJC.

Avis (800-633-3469; www.avis.com). BFL, BUR, FAT, LAS, LAX, OAK, ONT, RNO, SFO, SMF, SJC.

Budget (800-218-7992; www.budget.com). BFL, BUR, FAT, LAS, LAX, OAK, ONT, RNO, SFO, SMF, SJC.

Dollar (800-800-4000; www.dollar.com). BUR, FAT, LAS, LAX, OAK, ONT, RNO, SFO, SMF, SJC.

Enterprise (1-800-266-9565; www.enterprise.com). BUR, FAT, LAS, LAX, MMH, OAK, ONT, RNO, SFO, SMF, SJC. Enterprise is the only reasonably-priced car rental agency with locations in the Eastern Sierra: at Mammoth (Mammoth Airport; 760-924-1094), Bishop (187 W. Line St.; 760-873-3704), and Ridgecrest/Inyokern (437 N. China Lake Blvd.; 760-384-2816). To arrange for a convertible or SUV at these locations (you will want four-wheel drive in winter), call at least a month in advance.

Fox (800-225-4369; www.foxrentacar.com). BUR, LAX, OAK, ONT, SFO, SJC.

Hertz (1-800-654-3131; www.hertz.com). BFL, BUR, FAT, LAS, LAX, MMH, OAK, ONT, RNO, SFO, SJC, SMF.

Midway (866-717-6802; www.midwaycarrental.com). BUR, LAX. Specialty cars, convertibles.

National (1-877-222-9058; www.nationalcar.com). BFL, BUR, FAT, LAS, LAX, OAK, ONT, RNO, SFO, SJC, SMF.

Payless (800-729-5377; www.paylesscar.com). BUR, FAT, LAS, LAX, OAK, ONT, RNO, SFO, SJC, SMF.

Thrifty (1-800-847-4389; www.thrifty.com). BUR, LAS, LAX, OAK, RNO, SFO, SJC.

✳ Distances and Driving Times

Approximate distances are listed in miles for the shortest possible paved route between two locations. When summer routes are shorter than the corresponding winter detour, the former is listed first. Note: Given the radical topography of the region and the great variety of roads, the shortest route cannot always be counted on to be the fastest.

Driving times are impossible to estimate with any degree of accuracy. One might, for example, manage an average 60 miles per hour (or more) on US 395 between Mojave and Lee Vining, give or take a stop light or two in Bishop, and the same on CA 99 from Bakersfield to Fresno, depending on the volume of traffic, while on the Mineral King Road or Generals Highway or up the Old Priest Grade from Chinese Camp behind a smoking diesel, one might not clear 20 miles in one long hour. On the expensively

SEASONAL ROAD CLOSURES

Tioga Pass (9,943 feet) closes for the winter with the first major snowfall (generally by mid-November)—followed promptly by the closures of Sherman, Sonora, and Ebbett's Passes. The east and west sides of the range become essentially cut off from each other until snow can be cleared in late spring. In winter, the only way to get from Lee Vining to the Yosemite Valley (in summer an easy hour's jaunt), other than on skis or snowshoes, is by way of an epic 6-to-10-hour journey around the High Sierra: to the south via Walker Pass (5,250 feet) and Bakersfield; or north by CA 88 over Carson Pass (8,650 feet) to Jackson and Gold Country. Walker Pass will the best option in iffy weather (and for those making their way from Lone Pine and points south). In anything truly inclement, one may have to press north all the way to Carson City (to US 50) or to Reno (I-80). When Walker shuts down—more likely due to rockfall in the lower Kern Canyon than snow or ice—the next option is Tehachapi (3,793 feet).

SHERWIN MEADOWS, MAMMOTH LAKES AARON HOROWITZ

Winter closures in Sequoia-Kings include the Mineral King Road, the Moro Rock/Crescent Meadow Road, the Crystal Cave Road (and the cave itself), Panoramic Point, Redwood Mountain Road, and the Kings Canyon Scenic Highway (CA 180) from Hume Lake Junction to Cedar Grove. Generals Highway and CA 180 to Grant Grove are plowed and open all season, weather permitting.

All major roads into Yosemite from the west side are plowed in winter. Glacier Point Road is closed beyond the Badger Pass Ski Area and maintained, conditions permitting, for cross-country skiing.

ROAD CONDITIONS

Caltrans: 1-800-427-ROAD; www.quickmap.dot.ca.gov
Death Valley: www.nps.gov/deva/planyourvisit/conditions.htm
Sequoia-Kings: 559-565-3341; www.nps.gov/seki/planyourvisit/conditions.htm
Yosemite: 209-372-0200; www.nps.gov/yose/planyourvisit/conditions.htm

A NOTE ON TIRE CHAINS

Buy them at lower elevations (where they tend to be cheaper), and buy them before the storm. Steel chains are more durable and easier to work with, while cable chains are smoother-driving, slightly cheaper, and more likely to break. Either way, make sure they fit on your tires. Know whether your vehicle is front-or rear-wheel drive and install the chains accordingly (on the wheels that do the driving). Practice putting them on before you get to the snow, and carry them at all times.

Chains (or snow tires) are often required by law—i.e., when conditions get hairy—even for vehicles with four-wheel drive. P.S. When the roads are dry, you can take them off.

YOESMITE/SIERRA MILEAGE CHART

	Bakersfield	Fresno	Furnace Creek	Las Vegas	Lone Pine	Los Angeles	Mammoth	Reno	Sacramento	San Bernardino	San Diego	San Francisco	San Jose	Sequoia-Kings	Yosemite
Bakersfield		111	247	285	168	112	268	407	277	175	236	284	241	115	169
Fresno	111		357	396	278	215	189,365	299	164	278	339	185	151	57	60
Furnace Creek	247	357		121	107	288	207	373	435	244	350	459,532	452,491	361	240,415
Las Vegas	285	396	121		231	271	308	448	562	226	332	571	530	399	353,453
Lone Pine	168	278	107	231		209	100	259	329	191	297	352,453	345,412	282	133
Los Angeles	112	215	288	271	209		309	477	387	63	124	383	340	223	305
Mammoth	268	189,365	207	308	100	309		167	236	291	397	259,328	252,316	264,382	41
Reno	407	299	373	448	259	477	167		132	451	556	219	247	355	150
Sacramento	277	164	435	562	329	387	236	132		450	511	91	124	225	140
San Bernardino	175	278	244	226	191	63	291	451	450		109	446	403	280	368
San Diego	236	339	350	332	297	124	397	556	511	109		507	464	343	429
San Francisco	284	185	459,532	571	352,453	383	259,328	219	91	446	507		44	242	163
San Jose	241	151	452,491	530	345,412	340	252,316	247	124	403	464	44		208	165
Sequoia-Kings	115	57	361	399	282	223	264,382	355	225	280	343	242	208		113
Yosemite	169	60	240,415	353,453	133	305	41	150	140	324	429	163	156	113	

engineered Tioga Road there is a temptation to go faster than one should. Potential hazards include but are not limited to abrupt, unsignaled turnouts; cyclists; bear crossing; deer crossing; squirrel crossing; wilderness-dazed backpacker crossing; precipitous cliffs; and, of course, park rangers with radar guns.

FROM LAS VEGAS AND POINTS EAST

There are several perfectly reasonable ways to get from Vegas to Death Valley: north by US 95 to junctions at Lathrop Wells (NV 373 south to Death Valley Junction), Beatty (NV 374 to Furnace Creek and Stovepipe Wells), and, depending on road conditions, Scotty's Junction (NV 267 via Grapevine Canyon to Scotty's Castle)—the last affording, as W. A. Chalfant once put it, "the unusual experience . . . of driving into the mountains on a downhill slope most of the way." The most direct route—and on many levels the most interesting—follows the Blue Diamond Highway (NV 160) west from southeast Las Vegas, past Red Rock Canyon to Pahrump (gateway to the Brothel Art Museum, self-proclaimed "oldest tourist attraction in southern Nevada"), then due west across Ash Meadows Road and the Amargosa Valley to Death Valley Junction.

In summer, the shortest route to Yosemite is by US 95 northeast to Tonopah, west on US 6 to Benton, and finally CA 120 across to US 395. The trip to Mammoth Lakes is shorter by about 30 miles, taking NV 266 east from US 95 through Oasis and over Westgard Pass (7,271 feet) to Big Pine, but not necessarily any quicker than through Benton and across Long Valley on the Benton Crossing Road (open all winter to provide emergency escape in case of earthquake or volcanic eruption).

From Vegas to Sequoia, or to Yosemite in winter, the fastest route is most likely the least direct: south on I-15 to Barstow, east on CA 58 to Tehachapi and Bakersfield, and then north on CA 99.

FROM RENO

Take US 395 south through Carson City, Minden, and Gardnerville. At Topaz Lake, on the California-Nevada line, things start to get scenic, up the West Walker River to Sonora Junction, over Devil's Gate (7,519 feet) to Bridgeport, over Conway Summit (8,143 feet) to Mono Lake, Tioga, and the high Eastern Sierra.

FROM GREATER LOS ANGELES AND POINTS SOUTH

The two main routes from downtown Los Angeles to Furnace Creek (The Oasis)—up CA 14 and US 395 through Olancha or by I-15 via Baker to CA 127—are roughly equidistant. The former offers considerably less traffic, a glimpse of the airplane graveyard at Mojave, views of the southern promontory of the Sierra Nevada, the Inyo Range, and a heady crossing of the Panamints. The latter affords a snapshot of the "World's Largest Thermometer" at Baker and a sense of the historic '49er approach from the east. A third and considerably more desolate route approaches from the south, from Ridgecrest through Trona and up the salt flats of the Panamint Valley. (See Chapter 3 for descriptions of the various access routes into the valley.) Consider approaching by one route and leaving by another.

CA 14 and US 395 are the major arteries for access from points south to the Eastern Sierra, Mammoth Mountain and Mono Lake, and the Tuolumne Meadows region of Yosemite National Park (in summer). For fastest access to Sequoia National Park, take I-5 north to CA 99 to Visalia and CA 198. CA 65 north from Bakersfield, through

THE SOUTHERN SIERRA CONTAINS ONE OF THE TWO LARGEST ROADLESS AREAS IN THE LOWER 48, MOST OF WHICH IS
ACCESSIBLE ONLY ON FOOT OR BY PACK ANIMAL

Porterville, is considerably more scenic—through the oil fields and fruit orchards—but
also more time-consuming. The fastest route to Yosemite follows CA 41 due north from
Fresno, through Oakhurst and Wawona.

FROM SAN FRANCISCO/OAKLAND

The fastest route from the Bay Area to Yosemite—and to the Eastern Sierra and Death
Valley in the summer—follows I-580 to I-205, with a slight jog on I-5 to Manteca and,
finally, CA 120 to Big Oak Flat and Groveland. Follow signs to Yosemite. For a thrill-
ing demonstration of gravity, try the Old Priest Grade. To Sequoia-Kings, the most
direct route is by CA 180 due east from Fresno to the Big Stump Entrance. In winter,
with Tioga closed, the only way to Mammoth Lakes is by CA 50 to CA 89/88 through
Markleeville, weather permitting, or through South Lake Tahoe and Minden, Nevada.
A winter journey from the Bay Area to Death Valley is best achieved by way of Bakersfield and either CA 178 over Walker Pass or, when conditions are nasty, by CA 58 over
Tehachapi to Mojave.

FROM SAN JOSE/MONTEREY

From the South Bay, Salinas, or Monterey, the most direct shot across the valley follows
CA 152 over Pacheco Pass to the CA 99 corridor. CA 140 to Mariposa, El Portal, and
Yosemite can be reached by way of an excellent cutoff north of Chowchilla, through
Plainsburg and Planada. To get to Kings Canyon, take CA 99 south to Fresno and CA
180 east from there.

HURTLING TOWARD THE RANGE OF LIGHT

A Cross-California Bike-Packing Ramble in the Footsteps of John Muir

In my experience, most journeys worth the name begin not so much with that one first step prescribed by the ancient Chinese philosopher as with a series of trivial delays and procrastinations followed—finally, when there is no other option—by a mad dash. And so it was that on a clear Sunday morning in late June, in the company of an unflappable photographer named Osceola (after the famous mixed-blood Seminole war chief), I found myself sprinting through the streets of San Francisco on my old hard-tail mountain bike, with full camping and cooking kit and a week's supposed essentials in tow, harrowingly late for the Oakland ferry.

We leapt curbs and ran four-way stops, greatly exceeding the top speed recommended for our new cargo trailers. Finding Market Street closed to traffic for a parade—the sidewalks thronged from Castro to the Ferry Building—we blew past the traffic police and pedaled straight down the gullet of the route, cheered on by the crowds as though we were the warm-up entertainment. We hit the gate just as the boat was backpedaling in from its first cross-bay run, a lucky three minutes behind schedule.

Our plan was to ride our bikes across California, from San Francisco to Yosemite, following, as much as possible, the roads and trails John Muir had rambled along when he first made his way to the Sierra Nevada in the spring of 1868. We wanted to explore—and experience first-hand—the changes in the landscape. We wanted to see what was left, if anything, of "the great fresh unblighted, unredeemed wilderness" that Muir (like Thoreau before him) had hoped would be the salvation of the world. But also—and perhaps even more importantly—we wanted to travel as Muir had: free and unfettered, driven only by curiosity, listening to the birds and chatting idly with whatever characters we might meet along the way. Unfortunately, where Muir had allowed himself seven weeks to reach Yosemite, "drifting leisurely mountainward . . . by any road that we chanced to find; enjoying the flowers and light, 'camping out'

THE VIEW TO THE SIERRA NEVADA FROM PACHECO PASS, AS JOHN MUIR FIRST GLIMPSED IT   OSCEOLE REFETOFF

in our blankets wherever overtaken by night, and paying very little compliance to roads or times," the most we'd been able to wrangle for ourselves was seven days.

It was "about the first of April" when Muir stepped off a crowded Panama steamer in the Port of San Francisco. He would go on to become famous in his own time, and a legend in ours, as the scraggly-bearded Scot who regularly sauntered into the high country with nothing but a crust of bread and a handful of tea, who showed Ralph Waldo Emerson the "Range of Light" and hard-sold Teddy Roosevelt on the concept of the national parks. He would be a founder and first president of the Sierra Club, and in volume after volume of fervently descriptive prose would articulate a kind of deep metaphysics of wilderness that continues to drive and inspire nature lovers and conservationists worldwide. But that first spring in California, nigh upon his 30th birthday, he was just a young man with no particular prospects, a bright-eyed tramp with a plant press, a notebook, and a pocket map exploring the world.

Having no interest in the booming City by the Bay, his first action was to inquire of a passerby the quickest way out of town. "But where do you want to go?" the man asked. "To any place that is wild," replied Muir. "This reply startled him," Muir would remember later, describing a reaction with which we too would become familiar ("To Yosemite? On a bicycle!?"). "He seemed to fear I might be crazy and therefore the sooner I was out of town the better, so he directed me to the Oakland ferry."

And so we left that clapboard city of high-seas winds and fog, more or less as Muir had, left the street-art hipsters and megaphone evangelists, the ham-and-Gruyère pop tarts and "significant" avant-garde ice cream flavors—and landed in Oakland's Jack London Square. (So long New York. Howdy East Orange.) There was nothing terribly significant—culturally, geographically, or otherwise—in our own brief passage across the bay. But as we posed for snapshots with bedazzled parade-goers and answered the first in a long series of questions with regard to our provenance and destination, we began to feel a shift in perspective. We were now outside normal time and routine. We were on a journey, self-propelled and self-supported, rambling in the grand American tradition of which Muir was a prominent co-founder. The entire world was before us. And all we had to do—assuming we had it in us—was to sit in the saddle for at least 60 miles a day and pedal.

In 1868, the conventional (and quickest) route from San Francisco to Yosemite was by steamboat to Stockton, followed by another 16 hours' hard travel by stage (with multiple changes of horses) to Coulterville. From there, it was 3 or more days on horseback up into the famed Yosemite Valley. These days, the most direct route (I-580 E to CA-120 E)—the one Google Maps recommends—runs less than 200 miles nearly due east along a reliable course of gas stations, big-box stores, and In-n-Out Burgers, and takes about 4 hours in a car. True to form, Muir added more than 100 miles to the trip, first meandering southward between the bay and the Diablo Range, all the way to Gilroy, thence over Pacheco Pass to the San Joaquin Valley, and from there up along the Merced River to Coulterville. Luckily for us, a pair of artisan bookbinders from Santa Cruz, Peter and Donna Thomas, had retraced Muir's route in 2006—calling it the "Muir Ramble Route," or MRR—making numerous detours to avoid freeways, office parks, and other radical changes in the landscape, and to seek, whenever possible, the wildest way. It took them 34 days to cover the route on foot, and 4 years to publish their detailed walking directions. Theirs, it went without saying, was the route we would take.

Finding a farmers' market in full swing at our trailhead, beside Jack London's original Klondike cabin (moved from the Yukon to Oakland in 1970), we couldn't help but linger overlong, savoring our newfound rambledom. We bought asparagus, cherries, fresh linguine and pesto, a hunk of crusty wheat bread, and, in honor of Jack London's time in the Far North (and John Muir's before that), a good slab of smoked salmon. The cherries went into my handlebar bag for snacking, the rest into the dry-bag on the trailer for that evening's feast, wrapped in a plastic sack with a nugget of dry ice. Then, finally, we plugged into our respective soundtracks—Osceola's a world of "70's funk funk," mine leaning more toward Dylan and Townes Van Zandt and Ramblin' Jack Elliot—and rolled out along the railroad tracks.

Southward we rode, in and out of industrial backstreets, down long, flat glory-sections of officially-designated Bay Trail—paved or gravel paths through regional shoreline parks and pocket wildlife refuges, along drainage channels, sloughs, salt ponds, and wetlands in varying states of restoration. We learned to follow the Thomases' directions at about 10 times the speed intended. We saw feral cats and avocets, stacks of rusted flatbed trailers, dredging rigs and driving ranges, herons and blackbirds and Canadian geese. Along the sidewalks and chain-link fences grew wild proliferations of mustard and fennel. There were softball games and barbecues, kites, families out for afternoon strolls along the breakwaters, speaking languages from all over the world, and kids learning to ride bikes without training wheels.

"All this used to be fields," a local San Leandro man explained to his son, pausing beside a newly installed interpretive sign about migratory shore birds. For years, the Port of Oakland had been dumping fill into the marshes here, between the Oakland Coliseum and the airport. "People used to bring dogs out here to hunt rabbits. But then, as they say, progress." In 1986, the Sierra Club and other local organizations brought suit and earned a judgment of $2.5 million to restore the estuary, now an important stopover for shorebirds on the Pacific Flyway. The air was filled with the distant rush of the Nimitz freeway and the wail of train engines. The man looked out across the wetlands, hemmed in but still wild in its way. "But this is nice," he added, "that they did this."

On the south end of a place called Union City, across from a new subdivision, we were forced to halt briefly while a Mexican cowboy, on foot and backlit by the setting sun, drove a herd of cattle down off one of the many flood-control levees that keep the San Francisco Bay and its estuaries out of the fields and neighborhoods. We bedded down that night on a pair of picnic tables in Coyote Hills Regional Park on the site of an old dairy farm dating back to Muir's time, still less than 30 miles from the ferry dock in Oakland.

At first light, awakened by the chatter of local Buddhist monks out for a morning stroll, we ate gorp and cherries, applied cold chammy butter to our shorts to prevent saddle sores, and set off into the fog in search of a real breakfast. We rode over the top of the toll plaza for the Dumbarton Bridge and watched a hawk patrolling the marshgrass beside Pipeline #1 of the Hetch Hetchy Aqueduct, an unassuming little green tube silently bearing to San Francisco tens of millions of gallons of daily drinking and dishwashing water direct from Yosemite. (Muir had fought bitterly against the damming of the Tuolumne River within the boundaries of the national park, the only major battle he ever lost.) Over a locally recommended "3-Egger Breakfast" at All Star Burgers in Newark, on an old-town main street now swallowed by the suburbs of Fremont and San Jose, I looked at my map of California with a whole new sense of scale. I realized: (1) that we would need to pick up the pace if we were going to make Yosemite by the end of the week; and (2) that I would have to do this again someday with much more time to stop and linger along the way.

It took us two days to get from San Francisco to the heart of the Santa Clara Valley, leaving the southern estuaries of the bay, navigating the mowed and leaf-blown office mazes of Silicon Valley, spinning down into the center of Old San Jose and then back out again along a pleasant series of wild riparian corridors and leafy creekside pathways. It took another day to make a bitter, failed run at the Thomases' scenic overland shortcut across the Diablo Range, climbing a grueling 2,200 feet to the visitor center at Henry W. Coe State Park only to be turned back by an impending deluge and the overwhelming doubts of a lonely maintenance worker. (When we told him of our projected trek across 87,000 acres of rugged mountain wilderness, he ran his finger along a route across the park, lingering on a section where the contour lines pressed together in a thick band he called "the Wall." "What you're looking at is goat trails," he informed us. "And the goats are gone." Then he looked up at the darkening skies, hitched up his pants and went back to work.)

By late morning on our fourth day, we were at the summit of Pacheco Pass above the busy four-lane highway that connects the southern Bay Area with Los Angeles. We stood on the spot where Muir experienced his first glimpse of the Sierra Nevada rising some 70 miles distant ("like the wall of some celestial city") above a sea of yellow wildflowers. "A landscape was displayed," he would write over two decades later, "that after all my wanderings still appears as the most beautiful I have ever beheld." We were two months late for the flowers; the grasses and wild oats had already turned summer-gold. Across the San Luis Reservoir, the great Central Valley of California was now an intricate patchwork of industrial fruit and nut orchards, towns, dairies, and alfalfa fields. To our modern eyes the air seemed clear and pure, fresh-washed by the previous day's rainstorm, but it would be another day before we'd get our own first glimpse of the Sierra.

Across the valley we hurtled, spinning along irrigation canals and aqueduct service roads, past lonely, half-abandoned farmsteads—the historic 1930s house, the vintage '70s double-wide, the brand-new RV—past bright-eyed foals in flooded stalls and hedgerows of wild blackberries, stopping only occasionally to pluck goatheads and change tires. We found new additions to our running inventory of roadkill—fox, coyote, housecat, snake, dove, grasshoppers, miscellaneous winged creatures. How little I know of the taxonomy of flora and fauna, I thought (where Muir had known the common and Latin names for every organism he came upon).

Not far from where Muir had crossed the San Joaquin River at Hills Ferry, we came upon a pair of muleskinners, father and son, standing in their driveway, sorting gear for their annual Fourth of July pack trip up into the Sierra's Emigrant Wilderness. In daily life, they commuted to the Bay Area—more than an hour each way—to work for a big cement contractor. They shared with us a couple of their cold beers then sent us on our way with locally made sausages, zucchini, and fresh jalapeños from their garden. In the town of Snelling, at the first real tilt of the Sierra foothills against the Merced River, where Muir spent his first winter in California and secured his first gig as a sheepherder, we sat in the shade of a general store run by East Indians. We ate coconut ice cream bars, watched the exodus of boats and campers headed upcountry, and steeled ourselves for the 7,000-plus feet of climbing to come.

OSCEOLA REFETOFF FORDS SPRING RUNOFF ON THE FINAL APPROACH TO YOSEMITE

At Barrett Cove the next morning, we tried in vain to buy our way onto a water ski boat across Lake McClure to save ourselves the first major grade (encountering yet again those looks that said we must be mad). At the café in Coulterville, we savored our last burger and our last cold beer before heading up Dogtown Road into the Stanislaus National Forest, toward where the original stage road eventually peters out into brush-choked singletrack and the country remains much as Muir first came to know it: mostly untutored in the ways of human beings, teeming with butterflies, bears and squirrels, sugar pines, wild grapes, and thickets of poison oak.

Somewhere up there, late Saturday afternoon, 7 days and more than 200 miles from San Francisco, I came to enjoy one of the sweetest moments of my life, sprawled on the pine needles in the middle of the road, atop a now-forgotten grade that in its day must have killed its share of freight animals. We'd explored the still-wild fringes, bike paths, and backroads of central California, had slept on its ground, eaten its fruit, drunk its ales and pinots, and given our blood, here and there, to its mosquitoes. We'd felt the relentless press of civilization, but had also marveled at

THE AUTHOR IN YOSEMITE VALLEY AFTER 7 DAYS ON A BIKE OSCEOLA REFETOFF

its own valiant efforts to keep itself somehow in check, to try to preserve what was left, along its edges, or to restore what'd earlier been let go. And in any case to keep even the busiest roadsides remarkably clean of trash.

And now, here, there was birdsong in the trees and the buzzing of flies investigating the stains on my hat. I found myself wishing I could spend all summer like this. Maybe the rest of my life. Rambling from thicket to thicket across the land. And when I awoke—if indeed I was awake—I was in line at the convenience store at Crane Flat gas station, Yosemite National Park, on the busiest weekend of the year, cradling a cold six-pack of beer and a bag of honey-mustard potato chips, fuel for that last free-wheeling descent into the half-domesticated, happy-thronged paradise of the Yosemite Valley. Home. And nobody even cared to ask where I'd come from or how I'd got there.

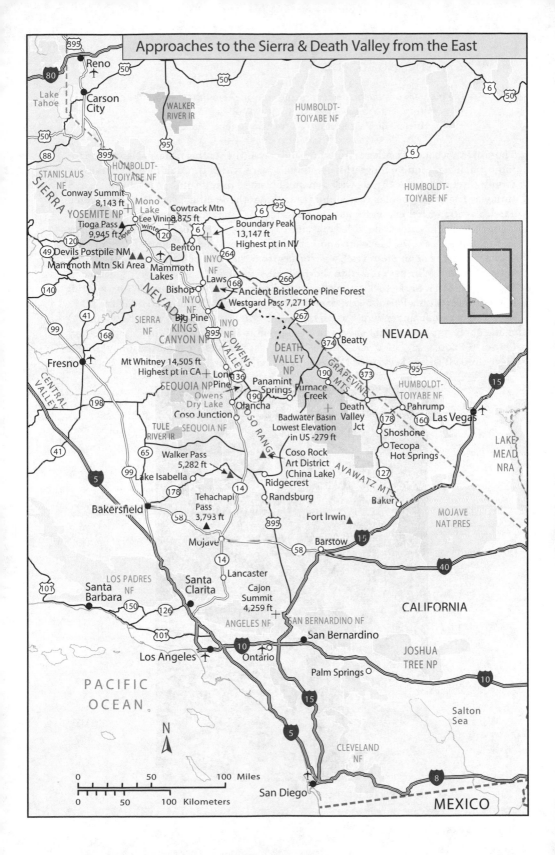

Approaches to the Sierra & Death Valley from the East

Reno
Carson City
Lake Tahoe
WALKER RIVER IR
HUMBOLDT-TOIYABE NF
HUMBOLDT-TOIYABE NF
STANISLAUS NF
SIERRA
HUMBOLDT-TOIYABE NF
Conway Summit 8,143 ft
Mono Lake
Lee Vining
Tioga Pass 9,945 ft closed in winter
YOSEMITE NP
Cowtrack Mtn 8,875 ft
Tonopah
Boundary Peak 13,147 ft Highest pt in NV
Benton
INYO NF
Devils Postpile NM
Mammoth Mtn Ski Area
Mammoth Lakes
NEVADA
Laws
Bishop
INYO NF
Ancient Bristlecone Pine Forest
Westgard Pass 7,271 ft
Big Pine
SIERRA NF
INYO NF
KINGS CANYON NF
OWENS VALLEY
DEATH VALLEY NP
NEVADA
Beatty
GRAPEVINE MTS
Mt Whitney 14,505 ft Highest pt in CA
Fresno
Lone Pine
Panamint Springs
Furnace Creek
HUMBOLDT-TOIYABE NF
Pahrump
Las Vegas
SEQUOIA NP
Owens Dry Lake
Olancha
Death Valley Jct
Shoshone
SEQUOIA NF
TULE RIVER IR
Coso Junction
Badwater Basin Lowest Elevation in US -279 ft
Tecopa Hot Springs
LAKE MEAD NRA
COSO RANGE
Coso Rock Art District (China Lake)
AVAWATZ MTS
Walker Pass 5,282 ft
Lake Isabella
Ridgecrest
Baker
Bakersfield
Tehachapi Pass 3,793 ft
Randsburg
Fort Irwin
MOJAVE NAT PRES
Mojave
Barstow
LOS PADRES NF
Santa Clarita
Lancaster
Cajon Summit 4,259 ft
CALIFORNIA
Santa Barbara
ANGELES NF
SAN BERNARDINO NF
San Bernardino
JOSHUA TREE NP
Los Angeles
Ontario
Palm Springs
PACIFIC OCEAN
CLEVELAND NF
Salton Sea
San Diego
MEXICO

N

| 0 | 50 | 100 Miles |

| 0 | 50 | 100 Kilometers |

✳ Where the Roads End

*The glaciers are the pass-makers and it is by them that the courses of
all mountaineers are predestined.*
—John Muir, "The Passes of the Sierra," *Scribner's*, March 1879

There are thousands of miles of trails into and across the southern Sierra Nevada, ranging from ancient native footpaths, sometimes mere traces through meadow grass, to
highly engineered stock trails with dynamite blasted granite staircases, bridges, and
tunnels. The most popular thoroughfares include: **the Pacific Crest National Scenic
Trail**, a section of which on its way from Mexico to Canada, traverses the range from
south to north, from its unheralded crossing of CA 58 to its busiest miles in the vicinity
of Tuolumne Meadows, thence to another mostly unheralded crossing of Sonora Pass
to the north; the **John Muir Trail**, which runs from the floor of Yosemite Valley to the
crest of Mount Whitney; the **High Sierra Trail**, westward from Crescent Meadow in
Sequoia National Park, also to the summit of Whitney; and the **Mount Whitney Trail**
itself, from Whitney Portal on the east side to the summit. Traffic on the Mount Whitney Trail is significant enough during the high summer season (May 1 to November 1)
that a quota has been established, with trail permits issued every February by lottery
(760-876-6200; www.fs.fed.us/r5/inyo). Wilderness permits are required for overnight
travel into all Forest Service or National Park lands in the Sierra and can be obtained

OFF PISTE IN THE EASTERN SIERRA PATITUCCIPHOTO

ACCESS AND AMENITY FEES

Access to public lands within the Inyo, Sierra, and Sequoia National Forests, including the southern unit of the Sequoia National Monument, is free, as is access to all lands managed by the Bureau of Land Management (such as the Alabama Hills). Amenity fees are generally assessed for use of developed campgrounds, picnic areas, high-use trailheads, and boat launches. Primitive camping, where allowed, is generally free. Campfire and wilderness permits are free (but generally required). Entrance fees to the national parks (Death Valley, Sequoia-Kings, and Yosemite) run $25-$30 per vehicle (for seven days), $20-$25 per motorcycle or $12-$15 per person on foot, bicycle, or bus, payable at entrance kiosks or park visitor centers. Annual Access Passes can be purchased at a rate of $60 for Yosemite and $50 for Death Valley or Sequoia-Kings. Children younger than 16 are admitted free. Depending on your plans, the best bet may be the interagency America the Beautiful–National Parks and Federal Recreational Lands Pass, which, at a cost of $80, provides the passholder and the occupants of his/her vehicle (not to exceed four adults) unlimited access to all federal lands and recreation sites for one year. Participating agencies include the National Park Service, the Forest Service, the Fish and Wildlife Service, the Bureau of Land Management, the Bureau of Reclamation, and the U.S. Army Corps of Engineers. For U.S. citizens or permanent residents age 62 or older, a lifetime Senior Pass is available at a one-time cost of $10; a free Access Pass is available for all U.S. 4th graders, active military personnel, volunteers with 250 service hours, and for U.S. citizens or permanent residents with documented permanent disabilities. These passes can be obtained at all park entrances and visitor centers, on the Internet at store.usgs.gov/pass, or by calling 1-888-ASK-USGS.

TIOGA ENTRANCE, YOSEMITE NATIONAL PARK BURKE GRIGGS

CONSIDERING THE DESERT (AND OTHER THINGS) AT LESS THAN 2 MILES PER HOUR

The needle on the temperature gauge pushed into the red. And then it kept going, like the needle on an old record player when the song ends.

We were at the foot of the wash, just out of cell range, still 3,500 vertical feet and 10 long miles from the crest of the Inyos. I wasn't terribly concerned. We had 11 gallons of water, a 12-pack of Mexican beer, ice, food, shade, propane, firewood, bicycles, sleeping bags, good shoes and hats, pens, notebooks, a new letter-stamp kit with red ink, and a library ranging from *Babar* to *Blood Meridian*.

Jasper was in the back, strapped to his booster seat, aged 4.99 and counting. The dog was curled up at his side. I'm gonna have to pull over, I said.

Jasper looked out the window, out across the sun-cracked arroyos of the planet Tatooine—deep Jawa country. He nodded and went back to his drawing. To let the engine cool, he said.

We were on our way to his fifth birthday convocation, to be held this year out at the Eureka Dunes, on the northwestern fringe of Death Valley National Park. We'd had a pleasant morning, rolling down the Owens against the northward exodus of fishermen and boats bound for opening day—Fishmas, they call it. (Good for business, said the woman at the gas station in Big Pine.) We'd picked up a hitchhiker on the way out of Mammoth. He was wearing a dark suit, a pressed white shirt and tie, and a porkpie hat. He held a document folder on which he'd written:

INDEPENDENCE (THE TOWN)

Independence is the county seat of Inyo, second largest and second least populated county in California, where, in 1969, Charles Manson was arraigned and jailed for possession of stolen vehicles after a California Highway Patrol officer found him hiding in a cupboard up in the Panamints. Aside from the Greek Revival courthouse (its fourth incarnation since the 1860s, due to earthquake and fire), this roadside hamlet is also home to a terrific little historical museum, a charmingly weathered 1920s motor hotel (for sale again), and an authentic Franco-Algerian bistro (open sometimes).

What, I asked, half-jokingly, you got a court appearance?

At 10, he said.

I looked at my watch. It was nearly 8:30. I think we might even get you there on time, I said.

He introduced himself as Robert. But most people call me Beto, he said. He slipped on a pair of Spy shades, settled in, and told us the story of how he and his buddy'd been busted building a bike jump out at the far end of Sherwin meadow, at the base of Mammoth Rock, on public land. We didn't even get to building the thing, he said. A hiker had tipped off the Forest Service, and for two days the rangers had watched and taken pictures from above as Beto and partner worked to divert a stream so they'd have water to wet down the jump when it got too dusty.

He said he hadn't known how things worked in these parts, that such a thing was illegal, and so forth. But he didn't harbor illusions his former ignorance would count for anything in court. With a certain amount of pride—pride I could understand and appreciate—he showed me the official document:

United States of America v. Robert M.

He'd been to court before; the reason he wasn't driving himself on this particular morning was the DUI he'd garnered not long ago. He wondered what this judge would be like, and if he'd ever get his shovels back. Jasper, for his part, kept silent all the way to Independence.

We dropped the accused across the street from the courthouse. He thumbed my email address into his Blackberry so he could let us know how it went.* Then we skirted the western shore of Owens Dry Lake, the poisonous surface of which, courtesy of a century's industrial-scale water diversion by the City of Los Angeles, was again in the process of blowing away to Nevada. We retrieved our old aluminum camping fuselage from its winter pasture in Olancha, turned around, and began the slow crawl back upriver to Big Pine and our road into the Inyos. Coming back through Independence, there was no sign of Beto.

The cap on the fluid reservoir popped before I could find a reasonable place to pull the whole circus off the road. Steam blew out from under the hood. I poured a couple gallons of good drinking water over the radiator, plus another gallon or so into the reservoir. We sat for a while, enjoying a breeze like midsummer at the shore—and the silence.

Eventually, the gauge crept back to normal. A local woman from the valley came by in a late-model Jeep and insisted on refilling my jerry can with water. I locked the hubs, shifted into four-wheel low, and pressed on. The worst that could happen, I figured, was that we'd have to abandon the rig a little ways up the road, consolidate our stuff, and hitch a ride with one of the truckloads of friends due out that way later in the afternoon. I could deal with all this steel and aluminum later, I thought.

But then I found that if I kept the heat blasting and the engine's revolutions down around 1,000 per minute—the speedometer flickering above zero like a cheap tea light in the wind, the truck barely ratcheting itself and its load uphill at about the pace a man might stroll beside a pair of oxen bearing his family and other worldly goods across a strange continent—I could keep the temp close to normal.

THE NORTH PASS TO SALINE

*It went like this: the judge found him guilty on all three counts: (1) construction without a permit; (2) making false statements (he'd tried to give a fake name—it'd worked on another occasion); and (3) threatening, intimidating, or interfering with a Forest Service officer. The prosecutor wanted $900 and 3 years' probation. The judge settled on a $450 fine and 50 hours of community service.

I was reminded of the time I drove from Tijuana all the way to Los Angeles in low gear, having shorn off my rear drive shaft in a late-night collision with an open manhole. And a certain long night's gear-grinding bus ascent of Morocco's Haut Atlas. And a slow climb from Batopilas to Creel with a French Canadian gambler, two Swedish girls, my brother, and a sick Tarahumara gentleman writhing atop the gear in the back.

There was time now, finally, to contemplate the whole great history of the wheel, the evolution from trail to road and beyond, the extraordinary technological leap in the newfound ability to ferry stones from here to there without necessarily resorting to slavery. It was a fine way to travel, especially out here where there was no traffic. I came to appreciate the sear of engine air on my toes.

Jasper gathered his books and stamp kit and drawing implements and climbed up into the front seat (*United States of America v. David Page*). We saw a total of four vehicles on the road that afternoon. In about as many hours. I had to look at the road occasionally, in case we had to work around some topographic feature, but otherwise we got a lot done.

We took turns reading to each other and looking out at the world as it crept not at all inexorably by. By the time our friend Deanna's spry little Volkswagen camper, the one containing my wife and other son, Beckett, happened upon us, still a long grind from the top—we'd drifted enough to one side that they were able to sneak around us—we'd done three rounds of The Tortoise and the Jackrabbit, studied hundreds of what we took to be swallows' nests in the road cuts, stamped out a thank-you note in red ink to Jasper's friend Noa, marveled at the Indian paintbrush, the tufty grass poking from dry sand, the crazy chandeliers of pink and white flowers exploding from thornbushes, the cries of seagulls on their way to Mono Lake, the spun-silk cocoons in the mesquite, the lizards, the all-but-erased mining roads cut in switchbacks against great ribs of slate running upwise and canted like the backbone of some scoliotic dinosaur.

We'd seen rusted-tin pop-tab beer cans in the bushes, a sun-bleached squeeze-bottle of Parkay margarine, a refrigerator, and an ancient coil of barbless fence wire. We'd seen Jawa caves from various tribes, and a witch's castle, flying monkeys bearing messages like passenger pigeons, and a herd of T-Rexes grazing in the Joshua trees. We'd relived the hunter shooting Babar's mother four times over and every goddamned time felt the emptiness of it.

You want to go with those guys? I said to Jasper (meaning with his mother et al. in the Volkswagen). They'll get to the dunes hours before we do.

Nah, he said. The birthday boy should always get there last.

"PRIMITIVE" CAMPING IN THE EUREKA BASIN

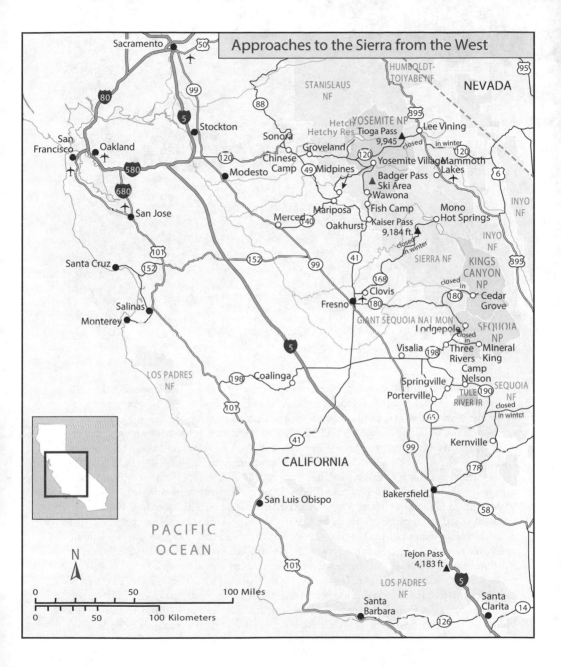

Approaches to the Sierra from the West

SPRING TRACKS ON SKIER'S ALTA, SEQUOIA NATIONAL PARK

from the nearest ranger station or visitor center. In winter these trails become the solitary domain of backcountry skiers, snowboarders, snowshoers, and pine martens.

For at least 180 years, people have been making their way into the High Sierra by horse and mule. Despite ongoing and highly contentious legal battles among a vociferous minority of hikers, the Forest Service, the Park Service, and the Backcountry Horsemen of America, pack animals are still a common sight on certain backcountry trails—and a unique way to explore the country. See the "Recreation" section in each regional chapter for detailed information on local pack outfits and services.

Mountain bikes, trail bikes, ATVs, and snowmobiles are, with specific local restrictions, allowed on appropriate trails and roads throughout national forest and Bureau of Land Management (BLM) lands, except within the bounds of designated wilderness areas, where all mechanized travel is prohibited. Within Sequoia and Yosemite National Parks, wheeled and/or motorized vehicles are not allowed beyond the pavement. In the remote canyons of Death Valley, on the other hand, hundreds of miles of old, suspension-brutalizing mining roads remain open to off-highway and four-wheel-drive enthusiasts, from Ballarat to Badwater, from the Ubehebe Crater to the Saline Valley. Please stay on existing roads, respect closures, and stay off dry lake beds.

DEATH VALLEY

DEATH VALLEY

The fascination of the desert is stronger in Death Valley than at any other place.
—Prospector Dismukes in Zane Grey's *Wanderer of the Wasteland*, 1923

Zane Grey, lion hunter, big-game fisherman, and millionaire author of *Riders of the Purple Sage* and other pulp Westerns, stepped off the Tonopah and Tidewater Railroad in March 1919. "It was sunset when we arrived," he wrote, "—a weird, strange sunset in drooping curtains of transparent cloud, lighting up dark mountain ranges, some peaks of which were clear-cut and black against the sky, and others veiled in trailing storms, and still others white with snow." Death Valley Junction was, in those days, not the desolate coming together of highways that it is now, but a bustling freight hub where the mainline T&T met the narrow-gauge Death Valley Railroad (DVRR), the latter bearing heavy tonnage of rough borax from the mines at Ryan, 21 miles to the west. Aside from the depot, there was a "dingy little store," a borax processing mill, and a sprawling collection of workers' tents and shacks. Where the hotel now stands was Tubbs' Saloon and Whorehouse. Grey spent his evening at the store, fraternizing with the locals: "I heard prospectors talk about float, which meant gold on the surface, and about high grade ores, zinc, copper, silver, lead, manganese, and about how borax was mined 30 years ago, and hauled out of Death Valley by teams of 20 mules."

It seems likely there were Mexican miners (and perhaps Mormons, too) working the region by the early 1840s, but tales of riches to be found in Death Valley got their true wings with that first fateful crossing in 1849–50. "Two or three of the party went to a range of hills a mile or two off the line of travel in search of water," P. A. Chalfant, prospector and fellow '49er (and W. A. Chalfant's father), wrote in 1872. "They came back and reported that they had found no water, but a mountain of something they believed to be silver." Since water was the more important element at that particular moment, they pressed on. Another version has Captain Townsend, of the Georgians, at some later date taking a piece of ore carried out of Death Valley to a gunsmith to have a new sight made for his rifle—and the ore turns out to be pure silver. In the fall of 1850, "while prospecting around Rough and Ready, Nevada County," Chalfant interviewed a Dr. McCormick, who had recently returned to Death Valley and come back with convincing samples. "He described the mountain as being in many places literally seamed with strings or wires of silver," wrote Chalfant, "that in many places the rock fairly glistened with silver."

The first problem: "It was situated in the midst of a most horrible desert some 300 miles in the wilderness, the nearest water being 25 or 30 miles distant, and that of such a degree of badness that it was wholly unfit for use when packed so far." The second: No one thereafter was ever able to locate the place.

"It was a valley where nature had been prodigal of her treasures, and terrible in her hold upon them," Grey wrote in 1923.

Another '49er by the name of Charles Breyfogle, who had once upon a time had a bit of luck in the Sierra foothills, was out looking for the "lost Gunsight Lode" when, one warm summer morning in 1864, probably somewhere in the Amargosa Valley, at Ash Meadows or at the edge of the Funeral Range, he awoke to find his horses and supplies

DEATH VALLEY JUNCTION

stolen, and—according to at least one account the heads of his traveling companions bashed in by Indians. Days later, delirious, blistering with sunburn, and clutching a piece of rock he had broken from a ledge somewhere, he was himself picked up by Indians. Whether these people made him a slave for the entertainment of their children or tied him up to keep him from drowning himself in a spring, whether he was saved by Mormon emigrants or given a horse and set on his way, "the crazy Dutchman from Reese River," as he was generally known, made it back to Austin, Nevada, with a nugget of gold impressive enough to drive thousands of so-called single-blanket jackass prospectors into the desert for many decades to come. (Prospectors these days are more likely to drive dirt bikes or ATVs than mules, and they have been known to supplement their shovel work with a certain amount of traffic in rare gems and fossils, and through the cultivation of marijuana in abandoned mine shafts.)

A silver strike in Surprise Canyon in 1874 brought the hasty construction of Panamint City, with its brief population of 2,000—often referred to as "the toughest, rawest, most hard-boiled little hellhole that ever passed for a civilized town." The place was abandoned in 1875 and destroyed the following year by flash flood. In 1898, the town of Ballarat had a population of 500 people and boasted "seven saloons, three hotels, a Wells Fargo station, post office, school, a jail and morgue, but not one church." The nearby Radcliffe Mine is said to have produced 15,000 tons of gold ore before it played out in 1903. A series of strikes in 1904–6—gold, silver, copper, and lead—brought fleeting settlement to places called Chloride City, Greenwater (where drinking water was sold for $15 a barrel), Harrisburg, Leadfield, Rhyolite, and Skidoo. Rhyolite peaked at 10,000 citizens, a three-story bank building, stores, bars, hotels, churches, a school, a hospital, and an ice cream parlor. Electricity came in 1907. In 1911, the biggest mill closed its doors. In 1916 the electricity was shut off—for good.

Other short-lived ventures in the region include one attempt at harvesting saltpeter (potassium nitrate) for fertilizer and gunpowder, and another at collecting sulfur for

PROSPECTOR'S CABIN, HARRISBURG FLATS, DEATH VALLEY NATIONAL PARK BURKE GRIGGS

making matches. An elaborate monorail was built to haul Epsom salts (magnesium) over the Panamint range, but the operation was suspended after only a few loads.

One night in the late 1870s, also near Ash Meadows, a prospector stopped off at the dirt-floor cabin of one Aaron Winters and his Mexican wife, Rosie. The man spoke of the money being made by those who had discovered borax in Nevada. He described the look of the stuff and related the process by which it could be identified. After he had gone, the couple made a journey to procure the necessary chemicals and supplies, and then they made their way to a place in Death Valley where Winters had once seen loads of something "answering to the description." Winters managed to sell his claim to onetime San Francisco vigilante William Tell Coleman for $20,000.

By 1883 Coleman's Harmony Borax Works was in full swing, with 40 men scraping "cottonball" (ulexite) from the playa near Furnace Creek and an array of cooling vats producing up to 3 tons a day of rough-processed borax. Borax, according to the U.S. Geological Survey, is "a common ingredient of soaps, cleansers, herbicides, soldering fluxes, gasoline antiknock compounds, pharmaceuticals, water softeners, food preservatives, and fire retardants . . . [and] in the manufacture of glass, pyrex, and porcelain enamels used on kitchen appliances, sinks, bathtubs, stoves, and other products." Borax is used as a pesticide and a wood preservative. Ulexite, specifically, is today a fundamental component of fiber optics. For six years the stuff was hauled out of Death Valley by the celebrated (and later trademarked) 20-mule teams—later 18 mules with a pair of horses as wheel animals—165 miles over the Panamints, at 16 to 18 miles a day, with 46,000 pounds of borax and 1,200 gallons of water (for the long days and nights between springs), to the nearest railroad at Mojave. The Greenland Ranch, for nearly a century known as the Ranch at Furnace Creek and now called simply The Ranch at Death Valley, was developed in the early 1880s to provide alfalfa for the teams and fresh meat, shade, and accommodations for the workers.

Coleman was broke 6 years later, forced to sell his extensive holdings to the Pacific Coast Borax Company. The ulexite operation at Harmony was abandoned in favor of colemanite mines in the Greenwater Mountains east of Furnace Creek. By the time

Grey arrived at Death Valley Junction, the famous mule teams had long since been replaced, first by a rather inept steam tractor, then by the railroads. The processing mill was, according to Grey, "getting out 2,500 sacks a day." A passenger could then board a train at the Santa Fe Depot in downtown Los Angeles (now an acclaimed school for architecture), transfer at Ludlow to the Tonopah and Tidewater, and in the space of about 16 hours, with Pullman service most of the way, step off the narrow gauge within hiking distance of the Greenland Ranch.

Grey and his traveling companion, a game and courteous Norwegian by the name of Nielsen, both ready, after a full day on the T&T and a night in Death Valley Junction, to be, as Grey put it, "lost to the works of man," opted to forego the DVRR and instead cover the last leg to Furnace Creek by mule. Near sunset they rounded a curve and caught their first glimpse of the great sink. While Nielsen continued down the canyon to set up camp—there were no tourist accommodations in those days—Grey lingered over a grand baroque spectacle of storm clouds and dying light. "When the sun had set," he wrote, "and all that upheaved and furrowed world of rock had received a mantle of gray, and a slumberous sulphurous ruddy haze slowly darkened to purple and black, then I realized more fully that I was looking down into Death Valley."

Perhaps because of Grey's less-than-flattering description of working conditions at Death Valley Junction (first in *Harper's Bazaar*, then in his travel memoir, *Tales of Lonely Trails*, published in 1922), and likely because of a sudden increase in tourism to the region (by just the sort of people who were likely to be reading Grey's gauzy descriptions of the desert), the Pacific Coast Borax Company, by then a subsidiary of British mining giant Borax Consolidated, Ltd., took it upon itself to buy the land beneath Tubbs' Saloon and Whorehouse in 1923 and build something more permanent. W. A. Chalfant, the son, described what was built as a "town under one roof": "Imagine a one-story adobe building occupying three sides of a square, and about 800 feet in length. The long roof sheltered offices, store, recreation places, barber shop, hospital

ORIGINAL 20-MULE-TEAM WAGONS, HARMONY BORAX WORKS

and accompaniments, and other places, even to a handsome little theater." Two years later, an enormous raw borax deposit was discovered in the Mojave Desert, significantly closer to major freight lines, and the whole operation—the mines at Ryan, the mill at Death Valley Junction—shut down.

In an effort to make good on some of its investments, the company renovated rooms at the junction to accommodate tourists, turned the defunct barracks at Ryan into the Death Valley View Hotel, and allocated $30,000 to start the construction of a first-class resort to be called the Furnace Creek Inn (now The Inn at Death Valley). The first guests arrived on February 1, 1927, by way of a gasoline-powered narrow-gauge passenger car on the old DVRR line. The room rate of $10 per night included private bath and three meals. Much of the staff came from the Old Faithful Lodge in Yellowstone National Park during its off-season from November to April. By the end of 1933, Death Valley had been designated a national monument, and two companies of Civilian Conservation Corpsmen had arrived to upgrade roads and build facilities. The DVRR was dismantled and shipped to Carlsbad, New Mexico, for service in a potash mining operation. The old trestle timber was used to build a kitchen and lounge for the inn.

Decades later, in 1969, Charles Manson was arrested in Death Valley National Monument. Another eight years down the road, George Lucas used the place as a stand-in for Luke Skywalker's home planet, Tatooine. Bill Clinton declared it a national park in 1994—the largest in the Lower 48—and in the same moment expanded its boundaries to include the northern end of the Panamint Range and Saline Valley. Ninety-five percent of the park's 3.3 million acres is designated wilderness.

✳ The Lay of the Land: Approaches and Logistics

Perhaps the most historic way to arrive in Death Valley would be to come in from the east, across the Amargosa, with oxen and enormous freight wagons bearing pianos and Louis XVI armoires. Or to come down Grapevine Canyon with a hand-drawn map on a cloth bar napkin depicting watering holes, most labeled with a skull and crossbones. Today, however, there are four well-asphalted routes into the valley from points east. From Vegas, CA 190 is the most direct (via the Blue Diamond Highway, then State Line Road from the north end of Pahrump, Nevada), following both the original emigrants' route into Furnace Creek (The Oasis) and the old railway bed of the DVRR (still visible on the south side of the highway from Death Valley Junction).

From Los Angeles, CA 178 from Shoshone over Salsberry Pass is the quickest way into the park—but proves not as speedy to Furnace Creek (The Oasis) as CA 190. For a hint of the way it used to be, try the well-graded gravel on the Greenwater Valley Road from CA 178 north to Ryan, or, from the north, try the fabulously underused Big Pine Road from CA 168 (Westgard Pass) to the Grapevine entrance, both manageable in a passenger car except during or immediately after any kind of inclement weather.

Note: The Park Service generally recommends high-clearance vehicles for travel off-pavement in Death Valley. Always check with a ranger for conditions. Bring plenty of water, extra tires (with a functioning jack and appropriate-size tire iron), and knowledge of the capacity of your equipment. Note also that smart-phone navigation apps cannot always differentiate between existing maintained roads and historic mining trails no longer passable by vehicle. Keep your head up and your common sense about you; people have died in recent years after following their devices into impossible situations.

The most common (and dramatic) access route from the east is by CA 190 from Olancha or Lone Pine via Father Crowley Point, Panamint Springs, Towne Pass, and

★ OTHER BOOKS TO SUPPLEMENT THIS CHAPTER

California Deserts Camping and Hiking, by Tom Stienstra and Ann Marie Brown (Moon Outdoors, 2012).
Death Valley: The Facts, by W. A. Chalfant (Stanford University Press, 1930).
Death Valley and the Amargosa: A Land of Illusion, by Richard E. Lingenfelter (UC Press, 1988).
Death Valley Photographer's Guide, by Dan Suzio (Nolina Press, 2011).
Death Valley SUV Trails: A Guide to 46 Four-Wheeling Excursions in the Backcountry in and around Death Valley National Park, by Roger Mitchell (Track and Trail, 2001).
Geology Underfoot in Death Valley and Owens Valley, by Robert Sharp and Allen Glazner (Mountain Press, 1997).
Hiking Death Valley: A Guide to Its Natural Wonders and Mining Past, by Michel Digonnet (Wilderness Press, 2016).

Eichbaum's old toll road to Stovepipe Wells. From Los Angeles or San Bernardino, a slightly more direct route follows the Panamint Valley north from Trona to CA 190. The Emigrant Canyon Road is a worthwhile, if slower, alternative, with a significant mountain pass and a brief potholed section in the heart of Wildrose Canyon.

The nearest full-sized grocery store to Death Valley is the Albertson's in Pahrump, Nevada (775-751-0160; 200 S. Hwy 160). There is expensive gas and free water available year-round at Furnace Creek (The Oasis), Stovepipe Wells, and Panamint Springs. There is a mechanic of some kind on general duty at the Furnace Creek Chevron (not necessarily on weekends)—and a AAA tow truck. There is no gas at Scotty's Castle. There is no gas at Death Valley Junction (try Mom's Convenience Store, 7 miles to the

ZANE GREY AT ZABRISKIE POINT, 1919 FROM *TALES OF LONELY TRAILS* BY ZANE GREY (1922)

WHEN TO GO

Death Valley is famous for being one of the lowest, hottest, driest spots on the planet. Less than 2 inches of rain fall here every year. Some years (1929, 1953), there is no rain at all. Other years (1942, 1976, 1984, 1988, 2004), it falls all at once, causing violent flash floods and debris slides across alluvial fans (such as that at Furnace Creek), washing out roads and buildings and scenic overlooks, floating cars, and filling vast, once-dry lakes. The asphalt on CA 190 gives out every time. In October 2015, 4 inches of rain fell on Scotty's Castle in two days, inflicting massive damage to structures, roads, and power infrastructure and causing the closure of the whole area until at least 2019 for reconstruction. Precipitation is most likely to occur in January, February, and March, and when it does occur, the wildflowers explode. Peak blooms generally begin at the lowest elevations around mid-February to mid-April (for more information check www.nps.gov/deva/learn/nature/wildflowers.htm). The hottest month is July, with an average high temperature of 115 degrees Fahrenheit.

The highest ambient temperature ever recorded in the United States was 134 degrees Fahrenheit, on July 10, 1913, at the Greenland Ranch (now The Ranch at Death Valley). For nine years this was the world record, until September 13, 1922, when a temperature of 57.7 degrees Celsius (135.9 degrees Fahrenheit) was recorded in Al'Aziziyah, Libya. (For some perspective, 140 degrees Fahrenheit is the temperature at which bedbugs, dust mites, and most bacteria will die; it is the minimum temperature to which hamburger must be heated in fast food restaurants; and it's the temperature at which coffee begins to present a significant burn hazard to human skin.) The Libya record was invalidated by the World Meteorological Organization in 2012, putting Death Valley back into the *Guinness Book of World Records*. But thorough analysis in 2016 has also called Death Valley's historic number into question. (There is informal contention that if a recording station were installed at the low point at Badwater [-282 feet] instead of at Furnace Creek [-214 feet], Death Valley would surely reign supreme.) In any case, according to extreme weather expert Christopher Burt, a reading of 129.2 degrees Fahrenheit, recorded at Furnace Creek on June 30, 2013 (and also at Mitribah, Kuwait, the following month), set a new bar as the hottest temperature ever "reliably measured."

When silent-film director Erich Von Stroheim took his cast and crew into Death Valley in August and September 1923, as reported at the time by the *Inyo Independent*, "the temperature was 130 degrees by a properly shaded thermometer, and the heat radiation from the scorching, sun-baked sand of the desert made the trousers of the men so hot as far up as their knees that many were compelled to wrap bandages around their calves to keep the cloth from touching the skin."

north and across the state line). Gas is sold at slightly more reasonable prices in Lone Pine, Olancha, Ridgecrest, Shoshone, and Beatty.

Listings within each section are organized from east to west, whenever possible, beginning with listings in the Amargosa Basin and Range, followed by those to the east of Death Valley, Death Valley proper, Panamint, and Saline. Recreation listings, toward the end of the chapter, are listed alphabetically.

✳ To See

AMARGOSA BASIN AND RANGE

Amargosa Opera House and Hotel (Death Valley Junction; 760-852-4441; www.amargosa -opera-house.com). By 1930, when W. A. Chalfant came through, he found the

The first people in the region, the Timbisha Shoshone, used to head for the high country in summer. Now they mostly go to Lone Pine. The early caretakers of the Greenland Ranch are said to have spent summer nights sleeping in irrigation ditches. "It's not hot until it hits 120," a park employee of five summers said during a recent 112-degree afternoon in May. The most pleasant time to visit, flash floods notwithstanding, is midwinter, when there is snow on the Panamints, the nights are cool at Furnace Creek (The Oasis), and the days are sunny and clear with temperatures in the high 60s and low 70s. The park tends to be busiest in March and April, then again in November. Those interested in experiencing the true extremes of the place—or saving money on this year's European vacation—should consider joining the automotive industry's car testers and the fleets of European tourists in the 24-hour-a-day scorch of July and August in Death Valley.

For detailed current conditions and a link to the NOAA forecast, check www.nps.gov/deva/planyourvisit/conditions.htm, or pick up a hard copy of the *Death Valley Morning Report* at the Death Valley Visitor Center.

HOT RAVENS, STOVEPIPE WELLS

once-bustling Borax headquarters "fallen into the doldrums." And thus Marta Becket, artist, musician, and Broadway dancer, found it in the spring of 1967 when she and her husband, after a week's camping in Death Valley, stopped here to have a trailer tire repaired. She found herself looking through a crack in the door of the old theater. It was in shambles, but it was a theater. "Peering through the tiny hole," she says, "I had the distinct feeling that I was looking at the other half of myself." For nearly half a century, until she died in 2017 at age 92, she gave nightly performances (in season), not merely to the screech of peacocks and to the colorful audience she once painted for herself, but often to a sold-out house of real people. Old prospectors came down from the hills; longtime Furnace Creek employees, uncertain tourists and retirees, French backpackers, and urban hipsters alike made the trek to the Junction for an evening of Marta's singing and storytelling. (In the final years, she was doing what she called "The Sitting Down Show," created after she hurt her back falling from a chair while hanging a curtain.) Year after year the season ended with a lengthy standing ovation, chocolate

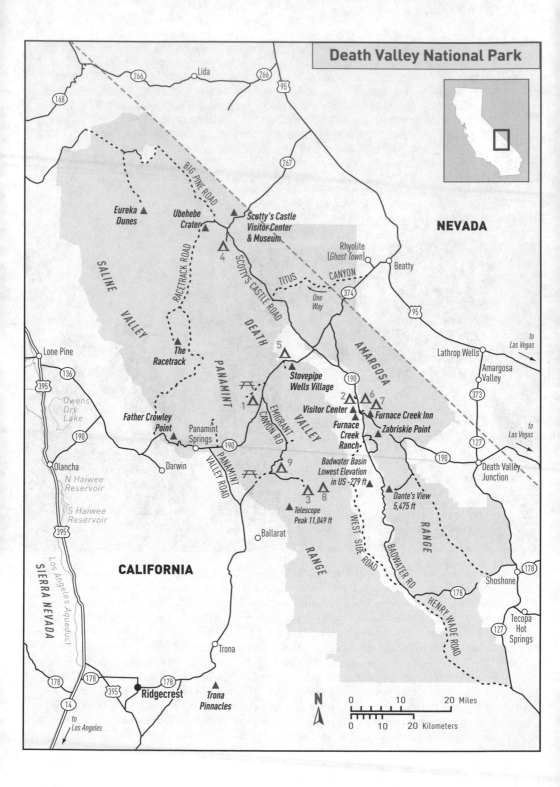

Death Valley National Park

NEVADA

CALIFORNIA

SIERRA NEVADA

SALINE VALLEY

PANAMINT VALLEY

DEATH VALLEY

PANAMINT RANGE

AMARGOSA RANGE

Eureka Dunes

Ubehebe Crater

Scotty's Castle Visitor Center & Museum

Rhyolite (Ghost Town)

Beatty

Lida

Lathrop Wells

Amargosa Valley

TITUS CANYON

One Way

The Racetrack

RACETRACK ROAD

BIG PINE ROAD

SCOTTY'S CASTLE ROAD

Lone Pine

Owens Dry Lake

Father Crowley Point

Panamint Springs

Darwin

Olancha

N Haiwee Reservoir

S Haiwee Reservoir

Stovepipe Wells Village

Visitor Center

Furnace Creek Ranch

Furnace Creek Inn

Zabriskie Point

EMIGRANT CANYON RD

PANAMINT VALLEY ROAD

Badwater Basin Lowest Elevation in US -279 ft

Dante's View 5,475 ft

Telescope Peak 11,049 ft

Ballarat

WEST SIDE ROAD

BADWATER RD

HENRY WADE ROAD

Death Valley Junction

Shoshone

Tecopa Hot Springs

Trona

Ridgecrest

Trona Pinnacles

Los Angeles Aqueduct

to Los Angeles

to Las Vegas

to Las Vegas

N

0   10   20 Miles

0   10   20 Kilometers

266

168

95

266

267

374

95

190

373

127

190

127

178

178

178

178

395

136

190

395

14

178

1

2

3

4

5

6

7

8

9

⊛ BEST MAPS TO SUPPLEMENT THIS CHAPTER

Each of these maps is available for purchase online or at most regional booksellers. For more information on map series, see Chapter 8.

"Eastern Sierra Guide Map," **AAA Explore!**
"Death Valley National Park," **AAA Explore!**
"Death Valley National Park," **Tom Harrison.**
"Death Valley National Park," **National Geographic Trails Illustrated.**

cake, and rum punch. Marta was survived by her cats Okie-Dokie and Domino ("the biggest cat in the world"). Revival shows featuring Marta's original choreography and costumes are still staged on occasion. An off-season visit is worthwhile for the murals and broken sidewalks alone. Whether you decide to stay the night may depend on the depth of your appreciation for the work of filmmaker David Lynch.

Ash Meadows National Wildlife Refuge (775-372-5435; www.fws.gov/refuge/ash_meadows). Ash Meadows, 23,000 acres of original, undeveloped desert oasis—the largest remaining oasis in the Mojave Desert—is a wildly popular stopover for migratory waterfowl and the native habitat of 24 unique plant and animal species—"a greater concentration of endemic life than any other local area in the United States," according to the U.S. Fish and Wildlife Service. No fishing, swimming (except in Crystal Reservoir), or camping. The visitor center is open 9:00 AM–4:30 PM daily. There are no entrance fees.

Devil's Hole. Across the northeast boundary of Ash Meadows NWR lies a tiny, isolated, rarely visited annex of Death Valley National Park. There is an overlook—an easy quarter-mile hike from the dirt road—where, through chain-link fence and razor wire,

PUPFISH V. VEGAS, DEVIL'S HOLE, DEATH VALLEY NATIONAL PARK

SAND STORMER

Testing the Jeep Wrangler Rubicon in the Death Valley Outback (from Hemispheres Magazine)

The largest U.S. national park outside Alaska, Death Valley is a wilderness of rocks and sand nearly the size of Connecticut, with topography as arid and mountainous as the Moroccan fringes of the Sahara. Since 1849, it's been notorious for waylaying travelers in wheeled vehicles. What better proving ground, then, for a factory-new 2012 Jeep Wrangler Rubicon?

We left the town of Lone Pine, California, late in the afternoon, outrunning the shadow of Mount Whitney—the tallest in the lower 48 states—on good pavement. My co-pilot, a photographer, snapped pictures through the open soft-top roof and played DJ as well, working the interface between his iPhone and the Jeep's onboard computer.

We'd been given the four-door model in a blend of yellow and orange dubbed "dozer" (a new color perhaps less reminiscent of heavy construction equipment than of artificial cheese), and we looked forward to giving it a respectable patina of dust. There was plenty of room in back for 10 gallons of water, a folding table and chairs, food, beer, and enough camping gear for two nights in the backcountry.

With its new six-cylinder engine—lighter and more efficient than its V-8 predecessors and, paradoxically, more powerful by 83 horses—the Rubicon (or "Ruby," as fans call it) hit its stride like a thoroughbred on the wide-open desert two-lane. It was wily on tight corners, of course, like a real Jeep. But I had to set the cruise control to keep my sporting impulses in check.

In the ramble-down former mining camp of Darwin, at pavement's end, we stopped to inquire about the road ahead. "You'll be fine—it's a Rubicon, toughest one they make," said a woman, who didn't appear to be in the pay of Chrysler Group, which owns Jeep. She gave it a final appraisal in the gaudy light of the setting sun. And then she had to ask: "What color is that?"

It wasn't until we'd forded a stream, climbed a steep pile of mine tailings, and performed a brush-crushing turnaround at a washout illuminated only by our headlights that we got a taste of what the Ruby could really do. Namely, what Jeeps have been doing for the past seven decades: jeeping. (What other brand in the history of vehicles can rightly claim its own verb?)

We overnighted at the Furnace Creek Inn (later re-branded The Inn at Death Valley), a luxe-vintage safari hotel set in a date palm oasis above the Death Valley salt pan, with a warm springs pool and a pith-helmeted bellboy. Then we lit out overland. Connecticut has roughly 21,000 miles of roads; Death Valley has 1,000, fewer than a third of which have been tamed

one can look down into the hole in the bedrock where the world's entire population of Devil's Hole pupfish lives. The fish themselves are not visible from the overlook, and they are only about an inch long, but they are responsible for the tens of thousands of acres of undeveloped landscape you will have driven across to get to within a quarter-mile of this spot. On a good year there have been as many 500 of the little Nemos going about their business down there in the 86-degree saltwater, for which the place was once called the Miner's Bathtub—all that's left of what was once (10,000 years ago) a vast lake. On a bad year, like 2006, there were 36. The Park Service and other agencies send in divers at least twice a year to do a count. Divers have been down 300 feet into the aquifer without finding its bottom, and at least two divers have gone in and not come out. The fish go as deep as 80 feet, but they do their spawning (and eating) near the surface, on a shallow shelf at one end of the hole. If the water level goes down a few feet, enough to expose the shelf, the species goes extinct. Which is why in 1976 the Supreme Court put an unprecedented kibosh on any further pumping of

with pavement. The other 700 range from suspension-busting washboard to barely discernible wilderness tracks best suited to cloven-hoofed animals. ("I hope you have good tires," a docent at the visitors center had remarked, showing us a dagger-edged rock sample from a typical "improved" road. "This is what the natives used to make arrowheads.")

On a single tank of gas and stock tires, we worked a 250-mile circuit that took us across four basins and three mountain ranges. We passed a Frenchman and a West African changing a shredded tire on an old Montero. We squeezed through a rock hallway that would have peeled the doors off a Hummer, and we descended a stepladder of dry waterfalls as smoothly as if we'd been in an inflatable raft—then, for fun, we crawled back up to do it again.

Grinding down a wagon-width grade into Saline Valley, we came grille to grille with a sibling Rubicon from '09, in silver. The vanity plates read "DV RUBY." We killed engines, cracked beers, and enjoyed a tour of the owner's $6,000 worth of after-market upgrades. Looking at ours, briefly, he wasn't so sure about the new color. But he did regret not having waited for the V6, and when he saw the AC power outlet built into the center console, his crest fell ever so slightly. "OK," he admitted. "Now that's slick."

CRUX NEGOTIATIONS ON STEEL PASS USCEOLA REFETOFF

groundwater—for agriculture or subdivisions or anything—anywhere near this place. Will the pupfish stop Las Vegas? Or will Las Vegas stop the pupfish? We'll see. Biologists are keeping a few hundred extra pups in refugee tanks at Ash Meadows and Hoover Dam just in case.

Goldwell Open Air Museum (Rhyolite, NV; 702-870-9946; www.goldwellmuseum .org). Big spooky sculptures in the desert and big views. Free. Open 24/7; visitor center and gift shop open sometimes.

Rhyolite. The ruins of what was once called, presumably by speculators in local real estate, "the Queen City of Death Valley." In its heyday (1905–7) it boasted a population of 10,000—roughly that of contemporary Sonoma or Mammoth Lakes on an average weekend; twice the size of Bishop or Aspen, Colorado; 10 times the size of nearby Beatty, Nevada. Most of the structures are on public Bureau of Land Management (BLM) land. It's 4 paved miles from Beatty and 35 miles from the Furnace Creek Visitor Center.

✪ **China Ranch Date Farm** (Tecopa; 760-852-4415; www.chinaranch.com). Follow the signs from the Old Spanish Trail (where the other '49ers passed) down the dirt road, through a narrow wash, and into a remarkable hidden oasis. Kit Carson and Alexis Godey of the 1843 Frémont party shot and killed two Indians here who may have been involved in carrying off two women and several horses from a nearby settlement at Resting Springs. A Chinese ex-Borax employee, "named either Quon Sing or Ah Foo" according to available sources, developed a productive farm here until he was driven off at gunpoint by another fellow by the name of Morrison. The date grove was planted in the 1920s and today produces some 26,000 pounds of fruit per season. Date samplers, shakes, bread, preserves, tchochkis, and a nursery of succulents and palm trees to go. It's a delightful, otherworldly place for a picnic. Open daily 9 AM–5 PM. Closed Christmas Day. Cynthia's tepees available for overnight guests.

✪ **Dante's View** (5,475 feet). At the gate of hell, Dante paused briefly over the following inscription: *Lasciate ogne speranza, voi ch'intrate* ("Abandon all hope, you who enter here"). And then he went in. One tires quickly, in these days of speed and chemically conditioned air, of all the glib-seeming references to the underworld in Death Valley. Coming from the east, let this be your first. Here is the perfect vantage from which to appreciate the scale of the place, with the sink at Badwater 5,757 feet below and the crest of Telescope Peak, across the basin, 5,575 feet above. The difference in elevation between the two—11,331 feet—represents the greatest topographic relief in the continental U.S. Stroll out beyond the parking lot, along the ridge, to where the road on the valley floor becomes visible. Appreciate also the temperature, often more than 30 degrees cooler than at Furnace Creek. Consider hiking north of the parking lot to the summit of Mount Perry (5,739 feet).

Zabriskie Point. Oft-photographed erosional badlands named for an early executive of the Pacific Coast Borax Company and made up of sediments from a long-gone lake. A justly popular place to take in a sunrise or sunset. Michelangelo Antonioni's 1970 film of the same name—either one of the worst films of all time or a misunderstood masterpiece—culminates here in a psychedelic orgy scene. The film is available on DVD and is especially notable for its marvelous array of rare (and rarefied) tracks from Jerry Garcia, Pink Floyd, The Youngbloods, and Patti Page (soundtrack available for download from iTunes).

THE SITE OF BENNETT-ARCANE LONG CAMP, WEST SIDE ROAD BURKE GRIGGS

FURNACE CREEK (THE OASIS) AREA

Borax Museum (Ranch at Death Valley). Housed in the oldest remaining structure from the early days of the Greenland Ranch—by one account the first Borax Company office, built in 1881 and moved to its current location in 1954—this museum is jam-packed with a fascinating collection of rocks, minerals, arrowheads, old photos, excerpts of journals by early visitors, and more. It also boasts a yard full of mining implements, railroad detritus, stagecoaches, wagons, and other early means of transportation. Open 9-ish to 2-ish most days. Free admission.

HOMELAND OF THE TIMBISHA SHOSHONE

When Zane Grey came through in 1919, he found "half a dozen families living in squalid tents . . . a ragged unpicturesque group." They collected firewood and did chores for the Greenland Ranch, when there was such to be done. Grey found their poverty depressing. He had never in his life, in all his travels, seen so many flies. He found these people resolutely less "Indian," less frugal and simple, than the Paiute and Navajo he had met. "With all that they were trying to live like Indians," he wrote, "these children of the open wore white men's apparel and ate white men's food; and they even had a cookstove and a sewing machine in their tent." Later they would do day labor for Borax Consolidated, making bricks for the original Furnace Creek Inn.

The Timbisha ("red rock") or Panamint Shoshone are descendants of the same Western Shoshone who, in 1863, signed a treaty of "peace and friendship" with the people and government of the U.S., by which the latter would be allowed to travel through, build upon, develop, and use the country however they saw fit, and the former would receive "as a full compensation and equivalent for the loss of game and the rights and privileges hereby conceded" 20 annual payments of $5,000 in provisions and clothing. Furthermore, according to Article 6:

"whenever the President of the United States shall deem it expedient for them [the Shoshone] to abandon the roaming life which they now lead, and become herdsmen or agriculturalists, he is hereby authorized to make such reservations for their use as he may deem necessary . . . and they do also hereby agree to remove their camps to such reservations as he may indicate, and to reside and remain therein."

In 1936, the Bureau of Indian Affairs and the Park Service drew up "a permanent residence area" of about 40 acres south of Furnace Creek and built nine adobe structures. The Civilian Conservation Corps (CCC) built a laundry, community center, and trading post. In the 1960s, under what today's Park Service calls "a less progressive administration," buildings that seemed vacant were "washed away with high-powered fire hoses." The tribe received official recognition by the secretary of the interior in the early 1980s—and an allotment of mobile homes.

TIMBISHA SHOSHONE VILLAGE, JUNE 2007 BURKE GRIGGS

In 2000, President Bill Clinton signed the Timbisha Homeland Act, setting aside for the tribe five separate parcels of land in California and Nevada, totaling 7,754 acres (a portion of which likely shares groundwater with the proposed Yucca Mountain nuclear waste repository). The tribe now has the right to negotiate a Class III gaming compact with the governor of either state (or both) for gaming on any of its land—except that within Death Valley. Its members also can now enter the national park without paying entrance fees.

DEATH VALLEY DATES AT THE RANCH AT DEATH VALLEY

Death Valley Dates (Ranch at Death Valley). Fifteen hundred trees, mostly deglet nour from Algeria, were planted here on 33 acres in the late 1920s, first from seed, then from cuttings. It never panned out as a commercial date farm, but today it provides a delightful place for an evening stroll with the coyotes and roadrunners, or, when the weather's mild, an afternoon picnic. Bring your own bocce. Barbecue facilities can be reserved at the ranch front desk or by calling 760-786-2345.

Wild Horse and Burro Corrals (adjacent to the Furnace Creek airport). Thousands of wild burros, and a few wild horses, have passed through here on their way out of the park.

SOUTH OF FURNACE CREEK AND THE OASIS

West Side Road. Easy graded-dirt road follows the west edge of the Badwater Playa; past the spot where the Bennett and Arcane families spent a month beneath their wagons (where later pioneers briefly tried alfalfa farming); past the grave site of Shorty Harris, founder of Harrisburg and Rhyolite, whose grave reads "single-blanket jackass prospector"; and past the remains of the valley's first and first-failed borax works—to reconnect with CA 178 just north of Ashford Mill.

Devil's Golf Course. Several thousand years ago, there was a lake here, 30 feet deep. Then the water evaporated, leaving a crust of salt (95 percent table salt) up to 5 feet deep. The pinnacles are diminutive, well-worn versions of those at Trona and Mono Lake. Imagine having to cross here, as the '49ers did, without a road.

Badwater. The lowest place in North America. A sign affixed to the side of the mountain, 274 feet above and to the east, indicates the level of the sea. A boardwalk has been constructed for one's strolling pleasure (to protect shoes from mud and mud from shoes). A short hike out across the tracked-up salt is a worthwhile adventure—especially when it's hot and dry. Bring good water.

Ashford Mill. Henry, Harold, and Louis Ashford sold their undeveloped interests in some dirt up the Black Mountains to a Hungarian count for $60,000 in 1914. The count, in turn, sold the claims for $105,000 to the McCausland brothers, who in turn built a state-of-the-art 40- or 50-ton mill that in the years since has produced mostly wildflowers.

NORTH OF FURNACE CREEK AND THE OASIS

Salt Creek. Home to another unique (endemic) species of pupfish, best spotted during high water in spring. The boardwalk covers a 1-mile loop to and from the parking lot. The water is not bueno for drinking.

Harmony Borax Works. Stabilized, oft-photographed ruins of Death Valley's first borax works. Original 20-mule-team wagons.

Stovepipe Well. Look east from the well—marked as it is today by the CCC—and see the century-old wagon tracks coming down the alluvial fan from Ryan. The original stovepipe is said to have once been displayed prominently at Eichbaum's resort. Note the eloquent grave of Val Nolan, victim of the elements. No water available.

Scotty's Castle (CLOSED UNTIL AT LEAST 2019 DUE TO FLOOD DAMAGE). One of the West's original million-dollar off-the-grid vacation homes, named for its some-time caretaker and inspiration, the compulsive liar, swindler, and circus cowboy Walter Scott. Tours of the place were offered as early as the 1930s. A modicum of political maneuvering took place when, Death Valley having been declared a national monument, it was suddenly discovered that the "castle" had been built on the wrong land. The place has been mostly painstakingly preserved as it was in the 1930s—except for the updating of the original swamp cooling system. The pipe organ alone is worth the visit. When it's open, popular fifty-minute-long living history tours begin hourly, every day, from 9 AM to 5 PM. So-called Underground Mystery Tours of the original cooling and waterheating systems are available by special request during summer and fall for those interested in infrastructure and historical engineering. Lower Grapevine Ranch

CROSSING THE DEVIL'S GOLF COURSE, 1926 COURTESY BANCROFT LIBRARY

THEY SHOOT WILD BURROS, DON'T THEY?

On his trip to Kansas in the 1540s, the unlucky Spanish conquistador Francisco Vasquez de Coronado brought with him 1,500 animals, including horses and burros—some of which managed to stay behind with the native peoples, or to found or join feral populations. Spanish missionaries in California rode burros and horses, and so did the fur trappers, cowboys and Indians, and '49ers. Burros and horses are together required to make mules, to this day the most effective means of transportation, after the helicopter, in the High Sierra. From 1849 to the early 1920s, the burro was the prospector's ride of choice. As mines played out and cars took over the business of getting people from one place to another, burros were left to fend for themselves, which they did quite successfully all across the Southwest, except for being frequently shot by government agencies or the public, or rounded up and sold to dog food canneries.

In 1971, in what became the Wild Free-Roaming Horse and Burro Act, Congress found and declared "that wild free-roaming horses and burros are living symbols of the historic and pioneer spirit of the West; that they contribute to the diversity of life forms within the nation and enrich the lives of the American people; that these horses and burros are fast disappearing from the American scene," and that they should therefore, on public lands, "be protected from capture, branding, harassment, or death." The tricky part, from the Park Service's point of view, was that wild horses and burros, like salt cedar, Washington palms, and other exotic species, were showing a capacity to out-compete the locals. In Death Valley they were trampling native plants and eating fodder that might otherwise have gone to native bighorn sheep, and they were multiplying. (The U.S. Geological Survey estimates that wild horse populations, "largely unchecked by natural predators," increase by 18 to 25 percent each year.)

The law was modified in 1976, and again in 1978, to allow for the removal or destruction of "excess animals"—at the discretion of the secretary of the interior—"in order to preserve and maintain a thriving natural ecological balance and multiple-use relationship in that area."

GATHERING WILD BURROS ON PUBLIC LANDS BLM PHOTO

NOT-SO-WILD BURRO, SALINE VALLEY, MAY 2017

One caveat: They were no longer to be used for commercial dog food. A 1987 article in the Los Angeles Times proclaimed the successful completion of a $1.4 million removal program: "Last of Wild Burros Removed From Death Valley." And yet some reports have Park Service staff or contractors shooting wild burros as recently as 1994.

By 1998, according to the BLM, the total wild horse population in the U.S., from a peak of about 58,000 head in 1977, had been reduced—by helicopter roundups, adoption programs, and "direct lethal means"—to 39,470. The total wild burro population had been reduced from 14,000 to 5,025. Still, in June 1999, various public land agencies, including Death Valley National Park, signed a strategic agreement that "recognized the overpopulation of wild burros on the desert" and outlined a policy for stepping up their removal.

In 2003 there were still an estimated 500 wild burros in Death Valley National Park, "primarily in the areas of Saline Valley, Butte Valley, and Wild Rose"—with small herds assumed to be migrating in and out of the park from adjacent BLM lands and the China Lake Naval Weapons Reserve. There may have been as many as a dozen wild horses. The plan was still to get rid of them all—"to achieve a zero population"—as much as possible by removal and adoption, then by lethal means if necessary, but by 2007 adoptions had lagged significantly, and lethal means had not been employed. There were field trials under way to see if a specific wildlife contraception agent might be used on wild burros—as it had in urban areas on squirrels and pigeons.

In 2017, Linda Manning, a wildlife biologist with the park service, estimated that there were still anywhere from 750-2,000 burros roaming free in Death Valley National Park, where they compete fiercely with native bighorn sheep. Park rangers have legal authority to shoot burros but find themselves generally reluctant to do so; most visitors consider the shaggy beasts part of the experience. The easiest place to see them is at the warm springs in Saline Valley, where they avail themselves regularly of food left unattended by campers, have been known to eat tires and Duraflame logs, and have also saved at least one lost hiker's life by leading him to water.

For information about how to adopt a wild horse or burro, go to www.blm.gov/adoptahorse.

NIGHT SKY OVER THE RACETRACK, DEATH VALLEY DAN DURISCOE, NPS PHOTO

tours are offered in winter. Meanwhile, during the closure, Flood Recovery Tours will be offered on a limited basis through the Death Valley Natural History Association (www.dvnha.org).

Ubehebe Crater. Two or three millennia ago, about the time the General Sherman tree began to sprout in what would eventually become Sequoia National Park (see Chapter 6), magma rose nearly to the surface here, flashing groundwater to steam and blowing off a sizeable chunk of the earth. Climb down into it if you want. Bring water.

✪ **Eureka Dunes**. The biggest sand dunes in California, Eureka is home to rare species and was oft-photographed by the likes of Ansel Adams. Off-limits to sand boarding and horseback riding. Primitive camping available.

✪ **The Racetrack**. One of the last great unexplained mysteries of the physical world. The Park Service officially recommends a high-clearance vehicle; check with a ranger to see if that might include a rental car. Bring spare tires.

PANAMINT AND SALINE

Emigrant Canyon Road. This paved road climbs up the backside of the Tucki Mountains to connect with decent graded-gravel side roads (the Park Service calls for high clearance) to the onetime town site of Skidoo and to Aguereberry Point. Of Skidoo (population 700), where, in 1907, the unfortunate barkeep Hootch Simpson was hanged twice (the second time to accommodate the press), not much remains other than the original desolation of the site and an interpretative sign. Water was piped here from a spring on Telescope Peak, at a distance of 23 miles and a cost of $250,000. Various structures and vehicles at Pete Aguereberry's camp of 40 years testify to the life and labors of another era. Aguereberry Point (6,433 feet) affords a vantage opposite Dante's View. In summer, temperatures are 20 to 30 Fahrenheit degrees cooler than in the valley below. In winter, they dip below freezing.

✪ **Wildrose Charcoal Kilns**. Some of the best-preserved charcoal kilns in the West, the Wildrose kilns were Swiss engineered and built by Chinese labor in 1876. Used to convert nearby pinyon trees to charcoal for the smelting of lead and silver ore 30 miles to the west, they were operated for 3 years, abandoned in 1879, restored in 1933 by the CCC, and restored again in 1971 by a crew of Navajo stonemasons. Note the similarity in masonry with structures in Chaco Canyon, New Mexico.

Trona Pinnacles National Natural Landmark. More than 500 tufa (calcium carbonate) spires, some up to 140 feet tall, are generally considered one of the best examples of tufa formations in North America. Like the tufa formations at Mono Lake, but more of them and bigger—and without the water. Recognizable as the location for the original and the 2001 remake of *Planet of the Apes*.

Trona (population 1,885). The Jayhawkers passed through here on their way out of Death Valley, only to find the water unpalatable. In 1862, John Searles discovered borax on the surface of the dry lake that would come to bear his name. Here was the terminus of the great, brief Epsom Salts Monorail from Death Valley.

Telescope Peak (11,049 feet). A good trail leads upward from Mahogany Flat (8,133 feet) and climbs its way through juniper and pinyon to the summit. The vertical drop from here to the Badwater Basin is twice the depth of the Grand Canyon. Cool alpine temperatures; views of Death Valley, the Panamint Basin, China Lake, the Argus, Coso, Slate, and Sierra Nevada ranges to the west; and views of the Amargosa and Spring ranges to the east—"not to be compared with any tawdry scene that needs the colors of vegetation to make it attractive," John R. Spears wrote in 1891. (See the "Skiing Death Valley" sidebar earlier in this chapter.)

Ballarat (population "more or less"). Named for a sister mining camp in Australia, this particular Ballarat is an abiding feature of a fast-disappearing American outback, conjuring images of Road Warrior and countless dystopian Westerns. It's the home of Seldom Seen Slim's grave and Tex Watson's Power Wagon. Once a bustling supply town of 400 permanent citizens in 1898, it now has population of two: Rocky Novak, prospector and mayor (he's been running the place since '04), and his father, George. The Outpost general store and historical museum is a last stop for cold drinks, hose clamps, and directions before heading up Goler Wash to look for wild burros and the last hideout of Charles Manson.

U.S. Naval Museum of Armament & Technology (760-939-3530; www.china lakemuseum.org). Old bombs, planes, missiles, and ordnance. Open to the public Monday through Saturday 10 AM–4 PM; closed Sunday and holidays. Call for information on how to get a guest pass to the base.

✪ **Last Chance Canyon Petroglyphs**. Said to be the largest concentration of Indian petroglyphs in North America, spanning 100 miles and many thousands of years of human history. Last Chance is on the National Register of Historic Places and is protected by no lesser institution than the U.S. Navy. U.S. citizenship is required for access. Contact the Maturango Museum (100 E. Las Flores Ave., Ridgecrest; 760-375-6900; maturango.org), Friends of Last Chance Canyon (760-377-4976; www.tflcc.org) or the Navy Public Affairs Office (760-939-1683) for information. (See "An Elegant Record" sidebar.)

ROCKY NOVAK, MAYOR OF BALLARAT, JUNE 2007 BURKE GRIGGS

THE NORTH ROAD TO CHINA LAKE WEAPONS RESERVE, DARWIN

BLM Wild Horse and Burro Adoption Facility (Randsburg Wash Road, off CA 178, Ridgecrest; 760-384-5765; www.blm.gov/wo/st/en/prog/wild_horse_and_burro .html). This preparation center for wild horses and burros gathered from public lands in the region is open Monday through Friday 7:30 AM–4 PM (closed federal holidays). Individual and group tours available. Viewing allowed from dirt perimeter road. Adoptions by appointment only.

Father Crowley Point. This gaping vista down Rainbow Canyon to the Panamint Dunes 4,000 feet below is worth getting out of the car for. It was named for John J. Crowley, "the Desert Padre," parish priest of Death Valley and Mount Whitney from 1919 to 1940 and one of the first great promoters of tourism in the Eastern Sierra.

Darwin. In 1876, Darwin (founded by prospector and man of adventure Dr. Erasmus Darwin French) boasted a thousand citizens, 200 frame houses, a raucous main street, and a pair of busy smelters. Today, with a population of 43 (down from 54 in 2011), the place is inhabited by ghosts, feral cats, vintage aluminum trailers, a handful of artists, and a registered sex offender.

✪ Saline Valley. One of the most isolated valleys in North America, Saline is higher than Death Valley by a thousand feet, but has similar topography. It's a haven for wild burros, rock hounds, nudists, and other contemporary misfits. Annexed by the National Park Service in 1994, it's frequently used by the U.S. military for million-dollar, low-altitude, upside-down flight training. The roads into the valley are long, rough, tire-shredding gravel washboards, not to be attempted frivolously or in wet conditions. Note the remains of nineteenth-century borax operations at the edge of the salt marsh, and the historic aerial salt tram over the Inyo Range to the west. The warm springs (alas, no longer any kind of secret), where Charles Manson and Family are said to have spent much time, are today a congenial oasis of fan palms, concrete tubs, a lending library, and shaded lawn, all spotlessly maintained by local residents—inheritors of an earlier counterculture settlement—in a kind of working truce with the Park Service. No gas; no services; no ice; no firewood; no disrespect. Camping is still free, clothing still optional. Pack it in, pack it out (unless it's cold beer or fresh vegetables, in which case the locals are likely to be happy to take it off your hands).

AN ELEGANT RECORD: VISITING THE ANCIENT PETROGLYPHS OF LAST CHANCE CANYON

A t 2 AM the wind was blowing 150 mph over the Sierra Crest, pounding at the stucco walls of the motel on Ridgecrest's main drag where I'd decided to camp for the night, less than a mile from the entrance to the Navy bombing range at China Lake. I wondered how long it would take such a wind to wear a town like Ridgecrest down to sand. Or to bury it—100 years? 1,000? 10,000?

Birthplace of the Sidewinder missile, the Tomahawk, and all manner of target-penetrating projectiles now being employed overseas, Naval Air Weapons Station (NAWS) China Lake comprises 1.1 million acres of Mojave desert, including, among other things, the largest concentration of ancient rock art in the Western Hemisphere. And by ancient I mean that some of it, depending on who you talk to, may date as far back as 16,000 years. Which is a while back: way before the Romans and Greeks, before the pyramids, before agriculture, before the bow and arrow, before pottery.

I was working on a bottle of pale ale and a paper container of dark-chocolate ice cream, reading about the deterioration of the cave paintings at Lascaux, in France, how even though the original chambers had been closed to visitors for nearly half a century, the artwork, or whatever it should be called—all those 17,000-year-old horses and reindeer and bison that

SOME OF THE IMAGES IN THE COSO ROCK ART DISTRICT MAY BE AS MANY AS 16,000 YEARS OLD BILL BECHER

had once caused Picasso to say of modern art that we had come no distance at all in nearly a thousand generations of human creativity—were now being consumed by some kind of latter-day, human-generated mold.

They'd tried everything. And it was getting worse. "We try to resolve one problem," the cave administrator told The Washington Post, "we create another."

In 1994, French spelunkers had come upon some even older paintings in a cavern a few hundred miles from Lascaux, which they dubbed the Grotte Chauvet. They found footprints in the sand—a human child's footprints—from more than 25,000 years ago, plain as if they'd been made the day before. Given the state of affairs at Lascaux, it was decided that the new cave would not, for the foreseeable future, if ever, be open to visitation.

Before I drifted off to sleep, I couldn't help but think: What will be left of us in another 25 millennia? They say it takes 1,000 years for a plastic bag to degrade into the earth, though no one really knows for sure. By the looks of some of the abandoned homesteads I've seen along the backroads of the Inyos and the Panamints, I'd guess that most modern artifacts—refrigerators, couches, bullet casings, tires, even whole vehicles—are unlikely to remain distinguishable from dirt for more than a couple of centuries. How long will a Picasso last out in the open air? Who knows?

Scientists researching the viability of long-term nuclear waste storage beneath Yucca Mountain made studies of conditions at Lascaux and Chauvet as natural analogues of what they might need—dry and dark—to keep spent fuel containers relatively leak-free for 30,000+ years. After which time, they figured, human beings would've either figured out a cure for cancer or died off from some other unforeseen calamity.

After dawn, clinging to a large Styrofoam cup of McDonald's coffee, I met up with photographer Bill Becher and professional archaeologist David Whitley, and together we slid into the pristine environment of Navy Civilian Public Affairs Officer Peggy Shoaf's personal minivan. We picked up a long-range two-way radio so that Shoaf could keep abreast of the day's bombings, and soon enough we were floating across the salt-crusted bed of what was once, from say 18,000 to 10,000 years ago, part of a system of interconnected saline lakes stretching from what is now Lancaster/Palmdale/Victorville to the basin now holding the remains of Mono Lake.

"You and I could go out there and walk around the edge of one of those big playas," Greg Haverstock, an archaeologist with the BLM's Bishop Field Office, would tell me later on the phone, "and within hours find fossilized bone from extinct megafauna: three-toed camels, dire wolves, mastodon. And right there on the same level find artifacts dating to 14,000 years ago. And some of those mastodon bones will exhibit wear from humans cutting them and making them into tools."

Accordingly to Whitley, there may be as many as 100,000 individual petroglyphs in the mountains above the China Lake basin, some that could date as far back as 12,000 to 16,000 years, others as recent as the mid-twentieth century. "There are so many up there," he explained, "that we don't even know how many there are."

Haverstock's not sold on the various techniques that have been used to try to date rock art. But based on the forty or so fluted-point projectiles (spear points) found over the years in the Owens Valley—projectiles being a common theme across human history—it's generally agreed that there've been people around here (maybe even five separate migrations of them) since the end of the last ice age.

We passed a turnoff marked EXPLOSIVE TRUCKS DELIVERY, followed by a sign for a WEAPONS SURVIVABILITY LAB. Across the flats we saw abandoned tanks, launchers, shipping containers with holes blown through their sides, a fleet of silica-white pickup trucks fresh-painted to match the playa. We worked our way up into the Cosos, past wild horses and Joshua trees. "That's some good-looking buckskin," said Whitley, referring to the horses. He talked about how the latest BLM culling policies had improved the herds. He talked about how the Miwok had once, briefly, had a horse culture to rival that of the Plains tribes. He talked about how stupid wild burros are, how they'll dig for water and then sully what they've found by wallowing in it.

We left the minivan beside a Park Service–style restroom 49 road miles inside the base's main gate. The air was still and cool, but the sun was warm. On foot we made our way down a path of soft sand, through a cut in the basalt to an enormous open-air rock art gallery with hundreds of stylized designs—human figures, bighorn sheep, abstract patterns, and the occasional more modern graffiti—etched into the oxidized cliff faces.

There are glyphs like these all up and down the ranges and canyons of the Eastern Sierra Nevada, and even the occasional painting too, from the El Paso Mountains above Red Rock Canyon to the dolomite formations above Swansea to the volcanic tableland beneath Casa Diablo. But nowhere is there such a dense concentration, spanning such a long stretch of time—from the Pleistocene into at least the 1940s—than in the Cosos. And nowhere else has the stuff been so thoroughly spared the general ignominies of bullet holes, looting, and vandalism that have for so many decades plagued other sites with easier public access. Perhaps there's something to be said for the kind of protections afforded "the resource" (as they say) by a well-funded, well-armed organization which also happens to run facilities in locations like the Persian Gulf and Guantánamo Bay.

As to what the images might mean, or why they were put here, there are nearly as many theories as there are individual images. Some see in them evidence of ancient hunting rituals; others see the hallucinations of shamans. "Iconography from another culture is fertile ground for people's ideas to run amok," said Whitley. "We've got people who are adamant that this was made by aliens."

The deeper you get into it, the more it seems that nobody really knows a damn thing—except that people have been out here scratching designs on the rocks for longer than we can really get our heads around. And some of it's really quite interesting to look at. "I remember the first time I came out here I just stood and looked," said Shoaf, who's been escorting visitors to the Coso Rock Art District for more years than she'd like to think about. "You can feel the past in this canyon. And I'm not that type of person."

Whatever it all means, and whatever it might eventually tell us—if anything—it's an elegant record. Perhaps the best we can hope for, down the road a few millennia, is that it's still here long after most of what we've done and left behind has disappeared.

Beta: Public tours of the Coso Petroglyphs are available through the Maturango Museum (100 E. Las Flores Ave., Ridgecrest; 760-375-6900; maturango.org). Visits also can be arranged through the Navy Public Affairs Office (760-939-1683). Reservations and proof of U.S. citizenship required in advance. No children under 10, no pets. All tours and visits subject to cancellation on short notice because of military testing, security concerns, or weather. For details and further restrictions, check www.cnic.navy.mil/ChinaLake/FamilyReadiness/PetroglyphTours/index.htm. For information on other local rock art sites on public land or the laws governing the protection of artifacts, check with the Bureau of Land Management (351 Pacu Ln., Bishop; 760-872-5000; blm.gov/ca/bishop).

✱ To Do

BIKING Bicycles are allowed on all of the same park roads as vehicles. Road biking is popular—and spectacular—from fall through spring, with epic out-and-back rides in all four directions from Furnace Creek. Off-pavement mountain biking is confined to dirt roads and Jeep trails and for the most part involves washboard surfaces and gravel. Basic bike rentals are available year-round from a stand adjacent to the **Ranch General Store** (760-786-3372). Nearest parts and services are in Las Vegas or in Bishop (Chapter 4).

Timber Tours (800-417-2453, 303-664-8388; www.timbertours.com) offers a six-day Death Valley Base Camp Tour that covers 269 fully-supported miles of paved road and 17,585 feet of climbing.

BIRD-WATCHING Desert salt marshes, springs, and oases are magnets for migratory waterfowl and havens for hundreds of endemic and nonnative species. Hoist your binoculars at the China Ranch Date Farm (www.chinaranch.com/birds.html), Ash Meadows National Wildlife Refuge (www.fws.gov/refuge/ash_meadows/), Saratoga Springs, or at the wildlife viewing platform off the Furnace Creek Golf Course.

DAWN AT FURNACE CREEK GOLF COURSE

GOLF Furnace Creek Golf Course (760-786-3373). The lowest all-grass course on the planet (214 feet), and a certified member of the Audubon Cooperative Sanctuary Program for Golf Courses. First opened in 1930, with ranch sheep keeping the greens trimmed. Expanded to eighteen holes in 1968. Redesigned by Perry Dye in 1997. Par 70. Various golf and lodging packages available. In summer the "Extreme Golf 6-Pack" includes nine holes of golf, club rental, cart, and bottled water for $25. For the least extreme experience, tee off at 6 AM, before breakfast.

HIKING Given the openness of the terrain and the sparse vegetation, opportunities for cross-country strolls are essentially limitless. Summertime "hikes" in the valley will most likely be limited to brief forays from the car to a given point of interest and back—in the shade of a broad-brimmed hat. In winter, day hikes of varying degrees of difficulty abound in side canyons up and down the basin. Popular, easy jaunts include the Golden Canyon Trail, Titus Canyon, and the Gower Gulch Loop. For something slightly more strenuous, try the Keane Wonder Mine Trail or Fall Canyon. The hike up Telescope Peak from Wildrose is a pleasant alternative to the deep-basin heat of mid-summer. Consult a ranger for suggestions and conditions. If you prefer a guided and supported experience, **Timber Tours** (800-417-2453, 303-664-8388; www.timbertours .com) offers a six-day Death Valley Hiking Tour that covers about 32 miles of trails.

HORSEBACK RIDING The horses at the Furnace Creek Stables (760-786-3339; www .furnacecreekstables.com) spend their summers working in the cool of the High Sierra and their winters (September–May) giving one-and two-hour trail rides on and around the old Furnace Creek Ranch. Wagon and carriage rides also available. Private horses are not allowed in developed campgrounds or on most valley trails, and are discouraged in steep canyons and ranges.

TENNIS There are six courts at Furnace Creek: two at the ranch and four at the inn. Rackets are available at the front desk. Bring low-altitude balls.

OFF-HIGHWAY DRIVING Of the 696 miles of maintained road in the park, only 243 are classified by the Park Service as "standard vehicle roads, or paved or unpaved that require no more ground clearance than a standard sedan." Visitors equipped with four-wheel drive, high clearance, and sufficiently beefy suspension will want to test their skills (and the strength of their tires) on the other 442 miles open to vehicle travel (the remaining 11 miles are service spurs, closed to the public). In order of ascending difficulty, start with popular Titus Canyon or Darwin Falls Roads, then try Goler Wash, from Ballarat to the West Side Road (past Charles Manson's last hideout), then finally Steel Pass, from the dunes at Saline to the much bigger dunes at Eureka (or the other way around). In all cases, six-ply tires (and at least two spares) will be appreciated. The miles of washboarded gravel on the Racetrack and Saline Valley Roads are generally passable, if not very pleasant, in a regular passenger car—except, that is, when there's snow on South Pass and/or flooding in the canyons, when all unpaved roads become quagmires or paths for debris slides. The erstwhile "road" to Panamint City, up Surprise Canyon, remains off-limits to motorized vehicles. **Farabee's Jeep Rentals and Tours** (877-970-5337, 760-786-9872; www.oasisatdeathvalley.com/activities/farabee-jeep-rentals) offers sturdy, late-model Jeep rentals and caravan tours. **Pink Jeep Tours** of Las Vegas (1-888-900-4480; www.pinkjeeptourslasvegas.com) offers a variety of air-conditioned and tinted-window backroad tours of, for example, Titus Canyon, the Wildrose Charcoal Kilns, and the Racetrack, complete with reclining leather captain's chairs, "artisan" lunches, and unlimited bottled water.

SKIING DEATH VALLEY

(Outtakes from the Men's Journal Expedition)

Once upon a time there was a certain utility to climbing mountains: to get the lay of the land, to see which way to run the wagons, to be the first to do it. That time is gone. And yet there we were, in the present, on a long haul to the top of the biggest mountain in the lower 48, in the dark, with skis on our backs.

1:05 AM: 1,609 FEET ABOVE SEA LEVEL; 1,891 FEET ABOVE BADWATER

I've been asleep for maybe 20 minutes when I smell coffee. We're into the second hour of March, at almost 1,900 feet above the lowest, hottest, driest basin in North America, and it's a balmy 65 degrees. The lights are on in Ryan Boyer's camper. Orion is still midway through his long, slow faceplant over the tail of the Panamints. A warm wind sweeps down-canyon, bearing only the faintest memory of winter.

John Wentworth arrives, racketing Paris-Dakar-style out of the dust and the moonless desert night. He's fresh from a day of epic, midwinter "pow" on the Four Gables in the High Sierra backcountry. (Later he will show us pictures on his phone, as if to reinforce the depth of our folly.) "Where's the snow?" he says.

"It's gonna be a bit of a walk," I say.

If I hadn't seen it with my own eyes, hadn't seen Boyer (our token redneck tele guy) and Bernie Rosow (our token jibber) posing with fat skis on their shoulders—at Dante's View, at Zabriskie Point, on the boardwalk at Badwater after breakfast yesterday, with the mercury already pressing 90 degrees Fahrenheit, the tourists looking on in disbelief, the snow-dusted crest of the range painted above our heads like some ineffectual wisp of cloud ("How d'ya get up there?" asked one; "What if someone breaks up?" asked another)—I wouldn't believe it existed. Much less that we might be able to ski on it.

PANAMINTS-BOUND ON WEST SIDE ROAD, DEATH VALLEY   CHRISTIAN PONDELLA

INTREPID SKIERS, FROM LEFT: DEVIN MCDONELL, DAVID SCHEMENAUER, BERNIE ROSOW, AND RYAN BOYER.
CHRISTIAN PONDELLA

The ranger at Furnace Creek had never heard of anyone doing it. "You mean like with crampons and an ice ax to the top and skiing down?" he said. "I think anyone you talk to is going to advise against it—that'd be pretty crazy."

Telescope Peak, at the summit of the desolate Panamint Range, is the highest point in Death Valley National Park, two dry ranges into the rain shadow of California's Sierra Nevada. From below sea level to where its crest grazes the troposphere, somewhere up there in the night sky, it offers more sustained vertical rise than any other peak in the Lower 48. Base to summit, it stands taller than any of Colorado's fourteeners, taller than the Tetons, taller than Whitney or Shasta or Rainier. By the Köppen Classification System, the summit of Telescope is a tiny oasis of cool "Mediterranean" climate (read: occasional snow) marooned atop a much larger island of so-called "arid mid-latitude desert," floating, in turn, in a vast sea-bottom of "arid low-latitude desert (hot)" that stretches from the Mojave to the Sonora and deep into Mexico.

> Telescope towers above the land at its foot as does no other peak in the
> United States.
> —W. A. Chalfant, *Death Valley: The Facts* (1930)

Looking at Telescope from a distance, which is your only choice if you want to take in the whole thing, it's nearly impossible to get perspective. The part of it that resembles other mountains, mountains you might ski on—the part with trees and snow, that is—is such a comparatively small part of the whole, it's hard to gauge. Early in the winter of 1849, a hardy Wisconsinite by the name of William Manly, scouting for a ragtag, dehydrated, half-starving convoy of California-bound emigrants, followed the distant vision of what he called "the lofty snowcapped peak" for 2 months, like the North Star, across the wasted basins and hard-rock ranges of southern Nevada, across what is now known as Area 51, across the unrelenting flats of the Amargosa Desert, through the Funeral Mountains, to the springs at Furnace Creek.

A hoard of twenty-dollar gold pieces could now stand before us the whole day long with no temptation to touch a single coin. . . . We would have given much more for some of the snow which we could see drifting over the peak of the great snow mountains over our heads like a dusty cloud.
—William Lewis Manly, *Death Valley in '49* (1894)

The day after Christmas—celebrated with boiled ox and coffee—he awoke to find the mountain, and the good water it might represent, still more than 20 miles away across the barely passable surface of one of the largest salt pans in North America. And even more of a barrier than he'd imagined. "Nothing could climb it on its eastern side," he wrote, "except a bird."

2:15 AM: 3,200 FEET ABOVE SEA LEVEL

We've crawled our two hardiest vehicles into the gutted, dust-dry larynx of Hanaupah Canyon's South Fork, in the dark, abandoning them when they could go no farther. We're on foot, picking our separate ways up the wash, eight men into the warm katabatic breeze, into the tangle of willows, into the riot of frogs up-canyon, on and up, headlamps bobbing and dipping across the night like drunken fireflies.

We've foregone the Park Service-recommended ice axes and crampons, have left behind our avy gear—shovels, probes, beacons—in the interest of traveling as light as possible (which is not very light, alas, with skis, skins, ski boots, food, winter clothing, and nearly a gallon of water each on our backs). My brother-in-law, Devin McDonell, whose headlamp is all but dead, claims the first spill: a turtle-dive flat on his face beneath the full weight of his pack. Joe Walker, former pro ski racer, accomplished world traveler, ski tuner for the World Cup, has forgotten his hiking shoes—but seems his usual happy self, dancing over cactus thorns in a pair of self-draining river moccasins. Rosow, with no headlamp at all, proves nimble enough in his low-top skate shoes.

3 AM: 3,400 FEET ABOVE SEA LEVEL

Schemenauer—"Shimmy," they call him, a onetime semi-pro big-mountain skier who now lives down in Reno but has made a point of skiing something every month of the year for the past 15 years—has the map (the entire quadrangle) graven on his brain. He sniffs out something of a game trail, a timeworn Shoshone path, leading straight up from the springs. He and Boyer angle for the ridge, trotting like a pair of wild goats.

Bulge on bulge rose the bold benches, and on up the unscalable outcroppings of rock, like colossal ribs of the earth, on and up the steep slopes to where their density of blue black color began to thin out with streaks of white, and thence upward to the last noble height, where the cold pure snow gleamed against the sky.
—Zane Grey, *Tales of Lonely Trails* (1922)

The rest of us clamber after, as best we can, the world now canted precipitously upward, the silhouette of the mountain rearing before us, an immense blue-black wall against the sky, against that ancient configuration of distant fires now and then shot through with a satellite, or a blinking jetliner on its way into or out of Los Angeles or the Bay Area or Vegas. Vegas spreads and grows behind us, like a stain, like dawn ever about to break. The track disappears into shale, then reappears. We make our way across broken fins of rock. The distant trickle of the springs, the cacophony of frogs far below, give way to silence—to the delicate clink-clink of gear, Walker's ski crampons lashed to the back of his pack, the scrabble of feet on scree, Rosow's whistling, and the general singing of bowels.

3:20 AM: 4,400 FEET ABOVE SEA LEVEL

The moon sneaks up behind us, a quarter moon, illuminating rabbit pellets, bleached coyote scat, carcasses of well-traveled party balloons, and the tracks of some big ungulate—a deer, perhaps, or a bighorn sheep.

3:35 AM: 4,930 FEET ABOVE SEA LEVEL

"Probably too early to say this," says Boyer, strolling along a flat ridgeline through sagebrush and half-dead juniper, "but this is downright civilized."

3:50 AM: 5,202 FEET ABOVE SEA LEVEL

There's an old fire pit on the ridge, the ground wet in patches where once, not long ago, there was snow. There are mosquitoes, and piñon pines, and mysterious bird-flutterings in the bushes. I think about Manly and his buddy John Rogers, marching 250 miles from Death Valley to what is now the edge of Los Angeles in early 1850—with no GPS, no maps, no real idea where they were or where they were headed, setting off with, as Manly put it, "seven-eighths of all the flesh of an ox . . . a couple spoonfuls of rice and about as much tea . . . [and] all the money there was in camp"—and then back, another 250 miles, to bring a little ration of flour, yellow beans, and hope to their compatriots.

Manly was 30, Rogers 27 or 28. What did they talk about? Did they have as nuanced a sense of humor as we did? Could their conversation move as deftly from the notion of ice on the planet Uranus all the way to the ingenious big-wall sanitation methods of Reinhold Messner?

Eleven years later, in April 1861, a Dr. Samuel George and one W. T. Henderson—prospectors for precious metals—were the first to climb to the summit of the Panamints. Henderson, who also happened to be no slouch at killing Indians, is said to have been the one who shot the horse out from under Joaquín Murrieta, who cut the bandit's head off to show his friends and then sold it for $35. Upon making the crest of the range, according to nineteenth-century correspondent J. R. Spears, the aging vigilante looked out across "such a landscape as can be seen nowhere else on earth," reached into the deep well of his creativity, and "because of the vast space which the eye could cover there" named the mountain after an optical instrument he'd neglected to bring along.

As many as 160 people a day—some 23,000 every year—climb Mount Whitney. Even in the dead of winter, you're likely to cross paths with other people on Whitney, to enjoy their uptracks or to have to ski across their lines on the way down. The vast country up the east face of the Panamints, by contrast, sees "maybe three to five groups a year, maybe ten to twenty people," according to veteran Death Valley ranger Charlie Callagan. And most, if not all, of those people will be traveling before the snow on the so-called Lowest-to-Highest Trail from Death Valley to Whitney.

The easiest and most popular way to the summit of Telescope is by the old mine road up the backside, from Wildrose Canyon past the charcoal kilns to Mahogany Flat, where, once upon a time, a fellow by the name of Thorndike envisioned building a ski resort. In summer, it's a moderate 7-mile hike up the ridgeline from road's end, at 8,133 feet, to the peak. In winter, the road is generally impassable beyond the kilns, except on skis or snowshoes. The ridgeline, they say, can be bulletproof ice, thanks to the relentless winds. I've heard anecdotes from a couple of folks who've skinned up that way, at one point or another, over the years, for the hell of it, and were either turned around by poor conditions, or made the top and skied back to the kilns "in great powder the entire time."

But that's the easy way. Which will undoubtedly be given more consideration next time, if any of us is ever to do this again. The way we're doing it, which for some reason had seemed purer, aesthetically—the clean, epic up-and-down of it, Hanaupah to the summit of Telescope and back—Michel Digonnet, in his classic hiking guide to the park, has dubbed one of the toughest treks in Death Valley: "Crossing the Grand Canyon in one day is much easier," he writes. "It's half as much climbing up and there's a trail." And then he adds: "Only a chosen few can do this in one day (I am not one of them, yet), and even fewer can cram the round-trip between sunrise and sunset."

4:20 AM: 5,453 FEET ABOVE SEA LEVEL

Snow! We begin to see tiny atolls of the stuff, scabbed-over like bits of discarded Styrofoam caught in the bushes. The ridgeline drops, rises again.

5 AM: 6,165 FEET ABOVE SEA LEVEL

Still crunching across brief allotments of wind-dried crust: Five or six ginger steps across the surface, then punch through to the knees. Then back onto dirt and rock. "This is awesome," says Rosow, only half sarcastically.

"Only six grand to go," says Pondella, working through a bag of dried tropical fruit medley, disappearing now and then to leave yet another gut-processed offering to the mountain. Walker trades his river shoes for his ski boots, and then he goes back to river shoes. Wentworth puts on his ski boots and disappears. We assume he's decided to sidehill down into the gully for good snow. We stay high, thinking it might be easier.

6 AM: 6,950 FEET ABOVE SEA LEVEL

Daylight coming up fast. A vertical mile and a half below us, the Wrangler Café is opening for breakfast. The first pack of diehard cyclists is setting out on the spring installment of the Death Valley Double Century. The Ansel Adams aficionados are in place on the boardwalk at Badwater, cameras on tripods, poised to get the shot: the first crack of sun across the snow-dusted wall of Telescope, more than 11,000 feet into the sky, reflected in the stagnant pool at the bottom of an extinct Pleistocene lake (named after William Manly), 282 feet below sea level.

Somewhere up there, invisible to the naked eye, maybe two-thirds of the way up, where the vast alluvial mess gives way to a peppering of trees and the first allotments of snow: That's us, with skis on our backs.

"I don't think I've ever been this awake for sunrise," says Rosow. "And sober!"

7:50 AM: 8,200 FEET ABOVE SEA LEVEL

A field of broken trees from an old slide, crisp little upslope wind. We've been on snow for more than an hour, alternately skinning and postholing. Devin McDonell drops a glove, has to climb back down for it. Then he drops a pole. "This is what they invented chairlifts for," he says. He is only half-kidding.

9 AM: 9,500 FEET ABOVE SEA LEVEL

The skis go back on the pack. A million little crystals slide past us across the surface, like rain on a tent. Heavy legs sink to the knees in the fast-warming slab. Still another 600 vertical feet to the ridge, more than 1,500 to the summit. If there's a crux to this marathon, I think, this is it. Pondella runs up and down the face, laughing, joking, taking pictures of human suffering and 3,000-year-old trees.

"I'd rather do an iron man," says McDonell (having done one). "It's easier."

11 AM: 11,049 FEET ABOVE SEA LEVEL; 11,331 FEET ABOVE BADWATER

Wentworth has beat us to the summit, having skinned up the main throat in the privacy of his iPod, without ever taking off his skis. He's already read and signed the summit register. (The previous entry was dated November 7—4 months earlier.) "Look yonder," he shouts, gesturing into the rising gale—the grand northward march of the Sierra 60 miles away; dust storms brewing across the China Lake Naval Weapons Station to the southwest; the innumerable ranges lined up to the east like islands in a great sea of clouds. Below us—more than 11,300 feet down and some 17 ragged miles overland—lies the barely fathomable Valley of Death, our trucks, and our cooler of cold Tecates.

> It was the picture of a desert, but if it be true that a picture is masterful in proportion to its power to stir the emotions, then the picture from that peak of the Panamints is not to be compared with any tawdry scene that needs the colors of vegetation to make it attractive.
> —John R. Spears, *Illustrated Sketches of Death Valley and Other Borax Deserts of the Pacific Coast* (1892)

We strip our skins, make fast our packs, make a brief series of calls home on Joe's satellite phone. Then, without any great ado, we drop in on 4,320 vertical feet of wide-open, wind-sifted velvet and five-star corn—nearly 100 feet more than the most lift-served vert in the Lower 48 (at Jackson Hole).

DAVID SCHEMENAUER SPRAYS VELVET 11,000 VERTICAL FEET ABOVE BADWATER CHRISTIAN PONDELLA

11:55 AM: 6,729 FEET ABOVE SEA LEVEL; 7,011 FEET ABOVE BADWATER

We're at the bottom of the tongue, chewing on salami—McDonell, Wenworth, and I—lounging on the dirt in the warm sun and the bittersweet glory, back in shorts and T-shirts, waiting for the cliffhuckers to come crashing through the brush.

It always goes too fast—the skiing down part. But such is the nature of it. Then you're onto the next thing, like a cold Tecate or a swim in a spring-fed pool. Like a queen-sized motel bed or a long drive back to Mammoth for a swing shift in a snowcat. One year, I think to myself, if conditions are ever right again (and the kids grow up and life slows down, etc., etc.), I'll haul some camping gear up to this spot—a lightweight sleeping bag, a stove, something good to cook—and set up a little early springtime beach-camp where the desert meets the snow, spend a week or so doing laps in the bowls, really explore the place.

For now, though, all that remains between ourselves and that next thing is another 5,000 vertical feet, 9 or 10 miles, and 4 long hours of stumbling, scree-slipping, kneetweaking descent, numerous cactus-stabs, a broken ski pole, one pair of shoes peeled clean of soles, a seam-split pack, a further and ever more sophisticated quotient of scatological disquisition, and a torn fingernail.

Like horses to the barn.

JOHN WENTWORTH DOES 10 MILES OVERLAND IN SKI BOOTS CHRISTIAN PONDELLA

RANGER AND INTERPRETIVE PROGRAMS An array of programs and tours is scheduled during peak season, from October to May. Consult the visitor center for a daily schedule.

ULTRA-RUNNING Every July, when the asphalt is fully molten, an elite crew of hardened distance runners and other masochists—by invitation only—set off from Badwater Basin in an attempt to run/walk/crawl the 135 miles from the lowest point in North America to the Whitney Portal at 8,300 feet (www.badwater.com/event/badwater-135/). Organizers call it the World's Toughest Foot Race, and there seems no reason to doubt the claim. In cooler seasons, you can run hundreds of miles all by yourself.

✳ Lodging

Coming from the east, there are simple accommodations at Tecopa Hot Springs and Shoshone, both with access to warm springs pools. There are motels and motel-casinos in Pahrump and Beatty, Nevada. The only accommodations worth consideration outside the park (in the Amargosa Basin) are Marta Becket's famed **Amargosa Hotel** (760-852-4441; www.amargosaoperahouse.com; inexpensive)—the location for David Lynch's *Lost Highway*, in the haunted old Pacific Coast Borax headquarters at Death Valley Junction—and **Cynthia's** (www.discovercynthias.com), whose empire now encompasses three safari-furnished tepees in the heart of the oasis at China Ranch as well as several stylish-eclectic guest rooms and a hostel in Tecopa (760-852-4580; www.discovercynthias.com; inexpensive to moderate, includes Wi-Fi and access to full kitchen and hot springs). The nearest accommodations west of the park are at Cerro Gordo or in Lone Pine (see Chapter 4), or to the south in Ridgecrest.

Within park boundaries, lodging is available at Furnace Creek (The Oasis), Stovepipe Wells, and Panamint Springs. Spring is the busiest season, especially during those weeks immediately following a splashy photo spread of desert wildflowers in the travel section of the Los Angeles Times. Accommodations at Furnace Creek (The Oasis) will frequently sell out on Friday and Saturday nights. Stovepipe Wells sells out less frequently, but it does happen. One weekend the park is sure to fill to capacity, during which you should steer clear or book many months in advance, falls during the Death Valley '49er Encampment in November. Otherwise, with fewer than a million visitors each year, most just passing through, Death Valley is still a place where silence and wind reign supreme.

✪ **The Inn at Death Valley** (formerly the **Furnace Creek Inn**). (CA 190, Death Valley; 800-236-7916; www.oasisatdeathvalley.com; very expensive; Elevation: -179 feet; Open: Mid-October to mid-May; Innkeeper: Xanterra Parks & Resorts; Pets: No; Wheelchair Access: Yes; Internet Access: Yes). Built from 1927 to 1935 by British mining conglomerate Borax Consolidated in the wake of pulling its mining business out of Death Valley, the Inn today ranks among the greatest—and most civilized—of the handful of great, historic, national park lodges still in operation in the U.S. The architecture and decor are a remarkable hodgepodge of mission, southwest, and art deco styles, with red Granada-tile roofs, sea green trim, porticos, painted brick, and abundant local stonework. Recent interior renovations have combined the latest in luxury bedding (plus televisions, hair dryers, and coffeemakers) with appropriately ponderous retro furnishings. The original charm of the place may suffer ever so slightly from an institutional proliferation of the Xanterra logo—on staff uniforms, on shrink-wrapped plastic cups in the bathrooms, shampoo bottles, and so on. But the real draw here is the *situation*: In a location where in 1926 you would find rocks and sand and borax, there is now a mature North African–style oasis of deglet nour date palms, spring-fed runnels and ponds, and shaded garden paths—favored on balmy evenings by coyotes and crickets—and a close-cropped lawn on which one thinks at any moment someone might begin a game of croquet. The pool is chlorine-free and perfectly delicious, fed by the same natural, 91-degree springwater that Mrs. Brier used to make her lifesaving coffee on Christmas Eve, 1849. A short list of many famous guests over the years includes Bette Davis, John Barrymore, Ronald Reagan, Peter Fonda, Dennis Hopper, and Anthony Quinn. Clark Gable and Carole Lombard had their honeymoon here in 1939.

Ranch at Death Valley (formerly the **Ranch at Furnace Creek**) (CA 190, Death Valley; 800-236-7916; www.oasisatdeathvalley.com; moderate to expensive; Elevation: -214 feet; Open: Year-round; Innkeeper: Xanterra Parks & Resorts; Pets: No; Wheelchair Access: Yes; Internet Access: Yes). When the Inn is closed for the season, or the budget so dictates, or the family's in tow, this is the place to stay. The property first opened to guests in 1933 as a rustic alternative to the Inn up the hill, after 50 years as a working stock ranch for mining operations throughout the region. The constructed pond (now a central feature of the golf course) has been serving migratory waterfowl since 1881.

Accommodations range from small, upgraded, Depression-era cabin units to spacious, midcentury, parkside motel rooms with sliding glass doors onto the lawn and pool area, all within a short salt cedar-shaded stroll of the stables, golf course, tennis courts, horseshoe pitches, restaurants, museum, general store, and saloon. The pool is a more utilitarian, family-friendly, slightly cooler, downstream version of the one at the Inn—fed by the same confluence of springs.

Stovepipe Wells Village (51880 CA 190, Death Valley; 760-786-2387; www.deathvalleyhotels.com; moderate; Elevation: Sea level; Open: Year-round; Innkeepers: Death Valley Lodging Co.; Pets: Yes; Wheelchair Access: Yes; Internet Access: Limited). Somewhere near here the Jayhawkers burned their wagons to smoke the meat of their last remaining oxen. Three-quarters of a century later, in 1926, a year before borax built the Furnace Creek Inn (The Inn at Death Valley), an electrical engineer and veteran of Rhyolite by the name of H. W. "Bob" Eichbaum got permission from Inyo County to build the first maintained road into Death Valley from the west, to charge a toll for travel on

THE SPRING-FED POOL AT THE HISTORIC FURNACE CREEK INN, NOW CALLED THE INN AT DEATH VALLEY

THE POOL AT THE RANCH AT DEATH VALLEY BURKE GRIGGS

it, and also to be the sole concessionaire. At the end of his road, across the dunes from the original Stovepipe Well, he built twenty modified tent houses, a restaurant, a pool, tennis courts, a landing strip, and a generator-powered Hollywood-style beacon to give pioneering motorists hope in the dark desert night. He called it Bungalette City. Its basic motel rooms have been upgraded within the last decade to include cotton sheets, coffeemakers, hairdryers (which seem superfluous), and galvanized steel waste buckets. The tennis courts are gone now. The landscaping—to this day not much has changed since the wagon burning, or since the end of the last little ice age—may be explained by a lack of free-flowing springwater. The pool, open until midnight, is filled with heated and chlorinated well water; showers feature extraordinary pressure; and drinking water is produced by reverse osmosis (or bottled elsewhere, trucked here, and sold in vending machines). Air-conditioning.

Panamint Springs Resort (40440 CA 190, Panamint Valley; 775-482-7680; www.panamintsprings.com; moderate; Elevation: 1,940 feet; Open: Year-round;

Innkeepers: The Cassells; Pets: Yes, for a small fee; Wheelchair Access: Yes; Internet Access: Free wireless via satellite). Panamint Springs had long gone to seed by March 2006, when the Cassell family—evidently not of quite the same depth of resources as the Xanterra Corporation—took a significant leap, purchased the historic inholding, and began its slow rescue. As best they could, given the logistical realities of being way out in the desert, some 40 miles from the nearest power lines and 5 miles from the nearest water source, they began replacing old plumbing and doing interior renovations (of the incremental "sweat-equity" variety), chipping away at the late-'70s-vintage veneer furnishings, ancient floral bedspreads, sea-green indoor/outdoor carpeting, fist holes in sheetrock, and so on. The old wooden windows, the sun-bleached shake roofs, the desert-pink cinderblock—that, together with the setting, give the place a dreamy, heat-induced hint of Old Mexico. The patriarch nurtures dreams of a beach-entry horizon pool with a swim-up bar and a grand sunset view across the dunes. In the meantime, the

ROOMS WITH VIEWS AT PANAMINT SPRINGS BURKE GRIGGS

word "resort" is difficult to apply except in the sense of a course of action adopted when no other presents itself. But the Cassells are a friendly and hospitable bunch, generous with their diesel-generated air-conditioning, their stuffed jackalope head, their wireless Internet, and their spectacular front porch—worth stopping in to visit, even if only for a fine burger, a cold microbrew or several, a landscape-defying mango-berry smoothie, or directions up the wash to nearby Darwin Falls.

CAMPING Camping on the desert is an experience not to be missed, especially in late fall and early spring, especially after the sun goes down and the stars come out. Nights on the valley floor can be cold in winter and unbearable in summer. Wildrose, Thorndike, and Mahogany Flat (in the Panamint Range) offer pleasant alternatives to the summer heat at lower elevations. There's not much to recommend the sun-seared, parking-lot-style campgrounds at Sunset, Stovepipe Wells, and Panamint Springs—except perhaps their proximity to concessions (and/or swimming pools).

Furnace Creek (The Oasis), though built to hold a small division of RVs, is by far the most pleasant, with an occasional salt cedar for shade and privacy (especially at some of the walk-in tent sites) and strict generator curfews to help keep evenings and early mornings focused on the big desert quiet. If you have a sturdy vehicle, the right equipment, and plenty of water, more secluded sites can be found along various backcountry roads, at the informal campgrounds at Eureka Dunes, and at the popular Saline Valley Warm Springs. Bring your own shade and avoid mine shafts. No campfires are allowed in undeveloped sites. Consult a ranger for up-to-date conditions and restrictions.

* Reservations: 1-877-444-6777; www
.recreation.gov

High clearance/four-wheel drive recommended

‡ Private concession: 775-482-7680

✳ Where to Eat

Keeping in mind the location—and the fact that, in the past century and a half,

XANTERRA?

It all began, perhaps, with an ambitious Englishman by the name of Frederick Henry Harvey, who in 1876, at the age of 41, opened the first of a highly successful series of traveler's eateries on the Atchison, Topeka & Santa Fe Railway. By the time old Fred died in 1901, the Fred Harvey Company was operating 47 restaurants, 15 hotels, and 30 dining cars, with trademark postcards and cheap Southwestern-themed curios at most locations selling even better than the hotcakes. For the spread of decent food, and for the courteous young "Harvey Girls" who served it, Will Rogers is said to have dubbed Harvey "the civilizer of the West." His descendants expanded the empire to include food service and hospitality in such glamorous locations as the Albuquerque airport, the Illinois Tollway, and, beginning in 1956, the U.S. Borax and Chemical Company's tourist properties in Death Valley.

To look at it from another angle, it begins even earlier, with a German fellow by the name of Heinrich Hackfeld, who, in 1849, opted not to go to California but to Hawaii. By the time Archduke Ferdinand was shot dead in the streets of Sarajevo in June 1914, H. Hackfeld & Company controlled about 60,000 acres of Hawaiian real estate, a significant portion of Hawaii's sugar trade, and a major dry goods chain named for Hackfeld's nephew, B. F. Ehlers. Four years later, at the height of the War to End All Wars, the U.S. government seized the company's assets—as it did those of many who had German names or relatives still in Germany—and sold them to a group of more overtly patriotic investors. The company's name was changed to American Factors, Inc. (later shortened to Amfac, Inc.), the dry goods business to Liberty House. In 1968 Amfac—which by then had begun to diversify into the parks and resorts business—bought the Fred Harvey Company.

Twenty years later, Amfac, after acquiring its rival, TW Recreational Services, sold itself for $920 million to a company called JMB Realty, subsidiary of an entity called the Northbrook Corporation. In 2002, the Amfac brand was changed to Xanterra, which, according to company literature, is a willful combination of Coleridge's mythical Xanadu ("an idyllic and beautiful paradise") and the Latin word terra, the composite therefore supposedly meaning "beautiful place on earth." Xanterra is today the officially contracted steward (along with the good old, chronically underfunded National Park Service) of such national treasures as Zion, Yellowstone, the Grand Canyon, Rocky Mountain National Park, the Everglades, Mount Rushmore, and Death Valley, with plausible claims to being the largest park management company in the U.S. And also the "greenest": Ask about the company's latest contributions to the environment.

Xanterra owns the golf course and buildings at The Oasis (formerly the Furnace Creek Resort), and the property beneath them, and the company runs them in cooperation with—but without any special restriction from—the Park Service. Stovepipe Wells and Scotty's Castle, on the other hand, are owned by the U.S. government and only operated by Xanterra. Park Service restrictions and pricing controls apply, accounting for differences in cost and service.

countless people (and beasts of burden) have starved to death in this place—there is surprisingly decent, if still limited, fare to be had in Death Valley and in the neighboring Amargosa Basin.

✪ **Amargosa Café** (HR-C 608, Death Valley Junction; 760-852-4432; www.amargosacafe.org; inexpensive). In 2016, veteran commercial photographer Bobbi Fabian, originally from Melbourne, Australia, took a break from Los Angeles and a globe-trotting career in order to bring back to life the old Depression-era diner on the south end of the Amargosa Hotel. With some hard work and a little help from some friends, she's reclaimed the classic lunch counter and turned the place into a surprising oasis of real fare in a vast landscape of saltbush, creosote, and packaged, industrially-processed fodder. The menu features produce and eggs from local

DEATH VALLEY CAMPING

	Elevation	Season	Reservations Accepted	Fee	Sites	Water	Agency
1. Emigrant (tents only)	2,100	Year-round	No	No	10	Yes	NPS
2. Furnace Creek*	-196	Year-round	Yes	Yes	136	Yes	NPS
3. Mahogany Flat **	8,200	Mar-Nov	No	No	13	No	NPS
4. Mesquite Spring*	1,800	Year-round	Yes	Yes	30	Yes	NPS
5. Stowepipe Wells	0	Oct-Apr	No	Yes	200	Yes	NPS
6. Sunset	-196	Oct-Apr	No	Yes	1,000	Yes	NPS
7. Texas Spring	0	Oct-Apr	No	Yes	92	Yes	NPS
8. Thorndike **	7,400	Mar-Nov	No	No	6	No	NPS
9. Wildrose	4,100	Year-round	No	No	30	Apr-Nov	NPS

* Reservations can be made online at www.recreation.gov or by calling 1-800-365-2267.

** High clearance/four-wheel drive recommended.

farms, seasonal fruit, house-baked biscuits, and fine Italian coffee. Proceeds benefit the ongoing restoration of the Amargosa Opera House. Breakfast and lunch served daily until 3 PM. Ask about special suppers served on Saturdays. BYOB.

✪ **The Inn Dining Room** (Inn at Death Valley; 760-786-2345; www.oasisatdeathvalley.com; expensive). In the spring of 1927, a dinner menu at the newly opened "Furnace Creek Inn" included such dry-country delicacies as pickled creosote buds, tarantula bullion,

AMARGOSA CAFE

SCORPION COCKTAIL (FROM THE INN DINING ROOM, THE INN AT DEATH VALLEY)

2 parts white rum
2 parts brandy
1 part lemon juice, freshly squeezed
1 part orange juice, freshly squeezed

Combine ingredients and shake with cracked ice. Strain into a frosted goblet. Garnish with a slice of orange and a maraschino cherry. Makes one cocktail.

gila monster à la king, and braised burro tongue, all of which could be washed down with a choice of scorpion cocktail, arsenic spring water, or hot borax tea. Of late, the most exotic thing on the menu may be the rattlesnake empanadas, made on the premises with nopalitos, cumin, garlic, red chile, lime, and imperceptible tidbits of serpent imported from Nevada or Texas. The date bread, with its accompanying selection of butters, is justly famous. But be sure to leave room for the duck. For breakfast, with the heat rising over the playa beyond, imagine fresh-iced melon and corn cakes with chile hollandaise. It's hard to eat anywhere else in Death Valley—unless you have no choice. Open mid-October to mid-May. Reservations recommended. No shorts or T-shirts.

Wrangler Buffet and Steakhouse (Ranch at Death Valley; 760-786-2345; www.oasisatdeathvalley.com; moderate to expensive). This bustling family-style supper house, with brass rails and comfortable booths done in airline-style upholstery, serves steak, ribs, chicken, and more. There's also a fine shrimp scampi, as if to remind a person why such an option abides. The lamb burger on rosemary focaccia with goat cheese, sun-dried tomatoes, and romaine is served with a steak knife, and the jalapeño poppers sell out fast. Progressive wine list; full bar. The copious buffets for breakfast and lunch are offered with upbeat Muzac versions of great Western film scores on the PA system. Open year-round (except at certain mysterious times of the year, when things are quiet and only the Forty-Niner Café is open). No reservations accepted. Gratuity included during summer (to help the Europeans).

49'er Café (Ranch at Death Valley; 760-786-2345; www.oasisatdeathvalley.com; inexpensive). Date shakes, pie, hamburgers, soups, salads, eggs, pancakes, biscuits and gravy, and a towering club sandwich with real sliced turkey and thumb-sized french fries. Diner-style, but with access to the full bar next door. Open daily October to May, and most days in summer too (except during certain mysterious weeks when things are dead-quiet outdoors and only the Wrangler is open).

Toll Road Restaurant (Stovepipe Wells; 760-786-2604; inexpensive). A standard cafeteria done up in vague mine-shaft accoutrements, with service reminiscent of a coffee shop in an old downtown Vegas casino. Highlights include breast of chicken smothered in barbecue sauce and topped with a bacon strip and melted cheddar cheese (with soup or salad, baked potato, fries, or rice). The menu expands slightly in winter. The breakfast buffet—crumbled egg-substance, melon cubes, etc.— evokes something recently reconstituted from ancient stores on the planet Tatooine. If you have water and fortitude enough to keep walking, keep walking. Open all three meals daily.

TAVERNS, SALOONS, AND ROAD-HOUSES **J & R Crowbar Café & Saloon**

SHOT IN DEATH VALLEY: A SHORT LIST

Greed (1923). Directed by Erich Von Stroheim; starring Gibson Gowland and Jean Hersholt. Skidoo, Stovepipe Wells dunes, Devil's Golf Course, and so on. Equipment and crew were hauled into the valley by mule. The film, considered a masterpiece at a running length of 10 hours, was never released theatrically.

Wanderer of the Wasteland (1923–24). Directed by Irvin Willat. Based on the novel by Zane Grey. Filmed in Technicolor; the last known print was found decomposed in the 1970s.

Twenty Mule Team (1940). Directed by Richard Thorpe; starring Wallace Beery and Leo Carrillo. Golden Canyon.

Yellow Sky (1948). Directed by William Wellman; starring Gregory Peck, Anne Baxter, and Richard Widmark. Near Furnace Creek.

Three Godfathers (1948). Directed by John Ford; starring John Wayne. Near Furnace Creek.

The Gunfighter (1950). Directed by Henry King; starring Gregory Peck. Opening titles only.

Spartacus (1960). Directed by Stanley Kubrick; starring Kirk Douglas, Laurence Olivier, Jean Simmons, and Tony Curtis. Ryan and Zabriskie Point.

One-Eyed Jacks (1961). Directed by Marlon Brando; starring Marlon Brando and Karl Malden.

The Professionals (1966). Directed by Richard Brooks; starring Burt Lancaster, Lee Marvin, and Jack Palance. Sand dunes, Stovepipe Wells, and Desolation Canyon.

Zabriskie Point (1970). Directed by Michelangelo Antonioni; starring Mark Frechette and Daria Halprin. Co-written by Sam Shepard. (Harrison Ford was considered for the lead, worked two days as an extra, and was eventually cut from the movie.)

Star Wars: Episode IV–A New Hope (1977). Directed by George Lucas; starring Mark Hamill, Carrie Fisher, and Harrison Ford. Between Stovepipe Wells and Death Valley Junction, Zabriskie Point, Ubehebe Crater, and Badwater.

Vacation (1983). Directed by Harold Ramis; starring Chevy Chase, Beverly D'Angelo, and Randy Quaid.

Star Wars: Episode VI–Return of the Jedi (1983). Directed by George Lucas; starring Mark Hamill, Carrie Fisher, and Harrison Ford.

The Hitcher (1986). Directed by Robert Harmon; starring Rutger Hauer, C. Thomas Howell, and Jennifer Jason Leigh. Shoshone and Death Valley Junction.

Star Trek V: The Final Frontier (1989). Directed by William Shatner; starring William Shatner, Leonard Nimoy, and DeForest Kelley. Trona Pinnacles.

The Doors (1991). Directed by Oliver Stone; starring Val Kilmer, Meg Ryan, Frank Whaley, and Kevin Dillon.

(CA 127, Shoshone; 760-852-4335). Established in 1920, built in the late '30s, and added onto in the '50s, J & R features a welded-steel railroad rail for a bar footstep. Burgers, steaks, enchiladas, and breakfast.

Corkscrew Saloon (Ranch at Death Valley). The best place for a cold draft beer or an ice-rimmed martini is the lounge or the terrace at the Inn, but when the Inn's closed—or too far up the hill, or when you can't be bothered to scrape the borax out from under your fingernails—the Corkscrew'll do. Sporting events on the television, a pool table, acres of functional oak veneer. Note the old mule-team yokes on the wall and the inexplicable 6-foot two-man log saw—more than 100 miles from the nearest tree of any significant size.

Badwater Saloon (Stovepipe Wells). The only watering hole within reasonable walking distance. There's not much to recommend the place: It has a terrific name but doesn't live up to it. Closes early if no one's drinking.

Lost Highway (1997). Directed by David Lynch; starring Bill Pullman and Patricia Arquette. Baker, Barstow, Death Valley Junction.

Dinosaur (2000). Directed by Eric Leighton and Ralph Zondag; starring D.B. Sweeney and Julianna Margulies. Trona Pinnacles.

Planet of the Apes (2001). Directed by Tim Burton; starring Mark Wahlberg and Helena Bonham Carter. Trona Pinnacles.

Gerry (2002). Directed by Gus Van Sant; starring Matt Damon and Casey Affleck.

Kill Bill, Vol. 2 (2004). Directed by Quentin Tarantino; starring Uma Thurman and Lucy Liu. Zabriskie Point.

Seraphim Falls (2006). Directed by David Von Ancken; starring Liam Neeson and Pierce Brosnan.

Tree of Life (2010). Directed by Terence Malick; starring Sean Penn and Brad Pitt.

Valley of Love (2015). Directed by Guillaume Nicloux; starring Gérard Depardieu and Isabelle Huppert.

GIBSON GOWLAND AND JEAN HERSHOLT IN ERICH VON STROHEIM'S SILENT MASTERPIECE, *GREED* (1923)

Panamint Springs (40440 CA 190; 775-482-7680). Fine burgers with avocado (in season), a notable selection of 150 microbrews, stone-oven pizzas, friendly folks, and the best roadside front porch in the Greater Death Valley region.

✳ Books, Maps, and Information

Shoshone Museum (118 CA 127, Shoshone; 760-852-4524). Originally built in 1906 as a union hall in the mining camp of Greenwater, the building was moved here in the 1920s, first to serve as a gas station, then as a rock shop, and now as a kind of homegrown museum run by the Death Valley Chamber of Commerce. Artifacts and photographs of early mining and exploration, some very old and mysterious local pachyderm bones (thought to be a mastodon of one kind or another), a good selection of local history and geology books and reports, plus the local cemetery guide. Open 9 AM–3 PM; closed Tuesdays.

Beatty Information Center (US 95, Beatty, NV; 775-553-2200). Basic exhibits on natural and cultural history of the region. Books, maps, and materials stocked by the Death Valley Natural History Association. Open daily 8 AM–6 PM, year-round.

✪ **Furnace Creek Visitor Center** (North of the Ranch; 760-786-3200; www.nps.gov/deva). Here lies the mother lode of Death Valley information. The designated historic Mission 66 midcentury-modern building—once home to a fabulous collection of 1960s-vintage dioramas that alas fell victim to a full-scale renovation in 2012–13—still houses a range of orientation programs, lectures, racks of helpful brochures and handouts, and a team of tireless, knowledgeable, map-wielding rangers, as well as a small selection of books, maps, collectibles, kid stuff, and imported drinking water stocked by the nonprofit Death Valley Natural History Association (760-786-2243; www.dvnha .org). Restrooms and water-refill stations. Open daily 8 AM–5 PM. Restrooms and water-refill stations. Open daily 8 AM–5 PM.

Scotty's Castle Bookstore and Visitor Center (Grapevine Canyon, NV 267; 760-786-2392). Exhibits on the history of the place, the old Staininger Ranch, the Johnsons, their friendship and patronage of the eccentric Death Valley Scotty, and so on. The bookstore is run by the Death Valley Natural History Association. If you're traveling with children, you might have better luck with the living history tour than with the underground lecture on utility tunnels. CLOSED UNTIL 2019 DUE TO FLOOD DAMAGE.

✪ **Eastern Sierra Interagency Visitor Center** (US 395 and CA 136, Lone Pine; 760-876-6200). Death Valley National Park is one of the cooperating agencies, so a full range of Death Valley materials is available here. Plus a selection of books, maps, and more, stocked by the Eastern Sierra Interpretive Association (esiaonline.com). Open daily 9 AM–5 PM;

8 AM–5 PM in summer. Closed Thanksgiving, Christmas, and New Year's Day.

Old Guest House Museum (13193 Main St., Trona; 760-372-5222; www1.iwvisp.com/svhs). Run by the Searles Valley Historical Society, the museum includes photos and artifacts from the glory days of prospecting and chemical extraction, including John Searles's coat. Open most mornings (except Sunday) or by appointment. Also run by the society are the **Trona Railway Museum and Caboose** and the **History House** (83001 Panamint St.; open by appointment only). Free admission.

Maturango Museum and Death Valley Tourist Center (100 E. Las Flores Ave., Ridgecrest, across from Home Depot; 760-375-6900; www.maturango.org). Exhibits, maps, books, videos, and information about the Upper Mojave Desert and neighboring Death Valley. Free admission to store and lobby; exhibit hall is $4 for adults. Open daily 10 AM–5 PM; closed on major holidays.

✱ Shopping

SUNDRIES AND SOUVENIRS **Amargosa Hotel Gift Shop** (Death Valley Junction; 760-852-4441; www.amargosa-opera-house.com). Peacock feathers, coffee mugs, cold sodas, ice cream, and books. Largest selection of Marta Becket performance videos in the world.

Inn Gift Shop. Southwest-themed gifts, apparel, accessories, Arizona-style Native American jewelry, and souvenir terry-cloth bathrobes. Open only in winter season.

Nugget Gift Shop (Stovepipe Wells). Jewelry, crafts, trinkets, dreamcatchers, and curios.

SPORTING GOODS AND EQUIPMENT **Furnace Creek Golf Pro Shop** (Ranch at Death Valley; 760-786-3373). Balls, clubs, shoes, fashions, gifts, cart rentals, and more from "the world's lowest golf course."

GENERAL STORES **Charles Brown Company Market** (CA 127, Shoshone). Charlie Brown, state senator for 24 years, used to run the place when he wasn't in Sacramento. Now he's in the cemetery out back. Canned goods, crackers, liquor, last gas before the park, Lotto tickets, and cheap souvenirs.

Ranch General Store (Ranch at Death Valley; 760-786-2578). Minor groceries, snacks, shrink-wrapped sandwiches, beer, liquor, ice, margarita and Bloody Mary mix, books, curios, postcards, hats, and sunscreen. Road-soundtrack selections on CD by Marty Robbins and Frank Corrales. Multistage purified bottled well water from Irvine, California.

Scotty's Castle Gift Shop (760-786-2325). Curios, postcards, trinkets, snack bar, books, cold drinks. Open daily 8:30 AM–5:30 PM. CLOSED UNTIL 2019 DUE TO FLOOD DAMAGE.

Stovepipe Wells General Store (760-786-2387). Curios, T-shirts, basic lunch and snack supplies, ice, a selection of books, cheap hats and shades, Fred Harvey signature socks, beer, liquor, wine, gas. Note the photo panel of Bungalette City in 1926.

The Outpost (Ballarat; no phone). More a point of interest (see below) than a place to stock up on essential goods and equipment. Still, if you're out this far and find yourself in need of something, this is all there is. Cold sodas and beers, motor oil, T-shirts, running water, black-powder gun trials (when there's powder). Stories, information, and shade.

✳ Special Events

January: **Furnace Creek Invitational Golf Tournament** (www.oasisatdeathvalley.com).

February: **Bald eagles often observed** (Ash Meadows National Wildlife Refuge). **Death Valley History Conference** (www.dvnha.org).

March: **Spring waterfowl migration begins.**

FROM THE DAYS BEFORE THE PINK JEEPS   AARON HOROWITZ

April: **Pupfish breeding season begins. Wildflower Show** (Maturango Museum, Ridgecrest; 760-375-6900; www.maturango.org).

May: **Spring songbird migration peaks. Annual Season Finale at the Amargosa Opera House** (www.amargosa-opera-house.com).

July: **Hottest temperatures. Badwater Ultra-Marathon** (310-570-2613; www.badwater.com). Run 135 miles nonstop from Badwater to Whitney Portal. **Peak century plant boom.**

August: **Fall bird migration begins.**

September: **Fall Date harvest begins** (www.chinaranch.com).

October: **Fall Death Valley Century and Double Century** (www.planetultra.com/portfolio/death-valley-century). **Annual Season premiere at the Amargosa Opera House** (www.amargosa-opera-house.com). **Fall kick-off golf**

tournament (Furnace Creek; www
.oasisatdeathvalley.com). **Gem-O-Rama**
(Trona; call Jim or Bonnie Fairchild:
760-372-5356).

November: **Death Valley '49ers
Encampment** (www.deathvalley49ers
.org). Art, photography, mining, minerals, lapidary and craft shows; stringed
instrument, needlework, woodcarving, and horseshoe competitions;
cowboy poetry, gold panning, four-wheel-drive tours, videos, oratories,
wagon trains, and more. **Shoshone
Old West Days** (760-852-4524; www
.deathvalleychamber.org). **Hand pollination of female date trees begins** (www
.chinaranch.com).

December: **Ash Meadows Christmas
Bird Count** (www.esaudubon.org).

OWENS VALLEY & THE EASTERN SIERRA

OWENS VALLEY & THE EASTERN SIERRA

This section of US 395 penetrates a land of contrasts—cool crests and burning lowlands, fertile agricultural regions and untamed deserts. It is a land where Indians made a last stand against the invading white man, where bandits sought refuge from early vigilante retribution; a land of fortunes—past and present—in gold, silver, tungsten, marble, soda, and borax; and a land esteemed by sportsmen because of scores of lakes and streams abounding with trout and forests alive with game.
—WPA Guide to California, 1939

Sometime between church and noon on Sunday, November 16, 1924, a posse of displeased citizens began to show up at the Alabama Spillway, a few miles from Lone Pine, on the Los Angeles Aqueduct. Their contention was that the water had been stolen from the valley—and should be returned. By all accounts, they'd left their guns at home. A lone security guard in the employ of the City of Los Angeles stepped aside as some of the men worked to open the gates above the spillway, diverting the main flow of the Owens River away from Los Angeles, back into its original bed.

The sheriff showed up, took names. A local judge issued a restraining order, then canceled it, citing his own lack of authority in the matter. The press came. Food was delivered. Tom Mix, on location nearby, sent over some musicians to entertain the gathering crowds.

"Los Angeles men came and were courteously received," wrote W. A. Chalfant, then editor of the *Inyo Register*. "Their declarations were similar to that of a British commander in an early Revolutionary skirmish: 'Disperse, ye rebels,' and were no more effective."

The sheriff asked the governor to send in the National Guard. The governor declined. For four long days the residents of the valley controlled the river—and Los Angeles, which had by then secured for itself more water than it knew what to do with, made do without. For four days.

The local Indians had been diverting water from the Owens since long before Joseph R. Walker first came through in 1834. They used it to irrigate fields of native hyacinth and nutgrass. John Frémont officially surveyed the valley in 1845, along with Walker, Kit Carson, Richard Owens, and topographer Edward Kern. The names Kern, Carson, and Walker having already been liberally distributed in other watersheds, the glory here fell to Owens. Ranchers started bringing in cattle and sheep in the late 1850s to satisfy hungry mining camps at Virginia City, Aurora, and Mono Lake. The Indians did their best to resist encroachment, to make life difficult for the settlers, but by 1863 they found themselves rather forcefully persuaded to sign a treaty allowing for their removal from the valley. In the wake of their departure—998 people were marched by the U.S. Army from Independence to Fort Tejon—there was, as one correspondent put it, a "general scramble for land in Owens Valley." "Prospectors and families are flocking in," wrote another. "Large numbers of beef cattle are being driven across the mountains."

Indian troubles continued for a few years thereafter. Lawlessness abounded to a degree that would later inspire countless Hollywood Westerns (many to be shot on location in the Owens Valley). But by the mid-1870s—with 400 bars of rough-grade silver bullion daily coming down out of Cerro Gordo; with 4,800 citizens and 1,600 mules in that camp alone; and with new bonanzas every year (at Bodie and Mammoth, Lundy and Tioga) bringing successive waves of prospectors and settlers—farms, ranches, and orchards flourished up and down the valley. By 1878, large-scale irrigation was under way. Before long, local farmers would be pulling permits on eight separate dam sites for storage and control of the Owens River.

Meanwhile, down south, a fellow by the name of Fred Eaton—22 years old in 1878 and superintendent of the Los Angeles City Water Company since he was 19—hired a fellow by the name of William Mulholland, then 23, as a ditch digger. Eaton went on to serve briefly as mayor of Los Angeles from 1898 to 1900. During his tenure, he created the Los Angeles Department of Water and Power (LADWP) and put Mulholland at its head. Around the time Eaton left office, the city's population broke the 100,000 mark. By 1903, there were 175,000 people, with hundreds more arriving daily. By July 1904, the city was consuming more water—by more than 4 million gallons a day—than was being delivered by its own river.

That summer, while on an extended camping trip to Yosemite and Mono Lake (with a side trip to Bishop for supplies), in the company of one Joseph B. Lippincott of the U.S. Bureau of Reclamation, Eaton, now no longer a servant of the public, was thinking very seriously about the water in the Owens River—and about how Los Angeles might be able to use it. Lippincott and the boys from Reclamation had already begun surveying the Owens as a possible federal irrigation project and had set aside half a million acres for such a purpose. The project depended on the enthusiastic support of local farmers; there was no disagreement anywhere in those days that 37 million acre-feet of annual Sierra runoff ought to be "saved"—one way or another—from the

ALVORD, LATER RENAMED ZURICH STATION, WAS ESTABLISHED IN 1884 AS A FREIGHT AND PASSENGER STATION SOUTH OF LAWS ON THE CARSON & COLORADO RAILWAY ("THE SLIM PRINCESS"). IT WAS FINALLY ABANDONED IN 1960 CAT CONNOR

CALIFORNIA'S HIGHEST PEAKS

Every year some half a million people drag their Vibram soles up and down Colorado's fourteeners. Millions more pose for photographs beside interpretive highway signs with one or more of the famous mounds in the background: Pike's, Long's, Evans, Elbert, Mount of the Holy Cross, etc. Most Californians, by contrast, proud as they may be of their fractional ownership of the highest (and lowest) points in the contiguous States, would be hard-pressed to identify the apex in that towering lineup along 395, or to name even one other peak over 14,000 feet, (OK, maybe Shasta . . . but Split? Sill? Thunderbolt? Starlight?) much less make the epic slog from the beach to the top of such a thing.

MOUNT WILLIAMSON (14,370 FEET) AS SEEN FROM INDEPENDENCE

salty waste of Owens Lake. The only question was where the water would be used and who might benefit.

In the spring of 1905, according to a report made that summer by the Inyo County land office (to the secretary of the interior), "Eaton began to secure options on land and water rights in the Owens Valley to the value of about a million dollars." Whether the sellers were under the false impression that the lands were shortly to be condemned by the Reclamation Service, or they believed that the water was to be used to develop other lands in the Owens Valley, or they were simply happy to have the cash, or all of these, is now rather impossible to ascertain. The report went on:

> In June or July most of these options were taken up and the said purchaser now owns all the patented land covered by the government reservoir site in Long Valley, and also riparian and other rights along the river for about 50 miles. The well-known friendship between him and Lippincott and his

There is disagreement as to whether California can boast 13 true summits over 14,000 feet, or 15, or more. Of the four needles to the south of Mount Whitney, for example, each is higher than 14,000 feet, but none is considered a separate summit worthy of listing as a "fourteener." Starlight and Polemonium are sometimes listed as separate peaks, sometimes as subpeaks of the North Palisade. There is no disagreement that all of California's highest points—with the exception of Mount Shasta—are in the Eastern Sierra.

The only one that gets any traffic at all is Whitney. "Here you're talking there's no trails," says Chris Davenport, referencing the silence, the great trackless gullies and faces, the all-but-impenetrable bushwhacks, the epic contrasts in the landscape, the unparalleled vertical from capstone to desert—on average 2,000 to 3,000 more feet of solid vert than anything in the Rockies. "Here there's nothing. Here you have Mount Whitney and Mount Whitney." And even Whitney, crowded as it may seem with more than 20,000 visitors a year and as many as 150 hikers on the main mule-trail on an average Saturday in August, still sees less traffic than an average Colorado Front Range fourteener like Grays.

The other California summits, especially in winter, are mostly left for the ravens, the lions, a handful of bighorns and other plucky locals—and, sometimes, the occasional favored interloper from somewhere else.

	PEAK	ELEVATION	RANGE	NEAREST TOWN
1	Mount Whitney	14,494*	Sierra Nevada	Lone Pine
2	Mount Williamson	14,370	Sierra Nevada	Independence
3	White Mountain	14,246	Whtie Mountains	Bishop/Big Pine
4	North Palisade	14,242	Sierra Nevada	Big Pine
5	Starlight Peak	14,180	Sierra Nevada	Big Pine
6	Mount Shasta	14,162	Cascades	Mount Shasta City
7	Mount Sill	14,153	Sierra Nevada	Big Pine
8	Mount Russell	14,088	Sierra Nevada	Lone Pine
9	Polemonium	14,080	Sierra Nevada	Big Pine
10	Split Mountain	14,042	Sierra Nevada	Big Pine
11	Mount Langley	14,022	Sierra Nevada	Lone Pine
12	Mount Tyndall	14,019	Sierra Nevada	Independence
13	Middle Palisade	14,012	Sierra Nevada	Big Pine
14	Mount Muir	14,012	Sierra Nevada	Lone Pine
15	Thunderbolt Peak	14,003	Sierra Nevada	Big Pine

* See Mount Whitney sidebar, page 162.

having represented the supervising engineer for the government made it easier for these rights to be secured, as the people were generously inclined toward the project and believed Eaton to be the agent of the Reclamation Service. Mr. Eaton's own statements were that he had bought these lands for a cattle ranch.

The people of the City of Los Angeles, by a margin of 10 to 1, approved two bond measures: one for the purchase of most of Eaton's newly acquired rights in the Owens Valley; the other for the construction of a $25 million gravity-fed aqueduct to be built by Mulholland's water department. Reclamation handed its surveys over to Mulholland and stepped aside in favor of the city. In May 1907, President Teddy Roosevelt pitched in, securing a right-of-way for the city and "protecting the purity of the aqueduct supply" by withdrawing from settlement another 220,000 acres of the Owens Valley. Thus, large swaths of land on which the only trees, if any, were those planted by

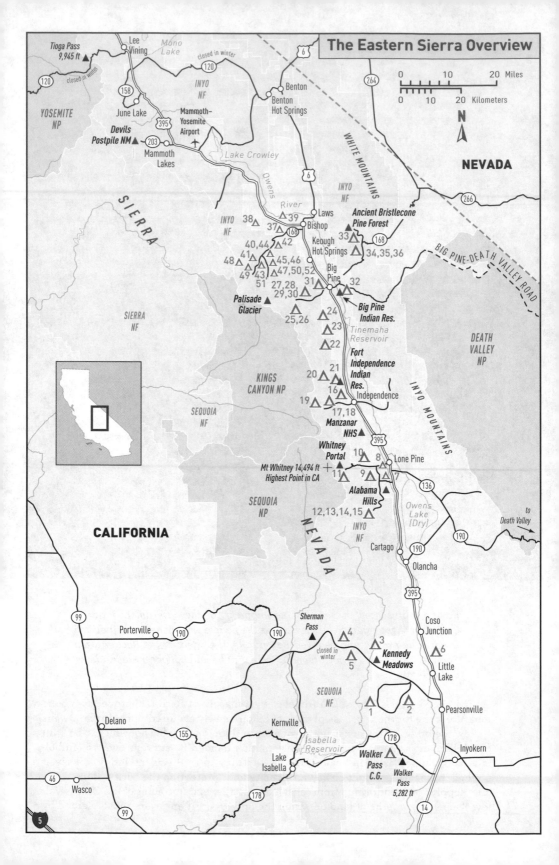

The Eastern Sierra Overview

settlers came to be called the Inyo National Forest. Roosevelt argued that it was the greatest good for the greatest number. "It is a hundred or a thousand fold more important to the state," Roosevelt said of the water in the Owens River, "and more valuable to the people as a whole if used by the city than if used by the people of the Owens Valley."

Construction on the aqueduct began in the fall of 1908. "Included in this work," read the water department's complete report, "were 215 miles of road, 230 miles of pipeline, 218 miles of power transmission line, and 377 miles of telegraph and telephone line." It was a project in scale second only to the Panama Canal. On a given day, there were as many as 3,900 laborers on the line, mostly Eastern Europeans and Mexicans, mostly working for $2.25 a day, minus a dollar a month for "medical, hospital, and surgical service when needed, except for venereal disease, intemperance, vicious habits, injuries received in fights, or chronic diseases acquired before employment." The Southern Pacific Railroad built a branch line from Mojave to Owenyo, near Lone Pine, to carry men and materials, including a thousand barrels of Portland cement a day. Six million pounds of blasting powder were used to bore 43 miles of tunnel. Steel pipe large enough to drive wagons through was shipped around Cape Horn from the East Coast (the canal was finished a year after the aqueduct).

On November 15, 1913, ahead of schedule and under budget, the Owens River reached the San Fernando Valley, and 30,000 people were there to meet it. Hundreds dipped cups and drank straight from the flow; hundreds more drank from bottles provided by the San Fernando Valley Chamber of Commerce. "There it is," said Mulholland to the mayor. "Take it."

"Do you have any idea what this land would be worth with a steady water supply?" remarked Jake Gittes (Jack Nicholson) in Roman Polanski's *Chinatown* (1974). "About $30 million more than they paid for it." And sure enough, a number of the city's most prominent citizens, including Harrison Gray Otis, publisher of the *Los Angeles Times*,

GUARDHOUSE, NINE-MILE CANYON SIPHON, LOS ANGELES AQUEDUCT

and Mulholland himself, made quick fortunes in newly irrigated San Fernando Valley real estate. The Owens, meanwhile, with its once-promising agricultural future, began a steady return to sagebrush and creosote.

In the five years it had taken to build the aqueduct, the population of Los Angeles had more than doubled—to 485,000. Between 1920 and 1930 the city climbed from tenth to fifth largest in the nation, with a population of well over a million. The population of all Inyo County during the same time period dropped from 7,031 to 6,555—down yet again from the 7,500 recorded in the 1880 census. Los Angeles had begun drilling wells on its land in the Owens Valley as early as 1918, supplementing the flow of the river by pumping groundwater into the aqueduct. Farmers still trying to irrigate at Aberdeen began to find the levels in their own wells subsiding. By 1924, after several years of less-than-average snowfall in the Sierra, Owens Lake—once plied by a pair of steamships—was as dry as the playa at Badwater in Death Valley.

"Ten years ago this was a wonderful valley with one-quarter of a million acres of fruit and alfalfa," famous Hollywood cowboy Will Rogers said in 1932. "Now this is a valley of desolation."

Dynamite was brought into play. The city men used it to clear what they saw as pirate dams and ditchworks. Locals used it to blast holes in the aqueduct. The city offered $10,000 for information leading to the arrest of local saboteurs, but no such information was forthcoming. It had been one more long, dry summer when the good people of the Owens Valley seized the Alabama Gates. Mulholland's response—so the story goes—was that he "half-regretted the demise of so many of the valley's orchard trees, because now there were no longer enough trees to hang all the troublemakers who live there."

The troublemakers dispersed on Wednesday and went home of their own accord, having achieved much favorable publicity worldwide and pledges of good faith on the part of the city toward some kind of equitable settlement. The city, in turn, resolved to buy up the rest of the valley. By 1933—after several more incidents with local dynamite and a brief period of armed guards searching cars on the highway—the city of Los Angeles had, by some chicanery but also by paying premium rates in the midst of the Depression, come to own 95 percent of all the agricultural land in the valley and 85 percent of its commercial and residential real estate. (Much of the latter was eventually leased or sold back to merchants and residents, sans water rights.)

Eaton and Mulholland had a dramatic falling out over the million dollars Eaton wanted to charge the city for rights to a potential storage reservoir in Long Valley (between Bishop and Mammoth), the construction of which was delayed into the 1940s. Meanwhile, in the spring of 1928, the alternate dam Mulholland built in the Santa Clarita Valley—the St. Francis dam—collapsed, killing 450 people and burying the town of Santa Paula in 20 feet of mud. Mulholland had inspected the dam that very morning and declared it safe. The disaster set the record for the worst American civil engineering failure of the twentieth century and ended Mulholland's career in disgrace. Mulholland assumed full responsibility, resigned, said he "envied those who were killed," and lived for another seven years. His onetime friend Eaton died a year earlier, in 1934, bankrupt and mostly forgotten. The city was finally able to purchase the reservoir site in Long Valley from his heirs.

The drying-up of Owens Lake, as early as the 1920s, was a boon to surface mining industries. U.S. Borax is still busily working to extract an estimated 70 million tons of trona from the playa. (Trona is a "double salt" used in the making of glass and as a feed additive for livestock.) In 1987, the EPA declared the southern Owens Valley in violation of National Ambient Air Quality Standards. By the late 1990s and into the first decade of the 2000s, the lake bed was considered "the largest source of coarse-particle

OWENS BASIN, THE INYO MOUNTAINS, AND WHITNEY PORTAL ROAD

air pollution in the country—second in the world only to the Sahara Desert," according to Jeffrey Anderson of *LA Weekly*. In 1998, the Great Basin Air Pollution Control District pushed the City of Los Angeles to begin mitigation efforts—shallow flooding, planting salt grasses on the playa, spreading gravel, and so on. Other methods, possibly less costly and more effective, were suggested and discarded. By March 2006 the city had spent $384 million of a projected $475 million and had achieved little more, by some accounts, than a general increase in the population of mosquitoes. As one Los Angeles city council staffer reportedly put it: "It's tough to grow grass in the desert."

But by 2017, after more than a decade of diverting water from its aqueduct—as much as half of the annual flow, or 80,000 acre-feet of water—back down the original Owens River channel to a heavily channelized and segmented lake bed, LADWP seems to have succeeded, under court order, in coming close to controlling the dust. In the process, accidental habitats were created for 100,000 migratory shorebirds that now use the Owens Playa as an important seasonal stopover (whereas, at the turn of this century, fewer than 1,000 would show up each year).

In any case, as Chalfant wrote in 1933, "Nature has written here, in bold strokes, studies more fascinating than the little affairs of humanity." Indeed, there is no topography in North America of such rugged and dramatic aspect. The Owens is one of the deepest valleys on the planet, with its floor on average less than 4,000 feet above sea level, bordered on either side by mountains more than 14,000 feet high. Consider, for example, the Tetons in Wyoming: The total rise from Moose Junction (6,500 feet) to the summit of the Grand Teton (13,770 feet) is 7,270 feet; from Lone Pine to the crest of Whitney is 10,795 feet. To put it another way, if you were to stack Yosemite's El Capitan—the largest granite monolith on earth (3,600 feet)—on top of the Grand Teton, you would see the approximate vertical scale of the Eastern Sierra at Mount

Whitney. And while the Teton Range is 40 miles long, the high crest of the Sierra stretches more than 150 miles.

And as remarkable as the topography itself is the way in which, thanks to the "little affairs of humanity"—specifically the enterprising spirit (and great thirst) of Los Angeles—the Owens Valley has remained essentially unmarred by patterns of urban and suburban development so common in other valleys across the American West. "The pollution and the destruction of habitats caused by such development have been avoided in the Owens Valley," writes Greg James, director of the Inyo County Water Department. In other words, instead of strip malls and ranchettes and suburban tract homes, the view here comprises vast, unbroken—and increasingly rare—landscapes of sagebrush and creosote, granite boulders and snowcapped mountains.

The 2010 census found 1.8 people per square mile in Inyo County, putting it on a par with some of the emptiest terrain in Idaho and Alaska. Of the county's 10,000 square miles, 94 percent—an area larger than the state of Vermont—is owned by citizens and managed by one branch or another of the government: the Park Service, the Forest Service, the Bureau of Land Management, the U.S. Navy, the State of California, the County of Inyo. Four percent is owned by the City of Los Angeles' Department of Water and Power, and less than two percent by private interests.

The remaining one-third of 1 percent remains in the hands of federally recognized Indian tribes. Fewer than 19 square miles are today under irrigation (or one-fifth of a percent)—not counting the 48.6 square miles of Owens lakebed undershallow flooding for dust-mitigation—compared to 117 square miles in 1920. The county of Imperial,

LAST OF THE DUANES (1930) STARRED GEORGE O'BRIEN, MYRNA LOY, AND MOUNT WHITNEY (RIGHT OF CENTER) COURTESY
MUSEUM OF LONE PINE FILM HISTORY

by way of contrast, which is half the size of Inyo, receives about the same amount of annual rainfall, and drains a significantly smaller watershed, has nearly 20 percent of its surface area under irrigation—and more than 100 golf courses. In the 10,000 square miles of Inyo County—from the summit of Mount Whitney to the Amargosa Basin—there are three golf courses: one at Furnace Creek (aka The Oasis at Death Valley), one at Lone Pine, and one at Bishop.

The scenery here—for the most part as wild as it was when Joe Walker first rode through in 1834—has provided the backdrop for hundreds of movies, television shows, and commercials. It has stood in for the Himalayas, for the Andes, for the High Atlas Mountains of North Africa, for distant planets, for the future, for the American West as it once was or might have been—or in this case still is. Ten thousand Japanese American citizens were interned here, for its supposed isolation, during World War II.

"Every cañon commends itself for some particular pleasantness," wrote author Mary Austin in Land of Little Rain (1904), "this for pines, another for trout, one for pure bleak beauty of granite buttresses, one for its far-flung irised falls; and as I say, though some are easier going, leads each to the cloud shouldering citadel."

✳ The Lay of the Land: Approaches and Logistics

"You may come into the borders of it from the south by a stage journey that has the effect of involving a great lapse of time," Austin wrote, "or from the north by rail, dropping out of the overland route at Reno." The Owens Valley can still be approached from the west by way of the ancient passes of the Sierra—on foot or by pack animal. Perhaps the best way to experience the full effect of the eastern scarp is to approach it from the east, as some of the '49ers did, coming over Townes Pass from Death Valley, or by Westgard into Big Pine. But the great majority of travelers in this part of the country come from the south, up US 395 from San Bernardino, Orange County, or San Diego; or up CA 14, as Eaton and Mulholland once used to do, along the aqueduct from Los Angeles, to join US 395 at Indian Wells.

The southernmost and lowest pass over the Sierra foothills is Tehachapi (CA 58), a major and historic shipping and transportation corridor, open year-round between Barstow and Bakersfield and thus between the southern cities and the Central Valley. It is historic in that the majority of automobile traffic from Los Angeles to the central and northern cities now crosses at a higher pass in the Sierra Madre to the west (at Tejon, otherwise known as the Grapevine). The railroad crosses at Tehachapi. Here, north of CA 58, across from the windmill farms, the Pacific Crest Trail leaves the Mojave basin and enters the high desert in earnest. The cement works here provided the bulk of materials for the Owens Valley–Los Angeles Aqueduct project.

Walker Pass (CA 178) is next, then Sherman (CR J41), the latter being the first true pass into the High Sierra (closed from the first substantial snow to late spring), offering a crossing of the South Fork of the Kern, paved access to various wilderness areas, and a roundabout passage to the Big Trees. From Sherman Pass to Tioga Pass, 180 miles to the north, there is no road crossing the Sierra.

The entrance to the Owens Valley proper is at Little Lake. US 395 (officially designated the Eastern Sierra Scenic Byway) is the main artery, the only continuously paved road south to north across the basin. Along it there are five main settlements: Olancha, Lone Pine, Independence, Big Pine, and Bishop, each with its own access spurs into the many hidden canyons of the Sierra. Lone Pine and Bishop provide the majority of travelers' services.

⭐ OTHER BOOKS TO SUPPLEMENT THIS CHAPTER

Cadillac Desert, by Marc Reisner (Penguin, 1993).

California Camping, by Tom Stienstra (Moon/Avalon Travel, 2009).

Farewell to Manzanar, by Jeanne Wakatsuki Houston and James D. Houston (Bantam Books, 1983).

Introduction to Water in California, by David Carle (UC Press, 2004).

Land of Little Rain, by Mary Austin (Houghton Mifflin, 1903).

The Laws Field Guide to the Sierra Nevada, by John Muir Laws (Heyday Books, California Academy of Sciences, 2007).

Sierra East, by Genny Smith, ed. (UC Press, 2000).

Sierra Nevada Natural History, by Tracy Storer, Robert Usinger, and David Lukas (UC Press, 2004).

Tales Along El Camino Sierra, by David and Gayle Woodruff (Eastern Sierra Publishing, 2017).

✳ To See

WALKER PASS TO SHERMAN PASS

Pearsonville (760-377-5446; www1.iwvisp.com/pville). Gas, water, franchise fast food, and Lucy Pearson's renowned hubcap collection.

Power Lines. Both of the parallel sets of towers and cables that run the length of the Owens Valley—sometimes next to, sometimes crossing over US 395—are managed by the Los Angeles Department of Water and Power (DWP), and both sets ship electricity southbound to the city. One set was completed in 1951 from DWP's three generating stations in the Owens Gorge north of Bishop. The other—the Pacific DC Intertie, completed in 1970 from stations on the Columbia River in Washington State—"carries a million volts for 846 miles," according to the Center for Land Use Interpretation, and is "the world's longest distance and highest voltage transmission line." The latter provides just under half of DWP's total supply of electricity.

Nine Mile Canyon (CR J41). A small sign on US 395, just north of Pearsonville, points the way to Kennedy Meadows. This road—the Sherman Pass Road—represents the quickest and one of the least-traveled routes into the Sierra Nevada from points south. At the mouth of the canyon, note the Owens River being siphoned toward the San Fernando Valley (this is not all of it; some passes unseen beneath the road by way of a second, underground aqueduct built in the 1970s). The land and waterworks are owned and maintained by the City of Los Angeles. The river's flow can be observed through vents in the pipeline. Note the radical change in ecosystems from an elevation of 2,500 feet at US 395 (at the northern edge of the Mojave Desert) to the lip of the Kern Plateau at more than 6,000 feet. In winter, the road is closed beyond Kennedy Meadows (6,500 feet). In summer, it continues over Sherman Pass (9,200 feet), thence to wind 6,000 feet back down to the Main Fork of the Kern River.

Joshua Trees. So named by early Mormon pioneers traveling the Old Spanish Trail to San Bernardino, these trees were made world famous in 1987 by Grammy Award-winning Irish rock band U2 (though the actual tree featured on the album cover is now dead and in a heap beside a concrete commemorative plaque in Death Valley's Panamint Basin). Frémont called them "the most repulsive tree in the vegetable kingdom," which seems also to be the general opinion of developers in contemporary Lancaster, Palmdale, and the greater Antelope Valley. In fact, they are not trees, but rather a kind of fibrous bush, a unique species of yucca (*Yucca brevifolia*) that grows only on certain plateaus and higher-altitude fringes of the Mojave Desert, between 2,000 and 6,000 feet up. The oldest are thought to be a thousand years old. "Tormented, thin forests of it stalk drearily in the high mesas," Mary Austin wrote in 1903, "particularly in that triangular slip that fans out eastward from the meeting of the Sierras and coastwise hills, where the first swings across the southern end of the San Joaquin." Good stands can still be seen on the eastern slope of Walker Pass (CA 178); across the uplift of Nine Mile Canyon (CR J41); along the base of the Coso Range, east of Haiwee Reservoir; along the southern promontory of the Inyos (between Death and Saline Valleys); and on the Big Pine-Death Valley Road above the Eureka Basin.

Kennedy Meadows General Store (1445 Kennedy Meadows Rd.; 559-850-5647). Generally manned by Ed McFarland, this is the last place for supplies of any kind. Through-hikers on the Pacific Crest Trail have caches of food mailed here. Most try to make it up here (out of the Mojave) by the first few weeks of spring—after the last snow in the high country, but before things get heated up below. Ice, propane canisters, cold beer, Gatorade, marshmallows, basic fishing tackle. Decent burgers. Local history. No gas. Note the extensive arrowhead collection. Open daily 9 AM–5 PM.

Bald Mountain Fire Lookout (9,430 feet). The highest lookout in the Southern Sierra, it was rebuilt entirely of steel in 1954. All the materials were hauled in by mule. Today's access is via a short, easy hike from the west side of the Sherman Pass crest. Big views of Kennedy Meadows and the Domeland Wilderness. Picnic table.

LITTLE LAKE TO OWENS LAKE

The Eastern Sierra Scenic Byway begins just south of Little Lake, once called Little Owens Lake, where at some point during the Pleistocene Era (more than 20,000 years ago), a great flow of lava sealed off the Owens Valley from its outlet to the Mojave. In the 1940s and '50s, a thriving hotel, store, garage, and post office could be found at Little Lake, serving sportsmen and motorists on their way to the Eastern Sierra. All that's left today is the lake.

Fossil Falls (3 miles north of Little Lake). This small canyon was carved into volcanic basalt by an ancient incarnation of the Owens River, extinct many thousands of years before the first brick was laid at the Pueblo of Los Angeles. Popular climbing spot. Abundant obsidian flakes. Campground.

Red Hill Cinder Cone (3 miles north of Olancha). Assembled by volcanic eruption some 10,000 to 14,000 years ago, Red Hill may have seen action as recently as the 1600s. Pumice and lava rock from Red Hill have been used in the making of cinder blocks, especially for sound-barrier walls along Los Angeles freeways. A borrow pit on the south flank provides cinders for Caltrans road maintenance.

Wild Burro Rescue (Falls Creek Rd., Olancha; 760-384-8523; www.wildburrorescue .org). In 2000, on the site of an old 1930s hunting club, Diane Chontos established a shoestring refuge for some of the wild burros captured in Death Valley. Today there are more than 200 burros—and usually a pack of rescued people and domestic animals, too—living up here on 140 acres with a brand new well. Visitors and volunteers welcome. Call or text for directions before you head up.

✪ **Owens Lake Trails** (North, Northeast and South shores, Owens Lake; www .esaudubon.org/owens_lake). Unveiled in 2016 as the result of hard-won compromises between the Los Angeles Department of Water and Power, the California State Lands Commission, the Great Basin Unified Air Pollution Control District, the Paiute-Shoshone Tribes, the Eastern Sierra Audubon Society, and other local stakeholders, this inspiring series of public access overlooks, interpretive paths, and art installations tells the story of more than a century of grand-scale human interventions on the surface and ecosystems of the Owens Basin and provides opportunities, in season, for viewing over one hundred different species of migratory shorebirds and waterfowl. Download maps and brochure online or ask for information at the Interagency Visitor Center in Lone Pine.

Cartago (3 miles north of Olancha). As the great historian, photographer, and water attorney Burke Griggs reminds us, Carthage was defeated by Rome (c. 146 BCE), thereafter to suffer the salting of its farmland. So the story goes. Once upon a time, at this Cartago, the steamers Bessie Brady and Mollie Stevens unloaded the silver bullion that helped build the Port of Los Angeles. When Los Angeles salted the lake, as it were, the American Potash Company established a surface mining operation here, of which nothing now remains but ruins, heavy metals, and a gleaming pile of soda.

Crystal Geyser Bottling Plant (1-800-443-9737; www.crystalgeyserasw.com). Here, at the base of Olancha Peak, in a 100,000-square-foot modular warehouse on the edge of the Owens Lake playa, one of the best-selling drinking waters in Southern California is pumped out of the ground, bottled, and hauled away on trucks. The company has also submitted plans to build a tea bottling plant up the hill along the old railroad grade. Meanwhile, Anheuser-Busch is reported to be pumping water from a ranch next door. "Olancha is the water capital of California," an Inyo County supervisor told *The High Country News* in 1996. The Crystal Geyser plant—"for insurance liability reasons and also for security"—is not open to the public.

Bartlett Glass Plant. Between the highway and the northwestern edge of the Owens Lake playa lie the silos and midcentury-modern ruins of the Pittsburgh Plate Glass Company's chemical plant, disused since the 1960s, now privately owned.

RED HILL CINDER CONE, OWENS BASIN

E ach of these maps is available for purchase online or at most regional booksellers. For more information on map series, see Chapter 8.

"*Eastern Sierra Guide Map,*" AAA Explore!
"*Mt. Whitney High Country,*" Tom Harrison.
"*Mono Divide High Country,*" Tom Harrison.
"*Kearsarge Pass–Rae Lakes Loop,*" Tom Harrison.
"*Bishop Pass,*" Tom Harrison.
"*John Muir Trail Map Pack,*" Tom Harrison.
"*Inyo National Forest Map,*" U.S. Forest Service.

EAST OF OWENS LAKE

Once upon a time—from prehistory into the 1890s—this was the busier side of the valley. There were fewer rivers to cross and much richer mineral deposits. Now it is home to various ruins, rusted equipment, and mostly abandoned settlements.

Keeler. The southern terminus of what was once the longest narrow-gauge railway in the West, the Carson & Colorado, from 1883. The long, slow decline began with the construction of a standard-gauge road from Mojave to Owenyo, up the west side of the lake, in 1910. Mining operations came and went until the 1950s. Today, it is the site of frequent alkali dust storms and is home to a few dozen ghosts and other reclusive characters.

Owens Lake Trails Plaza Route (see above).

Swansea. The embarkation point for Cerro Gordo bullion in the 1870s, before the business was taken over by Keeler. A sporadically maintained road to the east, into the hills, provides four-wheel-drive access to Cerro Gordo via the Swansea-Keeler petroglyphs (made between 300 BCE and 1200 CE—including ancient equinox markers and possible evidence of early Arabic and Celtic traders) and the remains of the Saline Valley Salt Tram, completed in 1913, which operated in fits and starts as late as 1936.

Dolomite Marble Mine. A pure white marble has been quarried here, at a site once called the Mountain of Marble, since the late 1800s. Deposits are said to extend for 6 miles at a thickness of at least 500 feet. The first two stories of the historic Mills Building in San Francisco (220 Montgomery) were built of this marble in 1891 and went on to survive the 1906 earthquake.

LONE PINE

In 1904 Mary Austin wrote of the pueblo Lone Pine as it once was: "At Las Uvas they keep all the good customs brought out of Old Mexico or bred in the lotus-eating land; drink, and are merry and look out for something to eat afterward; have children, nine or 10 to a family, have cock fights, keep the siesta, smoke cigarettes and wait for the sun to go down." Today the place is run by a breed that takes itself a bit more seriously. Still, it's a classic Western Main Street town in the lee of the highest crest of the Sierra, hub of contemporary tourist activity in the Owens Valley: motels, bars, restaurants, fast food, gas, basic shopping—a perfect base from which to explore the surrounding country. Sold out during the first weekend in October for the film festival.

⊛ **Alabama Hills.** So named by Confederate sympathizers in Lone Pine during the Civil War. The *Alabama* was a cruiser that had destroyed or captured as many as 60

EVACUEES OF JAPANESE ANCESTRY WAIT TO BOARD BUSES FROM LONE PINE STATION TO THE MANZANAR WAR RELOCATION CENTER, APRIL 1942   CLEM ALBERS, COURTESY BANCROFT LIBRARY

Northern vessels by 1864, when it was finally sunk off the coast of France by the USS *Kearsarge*. Union sympathizers in Independence gave the name *Kearsarge* to a number of local features, including the main trail over the Sierra to the Kings River. The boulders and wild rock formations are immediately recognizable as the backdrop of hundreds of movies, TV shows, and commercials. Stop by the Lone Pine Film History Museum for a self-guided drivingtour brochure, or for Dave Holland's *On Location in Lone Pine*, then head for the hills. The area has also become a popular rock climbing and bouldering spot, and it is supposed to be on a fast track to a National Scenic Area designation by Congress (the Alabama Hills National Scenic Area Establishment Act unanimously passed the bitterly divided House of Representatives in 2016). An easy loop can be made (in a passenger car) by following Movie Road north to Moffat Ranch Road, then back down to US 395 just north of the notorious Alabama Gates.

✪ **Whitney Portal.** The paved road west from downtown Lone Pine, built in the 1930s, climbs past the Alabama Hills, up a series of dramatic switchbacks to the Whitney Portal Store, campground, picnic area, and the main Mount Whitney Trailhead

OUTLAWS FOR A WEEKEND AT THE ANNUAL LONE PINE FILM FESTIVAL, HELD EVERY OCTOBER

ALABAMA HILLS, LAND OF *HOPALONG CASSIDY*, *THE LONE RANGER*, AND RIDLEY SCOTT'S *GLADIATOR*

at 8,360 feet. Busy in summer. See "Climbing Mount Whitney" sidebar for trailhead quotas and permit information.

Horseshoe Meadows/Cottonwood Lakes Road. Another exciting set of switchbacks with high exposure from the southern end of the Alabama Hills to the Cottonwood and New Army Pass trailhead at 10,040 feet. Likely the third highest paved road in California (after Rock Creek and Saddlebag Lake Roads—see Chapter 5), it roughly follows the trail John Muir rode on his first attempt at Mount Whitney in 1873. Closed in winter.

✪ **Manzanar National Historic Site** (US 395; 760-878-2194; www.nps.gov/manz). The site was named after the Spanish word for "apple orchard." The Owens Valley Piute were relocated from here by the U.S. Army in 1863. In 1942, the same U.S. Army leased the land from the City of Los Angeles for the relocation and internment of 110,000 Japanese Americans from all over the West Coast (including 12-year-old Larry Shinoda, who would go on to design the 1963 Corvette Sting Ray). Site open dawn to dusk daily. Maps, walking tours, exhibits, clean restrooms, and a wide range of information available at the Interpretive Center in the renovated camp auditorium, open daily 9 AM–5:30 PM in summer, 9 AM–4:30 PM in winter.

1872 Earthquake Grave. On the north side of town, a short trail leads up the highway embankment to a mass grave with a view.

Lone Pine Station. Located northeast of town along the old railroad grade. At the turn of the twentieth century it was owned by Quaker farmers, supposedly among the first to sell their land to Fred Eaton. Here, in 1910, at what was then called Owenyo, the Carson & Colorado narrow gauge met the Southern Pacific standard rail from Mojave. Materials for the Los Angeles Aqueduct were shipped through the depot here, as were thousands of Japanese Americans on their way to Manzanar during World War II.

THE LEGEND OF WINNEDUMAH

O nce upon a time, the Paiute people, who lived in the great valley of Wauco-ba (the Owens), were at war with their neighbors, the Diggers, from the other side of Pah-batoya (the Sierra). The Paiutes' war chief in those days was Tinemaha; Winnedumah, his brother, was a well-respected medicine man. One day, in a surprise attack, the Diggers came down out of the Sierra in great hordes. A battle raged through days and nights. "Never was there such a battle before, nor afterwards, between these primitive foes," wrote one Dan Rose in a 1927 issue of *Touring Topics*. "Hundreds fell in the first clash of arms. Locked in deadly embrace, they crashed each other's skulls with their stone tomahawks, neither giving way." Thousands were left dead or dying across the valley. The Paiutes, as bravely as they fought, were finally driven in retreat to the heights of the Inyo range. Winnedumah reached the crest "sorely pressed, exhausted, and alone," as W. A. Chalfant put it. His medicine had had little effect. His brother was dead. He took one last look across his beloved valley—the Digger warriors now nearly upon him—raised his arms to the sky, and invoked the Great Spirit. The sky cracked open; there was thunder and lightning; the earth shook; and in the great "convulsion of nature" Winnedumah was transformed into a pillar of granite. The Diggers freaked out, of course, and made their way as fast as they could back across the Sierra, never again to trouble the Paiutes. To this day, there atop the Inyos, a long scramble up and eastward from Mazourka Road, stands Winnedumah, "ever faithful."

INDEPENDENCE

County seat for the least populated county in the state of California, Independence was founded as a U.S. Army camp during the early period of white settlement, Indian trouble, and general violence between 1862 and 1877. Today it boasts a population of about 500, an authentic French Colonial bistro, a decent historic hotel, a gas station, a general store, an excellent historical museum, and the courthouse where Charles Manson was arraigned in 1969.

Inyo County Courthouse (168 N. Edwards St.; 760-878-0366; www.inyocounty.us). Designed by W. H. Weeks and built in 1922 in the Greek Revival style, this courthouse is fourth in a line of courthouses, the three previous lost to earthquake and fire. Here Charles Manson and family were jailed briefly and arraigned for possession of stolen vehicles in 1969—before Manson's indictment in the Tate-LaBianca murders.

Mary Austin House (253 Market St.). "If ever you come beyond the borders as far as the town that lies in a hill dimple at the foot of Kearsarge," Mary Austin wrote in 1904, "never leave it until you have knocked at the door of the brown house under the willow tree at the end of the village street, and there you shall have such news of the land, of its trails and what is astir in them, as one lover of it can give to another." Soon after the publication of *Land of Little Rain*, her most enduring work, she moved to Carmel to hang out with Jack London and George Sterling. Then she moved to New Mexico, where she would eventually collaborate with Ansel Adams on a book about the Taos Pueblo. The house is not open to the public.

✪ **Eastern California Museum** (155 N. Grant St.; 760-878-0258; www.inyocounty.us/ecmsite). Established in 1928 as a means of preserving the varied history and material culture of the Owens Valley, this museum features a variety of artifacts, from Shoshone and Paiute baskets to historic photographs to a collection of 1880s buildings, local mountaineering history, and a yard full of rusting equipment from the construction of the L.A. Aqueduct. The east wing houses temporary and traveling exhibits. No fee. Open daily 10 AM–5 PM.

1872 EARTHQUAKE GRAVE BURKE GRIGGS

✪ **Mount Whitney Fish Hatchery** (Oak Creek Rd., 2 miles north of Independence; 760-279-1592; www.mtwhitneyfishhatchery.org). M. J. Connell, state fish and game commissioner in 1915, wanted a hatchery "that would match the mountains, would last forever, and would be a showplace for all time." And so, the following year, this faux Tudor-style chateau was built of 3,500 tons of local granite. The landscaping is supposed to have been designed by a gardener from Golden Gate Park in San Francisco. The facility is now run by the Friends of Mt. Whitney Fish Hatchery and features interpretive wildlife and hatchery exhibits and fish-feeding ponds. Open daily.

BIG PINE

Gateway to the ancient bristlecone pines and the palisades, Big Pine was so named long before the giant sequoia—the so-called Teddy Roosevelt Tree—was planted on the north end of town to commemorate the opening of Westgard Pass to automobile traffic in 1923. Gas, motels, basic road food, world-famous barbecue, and an Indian reservation.

Owens Valley Radio Observatory (4 miles north on Leighton Lane, off CA 168, east of Big Pine; 760-938-2075; www.ovro.caltech.edu). The largest university operated radio observatory in the world. Studies include the sun and the origins of the universe. Public tours are given year-round at OVRO on the first Monday of every month except on holidays. If the first Monday is a holiday, the tour is held on the second Monday. All tours start at 1 PM and last about an hour. Reservations are not required and there is no cost. To arrange tours for schools and large groups call 760-938-2114.

✪ **Ancient Bristlecone Pine Forest** (760-873-2500; www.fs.fed.us/r5/inyo). What is likely the fourth-highest paved road in the state ends at the Schulman Grove (10,010 feet) and from there continues, unpaved, to the Patriarch Grove at more than 11,000 feet. From there the track continues past a locked gate—closed to vehicle traffic, except during one open-house weekend every August—to the top of White Mountain Peak, at 14,242 feet. The bristlecone pines are the planet's oldest living things, though in 2013 they were quietly, officially unseated by a cluster of spindly, 8,000- to 10,000-year-old spruce trees in Sweden. The oldest living individual, at more than 4,700 years old, is named Methuselah, after the longest-lived person in the Bible. The tree's exact location is, for its protection, a fairly well-guarded secret. An older specimen by the name of Prometheus (4,844 years old) was cut down by a graduate student in 1964. The new visitor center at Schulman Grove is open daily, June through September. Road closed in winter.

White Mountain Research Center Barcroft Station (at the end of White Mountain Road; 760-873-4344; www.wmrs.edu). Established in 1951 as a joint venture between the University of California at Berkeley and the Office of Naval Research, White Mountain's facilities and use permits were transferred by the Navy to UC in the 1970s. Facilities include an observatory on the Barcroft Plateau (12,500 feet) and a lab on the summit of White Mountain (14,250 feet). The latter facility is probably as close to Antarctica as a researcher can come without leaving the Lower 48. Ground has been broken here on the sexiest of topics: hypoxia, ventilation, hibernation, polarization of cosmic background radiation, holocene paleoecology in bristlecone pines, and climate change. Open house for the public on the first Sunday in August. Check website for scheduled community lectures. Bishop office at 3000 E. Line St.

✪ **Palisade Glacier**. "A more absurd theory was never advanced than that by which it was sought to ascribe to glaciers the sawing out of these vertical walls," the state's chief geologist, Professor Josiah Whitney, wrote in 1868. For the rest of his life, Whitney clung to the idea that there were no glaciers in the Sierra Nevada. John Muir, "ignorant sheepherder," proved him wrong. The Palisade glacier is the largest remaining in the Sierra Nevada and the southernmost in the US, dating back to the Little Ice Age some 700 years ago. It is thought to have been in retreat since the 1850s. These are tough times for glaciers—catch this one before it's gone. Visible from US 395 north

OWENS VALLEY RADIO OBSERVATORY BURKE GRIGGS

TULE ELK

In 1844 John Frémont found the western slope of the Sierra "crowded with bands of elk and wild horses." That same year, Lansford Hastings wrote, "It is very common to see herds of five or six hundred elk ranging from vale to vale, amid the oats, clover and flax, with which the plains and valleys everywhere abound." There were hundreds of thousands of tule or dwarf elk (*Cervus elaphus nannodes*) in California before the first great influx of population in the early 1850s. By the late 1860s they were nearly gone. "At its smallest," wrote naturalist Allan Schoenherr, "the population may have numbered fewer than 10." One forward-thinking (and/or nostalgic) rancher in Kern County established a private refuge for the handful that remained. In 1873, the state Legislature moved to protect them, and by 1914 there were too many for the refuge to sustain. The Department of Fish and Game began various attempts to introduce them elsewhere, but the only group of transplants that managed to thrive was the group that had been introduced to the Yosemite Valley. By 1933, the elk had come to be considered a problem in Yosemite, and all 26 of them were transferred to the Owens Valley, where they were not native. The following year these were joined by 28 from the Kern County refuge. Today the herd is kept at a number not exceeding 490. They range the length of the valley and can often be seen—depending on the kindness of local farmers and ranchers, who have been known to refer to the wandering outcasts as "welfare elk"—grazing on irrigated alfalfa along US 395 south of Big Pine, especially early in the morning and at dusk.

TULE ELK IN A PADDOCK, YOSEMITE VALLEY, PRE-1932 COURTESY NPS, YNP

THE DISAPPEARING SIERRA SUMMIT REGISTERS

On the trail of the fragile, valuable, and increasingly rare records of the Range of Light's climbing history (from Adventure Journal Quarterly, *No. 04):*

We drove up from California's Owens Basin with the rising sun still an hour behind the White Mountains. Our objective: to reach the summit of a certain pile of granite blocks amid a range of other such piles thrust more than 12,000 feet above sea level. Some years before, three young men had stood briefly upon that particular summit, and we hoped that we might find there, on this calm autumn day before the season's first snow, perhaps wedged into a crevice, a rusted tobacco tin or other receptacle, in which might be preserved a scrap of paper containing the climbers' names scrawled in pencil beside the year in which they'd made their pioneering ascent: 1934.

That had been eight decades ago—the year Bonnie and Clyde were gunned down on a Louisiana back road, the year Adolph Hitler became Germany's Führer, the year the Loch Ness monster was first spotted. It was also the year Hervey Voge, David Brower, and Norman Clyde bagged 32 first ascents in the Sierra Nevada during a productive 10-week "Knapsack Survey of Sierra Routes and Records." I'd never been much for adding my name to summit registers, myself. But to sit on a fin of granite in the same spot as like-minded men from another era, eating my bagel and cheese and chocolate and sipping a lukewarm pale ale in the sun—that seemed a pleasant enough way to interrupt a long day's march.

The tradition of summit registries is as old as mountaineering itself, perhaps dating back as far as the Middle Ages in the Alps. As a species, we seem to have a unique awareness of our brief time on the planet. Nowhere is this existential reality more palpable than atop a mountain, which does not care by which route we've come to be there, how inspiring the view is, or how excited we are to get back to a cheeseburger and a cold beer. And so, with that storm brewing over the next ridge, we give in to a deep impulse to leave a more lasting record of our passage: to erect crosses and cairns, to etch human figures onto basaltic cliff bands or carve our initials on aspen trees, to write our names on scraps of paper to be sealed in weatherproof containers for all eternity—or as much of eternity as can be managed.

There was a time when summit registers provided a record of conquest, serving as proof of the first human beings to reach those last remaining untrammeled places. Those days are gone. Nowadays they represent a loose, scattered folk archive in roughly the same genre as the guest books in backcountry ski huts and far-flung bed-and-breakfast cottages. The most recent entries may prove valuable to search-and-rescue teams in the event of a missing person. The oldest entries, or those of famous passersby, may have a certain historic value—indeed there is a published reference as early as 1933 to "souvenir hunters" stealing original registers from the pre-national park Tetons and others being brought down by guides for preservation in local museums. Otherwise, their value is essentially sentimental.

The tradition is also the source of controversy. Should such records be preserved in situ, as an enhancement of the experience of climbing a mountain, or should they be removed, either as blight or as important historical documents to be set aside for posterity? Opinions on such matters proliferate, as with most matters having to do with what we call wilderness.

Hervey Voge would later become known for his first definitive edition of *A Climber's Guide to the High Sierra*. Norman Clyde was a former schoolteacher and high school principal who'd been forced to retire after firing his pistol in the vicinity of a gang of students engaged in a Halloween prank. He'd recently achieved renown for having found the body of another young climber by the name of Walter A. "Pete" Starr Jr. on a high ledge on Michael Minaret the year before. Clyde was already well on his way to becoming one of the most prolific mountaineers of all time—both in numbers of peaks climbed and in words written about those climbs. Brower—later famously dubbed the Archdruid by writer John McPhee—would go on to make his mark as the first executive director of the Sierra Club, founder of the League of Conservation Voters and Friends of the Earth, and one of the principal architects of the Wilderness Act of 1964, thereby codifying the radical notion that there ought always to be some places on the ever-more-crowded earth where "the imprint of man's work" might remain forever "substantially unnoticeable."

Of all possible peaks, we'd chosen this one primarily because it seemed accessible enough to be done in one long day and because it seemed doable with dogs. On maps it has a name, which I will not share, but somehow it's not considered prominent enough, or emblematic enough, or otherwise notable enough, to figure on the Sierra Club's Sierra Peaks Section (SPS) list of 247 canonical peaks, nor even on the more extensive 344 Major Peaks list. And so it seemed likely to have been visited by fewer human beings. And might have a better chance, I figured, of harboring its original register.

During their whirlwind tour of summits, Brower, Voge, and Clyde added their names to existing registers and created new ones on peaks where they found no sign of previous climbers. They also found registers missing on peaks that should have had them and in turn felt compelled to remove others they felt might be in danger of being lost or taken—to instead preserve them in an archive. The Sierra, like other ranges, has a long history of having its summit registers disappear. They tend to be less durable than other human artifacts made of, say, obsidian, of which countless flakes and dart points dating back 15,000 years can still be found strewn about on the high passes. Even in the most benign conditions, paper falls apart. Metal rusts. Glass bottles break. Register pages blow away. Containers leak or get dropped into cracks or off cliff faces or get torched by lightning strikes. And the registers themselves, as it happens—especially the more coveted historical bits—are easily slipped into backpacks and carried away. And so it was also entirely possible that we'd find no record of those men.

According to Francis P. Farquhar's seminal *History of the Sierra Nevada*, the "first account of an identifiable mountain ascent in the Sierra" was Lt. John C. Frémont's 1844 winter climb of Red Lake Peak, from which the old commander and his mapmaker became the first white men to see Lake Tahoe. There's no mention in either man's diary of having left behind any kind of register. Nineteen years later, in 1863, William Brewer, a Yale-trained botanist and leader of the original California Geological Survey, placed the range's first summit register atop Mt. Dana. The following year, he and his topographer planted an American flag on a peak in the southern part of the range that would later bear Brewer's name. They scribbled their autographs on a piece of paper, sealed the paper in a glass bottle, and left them there for posterity—or for whomever might come next. "It is not at all probable that any man was ever on the top before," Brewer wrote in his published journal, "or that anyone will be again—for a long time at least." Brewer's original register was taken down to the Sierra Club's office in San Francisco for preservation in 1896, two years after the club, under the leadership of John Muir, began establishing official summit registers on peaks across the range. Ten years later, the office and all its contents were destroyed by the 1906 earthquake and fire.

One summer day in 1987, a photographer and trophy shop owner from Merced by the name of Robin Ingraham, Jr., an ardent campaigner against fixed climbing anchors in wilderness and a collector of rare books, made a roped first ascent up the south face of Midway Mountain with his friend Mark Hoffman. They'd read in Steve Roper's 1976 edition of *A Climber's Guide to the High Sierra* about an original 1912 register containing the signatures of Francis P. Farquhar and other Sierra Club pioneers William Colby and Robert Price. Their primary goal that day was to see those names in that register. Roper had claimed it was the oldest surviving register in the Sierra. "It was nearly a race," Ingraham wrote later, "to see who could hold the register first."

Hoffman got there first, but the old register book wasn't inside. A newer one—placed there in 1969, presumably because the old one was filled to capacity—contained an entry from 1979 by a cheeky bunch calling themselves the Purple Mountain Gang and claiming responsibility for the theft of the original book. The PMG, as Ingraham referred to them, had already achieved a certain notoriety for what they called a "register exchange program," in which as a kind of practical joke they would replace the summit register on a given peak with one they'd taken from another summit. In 1982, for example, Hoffman had found atop Mt. Dade the register from Colorado's Mt. Daly with a professional calling card from the PMG on which they described themselves as "an elite corps of imprudent snobs."

Hoffman and Ingraham threw themselves into a quest to find the Midway register, and, as Ingraham put it, to "bring the thieves to justice." They came to a series of dead ends, but after consultation with a number of old Sierra luminaries, including Brower, Voge, Farquhar, and Jules Eichorn, they formed an organization called the Sierra Register Committee (SRC) dedicated to removing historic registers for preservation in the new Sierra Club archives at the Bancroft Library in Berkeley. The removal campaign didn't sit well with people like R.J. Secor, Mountain Records Chair for the Sierra Peaks Section and respected author of the classic hiker's guidebook, *The High Sierra: Peaks, Passes and Trails.* Secor felt strongly that registers should not be removed from their original milieu for any reason—not even for preservation. "These two fellows came out of nowhere and took it upon themselves to remove these registers," Secor told the *Sacramento Bee* years later, in 2004, "when the general view of most climbers is: 'Leave them up there forever.'" (By coincidence, in the Eastern Sierra Museum in Independence, there is an old Sierra Club register from Mt. Langley that was donated by none other than R.J. Secor.)

Hoffman was killed in 1988 in an accident on the Devils Crags in the remote Kings Canyon backcountry. It was late afternoon. He and Ingraham were descending an open scree-and-talus-filled chute below Crag #8. According to his own harrowing account, Ingraham had watched helplessly as his friend was dragged over a cliff by a massive rockslide. He found Hoffman below, shattered and bloody but still conscious. Hoffman pleaded for his friend to stay with him. Ingraham felt he had no choice but to hike out for help. By the time he returned the next morning with a helicopter, after a night of light snow and rain, Hoffman was dead. Ingraham redoubled his efforts to save the most historic summit registers, but in 1994, weighed down by the loss of his friend and feeling alone in a protracted dispute with the SPS, Ingraham shuttered the SRC and abandoned climbing altogether. "Regarding the Purple Mountain Gang," he recently wrote to me in an email, "nothing ever turned up."

Registers continued to disappear. According to the Sacramento Bee, 19 register books were reported missing in 2004 alone, along with 10 containers. "The oldest, lost from Mount Barnard," wrote the reporter, "dated to 1936." Three years later, Ingraham found a post on the internet with a detailed description and pictures of the original register on Mt. Woodworth containing a signature from 1895. Worried it would be stolen, he called his friend Claude Fiddler on the east side of the range. Fiddler headed over Bishop Pass in six inches of fresh November snow and brought the register down to be stowed at the Bancroft.

In 2008, a young journalist from the Bay Area by the name of Andrew Becker tried for the summit of Black Kaweah. There'd been numerous online trip reports describing the original 1924 register ("fascinating," "out of this world") with Clyde's and Eichorn's signatures in it, as well as Pete Starr's from 1929, signed in legendary fashion—in blood drawn from a self-inflicted cut to his ear (for lack of a pencil). Becker ran into a group of climbers coming down Sawtooth Pass who assured him the register was still there. But night fell and he didn't make the summit. "That signature, still in an aluminum box on Black Kaweah's peak in Sequoia National Park," he wrote, "is one of the Sierra's treasures." But by the time veteran mountaineer and photographer Vern Clevenger went up there with his son three years later, it was gone. "We looked and looked and looked—and it's gone," Clevenger told the *Los Angeles Times*. "If anyone finds who took it, I hope they string him up. What kind of person would do something like that?

Harry Langenbacher is the man currently charged with the daunting task of documenting and keeping summit registers maintained all across the Sierra Nevada for the SPS. A retired electrical engineer based in Fullerton, he inherited the title and responsibilities of Mountain Records Chair from Secor, who suffered a massive brain injury from a glissading accident off the summit of Mt. Baldy in Southern California and never quite recovered. "My hand made the front page," Langenbacher told me recently, referring to the *L.A. Times* article that featured a photo of his hand turning the screw on a 1940's-era aluminum-cast Sierra Club register box. In the online comments, he recalled, there was a climber who took credit for having stolen the Black Kaweah register in order to address a personal score with Robin Ingraham over the question of fixed anchors in wilderness. (The article and comment thread are no longer available on the website.)

Despite a long cultural history in the West that assumes that collecting old stuff found lying about on the surface of our public lands is legal, the law—in particular the 1979 Archaeological Resources Protection Act (ARPA)—prohibits the removal without a permit of any "archaeological resource" that is more than 100 years old, "including, but not limited to, pottery, basketry, bottles, weapons, projectiles, tools, structures, pit houses, rock paintings, graves, and human skeletal materials." Confusingly, the law exempts coins and bullets "unless they are found in direct physical relationship with another archaeological resource." Arrowheads and other projectile points are generally exempted as long as they're found on top of the dirt. Horseshoes from more than a hundred years ago, on the other hand, are considered protected. Summit registers are not specifically mentioned.

According to the U.S. Department of Justice, "Beyond the obvious legal violations, some collectors do not understand the moral and historical implications of separating an item from where it was found and thus separating it from its historical context, its story." By this logic, and by the letter of the law, Fiddler's removal of the original Woodworth register could be considered a federal crime. The Black Kaweah register, on the other hand—less than 87 years old when it went missing, and in a cast-aluminum box that was younger by two or three decades—was, at least according to the law, fair game, no more protected than an errant bit of microtrash from a Clif bar wrapper.

"No one's really figured out what's happening to them," Langenbacher told me. There are stories of deliberate vandalism, he says. There are hardliners—backcountry park rangers maybe, or other self-appointed wilderness stewards—who feel that any sign of modern humans in the wilderness is essentially trash, detracting from the purity of the experience. And then, of course, there are the private collectors, some of whom may or may not eventually send their loot to the Sierra Club or some other historical archive. I asked Langenbacher if he'd ever been to see the collection at the Bancroft. "No," he said. And he didn't imagine he ever would. On his online registers page he compares archiving a summit register to putting a bighorn sheep in a cage: "I like to go see registers on peaks," he told me. But then he softened a bit: "I'd like to go see the old Woodworth one. It was gone before I had a chance to get up there."

I made a pilgrimage down to the Bancroft Library in Berkeley one day to have a look. The Sierra Club Mountain Registers and Records collection comprises 27 file boxes and other odds and ends. I left my bag in a coin-operated locker on the first floor, per regulations, made my way up the polished granite stairs to the reading room, past an unsettling life-size photo cutout on the landing of a Miwok woman carrying a bundle of firewood on her back. Register pages dated back to 1875, from several hundred peaks in the Sierra and beyond. The vintage containers included rusted tobacco and tea tins, a carved-wood Sierra Club box from Banner Peak dated 1963, and a mayonnaise jar "found on the east side of Mt. Shasta inside a 'cave'" in 1986—donated in 1991. After showing two forms of identification, I signed my name in pencil and ordered up Carton 10: Lower Cathedral Rock 1933 to Minarets 1933-1937.

Glen Denny, the master photographer and chronicler of the early Yosemite big wall pioneers, also a voracious endurance hiker and peak bagger in his day, had told me about seeing the poet Gary Snyder's signature in the summit register on the Matterhorn in Yosemite in the mid-1960s. Snyder had climbed the Matterhorn in 1955 with Jack Kerouac in an episode later made famous in Kerouac's *Dharma Bums* (Kerouac "bailed beneath the summit while Snyder went on alone to the top"). "I got kind of a charge out of seeing that," Denny told me.

When I pored through the Matterhorn file at the Bancroft, the earliest entries were from 1934. Earlier names, back to 1899—including Norman Clyde's in 1921—had been transcribed on the first pages. Mysteriously, the register skipped directly from October 1954 to August 1956. There were arrows drawn in pencil where, presumably, a researcher had noted the gap. Inside the cover of a later book, started in 1967, Snyder's entry had been transcribed—not in his hand: "10.23.1955 Gary Snyder here. Even the mountains shall become buddhas." The original was gone, as was Denny's entry from a decade later.

Still, in just this one file box, with its very incomplete scattering from just 18 summits, was a unique record. Thousands of people, the majority of whom were now long gone and mostly forgotten, had clambered their way upward to these rarified aeries, where they felt compelled to leave evidence of their passing: name, date, a note about the weather, a note about the route by which they got there and how long it took, a tone of reverence perhaps, some attempt to capture the unfathomable spiritual impact of being on top of a mountain, or otherwise to make light of it all. *This is to certify that the notorious Andy Ashurst landed his carcus [sic] on this bute [sic]. Sep. 5—1951.* Followed by: *This is to certify that Andy Ashurst can't spell.*

Made the ascent from the camp at head of Tuolumne Meadows in 4 1/2 hours, wrote Joseph N. LeConte, co-creator of the John Muir Trail, atop Mt. Lyell on July 8, 1897. *Perfectly clear day.* There are Victorian flourishes to the script. Without much effort, one can imagine the hobnail boots, the wool trousers, the neckerchief, the warmth of the rock, the blue sky. The paper is thin and fragile, sheathed in protective plastic. One more pleasant moment in the mountains briefly noted, long ago come and gone, removed from the elements, filed away.

The last file in the box was a manila folder containing five scraps of paper and a small envelope. It was noted on the envelope that the scraps had been "brought in by Jules Eichorn" from the Minarets, probably in 1954. The "rusty bouillon cube box" that had served as their container had been discarded. One of the scraps was a crumpled bit of newsprint on which Norman Clyde had written his name on June 28, 1928, to mark his first ascent of what would become known as Clyde Minaret. A Sierra Club party the following year had found the scrap laying loose and added to it a piece of folded green card stock that served as register for the next nine parties, through 1938. Perhaps the most remarkable entry on that card was that of "W.A. Starr," penciled on August 6, 1933, the day before he failed to meet his father at Glacier Lodge and 19 days before Clyde found his body on a ledge several hundred feet below the summit of Michael Minaret.

We hiked up into the wilderness on a well-worn path decorated with horse shit and the recent, irreverent treads of a mountain bike poacher. The aspen leaves were burnt out for the season. There was a thin fringe of ice along the edge of the stream. And then suddenly we emerged into a lovely sweet autumn day. The dogs settled into a more conservative pace. Above the upper lakes a thin trail gave way to fields of talus and a steep chute of scree and sand. We lost all trace of human beings. On one ledge we noted what might have been bighorn sheep tracks. Toward the top, the climb was more difficult than we'd anticipated, dipping into a handful of minor class-five moves requiring perilous dog portages.

A few days earlier I'd eaten dinner with Glen Denny and his wife Peggy at their house in South San Francisco. I'd shown them the photos I'd taken of the summit registers I'd found at the Bancroft earlier in the day. Among the many stories Denny told that night, there was the nameless scree-pile above the Goddard basin that he'd hiked up as a teenager in the mid-1950s. He'd been hoping for a first ascent; there were still some left then. "I remember the intense excitement I felt as I approached the summit," he said. "But when I got there, there was a small cairn on top. I was devastated: Goddammit, someone beat me to it!" It had been his first experience with "the game," as he put it. The next day he set his sights on a line of other minor peaks, where, finding no sign of previous ascent and thus considering them virgin territory, he erected his own cairns and left his name behind inside film canisters or whatever other containers he happened to have along.

On a busy summit like Mt. Whitney, national park employees haul, once a year, a stack of paper about an inch-and-a-half thick and containing many thousands of signatures down the mountain to be stored in the park administrative offices in Three Rivers. Grand Teton National Park has created a digital archive of summit registers from the late 1920s to the 1980s that can be browsed online. The Colorado Mountain Club, for its part, has begun working with land managers to phase out paper registers in favor of online digital registries, and a growing number of smart phone apps offer climbers a way to sign such registries from atop the peak itself and, as proof of accomplishment, to geotag the location. Whether there are or are not summit registers on mountaintops is of course immaterial to the places themselves. And on the long list of threats to the wilderness experience as conceived by Brower and his contemporaries—a list that now includes climate change, species die-offs, human population explosion, light and sound pollution, and new political maneuvers to dismantle basic protections such as those against mechanical travel—the human impulse to leave behind a written record seems of little consequence. It seems a shame to lose that sense of direct communion with those men and women who made it to these heights before us, especially those from an earlier, less technologically-driven age. But such is the way of things: some small part of our past will be relegated to museums and libraries and digital archives; the rest will be lost. The mountains, for their part, will abide long after we are gone.

Topping out, we immediately realized we'd made a mistake. Paying too little attention to the map, we'd climbed and heaved with our dogs to a false summit, perhaps a half mile from the official peak as a raven could fly it—over a jumble of massive boulders that would have taken the rest of our daylight to cross. There was no register there, of course. There was no cairn or any other evidence of human passage, and so, save for the contrails in the sky, all those people jetting to and from the ever-swelling San Francisco Bay Area, we were free to imagine ourselves lonely pioneers in a land without humans. But I had no illusions that we were the first to sit in that spot. Given the way the terrain looked from the lake below, ours was a natural mistake, one that even Voge, Brower, and Clyde might have made back in 1934.

And so we settled in to eat our lunches and enjoy the view. We told stories of other summits narrowly missed. And then we packed up our trash. We hauled our dogs back down to the scree, then leaped long-legged and careless down to the lakeshore, where the dogs could drink and the humans could empty their shoes of sand for the long walk out to the car.

KEELER MUNICIPAL POOL, JUNE 2007 BURKE GRIGGS

of Big Pine, plastered to a wall of granite needles, several more than 14,000 feet high (by either datum), the glacier itself can be reached by way of an 18-mile round-trip hike from the Glacier Lodge trailhead in Big Pine Canyon.

BISHOP

As the main population and supply center for the Eastern Sierra, Bishop is the only incorporated settlement in Inyo County. The town is named for Samuel A. Bishop, who brought cattle here in the 1860s, much to the chagrin of the locals. Today it's an internationally renowned climbing mecca and the uncontested mule capital of the world. Here you'll find motels, restaurants, hardware stores, banks, fast food, Chinese, Japanese, Mexican and Thai food, organic Greek frozen yogurt, craft beers, bagels, gas, groceries, and an Indian casino. Sold out Memorial Day weekend for Mule Days. Free high-speed Wi-Fi on Main Street.

Laws Railroad Museum and Historical Site (North on US 6 to Silver Canyon Road; 760-873-5950; www.lawsmuseum.org). Eleven acres of exhibits include the original 1883 Laws depot, post office, and agent's house, much as they were when the last train ran in 1960. Other buildings have been added to re-create the village of Laws as it was when the Carson & Colorado was in full swing. Non-railroad artifacts include antique cameras, photos, saddles, brands, wagons, old stoves, guns, bathtubs, telephones, and medical and printing equipment. It's also home to Death Valley No. 5, the gasoline-driven rail car once used to haul tourists from Death Valley Junction to the old Furnace Creek Inn (the Inn at Death Valley). Nice place for a picnic on a windless day in winter. Admission by donation. Open daily 10 AM–4 PM year-round.

Fish Slough Road. Head north from Bishop on US 6. At 1.3 miles, continue straight on Five Bridges Road. After another 2.3 miles, turn right on Fish Slough Road. Go 6.4 miles to the interpretive kiosk at the Owens Valley Native Fish Sanctuary, home to the last remaining population of Owens pupfish, declared extinct in 1948, rediscovered in the 1960s, and still hanging on today despite predation by bigger, badder non-native bass. On the right-hand side of the road, 4.6 miles later, behind a fence, note the Chidago Canyon Petroglyphs, etchings in volcanic rock dating from many thousands of years ago along with slightly less artful inscriptions from the late twentieth century. For information on local rock art sites on public land, and on the laws governing the protection of artifacts, check with the Bureau of Land Management (351 Pacu Ln., Bishop; 760-872-5000; blm.gov/ca/bishop).

❈ To Do

BISHOP

BIRD-WATCHING Countless creeks, reservoirs, marshes, and springs—from the Owens Gorge and tablelands north of Bishop to Little Lake—provide world-class birding. More than 320 known species frequent the valley floor. Check the Eastern Sierra Audubon Society's Web site (www.esaudubon.org) for hot spots. The "Eastern Sierra Birding Trail Map" is available online (www.easternsierrabirdingtrail.org) and through most local businesses and bookstores.

BOATING Leisurely tubing and kayaking are possible on certain remnant and newly re-established sections of the Owens River, from Bishop to below Lone Pine. Bishop Motosports (58 Commerce Dr., Mammoth; 760-934-0347; www.bishopmotosports .com) rents kayaks and inner tubes.

For an afternoon float on a High Sierra lake, bring your own craft or hire one at the following locations:

KAYAKING THE NEWLY RESTORED LOWER OWENS RIVER BILL BECHER

CLIMBING MOUNT WHITNEY

The tallest peak in the range was given its name in 1864, nine years before anyone managed to make the summit, by members of Josiah D. Whitney's Geological Survey. Its height was then estimated to be more than 15,000 feet above sea level. Clarence King, of that early survey, climbed a peak he thought was Whitney in 1871, only to discover two years later that he'd been on the wrong summit (today known as Mount Langley). By the time he'd heard the bad news, made his way back across the country from the East Coast, engaged an outfit from Visalia, and made the true summit, on September 19, 1873, he'd been beaten to the punch.

The first party consisted of three fishermen from Lone Pine who had erected a monument on the summit a month earlier and declared their mountain to be called "Fisherman's Peak." A slightly more scientific expedition, organized by Mortimer Belshaw of Cerro Gordo, made the top in early September and, using a barometer, measured its elevation at 14,898 feet. John Muir, hardy fellow, showed up a month after King.

Muir rode a horse south from Independence to Cottonwood Pass by himself. He left his horse in a meadow so as to climb what he thought was the highest peak, only to find himself, as King did before him, standing atop Mount Langley. But Muir, unlike King, actually noticed the higher peak 5 or 6 miles to the north. He ran down and moved his horse, and by sunset he was at the base of Whitney. He pressed on, and by midnight he made the base of the needles. "There I had to dance all night to keep from freezing," he wrote. And in the morning he bailed.

He retrieved his horse, returned to Independence, "ate and slept all next day," then, not to be deterred (Muir was no quitter, by the way), "set out afoot for the summit by direct course up the east side." He was standing at the fishermen's monument at 8 AM on the 21st of October, the first to climb Whitney from the east.

The good people of Lone Pine, who suffered no love for Whitney after he made absurd pronouncements on their little earthquake the year before, made a valiant attempt to make official the name "Fisherman's Peak"—even to the extent of introducing a bill in the state Legislature. But the mapmakers, natural partisans of Whitney, won out. The Wheeler Survey in 1875 penciled Whitney in at 14,471 feet. The first women to stand at that elevation did so in 1878. Loaded mules made the summit in 1881, and in 1883 a portion of the east side of the range—from Sheep Mountain to Williamson to the Alabama Hills—was set aside as the Mount Whitney Military Reservation, "ostensibly for military, in reality for scientific purposes." The trail was improved and a stone hut built on the summit during the summer of 1909. In 1926, the summit became the eastern boundary of the newly expanded Sequoia National Park.

The official elevation has changed a number of times over the years, from 14,522 (1881) to 14,515 (1903) to 14,502 (1905) to 14,496 (1928). "You're looking at the pride of the Sierras, brother—Mount Whitney," the gas station attendant says to Humphrey Bogart in *High Sierra* (1941), "14,501 feet above sea level." In the 1955 remake, *I Died a Thousand Times*, the guy says to Jack Palance: "You're looking at the High Sierras, mister. Mount Whitney's in there . . . 14,496 feet." AAA puts it down as 14,494, and the Park Service has it at 14,491. The Forest Service—the agency that issues the permits necessary to climb the thing—calls it 14,496 or 14,495.

"Determining the heights of peaks has always been a long and arduous calculation," says Mitch Adleson, Western Region cartographer for the U.S. Geological Survey. Modern instrumentation has helped the process considerably, but discrepancies still exist depending on the type and quality of the instrument used to do the measuring, the methodology, and—perhaps most importantly—where you decide sea level happens to be. That determination, as it turns out, is no small task.

The Sea Level Datum of 1929, aka the National Geodetic Vertical Datum of 1929 (NGVD29), by which all topographical elevations were thereafter supposed to be determined, was cobbled together from the observed mean sea level at 26 different tide gauges in the US and Canada, the theory being that as long as everyone's using the same starting point, however imprecise, everyone's numbers ought to come out about the same. But then, in 1991, to keep things interesting, the NGVD29 was replaced with a slightly adjusted datum, the North American Vertical Datum of 1988 (NAVD88).

"The difference between the two can, in California, be on the order of 2.5 to 3 feet," says Marti Ikehara of the National Geodetic Survey. The elevations referenced to NAVD88 are, as it turns out, higher than the old measurements. So, for people interested in ticking summits (or ski descents) off a list of 14,000-foot peaks, there's a potential complication: As Ikehara points out, there could theoretically be more fourteeners than there used to be, depending on whether the conversion's been made.

Anyway, back to Whitney, which by anyone's calculation is well over 14,000 feet and still the highest point of rock in the Lower 48, as well as an exceedingly popular hike for ambitious walkers from all over the globe. To keep the crowds down, all trails in the Whitney zone are subject to strict quotas between May 1 and November 1. Permits for the main Mount Whitney Trail are issued first by mail-in lottery in February, thereafter on a first-come first-served basis, as available, beginning at 11 AM on the day before the intended entry date. A variety of other, longer routes (from the west side or the Mountaineers' Route to the north) can get you there with greater effort but considerably less traffic. For more information, check www .fs.fed.us/r5/inyo/ or call the permit office at the Eastern Sierra Interagency Visitor Center at 760-876-6200.

WHITNEY CREST JOEL ST. MARIE

WINTER FLY-FISHING IN BISHOP PATITUCCIPHOTO

Lake Sabrina Boat Landing (Lake Sabrina; 760-873-7425; www.lakesabrinaboat landing.com). Fishing and pontoon boat rentals, canoes and kayaks. And good home-made pie with a view. April to October.

South Lake Boat Landing (South Lake, Bishop; 760-873-4177; www.parchersresort .net). Fishing and pontoon boat rentals, bait and tackle. June to October.

FISHING Fishing is open year-round below the Pleasant Valley reservoir. From there north the Owens boasts the earliest trout opener in the state, so you can get in there early for rainbow, brook, cutthroat, golden, and brown. As the season progresses, work your way up toward the Sierra along one of more than a dozen intensively stocked creeks. When the snow melts, hit the hatches in the upper lake basins. For the latest reports, maps, notes, news, stocking schedules, and other relevant links, check Mono County's fishing pages at www.monocounty.org/things-to-do/fishing/fishing-reports/. For more Eastern Sierra guide-service listings, see Chapter 5.

Note: A valid California fishing license is required for residents and nonresidents sixteen years of age or older on all public and private land outside and inside national park boundaries. Licenses can be purchased online at https://www.ca.wildlifelicense .com/InternetSales or through any authorized license agent (including most sporting goods outlets and local general stores). Always check with a park ranger, local outfitter, or visitor center staff for area- and species-specific quota and catch-and-release regulations.

Bishop Flyfishing Guide Service (760-387-2715; www.bishopflyfishing.com). Classes, seminars, full-service guide trips.

Pat Yaeger's Eastern Sierra Guide Service (760-872-7770; www.jaeger-flyfishing .com).

Sierra Drifters (760-935-4250; www.sierradrifters.com). Professionally guided year-round drift boat access to the Lower Owens River, plus summertime Bay Boat charters on Crowley and other Eastern Sierra Lakes.

Sierra Trout Magnet Fly Shop (2272 N. Sierra Hwy./CA 395; 760-873-0010; www
.sierratroutmagnet.com). Full-service outfitter and fly shop. Guide service from Independence to Bridgeport.

GOLF **Bishop Country Club** (1200 US 395 South; 760-873-5828; www.bishopcountry
club.com). Built in 1963. Eighteen holes, par 71. Pro shop, club and cart rentals, restaurant and bar. Open year-round for easy combination with mornings of powder skiing
in Mammoth.

    Mount Whitney Golf Club (2559 S. Main St.; 760-876-5795; www.mtwhitneygolfclub
.com). Built in 1959. Nine holes, medium length. Par 36. Open year-round. Bargain
greens fees and rentals; no tee times.

HANG GLIDING AND PARAGLIDING "Flying here can be categorized as extreme,"
notes champion pilot and multiple world record holder Kari Castle (760-920-0748;
www.karicastle.com), who also offers tandem flights, flying clinics, local guiding, and
instruction. "It's known for big air and world record flights—but also for turbulence."
The biggest air enthusiasts around have been known to launch themselves into the
atmosphere from Walt's Point, at 9,000 feet, on the Horseshoe Meadows Road.

HIKING AND TRAILRUNNING Every major tributary canyon offers a trail into the
Sierra wilderness. Each goes up first before it goes down. The most popular trailheads
are Whitney Portal (Mount Whitney Trail), Onion Valley (Kearsarge Pass), Big Pine
Creek (Palisades), and in the lakes basin at the head of Bishop Creek. Passes less
traveled include Haiwee, Olancha, Shepherd, Baxter, Sawmill, and Taboose. Also try
high-tundra striding up in the White Mountains. In midwinter, check out trails in the

KEARSARGE PASS FROM ONION VALLEY INTO THE JOHN MUIR WILDERNESS PATITUCCIPHOTO

SKIING CALIFORNIA'S FOURTEENERS

From a distance it looked perfect. Perfectly epic. But from the summit, with skis on, looking down at an enormous chockstone wedged into the trapdoor of a 55-degree couloir, 9,000 vertical feet above the trucks, a sliver's width passage to either side and only the thinnest of early-spring rot to look forward to, the prospect suddenly became, as Pondella would later recall, "frickin' dicey."

Davenport had flown out from Aspen a few days earlier, had rented a car in Reno and driven down to Mammoth to catch Pondella. The plan: to effect a quiet, personal, media-light tour of the highest peaks in California's High Sierra, to tick off as many fourteeners as time and conditions might allow, to get some sun, some good pics for the sponsors, to camp out in the sagebrush with friends, maybe do some bouldering, etc.—you know, easy, Eastside-style.

Having already bagged every last fourteener in Colorado—climbing and skiing off 54 summits in just under 12 months, and publishing a book about it—and having ticked off Rainier and Shasta soon thereafter, this was all that was left for ski alpinist Chris Davenport: fourteen more wind-battered patches of rock and snow (or 11, depending on your standards for topographical prominence) to complete the whole list for the Lower 48.

Although the pace would prove blistering by mortal standards—at least two big mountains for every three days—Davenport didn't seem in any real hurry to finish.

"The idea is just to submerse myself in the range," he said, like a man beyond last call contemplating the olive at the bottom of his martini. "It's like meeting a new girlfriend, just kind of figuring her out." As if to say: Hey, what's the rush? Let's put another quarter in that jukebox.

A RECON FLIGHT HAD SHOWN THE SOUTHERN PEAKS FAIRLY READY TO GO CHRISTIAN PONDELLA

In less than a month he'd be back to real business: helicopters, film crews, full entourage—and the pressure of getting it absolutely right down four of the most iconic and difficult lines in the Alps. "It's brutal," he would say later, on the phone. "But it's work. And I have to work."

Mammoth-based adventure photographer Christian Pondella had made an early season recon flight with Glen Poulsen, just before Christmas, which had shown the southern peaks fairly ready to go. The Palisades, where in a fat year a crew like this might be able to knock out a handful of summits from a single base camp, were all exposed rock and ice.

"We weren't sure about Whitney," recalled Pondella. "But we could see Langley was in, Split was in, Williamson was in. We weren't sure about White."

It seemed natural enough to start with Langley, at the south end, and work north from there. So they slept in the truck at the top of the moraine, right at snowline, and before dawn set out up the Tuttle Creek drainage toward the peak formerly known as Old Mount Whitney.

It was the third week in March and the Sierra was already deep into premature springtime. Snowpack was barely average. Still, the climb was straightforward and they were able to ski off the true summit on decent winter snow, dropping fast down the southeast couloir and all the way back to camp on fine corn. Up and back, they were the only two people in the world. And by the end of the day, they were blissfully bedding down in the parking lot at the Whitney Portal, requisite permits on their persons and a modest quotient of Tecate in their veins.

From the Mountaineer's Route they watched dawn splash bold across the east face. They crossed paths with two parties on the way up, the only other humans they would see in the backcountry that week: one, a pair of exceedingly well-encumbered gents, outfitted as if to spend three months besieging Everest ("as if they'd just robbed an REI store," said Davenport); and later a solitary European fellow who had summited early and though equipped for a few nights out was already on his way back, having forgotten to bring fire for his campstove. For the former party there was nothing to be done; for the latter a spare lighter was produced from Dav's first aid kit.

At the ridge they were surprised—and not a little pleased—to discover a thin tongue of perfect chalky snow right to the summit. It was an exciting rock-scramble for the last 300 vertical feet, and "definitely a no-fall zone coming back down," but they were able to ski the whole way. And still make the last hour of sun at the Buttermilks.

> We left the summit about noon and swooped to the torrid plains before
> sundown, as if dropping out of the sky.
> —John Muir, on his descent from Whitney to Lone Pine, *San Francisco Daily Evening
> Bulletin* (1875)

"It was one of the greatest days you could ever have," said Pondella. "To climb and ski Whitney, to watch the sunrise on the east face, across some of the most beautiful granite in the Sierras, and five hours later to be climbing up the granite boulders at the Buttermilks—there's not many places you could have it that good."

To cap it off they decided to forego the cozy intimacy of the truck in favor of "Jacuzzi, Internet, and nice beds" at Pondella's place up the hill. And the next day offered them a break, so they went down to the gorge for an afternoon's fingerwork on welded ash. But by moonrise that evening, having met up with John Morrison from Tahoe, they were back to work—with a good fire going and a plan for taking Williamson.

People have been skiing up and down this range—parts of it, anyway—for well over a century. There are accounts of early gold miners making their way through prodigious snows in Mammoth and Lundy on 12-foot-long so-called Norwegian snowshoes. In the 1880s, there was a local cabinetmaker and blacksmith by the name of Louis de Chambeau who ran a decent little side business fashioning slightly more manageable 9-foot planks for eastside locals at $8 a pair ($7 for women).

Pistol-packing Norman Clyde was skiing lines down big peaks all along the crest from at least the 1920s into the '40s. And it was Christmas Day 1928 when Orland Bartholomew, sometime stream-gauger for Southern California Edison, hitchhiked out of Lone Pine with a custom pair of laminated hickory boards to make the first winter ascent of Whitney, followed by a 300-mile ski traverse all the way to Yosemite Valley. A young Dave McCoy hitchhiked into Mammoth for the first time in 1935. Between backcountry jaunts surveying the snowpack for the City of Los Angeles, he started tinkering with rope tows and ski races, and pretty soon—70 years later—he sold a controlling interest in the company known as Mammoth Mountain Ski Area for $365 million.

From the summit of Williamson, Morrison dropped in first. "And as he was sidestepping in," Pondella remembered, "he took all the snow right down to the rock." Davenport tried the other way, around the right side, sidestepping down 3 or 4 feet and hopping into the air. "It was one of the sketchiest turns I've ever seen," said Pondella, "but he stuck it."

He also scraped the place clean, leaving the poor photographer to undergo what he would later describe as a "mini-epic."

Down where Davenport had made his hop-turn, Pondella found himself tips and tails on rock. "My skis were doing the bow-and-arrow-thing," he remembered. "I was sketching." The only option from there was to point it for 5 feet—then stop.

"THE LEAP IS A BASIC FORM OF JOY."—GASTON BACHELARD, *AIR AND DREAMS* (1946) CHRISTIAN PONDELLA

Alabama Hills, along the Owens River or Round Valley. Best source for local trails beta is Sage To Summit (see above). Wilderness permits (available free at local ranger stations) are required for overnight travel. See Chapter 5 for packers with stables and permits out of Mammoth and Mono County.

HORSEBACK RIDING AND MULE PACKING A variety of outfitters provides day trips, dunnage, spot trips, and full custom service from nearly every trailhead in the Eastern Sierra.

Bishop Pack Outfitters (Aspendell; 760-873-4785; www.bishoppackoutfitters.net). Mike and Tess Anne Morgan offer full pack and saddle service, including fly-fishing and photography trips and backpacker shuttles, to Sabrina Basin, Lamarck, Horton, Humphreys Basin, French Canyon, and Piute Pass from the North Fork of Bishop Creek, with four generations of experience. Horse and mule drives in fall and spring.

Cottonwood Pack Station (Horseshoe Meadows; 760-878-2015). Dennis Winchester, out of Independence, offers full service into Cottonwood Lakes, South Fork, Rock Creek, and the Mount Whitney Zone.

"And I'm like: I can't do that—this could be the last—I mess up, that's it, I'm done." Finally he slid his pack off, ever so gingerly, unhitched his crampons, threw his ax into the snow and managed to get one ski off. "Once I got that first crampon on I was fine."

Hemingway once tried to make the case that bullfighting was "the only art in which the artist is in danger of death." This in the days before high-powered energy drinks, before fat skis and alpine touring bindings and synthetic climbing skins, before Davenport & Co. The artistry of it, Papa argued, was in the matador's performance, in the degree to which he was able to control the amount of danger, to run it "exactly as much as he wishes"—without dying.

Surely this is also the measure of those few individuals who, with or without specific promises of financial remuneration, choose to leap from the planet's highest pinnacles on skis.

The line down the southeast face of Split—next on the list—was considerably less hair-raising. Still, it distinguished itself, off the top, with some of the worst so-called snow either man had ever skied. Redemption came swiftly, though, in the form of nearly 7,000 vertical feet of smooth, highgrade corn—enough of the stuff to cover the vertical drop from the high-altitude doughnut counter atop Pike's Peak to the Dunkin' Donuts on Colorado Avenue in downtown Colorado Springs. With, in this case, plenty of packaged chocolate mini-donuts waiting at the trucks.

Then the weather changed. By the following morning, by the time the sun hit the cold backside of White Mountain Peak, there was enough wind sluicing down the canyon that they found themselves shouting at each other.

"It's nuking up there!" yelled Pondella.

Davenport nodded. There was no arguing with the weather. So they turned around, punched their skis back out through the rabbit brush and scrub oak, drove up around Montgomery, took a nice long soak in one of the old tubs at Benton Hot Springs, and headed back down to the gorge: easy, Eastside-style—with the olive still marinating in the bottom of the glass.

Postscript: Over the course of about 10 days in April 2010, Davenport, Pondella, and friends knocked out eight more California fourteeners, including White and—with telemark maestro Ryan Boyer—a first ski descent, with two rappels in the middle of it, down a thin 45-degree couloir on the east face of Mount Muir. "There's raising the bar," wrote Hans Ludwig, senior editor of *Powder Magazine*, "and then there's breaking the bar."

Glacier Pack Train (Big Pine; 760-938-2538). M. A. Stewart offers full service to the Big Pine Lakes/Palisade Glacier area, Taboose Pass, John Muir Wilderness, and Sequoia/Kings Canyon National Parks.

✪ **McGee Creek Pack Station** (8-Mile Ranch, Independence; 760-878-2207 or 1-800-854-7407; www.mcgeecreekpackstation.com). Lee and Jennifer Roeser offer a range of wintertime trail and wagon rides in the Alabama Hills. In summer, they take the stock up to McGee Creek, 8 miles south of Mammoth (see Chapter 5).

Mount Whitney Pack Trains (Bishop/Rock Creek; 760-872-8331; www.rockcreek packstation.com). Full pack and saddle service into Sequoia-Kings, Golden Trout, and South Sierra Wildernesses from Sawmill, Shepherd, Taboose, and Olancha Pass trailheads. Popular multiday spring and fall horse drives between the Owens Valley and the High Sierra.

Pine Creek Pack Station and Sequoia Kings Pack Trains (Pine Creek/Independence; 760-387-2797 or 1-800-962-0775). Operated by Brian and Danica Berner. The oldest outfit in the Sierra (since 1872). Full service into the Inyo National Forest, Sequoia-Kings, and the Pacific Crest Trail from five trailheads.

Rainbow Pack Outfitters (5845 S. Lake Rd., Bishop; 760-873-8877; www.rainbow .zb-net.com). Run by the Allen family since 1924. The stables are at South Lake, behind Parcher's Resort. Full range of trips into Inyo National Forest and Sequoia-Kings.

MOUNTAIN BIKING Dirt roads abound in Inyo County, from flat gravel cruisers along the old railroad grades and the Owens River, to dozens of disused Jeep and horse trails from west of US 395 to the foot of the Sierra. Loop rides of varying difficulty are possible to the north and west of Bishop, especially in the Tungsten Hills, and west of Big Pine. For serious rough climbing, try Mazourka Canyon out of Independence or the Swansea and Yellow Grade Roads to Cerro Gordo. No vehicles of any kind, wheeled or otherwise, are allowed in wilderness areas. The best overall map of the region's back roads is the "Inyo National Forest Map," available at most bookstores and visitor centers. Also check in at Aerohead Cycles (312 N. Warren St., Bishop; 760-873-4151; www .aeroheadcycles.com) for detailed beta.

MOTOR SPORTS There are hundreds of miles of dirt roads and Jeep trails on public land, from the Alabama Hills to the Volcanic Tableland to the Inyo and White Mountains. The best overall map to the region's back roads is the "Inyo National Forest Map," available at most bookstores and visitor centers. Know the rules, stay on existing roads, and be courteous. No vehicles of any kind, wheeled or otherwise, are allowed in wilderness areas.

    Bishop Motosports (58 Commerce Dr., Mammoth; 760-934-0347; www.bishop motosports). Sales, rentals, service, accessories. ATVs, dirt bikes, Rhinos, Harleys, mountain bikes, and snowmobiles.

MOUNTAINEERING Bardini Foundation (Bishop; 760-873-8036; www.bardini.org). Founded in memory of the famous mountain and ski guide Allan Bard. Treks, ski tours, peak and wall climbs, a range of mountaineering courses. Guides: Tim Villanueva and Don Lauria.

    Sierra Mountain Center (200 South Main St.; 760-873-8526; www.sierra mountaincenter.com). Rock climbing, backpacking, ski touring, ice climbing, guide training, avalanche courses, Whitney ascents, and custom trips. Owned by veteran guides Robert "SP" Parker and Todd Vogel.

    ✪ **Sierra Mountain Guides** (760-648-1122; www.sierramtnguides.com). Owned and operated by veteran IFMGA/AMGA ski and mountain guides Howie Schwartz and Neil Satterfield. Ski mountaineering, backcountry skiing and snowboarding, rock climbing, ice climbing, alpine mountaineering, avalanche education, all forms of backpacking, and mountain running trips and courses throughout the Sierra Nevada and mountain destinations worldwide. All-star guide team includes Glen Plake and Peter Croft. Ask about their excellent kids' climbing courses as well.

    Sierra Mountaineering International (SMI) (236 N. Main St.; 760-872-4929; www .sierramountaineering.com). Rock climbing, peak climbing, ice climbing, backcountry skiing, backpacking, avalanche school, map and compass classes, technical training, and international expeditions. Gear rentals, too. Founder: Kurt Wedburg.

RANGER-GUIDED TOURS AND ACTIVITIES Check at the Interagency Visitor Center (760-876-6222) or the White Mountain Ranger Station (760-873-2500).

ROAD BIKING If you're looking for switchbacks and epic hill climbing, try Sherman Pass, Horseshoe Meadows Road, Whitney Portal Road, Westgard Pass, the first section of the Big Pine Death Valley Road, or the Bishop Creek Road. On a calm day in late fall or early spring, a tour of the Owens Lake playa makes a pleasant loop (60-plus miles). From Bishop, one of the Eastern Sierra's classic century rides follows the old Sherwin Grade Road north past Lake Crowley to Benton Crossing Road, east to Benton, then south along US 6 back to Bishop. The best easy cruising lies to the west and north of Bishop, as far as Round Valley. Contact Aerohead Cycles (312 N. Warren St., Bishop; 760-873-4151; www.aeroheadcycles.com) for detailed beta.

ROCK CLIMBING AND BOULDERING The Eastern Sierra has blossomed into one of the world's premier rock climbing and bouldering destinations. When the big alpine routes get too frosty, move down into the Owens River Gorge; try the Buttermilks, the Happy Boulders, or put up a new route in the Alabama Hills. Best sources for local beta and equipment are **Elevation** in Lone Pine (150 S. Main St.; 760-876-4560; www .sierraelevation.com), **Wilson's Eastside Sports** in Bishop (206 N. Main St.; 760-873-7520; www.eastsidesports.com), and **Mammoth Mountaineering** in Mammoth Lakes (361 Old Mammoth Road; 760-934-4191 or 1-888-395-3951; www.mammothgear.com). **The Rubber Room** (175B N. Main St., Bishop; 760-872-1363; www.rubberroomresoles .com) specializes in rock shoe resoles.

SPA, YOGA, AND MASSAGE **Belle Vous Day Spa & Salon** (125 W. Line St., Bishop; 760-872-3307). Full service. Hair, nails, and massage.

    Bishop Yoga & Pilates Center (150 Willow St., Bishop; 760-920-3764; www .bishopyogapilates.com). Yoga, children's yoga, dance, pilates. Classes daily. Drop-ins welcome. Full massage menu.

    Keogh's Hot Springs (Keogh's Hot Springs Road, 7 miles south of Bishop; 760-872-4670; www.keoughshotsprings.com). The largest hot springs pool around, built in the 1920s: 600 gallons per minute at 127 degrees. Warm and hot pools. Snack bar, picnic area, gift shop, massage, camping, and rustic accommodations. There is also a series of less developed, free tubs down the road, along the warm run-off stream below the power lines (watch for broken glass).

    ✪ **Benton Hot Springs** (760-933-2287; www.historicbentonhotsprings.com). Private outdoor soaking tubs available with advance notice. (See "Lodging" above.)

WINTER SPORTS Most will press on to the snow-season mecca of Mammoth Lakes (see Chapter 5), but those in the mood for more solitary backcountry tours will outfit themselves with snowshoes or backcountry skis (the latter with requisite climbing skins) and head for any Eastern Sierra trailhead—from Kennedy Meadows to Pine Creek.

    Wilson's Eastside Sports (206 N. Main St., Bishop; 760-873-7520; www.eastside sports.com) can provide the necessary equipment and information. See "Mountaineering" for local guide services.

✲ Lodging

There is no real destination lodging in these parts—nothing, that is, that rises too far above the strictly utilitarian. (OK, with one or two exceptions.) But there are plenty of places to get in out of the heat and the wind, and to get a decent night's sleep. Coming from the south, before the junction of CA 14 and US 395 at Inyokern, there's a clutch of half-abandoned scary-movie motels (many in the business of renting dry acreage to cell phone service providers)—as if to set the tone. There's something of a B&B, open only on weekends, in the former ghost town of Randsburg. There are basic franchise motels in Ridgecrest, catering mostly to those coming in or out of the China Lake Naval Weapons Station. The best, if you happen to be, say, on your way to or from the petroglyphs, is probably the **Best Western China Lake** (400 S. China Lake Blvd.; 760-371-2300; www.bestwestern.com). Otherwise, every town on US 395, from Olancha to Bishop, has at least two basic motels, some of which are remarkable examples of past booms in travel and tourism, first in the late 1920s and early '30s, then again in the post-war era. Many of these seem to have been neglected since the day they opened.

The **Winnedumah Hotel** in Independence is one of the oldest continuously operated lodgings on the road, along with the **Dow Hotel** in Lone Pine. Both are still a decent bet today (see full descriptions below). Accommodations at **Cerro Gordo** date back to the 1860s (see below). Lone Pine also boasts several AAA-rated lodgings and two late-model franchise motels, of which the Comfort Inn (1920 S. Main St.; 760-876-8700; www.choicehotels.com; moderate to expensive) is probably the best equipped, plus the excellent **Whitney Portal Hostel** (238 S. Main St.; 760-876-0030; www.mountwhitneyportal.com; inexpensive), managed by the owners of the Whitney Portal Store.

Bishop has more than 20 motels, many of recognizable brand names, and a wordly-eclectic adventure hostel (see below). The best bet for a quiet night's sleep is the recently upgraded **Creekside Inn** (see below). For B&B aficionados and those who appreciate the feeling of staying in someone else's home, try the ranch-style **Joseph House Inn** (376 W. Yaney St., Bishop; 760-872-3389; www.josephhouseinn.com; expensive). Note: Lone Pine sells out completely for the film festival during the first weekend in October; Bishop fills to capacity during Mule Days over Memorial Day weekend.

For old-school knotty-pine cabins at higher elevations, try **Glacier Lodge** (Big

Pine Creek Road, above Big Pine; 760-938-2837; www.jewelofthesierra.com; moderate)—the iconic old lodge burned down in 1998 but eight cabins remain—or **Parcher's Resort** (5001 S. Lake Rd., Bishop; www.parchersresort.net; 760-873-4177; moderate). North of Bishop on US 6, near the head of the Chalfant Valley, lies the locals' favorite hot springs getaway, the **Old House at Benton** (see below).

✪ **Cerro Gordo** (From Keeler, 7.5 miles and 5,500 feet of elevation up Yellow Grade Road; 760-876-5030; www.cerrogordomines.com; moderate; Elevation: 8,400 feet; Open: Late spring to early fall; Innkeeper: Robert Desmarais [caretaker] and Sean Patterson; Pets: Well behaved, on leash; Wheelchair Access: No; Internet Access: No). A handful of Mexican prospectors from Lone Pine found "color" here as early as 1865, but it wasn't until 1868 that the camp began to see serious action. As much as $17 million worth of ore was shipped down the grade by freight wagon to Swansea and Keeler, thence across the Owens Lake by steamship to Cartago, thence to the nascent Port of Los Angeles. Mortimer Belshaw and Victor Beaudry headed up the syndicate that built the road, the water system, an array of silver and lead smelters, and the American Hotel (1871), where by previous arrangement with the current owner visitors can enjoy a home-cooked meal and a microbrewed root beer. Accommodations include the two-bedroom, one-bath Belshaw House (c. 1868)—with private kitchen, indoor plumbing, a Franklin stove, and barely fathomable front-porch views across the Owens Playa to the Sierra—and the six-room Bunkhouse (1904), ideal for groups up to 12. The mines and structures are on private property; call before you head up the grade for road conditions, permission to visit, availability of lodging.

Dow Villa Motel (310 S. Main St. [US 395], Lone Pine; 760-876-5643;

800-824-9317; www.dowvillamotel.com; inexpensive to moderate; Elevation: 3,730 feet; Open: Year-round; Innkeepers: Lynne Bunn and Jeanne Willey; Pets: Allowed in motel section, some restrictions; Wheelchair Access: Yes; Internet Access: Free wireless). Walter Dow built the hotel in 1923 to house the movie companies working the Alabama Hills. Among the luminaries who have camped out in these rooms are Tom Mix, William Boyd (Hopalong Cassidy), Gene Autry, Roy Rogers, Errol Flynn, and, of course, John Wayne. The Duke first slept here in 1935. In 1978, while doing a commercial for Great Western Bank (his last appearance on film), he stayed in room 20 in the newer motel, now featuring wet bar and flat-screen TV. The expansive motel annex dates to 1958. Later restoration has brought carpets in homage to some abstract tropical broadleaf plant, silver-green on a field of royal purple, vinyl wall coverings, and trim work in surprising shades of turquoise. The exterior has been restored to its original faux-Spanish stucco glory. On opening night of the Film Festival (October), the lobby spills over with meticulously costumed bad men, buckaroos, and corseted ladies of, alas, questionable repute. The ghosts hang out where the real value is: in the old hotel. Rooms are available with private or shared bath. Upstairs front rooms offer grand Ansel Adams–style views of Lone Pine Peak and Mount Whitney over the Pizza Factory—at budget prices.

Winnedumah Hotel (211 N. Edwards St., Independence [across from the courthouse]; 760-878-2040; www.winnedumah .com; moderate [includes continental breakfast]; Elevation: 3,925 feet; Open: Year-round; Innkeepers: Frank and Celia Montoya; Pets: At innkeepers' whim; Wheelchair Access: Yes; Internet Access: Wireless). In 1927, Dow built the Winnedumah to catch the overflow

LONE PINE PEAK (12,944 FEET) DOMINATES THE TOWN OF THE SAME NAME; MOUNT WHITNEY IS ON THE RIGHT AND FARTHER BACK, ABOVE THE SHELL SIGN BURKE GRIGGS

from his hotel in Lone Pine, for those occasions when there was a movie shooting and it seemed that all of Hollywood had descended upon the Owens Valley. The Winnedumah, named for an 80-foot granite monolith in the Inyo Mountains to the east of town (see the "Legend of Winnedumah" sidebar), has thankfully suffered less intrusive renovation than its sibling in Lone Pine. The stucco façade and portico remain much as they were when it was first built—as the Dow's once was before it was treated to a set dressing of weathered barn wood. Many of the original details—bathroom tiles, the hearth in the lobby—remain unchanged, if a bit worn. Décor is haphazard and rooms are small by contemporary standards. Still, there's no better place to stay on the way up or down the old Kearsarge trail, or after a lamb couscous and a good bottle of Côtes du Rhone at the Still Life Café. Rooms available with or without private bath. Those at the back offer privacy and partial views of the Sierra. No TVs.

Creekside Inn (725 N. Main St., Bishop; 760-872-3044; www.bishopcreekside.com; moderate to expensive [includes hot breakfast buffet]; Elevation: 4,150 feet; Open: Year-round; Innkeeper: Western Inns Hotel Group; Pets: No; Wheelchair Access: Yes; Internet Access: Wireless). Significantly upgraded from its former life as a chain motel, the Creekside—which actually has a small perennial stream of water flowing through the grounds on its way to Los Angeles—is a dependably comfortable base camp for forays into the Eastern Sierra and White Mountains. All rooms have balconies or patios, some giving onto the landscaping and the creek, others (in the back) with views of the Sierra. Amenities include single-cup coffee makers, microwaves, mini-fridges, granite countertops, an outdoor hot tub, and a seasonal swimming pool. Bishop's

THE HOSTEL CALIFORNIA—AFFECTIONATELY KNOWN AS THC—IS TO THE CONTEMPORARY EASTERN SIERRA DIRTBAG CLIMBING SCENE WHAT CAMP 4 WAS TO YOSEMITE IN THE 1960S AND 1970S

Main Street dining and shopping is all within walking distance.

✪ **The Hostel California** (213 Academy St., Bishop; 760-399-6316; www.thehostelcalifornia.com; inexpensive; Elevation: 4,150 feet; Open: Year-round; Innkeeper: Matt; Pets: Yes; Wheelchair Access: Maybe; Internet Access: Wireless). In a twist that seems entirely appropriate to this still rough-edged frontier, the childhood home of legendary Owens Valley chronicler, newspaperman, and humanitarian W.A. Chalfant, built in 1898, has now become a vibrant hub for contemporary dirtbag climbing culture. Released in 2014 from its previous iteration as a creaky, earnest, lace-curtained bed and breakfast establishment, the old house and its sprawling annex and gardens, set on a quiet side street across from the public library, now hosts a revolving, sometimes fragrant, international cast of rock climbers, backpackers, Pacific Crest Trail through-hikers, itinerant musicians, and other latter-day hippies. The walls are adorned with maps and retired mountaineering tools. There's a lending library, an herb garden, a buzzing communal kitchen, a smoking courtyard (weed friendly), and a living room stocked for impromptu jam sessions with a range of guitars, percussion instruments, and an upright piano. Guests are welcome to borrow from a fleet of jalopy beach cruisers (rescued from Burning Man) and longboard skateboards for transportation to the mountaineering exchange or the brewery. A variety of dormitory bunks and private rooms are available. Stop in for a visit even if you ultimately decide to stay uptown at the Creekside.

✪ **The Old House at Benton Hot Springs** (CA 120, between Benton and US 395; 760-933-2287; www.historicbentonhotsprings.com; moderate (includes breakfast and hot springs access); Elevation: 5,626 feet; Open: Year-round; Innkeepers: Bill and Diane Bramlette; Pets: Yes; Wheelchair Access: Yes; Internet Access: No). For centuries, travelers of all stripes have been drawn out of their way, across windswept wastes of sagebrush and piñon, for the simple pleasure of a good soak in the hot springs at Benton. The water is without a doubt some of the most pleasant in the world. A village was established here in 1852 as a stopover between the booming settlements at Bodie and Aurora and points south—and as a destination in its own right. When gold was discovered in the surrounding hills in 1862, followed by silver, the place had its own boom, which lasted until 1889, brief and violent Indian skirmishes notwithstanding. All that's left of those days is a handful of weathered structures, some holes in the hillsides, assorted rusted implements, a graveyard—and, of course, the water. The town site and much of the surrounding ranchland has, for four generations, been owned by the Bramlettes, who have recently put a conservation easement on 900 acres and today run a quaint ranchstyle inn with springwater-heated saltillo tile floors and locally salvaged Victorian furnishings. The Old House from the 1880s is also now available for nightly rental, with three bedrooms, a kitchen, a porch, and its own private hot tub. Private tubs can be hired for day use, by the hour with advance reservations, and for overnight camping. BYOB. Nearest food (other than breakfast) is the small, Indian-run café at the gas station in Benton. Otherwise, it's all the way to Mammoth or Bishop.

CAMPING There are numerous developed campgrounds along the base of the range—west of US 395—managed by various agencies: Inyo County, the Bureau of Land Management, the U.S. Forest Service, the Los Angeles Department of Water and Power (LADWP), and the Fort Independence Indian Tribe. There is top-notch car camping at Kennedy Meadows (with a handful of sites, first-come first-served, along the South Fork of the Kern). The highest-elevation sites are at Cottonwood Pass, above Lone Pine, and

OWENS VALLEY / EASTERN SIERRA CAMPING

Sherman Pass	Elevation	Season	Reservations Accepted	Fee	Sites	Water	Agency
1. Long Valley	5,200	Year-round	No	No	13	No	BLM
2. Chimney Creek	5,900	Year-round	No	No	36	No	BLM
3. Kennedy Meadows	5,800	Year-round	No	Yes	38	Yes	USFS
4. Troy Meadow	7,800	Jun-Nov	No	Yes	73	Well	USFS
5. Fish Creek	7,400	Jun-Nov	No	Yes	40	Well	USFS
Little Lake to Lone Pine							
6. Fossil Falls	3,300	Year-round	No	Yes	12	Yes	BLM
7. Diaz Lake	3,700	Year-round	Yes*	Yes	200	Piped	DWP**
8. Portagee Joe	3,800	Year-round	No	Yes	15	Piped	DWP
9. Tuttle Creek	5,120	Mar-Nov	No	Yes	85	No	BLM
10. Lone Pine	6,000	Apr-Oct	Yes	Yes	43	Yes	USFS
11. Whitney Portal	8,000	May-Oct	Yes	Yes	43	Yes	USFS
12. Cottonwood Pass (walk-in)	10,000	May-Oct	No	Yes	18	Yes	USFS
13. Cottonwood Lakes (walk-in)	10,000	May-Oct	No	Yes	12	Yes	USFS
14. Horseshow Meadow (Eq.)	10,000	May-Oct	No	Yes	10	Yes	USFS
15. Golden Trout	10,000	May-Oct	No	Yes	18	Piped	USFS
Independence							
16. Independence Creek	3,800	Year-round	No	Yes	25	Creek	DWP
17. Lower Grays Meadow	6,000	Mar-Oct	Yes	Yes	52	Piped	USFS
18. Upper Grays Meadow	6,200	Mar-Oct	Yes	Yes	35	Piped	USFS
19. Onion Valley	9,200	Jun-Oct	Yes	Yes	29	Piped	USFS
20. Oak Creek	5,000	Year-round	Yes	No	22	Piped	USFS
21. Fort Independence	3,975	Year-round	No	Yes	25	Piped	Tribal
22. Goodale Creek	4,000	Mar-Oct	No	Yes	46	No	BLM
23. Taboose Creek	3,900	Year-round	No	Yes	56	Creek	DWP
24. Tinemaha Creek	4,400	Year-round	No	Yes	55	Limited	DWP
Big Pine							
25. Big Pine Creek	7,700	May-Oct	Yes	Yes	30	Yes	USFS
26. First Falls (walk-in)	8,300	May-Oct	No	No	5	No	USFS
27. Sage Flat	7,400	Apr-Oct	No	Yes	28	Yes	USFS
28. Upper Sage Flat	7,600	Apr-Oct	Yes	Yes	21	Yes	USFS
29. Palisade Glacier (group)	7,600	Apr-Oct	Yes	Yes	1	Yes	USFS
30. Clyde Glacier (group)	7,600	Apr-Oct	Yes	Yes	1	Yes	USFS
31. Baker Creek	4,000	Year-round	No	Yes	70	Yes	DWP
32. Glacier View	3,900	Year-round	No	Yes	40	Yes	DWP
White Mountain/ Bristlecone Forest							
33. Grandview	8,600	May-Oct	No	No	26	No	USFS
34. Ferguson (group)	7,200	May-Oct	Yes‡	Yes	1	No	USFS
35. Nelson (group)	7,200	May-Oct	Yes‡	Yes	1	No	USFS
36. Noren (group)	7,200	May-Oct	Yes‡	Yes	1	No	USFS
Bishop							
37. Millpond Recreation Area	4,400	Year-round	No	Yes	100	Yes	DWP
38. Horton Creek	4,975	May-Nov	No	Yes	53	No	BLM
39. Pleasant Valley Pit	4,500	Nov-May	No	Yes	75	No	BLM
40. Big Trees	7,500	Apr-Sep	No	Yes	9	Yes	USFS
41. Bishop Park	8,400	May-Oct	No	Yes	21	Yes	USFS
42. Bitterbrush	7,350	May-Oct	No	Fee	16	Yes	USFS
43. Forks	7,800	Apr-Oct	No	Yes	9	Yes	USFS
44. Four Jeffrey	8,100	Apr-Oct	Yes	Yes	106	Yes	USFS
45. Intake 2 (walk-in)	8,200	Apr-Oct	No	Yes	5	Yes	USFS
46. Intake 2 (upper)	8,200	Year-round	No	Yes	8	Yes	USFS
47. Mountain Glen	8,200	May-Oct	No	Yes	5	No	USFS
48. North Lake	9,500	Jun-Oct	No	Yes	11	Yes	USFS
49. Sabrina	9,000	May-Oct	No	Yes	18	Yes	USFS
50. Willow	9,000	May-Oct	No	Yes	7	No	DWP
51. Bishop Park (group)	8,200	May-Oct	Yes	Yes	1	Yes	USFS
52. Table Mountain (group)	8,500	May-Oct	Yes	Yes	1	Yes	USFS

Note: Reservations at USFS campgrouns, unless otherwise specified, can be made online at www.recreation.gov or by calling 1-877-444-6777

* For reservations at Diaz Lake, call 760-876-5656

** Los Angeles Department of Water and Power

‡ For group reservations at the Bristlecone Forest, call 760-873-2503.

CAMPING IN THE INYO RANGE, MARCH 2007

across the valley in the White Mountains. In general, the Forest Service campgrounds are the highest in elevation, offering the greatest access to streams, lakes, and high-country wilderness—and in the summertime the most coveted. Only on the busiest weekends in summer are campgrounds full to capacity. Leashed and attended pets are allowed at all campgrounds. Dispersed camping is permitted, with certain restrictions, anywhere on Bureau of Land Management and national forest land. The best spots include the Alabama Hills, the Inyo Mountains (i.e., up Mazourka Canyon Road), and the Sherman Pass area above Kennedy Meadows. Campfire permits are required outside developed campgrounds and are available at any district ranger station. A handful of private campgrounds from Lone Pine to Bishop are geared mostly toward users of recreational vehicles.

✳ Where to Eat

With few and notable exceptions, dining in this region is in the great American ground-beef-grain-and-potato tradition. But there are indeed exceptions. For squid ink pasta, oysters from the Sea of Cortez, dry muscat, and sweet potato gnocchi, press on to Mammoth. "And here is a hint if you would attempt the stateliest approaches," wrote Mary Austin, "travel light, and as much as possible live off the land. Mulligatawny soup and tinned lobster will not bring you the favor of the woodlanders."

WALKER PASS TO SHERMAN PASS

Joseph R. Walker likely drank at Indian Wells in 1834, having just discovered the low southern pass that would later bear his name. The Death Valley '49ers filled their canteens here more than once in the winter of 1850. "A more godforsaken, cheerless place I have seldom seen," wrote William Brewer, chief botanist of the Whitney Survey, having passed through in 1864, "a spring of water—nothing else." Contemporary boosters have determined it to be "the sunniest spot in the U.S." Today, the water is used chiefly in the making of an award-winning beer, distributed at

DINING HIGHLIGHTS

Alabama Hills Café & Bakery (Lone Pine): Best Breakfast (page 178)
Jake's Saloon (Lone Pine): Best Real-Deal Swinging-Door Saloon (page 178)
Still Life Café (Independence): Best Authentic French-Colonial Bistro (page 179)
Copper Top BBQ: Best oakwood barbecued tri-tip (page 179)
Bishop Burger Barn: Best locally sourced, hand-formed, grass-fed beef burgers (page 180)
Thai Thai: Best Airstrip-view Thai Food (page 180)

certain locations throughout Southern California. The steakhouse at the **Indian Wells Brewing Company** (2565 N. CA 14, Inyokern; 760-377-4290; www.mojavered.com), aka the Indian Wells Lodge, is the only place to eat along this stretch of highway, the sort of place where the choice is rice pilaf or baked potato, where garnish is a desiccated orange slice and a sprig of parsley—a place recommendable more for the view, the root beer floats, and the tall, cold Mojave Reds than for the steaks.

LITTLE LAKE TO OWENS LAKE

The Ranch House Café (US 395, Olancha; 760-764-2363; inexpensive). This charming old roadhouse, just north of the junction with CA 190, in the shade of hundred-year-old cottonwoods, is the only place to eat between Inyokern and Lone Pine. Basic truck-stop comfort food. Eggs and bacon, pie and coffee. Open daily for breakfast, lunch, and dinner.

LONE PINE

Bonanza Mexican Restaurant (104 N. Main St.; 760-876-4768; inexpensive). Naugahyde booths, counter service. The best chiles rellenos on the east side, home-fried tortilla chips, a mean enchilada with ranchera sauce, an array of respectable burritos, and a fresh salsa bar. Burgers and chicken-fried steak if you must. Beer and wine.

Merry Go Round (212 S. Main St.; 760-876-4115; moderate). Once an old standby for steaks and seafood, the Merry Go Round (formerly Margie's Merry Go Round) now serves a respectable selection of American-style Chinese and Mexican fare, still served in an intimate carousel-shaped dining room beneath the best neon sign in town. Dinner only, seven days a week. Outdoor dining in summer. Beer and wine.

✪ **Alabama Hills Café & Bakery** (111 Post St.; 760-876-4675; inexpensive). Friendly diner-style eatery with counter service and booths. House-made cinnamon rolls, pies, doughnuts, apple crisp, piled-high sandwiches to go. Breakfast served all day: a veggie scramble, a spicy sirloin skillet, peach pancakes, omelettes, an egg sandwich made to order on fresh, thick-sliced bread. Amusing cartoon murals of some of the rock formations up in the hills. Open for breakfast and lunch every day.

Totem Café (131 S. Main St.; 760-876-1120; moderate). Knotty-pine decor, antique skis, snowshoes, bows and arrows, and a bear trap. Autographs on the walls by John Wayne, Gary Cooper, Clint Eastwood, and others. Steaks, ribs, and fried chicken served family-style. Entrées served with a whole apple. Open every day.

TAVERNS, SALOONS, AND ROADHOUSES ✪ **Jake's Saloon** (119 N. Main St.; 760-876-5765). A favorite watering hole of bikers, dragsters, dust-mitigation contractors, German tourists, deputy sheriffs, film crews, clampers, and cowboys (real and ersatz). "We were in Vegas one year, going up to Lake Tahoe, shooting through Death Valley," says the Englishman in the black hat, the one with the authentic nineteenth-century

Peacemaker on his hip, "got here about 5 in the evening, it was getting dark, found somewhere to stay. Came in here for a couple of drinks, saw the saloon doors and thought: fantastic." Shuffleboard, pool table. Live music on the weekends. Brawls are infrequent but not unheard of. Beer and wine only; if you need it badly, the hard stuff is served across the street at the Double L.

COFFEE, TEA, ETC. Lone Star Bistro (107 N. Main St.; 760-876-1111). Passable local coffee joint, Internet.

GROCERIES Joseph's Bi-Rite (119 S. Main St.; 760-876-4378). Grocery shopping the way it used to be (since 1895). Deli counter, beer and wine, ice, charcoal, firewood, High Sierra pickled peppers, and local honey.

INDEPENDENCE

DINING ○ Still Life Café (135 S. Edwards St.; 760-878-2555; moderate to expensive). If, like the majority of travelers speeding up and down CA 395, you're in a hurry to get somewhere else—like to Mammoth for the weekend, or back down south in time for school and work on Monday—you may not appreciate what the Still Life has to offer. If, on the other hand, you have some time to slow down, to settle in with a glass or two of fine wine from the Old Continent, and to sample a few courses of traditional French country and Algerian cooking by the hand of an unassuming master (oh, and if the place happens to be open when you hit Independence), by all means park it and head inside. The moment you step through the door, you'll feel transported to some historic French colonial outpost in North Africa, or to some back-alley bistro in Marseilles or Toulouse a half-century ago. Malika Adjaoud runs the kitchen; her husband Michel pours the wine. Hours are capricious. Generally open Wednesday through Sunday for lunch and dinner, but call ahead. Some nights you'll have the place (and its owners) to yourself; other nights there'll be someone playing Harlem-style jazz improvisations on the piano and it'll be standing room only. Enjoy.

THE STILL LIFE CAFÉ IN INDEPENDENCE LAURA ALICE WATT

HANK OTTEN FIRING UP THE DAY'S TRI-TIPS AT COPPER TOP BBQ

BIG PINE

✪ **Copper Top BBQ** (310 N. Main St., Big Pine; 760-970-5577; www.coppertopbbq .com; inexpensive). Former tractor salesman Hank Otten and his son Matthew moved over from Bakersfield in 2013 to open a simple barbecue joint on Highway 395. In January 2015, their little roadside stand was named the best restaurant in the country on Yelp, a website and travel app that at the time boasted 135 million monthly visitors. Within a few days, the line for a plate of Hank's world-famous tri-tip or pork ribs stretched down the road. Things have calmed down since, but the meat is still especially tender and tangy, and draws travelers from all over the world to this handful of picnic tables with a view of the Palisades. House-made potato salad, coleslaw, green chili, and a selection of craft beers and sodas also available.

GENERAL STORES Carroll's Market (136 S. Main St.; 760-938-2718). Basic groceries, meats, produce, deli, ice, fishing licenses and tackle, ATM. Open daily.

BISHOP

DINING Amigos Mexican Restaurant (285 N. Main St.; 760-872-2189; inexpensive). Solid Yucatán-style Mexican food served in an assuming storefront location done up in bright primary colors. Carnitas in citrus marinade and lobster enchiladas with mango salsa.

Astorga's Mexican Restaurant (2206 North Sierra Hwy.; 760-872-3849; inexpensive). The best classic taqueria on the east side. Cold beer, good tortas, and real glass-bottle Coke. Pleasant outdoor patio for warm evenings. Look for their window at Mule Days and at the county fair.

✪ **Bishop Burger Barn** (2675 West Line St.; 760-920-6567; inexpensive). Bishop-raised grass-fed beef, locally-smoked bacon, house-baked buns, and other quality local fixings served through a drive-through pickup window to be eaten outdoors in the garden in a vinyl diner booth with an 8-track player. Dozens of milkshake options made from house-crafted cooked-custard ice cream. Tater tots. Popular with the bouldering crowd. Open every day except Tuesday.

Imperial Gourmet (930 N. Main St.; 760-872-1144; moderate). Because sometimes a body needs fried wontons, a decent plate of chow mein, crisp Chinese broccoli, and a fortune cookie. Delivery to local motels is available. Open daily for lunch and dinner; Sunday all-you-can-eat champagne brunch. No personal checks.

Schat's Roadhouse (871 N. Main St.; 760-873-0000; www.schatsroadhouse .com; inexpensive to moderate). Big 1/3-pound burgers, steaks, ribs, sandwiches, rotisserie chicken. Beer and wine. Live music some nights. Open for lunch and dinner every day except Wednesdays.

Thai Thai (703-C Airport Rd.; 760-872-2595;). "If there's something you want that's not on there, we can probably cook it," says owner Weng-Cheong Lim, handing me a menu that for my taste more than adequately covers the bases (I go for panang beef whenever and wherever I can get it). Lim—"like a leg," he explains—comes originally from Singapore by way of a long stint running another acclaimed Thai place up in Washington state. His business partner and chef, Alisa R. Khongnok, aka "Rung," comes highly decorated from her own restaurant on the west side of the Big Island. Mild, medium, or hot, everything is cooked fresh: fresh basil, fresh cabbage, fresh cucumber; even the egg rolls are made here. And of course it's all MSG-free. A hint of tasteful floral fabrics tones down the fluorescent lighting and dresses up the otherwise standard cafeteria atmosphere. "Forty seats and more than an acre of parking," says Lim. "No website, no Facebook page. Just good Thai food." Oh, and an unbeatable view out across the cracked tarmac to the well-anchored Cessnas and the great lumped-up massif of the White Mountains beyond. Credit cards accepted. BYOB encouraged. Dinner only. Live music and candlelight some nights. Closed Monday.

The Village Café (965 N. See Vee Ln.; 760-872-3101; inexpensive). Down-home country-style breakfast in a ramble-down cottage off the main highway.

Whiskey Creek (524 N. Main St.; 760-873-7777; www.whiskeycrk.com; moderate). The popular oak-and-brass saloon and steak house is back in business and is now part of the local Schat family empire. Sandwiches, burgers, steaks, and salads are served in the dining room, in the bar, or, when the weather's warm, on the patio.

Yamatani (635 N. Main St.; www.yamatanibishop.com; 760-872-4801; moderate to expensive). Robbie Tani's Yamatani serves teriyaki, tempura, miso, sushi, sake, and more. The specialty rolls are the best. It's not quite Nobu, but then Bishop is not quite Malibu. Family friendly. Full bar. Open daily at 5 PM.

TAVERNS, SALOONS, AND ROADHOUSES ✪ Mountain Rambler Brewery
(186 S. Main St.; 760-258-1348; www.mountainramblerbrewery.com). Ten original beers on tap, 600 barrels a year. Thai meatballs, lamb empanadas, jalapeño slaw, burgers, flatbread pizzas, locally-sourced arugula and hop shoots

served at picnic tables in a congenial mountain-industrial atmosphere. Open for lunch and dinner 7 days a week. Check schedule for quality live music.

Rusty's Saloon (112 N. Main St.; 760-873-9066). Classic Western saloon turned dive bar. Neon beer lights, pretzels, Elvira pinball machine, sporting events on TV, two pool tables, a mosaic in antique coins and poker chips. Check out the historic photos on the way to the back room. Bring your own food.

COFFEE, TEA, ETC. **Black Sheep Coffee Roasters**
(232 N. Main St.; 760-872-4142; www.blacksheepcoffeeroasters.com). Brick-walled, commercial shotgun flat hangout of local sculptors, climbers, photographers, would-be politicians, poets, and other aficionados of the well-crafted macchiato. Rigorously selected beans, artisanally roasted. Smoothies, breakfast sandwiches, and beer on tap. Free Wi-Fi.

Good Earth Yogurt (251 N. Main St.; 760-872-2020; www.goodearthyogurt.com) Soft-serve organic Greek yogurt on tap with topping bar, fresh pie, cheese, fine coffee, wine flights, and cold local beer. Perfect place to duck in out of the high-desert heat. Free Wi-Fi.

Looney Bean (399 N. Main St.; 760-872-2326). A friendlier local knockoff of the famous Seattle franchise with the

green logo. Beans are roasted in Mammoth. Baked items. Free Wi-Fi.

SANDWICHES AND SUCH ✪ **Erick Schat's Bakkerÿ** (763 N. Main St.; 760-873-7156 or 1-866-323-4854; www.erickschatsbakery.com). Legend has it that the Schat family fired up its first bakery in the Netherlands in 1893 (probably without the umlaut on the Y). A contingent of the clan made its way to North America in the 1950s, there to gain control of an old Austrian bakery in Bishop, already known for its authentic Basque-style sheepherder bread. Today, breads bearing the family name show up in supermarkets across California, and the vine-covered gingerbread-house outlet on Main Street in Bishop (built in 1979) is on any given day the busiest place in town. Pastries; doughnuts; sticky buns; machine-squeezed orange juice; turkey sandwiches assembled before your eyes from real roasted turkeys by a fleet of Mexican women; an array of gifty jams (from as far away as Maine); jerkies for the road; and, of course, racks and racks of bread, fresh from the oven.

Great Basin Bakery (275 S. Main St.; 760-873-9828; greatbasinbakerybishop.com). The Eastern Sierra's source for blue-ribbon breads, bagels, and pastries, Great Basin is where early-rising locals go for frosted cinnamon rolls, lemon scones, local artisan Black Sheep French roast, and the best wild, line-caught, King salmon lox bagels within 300 miles (without the lines and crowds of motor tourists you find up the street at Schat's). Try a sandwich, a bacon-and-egg Pino pie, or a slice of homemade cheesecake. Daily bread specials include Asiago sourdough and kalamata olive. Open 6 AM–4 PM Monday through Saturday and 6:30 AM–4 PM on Sunday.

✪ **Meadow Farms Country Smokehouse** (2345 N. Sierra Hwy.; 760-873-5311 or 888-624-6426; www.smokedmeats.com). Ham, bacon, sausage; a variety of top-quality beef, turkey, elk, buffalo, and salmon jerky; plus all manner of gifty condiments, preserves, and pickled items to take to your friends back home. Not cheap, but this isn't your average truck-stop leather. Stop in for generous free samples. Deli counter offers overstuffed breakfast burritos that'll last you well into the afternoon, and premium custom sandwiches to take in your pack for when the burrito wears off.

GROCERIES **Joseph's Bi-Rite Market** (211 N. Main St.; 760-873-6388). When the polish and gloss and selection offered by the "Safeway family of companies" is just too much—or when you prefer that your money stay in Bishop.

The Meat House (150 S. Main St.; 760-873-4990). Real-deal, old-school butcher shop. Call ahead for specialty cuts and family packages. Cheapest sandwiches in town, premade, po'boy-style.

Vons (1190 N. Main St.; 760-872-9811; www.vons.com). The works: deli, bakery, pharmacy, Starbucks, floral, liquor, produce, and gas. Cheaper, wider selection, and on busy weekends less crowded than the Vons in Mammoth. Open daily from 6 AM–1 AM.

✳ Books, Maps, and Information

LONE PINE

✪ **Eastern Sierra Interagency Visitor Center** (701 South Main St., Lone Pine; 760-876-9909). One-stop shop for regional information, sponsored by the full gamut of relevant federal, state, and local agencies. Wilderness and Mount Whitney Zone permits, displays on water infrastructure and history, good restrooms, and spectacular views of the sheer eastern scarp of the Sierra. Excellent collection of books, maps, and souvenirs sold by the Eastern Sierra Interpretive Association. Open daily, 8 AM–6 PM May through October, 8 AM–5 AM November through April.

✪ **Museum of Western Film History** (formerly the Lone Pine Film History Museum; US 395, south of McDonald's; 760-876-9909; www.museumofwesternfilmhistory.org). Mind-boggling collection of artifacts from the hundreds of movies and television shows filmed in and around Lone Pine: original costumes, guns, spurs, saddles, props, set pieces, and more. Exhibits span local film history from *Hopalong Cassidy* to *Iron Man*.

Highlights include the typewriter used to create the script of Gunga Din, the 1938 Plymouth Coupe in which Bogart drove to his demise in *High Sierra*, and Mary Austin and Zane Grey first editions. The gift shop sells Western-themed books, apparel, and an array of film festival memorabilia. Alabama Hills location maps and recreation guides available.

Lone Pine Chamber of Commerce Tourist Information Center (120 S. Main St.; 760-876-4444 or 1-877-253-8981; www.lonepinechamber.org). Books, maps, brochures, local and regional information. Ask for the free publication, *Motor Touring in the Eastern Sierra*.

✪ **Manzanar National Historic Site** (US 395; 760-878-2194; www.nps.gov/manz). The interpretive center features exhibits, photos (including some by Dorothea Lange and Ansel Adams), artifacts, and audiovisual presentations covering local history from 1885, with a focus on World War II relocation and internment, including a large-scale model of the camp crafted by former residents. Bookstore, theater, temporary exhibit gallery. Open every day except Christmas.

BISHOP

AAA (187 W. Pine St.; 760-872-8241; calif.aaa.com). Travel books, maps, Mexican insurance.

Bishop Area Chamber of Commerce and Visitors Bureau (690 N. Main St.; 760-873-8405 or 1-888-395-3952; www.bishopvisitor.com). Books, maps, brochures, general information, and trip planning.

Range and River Books (206 N. Main St.; 760-873-6882; rangeandriverbooks.com). Dynamic floor-to-ceiling selection of used, rare, and some new books with appropriate emphasis on Western and natural history as well as regional literature. Refreshing throwback to another era, when stories and knowledge were passed along by way of printed books, and passersby drifted in off the sidewalk to browse and be inspired. Check website for events, readings, and book signings. Open Monday through Saturday.

Spellbinder Books (124 S. Main St.; 760-873-4511; www.spellbinderbookstore.com). Well-curated selection of new books and some used: local interest, plus classic and new-release fiction and nonfiction. Pupfish Café coffee shop in the back. Open every day.

White Mountain Ranger Station (798 N. Main St.; 760-873-2500; www.fs.fed.us/r5/inyo). Books, maps, postcards, Inyo National Forest information, wilderness permits. Open daily May through November; Monday through Friday the rest of the year.

✳ Shopping

LONE PINE

SPORTING GEAR AND EQUIPMENT **Elevation Sierra Adventure Essentials** (150 S. Main St.; 760-876-4560; www.sierraelevation.com). Poor Jon Turner, white-water enthusiast, fell in love, and for the sake of a woman found himself high and dry, running a top-notch climbing and mountaineering boutique in Lone Pine—where the only whitewater for miles around (until you get over the hill to the Kern or the Tuolumne) runs inside a steel pipe on its way to Los Angeles. Stop by and tell him you feel bad for him, and pick up the latest fashions in Gore-Tex, down, and

SHOT IN OWENS VALLEY: A SHORT LIST

The Round-Up (1920). Directed by George Melford; starring Fatty Arbuckle and Wallace Beery.

The Virginian (1923). Directed by Tom Forman; starring Kenneth Harlan and Florence Vidor.

Greed (1923). Directed by Erich Von Stroheim; starring Gibson Gowland and Jean Hersholt.

Riders of the Purple Sage (1925). Directed by Lynn Reynolds; starring Tom Mix.

Blue Steel (1934). Directed by Robert Bradbury; starring John Wayne and Gabby Hayes.

Hop-Along Cassidy (1935). Directed by Howard Bretherton; starring William Boyd.

The Charge of the Light Brigade (1936). Directed by Michael Curtiz; starring Errol Flynn and Olivia de Havilland.

The Lone Ranger (1938). Directed by John English and William Witney; starring Chief Thunder-cloud and Silver King the Horse.

Where the Buffalo Roam (1938). Directed by Albert Herman; starring Tex Ritter.

Gunga Din (1939). Directed by George Stevens; starring Cary Grant and Douglas Fairbanks Jr.

High Sierra (1941). Directed by Raoul Walsh; screenplay by John Huston; starring Ida Lupino and Humphrey Bogart.

The Ox-Bow Incident (1943). Directed by William Wellman; starring Henry Fonda, Dana Andrews, and Anthony Quinn.

Tycoon (1947). Directed by Richard Wallace; starring John Wayne.

Yellow Sky (1948). Directed by William Wellman; starring Gregory Peck, Anne Baxter, and Richard Widmark.

The Lone Ranger (TV series, 1949–57). Starring Clayton Moore and Jay Silverheels.

The Gene Autry Show (TV series, 1950–56). Starring Gene Autry.

Rawhide (1951). Directed by Henry Hathaway; starring Tyrone Power and Susan Hayward.

The Long, Long Trailer (1954). Directed by Vincente Minnelli; starring Lucille Ball and Desi Arnaz.

Bad Day at Black Rock (1955). Directed by John Sturges; starring Spencer Tracy, Walter Brennan, Ernest Borgnine, and Lee Marvin.

---

fleece. Crampons, snowshoes, and lightweight bear canisters for rent.

Lone Pine Sporting Goods (220 S. Main St.; 760-876-5365). Of the hook and gun variety. Fish and game licenses. Open daily in summer.

SUNDRIES AND SOUVENIRS **Lone Pine Rock & Gift** (235 S. Main St.; 760-876-1010). Local rocks and minerals, gifts, and books.

Totem Trading Post (131 S. Main St.; 760-876-1120). Western apparel, hats, and knickknacks. Note the signatures on the walls, some recognizable.

GENERAL STORES **Lee's Frontier Chevron** (1900 S. Main St.; 760-876-5844). Lee used to drive a truck, so he knows about long hours: "Got to where 50, 60 miles would go by I wouldn't even remember." Standing at a cash register, he figures, there's less danger of a collision. Lee also knows what a body needs when it's on the road: free coffee, three choices of breakfast burrito, sandwiches, liquor, wine, beer, ice, bait, gas, and guns and ammo.

Whitney Portal Store (Whitney Portal; 760-876-0030; www.mountwhitneyportal.com). Earlene, Doug, and Doug Jr. have been supplying the hordes on the Whitney Trail for 20 seasons. It's the last stop for bear canister rentals, hiking poles, hats, water bottles, trail food, and postcards. Grill food, breakfast, lunch, and dinner are served. Don't miss the world-famous big pancakes, made with Krusteaz, vanilla, and cinnamon, and served family-style. Open May through October.

North to Alaska (1960). Directed by Henry Hathaway; starring John Wayne and Stewart Granger.

How the West Was Won (1962). Directed by John Ford, Henry Hathaway, and George Marshall; starring Henry Fonda, Gregory Peck, Debbie Reynolds, Jimmy Stewart, et al.

The Great Race (1965). Directed by Blake Edwards; starring Jack Lemmon, Tony Curtis, and Natalie Wood.

Nevada Smith (1966). Directed by Henry Hathaway; starring Steve McQueen.

Joe Kidd (1972). Directed by John Sturges; written by Elmore Leonard; starring Clint Eastwood and Robert Duvall.

Star Trek V: The Final Frontier (1989). Directed by William Shatner; starring William Shatner, Leonard Nimoy, George Takei, et al.

Tremors (1990). Directed by Ron Underwood; starring Kevin Bacon and Fred Ward.

Kalifornia (1993). Directed by Dominic Sena; starring Brad Pitt, Juliette Lewis, and David Duchovny

Maverick (1994). Directed by Richard Donner; starring Mel Gibson, Jodi Foster, and James Garner.

Star Trek: Generations (1994). Directed by David Carson; starring Patrick Stewart, et al.

G.I. Jane (1997). Directed by Ridley Scott; starring Demi Moore and Viggo Mortensen.

The Postman (1997). Directed by Kevin Costner; starring Kevin Costner.

Gone in 60 Seconds (2000). Directed by Dominic Sena; starring Nicolas Cage, Giovanni Ribisi, and Angelina Jolie.

Gladiator (2000). Directed by Ridley Scott; starring Russell Crowe and Joaquin Phoenix.

Iron Man (2008). Directed by Jon Favreau; starring Robert Downey Jr., Gwyneth Paltrow, Jeff Bridges, et al.

Django Unchained (2012). Directed by Quentin Tarantino; starring Jamie Foxx, Leonardo DiCaprio, and Samuel L. Jackson.

The Lone Ranger (2013). Directed by Gore Verbinski; starring Johnny Depp and Armie Hammer.

Godzilla (2014). Directed by Gareth Edwards; starring Ken Watanabe, Juliette Binoche, and David Strathairn.

BISHOP

CLOTHING AND FASHION The Toggery (115 N. Main St.; 760-872-3211). For all your classic High Sierra and Western fashion needs: boots, hats, belts, moccasins, Pendleton blankets, Carhartts, and Levi's.

SPORTING GEAR AND EQUIPMENT Aerohead Cycles (312 N. Warren St.; 760-873-4151; www.aeroheadcycles .com). The only professional bike shop in the Owens Valley. From custom beach cruisers to high-end road bikes to full-suspension downhill combat vehicles, these guys will do what it takes to get you rolling. Stop by for details on local rides. Closed Sunday.

Allen Outdoor Products, Sierra Saddlery & Feed (600 S. Main St.; 760-873-5903; www.allenoutdoor.com). If a person were planning to ride off into the sunset for an extended period of time, Jedediah Smith style, this would be the place to gear up. Full range of backcountry clothing, gear, and accessories of the cast-iron, wool, and leather variety, as well as cots, tents, range tepees, stoves, lanterns, chuck boxes, and snowshoes for rent. Look for the red horse and the fleet of U-Haul trailers.

Mammoth Mountaineering Gear Exchange (298 N. Main Street; 760-873-4300) Wide range of light- to heavily-used mountaineering, climbing, and backcountry ski gear, as well as clothing on consignment. Some new items at discount prices. Open daily.

Sage to Summit (312 N. Main St.; 760-872-1756; www.sagetosummit.com). The only dedicated running, trailrunning,

CHARLIE BARRETT SCALES BARDINI BOULDER, BUTTERMILKS CHRISTIAN PONDELLA

fitness, and fastpacking store in the Eastern Sierra. The latest in shoes, clothing, accessories, and beta for moving swiftly and efficiently on local trails. Also offers rentals on tents, hyperlite backpacks, bouldering crashpads, and crampons. Open daily.

⊕ **Wilson's Eastside Sports** (206 N. Main St.; 760-873-7520; www .eastsidesports.com). Well-curated selection of quality gear and clothing for self-propelled mountain and desert aficionados. Full range of backpacking, camping, climbing, snowshoeing, and ski touring equipment and rentals. The best source for local bouldering, climbing, and general dirtbagging info. Open daily except Thanksgiving and Christmas.

GALLERIES ⊕ **Mountain Light Gallery** (106 S. Main St.; 760-873-7700; www .mountainlight.com). It's often said that what Ansel Adams made of this landscape in silver salts and gelatin, Galen Rowell followed in color. Rowell was never the obsessive technician that Adams was. He was above all a consummate and highly accomplished mountaineer—with more than 100

technical first ascents in the Sierra Nevada alone—who also carried with him a 35 mm film camera and knew how to use it. "Photography," he wrote, "was a means of visual expression to communicate what I had seen to people who weren't there." At 1:23 AM on August 11, 2002, "on a dark, moonless night" (according to the National Transportation Safety Board report), Rowell and his wife, Barbara, also a photographer, were killed when a routine charter flight from Oakland collided with the Owens Valley less than 2 miles from the runway at the Bishop airport. "I've known all along that more of what I am seeking in the wilds is right here in my home state of California," he had written just the year before. "I couldn't say it with authority until I had all those journeys to Tibet, Nepal, Pakistan, China, South America, Antarctica, and Alaska behind me." The gallery features prints, books, posters, calendars, Rowell signature graduated neutral density filters, workshops, and rotating guest photographer exhibitions. Open daily.

PHOTOGRAPHY SUPPLIES **Phillips Camera House** (186 N. Main St.;

760-872-4211). Serving photographers since 1933. Compact flash cards, filters, batteries, lens cleaners, tripods. Now primarily a retailer for Verizon Wireless.

✳ Special Events

March: **Banff Mountain Film Festival** (Bishop; www.banffcentre.ca). **Early Opener Trout Derby** (Lone Pine; 760-876-4444; www.lonepinechamber .org). **Sage to Summit 5-10k Winter Race Series** (www.sagetosummit.com/ bishop-mammoth-running-races).

April: **Pilgrimage to Manzanar** (760-878-2194; www.manzanarcommittee .org). Special programs, music, and exhibits. No admission fee. **Wild, Wild West Marathon** (Lone Pine; 760-876-4444; www.lonepinechamber.org). **General trout opener** (statewide; www.ca.dfg .gov).

May: ✪ **Mule Days** (Bishop; 760-872-4263; www.muledays.org). The world's premier celebration of this hardest-working equine half-breed, Mule Days includes five days of family-friendly events and high patriotism. Barbecues, concerts, slightly off-standard rodeo, and parade. Saturday night sells out. Highlights include mutton bustin', chariot roping, and the highly competitive team pack scramble. Memorial Day. **Wild Wild West Marathon and Ultras** (Lone Pine; http://lonepinechamber.org/wild-west-marathon/). Increasingly popular 10-mile, 26-mile, 31-mile and 50-mile footraces in the Alabama Hills and on the Mount Whitney moraine. First Saturday in May. **Eastern Sierra Gem & Mineral Show** (Bishop; 760-873-3588; www .tricountyfair.com).

June: **California High School Rodeo State Finals** (www.tricountyfair.com) **Concert in the Rocks** (Alabama Hills; 760-876-9103; www.lonepinechamber .org/event/concert-in-the-rocks). **Lone Pine Time Trials** (Manzanar Airstrip; lonepinetimetrials.com). Non-sanctioned autocross benefit. **Mount Whitney Rally**

and **Poker Run** (try Jake's Saloon for information: 760-876-5765).

July: **Badwater Ultra-Marathon** (www.badwater.com). Death Valley to Whitney Portal: 135 miles uphill in temps up to 130 degrees. **Independence Day Celebration** (Independence; www .independence-ca.com).

August: ✪ **White Mountain Research Station Open House** (760-873-4344; www.wmrs.edu).

September: **Eastern Sierra Tri-County Fair** (Tri-County Fairgrounds, US 395, Bishop; 760-873-3588; www.tricountyfair .com). Highlights include cooking contests, carnival rides, truck pull, extreme bulls and broncos, and destruction derby. **Mount Whitney Classic** (Death Valley to Whitney Portal; www.summitadventure .com/whitney-classic/). A hard-core cycling endurance event. ✪ **Millpond**

VOLCANIC TABLELANDS AND ANCIENT PETROGLYPHS PATITUCCIPHOTO

Music Festival (Bishop; www.inyo.org/millpond). Three days of great live music, food, camping, and hanging out on the big lawn. **Good Ole Days** (Laws; 760-873-5950; www.lawsmuseum.org). Celebration of days gone by. Costumes, games, food, and craft displays. **Annual Pow Wow and California Indian Day Celebration** (Bishop, adjacent to the Paiute Palace Casino; 1-888-3PAIUTE; www.paiutepalace.com).

October: **Fall Colors Cruise and Car Show** (Tri-County Fairgrounds, Bishop; 760-920-3666 or 760-873-3901; www.owensvalleycruisers.com). ✪ **Lone Pine Film Festival** (Lone Pine; 760-876-9103; www.lonepinefilmfestival.org). A celebration of the millions of reels of film shot in and around Lone Pine. Panel conversations, location tours, autograph signings, live music, barbecues, parade. Bring your six-shooter and spurs.

November: **General trout season closes** (statewide; www.ca.dfg.gov).

December: **Christmas Bird Count**.

MAMMOTH LAKES & MONO COUNTY

MAMMOTH LAKES &
MONO COUNTY

*Were the painter, the novelist, the tourist, or the geologist, naturalist or
any other scientist, to search the world over for a point, easy of access,
that combined most wonderfully in the domains of nature all elements
of the sublime, immense, picturesque, curious, weird and varied in
forms, colors and startling contrasts, and extent of mountains, valley
and lake scenery, he would not be far wrong to locate it on one of the
highest granite or lava peaks near the new mining town of Mammoth
City.*
—James W. A. Wright, 1879

In 1851 or '52, three young Germans, half-starving and delirious, made their way westward across the Great American Desert. The rest of their party had been massacred
by Indians, but these three—they were brothers—had somehow managed to get away,
abandoning their gear, blazing their own haphazard path across the sagebrush toward
the headwaters of the Owens River. Twenty years later, Mark Twain would retell the
tale in *Roughing It*, giving it (the story, that is) considerable legs. "And in a gorge in the
mountains they sat down to rest," he reported, "when one of them noticed a curious
vein of cement running along the ground." Nowadays, consensus seems to locate this
occasion, to whatever degree it actually happened, somewhere in the pumice-coated
landscape above what is now the town of Mammoth Lakes.

"The vein was about as wide as a curbstone," wrote Twain, "and fully two-thirds of
it was pure gold."

Only one of the brothers made it across the Sierra alive—"exhausted, sick, and his
mind deranged by his sufferings." But on his person were samples of a reddish cement
of such miraculous assay that, every summer for more than a quarter-century thereafter, the peaks, canyons, and volcanic badlands south of Mono Lake were fairly overrun
with prospectors looking for "The Lost Cement Mine." Through the 1860s there were
rumors of mines developed in secret, ores smuggled out in the black of night. Here and
there a Paiute Indian would produce a nugget of pure yellow metal from his pocket,
smile, and then refuse to divulge a source. One poor fellow by the name of Hume
had his head cut off and left beneath a pile of stones in Deadman Creek, presumably
because he had information his partner preferred to keep to himself. Then one day in
1877, finally, up on Mineral Hill, at about 11,000 feet, with a fine view across Lake Mary
at a big dormant volcano called Pumice or Mammoth Mountain, a party of prospectors
found something vaguely promising.

The rough-and-ready camps at Mammoth, Mill, and Pine Cities had, by the summer
of 1879, a combined population of 2,500 people (about one-third of today's year-round
population), with a brand new 20-stamp mill, two semi-weekly newspapers (today
there are two weeklies), and a 54-mile toll trail all the way through to Fresno Flats
(Oakhurst). The price to use the trail was $15 each way, with 20 pounds of free freight,
8 cents a pound thereafter. Of actual ore there had as yet been no real sign. Of publicity there was plenty. San Francisco mining correspondent James W. A. Wright felt

he could safely report "in that grand and wonderful, almost enchanting, mountain region" the recent discovery "of more than 200 valuable mineral ledges, chiefly silver, but nearly all with some gold."

Then it started snowing.

Those who managed to dig their way out skedaddled—strapped barrel staves to their feet and went back to Bodie or Virginia City, or sold their picks and shovels and moved to San Diego. Of those who stayed, three froze to death. By the end of the following summer, with not a grain to show for three short seasons' blasting and drilling, everyone was gone. For decades to come, Lakes District, as it had been called, would be the peaceful domain of cattle ranchers, sheepherders, bears, coyotes, Indians, bighorn sheep, and a slow trickle of summertime home-steaders from down south. Into the 1920s, the keeper of one rustic lodge at Mammoth Camp was still burning firewood from enormous piles cut and stacked 40 years earlier for use at the stamp mill.

"Certain it is that if the Cement Mines exist they have remained undisturbed during all these years," W. A. Chalfant wrote in 1942, "and it is probable that somewhere in those hills of summer plea-

MAMMOTH FOUNDER DAVE MCCOY SKIING OFF THE TOP, 1950s PHOTO COURTESY MAMMOTH RESORTS

sure fortune awaits a claimant." Fortune would come, eventually—not in minerals, alas (though there are still actual gold prospectors here and there, living out of the backs of old Toyota pickup trucks and bathing in the hot springs out Whitmore Tubs Road), but in a substance considerably more plentiful: snow.

William Mulholland spent some days in Mammoth during the summer of 1907, taking snapshots of the impressive snowpack that would, in a few years, feed his aqueduct. With the aqueduct would come incidental improvements in transportation from Los Angeles to the High Sierra—overnight Pullman-car rail service to Bishop (with a change of trains in Lone Pine); then pavement from Lancaster to Mojave, and again in sections all the way up the Owens Valley. By the mid-1920s, a second boom was underway, with summer cabins and rustic knotty-pine fishing resorts sprouting up at every major drainage from Tom's Place to Virginia Lakes.

During the epic winter of 1935–36, a 21-year-old kid from El Segundo by the name of Dave McCoy, with a couple of buddies who happened to work as snow surveyors for the Los Angeles Department of Water and Power, started experimenting with motor-serviced downhill skiing. They made the skis themselves and improvised bindings. They found a hill and rigged a rope from the jacked-up back axle of a Model A Ford pickup truck. With one fellow on the gas pedal, the other two hanging on for the ride—off they went. In the spring, they left behind their machine, took to the backcountry, and explored the terrain from Lake Mary to the north flank of Mammoth Mountain: terrain where one day, nearly 70 years later, McCoy would make his fortune.

WILDASINN'S STORE, MAMMOTH MEADOW, JULY 1907 PHOTO BY WILLIAM MULHOLLAND; LIPPINCOTT COLLECTION, WATER RESOURCES CENTER ARCHIVES–UNIVERSITY OF CALIFORNIA, BERKELEY

A fellow by the name of Jack Northrop, a budding engineer and soon-to-be founder of the company that would become aerospace giant Northrop Grumman, installed a fixed rope tow, first in his backyard in Old Mammoth—which proved too much of a pain to get to in winter—then at McGee Creek, right on US 395 (across from Fred Eaton's old ranch, where Crowley Lake was soon to be made). Funding came from a wealthy Southern California ski enthusiast by the name of Cortlandt Hill, and technical assistance from McCoy. By 1940 hundreds of skiers were making the long drive up from the city every weekend. "All along High-way 395 north of Bishop is ski country," wrote a columnist from the Los Angeles Times. "There is a hundred-mile stretch of it that has been likened to the Tyrolean Alps. You can get out of your car and ski anywhere."

There were races on weekends, a Swiss-run ski school, cameo appearances by such stylish Hollywood celebrities as Henry Fonda and Gary Cooper, and all manner of rustic après-ski shenanigans. The place seemed poised for an unprecedented boom.

Then the war hit—and with it, gasoline rationing.

McCoy worked through the 1940s surveying the snowpack for the water department. He got married, had five kids, and supplemented his meager income with odd jobs—selling cordwood, guiding fishermen on Crowley Lake. He

MCGEE CREEK ROPE TOW, 1930s. THE GLASS MOUNTAINS ARE IN THE BACKGROUND COURTESY MAMMOTH RESORTS

secured a temporary "roving permit" from the Forest Service and built a portable rope tow he could drag around and set up on any given weekend, wherever the snow was best. The big snow along US 395 in the late 1930s turned out to have been anomalous. Season after season the best conditions in the Southern Sierra, and the best terrain to go with it, McCoy found on the north flank of Mammoth Mountain (above where Main Lodge now stands). Here big, wet winds off the Pacific funneled through a uniquely low saddle in the Sierra Crest—11,000 feet at San Joaquin Ridge—crashing headlong into the volcano, dumping payloads that regularly buried roads, cars, cabins, and Greyhound buses.

As the American economy boomed in the postwar years—especially in Southern California—so did the ski business. "After the war things picked up very fast," McCoy told Martin Forstenzer, author of *Mammoth: The Sierra Legend*. "We would have a hundred buses parked out here in the late '40s and '50s." Still, McCoy kept his day job. He put whatever he earned, and all his free time, into improvements—with no guarantees from the Forest Service as to how long he might be able to operate. With hand tools and a small crew working mostly for the fun of it, McCoy cleared trails and built a small warming hut. He bought tanklike war-surplus vehicles (Studebaker Weasels) for hauling folks from town to the base of the mountain. He put big diesel engines on his rope tows, earning an early reputation for running more people faster to the top of the slope than anywhere else in the country.

As early as 1945, the Forest Service had begun to consider the possibility of developing one or two major European-style ski resorts in the Southern Sierra. Mineral King (now in Sequoia National Park; see Chapter 6) was one site deemed to have excellent potential. Mammoth was another. "Mammoth Mountain is impressive in its ski potentialities," wrote Forest Supervisor Jim Gibson. "It seems beyond any question that proper development can make this mountain one of the top ski areas of the West."

MAMMOTH MT. MAMMOTH LAKES, CALIF.

PREESSEN STUDIO

THE ROAD INTO MAMMOTH IN THE 1950S COURTESY MAMMOTH RESORTS

⊛ OTHER BOOKS TO SUPPLEMENT THIS CHAPTER

Backcountry Skiing California's Eastern Sierra, by Nate Greenberg and Dan Mingori (Wolverine, 2014).

Mammoth Lakes Sierra, by Genny Smith, ed. (Genny Smith Books, 1993).

Geology of the Sierra Nevada, by Mary Hill (UC Press, 2006).

The Laws Field Guide to the Sierra Nevada, by John Muir Laws (Heyday Books, California Academy of Sciences, 2007).

Sierra Nevada Natural History, by Tracy Storer, Robert Usinger, and David Lukas (UC Press, 2004).

Tracks of Passion, by Robin Morning (Mammoth Ski Museum, 2008).

Yosemite and Mammoth Lakes Camping and Hiking (Moon Spotlight), by Tom Stienstra and Ann Marie Brown (Moon Outdoors, 2012).

In 1952, the Forest Service paved the road to McCoy's warming hut and, expecting at least a quarter-million-dollar investment in facilities—such as a chairlift, a T-bar, a full-service modern lodge, and more—opened the bidding.

"I thought somebody with money was going to come in and I'd be out in the cold," McCoy told Forstenzer years later. But nobody was willing to take the risk. Even McCoy's friend, Cortlandt Hill, who had financed the first rope tow at McGee Creek, thought Mineral King was a safer bet. "They said it was too far from a metropolitan area—it was too high in altitude, it was too remote," explained McCoy. "They said it wasn't what people were accustomed to—too much snow, too windy, too rugged."

And so by default McCoy found himself holding a 25-year lease on Mammoth Mountain, with not just the go-ahead to build a full-fledged resort, but the obligation to do so. He quit his job with the water department. He pulled his crew together, scrounged materials, and built the first wing of what would eventually become the sprawling Main Lodge complex. He procured a brand new double chairlift from a fledgling tramway company in San Francisco—on credit—and started putting in towers. He raised the price of an all-day lift ticket from $2.50 to $4. By Thanksgiving morning 1955, 3 feet of fresh powder had accumulated under the wide-open blue sky, and 250 skiers were lined up for the inaugural ride up Chair 1 (now a highspeed quad dubbed Broadway Express). The next boom was on.

"During the past couple of years," Wolfgang Lert wrote in Ski Magazine in 1958, "a ski area hidden away in California's Eastern Sierra Nevada has jumped into national prominence. Skiers who have visited it rave not only about the beautiful slopes and incredible snow, but also about the spirit of friendliness, of fairness, of trying to do the best for the skier, which pervades the whole place." In this spirit, McCoy managed to run the place for another half-century, weathering droughts, earthquakes, economic slumps, energy shortages, buyout offers from Disney and Universal Studios, repeated failures to secure regular commercial air service, and fears of volcanic eruption (generally thought to be unwarranted). A gondola-serviced "Village" opened for business in 2003, built in the style of similar "villages" at Whistler and Squaw Valley by Canadian real estate conglomerate Intrawest ULC, back before that entity began liquidating huge chunks of its worldwide assets. In 2005, exactly 50 years after the opening turn of Chair 1, McCoy sold his controlling interest in the mountain to Barry Sternlicht's privately held Starwood Capital Group—for $365 million.

In the late 1950s, Mammoth claimed about 200 year-round residents. By the end of the 1960s, the number had grown to 1,000, and a little village of A-frame ski cabins and faux Swiss chalets had sprung up in the woods within trudging distance of CA

203. Today there are more than 8,000 year-round residents enjoying all four seasons in the incorporated town of Mammoth Lakes. The ski area—a majority stake of which was purchased in 2017 by a partnership between Aspen Skiing Company and Denver-based KSL partners, but is still run by McCoy's hand-picked successor, onetime lift operator, now part owner Rusty Gregory—is regularly ranked among the top 10 winter resorts in North America for its huge size, the variety of its terrain, the quality of its snow, its dramatic scenery, its ski and snowboard school, its snowmaking and trail grooming, its radical terrain parks, its access to big backcountry, its on-mountain services, and its enormous number of skier-days per year. In winter, one can ski in the morning and, in the afternoon, go rock climbing in the Owens River Gorge, soak in a hot spring, or play golf in Bishop.

There is ice skating and sledding and snowmobiling, and an extensive network of groomed trails dedicated only to snowshoeing and cross-country skiing. On the best years, there is downhill skiing (and all manner of wet, costumed outrageousness) on July Fourth, between a parade and fireworks. When the snow melts, there is lift-serviced mountain biking with hundreds of miles of dusty trails both on the mountain and beyond, and there is world-class trout fishing, rock climbing, road biking, camping, skateboarding, hiking, backpacking, and more.

The town itself offers none of the typical main-street charm of the famous Victorian mining/ski towns of the Rocky Mountains, or of old ranch-supply towns like Steamboat Springs or Jackson Hole, or even nearby Bishop. All that remains of Mammoth's early days are a handful of old ruins above Lake Mary, a few log cabins along Mammoth Creek, the ruins of a stamp mill (closed in 2017 as a toxic waste site), and a

CHAIR 3 AND THE NEW TWO-STAGE GONDOLA TO THE SUMMIT, 1969 TOM JOHNSTON, COURTESY MAMMOTH RESORTS

rusted-iron Knight Wheel hauled up from Mojave in 1879 to drive the stamp mill—now almost entirely engulfed by the latest stages of the Snowcreek real estate development. Mammoth today bears certain unfortunate hallmarks of its historic association with metropolitan southern California—in the form of strip malls, outlet shopping, and a proliferation of cheap, uninspired condo developments and suburban-style tract homes (built mostly in the 1970s and '80s). But what Mammoth lacks in antique architectural charm it more than makes up for with the quality and friendliness of the community, and with its unparalleled setting.

The forest here—unlike at Tahoe, for example, or along the west side of the range—was never clear-cut. There are trees in and around Mammoth from the days of the last Norse settlements in Greenland—old-growth firs taller than 20-story buildings, from when the Moors were still running Spain and the Catholic kings were still hiding out in the Pyrenees, refusing to bathe. There are Jeffrey pines with trunks as thick as a man is tall. And where so many other resort towns across the West have found it impossible to resist the urge to sprawl, Mammoth—hemmed as it is into just 4 square miles by its boundaries with the Inyo National Forest and with land owned by the Los Angeles Department of Water and Power—has been successfully held in check.

A number of quarter-acre parcels of old red fir and pumice have given way to sturdy, multimillion-dollar, neo-craftsman-alpine-mission-barn-revival vacation lodges, and many of the old tumble-down A-frames and shag-carpet condominium complexes have been torn down, refaced or otherwise fixed up, and brought into the twenty-first century. A few have been left fallow to slouch a little more with each season, waiting for the next infusion of capital. But somehow, from year to year, through boom and relative bust, the town continues to feel ever more vibrant, with an ever better sense of itself, of what it is and how it hopes to be a model high-Alpine recreation community in the twenty-first century.

Mammoth has become renowned as North America's premier high-altitude training center for runners and endurance athletes. The summer is chockablock with live music; wine, craft beer, Shakespeare festivals, and food-tasting festivals. Winter events include the Night of Lights torchlight ski parade and fireworks extravaganza in December, international biathlon and cross-country ski races, ski and snowboard invitational events, and the much-anticipated wackiness of the Pond Skim in spring. But even on a Thursday night in late September, deep shoulder season, when in years past the town would've been cleared of all but the rummaging bears and the ground squirrels doing their last-minute hoarding for winter, the bar at Petra's is elbow-to-elbow, ringing with tales of adventure, clinking goblets, and the scraping of multiple spoons at the last of an organic peach flourless upside-down cake.

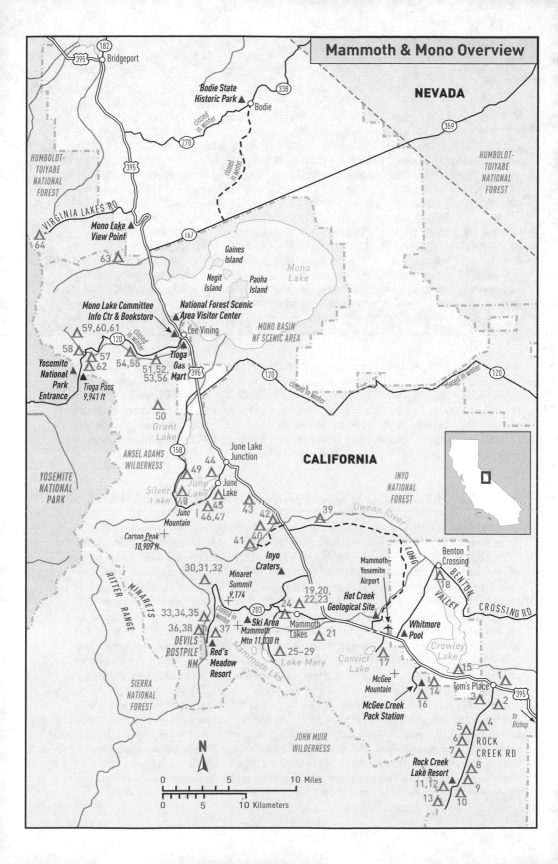

A NOTE ON SEASONS

Nearly 100 percent of annual precipitation falls between November and April, the majority of it in the form of snow. Average seasonal snowfall is more than 33 feet. The usual scenario is for a storm to hit hard and fast, dumping several feet of powder, then move on, leaving clear skies and soon-to-be-tracked slopes in its wake. Plausible claims are made that there are more than 300 days of sunshine per year. The coldest months are December and January, with average temperatures in the town of Mammoth Lakes, at 8,000 feet, lying between 20 and 40 degrees Fahrenheit. Very rarely does the mercury dip below zero.

Summers are dry and warm—hotter on the flats in Long Valley, cooler as one travels up into the lakes basins and high country. A common adage among locals is that having come for the winter, one ends up staying for the summer. Temperatures rarely climb above the 80-degree mark. Afternoon thundershowers are rare and glorious events. When a heat wave hits—the temperature occasionally breaks into the mid-90s for a few days—there are hundreds of cold snowmelt lakes within striking distance for the rapid cooling of one's core temperature. The "shoulder seasons" of fall and spring—with visitation and room rates at their lowest—are often the most pleasant times of year in the High Sierra: the former offering crisp mornings, golden stands of Aspen, and empty trails; the latter, wildflowers and boundless slopes of corn snow.

And through it all, the country beyond abides—from the Mono Basin to the meandering trout waters of the Upper Owens, from Montgomery Peak to the Wheeler Crest to the wild eastern edge of Yosemite National Park. A person can still walk 200 miles from the porch at Tamarack Lodge without crossing a single road. In every direction, the profound sense of wide-open space remains essentially and uniquely unchanged from way back on that fateful day, a century and a half ago, when an unlucky German prospector happened to look down and notice a curious-looking piece of cement.

✳The Lay of the Land: Approaches and Logistics

Mammoth is one of the most geographically remote mountain resort towns in North America—but it is also the closest to Los Angeles (310 mostly arrow-straight miles). More and more people are discovering the pleasures of arriving by air, along some of the most scenic flight paths in the Lower 48 (from LAX and sometimes other destinations). But most visitors still arrive by automobile from the south, coming fast across the Mojave Desert and up the Owens Valley on US 395. The way is long—five-plus hours—but the road, now mostly freeway-style four-lane blacktop, is easy, uncongested, and extraordinarily scenic. Even in the most inclement of winter weather the pavement from the south is generally dry and clear—until the last few miles of the trip (see Chapter 2 for winter driving tips). Southern Californians, raised on the principles of the multiple-hour commute, will often make the journey from as far as San Diego even for a short weekend.

After Mammoth-Yosemite (MMH), the closest commercial airport is Reno (RNO), 167 miles to the north by way of the more mountainous sections of US 395. The closest big-box shopping is in Carson City (136 miles). Access to and from Las Vegas (308 mostly straight miles) is possible year-round by a variety of routes. In summer, access to and from the west side of the range is by the Tioga Road, through Yosemite's East Entrance (see Chapter 7), 10 miles above Lee Vining (Mono Lake) and 40 miles from downtown Mammoth. In winter, once Tioga Pass is closed, the only way in from the west side is by crossing at one of the lower-elevation northern passes (i.e., Carson or Donner) or by coming around the range from the south. This chapter is organized from south to north along US 395 (the Eastern Sierra Scenic Byway), from Rock Creek to Mammoth to Mono Lake.

✳ To See

ROCK CREEK TO CASA DIABLO

Lake Crowley (CA 395, 3 miles north of Tom's Place). For years, Mulholland refused to buy the ranch land here from his old pal Fred Eaton (at the rates Eaton wanted to charge). After both men were dead and gone, the City of Los Angeles finally acquired the place, and in 1941, the city built a storage reservoir named for Father John J. Crowley, "the desert padre," who was among the first to promote tourism in the Owens Valley (before he was killed in a 1940 automobile accident). Owens River water is here diverted into a pipeline with a drop of 2,300 feet to a series of power plants in the gorge below. On opening day of fishing season, despite fears of infestation by non-native mussels, the lake's surface is obscured by thousands of anglers attached to a variety of flotation devices. By midsummer, the lake sports a bright-green algae bloom that makes swimming not quite so pleasant here as in other lakes in the region. The biggest-budget fireworks show in the Eastern Sierra takes place here on July Fourth, complete with tailgate barbecues and patriotic music.

    McGee Mountain (1.5 miles south along frontage road from McGee Creek Lodge). A plaque, some rusted equipment, a Jeep trail, and an old cabin mark the site of the first fixed rope tow in the Eastern Sierra.

LAKE CROWLEY LOOKING SOUTH TOWARD THE WHEELER CREST BILL BECHER

Convict Lake (2.5 miles south of CA 395 on Convict Lake Road). The 1939 WPA guide to California aptly describes it as "a pellucid sheet of blue, fronted by a rustic resort for fishermen and backed by the imposing height of Mount Morrison (12,245 alt)." The lake is so named because of a gun battle that occurred here in September 1871 between a group of escaped convicts from the Nevada State Penitentiary and a posse of citizens from the nearby town of Benton. Robert Morrison, a merchant and member of the latter group, was shot and killed, thereby giving his name to the imposing peak. Three of the convicts were eventually captured south of Round Valley; two were hanged nearby from a hastily constructed scaffold. "I am prepared to meet my God," one of the convicts said, fitting the noose around his own neck, "but I don't know that there is any." **Convict Lake Resort** (7,600 feet; 1-800-992-2260; www.convictlake .com; expensive) remains essentially a resort for anglers (and their families), offering a range of older cabins with the most utilitarian of appointments (but at premium rates), as well as several newer suburban-style houses designed to accommodate large groups. The year-round forest-service concession also features a marina, a restaurant, a general store, and horseback riding.

Hot Creek State Fish Hatchery (121 Hot Creek Hatchery Rd., just north of the airport; 760-934-2664; www.wildlife.ca.gov/Fishing/Hatcheries/Hot-Creek). Established in 1936 to take advantage of year-round hotsprings-fed water, the hatchery is today one of the largest in the state and said to be one of the most important broodstock and production facilities in the West. It produces nearly 13 million fertilized eggs per year, as well as millions of fingerling rainbow, brown, and Kamloops rainbow trout for stocking streams and lakes across the state. Bring quarters for fish food. Open daily 7:30 AM–4 PM.

Hot Creek Geological Site (Hot Creek Hatchery Road, 2.5 miles past hatchery). A variety of hot springs, steam vents, and low-level turquoise-colored geysers boil up into the creek water here in a small canyon along the lower stretches of Mammoth Creek. Locations and temperatures of pools and springs vary, depending on stream flow and local earthquake activity. Once a popular—if not altogether relaxing—bathing site, the waters here have been "temporarily" closed to swimming ever since 2006, due to increased and possibly deadly geothermal activity. Especially eerie in winter.

For a slightly less challenging soak, try one of the semi-improved hot-springs tubs along Whitmore Tubs Road, lately featured on various national magazine covers, or at Little Hot Creek.

Casa Diablo (CA 203, south of CA 395; 760-934-4893; www.mammothpacific.com). Geothermal hot spot in the heart of the Long Valley Caldera, with source water at temperatures up to 350 degrees Fahrenheit. Once a favorite soaking spot for Indians, miners, and tourists. Geysers used to spring up here on occasion (e.g., in 1937 and again in 1959), with water shooting up to 80 feet in the air. Geothermal drilling began in the 1960s, causing a subsequent diminishment in surface spring activity. Mammoth Pacific Geothermal, now wholly owned by Israeli utilities giant Ormat Industries, operates

LONG VALLEY HOMESTEAD BELOW THE OLD SKI SLOPES AT MCGEE, JUNE 2007 BURKE GRIGGS

SHOT IN MAMMOTH AND MONO: A SHORT LIST

The Trail Beyond (1934). Directed by Robert N. Bradbury; starring John Wayne. Snowcreek.

The Call of the Wild (1935). Directed by William Wellman; starring Clark Gable.

The Road to Utopia (1946). Directed by Hal Walker; starring Bing Crosby and Bob Hope.

North to Alaska (1960). Directed by Henry Hathaway; starring John Wayne. Hot Creek.

Ride the High Country (1962). Directed by Sam Peckinpah; starring Randolph Scott and Joel McRea. Mammoth Lakes Basin.

Nevada Smith (1966). Directed by Henry Hathaway; starring Steve McQueen. Hot Creek, Snowcreek, Oh! Ridge.

Caprice (1967). Directed by Frank Tashlin; starring Doris Day and Richard Harris.

High Plains Drifter (1973). Directed by Clint Eastwood; starring Clint Eastwood. Mono Lake, Inyo National Forest.

The Other Side of the Mountain (1975). Directed by Larry Peerce; starring Marilyn Hassett and Beau Bridges. Based on the true story of ski racer Jill Kinmont-Boothe.

First Monday in October (1981). Directed by Ronald Neame; starring Walter Matthau and Jill Clayburgh.

Indiana Jones and the Temple of Doom (1984). Directed by Steven Spielberg; starring Harrison Ford and Kate Capshaw. Mammoth Mountain.

Perfect (1985). Directed by James Bridges; starring John Travolta and Jamie Lee Curtis.

The Golden Child (1986). Directed by Michael Ritchie; starring Eddie Murphy. Snowcreek, Mammoth Mountain.

Born on the Fourth of July (1989). Directed by Oliver Stone; starring Tom Cruise.

Revenge (1990). Directed by Tony Scott; starring Kevin Costner, Madeleine Stowe, and Anthony Quinn.

For the Boys (1991). Directed by Mark Rydell; starring Bette Midler and James Caan.

The Scorpion King (2002). Directed by Chuck Russell; starring Dwayne Johnson, aka The Rock.

XXX (2002). Directed by Rob Cohen; starring Vin Diesel, Asia Argento, and Samuel L. Jackson.

Oblivion (2013) Directed by Joseph Kosinski; starring Tom Cruise and Morgan Freeman.

a series of power plants here, with eighteen wells on 10 acres. Hot water is pumped through heat exchangers to produce a gas vapor that in turn drives a series of eight turbines, making enough electricity to power 40,000 homes—all of which is sold to Southern California Edison, then resold to consumers in Los Angeles (and in neighboring Mammoth Lakes). No water is lost in the process. Call to arrange a tour. Behind the power plant looms what is called a "resurgent dome," a convenient placement for radio and cell towers and a feature that continues to rise (by as much as 80 centimeters in the past three decades) with the continued rising of the magma below. Call to arrange a tour.

MAMMOTH LAKES

The town's main business district sprawls west and uphill along "Main Street" (CA 203)—a road built at the convenience of the state transportation authority in 1937, at some distance from the original center of affairs at Old Mammoth—and south along what is now called Old Mammoth Road. Along these two vectors, you will find restaurants, coffee joints, sporting goods stores, gas, a full-size grocery store, a franchise drug store, a hardware store, an excellent toy and novelty boutique, a specialty food purveyor, restaurants, and a variety of motels. The **"Village"** (www.villageatmammoth .com) is just off the upper end of Main Street to the north, along Minaret Road, in the direction of Main Lodge and Devils Postpile National Monument, and offers lodging,

COMING HOME TO MAMMOTH

A family's deep roots in skiing and the Eastern Sierra

Jimmy Morning slouches back into the sofa and puts his feet up on the coffee table. He's wearing blue socks, jeans, and a faded grey zip-front sweatshirt. His hair is thick, the color of weathered barn wood. He rakes it upward from his forehead with his fingers and looks out over the top of his glasses. "I just got out of a session," he tells me. "We were doing some maintenance on the hot tub."

His son Peter, on break from a photo shoot at the golf course, doubts this. "You mean you were *using* the hot tub," he ribs.

The tub in question is one of the primitive geothermal tubs out in Long Valley, out past the airport and the Green Church. "The one he owns," quips Jimmy's younger sister Robin. Jimmy's up at 5 AM most mornings—he couldn't sleep later if he wanted to. He loves to start his day with a cup of coffee and a drive out for an early soak with a view of Mt. Morrison. He's part of a small crew of local hot springs aficionados who help keep the hand-built concrete tub clean and functioning properly. "There was a clog in the drain," he explains, "so we had to dig down about two feet and replace part of the pipe."

I've been invited over on this blustery fall afternoon to listen to the Mornings talk about legacy, ski racing, how Mammoth has changed—and how it hasn't. The Mornings are one of Mammoth's founding families. They've all been coached at one point or another by Dave McCoy, the legendary founder of Mammoth Mountain. Jimmy skied with the U.S. national team in the mid-1960s, and he is still one of the most beloved coaches in Mammoth's race department; Robin was on the Olympic team in 1968; Katie, the baby sister, was a pro racer and a pioneer women's freestyler in the mid-1970s, sponsored by Rossignol. Katie, who has recently moved back to Mammoth after nearly three decades in Connecticut, arrives bearing a platter of cold cuts and cheese. Robin has made a poppy seed cake. Susan, Jimmy's wife and Peter's mom, longtime photographer for the *Mammoth Times*, opens a bottle of red wine.

THE MORNING FAMILY CLIMBS WHAT IS NOW THE FACE OF 3 (BEFORE CHAIR 3 WAS BUILT) COURTESY ROBIN MORNING

The cabin is a ramble-down affair—logs and chinking stacked on a stone foundation; a covered entry that doubles as snow tunnel and wood shed; a main room which is at once kitchen, sitting room, meeting hall, and guest dormitory; an old wooden water tower in the yard reminiscent of a refilling tank on a narrow-gauge railroad line—all of which Peter characterizes as "legit." "It feels like home," says Katie, remembering Christmases past with presents strapped to the top of the Oldsmobile, pancakes in the morning, and skiing in the afternoon. "Everybody's had their time here," says Jimmy.

Nobody's quite sure when the cabin was built. Jimmy says the 1920s. Robin, who has written the definitive history of Dave McCoy and the early development of Mammoth Mountain Ski Area, says it was probably the 1950s. Their parents, Betty Jane and Sylvester, bought the place in '62 or '63. "It's not easy to heat," says Jimmy, citing the high ceiling, the non-functioning stone fireplace, and the castoff front window gleaned from a job site sometime in the 60s to replace the one a bear came through. "When it gets snow around the outside," he adds, "it's nice and cozy."

The first time Jimmy came up to the Eastern Sierra he was six years old. It was 1951. Dave and Roma McCoy were running a rope tow on McGee Mountain. That first morning, little Jimmy was the first out of the rental shop. He grabbed the rope, hung on tight. He watched the skiers making graceful turns on the way back down. At some point he let go of the rope and pointed the long boards toward the bottom of the hill. Then he realized: he had no idea how to turn or stop. He crashed into the line of people at the bottom, sprained his ankle, and spent the rest of the vacation in the trailer they'd rented down at Tom's Place.

Betty Jane and Sylvester had moved out from Colorado to Santa Monica after the war. There was a housing boom on, and they started a series of businesses: washing windows, doing construction cleanup, installing carpets. Pretty soon there were four kids (there's a third sister, named Jody, who became an artist and is now living in Tunisia). At first they skied mostly in the San Gabriels; at Snow Summit, Snow Valley, Mt. Baldy, or Holiday Hill. "Skiracing is what really got us," says Robin. "We went to a race at Snow Valley one weekend and from that time on we were just all about ski racing." Every weekend, they'd drive to the mountains, sleep in the car—all six of them in the back of the station wagon—and ski.

Betty Jane wasn't the greatest skier, Katie explains, but eventually she had a different Bogner outfit and a different Meggi sweater for every day of the week. In 1958 she founded the Junior Skiers of Southern California to help kids offset the costs of training and races. Eventually she and Roma McCoy would become close friends, fashion confidantes, and shopping partners.

In '59, Dave McCoy held a training camp at McGee for kids from all over California, in part to choose a Far West Junior National team. Jimmy made the team; Robin made alternate. McCoy was the coach. He provided lift tickets and meal tickets for the races. "We just had to find a place to stay," says Robin. The family was up and down financially, but Jimmy and Robin were in Mammoth every weekend.

Often it was Jimmy, aged 16, driving the 600 miles up and back at 45 miles an hour in his Volkswagen bus, while Robin slept in the back. They stayed wherever they could: at the trailer park, in the patrol room at Main Lodge, or at the coal-heated quonset hut out at Whitmore. "After that we were part of the Mammoth team," Robin tells me. "They couldn't get rid of us."

After high school, Jimmy went off to Colorado University. In '62 he spent a month in Europe with McCoy as part of a team of seven Americans, including Spider Sabich and Jimmie Huega. Huega would become one of the first two Americans, with Billy Kidd, to win an Olympic medal in Alpine skiing. Sabich would go on to make the '68 Olympic team. (Jimmy narrowly missed qualifying in '68, due—according to Robin—to the failure of the timing system on a winning slalom run.) Sabich was the partial inspiration for James Salter's 1969 film *Downhill Racer*, starring Robert Redford. In '74, he made the cover of GQ as "pro-skiing's richest racer." Then he was fatally shot in the bathroom of his house in Aspen, under mysterious circumstances, by his girlfriend, the singer and actress Claudine Longet.

Jimmy has fond memories of that first trip to Europe. "We were supposed to race but we didn't," he says. "We just skied everywhere." At one point, he was driving another Volkswagen bus from Switzerland into France. It was full of people and luggage and skis. Franz Kneissel had just given each of them a brand new pair of White Stars. The border, says Jimmy, wasn't very clear. There was just a little hut, which he drove right past—and suddenly they were surrounded by the army. "They thought we were smuggling skis." Huega's dad, who was French, managed to talk the soldiers down. When Jimmy came home at the end of that season, his parents had bought the log cabin in Old Mammoth.

Katie was 12 or 13 when she traveled to France with Betty Jane and the McCoys to see her big sister race in the Olympics. The day they arrived in Grenoble, they found Robin in a military hospital (the Olympic hospital was still under construction), in a bed next to an injured Chilean ski racer. She'd broken her leg in a final training run the day before the opening ceremonies. Her toes were black; her cast had to be cut off and redone. Betty Jane wheeled the Chilean down the hall and moved into the room with her daughter. "Everyone stunk of French cigarettes," Robin remembers. The next day, the McCoys' daughter Candy got hit in the head by an elevator and moved into another hospital across town. Katie remembers staying at the hotel by herself, commuting by bus between the two hospitals and the ski hill, where she watched the Olympic races and skied with her sister's credentials.

Throughout the '60s and early '70s, the kids were part of a small, tight-knit local community. There were the Thompsons, the Bachelders, the Manns, the Agees, the Stewarts, and the McCoys. Sylvester was often too busy with work down south, so the trips to Mammoth fell more and more to Betty Jane. During summer training, the kids lived in the dormitory at Main Lodge. For a year or two, Katie and Jody went to school at the tiny Mammoth Academy, where Robin got a job as a teacher so she could take care of her sisters. "It was crazy," says Katie. "We had no parental guidance. We were running loose."

The Morning cabin became central to the culture of California ski racing. "This house had a bit of a reputation," Robin explains. Betty Jane liked to host parties, and it was known that any racer on the circuit who needed a place to stay was welcome to crash at the Mornings'. During the annual California spring races the place was packed. People slept on fold-out couches and on the floor. There were spaghetti fights in the rafters and riotous games of "Are You There

dining, shopping, and regular live entertainment, as well as gondola access to the mountain (in winter) and shuttle service to the bike park (in summer).

On mid-winter weekends when conditions are good, the town is busy. On holiday weekends—Martin Luther King Jr. Day, Memorial Day, July Fourth, and during Bluesapalooza in August—the town hops. Still, with some 4,700 rental units, there are always plenty of beds to go around. Until the holidays. If you want to experience what Joseph and Mary went through on that famous trip to Bethlehem, try visiting Mammoth around the same time of year without making reservations. During the last two weeks of December (and again during Presidents Day Week, when all of Orange County is blessed with some kind of midwinter break), the valley fills to beyond capacity: The population of Mammoth Lakes explodes from 7,500 people to more than 35,000.

The result: Freelance snow-chain installers in arctic foul-weather gear make small fortunes on the Sherwin Grade or at the bottom of CA 203; oversized two-wheel-drive SUVs decorate the town's snow banks; the grocery store struggles to keep its shelves stocked with spaghetti and toilet paper; lines at restaurants spill out into the streets; lodging becomes impossible to come by (unless booked months in advance), even at double the usual peak-season rates, even in Bishop and June Lake; and parking, not just within striking distance of ski lifts but anywhere in town, comes at a premium.

Moriarty?", a dryland version of Marco Polo, wherein blindfolded seekers attempt to beat each other with clubs made of rolled-up newspaper.

It didn't last forever. After college and a stint in the army, Jimmy ended up back in Southern California building houses with his dad. He got married, started having kids. Robin moved to Colorado and got married. Later she got remarried and moved to San Diego to teach school. Katie got married and moved back east. In 1982, Jimmy and Susan made a play to purchase Kratka Ridge, a single-chair ski hill just down the Angeles Crest Highway from Mt. Waterman. But the forest service wouldn't commit to letting them develop snowmaking, so the deal fell through.

When Peter was born, in 1985, Jimmy named him after his old friend Spider Sabich, whose full name was Vladimir Peter Sabich, Jr. After Sylvester and Betty Jane passed away, Jimmy and Susan moved their brood—Peter, his older brother Matt, and their twin sisters K. C. and Kelly—to Reno for a job. It wasn't where they wanted to be. "The house was calling," Jimmy tells me. "I was always trying to get up here and stay longer." And so in 1991 they finally made the leap.

Their kids grew up ski racing and going to Mammoth High School. Susan has continued the open-house tradition at the cabin. Peter made the Junior Olympic team every year he was eligible. His siblings have moved elsewhere for school or work, but Peter's still in Mammoth, working as brand photographer for the ski area. Robin teaches adult Nordic skiing at Tamarack and writes. Katie cooks dinner four nights a week for Dave and Roma McCoy—Dave has just turned 101—and teaches beginners at Tamarack on weekends. "It's so amazing to go up and ski for two hours and then go to work," says Katie. "It's incredible. That's the way it used to be."

They still feel the generosity and graciousness of McCoy deep in the fabric of the local community. "It's diluted some now," says Robin, "but it's still there." There's still this feeling that people know each other and take care of each other. Jimmy even gets a little teary when he talks about the kids he coaches, how well they work together, how good they are to each other. And at the root of it all, somehow, is the place itself.

"I always feel better when I'm coming back here," says Jimmy. He used to have a dog named Easy, he says, a crazy dog who used to ride in the back of his truck and would get up on the roof of the cab when Mammoth Mountain came into view. Katie and Peter chime in: You see the Minarets, you roll down the window and get that first shot of cold fresh air, the smell of sagebrush. "When I pass Conway Summit, or coming the other way," says Jimmy, "I feel like, 'Ah . . . I'm home now.'"

Tickets for New Year's Eve events sell out across town at prices well over $100 a head. If, as with most folks, holidays are the only time off you get, make reservations as many months in advance as you can muster. Most properties will accept reservations a year in advance. Most will require a minimum stay of at least three nights, others as many as seven. The earlier you make plans, the more you'll have a chance to shop around.

If, on the other hand, you happen to be one of the lucky few with a more flexible calendar—or a more flexible work ethic—come up midweek, any time after about January 2. Not only will you save loads of money, you'll find yourself sharing one of the biggest ski mountains in North America with a handful of crows and coyotes and, depending on conditions, a few lonely, powder-glazed locals.

Earthquake Fault (off Minaret Road, CA 203, between the Village and Main Lodge). An impressive fissure in the underlying rock, running from the tennis courts at Mammoth Ski & Racquet Club, north-south across CA 203, and up the slopes of so called Earthquake Dome. C. Clarke Keely tells of pushing an old truck up here in summertime in the early 1920s, before there was a road, to get ice for the making of ice cream. "We would go down in the earthquake crack and fill big gunny sacks . . . the snow was practically solid ice and you had to pick it." There is some controversy among geologists as to whether this is actually an earthquake fault (the Paiutes have stories of a Big

LIVING VOLCANO COUNTRY

In July 1863 William Brewer and Charles Hoffman of the Whitney Survey took a side trip south of Mono Lake ("that American Dead Sea," as Brewer put it) to explore a chain of apparently extinct volcanoes. "The rocks of these volcanoes are a gray lava pumice stone so light that it will float on water, obsidian, or volcanic glass," Brewer observed in his journal. Not without difficulty in this loose and porous gravel they climbed to a height of 9,700 feet. "The scene from the top is desolate enough," he wrote, "barren volcanic mountains standing in a desert cannot form a cheering picture." Beneath much of this country—from the Lakes Basin south of Mammoth Mountain to Mono Lake—lies a vast reservoir of molten rock, or magma. One cataclysmic eruption about 760,000 years ago spewed as much as 130 cubic miles of the stuff across the landscape, causing the land to subside at what is now called the Long Valley Caldera ("cauldron" in Spanish). Mammoth Mountain—considered a quiescent, or dormant, volcano—was formed by a series of eruptions between 220,000 and 50,000 years ago. The Mammoth Knolls, to the north of town, were made about 100,000 years ago, the Inyo Craters and Deadman Dome as recently as 550 years ago. "During the last 5,000 years," according to the U.S. Geological Survey (USGS), "an eruption has broken out somewhere along this chain every 250 to 700 years." The most recent occurred about 250 years ago at Paoha Island in Mono Lake. In the past two decades, a series of earthquake swarms, tree die-offs at Horseshoe Lake, and increased geothermal activity in the Long Valley Caldera has led to concerns that another eruption may be on the horizon. The Mammoth Lakes Scenic Loop was paved in the 1980s to provide an alternate route to CA 395 in the event of significant volcanic activity (some locals wryly refer to it as the Mammoth *Seismic* Route). The Benton Crossing Road, from the green church (just south of the airport) to the town of Benton, is plowed and maintained throughout the winter for the same reason. "The probability of an eruption occurring in any given year," according to the USGS, "is somewhat less than 1 percent per year or roughly one chance in a few hundred in any given year." Which is about the same probability given for the occurrence of a major earthquake along the California coast, or for the eruption of a more active volcano in the Cascade Range, such as Mount Shasta or Mount Rainier. "Future eruptions will occur," says the USGS, but they are likely to be "small and similar to previous eruptions during the past 5,000 years"—and far enough from population centers that their impact is likely to be more of an inconvenience (in the form of falling ash) than a threat to life or property. Whatever happens, it seems fair to say that it's bound to be interesting. "Reading these grand mountain manuscripts displayed through every vicissitude of heat and cold, calm and

One having occurred here sometime back in the late 1700s), or merely a crack resulting from the cooling of lava or a monster landslide. The stairs down into the crack were closed briefly after a 6.0-magnitude tremor in 1980, then reopened. Here are some of the oldest trees in the region. Access by cross-country skis or snowshoes in winter.

Hayden Cabin/Mammoth Museum (on Mammoth Creek, off Sherwin Creek Road; 760-934-6918). Mapmaker Emmet Hayden built this cabin on the shore of Mammoth Creek in 1927. Today it is a repository for old mining equipment, artifacts, and memorabilia from the early days at Mammoth Camp, curated by the Mono County Historical Society. Open daily in summer; closed in winter. Equipment demonstrations held on weekends.

Horseshoe Lake Tree Kill (north shore of Horseshoe Lake, above Lake Mary). After a "swarm" of small tremors in 1989, Forest Service rangers began noticing a localized die-off of trees above the shores of Horseshoe Lake on the backside of Mammoth Mountain. The first and most obvious thought: drought and beetle kill. Then a ranger nearly died of carbon dioxide poisoning after breathing the air in a nearby snow-covered cabin. Scientists from the U.S. Geological Survey have measured levels of carbon dioxide in the soil comparable to those at Mount St. Helens and Kilauea "during

storm, upheaving volcanoes and down-grinding glaciers," John Muir wrote in *My First Summer in the Sierra*, "we see that everything in Nature called destruction must be creation—a change from beauty to beauty."

For more information, ballistics, eruption scenarios, and the latest conditions, check the USGS Volcano Hazards Program's Long Valley Observatory at www.volcanoes.usgs.gov/volcanoes/long_valley.

HOT CREEK GEOLOGICAL SITE, CLOSED TO SWIMMING IN 2006 DUE TO INCREASED VOLCANIC ACTIVITY   CHRIS FARRAR, USGS

periods of low level eruptive activity." The escape of gas here is thought to be the product of movement in the magma chamber below. By 1999, there were more than 100 acres of dead trees. Camping not allowed. In summer, the beach is popular with swimmers and dogs.

Inyo Craters (short day hike or cross-country ski from Mammoth Scenic Loop). Formed by a series of small but violent steam-blast eruptions, with mechanics similar to those that made the much older Ubehebe Crater in Death Valley. The most recent eruption in the region occurred here about 600 years ago, blanketing Mammoth with several inches of ash and adding to native stockpiles of obsidian for weaponry.

Knight Wheel (Old Mammoth Road, a half-mile west of Minaret Road). Hauled by mule teams from Mojave in 1878 to drive the Mammoth Mining Company's state-of-the-art 20-stamp mill (alas, it was never used to crush ore). The wheel was moved to its current location in 1902, where it was rigged as a Peltason water wheel to make electricity at the old Wildasinn Hotel. In the 1920s, Charlie Summers used it to power, among other things, an ice cream freezer. "Lights used to fluctuate as the voltage rose and fell and sometimes it would cut out entirely due to a trout getting in the nozzle," wrote C. Clarke Keely, "and Lloyd or Charlie would have to get out there with a rod and

ALTITUDE

The town of Mammoth lies between 7,500 and 8,500 feet above sea level, with Mammoth Mountain Inn nestled in at 9,000 feet. The air is thinner up here, with less oxygen and less humidity than at sea level. If you're coming up from the coast, no matter how strong you are, you might feel some effects of altitude sickness: muscle fatigue, insomnia, mild headaches, or slight shortness of breath. Some visitors are affected more than others—there doesn't seem to be much rhyme or reason to it. Dehydration is the primary complaint. It feels like a hangover. So go easy on yourself the first day: Drink loads of water (the tap here is closer to the source than anything you can buy in a bottle), take a dose of ibuprofen, keep the booze to a minimum the first night, and don't be afraid to take naps—after all, you're on vacation! Also: The sun doesn't play games up here. There's less gunk in the atmosphere to filter out the ultraviolet (UV) rays, so you'll want to wear those shades and slather on the highest SPF sunscreen you can find.

clean it out so the water would squirt on the buckets again." Today, the old wheel is surrounded by the latest "Creekhouse" phase of the Snowcreek development.

Mammoth Mountain Fumarole (north side of the ski mountain, near Chair 3). A fumarole is a vent hole to the magma chamber beneath a volcano. In April 2006, in a highly-publicized accident, three ski patrolmen died here of carbon dioxide exposure. Two of them were working to adjust the fence around the steamy sulfurous abyss when the snow gave way beneath them. Another saw them go and went in after. A monument was dedicated to all three at the top of the mountain on August 25, 2007—with big views from the crest of Hangman's Hollow.

EMMET HAYDEN'S CABIN, BUILT CIRCA 1927, NOW A POPULAR SPOT FOR SUMMER WEDDINGS

Town of Mammoth Lakes

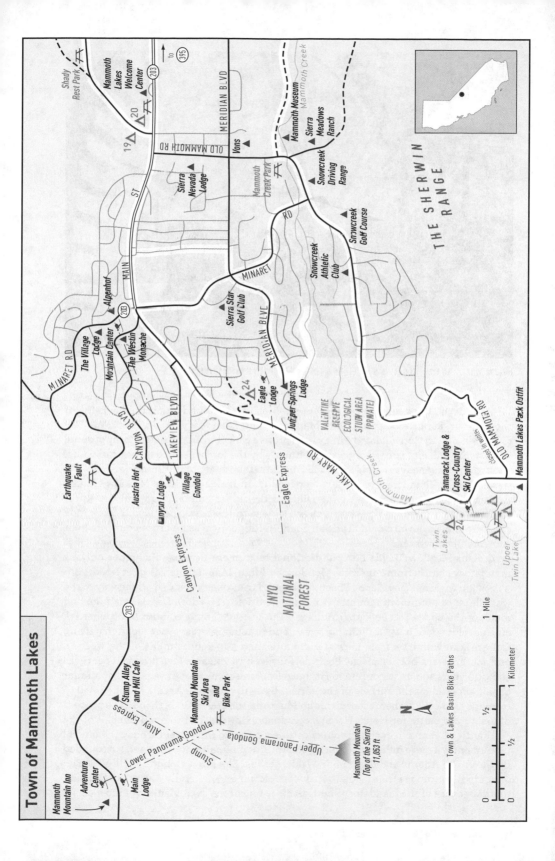

Mammoth Mountain Inn

Adventure Center

Main Lodge

Stump Alley and Mill Cafe

Alley Express

Mammoth Mountain Ski Area and Bike Park

Lower Panorama Gondola

Upper Panorama Gondola

Stump

Canyon Express

Mammoth Mountain (Top of the Sierra) 11,053 ft

INYO NATIONAL FOREST

Earthquake Fault

Austria Hof

Canyon Lodge

Village Gondola

MINARET RD

CANYON BLVD

LAKEVIEW BLVD

The Village Lodge

Mountain Center

The Westin Monache

Alpenhof

MAIN ST

Sierra Nevada Lodge

to 395

Mammoth Lakes Welcome Center

Shady Rest Park

△20

△19

203

OLD MAMMOTH RD

MERIDIAN BLVD

Mammoth Creek Park

Mammoth Creek

Mammoth Museum

Sierra Meadows Ranch

Vons

Snowcreek Driving Range

Snowcreek Golf Course

RD

MINARET

MERIDIAN BLVD

Sierra Star Golf Club

Snowcreek Athletic Club

△24

Eagle Lodge

Juniper Springs Lodge

Eagle Express

LAKE MARY RD

VALENTINE RESERVE ECOLOGICAL STUDY AREA (PRIVATE)

Mammoth Creek

Tamarack Lodge & Cross-Country Ski Center

OLD MAMMOTH RD

closed in winter

Mammoth Lakes Pack Outfit

Twin Lakes

Upper Twin Lake

△24

THE SHERWIN RANGE

N

Town & Lakes Basin Bike Paths

0   ½   1 Mile
0   ½   1 Kilometer

KNIGHT WHEEL, SITE OF WILDASINN'S HOTEL, NOW THE CREEKHOUSE AT SNOWCREEK

Mammoth Mines (off Lake Mary Road). Sites can be found along the backside of the Sherwin Range along upper Old Mammoth and Lake Mary Roads, from Mill City to the Mammoth Consolidated Mines Interpretive Site above Coldwater Campground. In 2017, the mill city site was closed indefinitely by the forest service for toxic cleanup, due to lingering heavy metals and such from nineteenth-century mining activity.

✪ **Minaret Vista** (crest of CA 203, between Main Lodge and Reds Meadow). Excellent easy-access viewpoint over the wilds of the upper San Joaquin and the Ritter Range, and back across the Long Valley Caldera to the east. Spectacular low-grade stroll from here upward along the San Joaquin Ridge. Access by cross-country ski or snowmobile in winter.

✪ **Reds Meadow/Devils Postpile National Monument** (access in summer only by mandatory shuttle from Panorama Gondola building, Main Lodge, Minaret Road; 760-934-2289; www.nps.gov/depo). Yosemite's boundaries once extended all the way to the west flank of Mammoth Mountain and included Reds Meadow, Devils Postpile, and much of the upper San Joaquin drainage. "But in 1905," ranger-naturalist Richard J. Hartesveldt wrote in 1952, "mining, water, and grazing interests succeeded in getting Congress to withdraw from park status more than 500 square miles of the western and southeastern portions." The Postpile, formed by a volcanic lava flow as recently as 100,000 years ago, is, according to Hartesveldt, "one of the best examples of columnar basalt exposed on the surface of the earth." By 1910 the whole area was scheduled to be made into yet another reservoir. John Muir and the Sierra Club, then in the process of losing the battle for Hetch Hetchy, convinced Howard Taft to avail himself of the Antiquities Act and to declare Devils Postpile a national monument. Today the official monument is a mere mile and a quarter square, but it remains above water, surrounded by the Ansel Adams and John Muir Wildernesses. Elevation along the still-wild San Joaquin River ranges from 7,800 to 7,100 feet—lower and generally warmer than Mammoth. Because of the mandatory shuttle, this is one of the least-visited yet most easily accessed wilderness areas in the Sierra Nevada. Rainbow Falls is a very worthwhile short hike through an old burn area (2.5 miles round-trip). **Reds Meadow Resort** (760-934-2345; www.redsmeadow.com), at the last shuttle stop, has a general store that is very popular with Pacific Crest Trail through-hikers, offering cold beer, a café with good root beer floats, a pack outfit, mineral-spring-fed hot showers, and rustic cabins. Campers, resort guests, fishermen with float tubes, and people with disabilities can bring in their own vehicles. The road and all facilities are closed in winter.

✪ **Top of the Sierra Interpretive Center**. Ride the scenic Mammoth Mountain gondola from the Adventure Center all the way to the summit, at 11,053 feet. Tour a variety of indoor exhibits on geology, volcanic history, seismology, weather patterns, and cultural heritage, plus unparalleled views stretching from Mono Lake to the Minarets and across the Upper Owens Valley to 14,252-foot White Mountain Peak, the third highest point in California. Snack bar.

Valentine Reserve (Between Juniper Springs and Old Mammoth Road; 760-935-4356; vesr.ucnrs.org). A 156-acre field research station and natural reserve administered by the University of California, Santa Barbara, protected from grazing and entry since the end of the 1900s. Some neighbors grumble that the forest here is overgrown to the point of being Mammoth's biggest fire hazard. Check the Web site or local papers for upcoming tours, summer camps for kids, and community outreach events.

JUNE LAKE LOOP

June Lake is a sleepy fishing-resort village of mostly middle-class Southern California heritage, whose glacier-carved setting has, for reasons that become immediately apparent upon cresting so-called Oh! Ridge, been compared with the Tyrol and the Italian Lakes District. There are three natural lakes along CA 158, otherwise known as the June Lake Loop: June, Gull, and Silver. In 1916, Roy and Nancy Carson established a rustic fishing camp on the shores of the last, where today the **Silver Lake Resort** (CA 158; 760-648-7525; www.silverlakeresort.net)—owned and operated by the Jones family—still offers a variety of basic cabin and guest house accommodations, a popular home-style café with what some locals consider the best breakfast in the Eastern Sierra, and a general store. Below Silver Lake, to the north along Rush Creek, is Grant Lake, a storage reservoir completed in 1941 by the Los Angeles Department of Water and Power to contain the flow of the various feeder creeks into Mono Lake. The now-faded June Lake Lodge was once a popular stopover for Hollywood celebrities (Charlie Chaplin, Buster Keaton, Ingrid Bergman, Samuel Goldwyn). June Lake

DEVILS POSTPILE, 1939. TO GET A SENSE OF THE SIZE OF THE SITE, NOTE THE MAN SITTING IN THE LOWER LEFT CORNER R.H. ANDERSON, COURTESY NPS, YNP

proper is ideal for swimming and boating in summer. In 1961, Bud Hayward put in the beginnings of a ski area at the southwest end of Horseshoe Canyon—later to be purchased by Dave McCoy. Now run by the same folks who run Mammoth, the June Mountain Ski Area is a delightfully low-key, family-style place which also happens to have direct access to some of the biggest big-mountain backcountry skiing in the continental U.S. At its northern end, CA 158 rejoins CA 395 at the Mono Craters.

MONO LAKE AND LEE VINING

> *This is the most remarkable lake I have ever seen. It lies in a basin at the height of 6,800 feet above the sea. Like the Dead Sea, it is without an outlet. The streams running into it all evaporate from the surface, so of course it is very salt—not common salt. There are hot springs in it, which feed it with peculiar mineral salts. It is said that it contains borax, also boracic acid, in addition to the materials generally found in saline lakes. The waters are very clear and very heavy—they have a nauseous taste. When still, it looks like oil, it is so thick, and it is not easily disturbed. Although nearly 20 miles long it is often so smooth that the opposite mountains are mirrored in it as in a glass. The water feels slippery to the touch and will wash grease from the hands, even when cold, more readily than common hot water and soap. I washed some woolens in it, and it was quicker and easier than any "suds" I ever saw. It washed our silk handkerchiefs, giving them luster as if new.*
> —William H. Brewer, 1863

Joseph Walker passed by here any number of times, but didn't think much of the place. Lt. Tredwell Moore, United States Army, chasing Tenaya's band of renegade Indians out of Yosemite in 1852, saw the lake and named it for the Indians who lived there—and also found some gold flakes. Leroy "Lee" Vining was among the first to come over the pass the following year. The name Mono is a variant of the Yokuts word *Monache*, or "people of the flies," so named because they made their primary living harvesting and eating the larvae of the alkali flies that to this day swarm and breed, by the millions, along the edge of the lake. "The Indians come from far and near to gather them," wrote Brewer. "The worms are dried in the sun, the shell rubbed off, when a yellowish kernel remains, like a small yellow grain of rice. This is oily, very nutritious . . . it does not taste bad, and if one were ignorant of its origin, it would make fine soup. Gulls, ducks, snipe, frogs, and Indians fatten on it."

Vining never found much gold, but others did, and before long he was making good money milling lumber and selling it to miners in Lakeview and Aurora. Samuel Clemens spent some time in Aurora in the 1860s before he landed a reporter's gig at the Territorial Enterprise in Virginia City and started using the pseudonym Mark Twain. Of Mono Lake he would later write: "It is one of the strangest freaks of Nature to be found in any land."

Vining was over in Aurora one day, having made a lumber delivery there; he got drunk at the Exchange Saloon and sometime thereafter met his demise when his own loaded pistol went off in his pocket. "Borax" Smith made his first million near here, mining the very detergent that Brewer used to wash his hankies in Mono Lake—the stuff that would eventually make Death Valley and Ronald Reagan (host of the popular Boraxo-brand TV series *Death Valley Days*) famous. The town of Lakeview got a post office in 1928, renaming itself Leevining (one word) after its unlucky founder, so as to avoid confusion with another Lakeview down south in Riverside County. In 1957, the

FROM ABOVE THE TIOGA GAS MART, LOOKING NORTH TO THE BODIE HILLS AND THE SWEETWATERS CAT CONNOR

United States Board on Geographic Names declared that the town should be called Lee Vining (two words).

Beginning in 1941, with the completion of Grant Lake, Crowley Lake, and a series of diversion tunnels beneath the Mono Craters south of Lee Vining, the City of Los Angeles began siphoning the water from Mono Lake's feeder streams and thus set about creating another Owens-style dry lake. By 1962 Mono had dropped 25 vertical feet. By 1982 it had fallen another 20—to an all-time low of 6,372 feet. Salinity levels doubled, algae photosynthesis lagged, brine shrimp had difficulty reproducing, tufa formation stopped, previously safe bird-nesting sites were suddenly accessible to coyotes, the air filled with poison dust and particulates, and so on. In 1978, an ornithologist by the name of David Gaines formed the Mono Lake Committee, took Los Angeles to court, and 16 years later—in 1994—won.

The city continues to divert into its aqueducts approximately 16 percent of water that would otherwise go to the lake, but the lake is coming back. The plan is to return it to a level of 6,391 feet. By the spring of 2017, after four years of severe drought and one record winter, the lake was still about 10 feet shy of the target.

South Tufa (Mono Lake Tufa State Reserve, south of Lee Vining off CA 120 East; 760-647-6331). Boardwalk stroll to the beach, signage showing historic subsidence of the lake and projected goals for its restoration. See the progress since Pink Floyd's *Wish You Were Here* album cover was shot here in the early 1970s. See the flies. Open every day, all year. Guided tours in summer. Bring drinking water. Lovely cross-country skiing when conditions permit.

High Sierra Brine Shrimp (54872 CA 395; 760-647-6122; www.hsbrineshrimp.com). Quantities of rare brine shrimp (*Artemia monica*) are harvested, frozen, enriched, and packaged here for use as a tropical fish food. It's the world's only supplier of the stuff.

Old School House Museum (Hess Park off CA 395; 760-647-6461; www.mono basinhistory.org). Artifacts, implements, photos, books, and maps documenting the cultural history of the Mono Basin, including the old paddle wheel from the 1930s pleasure boat *Venita*. Outdoor exhibits include Mellie Bly O'Bryan's visionary Upside-Down

ON SAFARI IN THE BODIE HILLS

We bounced into Bodie the way most of the lumber and firewood once did, up from the shores of Mono Lake on the old Cottonwood Canyon wagon road. It was mid-July, but up here where the Sierra Nevada meets the Great Basin, summer had only just taken hold. Beckett (3) slept in his car seat in the back, slumped over on a pillow against the door. Jasper (6) looked out at the hills. The dog, his head out the front window, gulped air spiked with sweet phlox, bitterbrush, and sage, and surveyed the landscape for jackrabbits.

The infamous Wild West town site—since 1962 preserved in a state of "arrested decay"—was at its fit-for-the-big-screen best, with cumulous clouds over the western ridges and great sidelong shafts of late-afternoon sun on antique timbers and spring-green hills. Even at five minutes to closing, the parking lot overflowed with dusty RV's and rental cars. But less than a mile down-canyon, along the trickle of Bodie Creek, what was once the main (and notoriously bandit-infested) stage road to Aurora turned rutted and wild—and empty.

At the edge of a meadow thick with wild daisies, before the Nevada state line, we turned onto a lonely, two-track Jeep trail. I locked the hubs and shifted into 4-wheel-drive.

Up we climbed into the heart of the Bodie Wilderness Study Area (WSA), one of three such designated areas surrounding the state historic park that together make up nearly half of the Bureau of Land Management's 200,000-acre Bodie Hills Complex. Because of the primeval nature of the landscape, the exceptional biodiversity, the critical water sources and habitat (including for threatened species like the greater sage grouse and the Lahontan cutthroat trout), the possibilities for solitude, and the outstanding geological, cultural, and scenic value of these areas, they were inventoried by the BLM back in 1979 as having potential for wilderness designation.

Since then, the BLM has had to toe a delicate line while waiting for Congress to decide whether to protect these areas or release them so they can be developed. On the one hand, the agency is required to honor historical activities such as mining (with valid claims) and off-road vehicle use (on existing roads and trails). On the other hand, by law, it must manage the areas "in a manner so as not to impair [their] suitability for preservation for wilderness."

We pitched our camp with some friends at an old fire ring at the edge of Dry Lake, at about 8,000 feet, on a high plateau. A band of pronghorn frolicked beside the cows on the stubble grass playa. To the east rose the Beauty Peak cinder cone; to the west rose the twin summits of Bodie Mountain and Potato Peak, dark colonies of willow and quaking aspen clustered in their folds.

With the day's last light fading over the snow-dappled Sweetwater Range, the boys watched their first satellite run across the sky. A barn owl hovered for a minute or two over our little campfire, as if to study marshmallow roasting techniques. Later, when the boys were zipped into their bags, the coyotes—dozens of them, it seemed—began a round of yipping and shrieking out in the darkness, all around us. The next morning, along the edges of the basalt flows, we came upon ancient petroglyphs and chippings of obsidian. We found bleached cow bones, pincushion phlox, pennyroyal, waist-high thickets of red columbines, and Basque sheepherder inscriptions dating back to 1913.

"You can see them sitting here," said our friend John Dittli, a photographer, noting how radically the outside world had changed in a century. This place, by contrast, was still essentially the same as when the first people came though 10,000 years ago.

In the afternoon we made our way back through Bodie. Our vehicles climbed up along the flanks of Potato Peak to the headwaters of Rough Creek—one of two streams in the Bodie Hills determined by the BLM to be eligible for federal Wild and Scenic River status. We splashed in the cool, clear water, walked barefoot in the grass, and strolled through fields of wild iris

SPRINGTIME IN THE BODIE HILLS JOHN DITTLI

and onion to drink from the springs. Then, before heading down Aurora Canyon, back to civilization and pizza at the Virginia Creek Settlement, we stopped off to explore the abandoned Paramount mercury mine.

The Paramount site, its fifty-year-old mine works and tailings piles now in the early stages of reclamation by wild aspen groves, "is rated as having a high potential for occurrence of gold, silver and mercury," according to a recent BLM report, and is of great interest to Electrum, a gold mining company that already has begun exploration. "Developing a gold mine here," says The Wilderness Society's Sally Miller, "would cut out the ecological heart of the Bodie Hills. Mining would pollute the water, harm wildlife, and forever scar the landscape."

To secure permanent protection for this special place, The Wilderness Society and other organizations formed the Bodie Hills Conservation Partnership (bodiehills.org). "We are developing a plan with other stakeholders to protect the area's outstanding natural and cultural values, enhance recreational opportunities, and help boost the local economy," Miller explains.

With legislation floated in Congress to drop protection of all remaining WSA's across the country, including in the Bodie Hills, the future of this unique landscape is far from certain.

TUFA, MONO LAKE JOEL ST. MARIE

House. Open in summer only. The park is an excellent place for a picnic, supplied by the Mono Mart or Tioga Toomey.

○ **Bodie State Historic Park** (CA 270 south of Lee Vining, 13 miles east of CA 395; 760-647-6445; www.parks.ca.gov/bodie). Waterman Body (or William Bodey) discovered small amounts of gold here in the 1860s, back in the days when spelling was an arcane form of necromancy. Not much came of the place until the Standard Company found a big vein in 1877, and before long 10,000 people were trying to make a go of

BODIE HILLS JOHN DITTLI

it here. Timber for building was brought by Chinese-built rail from Mono Mills on the south side of Mono Lake. There were two banks, a Chinatown (complete with opium dens), a red-light district, a school, churches, electricity (from 1893), and several dozen saloons. Many volumes of Wild West stories and $100 million in gold bullion came out of this place. Much of the town burned down in 1932; what remained was abandoned not long after. Designated a National Historic Landmark in 1961 and made a state park the following year, the whole area is now preserved in an interesting state of "arrested decay," which means that dust is allowed to collect on the array of valuable artifacts left behind, but buildings are kept from collapsing. No camping, no collecting. Both roads in are generally closed in winter due to drifted snow, but the park is always open and staffed by at least one ranger (9 AM–6 PM in summer; 9 AM–4 PM in winter). Winter access is by snowmobile or cross-country skis.

✳ To Do

BACKCOUNTRY SKIING, CLIMBING, AND MOUNTAINEERING From Rock Creek to Virginia Lakes, every side canyon offers access—by skin or by boot—to the heights of the John Muir and Ansel Adams Wildernesses. Big peaks abound. And granite crags. And tight couloirs for fast, steep descents. And out of Mammoth and June Lake, some of the best, easiest-access front-country stashes in the Lower 48. Get a copy of Dan Mingori and Nate Greenberg's definitive and heavily field-tested *Backcountry Skiing California's Eastern Sierra* (Wolverine, 2014), or, better, yet download the rakkup app for your smart device (on iTunes and Google Play). Check the Eastern Sierra Avalanche Center (www.esavalanche.org) for snow conditions. Chat with the folks at Mammoth Mountaineering (361 Old Mammoth Rd.; 760-934-4191; see above) to make sure that you have everything you need. Be prepared; be careful; know what you're doing; bring a beacon, a shovel, and a probe; go with a guide.

    Sierra Mountain Guides (June Lake; 760-648-1122; www.sierramtnguides.com). Rock climbing, ice climbing, mountaineering, backcountry skiing. Technical and avalanche courses. Veteran internationally-certified guides Howie Schwartz, Neil Satterfield, and friends.

    For Bishop-based guides offering services throughout the High Sierra, see Chapter 4.

BIRD-WATCHING Mono Lake is said to be the birthplace of nearly every gull in California. It's a major staging area for huge populations of migratory shorebirds, such as the unique Wilson's phalarope. The many hot springs and warm-water tributaries of the Upper Owens River provide unique habitat for hundreds of species. Check the Eastern Sierra Audubon Society's Web site, www.esaudubon.org, for hot spots as far north as Crowley Lake. The "Eastern Sierra Birding Trail Map" is available online (www.easternsierrabirdingtrail.org), and through most local businesses and bookstores. Also consult the Sierra Nevada Aquatic Research Lab's online list of local species at http://vesr.nrs.ucsb.edu/snarl/natural-history/birds-snarl.

BOATING Hundreds of alpine and subalpine lakes, as well as two large Los Angeles Department of Water and Power reservoirs (Crowley and Grant) provide opportunities that range from kayaking to kiteboarding, from stand-up paddling to puttering around some distant shore in an outboard-driven aluminum dinghy. A variety of marinas and independent outfitters offer hourly, half-day, and full-day rentals throughout the summer season.

CANOEING ON LAKE MARY

PADDLING AFTER MARK TWAIN

It was already well past dawn when we shoved off the sand and slipped out onto the quicksilver surface of Mono Lake. It was like floating on a sea of photographic fixer, across perfectly resolved upside-down images of surreal carbonate towers, the snow-ribboned wall of the Eastern Sierra Nevada, hundreds of gulls strewn about, in double, like so many half-flat beach balls left in the pool after a busy holiday, the cloudless sky.

There were three of us that morning, the only ones on the lake: Brant Miller and myself in Brant's old canoe and fearless Andy Bourne on his stand-up paddle board. We'd driven the quick half hour up from Mammoth, the sun rising over the craters and the old-growth pine forests, to meet at Navy Beach. The original notion had been for all three of us to head out on paddle boards and hopefully—conditions permitting—make a quick passage across to explore Paoha, an uninhabited island of clay and ash and vaporous fumaroles three nautical miles off the south shore.

In the 1860s Mark Twain had undertaken to pull out there in a rowboat, with his friend Higbie, and had survived to write about it. There'd seemed no reason we couldn't, all these years later, do it on late-model stand-up paddleboards. Then we began to hear stories of sudden, violent squalls, of gale-whipped waves, of swamped canoes, alkali burns, and killer foam.

Mono Lake is considered one of the oldest lakes in North America. It's all that's left of a once-vast prehistoric inland sea that geologists refer to as Lake Russell, after the pioneering nineteenth-century geologist Israel Russell, who, in 1889, described the strange remnant, some 70 square miles in extent, as "a wide sheet of burnished metal" resting on the desert plain. "No one would think," he continued, "that the water which seems so bright and enticing is in reality so dense and alkaline that it would quickly cause the death of a traveler who could find no other with which to quench his thirst."

The lake is fed by freshwater streams straight from the High Sierra. But it has no outlet—except by evaporation. In Russell's day, the water was about thirty percent saltier than the ocean. Today, after sixty years of diversion of its feeder streams by an ever-thirstier City of Los Angeles, more than 300 miles to the south, Mono Lake is more than three times as salty as the Pacific Ocean. It also contains fluoride, sulfur, arsenic, uranium, and no small amount of boron, which last is used to make all manner of household conveniences, from laundry detergent to insecticides to fiberglass insulation. The botanist William Brewer, in 1863, found the lakewater cleansed the grease from his hands "more readily than hot water and soap," and made washing clothes "easier and quicker than in any 'suds' I ever saw." Twain washed his clothes in it too, with relish, but did not recommend swimming in it (or capsizing in it), "for that venomous water would eat a man's eyes out like fire," he claimed, "and burn him out inside, too."

There are two shops in Mammoth—Wave Rave and Footloose—that rent stand-up paddle boards for use on any of the dozens of road-accessible freshwater lakes in the region, from Rock Creek Lake to the Mammoth Lakes Basin to Lake Tenaya up in Yosemite National Park. In recent summers I've stood and paddled on Mary and Horseshoe and June and Grant, and only soaked myself in cold Alpine water twice—once in high winds and another trying to paddle up a creek against rising whitewater. But neither establishment had any interest in letting me paddle one of their boards on Mono Lake. And so we went with Brant's canoe, reasoning that we'd thus have more capacity to bring supplies in case of emergency. And that if when we got out there we deemed conditions even remotely threatening, we'd be content with a simple paddle along the shore.

The source of inspiration for this foray was a guided kayak tour I'd been on a few weeks earlier with Stuart Wilkinson and his wife Sue Johnston, owners of the longstanding outfitter Caldera Kayaks. That morning too had been so fine, the air so still and silent, the whole great bowl of the Mono Basin so perfectly tame, that even the concept of wind seemed—at least at the outset—implausible. Collectively, our little group boasted kayaking experience ranging from the Sea of Cortez to Long Island Sound. We'd begun that day's adventure in the gravel parking lot in the fast-warming sun, listening to the chatter of blackbirds in the rabbit brush, reviewing paddlestroke techniques and rescue options. "Hang onto the kayak," Stuart advised with a wry smile. "Or we'll be forced to choose between you and the boat."

We followed Sue and Stuart out through the tufa formations (made famous at the height of L.A.'s water diversion by a photograph on the inner sleeve of Pink Floyd's 1975 album *Wish You Were Here*). We paddled and drifted over bubbling underwater springs, saw first-hand how the mineral towers were built. We learned about scuba-diving alkali flies, how the local tribe's kids, back in the day, used to wade out into the water to harvest the pupae, like so many kernels of oily rice, to be ground into a kind of flour. We watched an osprey returning to its nest with a fresh-caught rainbow trout in its talons. We scattered before us whole rafts of willets and grebes and red-necked phalaropes. We learned that the phalaropes were on layover, eating flies and doubling their weight before continuing on to South America for the winter, and that the grebes arrive and leave under the cover of darkness. We learned about the commercial value of brine shrimp, about the public trust doctrine in its application to water use, about polyandry and reverse osmosis and acoustic transparency. We saw thousands of gulls feeding at the freshwater inlet of Rush Creek.

Rounding a minor nub of land known as Windy Point, on our outbound run, Sue had remarked with a wink: "Hopefully we won't get to see why it's called that." Indeed, it wasn't until later, a little before noon, as we were making our last few strokes back to the landing, with a telltale midday test cloud rising from the U.S. Army Depot over in Hawthorne, Nevada, that the first squall patterns appeared on the water.

When we came back three weeks later, the phalaropes were gone. The grebes were gone. The fledgling ospreys had taken flight. We held a brief floating conference out among the tufa. We looked at our watches. We looked across to the island.

It couldn't take more than an hour to paddle across at full tilt, ventured Brant.

As long as we can make it back by noon, I said.

We were not at all prepared for the worst. We had about a liter of water between us, a couple of home-made sandwiches, and sandals for exploring in. But as Mark Twain had put it nearly a century and a half earlier: "the morning was so quiet and sunny, and the lake so smooth and glassy and dead, that we could not resist the temptation." And so we dug our paddles into the heavy water and pulled—hard.

It was only about 300 years ago—around the time of the founding of St. Petersburg by Peter the Great and that of New Orleans by the French Mississippi Company—that Paoha Island rose from the waters, the youngest in a local chain of volcanic hotspots that is itself the youngest volcanic range in North America. Stretching from south of Devils Postpile National Monument and Mammoth Mountain (itself a dormant volcano) to the northern edge of Mono Lake, this archipelago of domes and craters, basaltic columns, outcroppings of pure volcanic glass, hot springs, and fumaroles has been referred to as a sister to Yellowstone. The Long Valley caldera, which stretches from Mammoth to the Glass Mountains, is a massive crater formed 760,000 years ago in an eruption that sent ash across what is now the western United States, as far as Nebraska. It is nearly fifty times the size of Kilauea's caldera on the island of Hawaii.

One of the best ways to get an overview of the region's volcanic points of interest is to take a scenic ride up Mammoth Mountain's main gondola from the Adventure Center to the Top of the Sierra at 11,053 feet. Inside, there are exhibits on glaciation, plate tectonics, earthquakes, and volcanism. On a fair day (as most are in the summer), you can walk out along the ridge and look north across the Inyo-Mono craters to Mono Lake, thirty miles to the north. Another option is to sign on for a sunrise hot air balloon flight with veteran pilot Dave Metcalf of Mammoth Balloon Adventures. Rising gently from the sagelands at the heart of the caldera, you get an unparalleled view of the geology of the basin: the numerous hot springs, pools, and geothermal vents, the resurgent domes, and the blue-ribbon trout waters and glistening oxbows of Hot Creek and the Upper Owens River.

Paddling for our lives, well-splashed with salt and stinging water, we made the shore of Paoha in just under half an hour. It was almost too easy. And yet the piles of yellowish foam along the beach gave testimony to yesterday's wind, and to the hard fact that if and when the breeze came up we would be working against it all the way home. Our exploration of the island would need to be brief. We pulled our craft up onto the bank of dried clay, above the flies. There was no sign of Andy. (Later we would learn that he'd made it almost to the island, paddling on his knees for speed and stability, but then had had to turn back to go to work.) We drank most of our good water right there on the beach, put the dregs in a daypack along with the sandwiches, and took off overland, jogging, in search of hot springs and freshwater.

We climbed a mountain of ancient, powdery ash, followed a ridgeline, leaped like goats down a brush-choked canyon, across a cove of white sand ending in a steaming, belching, sulfurous knob. Here, it seemed, was the source of the word Paoha, which, as Stuart had explained on the kayak tour, derives from a native word meaning, roughly, "diminutive long-haired wavy spirits rising from hot springs." Here Twain, having brought no food or water, had mused about the possibility of cooking gull's eggs in boiling mineral water.

We bushwacked our way back up from the cove, through a dusty clawing jungle of grease-wood, to a pair of concrete ruins where one pioneer family is said once to have run 300 head of goats, raised corn ten feet tall, and dreamed of a hot springs resort. Sunburnt, thirsty, scraped-up, and tired, I found myself drifting into nostalgia for simpler adventures of previous weeks: the stroll across the green meadows of the Upper Tuolumne in Yosemite with my boys, the geology talk in the cool shade of Parson's Memorial Lodge, the electric-bicycle cruise up the new Mammoth bike path to Horseshoe Lake with my mother. Eventually we emerged into a marsh and fought our way through the reeds to the edge of the island. Easing our legs burning and raw into the lake, we bent and drank the cool, sweet water pouring from the rocks.

Twain and Higbie, whether in fact or for the sake of narrative, had worse luck. They never found fresh water. And by the time they got back to their landing spot it was late in the afternoon. The wind was up and their boat was drifting loose down the shore. Higbie swam and managed to recover the boat, but the crossing was brutal: he recounted that "the billows ran very high and were capped with foaming crests, the heavens were hung with black, and the wind blew with great fury."

Brant and I, on the other hand, found the canoe right where we'd left it. We shoved off just before noon into only the slightest breath of breeze off the Sierra. Paddling with considerably less alacrity than we had that morning, we nevertheless made it to the shore—and to cold beers—in less than three quarters of an hour. Over glorious burgers and fries at the Mono Cone in Lee Vining, we celebrated our return to the mainland as if we'd been gone for months. And then we began to plot our next foray.

Caldera Kayaks (Mammoth Lakes; 760-934-1691; www.calderakayak.com). Variety of kayaks for use on Crowley and Mono Lakes. Guided natural history tours of Mono Lake's rookeries, springs, and ancient tufa formations, including kayaks and gear. Bring your own water and lunch. See sidebar above.

Crowley Lake Fish Camp Marina (off CA 395; 760-935-4301; www.crowleylake fishcamp.com). Fishing boats, 15 and 30 horsepower. Tackle shop.

Convict Lake Marina (Convict Lake; 760-934-3800; www.convictlake.com/activities /marina.html). Fishing boats, pontoon boats, canoes, and kayaks.

Gull Lake Marina (June Lake Loop; 760-648-7539). Pontoon boats, flat-bottom boats, canoes.

June Lake Marina (June Lake; 760-648-7726; www.junelakemarina.net). Valcos with Evinrudes. Bait and tackle shop.

Lake Mary Marina (Lake Mary Road, Mammoth Lakes; 760-934-5353). Fleet of fishing dinghies, some with motors, some without. Store.

Mammoth Kayaks & Paddleboards (760-924-3075; mammothkayaks.com). Sit-on-top kayaks and stand-up paddleboards for rent on the beach at June Lake. $25 per hour.

Pokonobe Resort (Lake Mary, Mammoth Lakes; 760-934-2437; www.pokonoberesort.com). Pontoon boats, motorboats, rowboats, canoes, kayaks, and pedal boats. General store.

Silver Lake Resort (Silver Lake, June Lake Loop; 760-648-7525; www.silverlakeresort.net). Fishing boats with outboard motors; canoes and kayaks.

Twin Lakes Store (off Lake Mary Road beyond Tamarack Lodge, Mammoth Lakes; 760-934-7295). Rowboat and canoe rentals, general store.

Woods Lodge (Lake George, Mammoth Lakes; 760-934-2261). Motorboat and rowboat rentals. Tackle and snack shop.

CROSS-COUNTRY SKIING AND SNOWSHOEING The Mammoth Lakes Nordic Trail System includes 7 miles of groomed trails in and around town, with a new trail under construction that will link the town with Tamarack and the Lakes Basin. The Inyo National Forest also offers a network of trails off the Mammoth Scenic Loop to the north of town. Pick up a "Winter Recreation Map" at the Welcome Center. Also see Rock Creek Lodge, above.

Tamarack Cross Country Ski Center (Twin Lakes; 760-934-2442; www.tamaracklodge.com). Package rentals: striding and skating skis, snowshoes. Lessons and guided tours. More than 20 miles of expertly groomed trails.

SKATE SKIING AT HORSESHOE LAKE, TAMARACK BRAD PEATROSS, COURTESY MAMMOTH RESORTS

ON THE MOUNTAIN: ACCESS, SERVICES, AND LOGISTICS

Mammoth Mountain Ski Area Mammoth Resorts (referred to by locals as simply The Mountain) operates 29 lifts—including two high-speed "six-packs," nine high-speed "quads," and two gondolas—which together accommodate 50,000 rides per hour, serving 3,100 vertical feet and more than 3,500 acres of skiable terrain. Even on the busiest days of the season, there is likely to be more traffic at mid-mountain than at the bottom. During big storms, the top of the mountain and all upper lifts will close, then re-open at some highly anticipated but impossible-to-predict moment—not just when the sun comes out, but after the completion of avalanche control. There are four main access points to the mountain—**Eagle Lodge**, **Canyon Lodge** (served by the Village Gondola), **Stump Alley** (The Mill), and **Main Lodge**. There are dining facilities at each, as well as at mid-station (McCoy's), at the top of the mountain (Top of the Sierra), and, conditions permitting, at the bottom of Chair 14 (The Outpost).

Lift tickets can be purchased at any of the four day lodges, or at the bottom of the Village Gondola. Chairs 1 and 2, out of Main Lodge and Stump Alley, respectively, are the first to open each season and the last to close. Eagle, on the opposite side of the mountain, has the shortest season.

Canyon Lodge, because of its proximity to the Village and to a majority of condominium complexes, tends to be the most congested. Mammoth's ski and snowboard school operates out of Eagle, Canyon, and Main Lodge, with full-service child care available at Main Lodge only. The only lift service in summer—for scenic rides and bike park access—is from Main Lodge. For general information and reservations, call the Mammoth Mountain Ski Area at 760-934-0745 or 1-800-MAMMOTH.

Mammoth ski and snow report: 760-934-6166 or 1-888-SNOWRPT; www.mammothmountain.com

Avalanche and snowpack information: patrol.mammothmountain.com
Local weather: 760-934-7669
Road conditions: 1-800-427-ROAD
Race department: 760-934-0642
Winter on-mountain naturalist tours: 760-924-5500

MAIN LODGE (8,909 FEET)

The original base lodge, often the least crowded lunch spot on the mountain. Bar, food court, sundeck barbecue, coin-operated day lockers, first aid, preferred parking, ticket sales, equipment rentals, sport shop, host services. Ski and snowboard school combined with child-care backup (if your kid decides to quit ski school, you may not have to come to the rescue).

Adventure Center (Gondola building, summer only): 760-934-0706
Bike Repair (Gondola building, summer only): 760-934-2571, ext. 3269
Broadway Marketplace Food Court (third floor): 760-934-2571, ext. 3265
Lost and Found/Basket Check (second floor): 760-934-0667
Mammoth Moments Photo Service (third floor): 760-924-8395
The Mountain Shop (second floor): 760-934-0677
Performance Demo Shop (second floor): 760-934-2571, ext. 3280
Rental Shop (first floor): 760-934-2571, ext. 3270
Security (first floor): 760-934-0697
Small World Child Day Care (downstairs at Mammoth Mountain Inn): 760-934-0646
Ski Patrol (first floor): 760-934-2571, ext. 3276
Ski and Snowboard Repair (second floor): 760-934-2571, ext. 3280

Ski and Snowboard School (Schoolyard): 760-934-2571, ext. 3185
Ticket Office (first floor): 760-934-2571, ext. 3671
Tusks Bar (third floor): 760-934-2571, ext. 3227
Woollywood Kids (Schoolyard): 760-934-2571, ext. 3285
The Yodler (across parking lot from Main Lodge): 760-934-2571, ext. 2234

STUMP ALLEY (8,790 FEET)

Small day lodge, café and bar, sundeck, ticket sales. No other services. Easy-access parking;
a favorite for dog owners and RVs.
Mill Café: 760-934-2571, ext. 3675

CANYON LODGE (8,343 FEET)

Still known as Warming Hut II by longtime Mammoth diehards, Canyon is now the busiest of all
four day lodges. Find a parking spot early in the morning, pay for preferred parking, walk, or
arrive by shuttle or Village Gondola. Bustling après-ski bar, food court, outdoor "beach" barbecue (endless-loop classic rock on the public address system), coin-operated day lockers,
first aid, ticket sales, equipment rentals, sport shop, host services. Coffee, doughnuts, and
pretzels on the third floor. Excellent adult and kid ski and snowboard school with the most
varied beginner terrain on the mountain, but without child-care backup as offered at Main
Lodge (i.e., if your kid decides to quit ski school here, you have to come to the rescue).
Canyon Kids (second floor): 760-934-2571, ext. 3312 or 3398
Grizzly Bar (fourth floor): 760-934-2571, ext. 3226
Grizzly Square Food Court (fourth floor): 760-934-2571
Rental Shop (third floor): 760-934-2571, ext. 3370
Repair and Demo Center (second floor): 760-934-2571, ext. 3381
Security/Lost and Found/Basket Check (third floor): 760-934-2571, ext. 3367
Ski and Snowboard School (third floor): 760-934-2571, ext. 3389
Sports Shop (third floor): 760-934-2571, ext. 3377
Ticket Sales (third floor): 760-934-2571, ext. 3771

EAGLE LODGE (7,953 FEET)

Groundbreaking on the construction of a permanent Eagle Lodge is on indefinite hold, though
new ownership and financing deals have brought it back to the top of the slate. In the meantime, it all happens inside a high-tech Quonset hut dubbed "Little Eagle." Ticket sales, equipment rentals, sport shop, bar and restaurant. Adult and kids' ski and snowboard school, no
child-care backup (i.e., if your kid decides to quit ski school, you have to come to the rescue).
Eagle Sports: 760-934-0725, number 4
Rental Shop: 760-934-0725, number 3
Talons Bar: 760-934-0725, number 1
Ticket Sales: 760-934-0725, number 2

THE MOUNTAIN CENTER AT THE VILLAGE GONDOLA (8,100 FEET)

Ticket sales, equipment rentals, and sport shop. Overnight ski storage available under the
Village Gondola.
Family Center (third floor): 760-934-2571, ext. 2071
Skier Services (sport shop, rentals, repairs; first floor): 760-934-2571, ext. 3057

McCOY STATION (9,630 FEET)

Midstation on Panorama Gondola offers busy food-court dining, indoor and outdoor bars, a bakery and waffle counter, as well as exclusive European-style table service at Parallax Restaurant (reservations recommended).

Marketplace Food Court: 760-934-2571, ext. 3209

Parallax Restaurant: 760-934-2571, ext. 3118

Sports Shop: 760-934-2571, ext. 3330

Steeps Bar: 760-934-2571, ext. 3374

TOP OF THE SIERRA (11,053 FEET)

At the top of Panorama Gondola; interpretive exhibits, 360-degree views of the High Sierra and beyond, café/snack bar, professional photography, and ski patrol.

Café: 760-934-2571, ext. 3755

OUTPOST 14 (9,320 FEET)

Mammoth's "backside" open-air sundeck, recently offering panini sandwiches and not much for kids.

Grill: 760-934 2571, ext. 3214

THE TOP OF THE SIERRA (11,053 FEET), WITH A STORM BREWING OVER THE RITTER RANGE

DOGSLEDDING A French Canadian ex-bootlegger by the name of Tex Cushion ran a team of dogs here in the late 1920s, providing passenger and freight service for the tiny hamlet of Mammoth Camp. You can see what that might have been like with the help of **Mammoth Dog Teams** (760-914-1019; www.mammothdogteams.com). Half-hour and one-hour rides leave from Smokey Bear Flat off CA 395, weather and trail conditions permitting. Kennel tours and overnight trips can be arranged.

DOWNHILL SKIING AND SNOWBOARDING **Mammoth Mountain** (1-800-MAM-MOTH; www.mammothmountain.com). See the "On the Mountain" sidebar.

June Mountain Ski and Snowboard Resort (CA 158; 760-648-7733 or 1-888-JUNEMTN; www.junemountain.com). Laid-back, uncrowded, family-style ski area. Good bet for beginner and intermediate skiers, for powder days when the top of Mammoth is shut down, and for access to the steep and deep backcountry. Sports school, rentals and demos, on-mountain dining. Mammoth lift tickets and passes valid here.

FISHING There are countless lakes, reservoirs, rivers, spring streams, and high alpine brooks, most stocked by the Department of Fish and Game (760-934-2664; www.dfg.ca.gov) with hand-fed Alpers trout. Mono County fishing season runs from the last

MAMMOTH DOG TEAMS BILL BECHER

Saturday in April to November 15. From bait-trolling to traditional dry fly casting, this part of the Eastern Sierra offers some of the best trout fishing in the world. To prevent the spread of New Zealand mudsnail, wading is discouraged. If you want the latest insider tips, there are as many local guide services as condominium rental agencies, and at least as many guides as there are productive places to fish.

Note: A valid California fishing license is required for residents and nonresidents 16 years of age or older on all public and private land outside and inside national park boundaries. Licenses can be purchased online at https://www.ca.wildlifelicense.com/InternetSales or through any authorized license agent (including most sporting goods outlets and local general stores). Always check with a park ranger, local outfitter, or visitor center staff for area and species-specific quota and catch-and-release regulations.

Eastern Sierra Guide Service (760-872-7770; www.jaeger-flyfishing.com). Guide service and clinics.

David Moss Fly Fishing (760-937-4168). Guide service.

Performance Anglers (760-965-0049; www.performanceanglers.info). Shop, rentals, guide service.

Kevin Peterson's Fly Fishing Adventures (760-937-0519; www.kevinpeterson flyfishing.com). Guide service and backcountry pack trips.

Sierra Drifters Guide Service (760-935-4250; www.sierradrifters.com). Guide service and outfitting.

The Troutfitter Flyshop (Shell Mart Center, Main Street, Mammoth; 760-924-3676; www.thetroutfitter.com). Shop, rentals, guide service.

GOLF **Sierra Star** (2001 Sierra Star Parkway; 760-924-4653; www.mammoth mountain.com). California's highest-altitude 18-hole course (8,000 feet).

RAINBOW TROUT BILL BECHER

FLY-FISHING THE UPPER OWENS BILL BECHER

Regulation, medium length, par 70, built in 1999, Cal Olsen design. Meadows and great narrow corridors through the woods. Club and cart rentals, lessons, midweek specials. Call or book tee times online.

Snowcreek Golf Course (Fairway Drive, off Old Mammoth Road; 760-934-6633; www.snowcreekresort.com/golf.htm). Nine holes, par 35, in the meadow where Steve McQueen's Nevada Smith tracked down his last victim. Built in 1991, Ted Robinson design. Big views, water features. Clubhouse, café (sandwiches and snacks), accessories, and apparel. Lessons available. Collared shirts required. No metal spikes, no club rentals. Wide-open driving range.

HIKING Numerous popular hikes—from short strolls to day hikes to overnight trips— set off from trailheads in the Lakes Basin at the end of Lake Mary Road. From Coldwater Campground, try Duk Pass (local packers say you can see the letters D-U-K in the rocks above the pass) to Arrowhead, Skelton, and Barney Lakes (10 miles round-trip to Duk Lake); or the trail to Emerald Lake (1.5 miles round-trip); or add a few miles and make a loop around the crest to Lake George. From Horseshoe Lake hike over Mammoth Pass, then down to Reds Meadow (6 miles one way), have pie, take the shuttle or hike back. Or take the shuttle to Agnew Meadows on the San Joaquin, and climb from there up to Shadow Lake and Lake Ediza (12 miles round-trip). Wilderness permits and bear canisters required for overnight trips. Talk it over with a ranger at the Welcome Center.

HORSEBACK RIDING Numerous outfitters provide day trips, dunnage, spot trips, and full custom service from every major trailhead in the region.

PIONEERING TIOGA: WHAT IT TAKES TO GET THE ROAD OPEN

Every spring, with the old orchards already blooming on the floor of Yosemite Valley, the squirrels and pine martens out and about in Tuolumne Meadows, Mammoth's Lincoln Mountain a private, hiker's-only stash of untracked corn snow, and the grass already green at the Mobil Mart in Lee Vining, the question begins to nag: When will the pass open?

Tioga is the only connection between east and west along a 200-mile length of the Southern Sierra Nevada, through the second largest roadless area in the Lower 48. The road is closed for an average of six months every year, from the first significant snowfall (generally in November) until late in the spring, when the snowplow crews manage once again to punch through—the Park Service working from the West, Cal-Trans from the east.

In the early days, the opening of the pass occasioned a festive fish fry on the shores of Mono Lake—native people from the west brought perch and salmon to trade with eastern tribes for pine nuts and obsidian. Later, it was the first mule trains of the season—provisions came east from civilization, and gold and silver headed the other way. These days, for west-siders and Yosemite locals, it means the season's first straight shot to the hot springs in Long Valley. For eastsiders it's a much-needed opening to wildflowers and waterfalls—and nearly two hours shaved from the drive to San Francisco.

If you're wondering what could be so hard about plowing old snow from a road in the middle of May, check out this NPS video about plowing across an avalanche path in early June 2005: www.nps.gov/yose/planyourvisit/upload/olmstedplowing.mov. For opening and closing dates since 1980, check here: www.nps.gov/yose/planyourvisit/tiogaopen.htm.

In the days leading up to Memorial Day, no one watches the road conditions with quite the keenness that Yosemite National Park's lead wrangler, J. R. Gehres, uses as he prepares his world-champion pack team for the annual Mule Days competition in Bishop on the other side of the range. Rumor has it that getting the team over the crest is the Park Service's primary motivation for plowing its share of the road as early as possible. If it gets done, Gehres can trailer his animals to Bishop in about 3 hours—compared to 8 or more if the project lags. As might be expected, there is a long-standing tradition by which no official predictions are made as to when the road might open—until the gate swings for the season. In the meantime, check here for the latest update on the plows' progress: www.nps.gov/yose/planyourvisit/tioga.htm.

CLEAR PASSAGE TO THE WEST SIDE: MOUNT GIBBS AND MOUNT DANA, LEE VINING CANYON

A SPOT TRIP OUT OF JUNE LAKE INTO THE ANSEL ADAMS WILDERNESS BILL BECHER

Convict Lake Resort (Convict Lake Road; 760-934-3803 or 1-800-992-2260; www .convictlake.com). Two-hour guided trips to the other side of the lake. Three times daily in summer.

Frontier Pack Train (June Lake; 760-648-7701 or 1-888-437-MULE; www.frontier packtrain.com). Scheduled and custom trips into the Ansel Adams Wilderness and Yosemite high country from Kent and Dave Dohnel's stables at June Lake.

Mammoth Lakes Pack Outfit (Lake Mary Road; 760-934-2434 or 1-888-475-8747; www.mammothpack.com). Hourly trail rides and full pack and saddle service into John Muir and Ansel Adams Wildernesses. Spring and fall horse drives, plus rides in the Bodie Hills.

McGee Creek Pack Station (8 miles south of Mammoth on McGee Creek Road; 760-935-4324 or 1-800-854-7407; www.mcgeecreekpackstation.com). Lee and Jennifer Roeser offer full pack and saddle service up spectacular McGee Canyon into the John Muir Wilderness. One- to two-hour, half-day, and full-day rides plus fishing rides and custom packing services. Wintertime trail and wagon rides available in the Alabama Hills.

Reds Meadow/Agnew Meadows Pack Stations (Reds Meadow; 760-934-2345 or 1-800-292-7758; www.redsmeadow.com). Day rides to Rainbow Falls. Full pack and saddle service to Yosemite, Ansel Adams Wilderness, John Muir Wilderness, and Mount Whitney. Bishop to Bodie trips, custom fishing trips, and packing school.

Rock Creek Pack Station (Bishop/Rock Creek; 760-872-8331; www.rockcreek packstation.com). Craig and Herbert London offer full pack and saddle service to Hilton Lakes, Little Lakes Valley, Pioneer Basin, and Mono Creek. Also into Sequoia-Kings, Golden Trout, and South Sierra Wildernesses from Sawmill, Shepherd, Taboose, and Olancha Pass trailheads. Spring and fall horse drives, photography trips, and wild mustang trail rides.

Virginia Lakes Pack Outfit (Bridgeport; 760-937-0326; www.virginialakes.com). Offering fill-pack and saddle service and all-expense gourmet camping trips into the Hoover Wilderness and remote northern Yosemite.

HOT AIR BALLOONING Float up and away with the sunrise over the Upper Owens Valley with the Glass Mountains and the High Sierra as backdrop. Contact Mammoth Balloon Adventures (760-937-8787) to reserve your space in the basket.

ICE SKATING When conditions are just right, in the late fall, after weeks of freezing temperatures and no snow, hundreds of high-country lakes become natural skating rinks. The Mammoth Lakes Town Ice Rink may or may not be back in operation by the time you're reading this sentence.

MOTOR SPORTS There are hundreds of miles of crisscrossing forest roads north of Mammoth and east of CA 395 open to off-highway vehicles and snowmobiles. Wilderness areas are off-limits to all vehicles.

DJ's Snowmobile Adventures (Smokey Bear Flat, CA 395, north of Mammoth; 760-9354480; www.snowmobilemammoth.com). Five hundred acres of rolling snowmobile range from Smokey Bear Flat to Bald Mountain. Tours, rentals, guided trips.

Mammoth Mountain Snowmobile Adventures (Top of Minaret, across from Main Lodge; 760-934-9645 or 1-800-MAMMOTH; www.mammothmountain.com). Tours and rentals. Reservations suggested.

Sierra Engine (58 Commerce Dr.; 760-934-0347; www.bishopmotosports.com). Rents, sells, and services snowmobiles, snowblowers, lawn mowers, log splitters, and ATVs.

MOUNTAIN BIKING Conditions can be dusty and soft, but the terrain is nearly limitless. In general, the best riding is from 8,000 feet to timberline in the woods. **Mammoth Mountain Bike Park** (Mammoth Mountain; 760-934-0706; www.mammothmountain .com) offers 100 miles of lift-accessed single track from 11,053 feet at the summit to 8,050 at the Village. Bike shuttle provided from the Village to the Gondola at Main Lodge. Downhill, an array of free-ride features and family-friendly, gradually looping descents. Bike rentals and tickets at the Mountain Center in the Village and at the Main Lodge gondola building. A full range of rentals, parts, and service also available at **Footloose Sports** (3043 Main St., corner of Old Mammoth Road; 760-934-2400; www .footloosesports.com). Consult the Welcome Center for maps of other national forest trails and dirt roads across the Long Valley Caldera.

ROAD BIKING Three great rides from the Village at Mammoth: up Lake Mary Road, around Lake Mary to Horseshoe Lake, and back (approximately 12 miles); down CA 203 to 395, north to Mammoth Scenic Loop, and back (approximately 14 miles); down CA 203 to 395, south to the Green Church, east on Benton Crossing Road to CA 120, north to 395, and back by way of CA 395 south and Mammoth Scenic Loop (100 miles—essentially the reverse of the High Sierra Fall Century). Also try the spectacular June Lake Loop (21 miles)—start and end at the Double Eagle Resort. For rentals, parts, service, and local beta, try Brian's Bicycles (3059 Chateau Rd., off Old Mammoth Road; 760-924-8566; www.mammothbikesandskis.com) or Footloose Sports (3043 Main St., corner of Old Mammoth Road; 760-9342400; www.footloosesports.com).

WILD ICE: BACKCOUNTRY LAKE SKATING IN THE HIGH SIERRA NEVADA

As seasons go, it's rarer and more ephemeral than even the annual wildflower bloom in Death Valley. It doesn't happen every year. But when conditions are right—generally in late November and early December, after a cold, dry fall, before the first big snows, with the ski resort manufacturing its own version of the white stuff and skiers once again studying weather patterns over the Pacific, performing rituals before arcane gods in hopes of bringing powder by Christmas—this is when the high lakes begin to resemble plate glass, reflecting the sky, and those in the know set off into the woods with hockey sticks and skates flung over their shoulders.

One year it was up at Virginia Lakes, by the full moon, a bonfire just offshore for the roasting of weenies and marshmallows, the occasional eerie twang of ice cracking beneath one's skates like a snapped bowstring. (They say it's a good thing, that such noises speak well of the tensile strength of the ice. I'm more accustomed to it now, but still not completely convinced.) Another year it was McCleod, up in the saddle of Mammoth Pass. We fought our way upwind against wisps of blowing snow, across ice black as slate, then sailed downwind to the east at double speed. Then it got warm and the ice on McCleod went slushy and broke up. A week later it got cold again and again we tried our luck, for starters, on the shallow pond of Emerald, above Coldwater.

I met Lorenza Walker on the trail. A native of Cortina d'Ampezzo, Italy, she's been skating on lakes her whole life. "I look at the cracks," she said, "How deep they are, how far down I can see bubbles. They say all you need is 2 inches. I go for a little more than that."

Her then-husband Joe banged on the ice with his hockey stick. We could see the dark shapes of rainbow trout gliding beneath the ice. "This is 4 or 5 inches thick," he said. "You could drive a car on it."

The next day we hiked up the Duk Pass trail, into the John Muir Wilderness, seeking something higher in elevation—and bigger. The first storm of the year was coming in fast and hard. The wind rose in the pines, bearing the first tiny crystals. "What'll happen now is these lakes that are frozen will get snow on them, and it's over," said Brian Ellison, owner of a small bike and cross-country ski shop in town. "Tomorrow we'll be skiing here."

We emerged from the woods at the shore of Skelton Lake, at 9,915 feet. We flaked out a climbing rope on the shore, just in case. The wind was driving hard now, sidelong, and the temperature was dropping fast. We cinched up our skates and slid tentatively onto the ice, with Bill Becher taking photos from the safety of the beach. "We'll just start slowly," said Brian, "and work our way out."

"Ice formation is affected by a number of things," Pete DeGeorge, a deputy with the Mono County Sheriff's Department, would tell me later in a telephone interview. There's the depth of lake, the strength of the currents from inlet to outlet, how much vegetation there is, if there are birds landing in the water. The ideal, of course, is a good succession of cold days and

ROCK AND ICE CLIMBING From the Owens Gorge to Warming Wall, from the Minarets to Lee Vining Canyon, from top-rope sport climbing to multi-pitch traditional ascents, there is enough good vertical here to keep a person busy through several dozen pairs of shoes.

Mammoth Mountain Adventure Center (Top of Minaret Road, Panorama Gondola building; 800-MAMMOTH; www.mammothmountain.com). Good place to get hooked. Features a 32-foot climbing wall with professional belay service for kids and adults. Zip line and junior ropes courses.

nights, with air temperatures below freezing, and no wind. "The water has to get to a pretty stable 39.9 degrees," he explained.

DeGeorge is the assistant coordinator of the county's search-and-rescue team. He was on the scene at Convict Lake in February 1990, when the ice broke open far offshore and swallowed three teenagers, two camp counselors, a forest ranger, and a volunteer firefighter.

"It's only a matter of minutes before you start to lose things like being able to grab with your fingers and communicate," DeGeorge said. "When people are in the water for a while, they know it's bad. They get that blank stare. They try to kick and crawl up onto the ice, the ice continues to break, and they get exhausted."

We were on our own out there, a long way from help. But the ice was thick, at least 6 inches and solid from one side to the other. Before long, we'd skated along the shore all the way to the inlet and back, passing a puck and shouting to each other in the wind, and had begun making looping forays out into the middle of the lake. Then Joe and Lorenza showed up, and Stu Need with his dog JoJo, and Dan McConnell. By then all fear had gone, and for an hour or so, before the lake began to disappear beneath the snow, we felt something of what it might be like to fly. And then it was over.

For current ice conditions, check the Eastern Sierra Backcountry Ice Skating page on Facebook: www.facebook.com/pages/Eastern-Sierra-Backcountry-Ice-Skating/180447440786.

HIKING FOR ICE IN THE MAMMOTH LAKES BASIN BILL BECHER

Sierra Rock Climbing School (1-408-833-8308; www.sierrarockclimbingschool.com) and **Sierra Mountain Guides** (1-877-423-2546; sierramtnguides.com) offer private guiding, lessons, classes, and trips, plus ice climbing.

SKATEBOARDING **Volcom Brothers Skatepark** (Meridian Boulevard near Commerce Drive; www.volcom.com). "California's best snowboard resort now boasts a world-class skatepark," a staffer wrote in *Snowboarder Magazine* in 2006, "super-smooth concrete right up to boulders. There's also a giant cradle, a Burnside wall, lumps, humps, a big ol' bowl, a love seat wall, plus zillions of different transfers and trannies, too. It's really epic; a new skate-asylum for southern California!" Tony Hawk skated here. Early mornings are less crowded, for obvious reasons. Bikes not welcome.

SPA, MASSAGE, AND YOGA **Belladonna Day Spa** (3236 Main St., at the Best Western High Sierra; 760-920-5158; www.belladonnamammoth.com). Full-service day spa and salon.

The Body Shop Gym (306 Laurel Mountain Rd., 760-934-3700). Recently renovated, the Body Shop has a solid fitness (free weights, equipment) and cardio setup.

Creekside Spa at Double Eagle Resort (5587 CA 158, June Lake; 760-648-7004; www.doubleeagle.com). Full-service spa and salon: massage, shiatsu, Vichy shower body therapies, hydrotherapy, and more. Leave time to linger.

Double Eagle Spa at Snowcreek (51 Club Dr., Mammoth; 760-934-8511; www.snowcreekathleticclub.com). Massages, facials, body treatments, manicures, pedicures, hydrating spray tanning treatment, yoga, cycle fit, tennis, pools, whirlpools, steam, cardio, weights, and more.

Healing Arts Center (645 Old Mammoth Rd., Sherwin Plaza 2; 760-924-3223; www.mammothhealingarts.com). Massage therapy, skin and body spa, chiropractor, yoga, Pilates, tai chi, and more.

Mountain Mobile Massage (by appointment; 760-914-0427; www.mountainmobilemassage.com). Music, table, oils, the works—brought to you. Reasonably priced.

SWIMMING AND SOAKING Most condos and hotels in Mammoth offer heated pools and Jacuzzis year-round. In summer, the swimming is world-class at most local lakes (the only body of water in the lower Mammoth Lakes Basin open to swimming is Horseshoe Lake). The most popular swimming beaches are at Convict and June Lakes. The adventurous will want to try one of the natural hot-springs tubs in Long Valley (via Hot Creek Hatchery Road or Benton Crossing; ask a local for information).

Snowcreek Athletic Club (51 Club Dr., Mammoth; 760-934-8511; www.snowcreekathleticclub.com). Features small indoor and outdoor pools for members and non-members for a nominal fee.

Whitmore Pool (Benton Crossing Road, just south of Mammoth Airport; 760-934-4222). A 25-yard pool with a huge view of the mountains, wading pool, restrooms, showers, lawn. Open mid-June through early October.

TENNIS For good courts with epic backdrops, check out the free **Mammoth Lakes Community Courts** (760-934-0150), kitty-corner from the Village, or head over to the **Snowcreek Athletic Club** (760-934-8511; snowcreekathleticclub.com) in Old Mammoth. For tennis lessons contact Russ Chessler at 760-934-8511.

TUBING AND SNOWPLAY **Woolly's Tube Park** (Minaret Road; 760-934-7533). Rope tow, tube rentals, groomed slopes.

✳ Lodging

When a young man by the name of C. Clarke Keely first visited the region with his family in July 1920—later to become a surveyor on the Los Angeles Aqueduct and one of the early summer-homestead pioneers of Old Mammoth—the place to stay was Charlie Summers's ranch, at what had once been the old Wildasinn Hotel. "The accommodations consisted of three or four little board cottages," Keely would remember, years later. "Then there was what was called the lodging house. It was a long, two-story building with a tub, wash basin and toilet at each far end of the corridor. The water was heated with an old boiler they had brought down from one of the mines." A host of accommodations of this sort was put up in subsequent years, throughout the 1920s and '30s, from Rock Creek to Lake George, from Reds Meadow to Virginia Lakes. In the 1950s and '60s modern A-frame cottages sprouted beside their older board-and-batten counterparts. Many of these so-called resorts still serve as rustic summertime fishing camps. Most are boarded up and inaccessible in winter, but some—as at Rock Creek, Convict Lake, and Lake Mary—have been fixed up and winterized in order to provide lodging for cross-country skiers and other snow-play enthusiasts. The town of Mammoth Lakes now offers the widest range of accommodations in the Southern Sierra—from boutique to luxury-corporate, from vintage shag to the latest three-story neo-Craftsman vacation home with golf course views, giant flat-screen TVs, and acres of polished-granite countertop. June Lake boasts the only real destination spa in the region, open year-round. In Lee Vining, there are a couple of motels worth consideration, both conveniently located for day-trip forays to Mono Lake, Bodie, and the Yosemite High Country. For

⬤ LODGING HIGHLIGHTS

Hot Creek Fly Fishing Ranch: Best On-the-River Dry-Fly Fishing Cabins (page 236)
Tamarack Lodge & Resort: Best Up-to-Date Lakeside Cabin Resort (page 238)
Westin Monache Resort: Best Name-Brand Resort Hotel (page 240)
Mammoth Mountain Inn: Most Convenient Slopeside Hotel (page 247)
Double Eagle Resort and Spa: Best Laid-Back Destination Spa (page 243)

accommodations on the Tioga Road and at Tuolumne Meadows, see Chapter 7.

Holiday lodging rates, especially within the town of Mammoth Lakes, can spike to as much as double the average peak season rate. Peak season here generally coincides with ski season. (In fact, the town sees more visitors overall in summer, but a significant number is absorbed by the campgrounds.) The lakeside resorts and the motels in Lee Vining have their peak seasons in summer. Rates are often significantly reduced midweek and during the quiet shoulder seasons of spring and fall. Check for package deals.

CAMPING In developed recreation areas—Rock Creek Canyon, McGee Creek Canyon, Convict Lake, Reds Meadow, Mammoth Lakes, June Lake, Lee Vining Canyon, Lundy Canyon, and the Mono Basin Scenic Area—camping is permitted only in developed campgrounds. On certain busy summer weekends (e.g., July Fourth), campgrounds will fill to capacity, especially those at lakeside and streamside locations. Primitive dispersed camping is allowed on national forest and Bureau of Land Management land outside these areas, especially in the Inyo Craters, Deadman, Bald, and Glass Mountain areas of the Long Valley Caldera. A California campfire permit—available at any ranger station or visitors center—is required for the use of any open flame (including gas

MAMMOTH CAMPING

Rock Creek to Convict Life	Elevation	Season	Reservations Accepted	Fee	Sites	Water	Agency
1. Tuff	7,000	Apr-Oct	Yes	Yes	34	Yes	USFS
2. Holiday (overflow)	7,500	As needed	No	Yes	35	Yes	USFS
3. French Camp	7,500	Apr-Oct	Yes	Yes	86	Yes	USFS
4. Aspen Park (group)	8,100	May-Oct	Yes	Yes	1	Yes	USFS
5. Iris Meadow	8,300	May-Oct	No	Yes	14	Yes	USFS
6. Big Meadow	8,600	May-Oct	No	Yes	11	Yes	USFS
7. Palisade	8,600	May-Oct	No	Yes	5	Yes	USFS
8. East Fork	9,000	May-Oct	Yes	Yes	133	Yes	USFS
9. Pine Grove	9,300	May-Oct	No	Yes	11	Yes	USFS
10. Upper Pine Grove	9,400	May-Oct	No	Yes	8	Yes	USFS
11. Rock Creek Lake	9,600	May-Oct	No	Yes	28	Yes	USFS
12. Rock Creek Lake (group)	9,700	Jun-Oct	Yes	No	1	Yes	USFS
13. Mosquito Flat (walk-in)	10,100	May-Oct	No	Yes	10	No	USFS
14. Crowley Lake	7,000	Apr-Nov	No	Yes	47	No	BLM
15. Crowley Lake South Landing	7,000	Apr-Nov	Yes*	Yes	19	Yes	DWP**
16. McGee Creek	7,600	May-Oct	Yes	Yes	28	Yes	USFS
17. Convict Lake	7,800	Apr-Oct	Yes‡	Yes	85	Yes	USFS
18. Brown's Owens River	7,000	Apr-Oct	Yes**	Yes	75	Yes	Private
Mammoth Town Area							
19. New Shady Rest	7,800	Apr-Oct	Yes	Yes	92	Yes	USFS
20. Old Shady Rest	7,800	Jun-Sep	Yes‡	Yes	46	Yes	USFS
21. Sharwin Creek	7,800	Apr-Sep	Yes‡	Yes	85	Yes	USFS
22. Pine Glen (overflow)	7,800	As needed	Yes‡	Yes	10	Yes	USFS
23. Pine Glem (group)	7,800	May-Sep	Yes	Yes	7	Yes	USFS
24. Camp High Sierra	8,100	Jun-Sep	Yes***	Yes	40	Yes	DWP
Mammoth Lakes Basin							
25. Twin Lakes	8,600	May-Oct	Yes‡	Yes	92	Yes	USFS
26. Pine City	8,900	Jun-Sep	No	Yes	10	Yes	USFS
27. Coldwater	8,900	Jun-Sep	Yes‡	Yes	77	Yes	USFS
28. Lake Mary	8,900	Jun-Sep	No	Yes	46	Yes	USFS
29. Lake George	9,000	Jun-Sep	No	Yes	16	Yes	USFS
Reds Meadow & Devil's Postpile							
30. Agnew Meadows	8,400	Jun-Sep	No	Yes	21	Yes	USFS
31. Agnew Meadows (groups)	8,400	Jun-Sep	Yes	Yes	4	Yes	USFS
32. Agnew Meadows Horse	8,400	Jun-Sep	No	Yes	3	Yes	USFS
33. Upper Soda Springs	7,700	Jun-Sep	No	Yes	28	Yes	USFS
34. Pumice Flat	7,700	Jun-Sep	No	Yes	17	Yes	USFS
35. Pumice Flat (group)	7,700	Jun-Sep	Yes	Yes	4	Yes	USFS

stoves, lanterns, wood fires, charcoal fires, or smoking) outside of a developed campground. For up-to-date fire conditions and restrictions, call 760-873-2555. Wilderness permits are required for overnight backcountry travel in the Ansel Adams and John Muir Wilderness. Trail quotas apply in summer. If you've always wanted to spend a weekend in a private aluminum-and-plastic lakeside guest suite but don't feel up to hauling one behind your own vehicle, the folks at **Adventure in Camping** (1-800-417-7771; www.adventure incamping.com) will take the adventure right out of it, providing you a late-model travel trailer and then parking it for you in the campground of your choice, anywhere from Rock Creek to Virginia Lakes.

REDS MEADOW & DEVIL'S POSTPILE *CONTINUED*	ELEVATION	SEASON	RESERVATIONS ACCEPTED	FEE	SITES	WATER	AGENCY
36. MINARET FALLS	7,600	Jun-Sep	No	Yes	27	Yes	USFS
37. REDS MEADOW	7,600	Jun-Oct	No	Yes	52	Yes	USFS
38. DEVIL'S POSTPILE****	7,560	Jun-Sep	No	Yes	21	Yes	NPS
CRESTVIEW (NORTH OF MAMMOTH LAKES)							
39. BIG SPRINGS	7,300	Apr-Nov	No	No	26	No	USFS
40. OBSIDIAN FLAT (GROUP)	7,800	Jun-Oct	Yes	Yes	1	No	USFS
41. DEADMAN	7,800	Jun-Nov	No	No	30	No	USFS
42. GLASS CREEK	7,600	Apr-Nov	No	No	50	No	USFS
43. HARTLEY SPRINGS	8,400	Jun-Oct	No	No	20	No	USFS
JUNE LAKE							
44. OH! RIDGE	7,600	Apr-Nov	Yes	Yes	144	Yes	USFS
45. JUNE LAKE	7,600	Apr-Nov	Yes	Yes	28	Yes	USFS
46. GULL LAKE	7,600	Apr-Nov	No	Yes	11	Yes	USFS
47. REVERSED CREEK	7,600	May-Oct	Yes	Yes	17	Yes	USFS
48. SILVER LAKE	7,200	Apr-Nov	Yes	Yes	63	Yes	USFS
49. AERIE CRAG (OVERFLOW)	7,200	As needed	No	Yes	10	No	USFS
50. BLOODY CANYON	8,400	May-Nov	No	No	1	No	USFS
LEE VINING AREA							
51. LOWER LEE VINING	7,300	Apr-Oct	No	Yes	54	No	USFS
52. MORAINE	7,350	Apr-Oct	No	Yes	27	No	USFS
53. CATTLEGUARD	7,390	Apr-Oct	No	Yes	100	No	USFS
54. ASPEN	7,490	Apr-Oct	No	Yes	56	Yes	USFS
55. BIG BEND	7,800	Apr-Oct	No	Yes	17	Yes	USFS
56. CATTLEGUARD	7,325	Apr-Oct	No	Yes	16	No	USFS
57. ELLERY LAKE	9,500	Jun-Oct	No	Yes	21	Yes	USFS
58. JUNCTION	9,600	Jun-Oct	No	Yes	13	No	USFS
59. SAWMILL	9,800	Jun-Oct	No	Yes	12	No	USFS
60. SADDLEBAG LAKE	10,000	Jun-Oct	No	Yes	20	Yes	USFS
61. SADDLEBAG TRAILHEAD (GROUP)	10,000	Jun-Oct	Yes	Yes	1	Yes	USFS
62. TIOGA LAKE	9,700	Jun-Oct	No	Yes	13	Yes	USFS
63. LUNDY CANYON	9,700	Jun-Oct	No	Yes	60	No	USFS
64. TRUMBULL LAKE	9,500	Jun-Oct	Yes‡	Yes	45	Yes	USFS

Note. Reservations at USFS and NPS sites, unless otherwise specified, can be made online at www.recreation.gov or by calling 1-877-444-6777.

‡Some sites first come, first served. *Call 760-648-1189. Seven full hookups, 12 dry camps.

Los Angeles Department of Water and Power * Call 760-924-2368. Reservations available nine months in advance.

****Located within the park.

ROCK CREEK TO CASA DIABLO

Before US 395 was rerouted from lower Rock Creek Canyon to the Sherwin Grade in the late 1930s, **Tom's Place** (US 395 and Rock Creek Road; 760-935-4239; www.tomsplaceresort.com) was the place to stop—for fuel, radiator water, cold beers, lodging, and après-ski camaraderie. When the timing is right, it's still a good bet for a cold beer, a milk shake, and a roadhouse-style hamburger. Upper Rock Creek Road, a serious contender for the honor of highest paved public road in California, leaves the highway here and threads its way southwest up the canyon 11 miles, past a series of small lakes and aspen groves, to its dead end at the Mosquito Flat trailhead (10,300 feet). It's a worthwhile side trip in summer, not merely for the scenery and myriad opportunities for recreation, but also for an Angler sandwich and a big tranche of Sue King's renowned homemade pie or other deserts at ✪ **Rock Creek Lakes Resort** (Upper Rock Creek Road; 1-877-935-4311; www.rockcreeklake.com; inexpensive)—no longer known as Pie In The Sky. In winter the road is closed at East Fork, 6 miles up from Tom's Place, and groomed thereafter for cross-country skiing. North along US 395, beyond Tom's Place and Little Round Valley, the country opens up into the high sagebrush tableland of the Long Valley Caldera, with volcanic formations as old as 760,000 years and as young as 600. More recently, in 1941, the valley was flooded at its south end by the City of Los Angeles to form a storage reservoir at Lake Crowley.

Rock Creek Lodge (Upper Rock Creek Road; 1-877-935-4170; www.rockcreeklodge.com; moderate (summer)/expensive (winter); Elevation: 9,373 feet; Open: Year-round (winter recommended); Owner: Bobby Tanner; Pets: No; Wheelchair Access: Limited; Internet Access: Wireless in main lodge). Established in 1927 and added onto over the years with varying degrees of aesthetic inspiration, Rock Creek Lodge is one of several popular rustic-cabin summer resorts in the canyon and provides a good base camp for fishing, hiking, biking, and horseback riding in the High Sierra. Its true charm emerges in winter, however, when the road is closed, the lakes are drifted over, and the campgrounds and parking lots are buried in snow. Arrange to have your bags hauled up the hill by snowmobile while you enjoy the reasonable 2-mile ski-in. Equipment rentals available. Spend your days skate-skiing around the adjacent meadow, skinning up and practicing telemark turns, or making extended forays up-canyon into the backcountry. The price is high but includes three excellent meals daily (see "Dining") and unlimited access to the sauna. Newer, modern cabins are slightly less romantic but worth the extra few dollars for the private

bathroom/shower and thermostat-controlled electric heat. Reservations should be made far in advance, especially on moonlit weekends, and conditions confirmed before departure. The lodge also maintains a budget yurt-style ski hut at Mosquito Flat at road's end.

✪ **Hot Creek Fly Fishing Ranch** (85 Hot Creek Hatchery Road, east of US 395, past the hatchery; 760-924-5637 or 1-888-695-0774; www.hotcreekranch.com; very expensive; Elevation: 7,100 feet; Open: April to November; Riverkeeper: Bill Nichols; Pets: No; Wheelchair Access: Limited; Internet Access: Wireless). Zane Grey, having covered a good deal of country, is supposed to have found this place "the most beautiful in the Eastern Sierra that I have seen yet." Padding through thick meadowgrass, the snap of sage in the air, steam rising from the creek, the first splash of dawn on the wall of mountains beyond, one cannot help but wonder at the extraordinary restraint of such a comment. A fellow by the name of Tom Poole, part Paiute, built a cabin here in the late 1800s, where his ancestors had spent their summers. And when Fred Eaton came around buying land and water rights for the City of Los Angeles, Tom told him just where he could put his money. The result is one of the only pieces of private land in the valley: 300 acres with a cold, clear, spring-fed creek meandering through the heart of it—teeming with wild trout. Simple electric housekeeping cabins have kitchens, barbecues, porches, and views across the meadow. No phones, no TVs. Catch-and-release, dry fly-fishing only. It doesn't get much more old school than this. Fly shop; guide service available.

MAMMOTH LAKES

Not long ago there were three types of lodging for hire in Mammoth: rustic lakeside resort cabins; crappy, over-priced motel rooms; and cheesy, beat-up, overpriced condominium units. These options are still available, of course, for those whose aesthetic priorities don't stray far from the essential—or whose nostalgia (or sense of irony) happens to extend to shag and mirrors and creamsicle-colored Formica. But the fact is that times have changed. A number of luxury hotel-resort properties have recently come online, or come into their own, with several more approved and slated for the next infusion of capital and pending market conditions. Many offer the same kind of amenities as condos—kitchens, fireplaces, pools, and Jacuzzis—but with an entirely improved level of design and service. Also, real estate values have generally rebounded enough in the years since the last bubble burst in 2008, along with new incentive generated by Airbnb and the like, that many condo and vacation rental owners have found the wherewithal (and the inclination) to fix up their old places. Or at the very least to change the carpets and countertops. The best franchise motel accommodations are probably at the **Best Western High Sierra** (3228 Main St.; 760-924-1234; www .bestwesterncalifornia.com), though the **Motel 6** (3372 Main St.; 760-934-6660; www.motel6.com) has its devotees.

For unique and still relatively inexpensive family-run motor lodgings, try the Schaubmayers' **Alpenhof Lodge** (6080 Minaret Rd.; 760-934-8330 or 1-800-828-0371; www.alpenhof-lodge .com), conveniently located above **Petra's Bistro** and the **Clocktower Cellar** and across the street from the **Village Gondola**; Jim and Nancy Demetriades's centrally-located motel-resort **Sierra Nevada Resort & Spa** (164 Old Mammoth Rd., behind Rafters; 760-934-2515, 1-800-824-5132; www.sierranevadalodge.com); or the **Austria Hof** (Top of Canyon Boulevard; 760-934-2764; www.austriahof .com), located across the parking lot from Canyon Lodge.

HOTELS AND RESORTS The Mammoth Mountain Inn (CA 203, at Main Lodge; 760-934-2581 or 1-800-MAMMOTH;

A QUIET WEEKDAY MORNING ON THE MOUNTAIN BRAD PEATROSS, COURTESY MAMMOTH RESORTS

www.themammothmountaininn.com; expensive to very expensive; Elevation: 9,000 feet; Open: Year-round; Innkeeper: Mammoth Resorts; Pets: With fee and deposit; Wheelchair Access: Yes; Internet Access: Wireless). Dave McCoy's original A-frame ski lodge first opened for business in 1958, and it was renovated in the late 1990s with all manner of neo-Craftsman detailing, varnished wood, leather, and granite. A short stroll to the gondola, a short stumble home from après-ski at The Yodler, and, in the morning, the easiest schlep-free access to Small World Day Care or the Discovery Chair, the Mammoth Mountain Inn is by far the most stress-free place to leave the car behind and focus on the family ski vacation. There's also no better place to get snowed in with a pair of fat skis on reserve at the rental shop downstairs (and a pair of climbing skins in case the storm's so huge they can't get Chair 1 open). Historic black-and-white prints from the 1950s and '60s bring back the glory days of slow center-pole chairs, long lift lines, wool trousers, and hot toddies on the sundeck. Avoid the older rooms in the back. Rooms in the front building are spacious, ranging from upgraded motel-style suites to modern, fully equipped condominium units. Patios with big views of the mountain, an in-house bar, a restaurant and convenience store, an indoor Jacuzzi, a heated outdoor pool, underground parking, ski and snowboard rental, on-site child care, guest shuttle service to and from town—which at 4 miles can seem pleasantly distant on a busy weekend, or if you require nightlife, an arduous commute. In summer, these are the closest accommodations to the Adventure Center, Mountain Bike Park, and the Devils Postpile shuttle.

✪ **Tamarack Lodge & Resort** (At Twin Lakes, off Lake Mary Road; 760-934-2442 or 1-800-MAMMOTH; www .tamaracklodge.com; expensive to very expensive; Elevation: 8,600 feet; Open: Year-round; Innkeeper: Mammoth Resorts; Pets: Summer only (fee); Wheelchair Access: Limited; Internet Access: Wireless in lodge). Built in 1924 as a rustic fishing retreat for vaudeville star Eddie Foy and his family, Tamarack is the oldest continuously operated lodge in Mammoth and remains one of the classiest of its genre anywhere in the Sierra. Skiing through a blizzard on Mammoth Pass, or on the far side of Lake Mary, one's mind tends to reconstruct the coziness of the place: its warm wood paneling; its bark-trimmed ceiling; its decor of old skis, handsaws, and brass lanterns; wool socks drying before the granite fireplace; kids in long underwear playing checkers with chess pieces; the smell of hot cider from the bar. A handful of guest cabins was added in 1927. In the 1960s, the resort began to stay open year-round as a base for cross-country skiing into the world-class wonderland of the Lakes Basin. Today the Ski Center, adjacent to the lodge, maintains 19 miles of corduroy for skate-skiing, track-skiing, or

MAMMOTH LAKES BASIN ABOVE TAMARACK RESORT JOEL ST. MARIE

THE PEACEFUL WEST SIDE OF THE VILLAGE AT MAMMOTH

snowshoeing, and is poised for a significant expansion of facilities. Skate- and track-ski rentals and lessons available. A series of tastefully appointed "deluxe" cabins has been built in the past decade, with gas fireplaces and modern kitchens, and all of the older cabins have been refurbished. Rooms are also available upstairs in the lodge, with shared or private baths. On the right night, in the right mood, the Lakefront Restaurant is one of the best restaurants in the Southern Sierra.

The Village Lodge (1111 Forest Trail; 760-934-1982, 1-800-MAMMOTH; www .thevillagelodgemammoth.com; expensive; Elevation: 8,050 feet; Open: Year-round; Innkeeper: Mammoth Resorts; Pets: No; Wheelchair Access: Yes; Internet Access: Wireless). It may take a certain amount of geological time before the so-called Village—fabricated in the late 1990s, using the same basic mold as Whistler, Squaw Valley, and other latter-day mountain resorts—begins to feel organic to the landscape. At midweek and during the off-seasons, the wind still populates the cobbled alleyways here with much the same relentless silence as at the ruins of Pine City or Bodie. But during holidays, and on average summer weekends, thanks to rigorous entertainment programming, the place comes to life. People park their cars (if they can find a spot), shop, and dine and stroll about in finery—just like in the original artist's renderings. Accommodations are condo-hotel style, with a variety of individually owned units offering up-to-date kitchens, gas fireplaces, TVs, and balconies—plus 24-hour reception, bell service, and daily housekeeping. Ski and snowboard rentals available for guests. Noise can be a problem on busy weekends, especially in the White Mountain Lodge buildings, situated directly over two nightclubs. Your best bet is to book a unit on one of the upper floors of the main Village Lodge building (formerly Grand Sierra Lodge) or Lincoln House, looking out toward the street rather than in toward the courtyard. Heated pool, Jacuzzi, workout rooms, free underground parking, convenient access to and from the mountain by way of the Village Gondola, the Ski-Back trail from the top of Chair 7, and in summer, the Uptown/Downtown mountain bike trails.

Juniper Springs Resort (4000 Meridian Boulevard; 760-924-1102 or 1-800-MAMMOTH; www .mammothmountain.com; expensive to very expensive; Elevation: 7,953 feet; Open: Year-round; Innkeeper: Mammoth Resorts; Pets: No; Wheelchair Access: Yes; Internet Access: Wireless). Built in the last days before the Village (by the same people), Juniper Springs—including the newer Sunstone and Eagle Run complexes—offers essentially the same amenities: condo-hotel units with kitchenettes/kitchens, outdoor heated pools, Jacuzzis, underground parking, in-hotel ski rental shop, and so on. What it lacks in convenience to shopping and dining, it generally makes up for in sunshine and views—and quiet. Its slopeside location is a big plus in midwinter, especially with the Chair 9 express 6-pack providing fast access from the east side to mid-mountain—but keep in mind that Eagle Express, because of its low elevation and exposure to sun, is among the last lifts to open in the early season and among the first to close in spring. Convenient access in summer to Mammoth Creek, the Lakes Basin, the town bike path, the popular Juniper mountain bike trail (which connects by single-track all the way to Main Lodge), and the Sierra Star golf course.

✪ **The Westin Monache Resort**
(50 Hillside Dr.; 760-934-2526; www .westinmammoth.com; expensive to very expensive; Elevation: 8,100 feet; Open: Year-round; Innkeeper: Starwood Hotels and Resorts; Pets: Yes; Wheelchair Access: Yes; Internet Access: Wireless) Seventy-five heated steps above the Village Gondola, close enough and also just far enough away, is Mammoth's newest, tallest, most hyper-modern building, boasting 230 "upper-upscale" units—one-room studios to two-bedroom, full-kitchen deluxe suites—the best of which have private patios and views stretching from Chair 9 to Long Valley. Really, it's Mammoth's only full-service resort hotel. The lobby and hallways are artistically lit, detailed with varnished plywood and a variety of nods to the local environment, e.g., a scale version of basaltic columns behind the reception kiosks, or twig motifs in the carpets and chandeliers. The units feel a bit cramped for the price, but they offer all the amenities and services Westin aficionados have come to expect: the trademarked "Heavenly Beds" (also provided for pets); high-definition TVs; deep soundproofing; 24-hour room service; kitchens/kitchenettes with granite countertops, dishwashers, and stainless-steel toasters; gas fireplaces; and windows that actually open to the mountain air. Features underground parking, ski valet and rental shop, workout room, Kids Club, year-round outdoor heated pool, hot tubs, and evening "unwind" rituals involving libations and light entertainment. The pool and hot tubs are open to the public for a fee.

CONDOS, TOWN HOUSES, AND VACATION RENTALS Renting a condominium or a town house can be an economical and convenient option, especially for families or large groups. The trick is finding a nice one in a good location and at a decent price—with functioning appliances, heat, and the right number of sheets and towels. Units are individually owned and decorated, and therefore run the gamut of aesthetic possibilities. In the old days (as recently as the early 2010s), the only option was to wade into a morass of generally mercenary property management/rental agencies (listed below for old-schoolers). Nowadays, most travelers prefer the simplicity of Airbnb, Vacasa, VRBO, HomeAway, and other online reservation-by-owner services, which have been a boon to guests and second-home owner income streams alike but—until someone comes up with a solution—devastating to seasonal employee housing stock.

For a taste of the historic complexity of making arrangements for accommodations in Mammoth, try: **Mammoth Reservations** (1-800-223-3032; www.mammothreservations.com); **Mammoth Reservation Bureau** (1-800-462-5571; www.mammothvacations .com); **Mammoth Mountain Reservations** (1-888-204-4692; www .mammothres.com); **Mammoth Mountain Vacations** (1-866-443-9686; www.mammothmountainvacations .com); **Mammoth Sierra Reservations** (1-800-325-8415; www .mammothsierraonline.com); and **Grand Mammoth Resorts** (1-888-626-6684; www.1888mammoth.com), **Mammoth**

Front Desk (1-888-451-0156; www
.mammothfrontdesk.com), **Mammoth
Accommodation Center** (1-800-358-
6262; www.mammothaccommodations
.com), **Mammoth Five Star Lodging**
(1-866-626-6684; www.fivestarlodging
.com), **101 Great Escapes** (1-877-754-
6688; www.101greatescapes.com), and
Grand Havens (1-866-464-4726; www
.grandhavens.com).

Each of these agencies manages individual units for individual absentee owners in a variety of different complexes—in exchange for a significant percentage (as much as half) of the rental income. Some charge visitors a reservation fee; others do not. Some provide a decent service, with a variety of concierge-style perks (be sure to study the online pictures and location map and ask for guarantees that the specific unit you reserve will be the unit you end up with, and check your confirmation closely). Others, especially when it gets busy, will do little more than leave a key in a lockbox somewhere and a note wishing you the best of luck. The best bet is to first narrow your search to one or more of the better complexes—i.e., those with the best location (walking distance to lifts or a golf course) and/or the least deferred maintenance—and whenever possible book directly through individual owners or on-site management. Prices vary wildly, based on location, season, size, and condition of the individual unit.

The 1849 (826 Lakeview Blvd.; 760-934-7525 or 1-800-421-1849; www .1849condos.com). Possibly the apex of Mammoth's disco-era funk, though recently treated to something of a facelift. Mammoth's founder, Dave McCoy, lived in the penthouse here for 10 years back in the day. Still one of the best (and busiest) locations in town during ski season: across the parking lot from Canyon Lodge. Views of Lincoln Mountain, heated pool, Jacuzzi, tennis (in summer), fully equipped kitchens, underground parking, video rentals, wireless Internet, and private sledding hill. Enormous

A REGULAR BIKE PARK SHUTTLE RUNS THROUGHOUT THE
SUMMER SEASON FROM THE VILLAGE/WESTIN TO THE MAIN
LODGE ADVENTURE CENTER BILL BECHER

units. If you're looking for contemporary upscale, this is probably not it. But for a good-value, hassle-free family vacation, it's hard to beat. Also available through a variety of rental agencies.

The Bridges (Lake Mary Road, above Eagle Lodge; no on-site booking). Built in 1984. Ski-in/ski-out through the woods for intermediate and advanced skiers only. Big views to the Sherwins and Long Valley. Private decks and garages. Some private spas. Some units more upscale than others. Units available through a variety of rental agencies.

Eagle Run (4000 Meridian Blvd., above Eagle Lodge; no on-site booking). Built around the turn of the latest century, with contemporary maple cabinets, granite countertops, hardwood floors, and stainless-steel appliances. The only real slopeside units on the mountain. Walk to Sierra Star Golf Course. Some available through Mammoth Mountain (1-800-MAMMOTH; www.mammothmountain.com), others through a variety of rental agencies.

Mammoth Ski & Racquet Club (248 Mammoth Slopes Dr., near Canyon Lodge; 760-934-7368 or 1-888-762-6668; www.mammothdirect.com). Another funky vintage classic, but with good southern exposure and views. Short hike to lifts, ski back. Best access to summer mountain bike trails. Tennis, pool, Jacuzzi, wireless Internet, balconies, propane fireplaces, TVs, DVD players, free telephone calls, garage parking. "Deluxe" and "premium" units have been upgraded. Units also available through a variety of rental agencies.

Snowbird Condominiums (414 Rainbow Ln., across from Canyon Lodge; 760-934-8270 or 1-877-934-8270; www .1849condos.com). A smaller, quieter, slightly classier sibling to the 1849. Short walk to lifts. Outdoor Jacuzzi, free wireless Internet, fully equipped kitchens. Units also available through a variety of rental agencies.

Snowcreek Resort (1254 Old Mammoth Rd.; 760-934-3333 or 1-800-544-6007; www.snowcreekresort.com). Mammoth's largest, most sprawling condominium and townhouse project, and one of the originals, begun in the 1970s by construction-worker-turned-developer Tom Dempsey on 450 acres of ranchland that once included Charlie Summers's hotel. As a location, Snowcreek is probably best suited for summertime, with its own nine-hole golf course and driving range, along with convenient access to creeks, meadows, aspen groves, and the old road to the Lakes Basin. In winter, despite regular

THE NIGHT OF LIGHTS TAKES PLACE EVERY DECEMBER AT CANYON LODGE, WITH LIVE BANDS, STUNTS, AND ALL MANNER OF PYROTECHNICS CHRISTIAN PONDELLA

free shuttle service to the mountain, plentiful opportunities for snowshoeing or cross-country skiing exist, as well as direct access to the frontcountry powder stash that is the Sherwins Range, Snowcreek can feel rather remote—which has its advantages and disadvantages. Phases I, II, III, and IV, set in the woods between Minaret and Old Mammoth Road, are the oldest and most dated, but they are also the best value. Phase V is a classic Orange County–style suburban subdivision on the far side of the golf course. Phases VI and VII (the Lodges and Creekhouse, respectively) are the latest and most attractive, with collections of town houses built by the Chadmar Group of Santa Barbara in a style vaguely evocative of Western barns and old mining buildings (but with the latest in floors, countertops, and appliances). Units also available through a variety of rental agencies.

The Summit (3253 Meridian Blvd., across from Eagle Lodge; 1-800-255-6266; www.summitcondominiums.com). Short hike to Eagle Lodge or Sierra Star Golf Course. Built in the 1970s. Many units and most facades upgraded in recent years. Tennis, pools, Jacuzzis, patios, fitness center. Units also available through a variety of rental agencies.

Obsidian Residence Club (2610 Meridian Blvd.; www.obsidianrc.com; no on-site booking). Built in 2005 as a gated, fractional-ownership, private residence club (also available for nightly rental), the development formerly known as Tallus is probably the most architecturally remarkable project of Mammoth's early twenty-first century building boom, with glass-and-timber towers, hand-cut stonework, and detailing in red cedar and mahogany. Private terraces and hot tubs, Viking kitchens, radiant floors, digital screening rooms, and more. Full-service concierge; private, on-demand, four-wheel-drive shuttle service; indoor heated pool and spa; clubhouse.

Timber Ridge (671 John Muir Rd., above Canyon Lodge; no on-site

booking). Best views in Mammoth. Ski-in/ski-out through the woods and private powder stashes to either Canyon or Eagle Lodge. Direct access to mountain biking. Pool, indoor Jacuzzi, private garages. Chains and/or four-wheel drive required for access in winter. Some units upgraded; available through a variety of rental agencies.

The Timbers at Sierra Star (Meridian Boulevard and Sierra Star Parkway; no on-site booking). Among the most deluxe townhouse rentals in town, with all the latest features: granite countertops, hardwood and slate flooring, private spas, private two-car garages, flat-screen TVs, leather furniture, Craftsman-style detailing, and more. On the seventeenth fairway. Shuttle bus to Eagle Lodge. Units available through a variety of rental agencies.

Val d'Isere (194 Hillside Dr., above the Village; no on-site booking). Across the street from the Village Lodge. Short walk to the gondola, potential ski back, national forest access. On the uptown/downtown mountain bike trail. Many units upgraded, some with views; available through a variety of rental agencies.

Viewpoint Condominiums (3852 Viewpoint Rd., off Main Street; 760-9343132 or 1-800-826-6680; www.viewpointcondos.com). Short walk through the woods to the Village and to restaurants along Minaret. Fireplaces, fully equipped kitchens. Some units upgraded. Jacuzzi, pool, tennis court (seasonal). Outdoor parking. Excellent value.

JUNE LAKE LOOP

✪ **Double Eagle Resort and Spa** (5587 CA 158, west of town and June Mountain Ski Area; 760-648-7004; www.doubleeagle.com; expensive (includes breakfast and spa access); Elevation: 7,500 feet; Open: Year-round; Innkeepers: Ron and Connie Black; Pets: Yes (fee); Wheelchair Access: Yes; Internet Access: Free wireless). This is not your typical rustic mountain resort. In fact, the only thing rustic about it is the setting: between the outrun of Devil's Slide and the curtain-drop of Horsetail Falls, with Reverse Creek gurgling its way backward across the property and Carson Peak looming 4,000 feet overhead. Accommodations range from two-bedroom knotty-pine guest cabins with fully equipped modern kitchens, decks, fireplaces, woodstoves, TV/DVD setups, and wireless Internet to luxury hotel-style rooms arranged in four-plexes around a fly-fishing pond. Extraordinary hiking, fishing, and access to lakes in summer. Cross-country, downhill, backcountry, and big-mountain skiing in winter—and ice skating on the pond. Begin and end your day with a soak, a swim, and a treatment or two at the Creekside Spa. On-site restaurant and bar, fly shop, guiding services, and daily fitness activities. Open year-round.

MONO LAKE AND LEE VINING

El Mono Motel (51 CA 395, at Third Street; 760-647-6310; www.elmonomotel .com; inexpensive to moderate; Elevation: 6,781 feet; Open: April/May through late fall; Innkeepers: Kelly Miller and friends; Pets: No; Wheelchair Access: Yes; Internet Access: Wireless). Built in the 1920s as one of the first true motels on El Camino Sierra (later CA 395), El Mono today is the best value lodging on the east side of the Sierra Crest. It has been tastefully, artfully redone by the current owner, with desert-tone paint schemes, feather comforters, and framed prints by local artists and photographers. Every room is unique. Some have two rooms and private baths. Others are small, but still more than adequate for sleeping in, with shared bathing and toilet facilities (and budget prices). Garden-side rooms offer a view of the sunflowers, but they see a higher degree of foot traffic by fellow guests. Upstairs, Rooms 10 and 11 share a bath but offer more privacy—plus views across the highway to the lake. The proprietors offer a wealth of insider beta on the region. Lobby doubles as a cozy coffee joint (see below).

Tioga Lodge (54411 CA 395; 760-647-6423; www.tiogalodgeatmonolake.com; moderate; Elevation: 6,400 feet; Open: May through October; Innkeepers: Gloria Ma; Pets: No; Wheelchair Access: Limited; Internet Access: Wireless). An enterprising gentleman by the name of J. P. Hammond had a couple of old buildings moved over from Bodie and another from Lundy in 1897. He installed one of the first telephones in the region, charged a toll for use of the old Indian road around Mono Lake (today CA 395), and offered travelers a popular menu of whores, poker, whiskey, and cold beer. The beer was kept in the creek that ran beneath the saloon, retrieved through a trap door in the floor. When Hammond sold to the Cunninghams in 1918, the place went fancy: rose gardens, Chinese waiters in white jackets, a dancing pavilion, a marina, a pleasure steamer named *Venita*, and a gas pump. It was all pretty well swept away in a flood in 1955 to be rescued 40 years later by the Vints, who did a decent job not just of bringing the place back to life, but also of giving it new character (despite an increase in highway noise since back in those early days). The main buildings are whitewashed board and batten with weathered-plank decks overlooking the road and the lake. Cabins and basic motel rooms are individually, sparingly decorated with wood or Saltillo tile floors, cotton quilts, painted-clay washbasins, and windows that open to dawn over the lake. On-site dining. No TVs, no telephones, no AC.

✳ Where to Eat

"Be sure to take a good solid lunch with you," James W. A. Wright wrote in the days of hardtack and canned beans, "for the bracing mountain air and the exertion will give you ravenous appetite." About this particular phenomenon,

⭐ DINING AND DRINKING HIGHLIGHTS

Base Camp Café: Best West Coast Reuben Sandwich (page 246)
Clocktower Cellar: Best Classic Ski Bum Basement Bar (page 248)
The Good Life Café: Best Healthy Breakfast (page 246)
Mammoth Tavern: Best Cocktails (page 249)
Petra's Wine Bar: Best Cal-Mountain Bistro (page 249)
The Restaurant at Convict Lake: Best Hearty Country French Dining (page 245)
Restaurant Skadi: Best Fine Nordic/Alpine Dining (page 247)
Whitebark Restaurant: Best Late-Night Happy Hour (page 248)
Mammoth Brewing Company Tasting Room & Eatery: Best Upscale Pub Food (page 249)
Gomez's Restaurant and Tequileria: Best Margaritas (page 246)

nothing much has changed in all the intervening time. Except, that is, for the ability of Federal Express to deliver—even to the very edge of the wilderness—healthy, living crustaceans from the coast of Newfoundland, asparagus from South America, or cuts of freshly slaughtered red deer from Australia. From oysters to elk medallions, from baked chèvre salad to lobster-claw gnocchi, from New York–style pizza to Philly cheesesteak pita wraps to Nutella and fresh strawberry crêpes, the greatest range of well-prepared sustenance in the Southern Sierra can today be found in Mammoth (in town, on the mountain, or within a half-hour's drive of the No Shooting zone). The cost undoubtedly reflects not only the quality of the food served, but also the distance most ingredients have had to travel, as well as the long, quiet off-seasons (and midweek slumps) that restaurants here find themselves forced to endure between holiday rushes. Many establishments close for a week or more in October, and again in May, depending on snow conditions and seasonal events—so that owners and staff can go to Hawaii or Aruba and get their beach fix. Nowhere in town will a person feel obliged, except by personal preference, to upgrade his or her attire from the day's sap-stained cargo shorts or Merino long underwear. Note: The quality of dining at some of the establishments in this region can be subject to the vicissitudes of a seasonal labor force.

ROCK CREEK TO CASA DIABLO

East Side Bake Shop (1561 Crowley Lake Rd., McGee Creek; 760-914-2696). Elizabeth McGuire's home-made baked goodies, quiche, salads, and other natural fare. Outside seating with big views up McGee Canyon. Fireside acoustic jam sessions on Sunday afternoons. Closed in winter.

Rock Creek Lodge (Upper Rock Creek Road; 1-877-935-4170; www.rockcreek lodge.com; expensive). Impressive quantities of home-cooked comfort fare served up ski-lodge-family-style and only in winter—marinated pork tenderloin, spinach lasagna, soup, salad, fresh baked bread, and more. Hard to imagine a better place to hole up on a cold midwinter's eve, 2 miles from the nearest plowed road. Beer and wine available for purchase, or bring your own. Meals served to overnight guests and day skiers alike. Make reservations in advance for dinner and/or snowmobile shuttle service. One seating per evening: Don't be late. Sack lunches available for the trail.

The Restaurant at Convict Lake (Convict Lake Road; 760-934-3803 or 1-800-992-2260; www.convictlake.com; expensive). Ten miles from Mammoth Lakes—an easy 15-minute drive in clear conditions, an epic adventure in a blizzard—the restaurant at Convict Lake is a world apart. Pine-paneled cocktail lounge with leather and Craftsman-style furnishings; fish and game motifs; a touch of taxidermy; an open sheet-copper fireplace; linen tablecloths; views of the aspen trees, the lake, and the surrounding granite walls. Specialties are generally rich, saucy, French/California-style—a classic wild mushroom beef Wellington, duck, lamb, local farm-raised rainbow trout in toasted almonds and butter—with a list of good, hefty wines to match. Popular outdoor seating under the aspens in summer. Open seven days a week during peak seasons, summer and winter. Lunch, dinner, pizzas to go, and Sunday brunch. Reservations highly recommended, especially on weekends and during holidays and wedding season.

MAMMOTH LAKES

Austria Hof (Top of Canyon Boulevard; 760-934-2764; www.austriahof.com; moderate to expensive). Chalet food—schnitzel, sauerbraten, bratwurst, and more—in an authentic basement rendition of Kitzbuhel in the early 1970s. Good happy hour drink specials and free appetizers. Dinner only.

✪ **Base Camp Café** (3325 Main St.; 760-934-3900; www.basecampcafe .com; inexpensive). Locals' favorite for cheap breakfast specials, sandwiches (including the best Reuben in town), and friendly wait staff. Great brown-bag specials made for the trail. Open most days for breakfast, lunch, and dinner.

Campo (In the Village; 760-934-0669; moderate). Quality, congenial rustic Italian with origins in Reno. James Beard-nominated chef. House-made pastas and stone-oven pizzas. Lunch (in season) and dinner daily. Variable happy hour. Outside seating in summer.

✪ **Gomez's Restaurant and Tequileria** (In the Village; 760-924-2693; www.gomezs.com; moderate). Highest-altitude tequileria in the world, with 500 labels of distinctive fermented agave professionally sampled, selected and imported by owner Michael Ledesma.

Best margarita options. Quality carnitas. Lunch and dinner every day. Happy hour 2–5 PM daily. Outdoor patio dining in summer. Tequila tasting events, summertime margarita festival, and Chihuahua races.

✪ **The Good Life Café** (Old Mammoth Road; 760-934-1734; www .mammothgoodlifecafe.com; inexpensive). A local favorite for healthy breakfast and lunch. Whole-wheat pancakes, overstuffed omelets, machaca burritos, and Monte Cristo sandwiches served with fries or zucchini. Kids' menu. Open every day. All-you-can-eat lunch special weekdays only. No reservations accepted. In summer, eat on the patio in the sun, overlooking the parking lot.

Jimmy's Taverna (248 Old Mammoth Rd.; 760-934-9432; www.jimmystaverna .com). Greek and Mediterranean variations served in owner Jim Demetriades' lofty, cobbled dining space evocative of an Aegean seaside café. The oak-grilled loupe de mere is a favorite. Marble bar, open kitchen. Breakfast, lunch, and dinner.

The Lakefront Restaurant (at Tamarack Lodge, Twin Lakes, off Lake Mary Road; 760-934-3534; www .tamaracklodge.com/dining; expensive). Less than 3 miles out of town, tucked in the back room of Tamarack's original 1924 log lodge, Lakefront isn't what it once was under Chef Fred Pierrel (now Executive Chef at the Brasserie above Mammoth Rock and Bowl, see below), but it's still a fine choice for an intimate, romantic evening away from the crowds. Reservations required. Full bar. Lunch served seasonally, including an excellent hand-formed burger and catch-your-own trout amandine, served either inside or on the terrace.

Mammoth Rock Brasserie (3029 Chateau Rd., above Mammoth Rock & Bowl; 760-934-4200). Run by slumming former Lakefront Restaurant chef Frederic "Fred" Pierrel in a space reminiscent of an airline frequent-flyer lounge. Great views of the Sherwins, repectable martinis, excellent straight-up steak frites.

Morrison's (3516 Main St.; 760-934-7427; inexpensive to moderate). Scaled-up version of the classic knotty-pine rib joint formerly known as Angel's, still serving steaks, burgers, salads, and ribs—plus house-made pastas and brick-oven pizzas—all with a broader range of ingredients and creative flare, and a higher price point. Three-course prix-fixe menu on Wednesdays. Open daily at 4 PM for happy hour and dinner. Reservations accepted.

Mountainside Bar & Grill (top of Minaret Road at Main Lodge, Mammoth Mountain Inn; 760-934-0601; www .mammothmountain.com; expensive). If you're staying at the inn for more than one night without a kitchen, and need a break from the pub food over at The Yodler (or the dark, icy road into town), you'll probably end up eating here. The menu is generally creative—within the obvious corporate framework—but quality of food and service are variable, tied as they seem to be to the vagaries of snowpack, seasonal staffing, and overall corporate morale. Breakfast, lunch, and dinner daily. Reservations requested.

Nevados (Main Street and Minaret Road; 760-934-4466; www .nevadosrestaurant.com; expensive to very expensive). Before the latest boom and subsequent influx of chef-driven restaurants and serious wine lists, this was one of two or three places in town to throw down some money on good, handcrafted food. Local muleskinners still come to this low-key, locals-friendly bar to hobnob with ski patrolmen and movie producers over top-grade rye and appetizers, and the three-course prix fixe menu is still an excellent bet for ski-town romance. Open for dinner nightly. Reservations recommended.

✪ **Petra's Bistro & Wine Bar** (6080 Minaret Rd., in the Alpenhof Lodge; 760-934-3500; www.petrasbistro.com; expensive to very expensive). Owners Kirk and Robert Shaubmayer, chef Rad Williams,

sommelier Mitch Cahoon, and friends continue to build on the traditions that have made this casual off-Village bistro a beacon for lovers of fine wining and dining. Start with fresh crusty bread and artisan olive oil, a heaping bowl of mussels and clams in red-curry broth, accompanied by fries, garlic aioli, and a dry Portuguese muscat; move on to the venison loin and whatever's just come of age in red from South Africa. Have your partner do the quail, then the scallops. Be sure to tour the cheeses before stepping off at a chocolate pot de crème or a wheel of organic peach upside-down cake à la mode. Menu evolves daily. Extensive selection of craft cocktails and cruvinet-fresh wines by the glass. Eat at a table, at the bar, or on couches beside the fire. Open for dinner Tuesday through Sunday; closed Monday. Reservations recommended.

Rafters (202 Old Mammoth Rd., at the Sierra Nevada Lodge; 760-934-9431; www.raftersmammoth.com; moderate to expensive). Jim and Nancy Demetriades rescued this classic late-'60s Mammoth landmark from slow decay in 2010, and have made it a centerpiece of Mammoth nightlife. Nouvelle Italian and American cuisine served in intimate high-back booths or by the fireplace in the lounge. Open daily for breakfast, lunch, and dinner. Happy hour with half-price lounge food. Popular Karaoke scene on Tuesday nights. Live music on weekends. In summer, the deck overlooks the action on Frosty's miniature golf course.

Roberto's Cafe (271 Old Mammoth Rd.; 760-934-3667; moderate). Best South Bay-style rice-and-beans Cal-Mex: over-stuffed wet machaca burritos, mahi mahi tacos, chiles rellenos, duck quesadillas, chipotle wings, saucy enchiladas. Good margaritas. Sports bar upstairs, booth seating downstairs. No reservations accepted—the wait can be epic on busy weekends, but it can also be eased significantly with a basket of chips and a sloshing bucket of tequila and lime juice.

Open daily for lunch and dinner. Take-out available.

Restaurant Skadi (94 Berner St. Suite A; 760-914-0962; www.restaurantskadi .com; expensive). Named for the Norse goddess of skiing, Skadi presents a surprisingly elegant postmodern ski-lodge-inspired atmosphere in a converted warehouse space on Berner Street. Re-inspired in its new location, with exceptional attention to every detail by owner/chef Ian Algerøen. The menu still very much earns its umlauts and other diacritic marks (spätzli, røsti, rødkål, etc.). Solid bets include the wild mushroom duxelle crepes and the lingon-and-juniper-berry-slathered duck. Open for dinner nightly. Closed Tuesdays. Reservations highly recommended.

Slocum's Grill (3221 Main St.; 760-934-7647; moderate). Classic steakhouse fare in an authentically weathered Victorian atmosphere. Open for dinner nightly. Hickory-smoked ribs Friday and Saturday nights while they last. Popular happy hour, 4–6 PM, with steamed mussels and prime rib sandwiches. No reservations accepted.

Smokeyard BBQ and Chop Shop (In the Village; 760-934-3300; www .smokeyard.com; moderate to expensive). Brothers Alon and Guy Ravid, originally from South Africa, have kept the fire flaming beneath this cornerstone Village location built out in a blend of stainless steel, wood, and gallery-style lighting. Quality cocktails and thin-crust, wood-fired pizzas, plus all manner of burgers, chops, and an authentic South African potjiekos worked up in an exhibition kitchen. Happy hour specials include half-price pizzas. Open for dinner every night. Lunch on weekends only. Outdoor seating in summer.

The Stove (644 Old Mammoth Rd.; 760-934-2821; www .thestoverestaurantmammoth.com moderate). Old-standby for hearty, greasy, country-style breakfasts and family-friendly, knotty-pine atmosphere. Busy on weekends. Open daily for breakfast and lunch. No reservations accepted.

Sushi Rei (6201 Minaret Rd.; 760-934-0774; www.sushirei.com; expensive). Hipster snowboard-style sushi fusion bar. Prices reflect the distance from here to the other side of the Pacific Ocean. Beer and hand roll happy hour. Full bar, infused sakes. Open for dinner daily.

❂ **Whitebark Restaurant** (50 Hillside Dr., at the Westin; 760-934-0400; expensive). Named for the gnarled old conifers that have somehow survived for centuries at the timberline along the Sierra Crest. Vietnamese pork sandwiches and slider burgers. Breakfast, lunch, dinner, and lounge food selections. Or sit at the sushi bar for decent raw fish concoctions. Full cocktail bar with highly popular late-night happy hour (reduced-price food items) after 10 PM. Open daily. Reservations recommended in season.

DELIVERY Doorstep Deliveries (760-934-DINE; www.doorstep-deliveries .com). Delivers from some of the above restaurants in season for a small fee.

TAVERNS, PUBS, AND APRÈS SKI **Clocktower Cellar** (6080 Minaret Rd., basement of the Alpenhof Lodge; 760-934-2725). Underground hangout of choice for lift ops, snowcat drivers, local journalists, beer snobs, and terrain-park engineers. Darts, pool, foosball, big-screen TV. Mammoth's best and most international selection of beers in bottles and on tap. Spicy wings, beer-soaked pastrami, and other real-deal pub food available. Juke box, full bar.

Dry Creek Bar (Top of Minaret Road at Mammoth Mountain Inn, Main Lodge; 760-934-0601). When Main Lodge and The Yodler are slammed and you don't feel like fighting for a beer (much less a place to take your boots off), this is the quiet choice for slopeside après ski. Big A-frame windows onto the mountain, comfortable furniture, huge sundeck, soups, sandwiches, salad bar. If you're going to pay top dollar for a Mexican coffee, you might as well do it in your socks. Also a pleasant alternative to the high-noon lunch-tray hustle across the way.

Grizzly Bar (upstairs at Canyon Lodge; 760-934-2571, ext. 3226). First stop after the slopes or between runs. Standing room only on Saturday. Don't miss the last Village Gondola at 5 PM.

Lakanuki (6201 Minaret Rd., in the Village; 760-934-7447; www.lakanuki .com). Opened in 2003 by globe-trotting Kiwi/Vail veteran Stuart Need and posse during the latter days of urban ski-parka fashion. Laid-back South Bay tiki-style decor, with formidable Mai Tais and Hurricanes in plastic cups, a private security force, and wristbands on weekends. Locals nights, Texas hold 'em tourneys, karaoke, DJs, and occasional lingerie parties featuring men in boxer shorts and bathrobes and professionals dancing on tabletops. Decent pub food, terrific happy hour prices. Outdoor seating in summer. Open every day.

✪ **Mammoth Brewing Company Tasting Room & Eatery** (18 Lake Mary Rd.; 760-934-7141; www.mammothbrewingco .com). It's not exactly a bar, but on any given day, winter or summer, this loft-style brew-pub-with-a-view is one of the most congenial places in town to get your first beer on. Stop by to try the whole lineup, from Golden Trout to the gold-medal-winning Double Nut Brown to a rotating array of seasonals and other experiments. Talk to the craftspeople on duty, fill your growler, or stock up on limited-edition bottles of your favorite flavors. Classy MBC jockwear and merchandise for sale, plus kegs and ice to get the party going at your place. Brandon and Theresa Brocia's **Eatery** offers an inspired selection of haute pub food to complement the beers and to keep you going into the evening. Popular outdoor beer garden whenever the sun's shining.

✪ **Mammoth Tavern** (587 Old Mammoth Rd., #10; 760-934-3902; www .mammothtavern.com). Best, most interesting craft cocktails in town, served with upstairs views of the Sherwins and Mammoth Crest. Excellent whiskey selection. High-end, creative pub food. No reservations. Get there early if you want a table.

Petra's Wine Bar (6080 Minaret Rd., in the Alpenhof Lodge; 760-934-3500; www.petrasbistro.com). Extensive selection of cruvinet-fresh wines by the glass, plus an inspired assortment of classic and newly hatched mixological creations. Try, for example, the classic Sazerac or the Tonopah Low.

Side Door Bistro (100 Canyon Blvd., across from the Village Gondola; 760-934-5200; www.sidedoormammoth.com). Quiet, civilized, back-room wine bar and retail wine shop. Front room is a crêperie with a coffee and panini counter offering Mammoth's only real espresso, served in a demitasse with sugar cube (rather than in a paper cup). Convenient, uncrowded place to meet up with friends at the end of a day's skiing. Open daily.

Tusks Bar (1 Minaret Rd., Main Lodge, third floor, 760-934-2571, ext. 3227). Booth seating, fireplaces, view from the bar to the terrain park. Not as crowded as at Canyon. Closes at 5. Start here, then move across the street to The Yodler.

The Yodler (Minaret Road, next to Panorama Gondola building; 760-934-0636; www.theyodlermammoth.com). Legend has it that this Swiss après ski chalet was actually built in Switzerland sometime in the 1950s and then transported to Mammoth. The date on the facade is 1959. Its only drawback these days, if you don't happen to be staying next door at the inn, is the long bus ride back to town—let it not be a drive—at the end of a session. Outdoor sundeck; fireside lounge; full bar. Sausage sandwiches, burgers, schnitzel, and other hearty Bavarian-style pub fare. Occasional live music. Open for lunch and dinner in season.

COFFEE, TEA, ETC. **Black Velvet Coffee** (3343 Main St. Suite F; www .blackvelvetcoffee.com). Family owned and roasted artisan pour-over and

THE YODLER RESTAURANT AND BAR, IMPORTED FROM SWITZERLAND IN THE 1950s

espresso joint. Hipster industrial-style hangout and meeting place. Free Wi-Fi, cold-brew, waffles, and wine tastings. Retail whole-bean coffee by the ¾ pound.

Looney Bean (26 Old Mammoth Rd., in the Rite Aid shopping center; 760-934-1345; www.looneybean.com). Long-standing locals' favorite laundry break and office-away-from-home, tucked into the corner of the town's second-busiest strip mall (after Vons). Beans roasted on the premises. Gas fireplace. Baked goods. Free wireless Internet. East-facing outdoor seating in summer.

Stellar Brew and Natural Café (3280 Main St., next to Napa Auto Parts; 760-924-3559; www.stellarbrewnaturalcafe.com). Andrea Jones's breakout alternative to the above, set in the same charming, little, sky-blue shack that gave Looney Bean its start. Coffee, tea, pastries, beer, smoothies, breakfast burritos, healthy sandwiches, and comfy secondhand furnishings. Free Wi-Fi and occasional open-mike sessions. Popular south-facing sun deck for all seasons. Open 5:30 AM to 5 PM.

GROCERIES ✪ **Bleu Handcrafted Foods** (3325 Main St.; 760-914-2538; www.bleufoods.com) Specialty meats,

wild-game charcuterie, fresh bread, farmstead cheeses, olive oils, wines, and craft beers—all lovingly curated by Brandon and Theresa Brocia. Ask about private chef dinners and other catering options.

Busy Beez General Store (6201 Minaret Rd., street level at the Village; 760-9242899). Once upon a time, before this century, there was a venerable little village store called the Pioneer Market that, in its later years, provided hordes of snowed-in condo dwellers with everything from milk and raisin bran to goat cheese, arugula, and candied walnuts. Now a private residence club looms quietly, somewhat ominously, in its stead, and just up the street this putative general store hawks all there is for last-minute supplies at this end of town: milk, beer, bread, wine, cereal, top-shelf liquor, pasta sauce, candies, magazines, the *L.A. Times,* olive oil, smoked salmon, canned pumpkin, maybe a banana, maybe an onion. No goat cheese, no arugula, no candied walnuts. Open every day.

Sierra Sundance Earth Foods (26 Old Mammoth Rd.; 760-934-8122). Recently expanded. Vitamins, Tasty Bite Indian cuisine, carob malt balls, yogurt pretzels, hemp granola, organic chocolate, organic produce, organic free-range turkeys for Thanksgiving, bulk yerba maté, sprouted bread, bulk soups and cereals, and trail bars.

Vons (481 Old Mammoth Rd.; 760-9344536). Full-service big-city grocery store built for crowds and rumored to be the top-grossing Vons in California. If possible, avoid Friday nights and the second half of December. Deli (sushi, rolled fresh daily, plus sandwiches and grilled panini), bakery (the olive bread is the stuff of legends and sells out early), butcher and fish counter, pharmacy, Starbucks, flower shop (and balloons), beer, wine, liquor, produce section with hardwood floors (arugula and avocados are available even with 15 feet of snow in the parking lot). If they don't have it, they'll be happy to order it for you. Plastic bags available for a fee. Open daily 5 AM–1 AM.

SANDWICHES, TACOS, AND SUCH **Latin Market Taqueria** (1566 Tavern Rd.; 760-934-7120). Authentic Mexican grocery offering dried and fresh chiles, pan dulce, sopes, Mexican candies, Mexican shampoo, tamarind, and other sundries from south of the border. Adobada tacos and burritos made to order. Eat at picnic tables outdoors in summer. Open daily.

Nik-N-Willie's (76 Old Mammoth Rd., next to Radio Shack; 760-934-2012). Classic pizza and sub joint. Mammoth's best hot Italian sandwich. Beer on tap or by the bottle. Dine in or take out. Weekday specials. Discount for take-'n'-bake pizzas. Open daily.

Old New York Deli & Bagel Co. (6201 Minaret Rd., streetside at the Village; 760-934-DELI; www.oldnewyork.com). A scaled-down version of So Cal-favorite Jerry's Deli, with a full breakfast menu, matzo ball soup, heaped-up pastrami sandwiches, fresh-squeezed orange juice, and more. And bagels, of course, boiled on the premises. Prices are heaped-up, too, but when you need a good scallion or sun-dried tomato schmear, what're you gonna do? Other locations in Camarillo

and Newbury Park, where the prices are the same, but the smell of pine and access to powder is wanting. Free Wi-Fi for customers; $5 burger special during shoulder seasons; sidewalk dining in summer. Open daily (in season) from 6 AM for breakfast, lunch, and dinner.

The Pita Pit (6201 Minaret Rd., streetside at the Village; 760-924-PITA; www.pitapitusa.com). The Canadian franchise with headquarters in Idaho. Have your pita-wrapped sandwich built before your very eyes: breakfast pitas; falafel pitas; late-night Philly cheesesteak pitas. Dine in or take out. Delivery available for a fee.

Shea Schat's Bakkerÿ (3305 Main St.; 760-934-6055). They got divorced. He got the one in Bishop; she got this one. Still, we get the same (or indistinguishably similar) great sheepherder bread, the same great roast turkey sandwiches (served with pickle wedge and cookie), and the same great pastries and donuts. Open every day. Long lines on weekends.

Salsa's Taqueria (588 Old Mammoth Rd.; 760-924-0408). Mammoth's best catering-truck-style Mexican food. Tacos, tortas, burritos, horchata. Eat in or take out. Open daily for lunch and dinner.

SWEETS **Mammoth Fun Shop** (3131 Main St.; 760-934-1111; www.mammothfunshop.com). Premium selection of craft ice cream, hand-made waffle cones, milkshakes, and root beer floats. Polish off a Fundae—13 scoops of ice cream with toppings—and get your picture on the wall of fame!

Rocky Mountain Chocolate Factory (Two locations: at the Village, 760-934-6962; 437 Old Mammoth Rd., next to Vons, 760-934-6269; www.rmcf.com). Colorado's favorite franchise chocolate shop is right at home in the High Sierra. Boxed assortments, hot cocoa mix, fudge, caramel apples.

JUNE LAKE LOOP

Eagle's Landing (5587 CA 158; 760-648-7897; www.doubleeagle.com;

expensive). Start the day with an epic Bodie breakfast burrito or thick slices of Hawaiian-style French toast. The Alpers smoked-trout club makes a lunch worth coming in out of the cold for. Dinner is scaled-up chop house fare. The real attraction in this lofty, casual, fir-paneled dining room is the way the light slides from Carson Peak. Full bar. Box lunches available. Open daily from 7 AM.

TAVERNS, SALOONS, AND ROAD-HOUSES **June Lake Brewing Tasting Room** (131 Crawford Ave., June Lake; 858-668-6340; www.junelakebrewing .com). This is the hub of June Lake's newly vibrant social scene, especially in summertime. Stop by to try or purchase for carry-out any or all of a dozen award-winning local beers. Hawaiian food truck in the parking lot.

The Tiger Bar (Main Street, CA 158, center of June Lake Village; 760-648-7551; www.tiger barcafe.com). Established in 1932, the Tiger is an old standby for beer, bloodies, burgers, and pool.

COFFEE, TEA, ETC. **June Lake Junction Cafe** (CA 395 and CA 158, June Lake Loop; 760648-7509). Basic Shell gas mart, plus coffee bar, milk shakes, smoothies, breakfast burritos, fresh-baked cinnamon rolls, and deli sandwiches to go.

MONO LAKE AND LEE VINING

Mono Cone (CA 395, Lee Vining; 760-647-6606). Classic roadside burger and soft-serve ice cream stand. Chocolate-dipped vanilla/chocolate twist, of course. Picnic tables in the shade around back. Open spring to fall.

Whoa Nelly Deli (aka the Mobil station, aka Tioga Gas Mart, aka the Mo' Mart, 22 Vista Point Rd., at the junction of CA 395 and CA 120; 760-647-1088; www.whoanelliedeli.com; moderate). Back in the day, people wondered why chef Matt Toomey left a decent job at Mammoth's old Whiskey Creek restaurant to work the sandwich counter at the

gas station in Lee Vining. That is, until folks saw what he was able to do with the place. He's since moved on—to his own signature restaurant below 80/50 in Mammoth—but the crew still makes surprisingly excellent full-plate meals catering to the summer onslaught of bikers, climbers, backpackers, firefighters, European tourists, truckers, geologists, park rangers, water department stooges, kids, and dogs coming and going from the Yosemite high country. The fish tacos and lobster taquitos, each served with black beans and some version of exotic-fruit salsa, are still legendary, and the brick o'buffalo meat loaf and the apricot-wild-berry-glazed pork tenderloin still deserve respect. Order at the counter, grab a picnic table with a view of the lake, and wait for your number to be called. Beer and wine from the cooler; glasses provided. Open daily, May to October (when Tioga Pass is open). Hopping live music on the lawn most Thursdays and Sundays through the summer.

COFFEE, ETC. **Latte Da Coffee Cafe** (51 CA 395, at the El Mono Motel; 760-647-6310; www.elmonomotel.com). Cozy, fair-trade, organic coffee shop with a handful of tables and a fireplace. Local information and stories. Wireless Internet. Front porch with views across the highway to the lake.

GENERAL STORES **Mono Market** (51303 CA 395; 760-647-1010). Surprisingly extensive stock for its small, convenience-store size: meat, organic produce, beer and wine, spices, tortillas, natural foods, ice cream, office supplies, chocolate, cheese, trail mix, and batteries. A variety of deli-counter foods for take-out, including quiches, sandwiches, homemade "Lizzagna" (named for owner and veteran Mammoth ski patrolman Chris Lizza), and hefty black-bean breakfast monoritos, made fresh every morning with bacon, chorizo, or vegetables. Open every day, even in winter.

Tioga Gas Mart (at the Mobil station, aka the Mo' Mart, 22 Vista Point Rd. at the junction of CA 395 and CA 120; 760-647-1088). Beer, wine, soft drinks, snack food, souvenirs, postcards, stuffed bears, books, fish tacos (see above). Open daily in summer. Popular live music venue, Thursdays and Sundays. Closed in winter, except for gasoline.

✳ Books, Maps, and Information

MAMMOTH LAKES

⊕ **Booky Joint** (Minaret Mall, 437 Old Mammoth Rd.; 760-934-5023; www .bookyjoint.com). Mammoth's only complete bookstore. Independent, locally owned, and friendly. Best-sellers, classics, and children's books, plus a full magazine rack. Excellent selection of local-interest books, maps, and guides. Plus toys, puzzles, Legos, and craft kits.

⊕ **Mammoth Lakes Welcome Center** (2500 Main St., CA 203; 760-924-5500; www.visitmammoth.com). Jointly operated by the Inyo National Forest, the Town of Mammoth Lakes and Eastern Sierra Interpretive Association. Worthwhile first stop on your way into town. Excellent selection of local-interest books, guides, recreation and topo maps, brochures, bear canisters. Rangers and volunteers on hand for latest trail and fire conditions, camping information, wilderness permits. Open daily year-round.

MONO LAKE AND LEE VINING

⊕ **Mono Basin Scenic Area Visitor Center** (CA 395, a quarter-mile north of Lee Vining; 760-647-3044). Airy, fortress-like building built in 1992 on a promontory overlooking the lake. Interactive displays on the region's natural and human history. A 20-minute film, *Of Fire & Ice*, provides a good overview. Interpretive tours, lectures, rotating art and photo exhibits, and a very cool large-scale model of the entire basin. Bookstore

and gift shop run by the Eastern Sierra Interpretive Association (760-934-3042). Closed in winter.

⊕ **Mono Lake Committee Bookstore** (CA 395 and Third Street; 760-647-6595; www.monolake.org). Home of the friendly folks who never stop working to save Mono Lake and other scenic treasures. Tourist information, T-shirts, travel mugs, gifts, gallery with rotating art exhibits, one of the best selections of local and environmental books in the Sierra. Closed Tuesdays and Wednesdays.

✳ Shopping

MAMMOTH LAKES

CLOTHING, FASHION, AND GIFTS First Street Leather (6201 Minaret Rd., street level at the Village; 760-934-8515; www.firststreetleather.com). High-quality, high-dollar leather, fur, wool, and sheepskin for men and women. Bags, boots, belts, gloves, hats, coats, slippers, accessories. Good place to rack up miles on the credit card. Open daily.

⊕ **Mammoth Fun Shop** (3131 Main St.; 760-924-1111; www.mammothfunshop .com). Locally-owned, meticulously curated toy, gift, and novelty boutique for all ages. Magic kits, juggling supplies, Pokémon cards, guitar strings, gag gifts,

BODIE IN EARLY SPRING BURKE GRIGGS

STORM RIDING ON BARDINI RIDGE IN THE SHERWINS PATITUCCIPHOTO

funny socks, classic toys, seasonal items. Plus hand-scooped ice cream, root beer floats, and milkshakes (see above). Open daily in season.

Tonik (501 Old Mammoth Rd.; 760-924-7727; www.tonikstyle.com). Swank hipster boutique run by locals: high-art jeans, Dr. Seuss T-shirts, knee-length sweaters, caps, shoes, boots, jewelry, full-face sunglasses. Inventory changes frequently. Sale rack. Open daily.

GALLERIES Vern Clevenger Gallery (220 Sierra Manor Rd., Unit 4; 760-934-5100; www.vernclevenger.com). Classic, collectible large-format landscape photography of the Sierra Nevada and beyond by Vern Clevenger, world-class rock climber and mountaineer and long-time Mammoth local. Prints, posters, cards, professional lab service, and seasonal photography workshops.

GENERAL STORES Mammoth DIY Center (26 Old Mammoth Rd., next to Rite Aid; 760-924-7112; www.doitcenter.com). Hardware, tire chains, space heaters, light bulbs, Christmas tree stands, kitchen accessories, batteries, toilet plungers, folding chairs, barbecues, and propane canisters.

SPORTING GEAR AND EQUIP-MENT The Alpine Approach (6201 Minaret Rd., streetside at the Village; 760-934-6373; www.mammothgear.com). Upscale little sister to Mammoth Mountaineering (see below), with emphasis on wearable outdoor gear: puffy outerwear, sunglasses, Arcteryx pants and jackets, delicious Icebreaker merino wool long underwear. Open daily in season.

Brian's Bicycles and Cross Country Skis (3059 Chateau Rd., off Old Mammoth Road; 760-924-8566; www.mammothbikesandskis.com). Boutique-sized pedal shop in summer; track- and skate-skiing equipment in winter. Rentals, repairs, and personalized service by Brian himself. Open daily in season.

Footloose Sports (3043 Main St., corner of Old Mammoth Road; 760-934-2400; www.footloosesports.com). Full-service alpine ski and bike shop since 1981. Ski, snowboard, and bike rentals; performance demos; custom boot fitting; and repairs. Less expensive than on the mountain, better selection.

Helmets, snowshoes, and sleds also available in season. Open daily.

McCoy Sports (in the Village; 760-924-7070). High-fashion snow and sun wear, genuine Mammoth Mountain souvenirs, resort logowear, and accessories. Ski rentals for Village Lodge guests. Open daily.

✪ **Mammoth Mountaineering** (361 Old Mammoth Rd.; 760-934-4191 or 1-888-395-3951; www.mammothgear.com). Full range of alpine ski touring gear, climbing equipment, ropes, shoes, boots, tents, bags, backpacking accessories, books, maps, and functional outdoor fashions. Friendly, knowledgeable staff; one of the best sources around for local backcountry beta. Equipment rentals, performance demos, tuning, and repair. Open daily.

P-3 (3325 Main St.; 760-934-9500; www.p3mammoth.com). Picks up where traditional ski and bike shops leave off for parks, pipes, and powder. Specializing in terrain park, freestyle, and half-pipe gear; twin-tip, slarvy fat skis; free-ride and downhill bikes; skateboards; and accompanying fashions. Open daily.

Surefoot (6201 Minaret Rd., street level at the Village; 760-924-8333; www.surefoot.com). World-renowned custom boot-fitting shop with locations from Mammoth to Aspen to London to Verbier. Open daily in season.

✪ **Wave Rave** (3203 Main St.; 760-934-2471; www.waveravesnowboardshop.com). Setting and spreading knuckle-dragging trends since the late '80s, owned and operated by local snowboarders. Rentals, demos, repairs, fashion.

JUNE LAKE LOOP

GENERAL STORES **June Lake General Store** (1 Main St.; 760-648-7771). Basic small-town grocery with beer, liquor, ice, fishing tackle, canned goods, packaged pastries, camping supplies, hardware, charcoal, firewood. Open Daily 8 AM–8 PM.

Silver Lake General Store (Silver Lake Resort; 760-648-7525; www

SOAKING IN LONG VALLEY'S VOLCANO-HEATED WATERS PATITUCCIPHOTO

.silverlakeresort.net/store.htm). Basic groceries, beer, wine, ice, camping and fishing supplies, canned goods, sunblock, books, postcards, curios, and crafts.

SPORTING GEAR AND EQUIP-MENT Ernie's Tackle & Ski Shop (2604 CA 158; 760-648-7756; www.ernies tackleandski.com). Classic tackle and bait shop since 1932. In winter, it becomes a basic ski and snowboard shop with a range of accessories and rentals.

SUNDRIES AND SOUVENIRS Sierra Wave T-Shirt Co. (36 CA 158; 760-648-7161; www.sierra-wave.com). Bears, mugs, curios, T-shirts, jellies, and honey.

Creekside Corner at Double Eagle (5587 CA 158; 760-648-7004; www.doubleeagle.com). Cards, candles, fancy soaps, bath salts, bathrobes, teddy bears, and spa products.

✳ Special Events

February: **Presidents Day Week**. Second-busiest week in Mammoth, after the December holidays.

March: **Mammoth Winter Biathlon** (at the Tamarack Nordic Center; www.mammothbiathlon.org). Shooting and skiing. The largest winter biathlon race in North America, including pre-race clinics and kids' events. **Elevation Gay Ski Week** (www.mammothgayski.com).

April: **Mammoth Invitational** (Mammoth Resorts). Popular fundraising weekend pairing philanthropists with professional ski racers and other high profile characters to benefit the nonprofit Mammoth Community Foundation. **Ezakimak Challenge** (Mammoth Mountain) 5K race with 2,000 feet of elevation gain from the base to the summit of Mammoth Mountain on snowshoes, skis or fat bikes. **Pond Skim** (1-800-MAMMOTH; www.mammothmountain.com).

DR. MIKE KARCH, ORTHOPEDIST, DRILLS THE TARGET DURING THE ANNUAL MAMMOTH WINTER BIATHLON JIM BOLD

Average Closing, Tamarack Cross Country Ski Center. Fishing season opening day.

May: **Spring Fest** (1-800-MAMMOTH; www.mammothmountain.com). **Sierra Star Golf Course opening** (760-924-4653; www.mammothmountain.com). **Mammoth Lakes Film Festival** (www.mammothlakesfilmfestival.com). **Average Tioga Pass opening** (209-372-0200; www.nps.gov/yose/planyourvisit/conditions.htm).

June: **Mammoth Motocross** (Mammoth Lakes; www.mammothmotocross.com). **Mammoth Mountain Bike Park opening** (1-800-MAMMOTH; www.mammothmountain.com). **Mammoth Half Marathon. Mono Lake Bird Chatauqua** (www.birdchautauqua.org). Birds, science, art, music, field trips. **Pamper Pedal Road Bike Ride** (www.eastsidevelo.org)

July: **Fourth of July Parade** (Mammoth Lakes). **Fourth of July fireworks** (Crowley Lake). **Mammoth Food & Wine Experience** (www.mammothfoodandwine.org). **June Lake Triathlon** (www.highsierratri.org). **Unbound Chamber Music Festival** (www.felicitrio.com/cmu.html).

A FISH FRY NEAR MONO LAKE, CELEBRATING THE ANNUAL OPENING OF TIOGA PASS, 1920S COURTESY NPS, YNP

August: **Mammoth Festival of Beers & Bluesapalooza** (Sam's Wood Site, Minaret Road; www.mammothbluesbrewsfest .com). Three days of music and beer in the woods. 200 craft beers. Grand tasting Saturday afternoon. **Mammoth Margarita Festival** (www .mammothmargaritafestival.com). **Mammoth Rocks & Taste of the Sierra** (www .mammothrocks.net). **Shakespeare in the Woods** (www.sierraclassictheatre.com).

September: **Annual Labor Day Festival of the Arts** (www.monoarts.org). Local craft fair in the woods. **Mammoth Rock N Rye** (www.mammothrocknrye .com). **Troutstock Eastern Sierra**. Million-dollar fishing derby, kids' activities and entertainment. **Tioga Pass Run** (Lee Vining; www.monolake.org). **Hop 'N' Sage Harvest Festival** (www .mammothbrewingco.com). **Mammoth Gran Fondo** (Mammoth Lakes; www .fallcentury.org). The most beautiful 100-mile ride in the world, **Autumnal equinox. Graniteman Challenge** (www .highsierratri.org). **Mammoth Kamikaze Bike Games** (www.kamikazebikegames .org). **Mammoth Oktoberfest** (Mammoth Lakes; www.villageatmammoth .com). **Mammoth Mountain Bike Park**

COOPER WEBB, AGE 11, RACES IN THE RED BULL JUNIOR AMATEUR JAMS, PART OF THE ANNUAL MAMMOTH MOTOCROSS CHRISTIAN PONDELLA

closing (1-800-MAMMOTH; www
.mammothmountain.com).

October: **Average peak fall colors.**

November: **Average Tioga Pass
closing** (209-372-0200; www.nps.gov/
yose/planyourvisit/conditions.htm).
**Mammoth Mountain Ski Area open-
ing day** (1-800-MAMMOTH; www
.mammothmountain.com). **Thanksgiving
Day Turkey Trot. Tamarack Cross Country Ski Center opening** (Lakes Basin).
Masters Race Camp Week (Mammoth
Mountain).

December: **Volcom Peanut Butter and Rail Jam** (1-800-MAM-
MOTH; www.mammothmountain
.com). **Mammoth Film Festival** (www
.mammothfilmfestival.com). **ULLR
Festival** (www.villageatmammoth
.com). **Night of Lights** (Canyon
Lodge; 1-800-MAMMOTH; www
.mammothmountain.com). Big-bud-
get fireworks display, torchlight ski
parade, food, and live music. **June
Mountain Ski Area opening** (June
Mountain).

SEQUOIA, KINGS CANYON, & THE GREAT WESTERN DIVIDE

SEQUOIA, KINGS CANYON, & THE GREAT WESTERN DIVIDE

Such a landscape! A hundred peaks in sight over 13,000 feet—many very sharp—deep canyons, cliffs in every direction almost rival Yosemite, sharp ridges inaccessible to man, on which human foot has never trod—all combined to produce a view of sublimity of which is rarely equaled, one which few are privileged to behold.
—William Henry Brewer, *Whitney Geological Survey*, 1864

In August 1875, having just walked more than 300 miles—from the Merced to the Kings River, crossing the range at Kearsarge, climbing Mount Whitney a second time, then returning to Yosemite Valley via Mono Lake and Lee Vining Canyon—a young John Muir set out once again from Clark's Station (Wawona) in the company of a mule named Brownie. His goal: to survey "the sequoia belt, making special studies of the species and visiting every grove as far as its southernmost limit."

To Muir, the sequoia (*sequoiadendron gigantea*)—not to be confused with its taller, thinner cousin down on the coast, the California Redwood—was "the king of all the conifers" and "the noblest of the noblest race." Once upon a time the earth's surface was covered with them. They were the dominant life form of the Jurassic and Cretaceous Periods; the dinosaurs lived, reigned briefly, and died beneath them. As continents drifted apart, as mountains rose from the seas and the climate turned colder and drier, the Big Trees—most of them—went the way of the big reptiles. "No imperishableness of mountain-peak or of fragment of human work, broken pillar or sand-worn image half lifted over pathetic desert—none of these link the past and today with anything like the power of these monuments of living antiquity," Clarence King wrote of the ancient sequoias he'd seen on the Whitney Survey in 1864.

Today there are no more than 76 groves of native giant sequoias left in the world—all of them at an elevation between 5,000 and 8,000 feet on the southwestern slope of California's Sierra Nevada. They are the biggest living things on the planet. The biggest of all, the General Sherman Tree, now hulks above Generals Highway in Sequoia National Park at a height of 275 feet, with a diameter three times that of a standard trampoline and a volume comparable to that of two late-model 747s.

Muir found isolated groves of sequoias, in generally mixed forests of sugar pine, white fir, and incense cedar, as far south as the Great Western Divide and the slopes of the upper Kern. Along the way—in the "wild untrampled kingdoms of the Sierra"—he was also delighted by innumerable lakes and meadows, "stupendous rocks," granite domes, cliffs, and great, wide chasms many thousands of feet deep. The deepest of these, the canyons of the Middle and South Forks of the Kings (at their confluence a full 2,000 feet deeper than the Grand Canyon of the Colorado), Muir described with uncharacteristic understatement as "a rival to the Yosemite."

He was not so delighted, however, to see the trampling the country had already received. In one close-cropped meadow beside the Kings River, in the wake of a vast herd of sheep, he came upon a notice nailed to a tree: WE, THE UNDERSIGNED, CLAIM

THIS VALLEY FOR THE PURPOSE OF RAISING STOCK. MR. THOMAS, MR. RICHARDS, HAR-VEY & CO.

By Muir's count, there were already five commercial sawmills operating in the region, "all of which were cutting more or less of 'big-tree' lumber," to be used (because of the brittle quality of sequoia wood and the massive trees' tendency to shatter upon felling) for fence posts, grape stakes, roof shingles, and matchsticks. This at a time when the only portion of the Sierra Nevada that was in any way protected from commercial logging was the floor of Yosemite Valley. "Our forest belts are being burned and cut down and wasted like a field of unprotected grain," wrote Muir. "Unless protective measures be speedily invented and enforced, in a few years this noblest tree species in the world will present only a few hacked and scarred remnants."

Difficulties of transport more than anything—thanks to the severity of the topography—kept most serious logging interests away from the Big Trees. But in the fall of 1885, a group of utopian socialists calling themselves the Kaweah Colony filed 40 separate claims on 10 square miles of what is today known as the Giant Forest. That spring, despite delays in the processing of their claims, the colonists began work on a wagon road to the Big Trees. Five years later, through an almost miraculous combination of activism, unholy alliances, and political subterfuge—the Southern Pacific Railroad perhaps playing a card to limit competition for its timber monopoly—legislation came before President Benjamin Harrison that by his signature, in the fall of 1890, created Sequoia and General Grant National Parks—the nation's second and third such parks, after Yellowstone. Several of the old sequoia groves, including those filed on by the Kaweah colonists, were thus permanently withdrawn from "settlement, occupancy, or sale" and placed under the protection of the U.S. Army.

ONCE THE LARGEST GROVE OF GIANT SEQUOIAS IN THE WORLD, THE CONVERSE BASIN WAS LOGGED TO A SINGLE TREE

The first detachment of cavalry arrived with the melting of snow in 1891. The Kaweah Colony fell apart. In 1893, Harrison proclaimed that another 4 million acres should be set aside as the "Sierra Forest Reserve" (now the Sequoia and Sierra National Forests), encompassing the majority of sequoia groves from the Kings River south to the Tule and the summit of Mount Whitney.

How these vast swaths of public land were to be managed, under what designation and by which agency, are questions that we continue to grapple with to this day. The general trend, with some glaring exceptions, has been toward the expansion of federally protected boundaries. In 1926, Sequoia National Park was stretched eastward to include the upper Kern Canyon and the Sierra Crest. In 1936, when it looked as if Kings Canyon might be submerged beneath a reservoir, Ansel Adams traveled to Washington bearing photos. Four years later, Franklin Roosevelt declared the Kings Canyon National Wilderness Park, combining it with the earlier Grant Grove reserve. During World War II, Sequoia and Kings Canyon National Parks were consolidated under a single management scheme that is still in place today. Cedar Grove and the Tehipite Valley were added to the system in 1965, and Mineral King was added in 1978.

As "an outstanding example of significant geological processes and biological evolution" with "superlative natural phenomena, and areas of exceptional natural beauty," Sequoia and Kings Canyon National Parks were together designated an International Biosphere Reserve in 1976 and subsequently nominated for status as a World Heritage Site (though it has not yet made the list). In 2000, by authority of the Antiquities Act of 1906, President Bill Clinton created the Giant Sequoia National Monument, thereby prohibiting any further removal of trees from much of the public land adjacent to the parks. Timber interests have continued to challenge the designation, but prohibitions against cutting were upheld in the federal courts as recently as 2006. In 2017, the monument was "under review" by President Trump's Secretary of the Interior for possible commercial exploitation.

JOHN MUIR—A SCENE IN THE KERN RIVER COUNTRY   HELEN LUKEN JONES, COURTESY NPS, YNP

⊙ OTHER BOOKS TO SUPPLEMENT THIS CHAPTER

Challenge of the Big Trees: A Resource History of Sequoia and Kings Canyon National Parks, by Lary Dilsaver and William Tweed (Sequoia Parks Conservancy, 1990).

Geology of the Sierra Nevada, by Mary Hill (UC Press, 2006).

The Laws Field Guide to the Sierra Nevada, by John Muir Laws (Heyday Books, California Academy of Sciences, 2007).

Sequoia & Kings Canyon Camping and Hiking, by Tom Stienstra and Ann Marie Brown (Moon Outdoors, 2012).

Sierra Nevada Natural History, by Tracy Storer, Robert Usinger, and David Lukas (UC Press, 2004).

For now, despite more than a century of extraordinary booms in population, industry, and industrial-scale agriculture in the valley below, the country Muir explored back in 1875 is still some of the wildest and least trampled in the Sierra. There are no more than a handful of roads that penetrate this part of the range, roads carved with shovels and dynamite into mountainsides, some of the most dramatic and drop-dead spectacular roads in the world. Engineered (mostly in the 1930s) as if expressly to test the mettle of the oversized recreational vehicle, these roads climb thousands of feet in steep, tortuous switchbacks to offer hundred-mile sunset glimpses across haze and smog to the coastal ranges and beyond to the Pacific Ocean, then plunge headlong into some of the deepest canyons on the continent. Not one crosses over the crest to the other side. Where the asphalt ends and the backcountry begins—encompassing more than 4,000 square miles of designated, unbroken, roadless wilderness—travel is still accomplished only by mule, on horseback, or at the expense of one's boot heels.

Traditional threats by logging, mining, and grazing have for the most part been replaced by concerns over diminishing air quality (the smog in the San Joaquin Valley has recently been rated on a par with Los Angeles), climate change, and the spread of invasive plant and animal species. Still, since the days of Whitney and Muir, since the spring of 1827, when Jedediah Smith first scrambled up these canyons in search of beaver, since the arrival of the ancestors of the Monaches some 10,000 years ago—the scenery has remained fundamentally unchanged.

Tourist accommodations, on the other hand, have generally improved. Today, there are excellent meals to be had, as well as fridge-cold microbrewed beer, decent wine, a wealth of interpretive signage, soy protein bars, mediocre pizza, curios, books, phone cards (if not always cell phone reception), and comfortable beds right at the edge of the wilderness.

The annual number of visitors to Sequoia-Kings Canyon National Parks, at around 1.5 million, is less than half the number of visitors to Yosemite. Road access and infrastructure are also limited in comparison. As a result, the tourist hubs at Moro Rock and the Giant Forest, Lodgepole, and Grant Grove areas can feel thronged in July and August. Walk a couple hundred yards up any trail, however, and the world quiets down in short order. Outside and between the parks—other than on the busiest summer weekends or at the opening of hunting season in the fall—the national monument and national forest have a peaceful air of abandonment.

In the fall and spring, when the days are still warm and the nights crisp, oncoming cars prove infrequent enough, even inside the parks, that drivers smile and wave at each other through their windshields. In the winter, when the roads to Mineral King and the Kings River are closed and barricaded, when rain is falling hard in Three

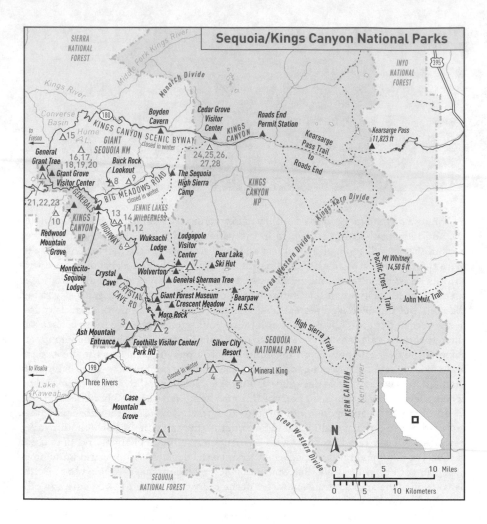

Sequoia/Kings Canyon National Parks

Rivers and the snow is piled higher than the restrooms at the Wolverton Ski Area, it's hard not to catch sight of, as John Muir once put it, "the clearest way into the Universe."

✳ The Lay of the Land: Approaches and Logistics

Travelers from Los Angeles and points south are most likely to enter the parks by CA 198, via Three Rivers, the only real gateway town to Sequoia-Kings Canyon. CA 245— connecting Visalia and points south with the northern entrance to Kings Canyon—is a lovely, forgotten little road, but it's no shortcut. For those making their way from Yosemite, San Francisco, and all other points north, the most direct route is CA 180, which shoots eastward from Fresno to the foothills, through the tough, hard-bitten agricultural towns of Minkler and Sanger, and then climbs in fairly short order to the Big Stump Entrance and the Grant Grove annex of Kings Canyon.

⭐ BEST MAPS TO SUPPLEMENT THIS CHAPTER

Each of these maps is available for purchase online or at most regional booksellers. For more information on map series, see Chapter 8.

"Sequoia and Kings Canyon: National Parks Guide Map," AAA Explore!
"Sequoia/Kings Canyon National Parks," Tom Harrison.
"Kings Canyon High Country," Tom Harrison.
"Mineral King," Tom Harrison.
"Mt. Whitney High Country," Tom Harrison.
"Golden Trout Wilderness," Tom Harrison.
"John Muir Trail Map Pack," Tom Harrison.
"Shaver Lake/Sierra National Forest," National Geographic Trails Illustrated.
Sequoia/Kings Canyon National Park, National Geographic Trails Illustrated.
"Sequoia National Forest Map (Includes Giant Sequoia National Monument)," U.S. Forest Service.
"Inyo National Forest Map," U.S. Forest Service.
"Sierra National Forest Map," U.S. Forest Service.

The only access from the east is by pack animal or on foot.

Gas is not sold within the parks' boundaries, but can be purchased—at a premium—at either Stony Creek Village (on Generals Highway) or from the antique gravity-fed pump at the Kings Canyon Lodge. The last major supply towns along these routes—for specialized outdoor equipment, cycling gear, sushi, relatively inexpensive gas, and more—are Visalia and Fresno, respectively. The farm stands at Sanger and Lemon Cove provide the last chance for fresh fruit and vegetables.

This chapter is organized into four main sections, according to the main access roads to the parks: (1) Three Rivers, primary gateway town to Sequoia National Park, and the foothills country off CA 198; (2) Mineral King; (3) Generals Highway and

MINKLER CASH STORE, ONE PLACE TO STOCK UP ON LUXURY ITEMS BEFORE LEAVING CIVILIZATION BURKE GRIGGS

LEAVE THE DRIVING TO THE PROS

Consider leaving the car, the stress, and the carbon footprint behind, instead heading up into the hills with nothing but a pack on your back and a credit card in your pocket. The Sequoia Shuttle (1-877-BUS-HIKE; www.sequoiashuttle.com) runs buses and vans up the hill several times a day, seven days a week, from Memorial Day through Labor Day, from points in Visalia, Exeter, and Three Rivers to the Giant Forest Museum in Sequoia National Park ($15 round-trip, includes park entrance fee). Advance reservations are required; check website for schedule and details. From the Giant Forest Museum, free park shuttles run every 15 minutes from 8:00 AM to 6:30 PM to Moro Rock and Crescent Meadow, and to the Sherman Tree and Lodgepole Visitor Center. The purple line runs every 30 minutes between Lodgepole and the Wuksachi Lodge and Dorst Creek Campground. The orange line runs between the General Sherman Tree and Wolverton.

For customized transport service and tour options, including special hiker/backpacker/skier shuttles, as well as transportation to and from the Hanford Amtrak station, contact Paul and Becky Bischoff at Sequoia Sightseeing Tours (559-561-4189; www.sequoiatours.com).

high-country Sequoia National Park; and (4) CA 180, the Kings Canyon Scenic Byway, from Grant Grove to Cedar Grove. Lodging, dining, services, points of interest, and recreation opportunities along each of these roads are listed geographically within the appropriate section.

Following these are general notes on two less-traveled but still highly worthy scenic byways to the south and north of Sequoia/Kings Canyon. First, to the south, the Great Western Divide Highway, also called the "Mighty 190," which meanders through the Southern Unit of the Giant Sequoia National Monument between Springville (south of Visalia, in the Central Valley) and Kernville (on the north end of Lake Isabella). Kernville also can be reached from Los Angeles and points south via CA 178 from Bakersfield, or—preferably, from a scenic standpoint—over Walker Pass from Inyokern and the Mojave Desert (see Chapter 4).

Finally, to the north of Kings Canyon, Kaiser Pass and the "Sierra Heritage Scenic Byway" (CA 168) climb up into the upper San Joaquin drainage (above Shaver and Huntington Lakes) to Mono Hot Springs and the Florence and Thomas Edison Reservoirs, with their unique ferryboat access to the John Muir Wilderness and the remote northern end of Kings Canyon National Park.

✳ To See

THREE RIVERS

A ramble-down, artsy-funky community of foothill cabins, second homes, ranches, and motels stretching for several miles along both sides of CA 198 (Sierra Drive), Three Rivers is home to what may or may not be the world's largest wood carving—of Paul Bunyan, of course. The South, Middle, and North Forks of the Kaweah River come together here before backing up into the Army Corps of Engineers' storage reservoir at Lake Kaweah.

Before the 1850s, some 2,000 Yokut and Monache Indians are supposed to have made their living in these valleys. Old grinding stones and campsites abound. As of the 2000 census, the population of Three Rivers was 2,248—down nearly 600 from five years earlier—of which less than 1 percent were categorized as Native American.

The grizzlies are gone, but the place still teems with wildlife: ground squirrels, tree squirrels, mule deer, opossums, raccoons, bobcats, mountain lions, black bear, coyotes, foxes, rattlesnakes, red-tail hawks, wild turkeys, turkey vultures, quail, bats, and scorpions. William Shatner and Anjelica Huston are said to own ranches in the surrounding foothills.

The first white settler, Hale D. Tharp, arrived and started ranching cattle and hogs in 1856 (eventually claiming summer pastures amid the giant sequoias at Crescent Meadow). From 1866 to 1891, an ambitious colony of socialists known as the Kaweah Co-Operative Commonwealth, or Kaweah Colony, maintained its headquarters and post office along the North Fork—until their timber claims were denied and a national park was declared where they had already built a road and a mill. In the early 1900s, in the wake of the Boer Wars, a handful of Rhodesian pioneers and British scouts are said to have built ranches here, the countryside perhaps reminding them of the Transvaal. The Hare Krishnas ran a boarding school here until the mid-1980s. With every little cabin and shack turned into short-term Airbnb lodging for tourists, year-round population has in recent years dropped from 2,000 souls to around 1,500 due to lack of affordable housing.

Most of the settlement of Three Rivers sits at about 800 feet in elevation. Summer temperatures frequently reach the high 90s to low 100s—a record-setting 118 degrees was recorded at Ash Mountain in July 2007—toasting the grass, testing the fortitude of radiator hoses, and generally making passers-through eager to jump in rivers or push up into the high country. With winter rains, the Kaweah booms, the hills turn back to a shocking hue of Irish green, and the town goes sleepy. The blooming of redbuds in early spring and the subsequent return of swallows to Pumpkin Hollow Bridge are spectacles worth traveling for. Basic tourist services, gas, grocery, crafts, curios, good coffee, sandwiches, home-crafted chocolate, and sit-down dining are available year-round.

Three Rivers Historical Museum (42268 Sierra Dr.; 559-561-2707; www.3rmuseum .org). Look for the 17-foot-tall Paul Bunyan, carved in 1941–42 from a 2,000-year-old giant sequoia. The "museum," run by the local chamber of commerce, houses a spare and eclectic collection of artifacts, books, and old photos. It gives a bit of flavor of the earlier days in Three Rivers. Highlights include a mountain lion pelt (with head) and a pile of news clippings on Disney's now-historic attempts to develop Mineral King.

Kaweah Colony Post Office (43795 N. Fork Dr.; 559-561-4745). The Kaweah Post Office was built in 1890 to handle mail for the burgeoning utopian settlement of Advance. The colony collapsed a year later. In 1910, the diminutive structure, complete with the original service window and brass post office boxes, was moved—probably by wagon—to its current location in the sleepy hamlet of Kaweah (population 480). In 1948, it was designated a California Historical Landmark and is now one of the smallest operating post offices in the United States.

Ash Mountain Entrance. Pay the fee and get a park map and newspaper here. Up the road, appreciate the ethnic confusion (if not the artistry) manifest in the historic Sequoia National Park sign, handcarved in the 1930s by an anonymous Civilian Conservation Corps (CCC) member from Arkansas. The Indian head was apparently patterned after the one on the old buffalo nickel, which, in turn, is supposed to have been a composite portrait of various Plains Indian chiefs. The word *sequoia*—the name given to the Big Tree and then the park—is generally considered to have been a nineteenth-century botanist's tribute to a half-German, half-Cherokee, Appalachian silversmith by the name of Sequoyah, or George Guess (or Gist), generally known for having invented, in his workshop 3,000 miles from the nearest Big Tree, the first practical syllabary for the Cherokee language.

KAWEAH COLONY POST OFFICE, ONE OF SMALLEST IN THE UNITED STATES

Hospital Rock Picnic Area. Ancestors of the Monache Indians were enjoying the shade and water here a hundred years before Columbus was born. By 1873, when a certain James Everton is said to have recovered here from a shotgun wound inflicted by a jury-rigged bear trap, the Monache were gone. Pictographs and acorn-grinding rocks remain as evidence of their tenure.

MINERAL KING

Climbing its sinuous way up along the East Fork of the Kaweah, through a full range of ecosystems (from chaparral to giant sequoia groves to broad subalpine meadows), the Mineral King Road is a genuine feat of engineering—especially considering much of it was built during a brief and failed series of mining booms in the 1870s. Don't be fooled by the sign at the junction on the north end of Three Rivers, proclaiming that there are 25 miles to go. These are likely to rank among the longest 25 miles you've ever traveled on pavement—or mostly on pavement (allow up to an hour and a half from Three Rivers, and don't let your mind lose track of the possibility of sudden down-coming traffic). The prominent peak to the east, at the head of the valley, is called Sawtooth (12,343 feet) for obvious reasons.

The current roadway was completed in 1915 to provide access to private summer cottages. Leases on these cottages are still held by the descendants of those who built them, six or seven generations later, and cannot legally be sold or transferred outside the family. In 1926, Mineral King was declared a National Game Refuge. Forty years later, in January 1966, Walt Disney Productions signed a multiple-use contract with the U.S. Forest Service to establish a major downhill ski resort in White Chief Bowl, with fourteen ski lifts, two large hotels, and a parking garage for 2,500 vehicles. A 13-year-long legal and public relations battle ensued, ending in 1978 with the defeat of the project and the annexation of Mineral King to Sequoia National Park. In October 2003, the collection of 66 off-grid summer cabins was promoted from Cultural Landscape District to an official listing on the National Register of Historic Places.

Note: There is no gasoline or alcohol available in Mineral King. The road is open only from late spring to the first major snowfall. In winter, the coveted bowls first touted by U.S. Ski Team coach Alf Engen in 1946 are accessible only to those on backcountry skis or snowshoes.

WATERMELON SNOW

Patches of reddish-pink snow on lingering High Sierra snowfields, known as "watermelon snow," are made by colonies of *chlamydomas nivalis*, or "snow algae." Some say the stuff tastes like watermelon, but the Park Service says the following: Don't eat it.

Atwell Mill and Skinner Grove. The old Hockett Trail, built in the 1860s as a resupply route from Visalia to Fort Independence and the Owens Valley, passes through here. The grove contains some of the highest-elevation old-growth sequoias in the Sierra. Kaweah colonists leased and partially logged the area in the early 1890s, after the creation of the national park, before a series of heated exchanges with the U.S. cavalry finally persuaded them to abandon the operation. Of their efforts, a steam engine and numerous big stumps remain. Lumber from this mill was used to build the flume to Mount Whitney Power Company's Kaweah Power House No. 1.

Honeymoon Point Cabin (across the street from the stables; no phone; www .mineralking.org). The old Crowley Resort, established in 1895, once boasted "a hotel, store, post office, butcher shop, stable, dance hall, and more than a dozen rental

CABIN AND SEQUOIA STUMP, ATWELL MILL, MINERAL KING ROAD, JUNE 2007 BURKE GRIGGS

cabins," according to local historian Louise Jackson. The place took a big hit in the San Francisco earthquake of 1906, was rebuilt, and took its final blow by avalanche in 1969. This small cabin survived and is today a humble museum maintained by the Mineral King Preservation Society.

GENERALS HIGHWAY AND HIGH-COUNTRY SEQUOIA

HONEYMOON POINT CABIN, MINERAL KING, JUNE 2007 BURKE GRIGGS

In just under 16 miles, between the Ash Mountain Entrance and the Giant Forest, Generals Highway climbs more than 6,000 feet in elevation to reach the largest sequoia groves in the world. The Mount Whitney Power Company built the first section of highway, from Ash Mountain to Hospital Rock, in 1898 as a service road for its flume along the East Fork of the Kaweah. The flume is still visible on the opposite side of the river. The section from Hospital Rock to the Giant Forest was completed in 1926, replacing the old Colony Mill Road as the main access route into the park's high country. The CCC came on board in the 1930s, adding a second lane, excavating so-called Tunnel Rock, building watering stations and native-stone guard walls, and extending the roadway—then called the Park-to-Park Highway—as far as Grant Grove.

Giant Forest Ex-Village. "This part of the Sequoia belt seemed to me the finest," wrote John Muir, "and I then named it 'the Giant Forest.'" By the 1930s, with the completion and subsequent improvement of Generals Highway, the grove became the hub of activity in the park. The Giant Forest Village eventually consisted of "four campgrounds, dozens of parking lots, a garbage incinerator, water and sewage systems, a gas station, corrals, and over 200 cabin, tent-top, dining, office, retail, and bathhouse structures," according to the official park service history. In the 1970s, with annual park visitation numbers topping a million, the gas station, post office, and campgrounds were transferred to the Lodgepole area. Full restoration of the groves and meadows began in 1997 with the painstaking removal of all remaining facilities, save the market and general store building (now the museum). Open year-round.

Moro Rock–Crescent Meadow Road. This worthwhile side road from the Giant Forest is now also serviced by a free shuttle. The original wooden stairs to the top of Moro Rock, built in 1917, were replaced with a stone stairway in 1931. Handrails were added by a CCC crew in 1933. In December 1937, an unnamed sequoia fell across the road, prompting the cutting of a tunnel through the log the following summer. Farther on is the parking lot for the High Sierra Trail, Crescent Meadow, and Hale Tharp's unique summer cabin. John Muir met Tharp here in 1875, had supper, and spent several days at this "noble den in a fallen sequoia . . . weatherproof, earthquake-proof, likely to outlast the most durable stone castle, and commanding views of garden and grove grander far than the richest king ever enjoyed." Even in the busiest days of summer, the meadow proves a delightful, peaceful place for a stroll through the wildflowers. Road closed in winter.

General Sherman Tree. This is the Big One: The world's most voluminous living thing. And it's still growing at an incredibly rapid rate—likely the fastest of any tree on the planet. Every year the thing puts on about 40 cubic feet of new wood, as much as what makes up an entire 60-foot-tall Douglas fir. Imagine the number of toothpicks. Park at the lot off the Wolverton road and enjoy a leisurely paved stroll down into the grove, replete with world-class people-watching opportunities (uphill on the way back). Near the bottom, note the cross-section of the General Sherman as represented on the pavement, with a surface area equivalent to that of 25 tournament-sized billiards tables. From the base of the tree itself, continue along the 2-mile **Congress Trail** (easy, paved) to various other named trees. If you'd prefer to do this in solitude, try during a snowstorm, at night, in the depth of winter. Or try a different grove.

Crystal Cave (559-565-3759; www.explorecrystalcave.com). One summer day in 1918, Walter Fry and another off-duty park ranger were scrambling down along Cascade Creek, wrestling their fly rods through thickets of poison oak, when one or the other stumbled upon the entrance to a cavern—with more than 3 miles of chambers and passageways, home to four or five unique species of invertebrate. "It is in this cave," wrote Fry, "that nature has lavishly traced her design in decorative glory." Of some 200 such caverns in Sequoia-Kings, Crystal and Boyden are the only two open to the public. The CCC built the pathway, rails, and stairs in 1939. The trail inside the cavern was paved in 1985 to keep dust from inhibiting the formation of crystals.

Bathrooms were removed from within the cave's entrance in 2000. Forty-five-minute guided tours are offered throughout the summer; tickets are available only at Lodgepole or Ash Mountain Visitor Centers. No tickets sold at the cave. Allow an hour and a half from the Giant Forest to the cave's entrance, and wear layers and practical shoes. "Wild cave tours" are available every Saturday in summer.

○ **Buck Rock Lookout** (559-336-9319; www.buckrock.org). A telephone line was strung from Pinehurst to a fire lookout platform on Buck Rock in 1914. The current wooden structure, built in 1923, is one of only three 4A-style cabs in existence today. The insane hanging stairway was built in 1942. Starting in 1997, after years of neglect, Kathy Ball and the nonprofit Buck Rock Foundation brought the lookout back into service. Access is via

PRACTICAL NOTE

If you're interested in visiting Crystal Cave (see page xxx), stop by the Foothills/Ash Mountain Visitor Center (47050 Generals Hwy.; 559-565-3135) to check the day's schedule and purchase tickets BEFORE heading up the mountain. Tickets are not sold at the cave. Tickets are also available at the Lodgepole Visitors Center (559-565-4436), but some backtracking will be required to get to the cave.

MORO ROCK: ON A CLEAR DAY YOU CAN SEE THE COAST RANGE BURKE GRIGGS

HOW THE REST OF THE WORLD CAME TO LEARN OF THE BIG TREES

Captain Walker and his men might be forgiven a degree of nonchalance when, in the fall of 1833, they happened to be the first Europeans to see the biggest trees in the world. They'd traveled some 1,200 miles from the Great Salt Lake, across what Walker described as "poor, sandy country," surviving mostly on buffalo jerky and rabbit, and ever imagining themselves surrounded by hostile Indians (and in their anxiety shooting and killing scores of them). They'd struggled for nearly four weeks across some of the roughest terrain in the High Sierra, their horses worthless in "the cold and famished region of snow"—except, that is, for the caloric content of their flesh. They had slightly more pressing things on their minds than the size of the local conifers. "It seemed to be the greatest cruelty," wrote Zenas Leonard, another chronicler of the expedition, "to take your rifle, when your horse sinks to the ground from starvation, but still manifests a desire and willingness to follow you, to shoot him in the head and then cut him up and take such parts of their [sic] flesh as extreme hunger alone will render it possible for a human being to eat."

Leonard did make the first brief printed mention of "some trees of the Red-wood species, incredibly large—some of which would measure from 16 to 18 fathoms round the trunk at the height of a man's head from the ground." The Indians had for thousands of years been pretty well versed in the great variety of local trees. In reference to the species we now call the giant sequoia (*Sequoiadendron gigantea*), the Tules are supposed to have made sounds along the lines of *Toos-pung-ish* and *Hea-miwithic*. The Southern Miwok word *Wa-wona* has been described variously as the word for "owl," or "guardian of the big trees," or simply "big trees." It took some years, however, before European Americans—generally preferring to discover things for themselves—began listening to the natives.

Two copies of Leonard's narrative survived a printing shop fire in Pennsylvania in 1839. News of the Big Trees failed to spread.

Frémont had passed without undue pause beneath "some trees extremely large" in 1846, probably on the North Fork of the Kings. A less renowned pioneer by the name of J. M. Wooster

Jeep trail—a nice day hike or horseback ride—from Big Meadows Road. On a rare clear day, the 360-degree views cover the whole of the country from the Monarch Divide to the Grapevine, from the Silliman Crest to the Coast Range. Open to the public 9:30 AM–6:30 PM in summer. Interpretive and environmental education programs on Friday evenings in summer.

Redwood Mountain Grove (Kings Canyon National Park). The overlook on the south side of Generals Highway, smog permitting, provides a rare overview of this largest grove of giant sequoias on the planet, with more than 2,100 Big Trees in 5 square miles. To lose oneself therein, descend the poorly marked dirt road opposite Quail Flat and Hume Lake Road to the Redwood Canyon trailhead.

GRANT GROVE AND THE KINGS CANYON SCENIC BYWAY

> *In the vast Sierra wilderness to the southward of the famous Yosemite Valley there is a yet grander valley of the same kind.*
> —John Muir, 1891

On the holy day of Epiphany in 1805, Lieutenant Gabriel Moraga and a small band of Spanish soldiers and missionaries made camp on the lower banks of a river they called El Río de los Santos Reyes (The River of the Holy Kings, today simply the Kings River).

may indeed, in 1850 (as he later claimed), have carved his moniker into the flank of a giant sequoia. But it was Augustus T. Dowd, Union Water Company employee from Murphy's, who started the real publicity storm. In 1852, on his way up the North Fork of the Stanislaus after a wounded bear, Dowd found himself suddenly face-to-face with the biggest living thing he'd ever seen. He went back to camp and told everyone who would listen—including the press. There seems to be no record of what happened to the bear.

Within a year, Dowd's "Discovery Tree" was felled, sawed into pieces, and shipped back to New York for exhibition. According to preeminent Sierra historian Francis Farquhar, it took "five men 22 days" to bring it down, "drilling by pump augurs through to the center from opposite sides." Its stump was used as a dance floor. The stump of another served time as a two-lane bowling alley. Other specimens had their bark stripped off, were marked in sections, and then were reassembled as far away as Chicago and London. Seeds were carried back eastward and planted, such that today there are individual sequoias dwarfing the local flora in Pennsylvania, Switzerland, Croatia, and New Zealand.

A COTILLION PARTY OF THIRTY-TWO PERSONS DANCING ON THE STUMP OF THE MAMMOTH TREE.

JULY 4 FESTIVITIES, 1854 FROM J. M. HUTCHINGS, *IN THE HEART OF THE SIERRAS*, 1006

"The river abounds with beaver and fish," Father Pedro Muñoz wrote in his journal. He estimated the number of natives living along the river to be more than 5,000. "It is a location suitable for a mission," he added, "although there would also have to be a presidio."

Twenty-two years later, with no significant resistance from the natives, Jedediah Smith and his crew harvested hundreds of pounds of beaver pelt along the lower stretches of the Kings and may have attempted to penetrate some distance into the canyon itself. There is no published account by the first white men to reach the head of the canyon. Captain Kuykendall, of the southern detachment of James Savage's Mariposa Battalion, came up the Kings in 1851 in pursuit of renegade Kaweahs. One of his men, also involved in the second expedition against Tenaya, remarked to a compatriot on that journey: "The King's river [sic] country, and the territory southeast of it, beats the Yosemite in terrific grandeur, but in sublime beauty you have got us."

By the time John Muir wandered through, first in 1873 and twice again in 1875, the meadows here were already well used by sheepherders and San Joaquin Valley stockmen, and the old Indian trail along Bubbs Creek, over what is now Kearsarge Pass, was already a popular thoroughfare to the east side of the range.

The General Grant Grove was set aside in 1893 as General Grant National Park. Of the neighboring Converse Basin Grove—once the largest grove of giant sequoia in the world, not so protected as the General Grant—every Big Tree was cut down and hauled off save one: the Boole Tree.

BUCK ROCK LOOKOUT WITH KINGS CANYON BEYOND

On average, the annual number of visitors to Kings Canyon comes in at just over half that of Sequoia (in 2006 the numbers were 552,766 and 954,507 respectively). In terms of total acreage, Kings Canyon is just over 10 percent larger than Sequoia. The obvious result, of course, from the point of view of the traveler entering the northern park after a day or two in the southern one, is fewer people per acre: i.e., less crowding, less traffic, more peace and quiet—especially when one strikes out beyond the Grant Grove area and into the depths of Kings Canyon proper.

The road from Hume Lake Junction to Cedar Grove, now a designated National Scenic Byway (closed in winter due to rock fall potential), was completed in 1939. The best time to visit the canyon floor is in early spring, when the road first opens, when the grasses are green, the flowers are abundant, and the black flies are absent. Or in midwinter, self-propelled. **Grant Grove Village**, cooler in summer, under snow in winter, is open year-round.

General Grant Tree. The second or third largest sequoia (once thought to be the biggest), depending on one's estimation of volume, this tree was designated the Nation's Christmas Tree by President Calvin Coolidge in 1926—at the behest of Charles E. Lee, then Secretary of the Sanger Chamber of Commerce. An annual "Trek to the Tree" ceremony is held here in December. President Eisenhower added to the tree's list of honorary titles in 1956, declaring it a living National Shrine to America's war dead. A paved stroll through the grove (0.3 mile) wanders its way past the Robert E. Lee tree, the Fallen Monarch, and many more of the approximately forty named trees in the grove.

✪ **Converse Basin, Chicago Stump, and Boole Tree**. Once the largest grove of sequoias in the world, the Converse Basin today provides the starkest possible contrast to the majestic Giant Forest and General Grant groves. A disused trail leads from Forest Service Road 13S03 to the so-called Chicago Stump, once the ancient General

THE WORLD'S TOP TEN BIGGEST TREES (ACCORDING TO WENDELL FLINT, *TO FIND THE BIGGEST TREES*, SEQUOIA PARKS CONSERVANCY, 2002)

	TREE	LOCATION	HEIGHT (Feet)	CIRCUMFERENCE (Feet)	VOLUME (Cubic feet)
1.	General Sherman	Giant Forest	274.9	102.6	52,508
2.	Washington	Giant Forest	254.7	101.1	47,850
3.	General Grant	Grant Grove	268.1	107.5	46,608
4.	President	Giant Forest	240.9	93.0	45,148
5.	Lincoln	Giant Forest	255.8	98.3	45,148
6.	Stagg	Alder Creek	243.0	109.0	42,557
7.	Boole	Converse Basin	268.8	113.0	42,472
8.	Genesis	Mountain Home	253.0	85.3	41,897
9.	Franklin (near Washington)*	Giant Forest	223.8	94.8	41,280
10.	King Arthur*	Garfield	270.3	104.2	40,656

*unofficial name

Noble Tree, which was cut down, taken apart, and shipped to Chicago for the World's Fair in 1893. "Through all the wonderful, eventful centuries since Christ's time—and long before that—God has cared for these trees," Muir wrote in 1897, "but he cannot save them from fools." Meanwhile, the Sanger Lumber Company, also in 1897, one step ahead of its creditors, set about felling and dynamiting the entire grove—an estimated 191 million board feet of brittle sequoia lumber, of which only about 20 percent is said to have made it to the mill in Sanger. The Boole Tree, the world's seventh biggest living thing, was spared. Wildfires in 1929 and 1955 cleared brush and remaining log debris and gave the grove a new start.

Hume Lake. The lake was built as a millpond for the Hume-Bennett Lumber Company, successor to the Sanger Lumber Company, and to supply water for what was once the longest log-transport flume ever constructed—to a planing mill at Sanger, some 70 miles distant. The dam itself, the first concrete multiplearch dam in the world, was completed in 1909 and today is a National Historic Landmark. Opposite the dam is a bustling Christian summer camp. Anglers and swimmers will enjoy the beaches on the east shore.

Junction View and Yucca Point. Thousands of feet above the confluence of North America's two deepest canyons, CA 180 makes its first switchbacks for the grand descent. Stop here for impossible pictures and unfathomable views.

There are more than 200 such passageways beneath these mountains. Yet

A NEAR-FORGOTTEN PATH TO A GHOST GROVE

SMALL ROAD, BIG COUNTRY: KINGS CANYON SCENIC BYWAY, TEHIPITE, AND KINGS CANYONS BURKE GRIGGS

another, dubbed Ursa Minor, was discovered as recently as the summer of 2006. Boyden is one of only two caves in Sequoia-Kings open to the public for visitation. Potential visitors often want to know which is better. The approach to Crystal Cave is down first, then up. The approach to Boyden is up first, then down. Both are paved, deliciously cool and dark on a hot afternoon, serve as impressive showcases of underground mineral formations and the human capacity for metaphor, and must be visited by way of a 45-minute tour led by a knowledgeable (and sometimes humorous) guide. A ticket to Crystal Cave is more expensive, by six or seven dollars, but the money goes to an educational nonprofit group rather than to something called the Sierra Nevada Recreation Corporation. Your call. Why not do both? Contact **Kings Canyoneering** (559-338-0959; www.kingscanyoneering.com) for information on canyoneering, cavern rappelling, and overnights in the cavern.

River Road. A brief stretch of scenic dirt road along the Kings River (3 miles). Try it on a bicycle.

Zumwalt Meadow. On a site formerly owned by Daniel Kindle Zumwalt (1845–1904), agent for the Southern Pacific Railroad, this meadow now features a 1-mile, self-guided nature trail and boardwalk.

✪ **Project Survival's Cat Haven** (38257 E. Kings Canyon Rd., CA 180; 559-338-3216; www.cathaven.com). An eminently worthwhile stop on the main road up to or back from Kings Canyon National Park, this open, park-like facility in the foothills 45 miles west of Fresno is home to an impressive collection of what founder Dale Anderson calls "ambassador cats"—representatives of some of the rarest and most endangered species on the planet, all rescued not from the wild but from zoos or private collections. There are four amur leopards here, for example, whose main job is to raise awareness of the plight of their 40 or so wild brethren still trying to make it in the backcountry of Primorsky Krai along the Russo-Chinese border (aided to some extent by armed ex-Russian-army game wardens). There are two Bengal tigers lounging in their own spring-fed pond, a cheetah named Tango who purrs like a house cat when visitors approach his enclosure, a Siberian lynx, a black jaguar (once native to California), a black leopard (of the same species Rudyard Kipling mistakenly called a black panther), a pair of well-spoken but poorly understood jaguarundi, and a Barbary lion (extinct in the wild) from a Moroccan sultan's private collection. May through September: open 10 AM–5 PM, with the last tour leaving at 4 PM; closed Tuesday. October through April: open 10 AM–4 PM, with the last tour leaving at 3 PM; closed Tuesday, Wednesday, and major holidays. Call ahead for group rates or golf cart tours.

KERNVILLE AND THE GREAT WESTERN DIVIDE HIGHWAY

From the old one-street ranching town of Springville, an easy hour or so south of Three Rivers, CA 190 climbs its way up the Tule River Canyon. The road was once part of a now-forgotten scheme to build a trans-Sierra highway from Porterville to Lone Pine. "Because of its comparative remoteness," old-school guidebook author Russ Leadabrand wrote of this road in 1964, back when much of it was still unpaved, "this island byway in the Sequoia National Forest high country is never heavily used." Today, the stretch of fine asphalt between Springville and the Johnsondale Bridge, to the great delight of those few cyclists, bikers, and sports car drivers who've made its acquaintance, remains one of the emptiest scenic byways in North America.

At Quaking Aspen the "Mighty 190" turns south and becomes "The Great Western Divide Highway," which in turn runs wide and fast for 20 miles through the ancient

THE OLD KINGS CANYON LODGE, JUNE 2007: ONLY THE 1920S VINTAGE GAS PUMPS SURVIVED THE 2015 ROUGH FIRE; THE TAXIDERMY COLLECTION IS GONE BURKE GRIGGS

forests and granite domes of the southern unit of **Giant Sequoia National Monument**. The road ends abruptly at a junction with CA 155. From here, one has the option to drop westward, back down to the foothills, via the historic waters at California Hot Springs, or south and east to the Kern River Canyon and Kernville (the latter route approximately 70 miles one way). It may have been here, in this southernmost part of the range, that the last California grizzly was shot in 1922 (then again, it may have happened north of Sequoia, at Horse Corral Meadow—or in Fresno County). It was here, near Johnsondale, on June 26, 2004, that 27-year-old Shannon Parker of Santa Monica lost her eye to a malnourished two-year-old mountain lion. Within hours, the lion was tracked down and shot by federal officials.

John Ford's *Stagecoach* was shot here in the late 1930s; in the mid-1940s, John Huston's *Treasure of Sierra Madre*. Here stands the largest unlogged grove of sequoias outside the national parks—the **Freeman Creek Grove**, home to both the **Castro Tree** and the **George Bush Tree**. Services along the road are as limited today as they were 40 or 50 years ago—if not more so. For overnight accommodations, there are a handful of campgrounds; several old Forest Service guard cabins (available by advance arrangement); a funky, half-renovated historic river-rock lodge; a pack station; and two road-house motels. Dining is generally best accomplished out of the back of one's vehicle.

The most popular section of this byway, to the south along the Kern River—from the Johnsondale Bridge to Kernville, every turnout and picnic area and campground—can be overrun in midsummer, when the population of Bakersfield comes upstream to bask in its own water supply. Kernville itself, southernmost of the true gateway towns to the

THE HUME LAKE DOCK AARON HOROWITZ

Sierra, is a mostly charming collection of picket-fence vacation cottages, river cabins, antique shops, and vintage motels—most charming when approached from upriver rather than from Lake Isabella (and most charming at any other time of year than in the furnace heat of summer). Many of the town's older buildings were moved here in 1953 from the site of Old Kernville, once a popular shooting location for Hollywood Westerns, now somewhere beneath the waters of the reservoir.

The Needles. Impressive granite formations offer world-class climbing and a fire lookout with a frightening, exhilarating, historic set of stairs and big views into the Kern River Canyon and Golden Trout Wilderness. The lookout was built by the CCC in 1937. Access is by a moderately steep trail (5 miles round-trip).

George Bush Tree. President George H. W. Bush, the father, signed a proclamation here on July 14, 1992, protecting all giant sequoias "in perpetuity, as unique objects of beauty and antiquity for the benefit and inspiration of all people." Efforts to cut down these trees were renewed under the son's administration. As recently as 2007, the trees were defended in the federal courts, but they were back under review in the early days of the Trump Administration. See 'em before they get turned into toothpicks.

A MOUNTAIN BIKE AND THE GEORGE BUSH TREE

Trail of 100 Giants. Paved stroll through the Long Meadow Grove, past more than 125 giant sequoias. Here President Bill Clinton signed his own proclamation in April 2000, designating 327,769 acres of forest to be protected as the Giant Sequoia National Monument. Interpretive walks at 10 AM and 2 AM every Saturday and Sunday in summer. For information, call the Tule River Ranger District at 559-539-2607.

Kern Valley Museum (49 Big Blue Rd., Kernville; 760-376-6683; www.krv historicalsociety.org). Extensive homegrown museum with evocative, piped-in, old-time pickin' music and friendly volunteer docents. On display: arrowheads, rocks, antique mining and farm implements, photos of Old Kernville (before Lake Isabella), artifacts from the early days of Southern California Edison, Hollywood memorabilia (including one of the stagecoaches used in the John Ford/John Wayne movie "Stagecoach"), and a collection of stereoscope photos of pack trips on the Upper Kern River (1922–26).

MONO HOT SPRINGS AND KAISER PASS ROAD

The **Sierra Heritage Scenic Byway** begins at Clovis, but it isn't until some 60 miles later—above the march of vacation-home subdivisions at Shaver and Huntington reservoirs, past developments with names like Apple Ridge and Meadow Ridge and Sierra Pines, past the ski area at Sierra Summit—that it begins to earn its designation. Abruptly, at a place called Badger Flat, CA 168 changes its tenor. Here the road becomes a remarkable single-lane mountain track, now rough-paved, built in the early 1920s as a service route over **Kaiser Pass** (9,200 feet) for workers on the upper waterworks of Southern California Edison's monumental Big Creek hydroelectric project—in those days the biggest such project ever undertaken. "Men, mules, plows, scrapers, and donkey engines were used to remove boulders and trees," writes local historian Carole Steele. "Juniper trees were spared whenever possible." A 6-mile spur to Mono Hot Springs was completed in 1927 and nicknamed the C&N, or "Cheap & Nasty," for reasons that will be immediately apparent to all travelers thereon.

Frémont likely passed through this country sometime in the winter of 1845–46, discovering "some trees extremely large" on the way up (perhaps at Dinkey Creek). From a flat granite ridge at 11,000 feet, he looked out at a small lake, far below, somewhere in the upper drainages of the San Joaquin. "I had grown, by occasional privation, to look upon water as a jewel beyond price," he wrote, "and this was rendered even more beautiful by its rough setting."

Today, three vast wilderness areas come together here—the Kaiser, the Ansel Adams, and the John Muir—separated only by the road itself and the limits of Edison's catchment reservoirs. In summertime, the highest of these "lakes," Florence and Thomas Edison, offer unique ferry access into the upper San Joaquin drainage and the remote northern end of Kings Canyon National Park. For a hilarious and lightly political survival guide to this road, with relevant tips on downshifting, see www.muirtrailranch.com/kprsurvival.html.

Note: There is no gas available above Huntington Lake.

Dinkey Creek (access from CA 168, before Shaver Lake). "Here is a grove of about 200 [sequoia] trees growing upon coarse flood soil," John Muir wrote in the San Francisco Daily Evening Bulletin in 1875. "This little isolated grove was discovered a few years ago by a couple of bear hunters, but on account of its remoteness from traveled roads and trails is hardly known." In all the years since—more than a century and a quarter—not much has changed but the occasional distant whine of a two-stroke engine.

✳ To Do

Outdoor recreation opportunities throughout the region include motor-boating, kayaking, white-water rafting, fishing, golf, hiking, backpacking, caving, rock-climbing, birdwatching, cross-country and backcountry skiing, sledding, mountain biking, road biking, and horseback riding. See the end of each regional section for how to get started.

THREE RIVERS

FISHING Bait fishermen and boaters line up along the shores of Lake Kaweah every morning to catch largemouth bass, catfish, and rainbow trout. Meanwhile, some of the best front-country wild-trout fly-fishing can be found along the Middle Fork of the Kaweah, inside Sequoia National Park. (See "Swimming" for river access issues.)

Note: A valid California fishing license is required for residents and nonresidents 16 years of age or older on all public and private land outside and inside national park boundaries. Licenses can be purchased online at https://www.ca.wildlifelicense.com/

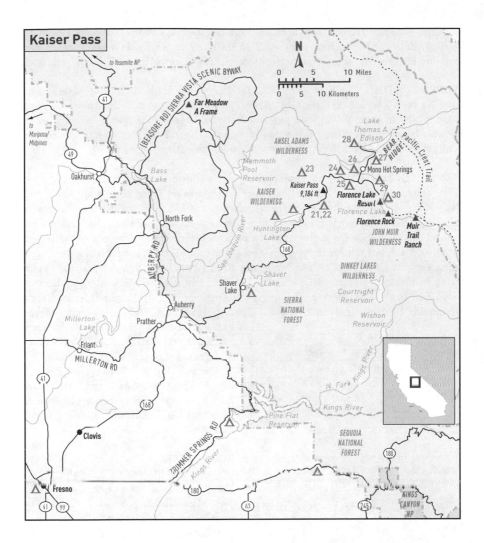

Kaiser Pass

InternetSales or through any authorized license agent (including most sporting goods outlets and local general stores). Always check with a park ranger, outfitter, or visitor center staff for area- and species-specific quota and catch-and-release regulations.

GOLF **Three Rivers Public Golf Course** (41117 Sierra Dr.; 559-561-3133). Nine holes, oak trees, ponds, deer, views up the Kaweah toward the high country. Open year-round.

HIKING There are hundreds of miles of good trail—most pleasant outside the raw sear of the summer months—to be accessed from the foothills region above Three Rivers. Centuries-old footpaths climb through chaparral and oak woodlands from trailheads at Potwisha and Buckeye Flat, just inside the park. From the end of North Fork Drive, one can hike up the Old Colony Mill Road, hand-built by Kaweah Colony socialists in the 1880s, as far as the road to Crystal Cave. Beware extensive colonies of poison oak. For secluded forays to lightly visited sequoia groves, head up into the Salt Creek and Case Mountain Areas (see "Mountain Biking," below, and www.blm.gov), or up the South Fork of the Kaweah to Ladybug Waterfall and/or Garfield Grove. In deep summer, you'll likely prefer to head for the high country above Mineral King or Lodgepole.

MOTORBOATING The motorboat and Jet Ski crowd flock to the flat waters of the Lake Kaweah Recreation Area (U.S. Army Corps of Engineers) and other area reservoirs, which in spring can flood parking areas and restrooms and by the end of the summer begin to show their full range of bathtub rings. Boat rentals and information available at **Kaweah Marina** (559-597-2526; www.kaweahmarina.com).

MOUNTAIN BIKING Off-pavement riding is not allowed within national park boundaries, except for along one brief section of scenic gravel along the Kings River, from Cedar Grove to Road's End. Mechanical travel of any kind—including bikes and other self-propelled vehicles—is prohibited in wilderness areas. That said, the National Forest and BLM holdings throughout the region offer hundreds of miles of fire roads, Jeep trails, and singletrack for the knobby-tire enthusiast. From Three Rivers, head up to Salt Creek and the BLM's **Case Mountain Area** (www.blm.gov). Access via Skyline Drive from Three Rivers or Oak Grove Road off the road to Mineral King. For trail maps and route descriptions, check www.mtbproject.com. Riding is intermediate to advanced. Hazards include mountain lions, poison oak, and occasional crossfire between DEA agents and backcountry marijuana farmers. (See "Blood, Guts, and Tarweed Burrs" sidebar.)

Sierra Bicycle Works (123 E. Main St., Visalia; 559-741-0700; www.sierra bicycles.com) is the locals' favorite for gear (road and mountain biking), service, and the latest trail beta.

CLIMBING GENERALS HIGHWAY, THE CCC'S FINEST
PETER AMEND

ROAD BIKING Cycling in this region is generally limited to epic alpine-style hill climbing of the out-and-back variety. The Mineral King Road (50 miles out and back), for all its 600 stubble-raising switchbacks and undeniably high scenic value, offers considerably less traffic than Generals Highway (plus homemade pie at Silver City). RVs and trailers are seriously discouraged. For a shorter, less vigorous cruise, try North Fork Drive through Kaweah to pavement's end. Team Garmin-Slipstream's CEO Jonathan Vaughters, in *Men's Journal*, called the 6-hour, 20-mile grind up CA 198 from Visalia all the way to the General Sherman Tree one of his five favorite rides in the United States. "Once you see the Sequoias," he wrote, "the burn quietly subsides."

For a truly heroic loop, start in the cool of dawn, ride down the Kaweah to Lemon

KAYAKING LAKE KAWEAH PETER AMEND

Cove, wind your way north along the foothills on J21 to Badger, and then climb into the parks via Pinehurst and the Big Stump Entrance. Return via Lodgepole and a final, mad, RV-slaloming descent of Generals Highway (82 miles, 6,000 feet of elevation).

SWIMMING Despite the abundance of swimming holes along the lower stretches of the Kaweah, public access is severely limited (and remains one of the most contentious issues in local politics). Without permission from a riverfront property owner (i.e., by staying at the Rio Sierra Riverhouse, the Buckeye Tree Lodge, or the Lake Elowin Resort), the only way down to the water is at the Slick Rock Recreation Area and by the Cobbleknoll Trail on the east end of Lake Kaweah. Access within the national park is limited only by the difficulty of the terrain. Try the trailheads at Potwisha, Buckeye Flat, and South Fork. Use extreme caution during periods of high water in spring and early summer: Drowning is the number one cause of death in Sequoia-Kings Canyon National Parks.

WHITEWATER RAFTING AND KAYAKING Dropping from its various headwaters above 12,000 feet to an elevation of less than 700 feet at the reservoir, the Kaweah is considered to be one of the steepest rivers in the country. Sections vary from moderate Class III to gnarly Class V boulder fields. Bill Pooley's **Kaweah River Page** (www .kaweahriver.org) is the one-stop resource for river runners, with detailed descriptions, flow graphs, gauge data, snowpack and weather reports, links, and a Web cam at Pumpkin Hollow Bridge.

Local outfitter Frank Root, with his **Kaweah Whitewater Adventures** (559-740-8251 or 1-800-229-8658; www.kaweahwhitewater.com), offers half- and full-day rafting trips on the Kaweah, on water ranging from Class III to Class V during the season.

MINERAL KING

FLY-FISHING Mostly brook trout in small lakes and streams, some rainbows. Goldens rumored in Silver and the Bullfrog Lakes on the far side of Farewell Gap. Beware rough

BLOOD, GUTS, AND TARWEED BURRS: MOUNTAIN BIKE DAWN PATROL ON THE OLD CRAIG RANCH

We meet at Mark Hirni's house at 7 AM sharp, at the top of Skyline Drive, above the village of Three Rivers. The morning is cool, as the sun is still procrastinating in the depths behind Case Mountain and the Great Western Divide beyond. A rafter of wild turkeys grazes on the neighbor's lawn.

I refuse to be intimidated by the locals' fleet of deluxe full-suspension rigs. They offer me a loaner. I decline. I'm used to being the only one on a hardtail from back at the end of the twentieth century. I like the way it climbs; I know how it handles in the narrows; I know exactly how much torque it takes, when I really need it, to get out of my clips. If nothing else, I trust my gearing. But when these guys saddle up and without equivocation point tires across a narrow ramp-feature right there in Hirni's front yard, I should (but don't yet) see my impending humiliation.

At the end of the street, we ride through the BLM gate and settle in for the long climb up the old Salt Creek fire road. It's 10 miles up to the first sequoias, but we're not going the whole way—not this time. Coming from Mammoth, at 8,300 feet, I feel strong and chatty, buoyed with extra oxygen. We talk about how the BLM picked up all this land in a series of trades with local ranchers beginning in 1979, how certain areas were highlighted for mountain biking only in the late 1990s. The entire complex comprises about 14,000 acres, rising from 1,200 feet of elevation at the gate, through a series of oak and chaparral ecosystems to six distinct sequoia groves, to the summit of Case Mountain at 6,818 feet and the southwestern edge of Sequoia National Park beyond.

Threading his way through coyote scat, Chip Chapman, an architect from Visalia, not winded in the slightest, recounts his inventory of local mammal sightings: horse, deer, bobcat, black bear, mountain lion. "You don't really want to see a mountain lion," he says.

TOM BROWN RIDES REAL SINGLETRACK PETER AMEND

Tom Brown is a contractor and woodworker. Aaron Cochran is an engineer for the phone company. They live down in Visalia too, but do their best to meet Hirn and others to exercise their mounts up here every Sunday morning—and every Wednesday night, too (the latter with full night-lighting equipment on their handlebars and helmets).

"The best time of year is late fall and early spring," says Tom, describing the bounty of waterfalls in the spring, the gnarly creek crossings, and the buckeye bloom. "The worst time is late spring, when the weeds are over your head and you can't see the trail." And, of course, there are certain days in July and August when it's just too hot to do anything but sit around and drink beers.

We pass the so-dubbed Three Amigos at a switchback where we trade the last of the cool, still morning for full sun exposure and a slightly mitigating down-canyon breeze. Phil Fortney, who is head of maintenance at a state mental hospital in Porterville and a die-hard member of the Skyline Dawn Patrol, shows off his glistening new drive train. "Check out the bling-bling," he says, describing his recent checkered past with a series of clunky, noisy chain rings. "Now I'm stealth, man." The only thing he spends more money on than his bicycle, he says, is his kids' private education.

At a picnic table at a place called the Corral, at 2,760 feet, beneath the shade of an oak, we regroup, drink water, look out at the valley and the mountains, and munch on energy chewies. From here on out, it's singletrack and fast. Chip and Tom are gone before I'm even clipped in. Aaron graciously plays sweep down the Cable Trail and back up to Bear Junction, at 3,000 feet, bareheaded and scornful of his helmet until it gets serious.

And then it gets serious.

Down we bounce along the Creek Trail, through jagged gullets of mossy granite, across upended meadows of blooming yellow tarweed, on trails little wider than a front tire, slipping and skidding on beds of dried oak leaves. I'm glad I'm not trying to follow a map. I'm on Tom's tail as he leaps through a cleft in the trunk of an ancient oak. "The Octopus, if you choose," he says. I choose not.

Then we're into a downhill minefield called Chutes & Ladders. Aaron watches me wrangle my rig back from a teetering nose-wheelie off a dry rapid—barely. But around the next corner, it's over. I catch a rut, landing hard on my helmet, in the weeds, with my bike on top of me. I have burrs by the hundreds in my hair, in my shorts, and in my socks. I've skinned my shoulder and have blood dribbling from my knee.

My nerve's gone and my equilibrium's shot, but I'm good. I wobble down to where the others are waiting. "That was awesome," I say. These guys and their buddies built these trails. They've been riding up here for nigh on 12 years. It's not fair. "I'm gonna have to come back and try that again sometime," I say, dreaming already of spring, when the grass is green and the world is softer.

After a while, we get through the unforgiving rock gardens and onto Old #1, the very first trail to be laid out for riding bikes on, back in the '90s, when the sport was still civilized. The old cowpath rolls and sidehills pleasantly through the grass at a nice 4 percent gradient, and then it jumps the road. We portage a barbed-wire fence, cross a dry creek on a narrow plank bridge, and eventually glide back down to the gate. I throw my bike in the truck, hosing some of the local landscape from my wounds. I'm well-chastened but also inspired. Then I drive down into town to meet Tom for coffee—and to talk about skiing.

Beta: Skyline Drive leaves CA 398 from the Veterans Memorial Building on the north end of Three Rivers. The BLM gate is at the end of the road. Parking is limited. Be respectful of the neighbors: Don't block driveways and don't leave trash. All trails are intermediate to advanced. A basic trail map is available for download at www.mtbproject.com, but I highly recommend trying to tag along with the locals first on Sunday morning. Keep an eye out for poison oak, mountain lions, and armed marijuana farmers. Bring spares, tools, and water. Yield to horses and hikers. Leave open gates open and closed gates closed.

GREAT HIKES: MINERAL KING

Mineral King is one of the top jumping-off spots for day hikes and extended trips into the High Sierra. Trails climb out of the bowl in every direction, follow tumbling snowmelt creeks to clear alpine lakes, and move onto the high ridges and peaks of the Great Western Divide, from which, on an extraordinary day, one might see east to Mount Whitney and west to the coastal range. Numerous multi-day loops are possible from here. A short 1-mile nature trail begins and ends at the Cold Springs campground. For guided walks and campfire programs, check in at the ranger station.

Monarch Lakes (8.4 miles round-trip, 2580 feet). Trailhead: Sawtooth Pass. Meadows, red fir forest, lakes, big views from Timber Gap to the Great Western Divide. Add 2.6 steep miles round-trip to Sawtooth Pass.

White Chief Trail (5.8 miles round-trip to the bowl, 1,400 feet). Trailhead: Eagle-Mosquito Lakes. One of the oldest trails in the valley, climbs past James Crabtree's ruined cabin from the 1870s to numerous mine shafts, sinkholes, and natural alpine cave entrances. "What White Chief is," says Ranger Len, "is the cobbling together of just about every formation the Sierra has that's not granite." Above is the bowl that Walt Disney once hoped to turn into a world-class downhill ski resort. Add another 1.2 miles and 800 feet to valley's end.

Timber Gap (4 miles round-trip, 1,600 feet). Mostly treeless along the old trail to the Empire Mine. Good views from the gap to Alta Peak and the Middle Fork of the Kaweah.

Note: All overnight trips require a wilderness permit, available at no charge from local ranger stations and visitor centers.

to nonexistent trail beyond the gap. Talk to the folks at Silver City Resort for specific up-to-date fishing beta.

Note: A valid California fishing license is required for residents and nonresidents 16 years of age or older on all public and private land outside and inside national park boundaries.

Licenses can be purchased online at https://www.ca.wildlifelicense.com/Internet Sales or through any authorized license agent (including most sporting goods outlets and local general stores). Always check with a park ranger or visitor center staff for area- and species-specific quota and catch-and-release regulations.

HORSEBACK RIDING The Mineral King Pack Station has been closed for regular commercial packing since 2004. Trips can be arranged, however, through Charley and Judy Mills at the **Horse Corral Pack Station** (559-565-3404; www.highsierrapackers .com) or through the **Cedar Grove Pack Station** (559-565-3464). Greg and Ruby Allen, of Bishop-based **Rainbow Pack Outfitters** (760-873-8877; www.rainbow.zb-net.com), have permits to run trips from the east side of the range into the backcountry of Sequoia–Kings Canyon National Parks.

GENERALS HIGHWAY AND HIGH-COUNTRY SEQUOIA

COURSES, SEMINARS, AND GUIDED ACTIVITIES For ranger-led walks and activities, check the bulletin boards at visitor centers, try the park hotline at 559-565-3341, or consult the latest copy of the park newspaper, *The Guide*, available at visitor centers or at park entrance kiosks. The **Big Trees Trail** and **Hazelwood Nature Trail**, both in the immediate vicinity of the Giant Forest Museum, provide excellent self-guided introductions to the history and ecology of the Big Tree groves.

For a full calendar of organized activities at extraordinarily reasonable rates, contact the Sequoia Field Institute (559-565-4251; www.exploresequoiakingscanyon.com).

Seminar topics include mammal tracking in snow, black bear management, bats, wildflowers, reforestation, and pottery. Field activities range from beginning cross-country skiing and kayaking to nature walks, ghost tours and overnight backcountry skiing expeditions. Or hire your own private naturalist.

FISHING There are good holes along the Marble Fork from Lodgepole to the falls. Even from the crowded bridge at the campground, rank amateurs have been seen landing healthy brook trout. Big Meadows Creek is said to be occasionally stocked with trout by the California Department of Fish and Game. Brookies and small, wild rainbows can be found in most alpine lakes and streams from the Jennie Lakes Wilderness to the Pear Lake tableland.

Note: A valid California fishing license is required for residents and nonresidents 16 years of age or older on all public and private land outside and inside national park boundaries. Licenses can be purchased online at https://www.ca.wildlifelicense.com/InternetSales or through any authorized license agent (including most sporting good outlets and local general stores). Always check with a park ranger or visitor center staff for specific quota and catch-and-release regulations.

HORSEBACK RIDING Even the great ambulator John Muir deigned to ride an animal on several of his long-distance romps in and around the Sierra. Horse Corral Pack Station (559-565-3404; www.highsierrapackers.com), at the end of the Big Meadows/Horse Corral Road, is run by Charley and Judy Mills, the last of their kind in Sequoia National Park. Their services include half- and full-day rides, extended pack trips, and spot-trip packing service for backcountry access. Call for reservations. Greg and Ruby Allen, of Bishop based Rainbow Pack Outfitters (760-873-8877; www.rainbow.zb-net .com), have permits to run trips from the east side of the range into the backcountry of Sequoia–Kings Canyon National Parks.

THE HOMEWATERS OF THE LEGENDARY CALIFORNIA GOLDEN TROUT LIE JUST OVER THE DIVIDE, A STURDY DAY'S HIKE (OR MORE) FROM MINERAL KING BILL BECHER

HOW OLD ARE THE BIG TREES?

Counting rings on the largest stump he could find in 1875 (in the Converse Basin), Muir "made a little over 4,000 without difficulty or doubt," thus placing the specimen's earliest years as a sapling sometime before the Amorite conquest of Ur, before the building of Stonehenge—more than a thousand years before the founding of Rome.

Sequoias do not die of old age or disease, Muir noted, but simply, finally, of toppling over. That they do not reach the towering height of their generally younger cousins, the coastal redwoods (*sequoia sempervivens*), is perhaps not so much the result of any genetic deficiency as it is of circumstance: the Big Trees poking their crowns, as they do, into prevailing winds and electrical storms at elevations up to 8,000 feet. "It is a curious fact," wrote Muir, "that all very old sequoias have lost their heads by lightning. Of all living things it is perhaps the only one able to wait long enough to make sure of being struck."

Muir's record-holding ring count has never been confirmed. Future parks superintendent Walter Fry is supposed to have spent five days with four buddies, sometime before 1912, sawing down a big sequoia and counting 3,266 rings on its stump. "Precise cross-dating of tree rings on cut stumps has shown that sequoias can reach at least 3,266 years in age," writes Nathan Stephenson of the current U.S. Geological Survey, "making sequoia the third longest-lived, non-clonal tree species known." The only trees older are the bristlecone pine (see Chapter 4) and the *alerce* of South America.

The world's largest living thing, the General Sherman Tree, is considered "a mere teenager" at somewhere between 2,000 and 2,500 years old. On a list of the top ten oldest tree species in the world, the western juniper and the foxtail pine, also found within the parks, are numbers four and seven, respectively.

HISTORY FROM THE POINT OF VIEW OF A VERY OLD TREE

MOUNTAIN BIKING Off-pavement riding is not allowed within national park boundaries, except for along one brief section of scenic gravel along the Kings River, from Cedar Grove to Road's End. Mechanical travel of any kind—including bikes and other self-propelled vehicles—is prohibited in wilderness areas. That said, the National Forest and BLM holdings throughout the region offer hundreds of miles of fire roads, Jeep trails, and singletrack for the knobby-tire enthusiast. The northern unit of the Giant Sequoia National Monument, north of Grant Grove from Converse Basin to Horse Corral Meadow to Hume Lake, offers hundreds of miles of old and not-so-old fire and logging roads for two-wheeled exploration. Consult Sequoia National Forest's Hume Lake Ranger District OHV maps, available online at www.fs.fed.us/r5/sequoia.

ROCK CLIMBING There is more good granite here—between the Domeland Wilderness and Bubbs Creek, between Moro Rock and Mount Whitney—than in all of Yosemite. It's just harder to get to (generally) and not as well known. The easiest-access climbing inside the park is the thousand feet of wall afforded by Moro Rock just off Generals Highway. Otherwise, pack your rack and overnight gear and enjoy the solitude on the Obelisk, the Grand Sentinel, Chimney Rock, or Angel Wings, whose 1,800-foot wall Galen Rowell is said to have been called "an alpine El Cap."

SWIMMING The **Marble Fork** offers a trove a good plunge both above and below Tokopah Falls, as does the upper **Middle Fork** from Bearpaw to the Kaweah Gap. One very popular series of slides and swimming holes can be found along **Stony Creek**, about a half-mile down a trail from the Stony Creek Lodge. At higher elevations, the park abounds with backcountry glacial lakes and forehead-numbing snowmelt creeks.

GOOD GRANITE OFF THE TOKOPAH FALLS TRAIL, LODGEPOLE   PETER AMEND

GREAT DAY HIKES: HIGH COUNTRY SEQUOIA

Along the Generals Highway section of Sequoia, one of the most popular (and easy) trails follows the clear pools of the Marble Fork from the Lodgepole campground to Tokopah Falls (3.4 miles round-trip, 500 feet). Other popular day hikes include the short climb to **Little Baldy** (3.4 miles round-trip, 700 feet), and the **Lakes Trail** from Wolverton to Heather (9.2 miles roundtrip, 2,100 feet) and **Pear Lakes** (13.4 miles round-trip, 2,300 feet), from which the most ambitious can make a run across the Tableland or at the worthy summit of **Alta Peak** (14+ miles round-trip, 4,000 feet) and loop back via Mehrton Meadow and Panther Gap. For paths slightly less traveled, head up into the **Jennie Lakes Wilderness** to Weaver Lake from the Big Meadows trailhead across from the old guard station on the Big Meadows/Horse Corral Road (8.4 miles round-trip, 1,420 feet), or to the summit of **Mitchell Peak** (6.4 miles round-trip, 2,265 feet) from the Marvin Pass trailhead near the end of the Big Meadows/Horse Corral Road. Loop possibilities abound. For custom hiker/backpacker shuttles, contact **Sequoia Sightseeing Tours** (559-561-4189; www.sequoiatours.com). All overnight trips require a wilderness permit, available at no charge from local ranger stations and visitor centers.

THE CCC-BUILT HIGH SIERRA TRAIL TRAVERSES THE HIGH BACKCOUNTRY OF SEQUOIA NATIONAL PARK, FROM CRESCENT MEADOW ALL THE WAY TO THE TOP OF MOUNT WHITNEY

WINTER SPORTS With proper equipment (and weather), the intrepid traveler can strike out across snow nearly anywhere in the Sierra's higher elevations, generally from 6,000 feet up. An overview map of the most popular cross-country ski trails, from Lodgepole to Moro Rock, can be purchased at park visitor centers. See above for information on the trek to the Pear Lake Ski Hut. For extended winter travel in the backcountry, consider a free-heel or Alpine touring (AT) ski setup with climbing skins, rather than snowshoes. Try them out before you get in too deep. All overnight trips require a wilderness permit, available at no charge from local ranger stations and visitor centers. Beware rapidly changing weather conditions (see the "Winter Travel in the Sierra" sidebar in Chapter 2).

WINTER SNOWSHOE EXPLORATION NEAR THE GIANT FOREST PETER AMEND

Montecito Sequoia Lodge (63410 Generals Hwy.; 1-800-843-8677; www.mslodge .com). Nearly 50 miles of groomed cross-country ski and snowshoe trails, three warming huts, equipment rental, and lessons. The Mountain Top Ski Shop also rents snowboards for groomed practice runs or backcountry powder. Tubing, sledding, dogsled rides, "snow biking," and ice skating.

Wolverton Ski and Recreation Area (Wolverton; 559-565-3435) The Wolverton Ski Bowl was developed here in 1921, and the last rope tows were removed in 1990. Today, 70 miles of quiet forest trails radiate from the meadow, with winter access to the General Sherman Tree and Giant Forest. Half- and full-day ski and snowshoe packages, lessons, sledding, telemark ski practice, and general snow play.

Wuksachi Ski Shop (Wuksachi Lodge; 1-888-252-5757). Cross-country ski and snowshoe rentals and lessons; snow play equipment for sale.

GRANT GROVE AND THE KINGS CANYON SCENIC BYWAY

CANYONEERING **Kings Canyoneering** (559-3380959; www.kingscanyoneering .com) offers a range of canyoneering tours for beginners, from 2.5 hours long to a full 12-hour epic. Learn basic climbing and rappelling techniques, explore the unique (and cool) world of polished-rock canyons, get wet. Tours are dependent on seasonal water levels and historic fire damage from 2015, but should run roughly from June to November.

FISHING "The upper section of the Kings in the Kings Canyon National Park has smaller fish," writes fly-fishing guru Bill Sunderland, "but lots of them." Note: A valid California fishing license is required for residents and nonresidents 16 years of age or older on all public and private land outside and inside national park boundaries.

THE SERVAL, *LEPTAILURUS SERVAL*, AN AFRICAN WILD CAT REVERED BY THE ANCIENT EGYPTIANS, IS AMONG THE LEAST ENDANGERED SPECIES AT PROJECT SURVIVAL'S CAT HAVEN

Licenses can be purchased online at https://www.ca.wildlifelicense.com/InternetSales or through any authorized license agent (including most sporting goods outlets and local general stores). Always check with a park ranger or visitor center staff for specific catch-and-release regulations.

HORSEBACK RIDING **Grant Grove Stables** (559-335-9292, operated by Delaware North) offers tame one- and two-hour trail rides in the Grant Grove and Sequoia Lake areas. Opens at 8 AM in summer; last ride leaves at 4 PM. Reservations recommended. **Cedar Grove Pack Station** (559-565-3464, operated by Delaware North), just up-canyon from Cedar Grove Village, runs 1-hour guided trips and full-day trips along the Kings River, as well as multiday pack trips into the high country. Call for information or reservations. From west of the park, the Clyde Pack Outfit (559-298-7397; www.dinkeystables.com) offers full outfitting services from Dinkey Creek into the John Muir Wilderness and the northern Kings Canyon National Park backcountry.

MOUNTAIN BIKING The northern unit of the **Giant Sequoia National Monument**, north of Grant Grove from Converse Basin to Horse Corral Meadow to Hume Lake, offers hundreds of miles of old and not-so-old fire and logging roads for two-wheeled

GRANT GROVE STABLES

GREAT DAY HIKES: KINGS CANYON

As in Yosemite, the valley floor around Zumwalt Meadow and Cedar Grove offers a civilized network of paths for easy strolls and loops through the woods and meadows along the river. From road's end, access to the wide-open backcountry—for day hikes and extended trips alike—is rivaled only by Mineral King's. The main difference here is the significantly greater elevation gain between the valley floor and the surrounding ridges and peaks. Day hikes include the Don Cecil Trail, the main access route to the valley floor before the completion of the road in 1939 (2 miles round-trip, 600 feet, to Sheep Creek Cascade), the Hotel Creek-Lewis Creek loop (8 miles, 1,200 feet), and the trip out and back along the South Fork to Mist Falls (9 miles round-trip, 600 feet). In midsummer, start early to avoid the heat. All overnight trips require a wilderness permit, available at no charge from local ranger stations and visitor centers.

FASTPACKING IN THE DUSY BASIN, NORTHERN KINGS CANYON NATIONAL PARK PATITUCCIPHOTO

exploration. Consult Sequoia National Forest's Hume Lake Ranger District Off-Highway Vehicle maps, available online at www.fs.fed.us/r5/sequoia. Off-pavement riding is not allowed within national park boundaries, except for along one brief section of scenic gravel down along the Kings River, from Cedar Grove to Road's End. Mechanical travel of any kind—including bikes and other self-propelled vehicles—is prohibited in wilderness areas.

ROAD BIKING An excellent loop ride can be made from Grant Grove to Hume Lake. Head north on CA 180 past the Converse Basin to Hume Lake Road. Descend to the lake, follow Tenmile Road (NF 13S09) past the Christian camp along the south shore of the lake, and enjoy the long climb up Tenmile Creek to Quail Flat. At the top, turn right onto Generals Highway, then right again at the "Wye" intersection with CA 180, through Wilsonia, and back to Grant Grove (20 miles total).

ROCK CLIMBING There is good hike-in, multi-pitch climbing along the Bubbs Creek Trail from Road's End. Look for the Charlotte and Charlito domes on the north side of the trail about 8 miles in.

SWIMMING Hume Lake is the best place to practice your triathlon starts within a short drive of Grant Grove. The best beach is on the east shore, on the opposite side of the Christian summer camp. Swimming in the fast-running Kings River is tricky business—and discouraged by the Park Service. The holes get better as the valley flattens out inside the park. Tributary creeks are best in early summer, before they dry up.

WHITEWATER RAFTING AND KAYAKING The South Fork of the Kings, from Bubbs Creek to the park boundary, is off-limits to watercraft of any kind. Die-hard wilderness kayakers have been known to haul their boats up the Middle Fork. For commercial trips below Kings Canyon (but above Pine Flat Dam), try **Kings River Expeditions** (1-800-846-3674; www.kingsriver.com) or **Zephyr Whitewater Expeditions** (1-800-431-3636; www.zrafting.com).

WINTER SPORTS The **Grant Tree Trail** loop is the only trail plowed for walking on in winter. All others are open for touring on snowshoes or cross-country skis. Rentals are available at the **Grant Grove Market** (559-335-5500). Panoramic Point Road and the many miles of logging roads in the Converse Basin and along the Big Meadows/Horse Corral Road, snow permitting, provide excellent terrain for winter touring. All overnight trips require a wilderness permit, available at no charge from local ranger stations and visitor centers. Beware rapidly changing weather conditions (see the "Winter Travel in the Sierra" sidebar in Chapter 2).

KERNVILLE AND THE GREAT WESTERN DIVIDE HIGHWAY

BIRD-WATCHING Along the South Fork of the Kern River, east of Kernville and above Lake Isabella, is California's largest lowland riparian forest, nearly 3,000 acres of which make up the **Audubon Kern River Preserve**. Home to 332 species, the area has been designated a National Natural Landmark and is one of Audubon's top 10 Important Bird Areas. Contact the Kern Valley Audubon Society (kern.audubon.org) for information on spotted owls, turkey vultures, peregrine falcons, and other winged creatures throughout the southern end of the Sierra.

FISHING The upper forks of the Kern offer some 75 miles of wild trout water through fabulously punishing wilderness, native habitat for the renowned and elusive California golden trout. Between the Johnsondale Bridge and Kernville, on the other hand, are 20 miles of stocked, easy-access trophy fishing. The excellent **Kern River Fly Shop** (11301 Kernville Rd.; 1-866-347-4876; www.kernriverflyshop.com) has all the gear and beta you need, plus classes, seminars, horse pack trips, and licensed guide service. Also try Kern River Fly Fishing Guide Service (www.kernriverflyfishing.com; 760-376-2040).

Note: A valid California fishing license is required for residents and nonresidents 16 years of age or older on all public and private land outside and inside national park boundaries. Licenses can be purchased online at https://www.ca.wildlifelicense .com/InternetSales or through any authorized license agent (including most sporting goods outlets and local general stores). Always check with locals for area- and species-specific quota and catch-and-release regulations.

HORSEBACK RIDING **Balch Park Pack Station** (559-539-2227; www.balchpark.com). Tim and Dianne Shew offer a full range of services to the Garfield-Redwood Grove of Big Trees (what John Muir called "the finest block of Big Tree forest in the entire belt"), the Golden Trout Wilderness, the upper Kern River, and the southern end of Sequoia National Park.

Golden Trout Pack Trains (above Quaking Aspen on the Great Western Divide Highway; 559-542-2816; www.goldentroutpacktrains.com). Steve and Rinda Day offer a full range of services to the Freeman Creek Grove and George Bush Tree, and into the Golden Trout Wilderness. Cabins and lodge meals available.

MOUNTAIN BIKING The southern unit of the Giant Sequoia National Monument, along the Great Western Divide Highway, has its own haphazard network of dirt roads and trails, including a smooth, whooping descent down good, solid, sequoia mulch to the George Bush Tree. But the real infrastructure is in and above the Kern River Valley. There's the Whiskey Flat trail along the Kern itself, the **Black Gulch Rabbit Ramble/Keyesville Classic** trails near Lake Isabella, and the epic **Cannell Plunge** with its 9,000-foot mostly singletrack descent all the way from the summit of Sherman Pass. There's even a BMX-style bike park, MTB pumptrack, and skills course next to the rodeo grounds (760-223-6165; kvbikepark.com). The hub of it all, of course (and so to speak), is the only bike store in town, **Mountain & River Adventures** (11113 Kernville Rd., Kernville; 760-376-6553 or 1800-861-6553; www.mtnriver.com), with all the local beta and last-minute gear, its own private campground right on the river, plus a terrific offering of bike shuttles to help you get right to the goods.

OFF THE GREAT WESTERN DIVIDE HIGHWAY

ROAD BIKING For a multi-day stage route of Tour de France proportions, consider riding from the Central Valley to the Mojave, over the Southern Sierra—from Springville via the Great Western Divide Highway and Sherman Pass (9,200 feet) to Pearsonville. Return by way of Walker Pass and the lower Kern Canyon. The **Bodfish Caliente Road**, CA 155, south of Lake Isabella, is one of the great, long-lost, traffic-free foothill passes in California. Avoid the hottest and coldest seasons. Wear sunscreen.

ROCK CLIMBING The Kern River Valley is well-stocked with good, sun-baked, Yosemite-style granodiorite. But there's also interesting limestone, basalt, and quartz. For great solitary wilderness cragging, head deep into the **Domeland Wilderness** off Sherman Pass (not recommended in the scorch of mid-summer). The most famous climbing in the area is higher up, on and around the Needles, between Johnsondale and Quaking Aspen off the Great Western Divide Highway. For gear and specific local beta, try either **Mountain & River Adventures** (11113 Kernville Rd., Kernville; 760-376-6553 or 1-800-861-6553; www.mtnriver.com) or **Sierra South Mountain and Paddle Sports** (11300 Kernville Rd., Kernville; 760-376-3745; www.kernriver.com).

SWIMMING The Tule and Kern rivers have abundant swimming holes, but tend to be crowded during the hottest part of the summer. The best plunge in the area—alas, no longer a secret—is at a series of natural water slides on a high tributary of the Kern above Johnsondale and below the intersection of Parker Pass Road with the Great Western Divide Highway. Head several miles north on Forest Road 22S83, look for the busiest turnout (on the right), and follow the locals (across the road) with their wheeled coolers. The hike in is hot and exposed. Wear a big sombrero and pack a picnic, plenty of cold beer, sunscreen, and water.

WHITEWATER The Kern has some of the most accessible and therefore busiest rapids in Southern California. All summer long, the place is lousy with boats and

TAKING IT FOR THE TEAM ON THE KERN RIVER BILL BECHER

floaters of all stripes. For outfitting, day trips, overnights, kayak rentals, private camping on the river, and detailed beta, try **Mountain & River Adventures** (11113 Kernville Rd., Kernville; 760-376-6553 or 1-800-861-6553; www.mtnriver.com). **Sierra South Mountain and Paddle Sports** (11300 Kernville Rd., Kernville; 760-376-3745; www.kernriver.com) provides stiff competition in the paddle sports racket with a good menu of day trips, overnights, lessons, and classes. They also sell new and used boats and equipment.

MONO HOT SPRINGS GENERAL STORE AND POST OFFICE BURKE GRIGGS

WINTER SPORTS **Ponderosa Lodge Ski Shop** (CA 190, Ponderosa; 559-542-2579) offers basic rentals, equipment, and local trails information. **Mountain & River Adventures** (11113 Kernville Rd., Kernville; 760-376-6553 or 1-800-861-6553; www.mtnriver.com) rents snowshoes, cross-country skis, and sledding equipment in season.

MONO HOT SPRINGS AND KAISER PASS ROAD

BOATING **Vermilion Valley Resort Ferry and Boat Rentals** (559-259-4000; www.edisonlake.com) has fishing boats, canoes, kayaks, bizarre-looking paddleboats, bicycle boats, and a pontoon boat for hire.

Note: Water levels are determined by Southern California Edison. Sometimes the "lake" comes right to the edge of the resort, and other times, such as when the water's needed downstream in late summer and fall, the landscape is one of sand dunes and puddles. The Florence Lake Ferry (www.florence-lake.com)—the Sierra Queen, in service since 1969—makes at least five trips a day, out and back, to the other side of the lake; more on Saturday. Check the website or the store for schedules, rates, and water levels. Also available for hire: 15-foot aluminum fishing boats with outboard motors and bailing buckets ($65 a day).

FISHING The sport here ranges from lazy trolling for leviathan rainbows in one or the other of the big high reservoirs to wild backcountry epics in search of mythical pan-sized delicacies. **VVR** (559-259-4000; www.edison lake.com) offers guided flyand ATVfishing trips. **Sierra Fly Fisher** (559-6837664; www.sierraflyfisher.com) hosts an annual wild trout camp in early October at Mono Hot Springs for the fall brown trout run up the San Joaquin.

Note: A valid California fishing license is required for residents and nonresidents 16 years of age or older on all public and private land outside and inside national park boundaries. Licenses can be purchased online at https://www.ca.wildlifelicense.com/InternetSales or through any authorized license agent (including most sporting goods outlets and local general stores). Always check with locals for specific catch-and-release regulations.

HORSEBACK RIDING John and Jenise Cunningham's **High Sierra Pack Station** (559-285-7225; www.highsierrapackstations.com) has stables at both Florence and Edison

FLORENCE LAKE FERRY TO THE JOHN MUIR WILDERNESS

Lakes, offering full packing and saddle service into the Ansel Adams and John Muir Wildernesses, the Evolution Valley, and the northern wilds of Kings Canyon National Park. The **Muir Trail Ranch** (209-966-3195; www.muirtrailranch.com) offers custom day rides and full pack services for guests.

MOUNTAIN BIKING The **Kaiser Pass** region offers some exploratory off-highway riding, but the competition is fierce with the motorized set.

ROAD BIKING The Kaiser Pass road would make a spectacular climb (and descent) were it not for the bounty of tree roots, frost heaves, potholes, and bottlenecked toy-haulers. Still, people do it.

SWIMMING The South Fork of the San Joaquin, off the Kaiser Pass, offers a host of good granite pools for plunging in—depending on the release and flow of water from upstream dams. There are pleasant, secluded beaches on Florence and Thomas Edison Reservoirs—the more pleasant and secluded the farther you hike. And, of course, there are the ancient hillside soaking tubs at Mono Hot Springs.

✳ Lodging

In the spring of 1899, Visalia ranchers Ralph Hopping and John Broder partnered up to establish the first commercial accommodations in the new Sequoia National Park. For $35 a head, they provided stage and pack service up the Old Colony Mill Road, a horse to ride on for the last 4 miles to Round Meadow, a week's lodging, and three meals a day. Camp Sierra, as the enterprise was called, consisted of a collection of simple platform tents at the edge of the Giant Forest. The operation was abandoned in 1908.

Accommodations of this sort are still available at Grant Grove, as well as at the historic **Bearpaw High Sierra Camp** and the newer, more deluxe Sequoia High Sierra Camp. Otherwise, lodgings within the parks range from modern, relatively upscale motel rooms to the ricketiest board-and-batten-style tourist cabins of the 1920s and '30s. There

LODGING HIGHLIGHTS

Silver City Resort: Best Historic-Rustic Mountain Cabins (page 304)
Bearpaw High Sierra Camp: Best Wilderness Base Camp (page 304)
Pear Lake Ski Hut: Best Winter Adventure Accommodations (page 305)
The Sequoia High Sierra Camp: Best Luxe-Boutique Eco Resort (page 307)

is not much to recommend lodging in Kings Canyon or along the Great Western Divide Highway—other than, of course, the scenery. Notes have been included here in case the scenery should prevail. As always, one's appreciation of the simpler amenities will improve significantly if one has first slept on the ground somewhere, or exhausted oneself on some dusty trail in the wilderness, or at the very least driven long hours on empty, winding mountain roads with the windows down and the music device cranked.

A TENT CABIN AT BEARPAW HIGH SIERRA CAMP, SEQUOIA NATIONAL PARK (11 MILES FROM PARKING)

SIERRA/KINGS CANYON CAMPING

Three Rivers/Foothills	Elevation	Season	Reservations Accepted	Fee	Sites	Water	Agency
1. South Fork*	3,600	Year-round	No	Yes	10	No	NPS
2. Buckeye Flat*	2,800	May-Sep	No	Yes	28	Yes	NPS
3. Potwisha*	2,100	Year-round	No	Yes	42	Yes	NPS
Mineral King							
4. Atwell Mill*	6,652	May-Oct	No	Yes	21	Yes	NPS
5. Cold Spring*	7,500	May-Oct	No	Yes	40	Yes	NPS
Sequoia National Park/ Generals Highway							
6. Dorst*	6,800	May-Sep	Yes	Yes	204	Yes	NPS
7. Lodgepole*	6,700	Year-round	Yes	Yes	250	Yes	NPS
Giant Sequoia National Forest/ Monument North							
8. Buck Rock	7,600	May-Sep	No	No	5	No	USFS
9. Big Meadows	7,600	Jun-Oct	No	No	25	Creek	USFS
10. Eshom Creek	4,800	May-Oct	No	Yes	23	Piped	USFS
11. Stony Creek	6,400	May-Sep	Yes	Yes	49	Yes	USFS
12. Upper Stony Creek	6,400	May-Oct	Yes	Yes	19	Piped	USFS
13. Fir (Group)	6,400	May-Sep	Yes	Yes	‡	Yes	USFS
14. Cove (Group)	6,500	May-Sep	Yes	Yes	‡	Yes	USFS
15. Princess	5,900	May-Sep	Yes	Yes	90	Yes	USFS
16. Aspen Hollow (Group)	5,200	May-Sep	Yes	Yes	‡	Yes	USFS
17. Logger Flat (Group)	5,300	May-Sep	Yes	Yes	‡	Yes	USFS
18. Landslide	5,800	May-Oct	No	Yes	9	Piped	USFS
19. Tenmile	5,800	May-Oct	No	Yes	13	Piped	USFS
20. Hume Lake	5,200	May-Sep	Yes	Yes	74	Yes	USFS
Grant Grove/Kings Canyon National Park							
21. Azalea*	6,500	Year-round	No	Yes	144	Yes	NPS
22. Crystal Springs*	6,500	May-Sep	No	Yes	66	Yes	NPS
23. Sunset*	6,500	May-Sep	No	Yes	119	Yes	NPS
Cedar Grove/ Kings Canyon National Park							
24. Moraine*	4,600	May-Oct	No	Yes	120	Yes	NPS
25. Sentinel*	4,600	May-Oct	No	Yes	83	Yes	NPS
26. Sheep Creek*	4,600	May-Oct	No	Yes	111	Yes	NPS
27. Canyon View*	4,600	Jun-Oct	No	Yes	23	Yes	NPS
28. Canyon View (Group)*	4,600	Jun-Sep	Yes	Yes	9	Yes	NPS

Note: Reservations at USFS and NPS Sites, unless otherwise specified, can be made online at www.recreaetion.org ot by calling 1-877-444-6777.

*Located within the park. ‡ Group Sites accommodate from 50 to 100 people. Consult reservation agency for specifics.

For a taste of the old school, consider spending a night in a decommissioned fire lookout or Forest Service guard station. For highest adventure, try an overnight midwinter ski expedition to the **Pear Lake Ski Hut**. For anything approaching real luxury accommodations, the traveler will have to press on to the Yosemite region.

CAMPING Options for car camping are abundant throughout the region, ranging from the most crowded and developed sites at Lodgepole to more secluded (and primitive) dispersed camping along Forest Service back roads, as along the Big Meadow/Horse Corral Road, where one can set up a temporary homestead nearly anywhere there is flat ground and a pre-existing fire ring. Reserve upper sites along the river at Lodgepole, or look to Dorst and Stony Creek. A campfire permit is required for fires outside developed campgrounds or designated recreation sites. Permits are available free of charge from any Forest Service, California Department of Forestry and Fire Protection, or Bureau of Land Management

(BLM) office. Camping in the foothills is most comfortable from late fall to spring, when the high country is under snow. In summer, heat and black flies will drive all but the most intrepid to cooler altitudes. The Upper Kern River, from Kernville to the Johnsondale Bridge, is a circus on summer weekends. Pets are allowed in all campgrounds, but must be on a leash and attended at all times. For solitude, secure a free backcountry permit from the nearest ranger station or visitor center and head for the backcountry.

THREE RIVERS

Three Rivers boasts motels, cabin resorts, chalets, and B&B cottages of varying styles and utilities, from franchise to funky—the best within earshot of the river. During peak season, great hordes of Sequoia-bound travelers cycle in and out of the 103 rooms at the **Comfort Inn & Suites** (40820 Sierra Dr.; 1-866-875-8456; moderate), where amenities include satellite TV, wireless Internet, in-room coffeemakers, and ironing equipment, plus a daily complement of breakfast cereals and pour-it-yourself waffles. Quieter, lazier, and more in tune with its surroundings is the **Lazy J Ranch**

LAKE ELOWIN RESORT HAS BEEN IN BUSINESS SINCE THE 1920S

Motel (39625 Sierra Dr.; 209-561-4449 or 1-800-341-8000; moderate) on the south side of town, with its spacious rooms and stand-alone brick cottages overlooking the lawn and swimming pool. Porches come equipped with plastic chairs. For more uncommon accommodations and/or better access to the river, consider one of the following properties on the north end of town.

Lake Elowin Resort (43840 Dineley Dr.; 559-561-3460; www.lake-elowin.com; moderate to very expensive; Elevation: 850 feet; Open: Year-round; Owner: Milton Melkonian; Pets: No; Wheelchair Access: Yes; Internet Access: No). After several hours in the presence of a golden Buddha in Thailand in 1976, Milton Melkonian had a vision. So, when he got home, he bought the Lake Elowin Resort. Old Herb Wilson had built the place back in the 1920s on the site of a watering hole where his Potwisha ancestors had once camped. Milton has worked hard to upgrade most of the cabins with knotty-pine paneling, wood floors, and modern kitchens. Peace and quiet abound to such a degree that Milt's famous friends from Hollywood and Nashville come here to get work done. The script for *Thelma and Louise* was finished in Cabin 2. The landscaping, consisting of periwinkle, pomegranate, citrus and banana, tall cedars, terraced lawns, and lily pads, all irrigated by two miner's inches of deeded flume water (by Milton's calculation, 64,000 gallons a day), is positively lush, especially in the dry heat of August. The "lake" is an artificial sandy-bottom pond, meticulously drained and aerated to keep the water just right for swimming. A private trail leads down to the river. Barbecues, coffee percolators, and kitchen implements provided. No phones, TVs, radios, car alarms, or sinking of canoes allowed. No smoking. Bring your own lawn chairs.

Cort Cottage Bed & Breakfast (44141 Skyline Dr.; 559-561-4671; www.cortcottage.com; expensive; Elevation: 1,200 feet; Open: Year-round; Owner:

Elsah Cort; Pets: No; Wheelchair Access: No; Internet Access: Wireless [via satellite]). Up at the end of Skyline Drive, an easy stone's throw from the entrance to the BLM's 440-acre Case Mountain Giant Sequoia Grove Complex, squats this one-bedroom cottage with its commanding views across the black-oak foothills to the mountains. The location is supreme, especially in winter and spring, when the hills are green, the mountaintops white, and the waterfalls running in the canyon. It feels very much like someone's private guest house—which it is. The owner, local collage artist cum feng shui consultant cum craniosacral therapist Elsah Cort, lives and works in the main house above—but the smaller home is thoroughly equipped and cozy and, because of its orientation and separate entrance, quite private. It's a perfect base camp for hiking or mountain biking in the foothills, or for just sitting around catching up with oneself. Full kitchen, books, board games, TV/DVD, air conditioning (in summer), and hot tub (in winter).

Rio Sierra Riverhouse (41997 Sierra Dr.; 559-561-4720; www.rio-sierra.com; moderate to expensive; Elevation: 800 feet; Open: Year-round; Owner: Margaret Roberts Mars; Pets: No; Wheelchair Access: No; Internet Access: Wireless). "L.A. is a state of mind," says Mars, the former TV-producer-turned-innkeeper now lounging in the shade above her own private beachhead on the Kaweah River. As it happens, it's a state of mind she's most successfully achieved by selling her duplex in Venice Beach and crafting what she calls an "L.A. hotel" right here in Three Rivers, just down the road from the entrance to Sequoia National Park. In the span of a few years, she's cleaned up and breathed life into what is now a charming blue-clapboard beach retreat with four units, wraparound porches, landscaped lawns, a firepit, cabanas, and white-sand beach access to one of the most coveted swimming holes along this stretch of the river. The Master Suite and River Studio open directly onto the rush and tumble. The so-called Garden Room, around back, leaves a bit to be desired with its low ceiling and highway frontage, but comes paired with its own private cabana on the river. All rooms have mini-fridges and coffeemakers. Available with or without breakfast.

Buckeye Tree Lodge (46000 Sierra Dr.; 559-561-5900; www.buckeyetree .com; moderate; Elevation: 1,300 feet; Open: Year-round; Owners: Dennis and Stacie Villavicencio; Pets: Yes; Wheelchair Access: Yes; Internet Access: Wireless [via satellite]). When Dennis Villavicencio left San Diego (and a career in securities law) to come home to Three Rivers, he thought he'd have more time to ride his bike. In 2005, he bought the Sequoia Village Inn (see below) and started fixing it up, and when the Buckeye—the old postwar motor lodge across the street—came up for sale, he couldn't help but buy that, too. The draw here is the river frontage: the spectacular jumble of boulders at the confluence of the Middle and East Forks, the swimming holes and kayaking run, the grassy lawn, the shade of native sycamores. Rooms are basic but feature fabulous porch and patio views across the canyon. The Ash Mountain Entrance is a quarter-mile up the road, and the Gateway Restaurant/Bar is next door. There's a bike-able trail from here to Mineral King, but with busy summers and an ongoing overhaul of rooms during the off-season, Dennis's fleet of bikes still mostly gathers dust. "Little by little," he says. Amenities include a swimming pool, barbecues, picnic tables, in-room refrigerators, and free long-distance telephone service. Larger kitchenette unit and private cottage also available.

Sequoia Village Inn (45971 Sierra Dr.; 559-561-3652; www.sequoiavillageinn .com; moderate to expensive; Elevation: 1,300 feet; Open: Year-round; Owners: Dennis and Stacie Villavicencio; Pets: Yes; Wheelchair Access: Yes; Internet Access: Wi-Fi). Across the road from the

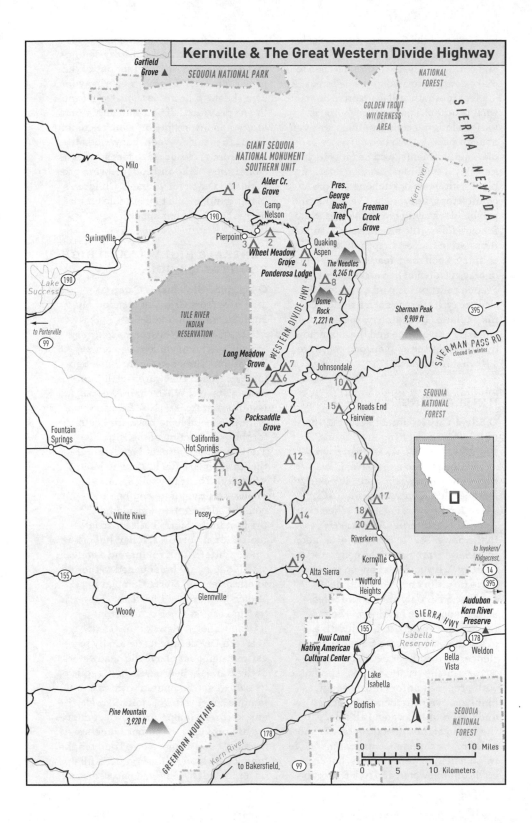

Kernville & The Great Western Divide Highway

Garfield Grove ▲

SEQUOIA NATIONAL PARK

NATIONAL FOREST

SIERRA NEVADA

GOLDEN TROUT WILDERNESS AREA

Kern River

Milo

GIANT SEQUOIA NATIONAL MONUMENT SOUTHERN UNIT

▲1

Alder Cr. Grove ▲

Camp Nelson

Pres. George Bush Tree ▲

Freeman Crock Grove

(190)

Springville

Pierpoint

▲3 ▲2

Wheel Meadow Grove

Quaking Aspen

Ponderosa Lodge ▲4

The Needles 8,245 ft

▲8

Dome Rock 7,221 ft

▲9

Sherman Peak 9,909 ft

(395)

to Porterville
(99)

Lake Success

(190)

TULE RIVER INDIAN RESERVATION

WESTERN DIVIDE HWY

Long Meadow Grove

▲7 ▲6 ▲5

Johnsondale

SHERMAN PASS RD
closed in winter

SEQUOIA NATIONAL FOREST

▲10

Packsaddle Grove ▲

Roads End
Fairview

▲15

Fountain Springs

California Hot Springs

▲12

▲16

▲11

▲13

▲17

White River

Posey

▲14

▲18
▲20

Riverkern

Kernville

to Inyokern/ Ridgecrest,

(14)
(395)

▲19

Alta Sierra

Wofford Heights

(155)

Glennville

Woody

SIERRA HWY

Audubon Kern River Preserve

Nuui Cunni Native American Cultural Center

Isabella Reservoir

(155)

Weldon

(178)

Lake Isabella

Bella Vista

Pine Mountain 3,920 ft

GREENHORN MOUNTAINS

Kern River

Bodfish

N

SEQUOIA NATIONAL FOREST

(178)

to Bakersfield,
(99)

0   5   10 Miles

0   5   10 Kilometers

Buckeye and the Gateway sits this eclectic collection of newly renovated chalets and cottages. The local Indians used to make camp here among the oak trees. An ancient footpath still leads from here into what is now the national park. Today, various lodging configurations are available for parties from two to twelve people. Appointments in some units include knotty-pine ceilings, bamboo floors, fireplaces, kitchens or kitchenettes, granite countertops, flat-screen TVs, VCRs, and private decks with gas barbecues. Note Stacie's folksy tile mosaics and Dennis's illustrative framed snapshots of the high country. Each room features a selection of teas, a coffeemaker, an assortment of French roast beans, and a grinder. "Rustic luxury, if there is such a thing," Dennis explains. Lounging by the pool, with a plastic cup of wine and the alpenglow dying across the canyon, one begins to see what he means.

MINERAL KING

✪ Silver City Mountain Resort (25 hard miles up Mineral King Road from CA 198; 559-561-3223; www.silvercityresort .com; moderate to expensive; Elevation: 7,000 feet; Open: Late May–early October; Innkeeper: High Sierra Conservation Resorts; Pets: No; Wheelchair Access: Yes; Internet Access: Wireless in the newer "Swiss chalets," after noon in general store [when the generator's fired up]). If you don't happen to have close ties with one of the original 65 families, your only choice for roofed accommodations in Mineral King is the Silver City Resort. Luckily, it's a great choice. For a true frontier experience, try a night or two in one of the 1930s-vintage "rustic cabins," appointed with propane and/or kerosene lamps, blankets, camp kitchens, barbecues, and cold running water. Fall asleep to the sound of the creek through the knotholes in the siding. "Comfy cabins" have wood paneling, refrigerators, hot and cold running water, and toilets. For the

latest in suburban comforts—laminate floors, composite decking, lofty ceilings, and wireless Internet, opt for one of the newer "chalets." In any case, bring your own sheets, pillowcases, and towels (no linens provided). If you plan on staying more than one night—or if you're coming up on Tuesday or Wednesday, when the restaurant is closed, save for the occasional slice of pie and coffee—bring groceries and cook for yourself. Children's playground, picnic tables, table tennis, horseshoes, and hammocks.

GENERALS HIGHWAY AND HIGH-COUNTRY SEQUOIA

✪ Bearpaw High Sierra Camp (11.5-mile hike from Crescent Meadow on High Sierra Trail; 1-866-807-3598; www .visitsequoia.com/bearpaw.aspx; very expensive (but includes two meals); Elevation: 7,800 feet; Open: June–September; Hosts: Delaware North Company; Pets: No; Wheelchair Access: No; Internet Access: No). Bearpaw was originally established as a crew camp for the construction of the High Sierra Trail between Crescent Meadow and the Kaweah Gap (on the way to Mount Whitney). The trail itself, a marvel of pick-and-dynamite engineering completed in 1931, is considered to be the first in the Sierra built for strictly recreational purposes. A handful of wood-platform tent cabins and a canvas-sided lodge were first opened to the public as a High Sierra Camp in 1934. Today, with its wood-fired hot showers; its timeless, weather-beaten front porch; its unparalleled views of the Great Western Divide; and its generally precarious perch far above the headwaters of the Kaweah, Bearpaw is in a league of its own—even compared with its more famous cousins in Yosemite. Towels, linens, kerosene lamps, and down comforters are provided. Generous home-style breakfast and dinner served daily in the main camp lounge. Reservations fill up on a first-call first-served basis starting at 7 AM on January 2 of each year (1-866-807-3598), but cancellations do happen. Plan at least two nights here—to allow a day of leisure, perusal of the camp's vintage lending library, and general exploration in the backcountry. Swimming holes and glacial lakes abound.

⊕ **Pear Lake Ski Hut** (6 miles and 2,000 feet above Wolverton Meadow; 559-565-3759; http://www.sequoiaparksconservancy.org/pear-lake-winter-hut.html; inexpensive; Elevation: 9,200 feet; Open: December–May (weather permitting); Hutkeeper: Sequoia Parks Conservancy; Pets: No; Wheelchair Access: No; Internet Access: No). Over the summers between 1939 and 1941, the CCC built this classic A-frame chalet of local timber and granite. One of the last examples of true rustic architecture in the parks, it is also,

according to park historian William Tweed, "one of the most environmentally successful alpine structures ever designed by the NPS." In summer, the building does time as a ranger station. In winter and early spring, surrounded as it is by thousands of acres of snowbound terrain—gentle bowls, glades, chutes, high ridgelines, and peaks over 11,000 feet with big views to the Great Western Divide—the place is paradise for snowshoers and backcountry skiers. Sunsets viewed from the front porch go on forever. Meals tend to be gourmet communal affairs (pack creatively; bring better than freeze-dried), with impromptu live music, storytelling, and deep snores around the pellet stove. Hut sleeps 10. Check the website for details and equipment list. Reservations by lottery, held in November, or check the calendar for

THE FRONT YARD OF PEAR LAKE SKI HUT, MARCH 2007

openings. Plan for at least two nights. The approach is no stroll in the park, but as hard as it is to get here, it's much harder to leave.

Wuksachi Lodge (64740 Wuksachi Way (off Generals Highway); 1-866-807-3598; www.visitsequoia.com; moderate to very expensive; Elevation: 7,200 feet; Open: Year-round; Innkeeper: Delaware North Company; Pets: No; Wheelchair Access: Yes; Internet Access: Wireless in main lodge only). As the last ramshackle cabins in the old Giant Forest Village were being hauled off and made to disappear (see "Points of Interest"), ground was broken on the next generation of lodging in Sequoia National Park. Opened in 1999—10 miles north of Giant Forest and 4 miles north of Lodgepole—Wuksachi Lodge consists of a series of detached motel-style buildings (walking distance from the parking lot) and a lodge of rather grand scale, also at some remove, for dining (see Dining). It's really nothing like a village, but, well, it's what there is—it's all there is, in fact, if you want to sleep in a hired bed near the hub of things in Sequoia National Park. Rooms are modern and spacious, done up with mission-style pine furnishings, comfortable beds, upholstered armchairs, and aluminum slider windows with pocket views of the woods and the cliffs of Tokopah Canyon. There's an easy hiking trail from here to Lodgepole (3 miles) and occasional fireside activities in the evenings, but the impulse at the beginning of the day is still to get in one's car and drive—somewhere else. Maybe one day they'll build a Yosemite-style bike path and the place won't feel quite so disconnected. The new shuttle, which drops by every 30 minutes in summer, is a step in the right direction.

Montecito Sequoia Lodge (63410 Generals Hwy., Sequoia National Monument; 1-800-227-9900 (reservations); 559-565-3388 (front desk); www.montecitosequoia.com; moderate to expensive (package rates including meals); Elevation: 7,500 feet; Open:

Year-round; Pets: No; Wheelchair Access: Limited; Internet Access: Wireless in lodge). If you ever wish you could go back to the glory days of summer camp, or if you never went and always wish you had, here's your chance: Pack the troop into the minivan and head for Lake Homovalo. Weeklong "summer family camp" packages include three meals a day, utilitarian lodging dating back to the early 1940s, and a profusion of activities for kids and adults: archery, tennis, kayaking, horseback riding, hiking, mountain biking, fencing, yoga, trampoline, gymnastics, and more. Hook your toddler up with a morning in the play yard while you go waterskiing. Let the surly teen learn horse-whispering while you lounge by the pool with the latest best-selling confessional memoir. Variety shows, night hikes, and, of course, campfire singalongs. Full bar, Starbucks coffee, and copious buffet-style meals. Mini-week summer sessions and Saturday-night-only rates also available. Winter brings cross-country skiing, sledding, dogsled rides, and ice skating.

Big Meadows Guard Station (Big Meadows Road, Giant Sequoia National Monument; 1-877-444-6777; www.reserveamerica.com (reservations); moderate (inexpensive for groups); Elevation: 7,600 feet; Open: June–October (weather permitting); Management: U.S. Forest Service (559-338-2251); Pets: Not inside; Wheelchair Access: Limited; Internet Access: No). Built in the mid-1930s by the CCC to house fire crews in the wide-open country between Kings Canyon and the northern edge of Sequoia National Park, the Big Meadows Guard Station is within convenient striking distance of all major points of interest in both parks. It's also far enough off the beaten path to give one the sense of having the whole place to oneself. Bathroom, kitchen, pots, pans, utensils, miscellaneous cleaning supplies, refrigerator, woodstove, living room with pull-out couch, bedroom stuffed with beds, and a desk. Sleeps six inside, with plenty of room to pitch tents in the yard. A stay here requires a bit more self-reliance than at a concessionaire-serviced cabin—as well as all the requisite leave-no-trace-style cleanup on the back end—but the payoff is savoring one's own home-cooked meal on a porch overlooking one's very own meadow. And after breakfast in the morning, you can stroll or ride a mountain bike on miles of dirt track. Bring your own bedding, towels, food and beverages, toilet paper, and firewood.

○ **The Sequoia High Sierra Camp** (Off Marvin Pass trail; 1-866-654-2877; www.sequoiahighsierracamp.com; very expensive (all meals included); Elevation: 8,500 feet; Open: June–September; Owners: Burr and Suzanne Hughes; Pets: No; Wheelchair Access: No; Internet Access: No). When Burr Hughes came out from Memphis and looked at Yosemite's famous High Sierra Camps, he knew he wanted to do something different. "Something like 6,000 people a year put in for 900 beds up there," he explains, "and you have to share a tent with strangers!" He scoured the maps, found the perfect inholding of private land between Sequoia and Kings Canyon National Parks—an even five hours' distance from either Los Angeles or San Francisco—and set about building a true eco resort along the lines of what he and Suzanne had seen at Maho Bay and the Estate Concordia Preserve on St. John in the Virgin Islands. The result is a tasteful collection of luxury tent cottages—with crown moldings, shuttered windows, throw rugs, down comforters, propane lanterns, and plush-top beds—terraced into a sloping grove of old-growth red fir. It's not nearly so arduous to get to as Bearpaw: You can bounce a low-slung hybrid to road's end (be sure to print out detailed directions before you leave home, and pay attention to your odometer along the way—your GPS unit may prove useless out here); the hike in is less than a mile, climbing

THE DAY WANES AND THE PROPANE BLAZES AT THE SEQUOIA HIGH SIERRA CAMP BILL BECHER

300 feet and winding through a rich meadow of wildflowers. With hazy sunset views across the distant rim of Kings Canyon, crackling fires, the deep sound of wilderness all around, and the most noteworthy and sophisticated food on the west side of the Sierra (see "Dining"), it's the sort of place one feels inclined to settle into for a few days. Hikes to Mitchell Peak, Seville Lake, Lookout Point—and even down into Cedar Grove—are among the emptiest in the parks. For maximum appreciation of such luxuries as hot showers, a glass of tawny port in the evening, and fresh-squeezed orange juice and a custom omelet station in the morning, consider walking here from Lodgepole (11 miles) or Cedar Grove (8 miles). Return shuttles can be arranged by calling the camp in advance.

GRANT GROVE AND THE KINGS CANYON SCENIC BYWAY

There is a considerable difference in the quality of services and facilities in Kings Canyon, compared to those in Sequoia. Most of the concessions in Sequoia (other than those in Mineral King or at the Sequoia High Sierra Camp) are operated by an enormous, hugely capitalized international hospitality and entertainment conglomerate—the various Delaware North Companies—with tentacles stretching from London's new Wembley Stadium to the Boston Bruins, from the Los Angeles Airport to the Kennedy Space Center, from Niagara Falls to the Grand Canyon. Concessions in Kings Canyon, on the other hand (and at the Stony Creek Lodge in Sequoia National Monument), are managed by a small local operator, the Sequoia–Kings Canyon Park Services Company, which has been running concessions here as far back as anyone can remember, but which, according to a company lawyer (as quoted in the year 2000), "has not been able to operate profitably."

All of which is not to say that one should write off the possibility of decent overnight accommodations in Kings Canyon. The more discriminating visitor may prefer to bring his own camping and cooking equipment, but there is a particular old school charm—and undeniable value—to the historic-rustic 1920s camp cabins at **Grant Grove Village** (1-866-522-6966; www.sequoia-kingscanyon .com; inexpensive to moderate). Many of the structures here, tobacco-brown paint and all, are designated National Historic Landmarks. Units available with or without private bathrooms; no cooking allowed. For more modern, franchise-motel-style accommodations with aluminum doors and windows, high-traffic carpeting, fireside wireless Internet access, and board games in the "lobby," try the adjacent **John Muir Lodge** (1-866-522-6966; www .sequoiakingscanyon.com; expensive), built in 1998. Open year-round. For a pair of motel-style queen beds within earshot of the rushing waters of the mighty Kings, nearly as deep into the rugged heart of the Sierra Nevada as one can get by automobile, there is no other option than the **Cedar Grove Lodge** (1-866-522-6966; www.sequoia-kingscanyon.com; moderate to expensive). Wood-veneer furniture, cottage-cheese ceilings, well-worn carpeting. When available, the three "patio rooms" are worth the extra few dollars. Closed in winter.

KERNVILLE AND THE GREAT WESTERN DIVIDE HIGHWAY

Among the least developed regions in the Sierra, this part of the **Sequoia National Forest** has the least to recommend by way of tourist accommodations. Between Springville and Kernville the only decent option is the lavishly renovated but still slightly spooky **Camp Nelson Lodge** (559-542-0904; www .campnelsonlodge.com; expensive; no alcohol allowed, but the very best in mattresses and log furnishings). In a pinch, very basic and inexpensive motel rooms with Wi-Fi can be had at

KERNVILLE/GREAT WESTERN DIVIDE/KAISER PASS CAMPING

Great Western Divide Highway/ Sequoia National Forest/ Monument South	Elevation	Season	Reservations Accepted	Fee	Sites	Water	Agency
1. Wishon	3,900	Year-round	Yes	Yes	39	Piped	USFS
2. Belknap	5,000	Apr-Nov	Yes	Yes	15	Piped	USFS
3. Coy Flat	5,000	Apr-Nov	Yes	Yes	20	Piped	USFS
4. Quaking Aspen	7,000	May-Nov	Yes	Yes	32	Yes	USFS
5. Holey Meadow (Group)	6,400	Jun-Oct	Yes	Yes	‡	No	USFS
6. Redwood Meadow	6,100	Jun-Oct	Yes	Yes	15	Piped	USFS
7. Long Meadow (Group)	6,000	Jun-Sep	Yes	Yes	1	No	USFS
8. Peppermint	7,100	Year-round	No	No	19	Creek	USFS
9. Lower Peppermint	5,300	May-Oct	No	Yes	17	Piped	USFS
10. Limestone	3,800	Apr-Nov	No	Yes	22	Creek	USFS
11. Leavos Flat	3,000	Year-round	Yes	Yes	9	Piped	USFS
12. Frog Meadow	7,500	Jun-Oct	No	No	10	No	USFS
13. White River	4,000	May-Sep	Yes	Yes	12	Yes	USFS
14. Panorama	7,500	Jun-Sep	No	No	10	No	USFS
Upper Kern River							
15. Fairview	3,500	Apr-Oct	Yes	Yes	55	Yes	USFS
16. Goldledge	3,200	May-Sep	Yes	Yes	37	Yes	USFS
17. Hospital Flat	3,000	May-Sep	Yes	Yes	40	Yes	USFS
18. Camp 3	2,800	May-Sep	Yes	Yes	52	Piped	USFS
19. Cedar Creek	4,800	May-Oct	No	No	11	Piped	USFS
20. Headquarters	2,800	Year-round	Yes	Yes	44	Piped	USFS
Kaiser Pass/Sierra National Forest							
21. Badger Flat	8,200	Jun-Oct	No	Yes	15	No	USFS
22. Badger Flat (group)	8,200	Jun-Oct	Yes	Yes	‡	No	USFS
23. Sample Meadow	7,800	Jun-Oct	No	No	16	No	USFS
24. Portal Forebay	7,200	Jun-Sep	No	Yes	11	No	USFS
25. Bolsillo	7,400	Jun-Oct	No	No	3	Yes	USFS
26. Mono Hot Springs	7,400	May-Oct	Yes	Yes	26	Yes	USFS
27. Mono Creek	7,400	Jun-Oct	Yes	Yes	14	No	USFS
28. Vermillion	7,700	Jun-Oct	Yes	Yes	31	Yes	USFS
29. Ward Lake	7,300	Jun-Oct	No	Yes	17	Lake	USFS
30. Jackass Meadows	7,200	Jun-Oct	No	No	8	Yes	USFS

note: Reservations at USFS and NPS Sites, unless otherwise specified, can be made online at www.recreation.org ot by calling 1-877-444-6777.

*Located within the park. ‡ Group Sites accommodate from 50 to 100 people. Consult reservation agency for specifics.

the **Pierpoint Springs Resort** (559-542-2423; www.pierpointsprings.com) and at the **Ponderosa Lodge** (559-542-2579; www.brewersponderosalodge.com). The most interesting—and economical—way to establish a base camp in the region, other than by pitching a tent or pulling up an RV, is to reserve one of several housekeeping-style Forest Service cabin or lookout rentals (559-539-2607; www.fs.fed.us/r5/sequoia/ recreation/rec_rentals.html; moderate). The **Quaking Aspen Cabin**, in particular, next door to the idyllic **Quaking Aspen Campground**, stands within easy striking distance of all the major points of interest along CA 190, sleeps up to six very close friends, and offers such luxuries as electricity, hot and cold running water, a fridge, a stove, a motley collection of kitchen implements, an outdoor fire pit, and a porch for entertaining the abundance of local wildlife. Check the website for other options farther afield. Be sure to call ahead and clarify directions.

In Kernville, where motor-court lodgings are plentiful, the quality of a given establishment can generally be estimated by the furnishings on its front porch. Try the **Whispering Pines Lodge** (760-376-3733; www.kernvalley .com/whisperingpines; moderate to very expensive; no pets), with its private cantilevered decks and poolside view of the river.

MONO HOT SPRINGS AND KAISER PASS ROAD

Mono Hot Springs Resort (CA 168; 559-325-1710; www.monohotsprings .com; inexpensive to moderate; Elevation: 6,560 feet; Open: May–November; Owners: The Winslow family; Pets: Yes;

KAISER PASS AND THE ANSEL ADAMS WILDERNESS BURKE GRIGGS

Wheelchair Access: Limited; Internet Access: Wireless [at the store]). A series of bathhouses has come and gone at the springs across the river, where once upon a time Mono Indians—and likely their prehistoric ancestors, too—made their annual summer camp. The soaking tubs remain. Walter Hill, a contractor and avid sportsman from Sanger, secured a permit from the Forest Service in 1939 to allow passenger cars up the road and to build a rustic summer resort. During all the short seasons between 1939 and 1947, Walter and his wife, Polly, literally cobbled this place together from local San Joaquin river rock. The Hill kids eventually sold to the Winslows, of which the third generation can today be seen scurrying about trying to keep the place standing (and the plumbing functioning). In late 2000, in a letter recommending that the resort structures be listed on the National Register of Historic Places, forest historian Thomas Nave cited the unique use of cobblestone, the influence of the Arts and Crafts Movement, and "Walter Hill's mastery of the vernacular bungalow style." With a handful of days, a carload of kids, and a trunkful of provisions, it's hard to imagine a more timeless and idyllic spot to set up housekeeping.

✪ **Muir Trail Ranch** (6 miles' walk (or trail ride) from the far end of Florence Lake Elevation: 7,600 feet; 209-966-3195; www.muirtrailranch.com; very expensive (includes meals); Open: June–September; Owners: Adeline Smith and family; Pets: No; Wheelchair Access: No; Internet Access: No). As the story goes, Karl Smith, professional trombone player, was traipsing through the High Sierra one summer with his friend, Sam Peckinpah—this must have been sometime in the 1940s—when, at some point, Sam, later to become a famous film director, fell and cut his hand. The fastest way out was via the old Diamond D Ranch. Sam got his hand fixed up proper, and Karl, after a soak in the hot springs and a good look around, set his sights on buying the place. He started by buying the boathouse and store on Florence Lake, and in 1953 he and his wife, Adeline, swung a deal for the ranch itself. Log cabins, tent cabins, tiled hot springs tubs, ranch-generated hydroelectric power, limitless hiking, horseback riding, fishing, swimming, and general lounging around. A popular resupply stop for hikers on the John Muir Trail. Getting here is no small endeavor: It involves a long drive, a ferry ride, time in the saddle, or a 6-mile hike—assuming you're coming in from the nearest road. But securing a reservation is the hardest part. Book the whole ranch for a week, or try for a shorter stay in spring or fall. Bring your own libations, towel, flashlight, and sleeping bag.

✻ Where to Eat

High cuisine has only recently begun to make forays into this part of the high country. Rare is the trained and innovative chef willing to forsake the bright lights of Vegas or San Francisco for a set of propane burners on a ledge of granite at 8,000 feet above the sea. Rarer still is the one willing to stick it out for more than a couple of seasons. Water is slow to boil up here, sauces quick to cool; fixings for the delicate palate—fresh-harvested shellfish, papaya, herbs, heirloom tomatoes, and such—tend to fare imperfectly on the arduous and refrigerated journey up the hill.

That said, hunger bred from exertion is one of the most powerful seasonings known to man. The food at Sequoia's two different High Sierra Camps, whether with boxed burgundy or a bottle of Sonoma's finest Zinfandel, by the light of the alpenglow, in the wake of hours-long knee-jarring descents from cold alpine lakes, has been known to open new glimpses into the sublime. But there is also decent roadside fare to be had, Mexican food at lower elevations, and in the gateway towns a host of options for

respectable steak-and-potato-style fare, all of which tend to be enhanced considerably by one's having spent long hours beneath a 60-pound pack eating nothing but energy bars. Breakfast and pie are prepared with appropriate reverence nearly everywhere.

Be forewarned, however: The longer one dallies along the scenic byways of the sequoia belt, the more difficult it becomes to avoid the concessionaires' ubiquitous shrink-wrapped deli sandwiches and microwave pizzas. It is eminently advisable, therefore, before proceeding into the hills—here more than in any other part of the Southern Sierra—to first make a stop at one of the farm stands in the valley (i.e., between Fresno and Sanger, between Visalia and Lemon Cove, or between Porterville and Springville), and to carry in the trunk of one's vehicle a well-stocked cooler and the means to whip up a decent roadside picnic.

THREE RIVERS

Buckaroo Diner (41695 Sierra Dr.; 559-465-5088; www.theolbuckaroo.com). A few years back, Three-Rivers-native Nicki French packed up everything she'd learned about food in San Francisco and moved her family back to the banks of the Kaweah to run a food truck. The food truck quickly expanded into the art-deco diner space next door, and now it's hands-down the best place to eat in the Southern Sierra foothills. Locally sourced organic veggies and herbs, grilled prawns and trout, slow-roated pork shoulder, fried chicken, bacon and eggs, cold craft beer. Eat inside in the AC or outside by the river. Open for dinner Thursday through Monday. Breakfast and lunch on weekends.

Gateway Restaurant (45978 Sierra Dr.; 559-561-4133; www.gateway-sequoia .com; expensive). Classic American fine dining of the steak/soup or salad/baked potato school. Red tablecloths, stemware, candles, and the locals' favorite tableside view of the Kaweah. Deviations into melted-cheese broccoli and gravy-esque red wine sauces do the trick and are sure to put heft in your step. The twice-baked stuffed potato is a highlight. Last full-service bar before the park.

TAVERNS, SALOONS, AND ROAD-HOUSES **Gateway Bar** (45978 Sierra Dr.; 559-561-4133; www.gateway-sequoia .com). Stop in for a $100 shot of Van Winkle family-reserve rye and local tales told by owner and long-time Santa Monica transplant Glenn McIntyre.

River View Restaurant & Lounge (42323 Sierra Dr.; 559-561-2211; inexpensive). Favorite watering hole of local artists, bikers, and park rangers on shore leave. Basic burgers, fries, pizzas, and the like served on the patio overlooking the river. Live music four nights a week.

GROCERIES **Three Rivers Village Market** (40869 Sierra Dr.; 559-561-4441). The only full grocery store this side of Visalia. Decent produce, deli and meat counter, basic wine and liquor selection, beer, ice, bread, Ben & Jerry's, and charcoal.

SANDWICHES AND SUCH **Anne Lang's Emporium** (41651 Sierra Dr.; 559-561-4937; www.threerivers.com/Anne Lang.htm). Old-fashioned soda fountain, wide selection of bulk teas and coffee beans, homemade soups, salads, and sandwiches. Take lunch to go or eat on the deck over the river. Espresso, full-service flower shop, and notary.

✪ **Sierra Subs and Salads** (41717 Sierra Dr.; 559-561-4810; www .sierrasubsandsalads.com). Best grilled sandwiches on the western slope can be found here, the local favorite lunch stop, owned and operated by the school principal's daughter and her husband. Try the Alta Peak Club, the Manzanita Melt, or the Tokopah Turkey. Fresh fruit smoothies, salads, and healthy box lunches available for picnics in the high country—about 1,000 times better than what you can get up in the park. Oh, and subs, too. Closed Mondays.

SWEETS **Reimer's Candies and Gifts** (42375 Sierra Dr.; 1-866-766-2263; www .reimerscandies.com). "Every man who

THIS SIGN ISN'T STRICTLY TRUE, OF COURSE. THERE IS GAS, MOST OF THE TIME, AT THE STONY CREEK LODGE, 35 MILES UP THE ROAD FROM THREE RIVERS. BUT IT IS YOUR LAST CHANCE FOR A GOOD GRILLED SANDWICH AND A WELL-MADE MACHIATTO

finds the time long and the atmosphere difficult to bear should comfort himself with a chocolate," wrote eighteenth-century French epicure Brillat-Savarin. Properly prepared and in its darkest form, this classic Mesoamerican delicacy has been shown to be an effective antidepressant, producing some of the same effects on the brain as heroin and cannabis. It may also help combat cholesterol, high blood pressure, hypertension, coughing, diarrhea—even altitude sickness. The Aztecs found that a man could walk all day with nothing but a piece of chocolate. At Reimer's, amid high patriotism, cuckoo clocks, and nutcrackers, the stuff is as real as it gets. There's also peanut brittle, toffee, licorice, and homemade blackberry ice cream—in a riverside setting all dressed up like a Bavarian teahouse. How can you not?

MINERAL KING

Silver City Restaurant & Bakery (559-561-3223; www.silvercityresort.com; inexpensive). Copious breakfasts served with local-roast French-pressed coffee, burgers, salads, and sandwiches with local-made cheese served family-style on knotty pine tables with benches (or out on the porch when the sun is warm), 8 AM–8 PM Thursday through Monday. Bring your own beer or bottle of wine from down in the valley. Root beer floats and the best homemade pie on the western slope of the Sierra Nevada, served on a pine board. Dinner specials on weekends. Restaurant closed for meals on Tuesday and Wednesday; pie and coffee served seven days, all summer long.

GENERALS HIGHWAY AND HIGH-COUNTRY SEQUOIA

✪ **Bearpaw High Sierra Camp** (meals for camp guests only). Late afternoon brings lemonade and brownies on the porch and the faint wafting of bluegrass from the solar-powered satellite radio in the kitchen. At 5:30 the call to dinner comes

DINING WITH A VIEW, BEARPAW HIGH SIERRA CAMP BILL BECHER

in the form of a cast-iron skillet rung with a metal spoon. If you're hiking in, be sure to leave the trailhead early enough that you make camp by dinner. One recent evening's fare included a layered asparagus salad, white pizza, "collapsed" tomatoes, pork tenderloin, and organic white bean "goop" with roasted garlic and fresh rosemary—all ingredients hauled in by mule—followed by camp-crafted chocolate ice cream, boxed red wine, ceramic-filtered spring water, and the rising and fading of alpenglow on granite. Full hot breakfast in the morning. Sack lunches available for a modest fee.

✪ **Montecito-Sequoia Lodge** (at the Montecito Lake resort; 1-800-843-8677; www.mslodge.com; moderate). The atmosphere is pure summer camp, with banged-up eight-top tables, aluminum folding chairs, and the general mayhem of kids on vacation in the woods, but the food—buffet-style vats of veggie lasagna, chicken cordon bleu, rice pilaf, baby-green salads, mashed potatoes, and such—is some of the healthiest and most satisfying in and around the parks. Milk, juice, and Sierra Nevada on tap. Homemade desserts and breakfasts to last through a full day of adventures. Dining hall open to the public year-round. Call ahead for mealtimes.

The Peaks Restaurant at the Wuksachi (64740 Wuksachi Way; 1-866-807-3598; www.visitsequoia.com; expensive). With its lofty post-and-beam construction and retro mission-style furnishings, the Wuksachi aims for the grandeur of parks lodges of bygone days, but can't quite mask its contempo corporate-generic heritage. Alas, it's still the best (read: only) place around to enjoy a snifter of Armagnac and check your e-mail in view of browsing mule deer and the granite cliffs of Tokopah Canyon. The staff has none of that banished-to-the-gulag aspect one finds down the road in Kings Canyon. The wine list is ample; the food comfortable (if dear). Along that last mile of dusty trail, imagine spring greens with prosciutto and feta saturated in pear vinaigrette, a craft beer, and a $20 slab of meat loaf with mashed potatoes. Rainbow trout flown in all the way from South America. Muffled acoustics help toe the line between family-friendly and civilized, but the piped-in techno-flamenco may keep you from lingering over the fruit cobbler. Dinner until 10 PM in high season. Reservations required. Half-decent steamer-warmed breakfast buffet.

✪ **The Sequoia High Sierra Camp** (65745 Big Meadow Rd.; 1-866-654-2877; www.sequoiahighsierracamp.com; meals for camp guests only). This is surely one of the most remote outposts in the world for classic Southern hospitality and a true epicurean experience. But rest assured: New Orleans veteran chef Fidgeir Helgason (originally from Iceland) and his crew of bright-eyed European college students deliver just that. Each evening brings a new multiple-course menu built on local, sustainably procured ingredients, served family-style on wrought-iron tables in an impressive acropolis-style dining pavilion, with a campfire crackling beyond and bats and jet trails in the sky. And when there's trout on the menu it comes from one of the nearby streams.

Conversation among the particular genre of world-savvy clientèle willing and able to adventure this far into the woods, and to pay for the experience, tends to be lively and inspired—and to linger well into the night's slow rotation of the Milky Way. Excellent wine and craft beer selection, or bring your own. Homemade muffins, fresh-cut fruit, and custom omelets for breakfast. Build your own sack-lunch picnic from the full sandwich bar. Open June–October.

GRANT GROVE AND THE KINGS CANYON SCENIC BYWAY

The **Grant Grove Restaurant** (Grant Grove Village), once vaguely reminiscent of so many roadside cafés along defunct sections of Route 66, has undergone major renovation, and still provides decent sit-down dining for three meals a day. The **Pizza Parlor** (Grant Grove Village) is open during the summer. Multiple-day visits to the Cedar Grove area may be limited by the quality of dining available at the **Cedar Grove Snack Bar** (shoes and shirts required), which is closed in winter.

KERNVILLE AND THE GREAT WESTERN DIVIDE HIGHWAY

Pierpoint Springs Resort (CA 190; 559-542-2423; www.pierpointsprings.com; inexpensive to moderate). Classic diner-style fare, vinyl tablecloths, beer, wine, cocktails, and the most reliable free wireless Internet between Springville and Kernville. Live music some weekends.

Ewing's On The Kern (125 Buena Vista Dr., Kernville; 760-376-2411; www.ewingsonthe kern.com; expensive). Serving up voluminous slabs of prime rib and "The World's Coldest Beer" with the best view in town. The beer is cold because the glasses are put in the freezer wet. Recent dinner specials included tempura eggplant with chipotle dipping sauce and chicken cordon bleu. Note the authentic bear and lion skins on the wall and, behind the bar, the diorama of pre-reservoir Isabella Valley showing the historical progression of means of transport (mule to horse to pack train to covered wagon to stagecoach). Dinner only. Closed Wednesdays.

TAVERNS, SALOONS, AND ROAD-HOUSES

Wellsville Saloon (CA 190, Cedar Slope; 559-542-2319). Owner Jim Wells's fine selection of tequilas may be the perfect antidote to the curves in the road. Clear the palate with a couple of dollar tacos (ground beef). Play a round of pool or just appreciate the craftsmanship in the wood floor and the organ-pipe-sized wind chimes on the deck. Press on.

Ponderosa Lodge (CA 190, Ponderosa; 559-542-2579; www .brewersponderosalodge.com). In summer, a favorite stop for the Harley-Davidson crowd, but still plenty friendly for spandex-clad cyclists and German tourists freshly emerged from the bowels of Rent-America RVs. Burgers and beers. Outside or in. Saturday night steak dinners. Fat Tire on tap. In winter, the place converts to a cozy cross-country ski lodge ministering bowls of chili and hot chocolate. Closed Tuesday and Wednesday in winter.

McNalley's Fairview Lodge on the Kern (CA 99, 15 miles north of Kernville; 760-376-2430; www .mcnallysfairviewlodge.com). Classic pine-paneled lounge and dining room beside the river, serving all manner of fried appetizers and oversized, professionally prepared slabs of beef. Various surf 'n' turf options and mud pie. Open daily for dinner. Popular outdoor

BASIC ACCOMMODATIONS AND PRIVATE RIVERVIEW PATIOS AT THE WHISPERING PINES, KERNVILLE

hamburger stand open Friday, Saturday, and Sunday. Basic cabins and motel rooms if you just can't bring yourself to get back in the car.

Kern River Brewing Company (13415 Sierra Hwy., Kernville; 760-376-BEER; www.kernriverbrewingcompany.com). Hand-drawn local and guest brews, from blonde to stout, plus burgers, brats, fish and chips. Live music most weekends.

Kernville Saloon (20 Tobias St.; 760-376-2500). Classic historic Western Saloon. Tin ceiling tiles, cowhide bar-stools. Moose antlers, pool table, and shuffleboard. Opens at 10:30 AM.

Sportsman's Inn (11123 Kernville Rd., Kernville; 760-376-2556). Where Kernville does its serious drinking. Where university-trained biologists studying owl habitat patterns in burnt-out forests might congregate with river guides and bikers to play pool and sip buckets of Red Bull with Crown Royal and peach schnapps.

MONO HOT SPRINGS AND KAISER PASS ROAD

The **River Rock Café** (at Mono Hot Springs; 559-325-1710; moderate). Lunch and dinner served alfresco on the shaded porch—most days, while supplies last, June through October. Try the corned buffalo Reuben.

Vermilion Valley Resort (West shore, Lake Thomas A. Edison; 559-259-4000; www.edisonlake.com; moderate). Affectionately known as VVR. Where else can you sit by a roaring campfire, in a grove of lodgepole pine, at the edge of the wilderness, talk shop with wild-eyed through-hikers on their way from Mexico to Canada, watch baseball on a TV powered by a diesel engine, check your email for $10 an hour ($20 a day), and gorge on stuffed pork chops, barbecued tri-tip, or fresh-caught rainbow trout piccata? Good beer and wine available from the camp store, plus rustic tent and trailer accommodations if you feel like hanging around for a few days.

✳ Books, Maps, and Information

THREE RIVERS

⊕ **Foothills/Ash Mountain Visitor Center** (47050 Generals Hwy.; 559-565-3135). This is Park Service headquarters for all of Sequoia–Kings Canyon. Displays and exhibits provide an introduction to the oak woodlands and wild chaparral of the Sierra Nevada Foothills, one of the most diverse—and increasingly endangered—ecosystems in North America. The bookstore, run by the venerable nonprofit **Sequoia Parks Conservancy** (559-561-4803; www.sequoiaparksconservancy.org), contains a thorough selection of titles on the cultural and natural history of the Sierra. A range of guidebooks, maps, bear canister rental, and Crystal Cave tickets are also available, as well as wilderness permits. Open 8 AM–5 PM in summer; 8 AM–4:30 PM after mid-November.

MINERAL KING

BOOKS, MAPS, AND INFORMATION **Mineral King Ranger Station** (559-565-3768). Books, maps, wilderness permits, first aid, and bear canister rental at 7,580 feet. Ranger Len is the go-to guy for practical information on the region: trail conditions, geology, flora and fauna, local lore. Open daily 8 AM–4:30 PM, June through early September.

GENERALS HIGHWAY AND HIGH-COUNTRY SEQUOIA

Beetle Rock Nature Center (across from Giant Forest Museum; 559-565-3081). According to Ansel Hall's Guide to Sequoia and General Grant National Parks (1930), "the rock was named in 1905 when a new species of beetle was there discovered by Ralph Hopping [the son], a government entomologist."

Today, the center houses interactive children's exhibits from the old Walter Fry Nature Center, and it also serves as an education and conference center run by the Sequoia Natural History Museum. For sale are children's books, puppets, stuffed animals, and science kits. Open in summer.

۞ Giant Forest Museum (559-565-4480). What was once the Giant Forest Market is now a beautifully tooled museum documenting the history of the Big Trees and their strange, historic interactions with humans. The bookstore, run by the Sequoia Parks Conservancy, offers essentially the same excellent selection of books and maps as Ash Mountain and Lodgepole Visitor Centers.

Lodgepole Visitor Center (559-5654436). A range of exhibits covers the natural and human history of the Southern Sierra. The movie *Bears of the Sierra* runs on a continuous loop in the theater. Books, maps, postcards, souvenirs, wilderness permits, rental bear canisters, first aid, and Crystal Cave tickets. Open daily, early spring through late fall.

GRANT GROVE AND THE KINGS CANYON SCENIC BYWAY

Grant Grove Visitor Center (Grant Grove Village; 559-565-4307). Range of bilingual exhibits on the history of Grant Grove and the natural history of Kings Canyon and the High Sierra. Excellent selection of books and maps stocked by the Sequoia Parks Conservancy. Wilderness permits, pay phone, first aid.

Cedar Grove Visitor Center (Cedar Grove Village; 559-565-3793). This 1932-vintage Forest Service cabin houses a tiny selection of books and maps and a retinue of friendly rangers to answer questions. Pay phone (cell phones do not work here) and first aid. Closed in winter.

Road's End Permit Station (at the end of the road in Kings Canyon; no phone). Maps, trail conditions, bear canister rentals, wilderness permits. Open 7 AM–4 PM in summer.

MONO HOT SPRINGS AND KAISER PASS ROAD

High Sierra Ranger Station (at Bolsillo Creek, east of Portal Forebay; 559-877-7173). Good selection of books, guides, wilderness maps, and general Sierra National Forest information. Wilderness and campfire permits available. Open daily June through August. Note the grave marker for three Alaskan sled dogs who in the early 1920s helped run mail and supplies to workers at Florence Lake.

✳ Shopping

THREE RIVERS

GALLERIES **The Arts Alliance of Three Rivers** (www.artsalliancethreerivers .org). Directory of local artists working in oil and acrylic, pencil, mixed media, gourds, wood, weaving, jewelry, clay, books, guitars, prints, and photography.

Colors Art Studio (41763 Sierra Dr.; 559-561-4493). World-class hand-painted furniture and colorful ceramics by Wendy McKellar and guests. Custom guitars by Wendy's son, Ryan Tate Johnson. Irregular hours. "If you ever find an artist who keeps regular hours," says the neighbor (a real estate agent), "how good could they be?"

Cort Gallery (41881 Sierra Dr.; 559-561-4036). Contemporary loft-style gallery space beside the river, designed by owner/architect Gary Cort. Rotating exhibits, dance and yoga classes, drum circles, lectures, and performances.

SUNDRIES AND SOUVENIRS **Heart's Desire Gifts** (42249 Sierra Dr.; 559-561-4401). In the shingled geodesic dome. Wind chimes, wind socks, craft jewelry and textiles, curios, photography, secondhand spiritual paperbacks, and a pot of coffee. Wi-Fi on the deck beside the river. Ask for the password.

GENERAL STORES **Kaweah General Store** (40462 Sierra Dr.; 559-561-3475).

Features a variety of unique things (stuffed rattlesnake?) plus a selection of hunting and fishing supplies, fish and game licenses, hardware, firewood, and basic groceries.

Three Rivers Mercantile (41152 Sierra Dr.; 559-561-2378). National franchise hardware store in a metal building. Coleman-style camping equipment, bait-fishing supplies, and fish and game licenses.

MINERAL KING

GENERAL STORES **Silver City General Store** (559-561-3223; www.silvercity resort.com). Books, maps, souvenirs, bug spray, sunscreen, toilet paper, T-shirts, canned goods, marshmallows, marmot wire rental, and transmission oil cooler hose. No fresh food, beer, wine, liquor, or dairy products. No ice or gasoline.

GENERALS HIGHWAY AND HIGH-COUNTRY SEQUOIA

GIFT SHOPS **Wuksachi Gift Shop** (Wuksachi Lodge; 1866-807-3598) has a small selection of books and souvenirs; Wuksachi and Sequoia logo wear; beer, wine, and soft drinks; and Native American–themed gifts. Open year-round.

GENERAL STORES **Lodgepole Market, Deli & Gift Shop** (63024 Lodgepole Rd., across from visitor center and post office; 559-565-3301). Built in 1975 as a means to pull the load away from the Giant Forest Village. Offers a half-decent selection of beer, wine, picnic supplies, books, curios, phone cards, and outdoor equipment. Deli, pizza, and burgers across the hall. Charcoal and firewood; ice, laundromat, and showers. Closed in winter.

Stony Creek Village (65569 Generals Hwy., 11 miles north of Lodgepole; 559-335-5500 or 1-866-522-6966). Convenience-style market and curio shop. The only modern gas pumps in the region. Basic motel rooms upstairs in

case you get stuck here. Open late May through October.

GRANT GROVE AND THE KINGS CANYON SCENIC BYWAY

GIFT SHOPS **Grant Grove Gift Shop** (Grant Grove Village; 559-335-5500). Eclectic selection of Sequoia–Kings Canyon souvenirs, postcards, T-shirts, tchotchkes, and nature-themed gifts.

GENERAL STORES Small purveyor of groceries, firewood, beer, wine, soft drinks, ice, limited fresh fruit and vegetables, basic picnic and camping supplies, and phone cards.

Cedar Grove Market (Cedar Grove Village; 559-565-0100). Basic convenience store, books, maps, souvenirs and postcards, ATM, and laundry facility.

KERNVILLE AND THE GREAT WESTERN DIVIDE HIGHWAY

GENERAL STORES **James' Store** (13432 Sierra Hwy., Kernville; 760-376-2424). Meat, produce, ice, bait and tackle, camping supplies, gas, liquor, and ammo.

Camp Nelson General Store (Camp Nelson; 559-542-3700). Basic grocery and hardware, video rentals, beer, and wine.

MONO HOT SPRINGS AND KAISER PASS ROAD

GENERAL STORES **Florence Lake Store** (Florence Lake; www.florence-lake.com). Books, toys, batteries, souvenirs, trail supplies, and ferry tickets sold beneath a one-of-a-kind log cupola. Owned and operated by the Muir Trail Ranch. No alcohol sold here.

Mono Hot Springs General Store (Mono Hot Springs; 559-325-1710). Basic staples, ice, ice cream, beer, wine, fishing tackle, microwave burritos, aspirin, Band-Aids, books, Adirondack chairs, and wireless Internet.

COLD PLUNGE IN THE JOHN MUIR WILDERNESS PATITUCCIPHOTO

Vermilion Camp Store (Vermilion, on the west shore of Lake Thomas Edison; 559-259-4000; www.edisonlake.com). Connoisseur's selection of microbrews, graham crackers, marshmallows, white gas, and other trail supplies.

✳ Special Events

January: **Polar Dip River Swim** (Gateway Restaurant, Three Rivers). **Chimney Rock Challenge Nordic Ski Race** (Montecito Sequoia Lodge, www.montecitosequoia.com).

February: **Whiskey Flat Days** (Kernville). Parade, carnival rides, frog-jumping contests, gold panning, epitaph contests, and line dancing.

March: **Return of swallows** to Pumpkin Hollow Bridge (Three Rivers; kern.audubon.org). **Three Rivers Artists' Studio Tour** (Three Rivers; threeriversartstudiotour.com). Three Rivers artists open their home studios to the public. **Keyesville Classic Mountain Bike Stage Race** (Lake Isabella; 541-490-0900; www.keyesville.com). Cross-country, downhill, short-track, trials events, kids' race and poker ride. On-site camping and catered food.

April: **Jazzaffair** (Three Rivers; www.jazzaffair.info). **Kern River Festival** (Kernville; www.kernfestival.org). **Lions Team Roping** (Three Rivers; 559-561-2222). Good, old-fashioned, small-town entertainment. Former roping chairman Van Bailey calls it "a champagne event at Pepsi-Cola prices." Highlights include dummy roping, barrel racing, and a pig scramble. **Springville Sierra Rodeo** (Springville; 1-866-763-3649;

www.springvillerodeo.com). Billed as "The Biggest Little Rodeo in the West." **National Park Week** (www.nps.gov/npweek). Free access to all national parks. **Kern Valley Spring Nature Festival** (Kern Valley; kern.audubon.org).

May: **Redbud Arts and Crafts Festival** (Three Rivers; 559-561-4417).

June: **Brewer's Mountain Style Chili Cook-Off** (Ponderosa Lodge, CA 190; 559-542-2579; www.brewersponderosalodge.com). Saturday of Memorial Day weekend.

July: **Buck Rock Lookout Annual Open House and Fourth of July Celebration** (www.buckrock.org). **Dark Sky Festival** (www.sequoiaparksconservancy.org)

August: **Kern Valley Hummingbird Celebration** (Kern River Preserve; kern.audubon.org).

September: **Celebration of Sequoias Festival** (Springville; 559-338-2251). **Kern River Valley Turkey Vulture Festival** (Kern River Preserve; kern.audubon.org).

October: **Springville Apple Festival** (Springville; www.springville.ca.us; 559-539-0619). **Springville Fat Tire Classic** (Springville; www.springville.ca.us; 559-781-6234). An 8-mile circuit race beside the Tule River. Fire road and singletrack combo, prizes, free lunch, kids' race.

November: **Pear Lake Ski Hut Lottery** (559-565-4222; sequoiahistory.org). **Kaweah Land & Arts Festival** (www.sequoiariverlands.org; 559-738-0211). The Kaweah River watershed in art and writing.

December: **Trek to the nation's Christmas tree** (Grant Grove; Sanger Chamber of Commerce, 559875-4575; www.sanger.org).

YOSEMITE

YOSEMITE

No photograph or series of photographs, no paintings ever prepare a
visitor so that he is not taken by surprise . . . no description, no mea-
surements, no comparisons are of much value.
—Frederick Law Olmsted, 1865

On March 28, 1864, four score and eight years after the founding of the nation, just as newly promoted Lieutenant General Ulysses S. Grant was preparing Union troops for an all-out springtime assault on Richmond, California Senator John Conness introduced a rather abstract piece of legislation in Washington. The idea was that the federal government would grant to the State of California—in those days still several hard months' travel to the west—a certain portion of the Sierra Nevada that no one in the building had ever seen in person; that only a few hundred Californians, and Indians, had managed to get to; and that had not yet even been surveyed. The proposal in itself was not remarkable: The bulk of the nation's territory, from the Mississippi to the Pacific Ocean, had in the space of 50 years been acquired on the strength of hand-drawn maps, rough sketches, and explorers' journals (with here and there an actual painting for color). What was remarkable in this case was the idea that the place—any place—might be so granted, as was proposed, "for public use, resort, and recreation . . . inalienable forever."

There were in those days, in sophisticated places like Paris and London, great urban parks for the recreational use of the citizenry. Charles I had opened Hyde Park to the public in 1637. Napoleon III had followed suit with the Bois de Boulogne in 1852. There were popular "pleasure gardens" such as Vauxhall (London), Tivoli (Copenhagen), and Prater (Vienna), with fountains and fireworks, music and merry-go-rounds. New York's Central Park—with its looping carriage roads and bridges, its artificial lakes, its soil and trees imported from New Jersey, its courteous and helpful "park keepers"—had been under construction since 1857 under the visionary guidance of its superintendent and architect-in-chief, Frederick Law Olmsted. The well-designed urban park was one of the great hallmarks of modern civilization. But there was as yet no such thing, anywhere in the world, as a government-protected public park in the depths of the wilderness. The idea was essentially counterintuitive.

Most of the legislators in the nation's capital that war-weary year, and surely President Lincoln as well, would have read about or at least heard of Yosemite, if not seen it represented in pictures. In the nine years since Thomas Ayres had made and published his first sketch of the place, in James Hutchings's *California Magazine*, the word had spread far and wide. The first edition of T. Richardson's best-selling *Illustrated Handbook of American Travel* (1857) had called the valley's scenery "perhaps the most remarkable in the United States, and perhaps in the world." Horace Greeley, the most influential newspaperman of his day, editor of the *New York Tribune* and founder of the Republican Party, had in 1859 made the trip overland to see it for himself. When he returned home, despite considerable suffering in the saddle and the fact that the much-touted Yosemite Falls had been stone dry (as it generally is in August), he wrote: "Of all the grandest sights I have enjoyed—Rome from the dome of St. Peter's, the Alps from the Valley of Lake Como, Mount Blanc and her glaciers from

Chamouni [sic], Niagara, and the Yo Semite—I judge the last named the most unique and stupendous."

Earlier that same season, when the waterfalls were still in fine form, Charles Weed and R. H. Vance had managed to haul all manner of equipment by mule over the rough trails to make the first photographs of the place. Thomas Hill, a landscape painter from Philadelphia, considered the last of the Hudson River School, set up a studio at Wawona in 1861. Carleton Watkins made the trek up from San Francisco with his stereoview and mammoth-plate cameras. His images of the valley, and of the Big Trees in the Mariposa Grove, were exhibited to much applause at the swank Goupil & Cie. gallery in New York. "Nothing in the way of landscapes can be more impressive," wrote a reviewer for the *New York Times*. Albert Bierstadt saw the show and the following summer was on his way west, easel strapped to his saddle, to make his first famous sketches of Yosemite. Where the earliest attempts to reconstruct actual giant sequoias in New York and London had generally failed to convince, Watkins's photos did the job. As Ralph Waldo Emerson put it, the images "made the tree possible."

In February 1864, Israel Ward Raymond, California representative of a New York steamship concern, shipped a set of Carleton Watkins prints across the country to John Conness, in Washington—"some views of the Yosemity [sic] Valley"—in order that the senator might have "some idea of its character." "No. 1," wrote Raymond, "is taken from a point on the Mariposa trail and gives a view of about seven miles of the Valley, and the principal part of it. You can see that its sides are abrupt precipices ranging from 2,500 feet to 5,000 feet high. Indeed there is no access to it but by trails over the debris deposited by the crumbling of the walls." Lest there be some debate, he was careful to add: "The summits are mostly bare granite rocks [and] in some parts the surface is covered only by pine trees and can never be of much value."

The matter came before the 38th Congress during the third week of May. It passed the Senate after a moment or two of discussion, Conness having assured his colleagues that the lands in question were "for all public purposes worthless" and would involve "no appropriation whatsoever." There were, as it happened, more pressing issues on the docket. Union troops were having bad luck in Virginia; in Louisiana they were on the run. It was hard to say what was going on with Sherman in Georgia, other than that it was very bloody. On June 3, Grant lost 2,000 men in 20 minutes at the Battle of Cold Harbor—a hundred miles from the federal capital. By June 12th he had disengaged, having lost 13,000 of his men to Lee's 2,500.

On the 29th, with not much ado, the Yosemite matter passed the House, to be signed the following day by Lincoln. Eleven months later, in April 1865, Lee surrendered to Grant at Appomattox, and at Ford's Theatre in Washington, D.C., John Wilkes Booth fired a .44-caliber slug 6 inches into Lincoln's brain, ending the possibility that the president might one day see Yosemite. Conness was a pallbearer at the funeral. Today, there is a sequoia tree named after Lincoln, not in Yosemite but in the Giant Forest in Sequoia. It is considered the world's fourth largest living tree, after the Sherman, Grant, and President trees. The name "Conness" went to a prominent peak (12,590 feet) above Tuolumne Meadows on the northeastern border of what is now Yosemite National Park.

What to do with the place was left to California. There were no specific guidelines. There were no precedents. There had been no money appropriated. The mandate was impossibly vague: "for public use, resort, and recreation." Should there be fun houses, platform carousels, and gravity railroads? Should there be bandstands and nightly fireworks displays? Should there be a grand public bathhouse on the banks of the Merced? First and foremost: Should roads be built and decent accommodations provided, such that the public could actually visit the place? What sort of accommodations? Who

CARETAKER GALEN CLARK'S CABIN IN MARIPOSA GROVE, BUILT IN 1857 GEORGE FISKE, COURTESY NPS, YNP

should do the work, provide services, manage the place? How should it all be paid for? If and when there was profit, how should it be allocated?

To study these issues and to come up with a preliminary report, the governor appointed a First Yosemite Commission of eight relevant gentlemen, including Raymond of the steamship concern; Professor Whitney, state geologist; and Galen Clark, the homesteader at Wawona who in those days ran the only lodgings on the trail to Yosemite and provided guide service to the Big Trees. Frederick Law Olmsted, then ex-superintendent of Central Park (today generally considered the father of American landscape architecture), was appointed chairman. Olmsted's vision for the park in New York, and his scruples, had for the time being exceeded those of his employers, causing him in 1863 to accept a job as manager of a vast mining estate in Mariposa County, California (on 18,000 acres that John C. Frémont had purchased for $10,000 after the close of the Mexican War). In this capacity Olmsted had occasion to explore not only the Mariposa Grove and Yosemite Valley, but also Tuolumne Meadows and some of the surrounding High Sierra. What he saw there was, as he wrote in a letter to his father, "far the noblest park or pleasure ground in the world." Olmsted spent the summer of 1865 on location, hiking around, having discussions with scientists (Whitney, Torrey, et al.) and artists (Watkins and Hill), entertaining visiting politicians and newspapermen, and hammering out not so much the specifics of how to proceed, but a general philosophy. The first order of business was to commission a survey and a map, which he did, engaging Clarence King of the Whitney Survey out of his own pocket. The next step, and by far the most challenging, was to determine—and as much as possible describe—what it was about the place that made it so unique and enjoyable and *necessary* to the public. What made the scenery here so great? What was so "peculiar to this ground," as Olmsted put it, that it should, by order of Congress, be treated "differently from other parts of the public domain"? And, anyway, what was so important about scenery in general that people should go so far out of their way not just to see it, but to protect it and/or develop it in such a way that others might see it, too—for all time?

The photographs, stereoviews, and paintings were extraordinary and served a certain purpose. They seemed no less than glimpses of Eden in the days of Genesis. But still, for those who had been there, for those who had slept on its ground and walked among its wonders, the images failed to get at the essence of the place. Words, too, tended to fall short. "By no statement of the elements . . . can any idea of that scenery be given," Olmsted wrote in his report, "any more than a true impression can be conveyed of a human face by a measured account of its features." Naturally, as others before him and so many after, he resorted to comparisons. "The stream is such a one as Shakespeare delighted in," he wrote, "and brings pleasing reminiscences to the traveler of the Avon or the Upper Thames." The "cabinet pictures," revealed in every side canyon, recalled "the most valued sketches of Calame in the Alps and Appenines." Yosemite Falls he declared to be "15 times the height of Niagara." And yet, he wrote: "There are falls of water elsewhere finer, there are more stupendous rocks, more beetling cliffs, there are deeper and more awful chasms, there may be as beautiful streams, as lovely meadows, there are larger trees."

What was it, then, about Yosemite? "I shall not attempt to describe it," Richardson would write in *Beyond the Mississippi* (1867), "the subject is too large and my capacity too small." Lafayette Bunnell, in his account of that first teary-eyed sighting in 1851, would mention "the vapory clouds . . . a weirdness to the scene . . . the conviction that it was utterly indescribable." Olmsted cited "the imperceptible humidity of the atmosphere and the soil . . . some temporary condition of the air, of clouds, of moonlight, or of sunlight through mist or smoke," lending the scenery in the valley its "indescribable softness and exquisite dreamy charm." More than a century later Ansel Adams, in his autobiography, put it this way: "It is easy to recount that I camped many times at Merced Lake, but it is difficult to explain the magic."

The bottom line, concluded Olmsted, was that people would have to experience the place for themselves, in person—if not for merely aesthetic reasons, then for their health. "It is a scientific fact," he wrote, "that the occasional contemplation of natural scenes of an impressive character, particularly if this contemplation occurs in connection with relief from ordinary cares, change of air and change of habits, is favorable to the health and vigor of men . . . that it not only gives pleasure for the time being, but increases the subsequent capacity for happiness and the means of securing happiness."

Built into Olmsted's proposal was a fundamental contradiction, one that to this day provides a never-ending challenge, not merely for the Park Service in managing places like Yosemite, but for all booming populations stuck between democratic ideals and diminishing natural resources. On the one hand, the place was to be preserved in as "pristine" a state as possible—"as a museum of natural science." On the other hand, facilities and access were to be improved, so that not only the rich but "the whole public" might enjoy the park. A decent road was to be built in place of what was then "a very poor trail," to reduce "the expense, time, and fatigue of a visit," but also for fire suppression, and to bring in timber and supplies for an increasing number of visitors without having to cut down the valley's trees or till its meadows. Strict regulations were to be devised, and enforced, against "injury to the scenery." Traffic patterns were to be considered; roads, trails, and structures built in such a way that they "should not detract from the dignity of the scene."

For the construction of a good access road into the valley, and of "30 miles more or less of double trail and foot paths," bridges, cabins, stairways, surveys, advertising, incidentals, and so on, and for two years' expenses already incurred, Olmsted proposed appropriations by the state Legislature to the tune of $37,000. After this admittedly lavish expenditure, he imagined, "the further necessary expenses for the management of the domain will be defrayed by the proceeds of rents and licenses which will be collected upon it."

In August 1865, five of the eight commissioners (all those present, not including Whitney and Raymond) endorsed the proposal. Olmsted went back to New York to resume his duties as architect and superintendent of Central Park (this time with greater leeway, and terms more favorable to his ambitions for the place). He would go on to design Prospect Park in Brooklyn and the landscapes of at least 16 other major urban parks across the country, as well as the grounds at the U.S. Capitol building and at Niagara Falls. In the 1880s he returned to California to design the campus at Stanford University, but he would never again return to Yosemite.

After Olmsted had gone, in November 1865, Whitney moved to suppress the report, fearing that the Legislature would balk at the cost—and/or that such a project would cut into the already limited budget for his own ongoing geological survey. The document was "lost," not to resurface until 1952. Yosemite's early infrastructure was, as a result, pieced together by private interests, leaseholders, and competing concessionaires, some well meaning, some otherwise, but without any kind of master plan and without any official precautions taken against "injury to the scenery." When a young John Muir ambled into the pleasure ground for the first time in 1868, three years after the disappearance of Olmsted's report, he was able to find employment first as a sheepherder, then as a foreman at Hutchings's sawmill at the base of Yosemite Falls.

Muir was on the one hand a great promoter and forceful advocate for public access. "Everybody needs beauty as well as bread, places to play in and pray in, where nature may heal and give strength to body and soul alike," he would write in his seminal narrative guide to the park, *The Yosemite*. But with equal force he would decry the people's despoilment of the cathedral. "Ax and plow, hogs and horses have long been and are still busy in Yosemite's gardens and groves," Muir wrote in *The Century Magazine* (September 1890). "All that is accessible and destructible is being rapidly destroyed."

On October 1, 1890, fast upon signing Sequoia and Grant Grove National Parks into existence, President Harrison put his name to another bill giving national park status to Tuolumne Meadows and a million acres of the Yosemite High Sierra (the valley and the Mariposa Grove would remain under the management of the State of California for another decade). African American troops from the U.S. Army's famed Buffalo Soldier regiments rode in from the now-quiet Indian frontier to drive out Basque sheepherders. The year 1892 saw the incorporation of the Sierra Club in San Francisco, with Muir as its first president. The group's mission was twofold: on the one hand, "to explore, enjoy, and render accessible the mountain regions of the Pacific Coast"; and on the other, to work for their preservation and protection. In 1903 Muir spent three days and two nights giving President Theodore Roosevelt a personal tour of the park's finer points and of the threats thereto. "The first night we camped in a grove of giant sequoias," the president wrote years later. "It was clear weather, and we lay in the open, the enormous cinnamon-colored trunks rising about us like the columns of a vaster and more beautiful cathedral than was ever conceived by any human architect."

Every year brought more tourists, more photographs, more stereoviews and photopostcards, more magazine articles and guidebooks promoting the salubrious aspects of a visit to the "wilds" of Yosemite and touting the great improvements in facilities. In 1906, at the urging of Muir and the Sierra Club, and with Roosevelt's support in Washington, the State of California agreed to give back to the federal government the original 1864 grant—the valley and the Mariposa Grove—such that the whole tract could be managed as a single national park. In 1914 civilian park rangers replaced the cavalry troops. In 1916—the same year 14-year-old Ansel Adams read Hutchings's *In the Heart of the Sierras* and made his first visit to Yosemite (later to serve for nearly three decades on the Sierra Club's board of directors)—Congress created the National Park Service. Its purpose: "to conserve the scenery and the natural and historic objects and the wildlife therein and to provide for the enjoyment of the same in such manner and by such means as will leave them unimpaired for the enjoyment of future generations."

"In God's wildness lies the hope of the world," wrote Muir, echoing Thoreau before him. There is still wildness in Yosemite, of a kind. Ninety-five percent of the park is roadless backcountry, legally designated and for the most part unmitigated "wilderness," serviced only by pack trains and dirt trails, populated by marmots and mountain lions, ancient whitebark pines, wildflowers, granite, and colorfully costumed backpackers in varying states of blissful dishevelment. Yosemite in our time is not generally a place for solitude, in the sense of being by oneself, without other people, in the way Muir and even Adams once experienced it. And yet with some effort it can still be found—atop certain unheralded subpeaks and nameless granite promontories; along certain disused, half-forgotten trails many miles from the valley, or from the Tioga Road, or from the popular John Muir Trail; or else midweek in midwinter, when lo, one might stand on one's skis at some untracked point along Horizon Ridge, utterly alone, looking across at the smooth black shoulder of Half Dome in the silence of new-fallen snow, and imagine oneself briefly (for a brief eternity) beyond the reach of time.

There is wildness in the valley, too, even in midsummer, when on a busy day the population can exceed 25,000 people. It is a carefree sort of half-civilized wildness—incomparable, indescribable—one that does not exclude humankind but rather indulges it. It is the wildness of blackberry thickets and creeping roses, of old apple orchards and tennis courts long untended, of squirrels and jays battling for picnic scraps, of deer grazing in parking lots, stone footbridges and impromptu float trips on plastic

PRESIDENT THEODORE ROOSEVELT AND JOHN MUIR RIDING IN YOSEMITE VALLEY, MAY 1903 COURTESY NPS, YNP

YOSEMITE'S FIRST RANGERS, THE 24TH INFANTRY, 1899 CELIA CROCKER THOMPSON, COURTESY NPS, YNP

rafts, and bicycles strewn beside a beach. It is the strange wildness of nature-paparazzi scurrying along overgrown footpaths after the quick-fading light; of boys and girls chasing bears through the canvas alleyways of Curry Village (recently renamed "Half Dome Village" due to a trademark dispute arising between the park service and the former concessionaire). "Yosemite Park is a place of rest," wrote Muir, "a refuge from the roar and dust and weary, nervous, wasting work of the lowlands, in which one gains the advantages of both solitude and society." The trick these days is to get out of the car long enough to let the engine cool, to get beyond the clutches of the corporate concessionaire, to strike out across a meadow on foot, or to stretch out in the shade beside the lazy Merced—long enough to allow the place, exactly as it is, and as it has been for thousands of years, to take hold.

✳ The Lay of the Land: Approaches and Logistics

There are four main roads into the park, all paved, all high-gear: (1) the Wawona Road (CA 41) from the southwest via Oakhurst; (2) the El Portal Road (CA 140, also known, for debatable reasons, as the All-Weather Highway) from the west via Mariposa and Midpines; (3) the Big Oak Flat Road (CA 120) from the northwest via Groveland; and the Tioga Road (CA 120) from Lee Vining across Tuolumne Meadows—this last being the only road into the park from the east, and open only in summer. Notes and listings in this chapter are organized geographically along these four gateway corridors. The final section is devoted to the Yosemite Valley itself. Hetch Hetchy is accessed via the Big Oak Flat Road.

There is a grocery store in Yosemite Valley with a decent, if expensive, selection of gourmet picnic and backpacking items—wine, cheese, packaged foods, and more. Best

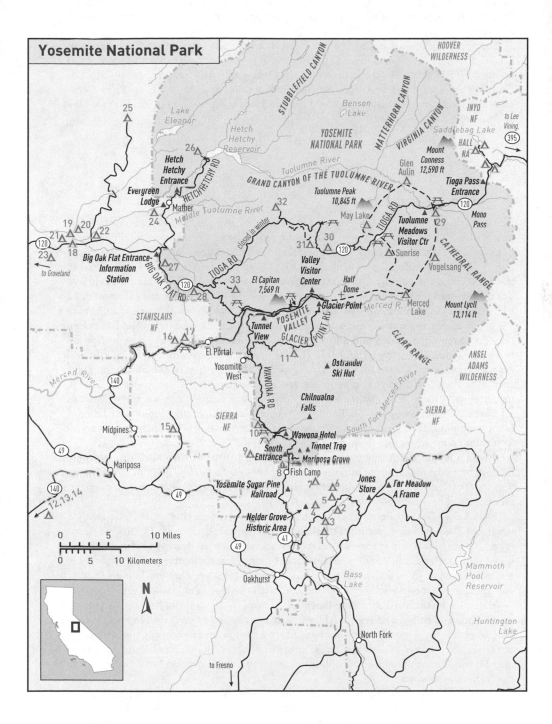

Yosemite National Park

STUBBLEFIELD CANYON

HOOVER WILDERNESS

Lake Eleanor

25

Benson Lake

MATTERHORN CANYON

INYO NF

to Lee Vining,

395

Saddlebag Lake

HALL NA

26

YOSEMITE NATIONAL PARK

VIRGINIA CANYON

Mount Conness 12,590 ft

Hetch Hetchy Entrance

HETCH HETCHY RD

Hetch Hetchy Reservoir

Glen Aulin

Tioga Pass Entrance

120

Evergreen Lodge

Tuolumne River

GRAND CANYON OF THE TUOLUMNE RIVER

Mather

24

Middle Tuolumne River

32

Tuolumne Peak 10,845 ft

May Lake

TIOGA RD

Mono Pass

Tuolumne Meadows Visitor Ctr

29

19 20

21

18

22

closed in winter

31

30

120

Sunrise

CATHEDRAL RANGE

120

23

Big Oak Flat Entrance-Information Station

BIG OAK FLAT RD

TIOGA RD

33

Valley Visitor Center

Vogelsang

to Groveland

27

120

28

El Capitan 7,569 ft

Half Dome

Glacier Point

Merced R.

Merced Lake

Mount Lyell 13,114 ft

STANISLAUS NF

16 17

Tunnel View

YOSEMITE VALLEY

GLACIER

POINT RD

CLARK RANGE

ANSEL ADAMS WILDERNESS

El Portal

11

Merced River

140

Yosemite West

WAWONA RD

Ostrander Ski Hut

SIERRA NF

Midpines

15

SIERRA NF

Chilnualna Falls

South Fork Merced River

49

Mariposa

140

SIERRA NF

10

Wawona Hotel

Tunnel Tree

9

South Entrance

Mariposa Grove

140

12,13,14

49

Yosemite Sugar Pine Railroad

8 Fish Camp

7

6

Jones Store

Far Meadow A Frame

5 4

2

Nelder Grove Historic Area

3

41

1

0   5   10 Miles

0   5   10 Kilometers

49

Oakhurst

Bass Lake

Mammoth Pool Reservoir

N

North Fork

Huntington Lake

to Fresno

bets for fresh produce and franchise-style value shopping are Oakhurst and Mariposa (or at the farmers' market in Groveland if you happen to be there on a Saturday morning in summer).

For sporting equipment before you head into the hills, stop off at **Herb Bauer** in Fresno (6264 N. Blackstone Ave.; 559-435-8600; www.herbbauersportinggoods.com) or the new **REI** (7810 N. Blackstone Ave.; 559-261-4168; www.rei.com). Exit CA 41 at Herndon Avenue, head west for less than half a mile, and go north on Blackstone. Last-minute items and basic equipment are available at a premium in Yosemite Valley and at Tuolumne Meadows.

✳ To See

THE WAWONA ROAD (CA 41)

The straightest shot from Los Angeles to Yosemite runs via Fresno and Oakhurst. If you're one of those who prefers to beat traffic out of the city, to throw the whole pile of gear from the last trip into the trunk and deal with provisions later, Oakhurst (population 18,000, elevation 2,300 feet) is your last best stop for cleaning out the mold in the cooler and restocking. Oakhurst is the sort of town J. M. Hutchings would have described—had it existed as such in the 1880s—as one "with all the usual accessories of business, amusement, and education." There are two bog-chain groceries, a bike shop, basic sporting-goods stores, banks, thrift shops, check-cashing outlets, Mexican and Japanese restaurants, and a range of franchise motels that serve as overflow on busy weekends when the park is full. (Be forewarned: There are nights in July and August when even Oakhurst is sold out down to the last flimsy cubicle at the Days Inn.) If there's credit on your plastic and you feel you deserve it, stop over for a meal, or better yet a night, a spa treatment, and an afternoon beside the pool at the **Chateau du Sureau**. Otherwise, press on. Between Oakhurst and the South Gate are 12 miles of fast pavement (fast except for on a Friday evening in summer). The deep woods begin around the first curve out of town.

There is lodging to be recommended near Fish Camp and at Wawona. From Wawona onward runs the oldest route into the valley—the way Jim Savage's bunch came in, the way most of Tenaya's people went out—and the oldest section of paved road in the park, since 1902.

Bass Lake (County Route 274). Hunter S. Thompson described it as "not really a town, but a resort area—a string of small settlements around a narrow, picture-postcard lake." It's about the same today, 40 years later, and worth a brief side trip if you're interested in motorized water sports, warm-water fishing, hydroelectric power generation, or the various ways in which the world has changed (and not changed) since Thompson spent a memorable holiday weekend here with the Hells Angels in 1965.

Yosemite Mountain Sugar Pine Railroad (56001 CA 41; 559-683-7273; www.ymsprr .com). Kids and full-grown train enthusiasts crowd aboard a converted logging train— "the logger"—for a good, old-fashioned, narrow-gauge chug through the woods (at contemporary prices). Snack bar, bookstore, gift shop, train museum. Runs daily from mid-March through October. Moonlight runs some Saturdays and Wednesdays. Limited schedule in winter.

✪ Mariposa Big Tree Grove (South Entrance). Part of the original 1864 grant, Mariposa is the most extensive of the three sequoia groves in Yosemite National Park and is home to the famed **Grizzly Giant**, subject of more than 150 years of painting and photography. There are several dozen other named trees as well, most christened in the

THOUGHTS ON YOSEMITE

It is but 16 years since the Yosemite was first seen by a white man, several visitors have since made a journey of several thousand miles at large cost to see it, and notwithstanding the difficulties which now interpose, hundreds resort to it annually . . . in a century the whole number of visitors will be counted by millions. An injury to the scenery so slight that it may be unheeded by any visitor now, will be one multiplied by these millions.
—Frederick Law Olmsted, 1865

When after a rest from the fatigues of the journey the tourist sets out from the hotel, armed with his instrument, to register, if may be, a few of those glorious scenes about him, that those at home might enjoy them, there comes a feeling of utter helplessness at the prospect before him. It is like going out to do battle with a toy pistol.
—Samuel Douglass Dodge, "A Day in Yosemite with a Kodak," *The New England Magazine*, 1890

After the initial excitement we may begin to sense the need to share the living realities of this miraculous place. We may resent the intrusion of urban superficialities. We may be filled with regret that so much has happened to despoil, but we can also respond to the challenge to re-create, to protect, to re-interpret the enduring essence of Yosemite, to reestablish it as a sanctuary from the turmoil of the time.
—Ansel Adams, 1960

1860s by the grove's original caretaker and guide, Galen Clark. "There are hundreds of such beauty and stateliness that intelligent travelers have declared that they would rather have passed by Niagara itself than have missed visiting this grove," Frederick Olmsted wrote in his 1865 report. The Yosemite Stage and Turnpike Company in 1881 carved what became known as the **Wawona Tunnel Tree** such that wagons and later automobiles could pass beneath and have their pictures taken. Photographs of this tree were featured in popular magazines and children's textbooks for three generations, even after the legendary snows of 1969 finally did it in—a millennium or two before its time. The **California Tunnel Tree** still stands, scooped out in 1895 for the same purpose, but never to make the big time. Somewhere here Teddy Roosevelt spent the night with John Muir in 1903, on the ground amid the "cinnamon-colored trunks." The **Mariposa Grove Museum** is open during the summer, well worth the modest climb, in a restored 1930s cabin in the upper grove on a site first built upon by Clark himself. Hiking opportunities abound, from short strolls to longer through-trips. In winter, the place can be explored in relative solitude on snowshoes or cross-country skis.

Pioneer Village and Yosemite History Center (Wawona; 209-375-6574). This collection of original structures—including a blacksmith shop, a Wells Fargo office, a jail, and the original Degnan's Bakery—was moved here at one time or another from locations elsewhere in the park. From July to Labor Day it is open as a "living" museum, staffed by costumed volunteers. The fastest tour of the place is by historic mud-wagon stage, with Burrel Maier, the only ranger/stage driver in the Park Service, at the reigns. Starts and ends at the covered bridge (the park's oldest, 1868–78).

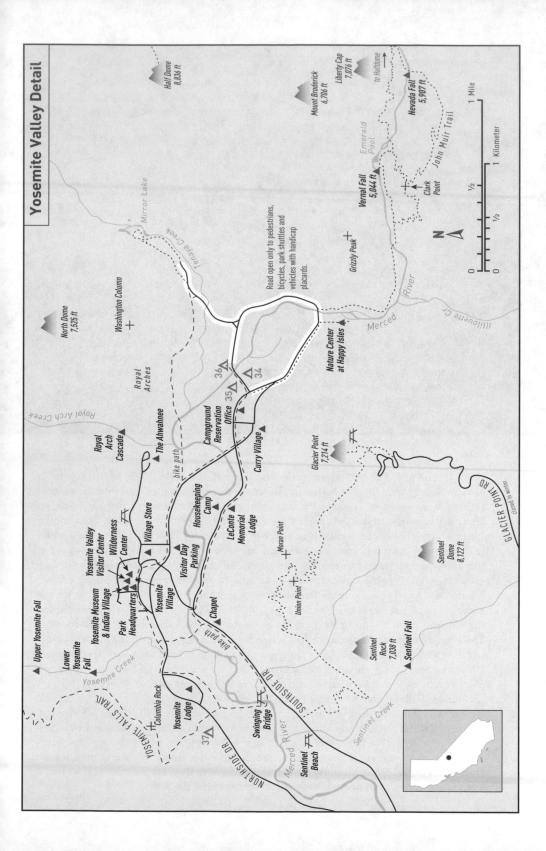

Yosemite Valley Detail

Half Dome
8,836 ft

Mount Broderick
6,706 ft

Liberty Cap
7,076 ft

to Halfdome

Nevada Fall
5,907 ft

Vernal Fall
5,044 ft

Clark Point

Emerald Pool

John Muir Trail

North Dome
7,525 ft

Mirror Lake

Tenaya Creek

Washington Column

Royal Arches

Royal Arch Creek

Royal Arch Cascade

The Ahwahnee

bike path

Campground Reservation Office

Curry Village

Village Store

Housekeeping Camp

LeConte Memorial Lodge

Wilderness Center

Yosemite Valley Visitor Center

Yosemite Museum & Indian Village

Park Headquarters

Visitor Day Parking

Yosemite Village

Chapel

Upper Yosemite Fall

Lower Yosemite Fall

Yosemite Creek

YOSEMITE FALLS TRAIL

Columbia Rock

Yosemite Lodge

NORTHSIDE DR

SOUTHSIDE DR

bike path

Swinging Bridge

Sentinel Beach

Merced River

Sentinel Creek

Sentinel Rock
7,038 ft

Sentinel Fall

Sentinel Dome
8,122 ft

GLACIER POINT RD
closed in winter

Glacier Point
7,214 ft

Moran Point

Union Point

Grizzly Peak

Merced River

Illilouette Cr.

Nature Center at Happy Isles

36

34

35

37

Road open only to pedestrians, bicycles, park shuttles and vehicles with handicap placards.

N

0   ½   1 Mile

0   ½   1 Kilometer

⭐ OTHER BOOKS TO SUPPLEMENT THIS CHAPTER

Geology of the Sierra Nevada, by Mary Hill (UC Press, 2006).

The Laws Field Guide to the Sierra Nevada, by John Muir Laws (Heyday Books, California Academy of Sciences, 2007).

The Complete Guidebook to Yosemite National Park, by Stephen D. Medley (Yosemite Conservancy, 2012).

The Yosemite, by John Muir (The Century Company, 1912).

Yosemite: Art of an American Icon, by Amy Scott (UC Press, 2006).

Sierra Nevada Natural History, by Tracy Storer, Robert Usinger, and David Lukas (UC Press, 2004).

Yosemite and Mammoth Lakes Camping and Hiking, by Tom Stienstra and Ann Marie Brown (Moon Outdoors, 2012).

The Road Guide to Yosemite, by Bob Raney (Yosemite Conservancy, 1989).

Glacier Point (terminus of Glacier Point Road). The first decent road from Chinquapin to Glacier Point was built in 1882 by Clarence Washburn, by then owner of Clark's Hotel at Wawona. Previously, the viewpoint was most commonly accessed by the so-called Four Mile Trail coming up from the valley (a mule trail improved in 1929 by legendary trail engineer John Conway). "Here we are on the edge of an abyss 3,257 feet deep," Hutchings wrote in 1886, "and although the great sweep of the northern rim of the Valley is before us, with its multitudinous crags and rents, the Half Dome, as omnipresent as ever, overshadows and eclipses every lesser object." For years—from the 1870s all the way to 1968—there was terrific entertainment to be had for those on the point, and also for some of those thousands of feet below, in the dropping of objects to the valley floor: stones, empty boxes, chickens, campfires, and so on. Such activity is no longer legal. The road is closed from The Yosemite Ski and Snowboard Area (aka Badger Pass) in winter but groomed for cross-country skiing. Gift shop and snack bar in summer. The once-famous Overhanging Rock, where automobiles and costumed Indians and ballerinas once posed for scary photographs, now hangs in relative obscurity, strictly off-limits, beyond the railing to the west.

EL PORTAL ROAD (CA 140)

While the other routes afford famous, last-minute, jaw-dropping panoramas of Half Dome and Bridalveil, the El Portal

MOTOR STAGE AT WAWONA TUNNEL TREE, 1927. THE TREE FELL IN 1969 COURTESY NPS, YNP

DITCH THE CAR, LEAVE THE DRIVING TO THE PROS

Mammoth Resorts CFO Mark Clausen once told me that every year he and his wife walk out their front door in Old Mammoth all the way to Yosemite Valley. It takes five days to cover the 70 or 80 miles. They bring a credit card, ship their dinner clothes, spend a night at the fancy hotel formerly known as the Ahwahnee, then catch the YARTS bus back to Mammoth. "If we ever sell our house," he added, "we can say it's walking distance to the Ahwahnee." Yosemite Area Regional Transportation System (YARTS) (1-877-98-YARTS; www .yarts.com) runs a bus once daily during peak summer season from the Mammoth Mountain Inn to the Yosemite Valley Visitors Center and back ($36 round-trip, includes park entrance fee), with scheduled stops in June Lake, Lee Vining, and Tuolumne Meadows. Weekends only in June and September, conditions permitting. YARTS also serves CA 140 from various points in Merced (including Amtrak and the Merced Airport), through Mariposa, Midpines, and El Portal to destinations in the Yosemite Valley. Check website for seasonal closures, routes, schedules, and fares.

Inside the park, Yosemite is one of a few places in the American West, between Chicago and San Francisco, where you don't need a car to get around. Yosemite Shuttle (209-372-0200; www.nps.gov/yose/planyourvisit/bus.htm) runs free hybrid buses every 10 to 20 minutes from 7 AM to 10 PM year-round, covering all major valley and village stops from Camp 4 to the day-use parking lot, Happy Isles, and Mirror Lake Junction. Another route, with buses running every half-hour (only in summer), serves the west valley, El Cap, and the Four Mile Trail. There are fee-based tours from Yosemite Valley to Tuolumne Meadows or Glacier Point in summer only. When the grove is open, a free shuttle has traditionally been available between Wawona and the Mariposa Grove (with shuttle riders guaranteed access to the grove even when the parking lot is full). In winter (December through March) there's a daily free shuttle from valley hotels to the old Badger Pass Ski Area (now called Yosemite Ski and Snowboard Area). Note: Park shuttles are popular and eminently useful tools for hikers interested in point-to-point rather than out-and-back treks, and are a much better option than driving around and trying to find parking.

Road, the least traveled overall but the main artery for commuting park employees and public transportation, starts the drama earlier in the journey. From Merced it climbs into the foothills normally enough, speedily enough, to the timeworn gold rush town of **Mariposa** (2,252 feet)—last stop for half-reasonable gas, Chinese food, bacon ranch burgers, truck tacos, not-so-cheap motels, antiques shopping, craft beers, and a fabled back-alley hole-in-the wall saloon. **Midpines** is a barely discernible collection of cabins and homesteads tucked away in the woods and locus of the venerable Yosemite Bug (see "Lodging"), after which the road drops fast and hard to Briceburg, deep in the lower canyon of the Merced. From 1907 to 1945, the Yosemite Valley Railroad bore passengers along the river from Merced to El Portal. The old railroad bed is visible along much of the route through the canyon, and in places it provides excellent minimal-grade mountain biking opportunities. CA 140 was once called the all-weather road into Yosemite, due to its low-elevation approach, but it is frequently subjected to damage from seasonal flooding and debris slides. In the big flood of 1997, the road was completely washed out in several places. In the spring of 2006 a section of the road 6 miles below El Portal was buried beneath a 300-ton rockslide. The road was closed for nearly four months, then reopened via a one-lane detour across the river and along the old railroad grade. The detour is still and indefinitely in place. Expect one minor but scenic stop-light delay: The rockslide is visible on the opposite bank. **El Portal**, once the transfer point from rail to stage, is populated almost entirely by Park Service or Aramark employees. Entrance to the park is through the so-called Arch Rock.

✪ **California State Mining and Mineral Museum** (CA 49 South, at Mariposa County Fairgrounds, Mariposa; 209-742-7625; camineralmuseum.org). More than thirteen thousand objects related to the history and geology of California's gold rush, including the famous 13.8-pound Fricot nugget, found in the American River in 1864. Site of a spectacular Hollywood-style heist in 2012, in which a band of robbers dressed as ninjas with pick-axes made off with $1.3 million in gold and gems in broad daylight. Five men were eventually arrested and put in jail. Few of the specimens were recovered. Hands-on displays, tours, kids' activities, mine tunnel. Books and gifts at the museum shop. Open Thursday through Sunday.

Mariposa Museum & History Center (5119 Jessie St., Mariposa; 209-966-2924; www.mariposamuseum.com). Sprawling collection of gold rush artifacts, displays and implements, including an authentic five-stamp mill. Bookstore and gift shop. Picnic area. Open daily year-round. Adults $5, kids free.

Mariposa County Courthouse (5088 Bullion St., Mariposa; 209-966-7081). Oldest working superior courthouse west of the Mississippi, built in 1854. Open during business hours. Tours given Saturday and Sunday, May through October. Call for details.

Site of Savage's Trading Post (West of El Portal). Historical marker on the site where James D. Savage had his first run-ins with Yosemite Indians in 1849.

BIG OAK FLAT ROAD (CA 120)

The earliest version of this road was punched through to the valley in 1874. Today it remains the most popular way in from the Bay Area, Sacramento, and points north—and generally it's the fastest, though it can be slow going on Friday afternoon of a busy holiday weekend, and impassable during a big snowstorm. The topography kicks in in earnest on the east side of the Moccasin Reservoir, after the junction with CA

BIG OAK FLAT ROAD AND BRIDALVEIL FALL, 1903 J. T. BOYSEN, COURTESY NPS, YNP

49. The main road, along with all heavy trucks, toy haulers, and recreational vehicles, follows the sinuous "New" Priest's Grade (completed in 1915) from an elevation of 910 feet to 2,450 about 8 miles later at the once-abandoned Priest's Station Hotel, recently re-acquired by fifth and sixth generation descendants of the original Priest Family pioneers, and opened as the **Priest Station Café and Store** (16756 Old Priest Grade; 209-962-1888; www.prieststation.com). The older grade, once called Moccasin Hill, or Rattlesnake Hill, climbs the same 1,540 feet in 2 miles. In earlier days travelers were obliged to walk while frothing beasts pulled empty stages. There is a spring midway up the hill where all—including fellow travelers, animals, Miwok families, ruthless highwaymen, and the like—could pause for shade and water. "It is no longer necessary to stop at the spring," wrote one local historian in 1955, who even then preferred the old grade to the new. "Any well-driven modern car in good condition can, in the cool of the day, go straight up." Not far from Priest's stood the large tree that gave the flat, and subsequently the road, its name. By the time the venerable old oak burned the first time, in 1863, it had already been undermined by gold-seekers carting dirt from its base. Its charred top fell off in 1869, and what was left burned a second time in 1900. Groveland is the newer, more genteel moniker for the old mining settlement once called Garrote, after the hanging from another oak of a Mexican fellow who may or may not have put his hands on $200 worth of someone else's gold. Groveland today is among the most charming of Mother Lode villages, and it's the last supply stop before Yosemite or Hetch Hetchy, boasting a brief main street, a pair of historic inns, an excellent restaurant, a nursery/coffeehouse/gallery/general store, gas, and groceries. Most of the forests here have been cut over at least once in the past century and a half. Note the difference in size of timber outside the park versus inside. Hetch Hetchy Road is open beyond Camp Mather from 8 AM to 7 PM only, gated at night. At Crane Flat, just below the Tuolumne Grove, the two loose ends of CA 120, east and west, come together for the final three-tunnel descent into the Yosemite Valley, affording along the way the same brief view over the Merced that Hutchings once described as "one of the most magnificent and comprehensive scenes to be found anywhere."

O'Shaughnessy Dam (Hetch Hetchy). The curved gravity dam that is said to have broken John Muir's heart. See it now. One day it may only exist in pictures.

Tuolumne Grove of Big Trees (north of Crane Flat). Historians generally agree that these must have been the trees—"of the Red-wood species, incredibly large"—of which Joseph Walker and his men took passing note on their way across the Sierra in the winter of 1833. "My first impressions of the Big Trees were somewhat disappointing," Joseph LeConte wrote nearly 50 years later, "but . . . a sense of their immensity grew upon me." Give them a chance. Linger. They are giants. This grove is smaller in terms of numbers of monarchs, but also much quieter and less frequented than the more famous Mariposa Grove on the south end of the park. Downhill hike in, uphill on the way out. Bring water.

TIOGA ROAD AND TUOLUMNE MEADOWS (CA 120)

> *It is a good deal like a roller coaster, only rougher! But if your car's in good shape and you are confident of your driving skill; if you are looking for an adventurous route and breathtaking scenery, there's no better place to find them than along the Tioga Pass Road.*
> —*Travel News Bulletin*, May 1947

The beginnings of a road had, by the late 1870s, been hammered and blasted up the east side of the range from Mono Lake. In 1881, by the impetus of the Great Sierra

TIOGA ROAD AND TENAYA LAKE, 1935 RALPH ANDERSON, COURTESY NPS, YNP

Consolidated Silver Company, surveying began for the construction of a wagon road from Crane Flat to the mines at Tioga. "Priest's powder gang, following the picks and shovels, reached Lake Tenaya Thursday," wrote the *Homer Mining Index* on August 11, 1883, "and will skip the heavy blasting along the margin of the lake for the present and follow up to the Tuolumne River, after which 100 blasters will be put on to finish the three fourths of a mile along the lake. It is believed that freight wagons will reach Tioga by or before the end of the month." Meanwhile, towns with official post offices had been thrown up at Dana City and Bennetville, and a tunnel had been punched nearly 2,000 feet into Tioga Hill. By 1884, the whole endeavor was a bust—with not an ounce of color to show. But the road—the great Sierra Wagon Road—was established. The east side sections of Tioga Pass were upgraded from 1899 to 1907. In 1915, the U.S. government purchased the roadway for $10. That summer 190 automobiles entered the park from the east side. By 1940, all but 21 miles had been widened, realigned, and paved. By June 24, 1961, the final 21 miles, including another round of dynamiting along the granite shore of Lake Tenaya (much to the chagrin of the Sierra Club), was complete. "NPS people should have been jailed for what they destroyed at Tenaya Lake," wrote David Brower years later. Sections of the original wagon road can still be driven on: from White Wolf to Yosemite Creek campground, and up the short spur along Snow Creek to the May Lake trailhead.

Tioga is said to be a Mohawk word, generally applied to a fork in a river, brought here from the East during the brief mining boom. Tuolumne (pronounced *too-all-lumee*) is considered the largest subalpine meadow in the Sierra. The word is said to be a gentle corruption of a local Miwok word *taa-walïmni*, or "place of the squirrels"—which it most certainly is. Basic supplies are available here. For gas, continue to Crane Flat or Lee Vining. After the first major snowfall of the season (October or November), the road is closed except for travel by cross-country skis or snowshoes. The springtime opening of the road is a much-anticipated event, impossible to predict. Lore has it that the Park Service does its best to get the road cleared by Memorial Day so that its award-winning pack team can make Mule Days in Bishop without having to go the long way around.

Tioga Pass Entrance Station (9,945 feet). The highest pass on the California state highway system. The station, constructed of peeled logs and granite boulders, was built in 1931.

✪ **Parsons Memorial Lodge** (20- to 30-minute stroll from Lembert Dome parking lot or Tuolumne Visitor Center, at the northern edge of Tuolumne Meadows; 209-372-4542). An Angora goatherd by the name of "Hermit John" Lembert homesteaded property here, next to the soda springs, beginning sometime in the early 1880s. Then he lost his goats in a snowstorm in 1890 and decided to make his way down to lower elevations, where in 1896, near El Portal, he was murdered. The property was bought and sold a couple of times, picked up by the Sierra Club in 1912, and finally sold to the National Park Service in 1973, as a management headache, for $208,750 dollars. The lodge, a small fortress of local rubble stone and peeled logs, was built by the Sierra Club in 1915—possibly designed by Berkeley architect Bernard Maybeck. Interpretive services, lectures, readings, slide presentations, and a fall poetry festival organized by the Yosemite Conservancy. Closed fall to spring.

Soda Springs (Tuolumne Meadows, next to Parsons Lodge). Cold, carbonated water bubbles up from the rusty mud within an old log enclosure. It's not quite Pellegrino, but it's pleasing, or at least interesting, for a sip or two—especially when you've been hiking all day and all you have left in your water bottle is sun-warmed dregs.

✪ **Lake Tenaya** (CA 120). Chief Tenaya was captured here on May 22, 1851. Lafayette Bunnell, feeling sorry for the old man, applied his name to the lake. Tenaya explained that the place already had a perfectly good name: Py-we-ack, or "Lake of the Shining Rocks." An Irishman by the name of John Murphy is said to have planted 52 brook trout from the lower Tuolumne River here in August 1878. Four seasons later, an east-side mining newspaper would claim: "The lake is swarming with fish, some already 2 feet in length." Today there's a lovely swimming beach, picnic tables, and a trailhead for the shortest hike to the summit of Cloud's Rest (13 miles round-trip).

✪ **Olmsted Point** (CA 120). One of the most popular turnouts in the park, named after the renowned landscape architect and first chairman of the board of commissioners for the Yosemite Grant, back in 1864. Interpretive signage and iconic views down Tenaya Canyon all the way to Half Dome. If you're not planning to stop here, beware sudden braking and wild, signal-free swerves by other drivers.

YOSEMITE VALLEY

> *At another turning of the road we look into the profound and haze-draped depths, and up toward the sublime and storm-defying heights, with feelings all our own, and behold Yo Semite [sic].*
> —J. M. Hutchings, *In the Heart of the Sierras*, 1886

All roads ultimately enter the valley from the west, from downriver, merging into a fine two-lane parkway along the south bank of the Merced, at the parking area for **Bridalveil Fall** (reached by way of a pleasant, if busy, stroll along a trail and series of rustic bridges built by cavalry troops around the turn of the twentieth century). "When carriages are introduced," Olmsted wrote in his 1865 report, "it is proposed that they shall be driven for the most part up one side and down the other of the valley, suitable resting places and turnouts for passing being provided at frequent intervals. From this trail a few paths would also need to be formed, leading to points of view which would only be accessible to persons on foot. Several small bridges would also be required." And so it is today, for the most part.

From Bridalveil, views of **El Capitan** opening on our left, we wind around past the turnoff for **Sentinel Beach**, past the trailhead of the historic **Four Mile Trail** to Glacier Point, past the popular swimming hole at the now quite-sturdy **Swinging Bridge** (glimpses of **Yosemite Falls**, in season), and past the New England–style **Yosemite Chapel** (209-372-4831). The chapel, still in service today, was built in 1879, moved to its current location in 1901, and is now all that remains of the original Yosemite Village (the rest of which was dismantled and/or moved to Pioneer Village at Wawona between the mid-1920s and 1980). **Sentinel Bridge**—shortcut to the new **Yosemite Village** (and day-use parking), the **Majestic Yosemite (aka Ahwahnee) Hotel**, and the **Yosemite Valley Lodge**—was the first bridge built by the National Park Service, in 1919. Many of the other bridges throughout the valley—Pohono, Ahwahnee, Happy Isles, Stoneman— were built in the 1920s and '30s.

Continuing west along Southside Drive, we pass **Housekeeping Camp** on our left and the handsome **Yosemite Conservation Heritage Center (formerly LeConte Memorial Lodge)** on our right before we arrive at the intersection with Northside Drive at **Stoneman Bridge**. From here, a right-hand turn takes us to the bustling hub that is **Half Dome (aka Curry) Village** (dining, budget lodging, recreation center, equipment rental, pool, day-use and trailhead parking for **Happy Isles**, the **Mist Trail**, **Panorama Trail**, **Half Dome**, and **Mirror Lake**). Going straight over the intersection takes us past the campground reservation office to the **Upper, Lower,** and **North Pines** campgrounds (parking available only for those with campsite reservations).

Crossing over the Merced River via Stoneman Bridge (popular put-in point for the leisurely float trip down valley), we angle back westbound on Northside Drive to the

THE AHWAHNEE BRIDGE, ACCESSIBLE ONLY ON FOOT OR BICYCLE, IS ONE OF EIGHT GRANITE-FACED CONCRETE ARCH BRIDGES BUILT BETWEEN 1921 AND 1933

main day-use parking lot at Yosemite Village (visitor center, museum, gallery, food, shopping, activities, auto repair, post office, medical clinic—no lodging). A side road to the right, past the **Village Store**, leads to the Majestic Yosemite (aka Ahwahnee) Hotel (lodging and dining, limited parking available). Continuing along Northside Drive, we reach, across from **Yosemite Falls**, the Yosemite Valley Lodge complex (lodging, dining, shopping, activities, and equipment rental), beyond which the parkway leads us back past El Capitan to all park exits, or to **Pohono Bridge** for another loop.

The best bet is to drive straight to the day-use parking lot, to leave your vehicle for the duration of your visit, and to strike out from there by alternative means. From Swinging Bridge to Happy Isles to the mouth of Tenaya Canyon, along the base of the Royal Arches to the village and beyond to Yosemite Falls, the valley is well served by 12 miles of easy-cruising, paved bicycle path—and an extensive network of walking trails, some of which are thousands of years old. The Yosemite Valley Shuttle runs a regular circuit, every 15 to 30 minutes, to all main points along the parkway.

✪ **Yosemite Conservation Heritage Center (formerly LeConte Memorial Lodge)** (Southside Drive; 209-372-4542; www.sierraclub.org/yosemite-heritage-center). Built of local granite and timber in 1903–4 by the Sierra Club as Yosemite's first public visitor center, LeConte was named for scientist, author, early Sierra advocate, and friend of John Muir, Joseph "Little Joe" LeConte (1823–1901). A teenaged Ansel Adams was a custodian here in 1919. Features include interesting pop-up presentations and displays about conservation history in the Sierra, as well as a comprehensive library, relief maps, and a children's play area. Open daily from May to September.

Mirror Lake. A seasonal lake at the mouth of Tenaya Canyon, Mirror Lake was given its name by Lafayette Bunnell in 1851, although he claimed to have been open to suggestions. One scholar in the 1950s found an old stereoview on which the lake was dubbed "the toilet glass of Yosemite." "The water is remarkably clear and placid," wrote John S. Hittell in one of the earliest Yosemite guidebooks (1868), "and the reflection of the Washington Column and of the South Half Dome on its surface is so nearly perfect that photographic views of them are frequently mistaken for upright views taken directly from the objects themselves." Carleton Watkins made the first famous photograph of Mirror Lake circa 1861. In it, one particularly tall conifer stands prominent against the sky between Mount Watkins and Cloud's Rest, and in the near-perfect reflection on the lake's surface. Over the years, similar views have been made in a variety of visual media by such luminaries as Albert Bierstadt, Charles Weed, Eadweard Muybridge ("the father of cinema"), George Fiske, and Ansel Adams, as well as by who knows how many millions of other Vibram-soled nature paparazzi. In all but the fantastical painting by Bierstadt, there is that same tree, ever taller and more ragged as time wears on. Some things have changed. In 1864, the total number of visitors to Yosemite National Park was 147. Nearly a century and a half later, the number has climbed to 4 million. The lake is now a grassy meadow for most of the summer and fall seasons, thanks to the quantity of sediment delivered annually by Tenaya Creek, and will soon disappear entirely. It was dredged for the last time in 1971. The place is now accessible only on foot. Bikes must be left at the bottom of the grade. A stone jetty, of sorts, has been built on the west shore of the meadow to accommodate tripods. The tree, reports park archivist Linda Eade, is "probably a ponderosa pine."

✪ **Majestic Yosemite (aka Ahwahnee) Hotel** (end of Ahwahnee Road). See the rustic porte cochère (a successful afterthought), the rubber-tile mosaics, the walk-in Rumford fireplaces, the concrete rafters formed to look like wood, the original kilims and tapestries, the Howard mural in the Writing Room, and the classic old photos in the Winter Sports Room in the opposite transept. Curl up in front of the fire and spend an afternoon in the heart of the Sierra with a good novel (or a rousing guidebook). Open

MIRROR LAKE AND MOUNT WATKINS, AS SEEN IN 150 YEARS OF PHOTOGRAPHS

to the public year-round. Wi-Fi only available to hotel guests. Free tours. See concierge or call 209-372-1426 for schedule.

Yosemite Museum and Indian Village (next to Yosemite Village Visitor Center; 209-372-0282). Features displays on Miwok and Paiute history and culture, baskets, beadwork, and a reconstruction of a traditional Indian village. Temporary and seasonal exhibits are generally excellent. Gift shop and art gallery. Cemetery guide available. Open daily.

Yosemite Cemetery (across the road from the Yosemite Museum). Galen Clark's body resides here "in the Sequoia-shaded grave which, after the tranquil fashion of those biblical patriarchs whom in simplicity of spirit he resembled, he had prepared himself years ago" (J. Smeaton Chase, 1911). J. M. Hutchings is here too, and the photographer George Fiske, as well as "A Boy," a "Frenchman," and a handful of Piute and Yosemite Indians. Open year-round.

Hutchings Orchard (between Yosemite Falls and the shuttle stop). Good place to see deer grazing among the ancient, long-untended apple trees that once upon a time provided good hard cider for weary travelers.

✳ To Do

There are few places in the world with such a high concentration of resources for outdoor recreation—150-plus years of local dedication to the subject—combined with such superlative terrain. If what you're looking for involves one or more of the following ingredients—rock, air, sunlight, fresh water, snow, ice, dirt, and/or gravity—you've come to the right place. Here is an overview of the possibilities.

ART AND PHOTOGRAPHY When people ask Howard Weamer, photographer and longtime caretaker of the Ostrander Ski Hut, how he got his famous 1989 shot, "Storm Light, Half Dome"—expecting, perhaps, to hear about aperture and shutter speed and the length of his lens—what he says is something to the effect of "Well, I guess I was in the right place at the right time." The ongoing effort to get a moment like that on film, or on canvas, is one of Yosemite's oldest and most enduring pastimes. And what better excuse to be out in the thick of it when the light is at its best?

Yosemite Art Center (Yosemite Village, next to Village Store; 209-372-4207; www .yosemiteconservancy.org/yosemite-art-center). Art supplies, paints, books, classes, and workshops. Open spring to fall and during holidays. For the latest schedule, check the current issue of *Yosemite Today*, available at all entrance kiosks and visitor centers, or check the website.

Ansel Adams Gallery (Yosemite Village; 650-692-3285; www.anseladams.com). Digital and traditional photography workshops. See website for schedule.

BICYCLE CRUISING The best way to really appreciate the valley is by cruising along the 12 miles of mostly deadflat bike path from Swinging Bridge to within a half-mile of Mirror Lake. Features include scenic bridges, beaches, meadows, boardwalks, forgotten carriage roads, and major trailheads. Old beat-up cruisers, child trailers, strollers, and wheelchairs for hire by the hour, weather permitting, at the **Yosemite Valley Lodge Bike Stand** (209-372-1208) and the **Half Dome (aka Curry) Village Recreation Center** (209-372-8319). Call ahead for reservations during the busy season, or bring your own.

BOATING AND FLOATING Perhaps the grandest, most carefree way to take in the Yosemite Valley is Tom Sawyer–style, from the half-deflated pontoon of an undersized inflatable raft. The Merced River is generally open for floating upon, from Stoneman Bridge to Sentinel Beach, from late May to sometime in July, depending on water levels. Bring your own non-motorized flotation equipment—raft, inner tube, kayak—or hire a four-to six-person craft from the **Half Dome (aka Curry) Village Recreation Center** (209-372-8319). Fees include paddles, life jackets, and return shuttle. Children must weigh more than 50 pounds. For more active adventure, consider a white-water trip below the park on the lower Merced (April through July) or the lower Tuolumne (April through September). Class IV. Not recommended for small children.

✪ **Sierra Mac River Trips** (Groveland; 1-800-457-2580; www.sierramac.com). Marty McDonnell, aka "Sierra Mac," is the guy who pioneered most of California's big white-water back in the '60s and '70s, including the spectacular Class V Cherry Creek-Upper Tuolumne run, now one of the most popular white-water trips in the American West. When the Forest Service finally agreed to open up the renowned Middle Fork of California's Feather River to commercial rafting, the only guy they trusted was Sierra Mac. As an outfitter, his specialty remains the Tuolumne, which is hands-down the best water in the Yosemite region. And it's not just about the thrills. When the late *New York Times* food critic Craig Claiborne found himself running a river with Sierra Mac back in 1986, he described the first evening's meal as follows: "[It] began with a mandala of seasonal vegetables with a tarragon dipping sauce and assorted domestic cheeses, followed by sausages flavored with aged tequila and a variety of mustards, deep-fried quail eggs with chili croutons, a filet mignon grilled over mesquite and served with a roast garlic butter, wild rice blended with chanterelle mushrooms and sun-dried tomatoes, buttered spinach, a string bean salad with hazelnuts and cream and, for dessert, fresh figs with raspberries." On a river trip? Luckily for us, attention to the finer details of time spent ashore continue to be as important to Sierra Mac as the safe passage of his guides and guests through the frothy runoff. Novice to expert rafting available. One-, two-, and three-day trips, plus a combination of Cherry Creek and the Main Tuolumne for an extended four-day, Class V epic.

American River Touring Association (ARTA) (24000 Casa Loma Rd., Groveland; 209-962-7873 or 1-800-323-2782; www.arta.org). This locally based nonprofit organization offers one- to three-day guided trips on the Tuolumne and Merced. Newcomer specials.

Zephyr Whitewater Expeditions (P.O. Box 510, Columbia 95310; 209-532-5249 or 1-800431-3636; www.zrafting.com). Half-, full-, and multi-day guided trips on the Merced and the Tuolumne. The Yosemite Whitewater Special includes one day on the Merced and two or three on the Tuolumne.

O.A.R.S. (P.O. Box 67, Angels Camp 95222; 209-736-4677 or 1-800-346-6277; www.oars.com). Variety of trips on the Tuolumne and Merced. Multisport tours include mountain biking, rock climbing, and white-water rafting.

FISHING Hutchings quotes an old adage: "It takes an Indian to catch a trout at Yo Semite." The fact is, before the mid- to late-1800s, there were no fish of any kind in the Yosemite High Sierra. The glaciers of the Little Ice Age killed them off, and after their retreat, the waterfalls made a rather impenetrable barrier. Then the miners and ranchers and Basque sheepherders began to stock high country lakes and streams in order to have a ready food supply in summer. Later on, the National Park Service picked up where they'd left off. It wasn't until the late 1970s that Park Service officials began to realize that non-native trout species (especially the hardy European browns) were having an adverse effect on native species (especially the yellow-legged frog). Since 1991 there has been no stocking of fish in the park. Nevertheless, the wily bastards still rise

TO THE TOP OF HALF DOME—AND BACK

To make the top of the valley's most prominent feature (8,836 feet) is for many park visitors a kind of rite of passage. (As many as 1,000 per day were making the trek on summer weekends in the years before the Park Service, in the summer of 2010, instituted an experimental quota system.) The thing does fairly scream to be stood on top of. A Scottish pioneer by the name of George Anderson, whose attractive floorless log cabin is nowadays on display at Wawona, took it upon himself in October 1875 to hand-drill a series of eyebolts and thus string 400 feet of rope up the near-sheer granite backside of Half Dome. John Muir, in the wake of that season's first snow, was among the first to use the ropes to make the summit. The next year Anderson was charging tourists for the privilege and dreaming of making a fortune with a staircase. In 1877 he took Hutchings up, and a photographer, and had his picture taken on the same overhanging ledge where today people wait in line to achieve similar immortality—striking fearless poses nearly 5,000 feet of gauzy air above the valley floor. By 1884 the ropes, and many of the bolts, had been destroyed by snow and ice—and Anderson had died alone, and broke, in his cabin. A system of fixed cables was installed in 1919, the essence of which is still in use today (with some improvement by the Civilian Conservation Corps in the 1930s). The Park Service takes the cables down every winter and puts them back up every spring. The most popular route—15 to 17 miles round-trip, at least 4,836 feet of elevation gain, a long day's trek not to be undertaken lightly or without adequate supplies—begins at Happy Isles and climbs to the Little Yosemite Valley by way of either the John Muir or the Mist Trail.

The cables take a bit of getting used to. They are eminently trustworthy—as long as you hang onto them. There is a pile of old gloves at the bottom, worth borrowing from, especially for the descent.

Look for a break in the crowd, keep your head, keep moving, and trust your feet. Don't try it if the rock is wet, or the cables aren't there, or if there's the vaguest possibility of lightning.

MISMATCHED GLOVES ARE PROVIDED TO PROTECT HALF DOME CLIMBERS FROM CABLE BURNS

Ten to twelve people die every year in Yosemite, mostly by drowning. From 1919 to 2007, not a single person had actually met his maker in an attempt at the cables on Half Dome. Then, on a typically spectacular June afternoon, with a standard 45-minute wait at the bottom, hundreds of people on the rock—everybody climbing over and under and around each other, some working their way up, some down, some just taking a moment, gripping both cables with crusty mismatched gardening gloves, working to retrieve wits, to trust feet, to remember why there was this notion to stand on top of Half Dome in the first place—with no ado whatsoever, without so much as a scream, a 37-year-old Japanese citizen by the name of Hirofumi Nohara slipped, lost his grip, and fell. One minute he was laughing and talking, the next he was silent, outside the cables and on his way down—fast. It was other people who did the screaming. "The last I saw him," said the guy who'd been right behind him on the way up, "he was backwards in a somersault going over the ledge."

Is the Park Service planning to retire the cables on Half Dome? Not anytime soon, says Scott Gediman, public relations ranger for Yosemite. "We wouldn't build them today," he says, "but now they're historic."

GEORGE ANDERSON ATOP HALF DOME, 1877 S. C. WALKER

Permits are required seven days per week when the cables are up for anyone planning to head above the sub-dome during cable season—weekends and weekdays alike. No more than 300 permits are issued for each day. Permits are distributed by lottery through the **National Recreation Reservation Service** (1-877-444-6777; www.recreation.gov), with one pre-season lottery with an application period in March, and daily lotteries for approximately fifty permits per day during the hiking season. Backpackers—including those who want to spend the night in Little Yosemite Valley—should apply for Half Dome permits with their wilderness permit. For more information and latest conditions, check www.nps.gov/yose/planyourvisit/hdpermits.htm.

Consider doing it on a weekday—Monday through Thursday, that is—when there's room to maneuver and permits are easier to secure. Or do it at night, with a couple of friends by the light of the full moon. Bring a headlamp. Make yourselves a cup of tea on the top, watch the sun rise over the Clark Range, and be off the mountain in time for a midday beer and lamb shank at the Majestic Yosemite (aka Ahwahnee).

For more information, check www.nps.gov/yose/planyourvisit/halfdome.htm.

to the hatch in streams and lakes from Hetch Hetchy to Chilhualna Creek to Tuolumne Meadows to the South Fork of the Merced.

One interpretive park ranger came padding, much like an Indian, into the Merced Lake High Sierra Camp one recent late-summer afternoon with a fly rod and at least six small trout in his creel for the evening fire. "Save the frogs," he said. "Catch as many as you can." For bigger fish, try for the native rainbows in the lower reaches of the Merced and the Tuolumne, below the park. Guide services and trips throughout the greater region available through the recreation desk at the **Evergreen Lodge** (33160 Evergreen Rd., off CA 120; 209-379-2606; www.evergreenlodge.com), **Rush Creek Lodge** (34001 CA 120; 209-379-2373; www.rushcreeklodge.com), and through **Southern Yosemite Mountain Guides** (North Fork; 1-800-231-4575; www.symg.com).

Note: A valid California fishing license is required for residents and nonresidents 16 years of age or older on all public and private land outside and inside national park boundaries. Licenses can be purchased online at https://www.ca.wildlifelicense.com/InternetSales or through any authorized license agent (including most sporting good outlets and local general stores). Always check with a park ranger, outfitter, or visitor center staff for area- and species-specific quota and catch-and-release regulations.

GEOCACHING Geocaching is not permitted within park boundaries, except during occasional special events, such as Earth Day cleanups. For newcomers to this increasingly popular means of making one's way, half-blindly, across the landscape, starter kits and GPS rentals are available at **Tenaya Lodge** (1122 CA 41, Fish Camp; 1-888-514-2167; www.tenayalodge.com) and at the **Evergreen Lodge** (33160 Evergreen Rd., off CA 120; 209-379-2606; www.evergreenlodge.com).

GOLF **Big Trees (aka Wawona) Golf Course** (CA 41, Wawona; 209-375-6572). An Audubon Cooperative Sanctuary, Wawona was built in 1918 as the first regulation course in the Sierra Nevada. Nine-hole, par 35, with alternate tee options for 18-hole, par 70 format. Pro shop, cart and club rentals, lessons.

Pine Mountain Lake Golf Club (12765 Mueller Dr., off CA 120, Groveland; 209-9628620; www.pinemountainlake.com). Eighteen holes, par 70, in the oaks and new-growth pines. Designed by Billy Bell in 1969. The public can reserve tee times up to 10 days in advance. Dress code.

GUIDED TOURS ✪ **YExplore** (209-532-7014;www.yexplore.com). Offering a wide range of guided hikes, family tours, Half Dome summit adventures, photography workshops, multi-day backpacking trips, and other custom tours. Year-round.

Yosemite Guided Bus & Tram Tours (888-413-8869; www.travelyosemite.com). A variety of bus and open-air tram tours is offered from spring through fall. The information comes to you by way of an amplifier, and someone else does the driving. Valley Floor, Glacier Point, Tuolumne Meadows (with hiker-shuttle option), a combination Grand Tour, wintertime tours, and a round or two on full-moon evenings, weather and sky permitting. For rates and schedules, check website or stop by one of the Tour & Activity Desks at Half Dome (aka Curry) Village, the Yosemite Valley Lodge lobby, or by the Village Store.

HIKING There are at least 840 miles of trails in Yosemite National Park, including some that have fallen off the modern maps and are worth rediscovering. The most popular (and easiest) strolls in the valley are those to the most famous points of interest—Bridalveil Fall, Happy Isles, Mirror Lake, and Yosemite Falls. The best bet is to get a

HEAD OF THE JOHN MUIR TRAIL (JMT), HAPPY ISLES

HIGH SIERRA LOOP TRAIL	MI	KM
VERNAL FALLS BRIDGE	0.8	1.3
TOP OF VERNAL FALLS	1.5	2.4
EMERALD POOL	1.6	2.6
TOP OF NEVADA FALLS	3.4	5.5
LITTLE YOSEMITE CAMPGROUND	4.3	6.9
GLACIER POINT	8.2	11.3
HALF DOME	8.2	11.3
CLOUDS REST	10.5	17.0
MERCED LAKE	13.1	21.0
TENAYA LAKE	16.4	26.0
TUOLUMNE MEADOWS	27.3	44.0
MOUNT WHITNEY VIA JOHN MUIR TRAIL	211.0	340.0

NO PETS ON TRAILS

decent topographic map (e.g., the Tom Harrison "Yosemite Valley" or "Yosemite High Country," available at local bookstores and visitor centers), pack a lunch and plenty of water, and strike out wherever your fancy leads you.

The **Mist Trail**—not a long hike (3 miles round-trip to the top of Vernal Fall), but steep—is worth a few hours, not just for the extraordinary cascade, but also for the world-class people-watching along the way. The **Valley Floor Loop** (13 miles round-trip) is a surprisingly peaceful alternative, and it's great for families with small children with plentiful options for bailing out early and taking the shuttle back to the hotel. For a good, strenuous day hike, head up the Panorama Trail to Glacier Point (8.5 miles, 3,200 feet) and return either by shuttle or by the steep and historic **Four Mile Trail** (4.8 miles, 3,200 feet), long ago the daily commute of Derrick Dodd's famous chicken (see "Derrick Dodd's Tough [Hen] Story" sidebar, page 371). For **Half Dome Trail** information, see "To the Top of Half Dome—and Back" sidebar, page 344.

From Tuolumne Meadows, the John Muir Trail and the trails that connect the High Sierra Camps are busy in summer and well rutted by stock travel. Whenever possible, consider side routes to no-name lakes. In the backcountry, note the century-old T's blazed by cavalry troops into the bark of pine trees to mark the way.

Trailheads off the Wawona and Glacier Point Roads and from Hetch Hetchy tend to be the least crowded during the busy season. But across the park, things tend to quiet down considerably after Labor Day, especially if you can get up during the week. In summer, use free park shuttles to your advantage (see "Ditch the Car, Leave the Driving to the Pros" sidebar, page 334): Wawona to the Mariposa Grove with a shuttle back (or vice versa); the **Four Mile Trail** from the valley floor to Glacier Point with a shuttle back; shuttle to the Yosemite Creek trailhead on the Tioga Road and hike down to the valley by way of trail-engineer John Conway's brilliant **Upper Yosemite Falls Trail** (or the reverse); or hike **Tenaya Canyon** from Mirror Lake to Olmsted Point with a shuttle back.

For current trail conditions, check in with a ranger at the **Big Oak Flat Station** (209-379-1899), **Tuolumne Meadows** (209-372-0263), **Wawona** (209-375-9531), the **Valley Visitor Center** (209-372-0299), or the **Wilderness Center** (209-372-0740). Wilderness permits are required for overnight travel in the backcountry. For guided hiking and backpacking trips, try the **Yosemite Mountaineering School** (Half Dome (aka Curry) Village or Tuolumne Meadows; 209-372-8344; www.yosemitemountaineering.com) or **Southern Yosemite Mountain Guides** (North Fork; 1-800-231-4575; www.symg.com).

HORSEBACK RIDING AND MULE PACKING Easy two-hour rides are offered from the **Big Trees (aka Wawona) Stables** (adjacent to Pioneer Village; www.travelyosemite .com). No children under 7 years old or 44 inches tall are permitted. Maximum weight is 225 pounds. Horseback riding is no longer offered in Yosemite Valley or Tuolumne Meadows. Saddle trips and pack service are available with High Sierra Camps reservations (see page 365). For trail and sleigh rides near the South Entrance, try **Yosemite Trails Saddle & Sleigh Company** (Fish Camp; 559-683-7611; www.yosemitetrails.com). See Chapters 4 and 5 for a variety of private pack outfits into the Yosemite National Park backcountry from the east side of the range.

INTERPRETIVE PROGRAMS AND ACTIVITIES Ranger-led walks, lectures, campfire programs, children's programs, slide shows, films, pioneer demonstrations, stargazing, writing and poetry workshops, live performances, and guided snowshoe walks in winter are offered at Pioneer Village at Wawona, Yosemite Village Visitor Center, Half Dome (aka Curry) Village Amphitheater, the Yosemite Valley Lodge Amphitheater, the LeConte Lodge, and Parsons Lodge in Tuolumne Meadows. Check out Lee Stetson's enduring and well-informed impressions of John Muir, or see Ranger Shelton Johnson as Sergeant Elizy Bowman of the 9th Cavalry, at the handsome new Yosemite Theater behind the Yosemite Village Visitor Center. Both personalities were recently made famous by filmmaker Ken Burns. For details and the latest schedule, check the current issue of *Yosemite Today*, available at all entrance kiosks and visitor centers.

MOUNTAIN BIKING Off-road cycling is not allowed within the park, but the Sierra and Stanislaus National Forests and the Merced River Recreation Area offer hundreds of miles of logging roads and trails through the woods. **Tenaya Lodge** (1122 CA 41, Fish Camp; 1-888-514-2167; www.tenayalodge.com) and **Evergreen Lodge** (33160 Evergreen Rd., off CA 120; 209-3792606; www.evergreenlodge.com) offer rentals and good beta on local trails. The **Yosemite Bug** (CA 140, Midpines; 209-966-6666; www .yosemitebug.com) is another good base camp, with year-round riding nearby. Bring your own bike. **Yosemite Bicycle and Sport** (40680 CA 41, Oakhurst; 559-641-2453; www.yosemitebicycle.com) is the nearest full-service bike shop to the park, offering rentals, guide and shuttle service, and beta for the extensive trails in the adjacent Sierra National Forest.

ROAD BIKING The topography is terrific, the scenic value extraordinary, the traffic very often a bummer. Early-morning fast laps in Yosemite Valley (almost year-round), the climb from Mono Lake to Tioga Pass, and the long, gradual descent from Tuolumne to Crane Flat (spring to late fall) are hard to beat. The best time to ride all roads into the park is late fall—October and November, weather permitting—when the air is cool, the roads still dry, and the RVs stabled down south for the winter. Outside the park, try the network of paved logging and recreation roads above Bass Lake. Again, talk to the folks at **Yosemite Bicycle and Sport** (40680 CA 41, Oakhurst; 559-641-2453; www .yosemitebicycle.com) for detailed information.

ROCK CLIMBING, BOULDERING, AND MOUNTAINEERING "Climbers through-out the world have recently been expressing interest in Yosemite," Yvon Chouinard (founder of Patagonia) wrote in the *American Alpine Journal* of 1963, "although they know little about it." Those days are gone. Today, Yosemite is the most famous rock-climbing destination on the planet. Why? In part because of the array of characters who made the first ascents and changed the way climbing was done. But ultimate credit must be given to the rock itself—to the vast quantity of it and to its quality. "Nowhere else in the world is the rock so exfoliated, so glacier-polished and so devoid of hand-holds," wrote Chouinard. The valley is best known for its big-wall crack climbing—on any given day one can pull off at the turnout on Northside Drive, set up a lawn chair, crack a cold beer, and peer through binoculars at some miserable pair of sods toasting in the sun 15 pitches up the west face of El Cap. If you're lucky, you can watch somebody do it without ropes.

Bouldering is popular in the shade along the base of the cliffs, especially between Camp 4 and the Majestic Yosemite (aka Ahwahnee). In summer, when the valley heats up, most climbers—and the headquarters of the Yosemite Mountaineering School—pack up and move to the glorious granite-domeland paradise of Tuolumne Meadows. For those not quite so technically inclined, the range here offers many hundreds of fine and dramatic peaks that can be bagged John Muir–style with no more equipment than a pair of shoes and two good hands.

Southern Yosemite Mountain Guides (North Fork; 1-800-231-4575; www.symg .com). Scheduled and custom trips, classes. Climbing, hiking, backpacking, ski tour-ing. Yosemite and points south.

Yosemite Mountaineering School (Half Dome (aka Curry) Village, Tuolumne Meadows, Yosemite Ski and Snowboard Area (aka Badger Pass); 209-372-8433; www .yosemitemountaineering.com). These are the people who trained Clint Eastwood for *The Eiger Sanction*, the same people who invented and thankfully continue to profit from the world-famous Go Climb a Rock T-shirt (available at stores throughout the park). Classes and trips are scheduled year-round, and private instruction and custom guiding are available. Rock climbing, hiking, backpacking, ski touring, hut trips, and equipment rental.

SPA AND MASSAGE ✪ **Spa Du Sureau** (at the Chateau du Sureau, Oakhurst; 559-683-6860; www.chateausureau.com/spa-sureau). Film-noirish, lavender-scented, art deco pleasure palace; open to the public. Dry sauna, hydrostorm, lavishly appointed couple's room, facials, footbaths, marine therapy, wild elderberry skin polishing, the works.

Ascent Spa (at the Tenaya Lodge, CA 41; 1-888-514-2167; www.tenayalodge.com/ spa.aspx). A whopping 10,000 square feet of spa and wellness center to match the hotel's vast conference facilities. Massage therapy, face and body treatments, yoga, dry saunas, steam rooms, Jacuzzis, indoor and outdoor pools, and a wall of waterfalls.

Health Spa at the Yosemite Bug (CA 140, Midpines; 209-966-6666; www .yosemitebug.com/spa.htm). Massage therapy, spa treatments, sauna, and a spring-fed stainless-steel hot tub. Tai chi, yoga, and dance classes with a view.

SWIMMING There are crowded outdoor swimming pools at the Lodge and at Half Dome (aka Curry) Village that may come into their own during times of extreme drought (open to non-guests for a fee) or very late in the season. Otherwise, with the crystalline water of the Merced and its plethora of swimming holes within strolling dis-tance, the pool may not be the place. The antique cold tank at Big Trees (aka Wawona) Lodge can hit the spot after a long drive up from the Central Valley on a hot day. The

SWIMMING IN THE MERCED RIVER BURKE GRIGGS

small pool at the Majestic Yosemite (aka Ahwahnee) is a convenient dip for hotel guests. It is illegal to put so much as a toe in San Francisco's water supply at Hetch Hetchy, but higher up in the watershed, up the Tuolumne to the meadows and beyond, there are thousands of ice-cold bodies of water waiting to shock your system.

TENNIS There are courts near the Majestic Yosemite (aka Ahwahnee)—like a secret garden, long-lost, neglected, and overgrown with vines—and behind the Big Trees (aka Wawona) Lodge. Non-guests play for a nominal fee. Bring your own rackets and balls.

WINTER SPORTS **Yosemite Ski and Snowboard Area (aka Badger Pass)** (Glacier Point Road; 209-372-8433; www.badgerpass.com), with its five lifts, lack of crowds, ultra-mellow groomed terrain, and old-school, laid-back atmosphere (the oldest ski area in California, since 1935), is a great place to work your telemark turns before heading into the backcountry, or to get the kids on skis without having to pull a third mortgage on the farm. There are ski and snowboard rentals (209-372-8438), acclaimed ski school (209-372-8430), telemark and cross-country ski rentals (209-372-8444), and snow tubing (209-372-8444). Season runs December to April, conditions permitting. Free shuttles daily to and from Half Dome (aka Curry) Village, the Majestic Yosemite (aka Ahwahnee), and the Yosemite Valley Lodge. For sledding, try Crane Flat. If you're lucky enough to be in the valley when it snows, snowshoes or cross-country skis can be hired from the **Mountain Shop at Half Dome (aka Curry) Village** (209-372-8396). Outdoor ice skating at Half Dome (aka Curry) Village (209-372-8341) has been a favorite tradition since the 1920s, though the rink is considerably smaller than in those days. Open daily, December through March (weather permitting). Skate rental and hot chocolate available.

MOUNTAIN GUIDE DOUG NIDEVER ON THE TIOGA ROAD IN WINTER BILL BECHER

SKATING AT CURRY VILLAGE, FEBRUARY 1939 RALPH ANDERSON, COURTESY NPS, YNP

✳ Lodging

It seems fair to say that everyone should, at least once in their lives, spend a night—or several—on the floor of Yosemite Valley. "If it is among the possibilities," wrote pioneer Yosemite hotelier J. M. Hutchings in 1886, "if you would make your visit healthful, restful, and thoroughly enjoyable . . . do not attempt any very fatiguing excursion the first day after arrival, [but rather] devote it to day-dreaming and rest . . . an easy jaunt among some of the attractive scenes not very far from the hotel." There is no substitute for settling in: for lingering over the fading alpenglow, watching the moon rise over Illilouette Canyon, sipping a cocktail beside the lawn at the hotel formerly known as the Ahwahnee, letting memories of the car and the road home slip into oblivion, and much later, after a good night's rest, stumbling onto the lodge porch in time for dawn to catch the crest of the falls. There are options for every budget.

Plan ahead as far in advance as practicable, as beds can be hard to come by (and often impossible to come by) at the last minute, especially in summer. If you prefer a modicum of silence and solitude, make it midweek in midwinter. An overnight trek to one or more of the historic High Sierra Camps is also an experience not to be missed (facilities only open in summer)—especially for those who might prefer to enjoy the wilderness without the full complement of camping gear borne upon their shoulders, and to let someone else do the cooking and the dishes. That said, there are excellent reasons for spending a night or two in some of the finer establishments along the gateway corridors: to break up the trip on the way in or out (or both); to get away from the crowds; to explore less-trampled country; to have a place for your pet to sleep; to go mountain biking or geocaching or to pursue any number of other activities not permitted within the national park;

to spend less money; to find relief from the inevitable institutional character of Park Service concessions; or because the park is full and you have no choice. For a memorable winter adventure, try an overnight ski trip to Glacier Point or to the historic ski hut at Ostrander.

CAMPING In the old days, a person could lay out his bedroll or pitch a tent anywhere he so desired. To a certain degree this is still possible along back roads in the Stanislaus, Sierra, and Inyo National Forests, and in the backcountry of Yosemite's High Sierra. (It is emphatically required, by terms specified on a backcountry permit, that a person camp only on ground previously used for that purpose, and at a certain distance from water sources, roads, and trails.) Permits are available at no charge from the ranger station or visitor center nearest the departure trailhead. During peak season (May through September), some trails in Yosemite are subject to quotas for overnight travel. Permit reservations may be made in advance for a small fee (209-372-0740; www.nps.gov/archive/yose/wilderness/reserve.htm). It is illegal to sleep in one's car or RV anywhere within Yosemite National Park, except in a designated campground.

WILDERNESS PERMIT STATIONS **Yosemite Valley Wilderness Center**, between the Ansel Adams Gallery and the post office in Yosemite Village. Open May through October. In winter, permits are available at the Valley Visitor Center.

Tuolumne Meadows Wilderness Center, off Tioga Road at the turnoff to Tuolumne Meadows Lodge. Open late May through October (conditions permitting). In winter, self-registration permits are available at the Tuolumne Meadows Ranger Station.

Big Oak Flat Information Station, at the Big Oak Flat Entrance. Open May through September (self-registration outside in winter).

Wawona Visitor Center at Hill's Studio, next to the Big Trees (aka Wawona) Hotel. Open May through September.

Hetch Hetchy Entrance Station, Hetch Hetchy Road. Open year-round.

Badger Pass Ranger Station, the A-frame across from the ski lodge. Open December through March. Self-registration on porch when open.

CAMPGROUND LOGISTICS Developed campgrounds in or within striking distance of Yosemite routinely fill up on summer weekends, and often during the week as well. More than anywhere else in the Sierra, reservations are highly recommended. Of the 13 car campgrounds inside the park, seven have sites that can be reserved in advance. Reservations can be made up to five months prior through the **National Recreation Reservation System** (1-877-444-6777; www.recreation.gov) beginning at 7 AM Pacific time on the 15th of the month. For example, reservation requests for campsites during the third week in July will be accepted beginning at 7 AM on March 15—and will likely sell out within minutes. Cancellations and no-shows do occur, with sites reassigned on a first-come, first-served basis starting at 8 AM at **campground offices**: at the edge of the Half Dome (aka Curry) Village parking area; at Wawona; at the Big Oak Flat Entrance Station; and at Tuolumne Meadows.

The only other camping in the valley available on a first-come, first-served basis in summer, with parking adjacent, is at Sunnyside (the old Camp 4), where a certain amount of walk-in square footage is rented cheap, per person, with six people to a site. "Camp 4 is the physical and spiritual home of the Yosemite climbers ... and other hard to classify and vaguely undesirable visitors," Doug Robinson wrote in 1969. And so it remains today. A much better bet, if you can carry your gear on your back or in a bike trailer, is the little-used backpackers' campground beneath the Royal Arches, across Tenaya Creek from the North Pines campground (wilderness permit required; parking at Half Dome (aka Curry) Village). Upper Pines is available on a first-come, first-served basis in winter. Pets are not allowed at Camp 4 (Sunnyside), Tamarack, or Porcupine Flat. For further information and the latest Yosemite camping policies, check www.nps.gov/yose/planyourvisit/campgrounds.htm or call the main campground office at 209-372-8502.

If you find yourself in Yosemite on July Fourth weekend and thoroughly stymied for a place to lay out your sleeping bag, head up 120 West to the Evergreen/Hetch Hetchy Road for the plentiful—if not always level—dispersed camping on the great public dirt of the Stanislaus National Forest.

TENT CABINS For camping-style exposure to the elements, but without the hassle of pitching your own tent and blowing up air mattresses, try **Housekeeping**

Camp (Southside Drive; 801-559-5000; www.travelyosemite.com; inexpensive). Best bet, if you can secure one, is a site right on the river—three concrete walls, a canvas roof, a patio, bunk beds, and a picnic table on the beach. Linen packages are available for a nominal fee. Traditional canvas tent-cabins are available for hire at **Half Dome (aka Curry) Village** (off Southside Drive, east end of the valley; 801-559-5000; www.travelyosemite .com; moderate)—which during peak season is reminiscent of a United Nations refugee camp—as well as at **Tuolumne Lodge**, **White Wolf**, and the **High Sierra camps** (see below). An interesting alternative for families visiting the Hetch Hetchy region is to book a cabin or tent site at historic **Camp Mather** (209-379-2284; www.campmather.com; inexpensive), which is owned and managed by the City of San Francisco Recreation and Parks Department (415-831-2700 or 209-379-2284; sfrecpark.org/destination/camp-mather), and which narrowly, miraculously escaped being destroyed by the 2013 Rim Fire. Summer reservations are assigned by lottery in February of each year.

THE WAWONA ROAD (CA 41)

❂ **Château du Sureau** (48688 Victoria Ln., Oakhurst; 559-683-6860; www .chateausureau.com; very expensive; Elevation: 2,300 feet; Open: Year-round; Owner: Erna Kubin-Clanin; Pets: With permission; Wheelchair Access: Yes; Internet Access: Wireless). California has its share of ersatz European castles: Hearst's, Scotty's, the Disney Castle in Anaheim, Vikingsholm at Tahoe. So it should come as no great surprise to find, even on the outskirts of a raggedy supply town like Oakhurst, a gracefully proportioned hillside European-style château—completed in 1991. And yet it does. Most surprising of all, however, is the way it seems always to have been here, with its ivy-clad stone tower, whitewashed walls, and terra-cotta roofs set into a hillside of coulter pines, elderberries,

YOSEMITE CAMPING

Wawona Road (CA 41)	Elevation	Season	Reservations Accepted	Fee	Sites	Water	Agency
1. Greys Mountain	5,400	Jun–Oct	No	Yes	26	No	USFS
2. Texas Flat (Group)	5,400	Jun–Nov	Yes	Yes	4	No	USFS
3. Soquel (Overflow)	5,400	Jun–Oct	Yes	Yes	11	No	USFS
4. Nelder Grove (Primitive)	5,300	May–Sep	No	No	7	No	USFS
5. Kelty Meadow (Equest.)	5,800	Jun–Oct	Yes	Yes	11	No	USFS
6. Fresno Dome	6,400	Jun–Oct	No	Yes	15	No	USFS
7. Big Sandy	5,800	Jun–Oct	No	Yes	18	No	USFS
8. Summerdale	5,000	Jun–Nov	Yes	Yes	29	Piped	USFS
9. Summit	5,800	Jun–Oct	No	No	6	No	USFS
10. Wawona*	4,000	Year-round	Yes**	Yes	93	Piped	NPS
11. Bridalveil Creek*	7,200	Jun–Sep	No	Yes	110	Piped	NPS
El Portal Road (CA 140)							
12. McCare Flat	1,200	Year-round	No	Yes	14	No	BLM
13. Railroad Flat	1,200	Year-round	No	Yes	9	No	BLM
14. Willow Placer (walk-in)	1,200	Year-round	No	Yes	8	No	BLM
15. Jerseydale	4,000	May–Nov	No	No	10	Yes	USFS
16. Dry Gulch (walk-in)	1,600	Year-round	Yes	Yes	4	Yes	USFS
17. Dirt Flat (walk-in)	1,600	Year-round	Yes	Yes	5	Yes	USFS
Big Oak Flat Road (CA 120)							
18. Lost Claim	3,100	May–Sep	No	Yes	10	Well	USFS
19. South Fork	1,500	Apr–Oct	No	No	8	No	USFS
20. Lumsden	1,500	Year-round	No	No	10	No	USFS
21. Lumsden Bridge	1,500	Apr–Oct	No	No	9	No	USFS
22. Sweetwater	3,000	Apr–Oct	No	Yes	12	Piped	USFS
23. Moore Creek (Group)	3,100	Year-round	Yes‡	No	1	No	USFS
24. Dimond "O"	4,400	Apr–Oct	Yes	Yes	36	Piped	USFS
25. Cherry Valley	4,700	Apr–Oct	No	Yes	45	Piped	USFS
26. Hetch Hetchy (Backpackers)*	3,800	Year-round	No	Yes	19	Piped	NPS
27. Hodgdon Meadow*	4,900	Year-round	Yes**	Yes	105	Piped	NPS
28. Crane Flat*	6,200	May–Oct	Yes**	Yes	166	Piped	NPS
Tioga Road (CA 120)*							
29. Tuolumne Meadows*	8,600	Jun–Oct	Half	Yes	304	Piped	NPS
30. Porcupine Flat*	8,100	Jun–Oct	No	Yes	52	Creek	NPS
31. Yosemite Creek*	7,659	Jun–Sep	No	Yes	40	Creek	NPS
32. White Wolf*	8,000	May–Sep	No	Yes	74	Piped	NPS
33. Tamarack Flat*	7,569	May–Oct	No	Yes	52	Creek	NPS
Yosemite Valley							
34. Upper Pines*	4,000	Year-round	Yes**	Yes	238	Piped	NPS
35. Lower Pines*	4,000	Mar–Oct	Yes	Yes	60	Piped	NPS
36. North Pines*	4,000	Apr–Oct	Yes	Yes	81	Piped	NPS
37. Camp 4 (Sunnyside Walk-in)*	4,000	Year-round	No	Yes	35	Piped	NPS

Note: Reservations at USFS and NPS sites, unless otherwise specified, can be made online at www.recreation.gov or by calling 1-877-444-6777.
*located within the park.
**first come, first served in winter.
*** For campgrounds east of the park, see chapter 5.
‡ For reservations call the Groveland Ranger District at 209-962-7825.

and manzanita—as if it had once been some nobleman's country estate and the town had only recently sprung up around it. Through the gates all notion of traffic disappears. There are fountains and koi ponds, herb gardens, rose gardens, a boccie court, a pool, a garage for one's collectible automobile. There are solicitous maids in traditional black-and-white uniforms, classical music and Campari in the salon, a music room, a chapel, a fireplace and balcony in every

HALF DOME (AKA CURRY) VILLAGE TENT-CABINS BURKE GRIGGS

room, and a discreet stand-alone villa for those attempting to elude the tabloid press. "Consider any individual at any period of his life," wrote Alexis de Tocqueville, "and you will always find him preoccupied with fresh plans to increase his comfort." No more so, perhaps, than when he is on his way in or out of the wilderness. Two-course European-style breakfast is served in the sunroom or *al fresco* in the courtyard; lunch is prepared by request. Multiple-course dinners are served next door at Erna's Elderberry House. Television available on request. Spa, customized excursions, limousine service, and gift boutique. The only officially designated Relais & Châteaux property between the California Coast and the Rocky Mountains.

✪ **Far Meadow** (Beasore Road (Sierra Vista Scenic Byway), 16 hard miles above Bass Lake; 310-728-6158; www .farmeadow.com; moderate to expensive; Elevation: 7,200 feet; Open: Year-round;

Owners: Heinz Legler and Veronique Lievre; Pets: Yes; Wheelchair Access: No; Internet Access: Wireless via satellite). Los Angeles-based designers Heinz Legler and Veronique Lievre—the creative team behind the boutique eco-spa Verana on the Mexican Costalegre—have breathed new life into the classic mid-century A-frame vacation hut genre. Set in a forest of lodgepole pines beside a small seasonal creek and a private meadow of wildflowers, and surrounded by the Sierra National Forest, three airy cottage-size A-frames and the neighboring log cabin are an inspired combination of off-the-grid simplicity and spare, IKEA-modern comfort. Lights, electrical outlets, and satellite Internet all derive ample juice from the sun. Though it's only 16 miles off the well-traveled Bass Lake Road tourist corridor (and much less as the crow flies), Far Meadow feels very far away indeed. Other than on midsummer weekends or during hunting season, several hours might drift away into birdsong between the passage of one car and another. Although it may look close on the map, it's not a very practical base camp for day trips into Yosemite National Park. A better strategy would be to stay several days, treat the immediate region as your own private Yosemite, making short forays by car or bicycle, utterly sans crowds and traffic, to half-forgotten points of interest such as Globe Rock (in the footsteps of the remarkably well-traveled Teddy Roosevelt) and Clover Meadow, to the Mammoth Pool reservoir on the San Joaquin, and to Fresno Dome and the silent Nelder Grove of Giant Sequoias. Bring groceries and supplies for all meals. Only basic sundries, sandwiches, and burgers available down the road at Lois and Vern Jones's store. If the A-frames are booked, try the log cabin or the vintage trailers. Or try the sister property, the **Old Yosemite Road Cabin**, between Oakhurst and the park entrance.

Narrow Gauge Inn (48571 CA 41, Fish Camp; 559-683-7720; www

.narrowgaugeinn.com; moderate to expensive; Elevation: 4,990 feet; Open: Year-round; Innkeeper: Aung Oo; Pets: Yes ($25 fee); Wheelchair Access: Yes; Internet Access: Wireless). Within earshot of the train whistle and a short walk up the hill from the depot is a series of terraced motel units offering a good value alternative to the deluxe corporate-run resort up the road. A variety of rooms and suites, each with some combination of wood paneling, pioneer-style and/or Victorian furnishings; a flat-screen TV; a private or semi-private shaded porch; a pair of Adirondack chairs; and a view into the woods across the tracks. The Mission Suite features rough-pine paneling, caribou antlers, a mini-fridge, and two bathrooms. Sleeps a family of five. Jacuzzi, pool, on-site dining, and bar. Two-night minimum on weekends between Memorial Day and Labor Day. Continental breakfast included.

Tenaya Lodge (1122 CA 41, Fish Camp; 1-888-514-2167; www.tenayalodge .com; very expensive; Elevation: 5,288 feet; Open: Year-round; Innkeeper: Delaware North Companies; Pets: Yes (with $75 canine concierge fee); Wheelchair Access: Yes; Internet Access: Wireless). Two short miles from the South Entrance and the Mariposa Grove, 35 long and scenic ones to Glacier Point or the valley, and convenient to The Yosemite Ski and Snowboard Area (aka Badger Pass), what is now Tenaya Lodge was built in the early 1990s as a Marriott resort. It was then purchased and treated to an extensive mountain-themed makeover by Delaware North—with granite floors, diamond-motif carpeting, antler chandeliers, chainsaw bears, Rocky Mountain elk heads, and piped-in music to keep you moving. The 294-room property is the deluxe, contemporary, corporate-retreat version of the Yosemite gateway hotel. Because of its size and price tag, it's often the last place to fill up on a busy weekend. Rooms are enormous, deeply soundproofed, and pleasingly lit. Beds are well dressed with high-thread-count

THE A-FRAME AT FAR MEADOW, SIERRA VISTA SCENIC BYWAY ABOVE BASS LAKE FARMEADOW.COM

sheets, channel-stitched cotton and goose down; water pressure is spectacular. Full-service spa, fitness center, indoor and outdoor pools, Jacuzzi, ice skating, mountain biking, geocaching, wall climbing, horseback riding, cross-country skiing, arcade, children's activities, and 15,000 square feet of indoor meeting space. Five options for on-site dining, including a pizzeria, deli, coffee shop, and convenience store. Babysitting services are available. Check for activity packages and discounted winter rates.

✪ Big Trees (aka Wawona) Hotel (CA 41, Wawona; 801-559-5000; www.travelyosemite.com; moderate to expensive; Elevation: 4,000 feet; Open: Year-round; Innkeeper: Aramark; Pets: No; Wheelchair Access: Yes; Internet Access: No). The second-oldest operating hotel in the West, the Big Trees (aka Wawona) is a handsome collection of glossy white clapboard buildings with the air of a grand old Victorian resort lost in the Adirondacks. It's artfully aged, generally thoughtfully maintained, and protected by National Historic designation as much from decay as from ambitious renovation. James Savage and his Mariposa Batallion camped here early in the spring of 1851, at a comfortable distance from the Indians. By 1856, the Indians had gone and Galen Clark had built a cabin on the west end of the meadow, from which he regularly served venison and trout to hungry travelers. Ulysses S. Grant stayed here in 1879, before the paint was dry on the new two-story building, followed by other such dignitaries as William Jennings Bryan, William Harrison, and the actress Lillie Langtry. The place is still a welcome refuge from road and trail and crowds—with its wide wraparound verandas creeping with hops, wicker chairs that prove on close inspection to be plastic, a lawn made for strolling, a cold swimming tank from the 1920s, a tennis court, a classy old-world golf course, and canvas awnings that come up in the evening to reveal the sun catching the crowns of ancient trees for which the place was named. Even the Park Service trash cans are painted white. "I do not know a more idyllic spot," J. Smeaton Chase wrote

THE ORIGINAL WAWONA HOTEL, 1880s THOMAS HILL

SKIERS LOOKING AT HALF DOME FROM GLACIER POINT, 1936 RALPH ANDERSON, COURTESY NPS, YNP

in *Yosemite Trails* (1911), describing the confluence of mountain, meadow, and forest. "If Yosemite has the greater glory, Wawona has the deeper charm." The newest building dates from 1918. Rooms are available with private bath or without. No TVs, no telephones. Don't miss Tom Bopp live at the piano every evening except Sundays and Mondays (since 1983).

Glacier Point Ski Hut (Glacier Point; 209-372-8444; www.travelyosemite.com; expensive to very expensive (includes guide and all meals); Elevation: 7,200 feet; Open: Winter, by reservation only; Innkeeper: Aramark, Yosemite Mountaineering School; Pets: No; Wheelchair Access: No; Internet Access: No). Dormitory-style winter accommodations are fashioned from what in summer is a bustling gift shop and snack bar. There was a grand hotel here once—Ansel Adams made publicity photos of it in the 1920s—but it burned down in 1969. Glacier Point is the most popular, most famous, and in summer most easily accessed and crowded vantage of Half Dome, the valley, and the High Sierra beyond. In winter, it is left to those select few who are willing—or rather, thrilled—to ski 11 miles out the smooth, groomed road from The Yosemite Ski and Snowboard Area (aka Badger Pass), and then eventually to ski 11 miles back, mostly mellow uphill. If you want to be there for sunset, moonrise, meteor showers, and dawn, but don't want to haul a tent, a bivvy sack, and cooking gear, your best bet will be to sign up for a guided Glacier Point Lodge trip. All meals are provided. Sleeping is dormitory-style; bring your own bag and pillow (or rent one at the hut). One- and two-night guided trips, self-guided options, equipment rental, and midweek packages are available. Good especially as a trial run for an Ostrander trip.

✪ **Ostrander Ski Hut** (Ostrander Lake, from Glacier Point Road; 209-379-5161; www.yosemiteconservancy.org/ostrander-ski-hut; inexpensive; Elevation: 8,500 feet; Open: Winter; Innkeepers: Howard Weamer, George Durkee, and Fritz Bagget; Pets: No; Wheelchair Access: No; Internet Access: Wi-Fi in the Annex). Hand-hewn of local granite and lodgepole pine and assembled by Civilian Conservation Corpsmen, the hut at

Ostrander Lake—started and completed in less than 10 weeks during the summer of 1940 with nothing but hand tools and a block-and-tackle—is one of the best and most enduring examples of rustic park architecture in the U.S. It was built expressly for ski touring. "From that center skiers could ski for days always on new terrain," wrote Badger Pass ranger Frank Givens in 1939. "The scenery is the best. Snow conditions are always good due to many different exposures." The hut is a 10-mile ski/snowshoe trek from the The Yosemite Ski and Snow-board Area (aka Badger Pass) parking lot, which, depending on conditions, can take from a few hours to all day. There's nothing technical about it, but neither is it recommended for beginners on skis. Maps, current conditions, and wilderness permits are available at the Badger Pass ranger station. The two significant uphill sections on the way in—with ever-improving views of the Illilouette drainage, the Clark Range, Cloud's Rest, and Half Dome—are best tackled with climbing skins on free-heel or randonée skis (something you can make rough turns on going down). No matter how light you travel, no matter what kind of shape you're in, or how spectacular the weather, you're always glad to smell the wood smoke from Ostrander. Stove, kitchen, pots and pans, unfiltered water, solar-powered light, thousands of acres of relatively avalanche-free intermediate to advanced terrain. Sleeps 25. Bring sleeping bags, hut slippers, and the best food and beverages you can carry. Stay at least two nights to allow for exploration, lounging, and telemark practice. See the website for details. Reservations are by lottery in early November, or by telephone after December 1. Discounted rates for Yosemite Conservancy members.

EL PORTAL ROAD (CA 140)

There's a full range of basic motels in Mariposa. None, with the possible exception of Vicky Lorenzi's popular 8-room **River Rock Inn** (4993 Seventh St.; 209-966-5793 or 1-800627-8439; www.riverrockncafe.com), is worth staying in town for. The rooms at the RiverRock, with their pumice-colored shag carpeting and cheap ceiling fans, fall a bit shy of claims to the "exquisite," but they're clean and comfortable. The grounds are, as a visiting young French intellectual recently put it, *sympat*. Plus there's an inviting hipster wine bar/café and live music in the garden most Friday nights in summer. And a quality continental breakfast in the morning.

✪ **Yosemite Bug** (6979 CA 140, Mid-pines; 209-966-6666 or 1-866-826-7108; www.yosemitebug.com; inexpensive to moderate; Elevation: 2,250 feet; Open: Year-round; Owners: Caroline McGrath and Douglas Shaw; Pets: Yes; Wheelchair Access: Limited; Internet Access: In the lodge). Yosemite Bug is by far the best place to stay on CA 140, not only as a stopover on the way to Yosemite (still 25 miles farther up the road), but as a destination in its own right. Terraced into an oak-shaded hillside in the foothills above Mariposa, it's summer camp meets college meets backpacking in Europe meets Yosemite. Accommodations include ultra-budget, youth-hostel-style dormitories; tent cabins (cheaper, quieter and more comfortable than those in the park); and some of the most interesting and elegantly appointed private motel rooms in the region. Dining is gourmet camp-style in the most congenial setting this side of the High Sierra Camps. Full range of activities, tours and classes, live music, a wealth of regional information. Massage therapy, spa treatments, sauna, and a stainless-steel outdoor hot tub. Easy access to swimming holes, local hikes, mountain biking trails, and the Merced River Recreation Area. Hot in midsummer, mild in winter. Public transportation–friendly (YARTS from Merced), plus three chartered "Bug Buses" weekly to and from San Francisco and custom Bug shuttles and tours into the park.

BIG OAK FLAT ROAD (CA 120)

Groveland Hotel (18767 Main St., Groveland; 209-962-4000 or 1-800-273-3314; www.groveland.com; expensive to very expensive (includes breakfast); Elevation: 2,800 feet; Open: Year-round; Innkeepers: Peggy and Grover Mosley; Pets: Yes (with small fee); Wheelchair Access: No; Internet Access: Wireless). The oldest part of the hotel was built of local adobe brick in 1849. The newer Queen Anne–style annex was added in 1914 to house bigwigs on the O'Shaughnessy Dam project at Hetch Hetchy. Today, with its wraparound porches and wicker chairs, its abundant floral patterns, quilts, feather beds, and period antiques, the place fairly creaks with old world charm. In-room coffeemakers, telephones, and wireless Internet generally seem to keep Lyle, the inn's resident ghost, at bay. Breakfast goes above and beyond the call for a B&B, with squeeze-your-own OJ and heaping, made-to-order skillet scrambles. Spa services, bathtubs, and romantic packages available. Fine dining in the evening. Historic, discreet back door to the Iron Saloon in case the romance goes awry. See the website for scheduled wine tasting events and summertime courtyard theater. And yes, Peggy did go to high school with Elvis Presley.

☉ Evergreen Lodge (33160 Evergreen Rd., Groveland (on the road to Hetch Hetchy); 209-379-2606 or 1-800-93-LODGE; www.evergreenlodge.com; moderate to expensive; Elevation: 4,550 feet; Open: Year-round; Owners: Lee Zimmerman, Brian Anderluh, and Dan Braun; Pets: No; Wheelchair Access: Limited; Internet Access: Wireless in recreation building). The Sierra is peppered with "rustic" cabin resorts of the kind that had their heyday in the decades of flapper skirts, touring cars, and moonshine. The majority of these have since fallen so far into disrepair—or worse, been subjected over the years to such haphazard shag-carpet-and-linoleum

BURREL MAIER AND THE MUDWAGON, PIONEER VILLAGE, WAWONA BURKE GRIGGS

surface renovations—that today the word *rustic* is less evocative of the simplicity of yesteryear than it is redolent of propane leaks and general mouse-infested squalor. The Evergreen is one of a select few that has been rescued from such a fate. Originally a post office and general store, later a brothel and speakeasy servicing workers on the O'Shaughnessy Dam project, briefly left for dead in the early 1970s, the Evergreen was expanded and brought back to even greater glory in 2004—to the tune of $10 million—and then expanded again (in 2009-10) by a team of creative and socially conscious investors from San Francisco. In 2012 they completed their trajectory toward being a full-scale mountain resort with a 2,000-square-foot outdoor swimming pool, hot tub, pool house and full-service poolside bar. Cabins are clean and spare, with tastefully retro furnishings, galvanized sconce lighting, personal satellite radios, and just the right amount of knotty-pine trim. The recreation building, with its crackling fire, cozy armchairs,

HETCH HETCHY: ONCE AND FUTURE MEADOW?

Once upon a time, after the glaciers receded, before any people showed up, both Yosemite and Hetch Hetchy Valleys were made into lakes, with meltwater backed up against dams of glacial moraine. Eventually the moraine eroded away, the lakes drained, and meadows and forests moved in. (The name Hetch Hetchy is said to come, for whatever reason, from the Southern Miwok word for *magpie*.) In 1906 the San Andreas Fault broke open beneath San Francisco, thousands died, and a good part of the city burned to the ground. The idea was circulated that if there'd been more water, the fires might have been stopped. All eyes turned to the Sierra, and to the 459-square-mile Tuolumne River watershed.

By the end of 1913, despite a fervent campaign by John Muir, Congress had adopted the Raker Act, which gave San Francisco City Engineer Michael "The Chief " O'Shaughnessy the green light to begin building his now-notorious curved gravity dam. Muir died the following year—according to legend, of a broken heart. "That anyone would try to destroy such a place seems incredible," he had written before the last round of congressional hearings, "but sad experience shows that there are people good enough and bad enough for anything."

Not everyone was so deeply opposed to the backing-up of the waters. William Randolph Hearst was a big fan, and William Jennings Bryan, and the nation's first chief forester, Gifford Pinchot, and Woodrow Wilson—and a good number of locals. "The lake which will soon be created," wrote University of California geology professor Andrew Lawson in Ansel Hall's *Handbook of Yosemite* (1921), "will be but a restoration on a larger scale of the lake which once existed there . . . [it] will seem very natural in its mountain setting." The dam was completed in 1923. The resulting reservoir, stretching 8 miles upstream into the Grand Canyon of the Tuolumne, off-limits to boating or swimming, now provides up to 85 percent of San Francisco's drinking water, at 220 million gallons a day, and clean power for 2.5 million people. For this resource the City of San Francisco pays the federal government rent, at the rate of $30,000 per year—plus another million or so to help pay for park rangers and trails and such.

As in the windblown aftermath of the great Owens Valley water grab on the other side of the range, there was at Hetch Hetchy an unintended consequence: silence. Where today the place might otherwise be filled with cars and tourist buses and hotels, it is instead the wildest, most rattlesnake-infested, least-visited part of Yosemite National Park.

In 1987, Ronald Reagan's interior secretary, Donald Hodel, proposed to study the feasibility of removing the dam and restoring the valley to an earlier state of affairs. "This is the worst idea I have heard since the sale of weapons to Iran," said Dianne Feinstein, then mayor of San Francisco. "There is no issue on which there is more controversy and concern than water in California." Reports were made and the idea dropped, but the wheels were turning. In 2006, in response to a flurry of proposals from academic and environmental sectors, the California Department of Water Resources, together with the Department of Parks and Recreation, took a good, hard look at the matter. There were many concerns: How would it be done? Diamond-saw cutting? Blasting? Hydraulic ramming? How long would it take the meadow to come back? Would the stains on the rocks go away? What about flood control? Where would

local-resource library, and wireless Internet, provides one of several congenial social hubs (others being the main plaza, the s'mores pit, the kids' game room and, of course, the tavern). A recreation concierge is on hand from early morning until late in the evening to help you earn your end-of-the-day libations. Activities include fly-fishing, mountain biking, white-water rafting, hiking, snowshoeing, pine-needle basket weaving, table tennis, geocaching, hammock- or pool-lounging, horseshoes, and massage.

 ○ **Rush Creek Lodge** (34001 CA 120, Groveland; 209-379-2373; www .rushcreeklodge.com; expensive; Elevation: 4,600 feet; Open: Year-round; Owners: Lee Zimmerman and Brian

San Francisco's water and power come from? How much would it cost? For every obstacle there seemed at least the possibility of a solution. The final recommendation was that further studies be conducted to the tune of $7 million. The Bush administration, in its 2008 budget proposal, included an item allowing for just such a study, to be paid for by the City of San Francisco.

"It would be a monumental mistake," said San Francisco Mayor Gavin Newsom. "It's a raid on San Francisco resources," said Feinstein, who, by that time, had become a U.S. Senator.

The study was dropped from the budget.

The debate continues over whether it'd be greener, at this point, to leave the dam in place or to tear it down. "Our goal is to focus not just on restoring Hetch Hetchy, but on creating more sustainable water management practices for the City of San Francisco," Mike Marshall, executive director of the nonprofit group Restore Hetch Hetchy (www.hetchhetchy.org), said in an interview with *The New York Times*.

HETCH HETCHY SPILLWAY

Anderluh; Pets: No; Wheelchair Access: Yes; Internet Access: Wireless). Sister property to the Evergreen Lodge (above), the 143-room Rush Creek Lodge resort opened in 2016 on the banks of Highway 120 just a half mile from the entrance to Yosemite. Without question the best park-adjacent accommodations, with ultra-modern hotel-style lodge rooms, suites and two-bedroom villas. Every room has a private deck overlooking the woods. There's a salt-water pool, two hot tubs, two bars, ping pong, shuffle-board, a comfortable reading lounge, and a full-service recreation planning desk. On-site dining is excellent and varied (see below), if a tad expensive. Grab-and-go lunch items available at the

General Store. Live music and events programmed throughout the season. The biggest issue with the place is that you may not find yourself terribly compelled to continue on to the park.

TIOGA ROAD AND TUOLUMNE MEADOWS (CA 120)

Tioga Pass Resort (TPR) (CA 120, 1 mile east of Tioga entrance; reservations@ tiogapassresort.com (no phone); www .tiogapassresort.com; moderate to expensive; Elevation: 9,641 feet; Open: Year-round; Pets: No; Wheelchair Access: Limited Internet Access: No). Known as Camp Tioga into the 1950s, TPR's first structures were built in 1914 by onetime trapper and prospector Albert Gardisky. Today the place offers a variety of yurts, roadside knotty-pine cabins with kitchenettes, four high-value motel rooms with private bathrooms and showers down the hall, and the best, most reasonable place to eat between Groveland and Lee Vining. Its current owners bought the place for its vintage snowcat and its spectacular ski terrain—what Hans Ludwig, in *Powder* magazine, once called "the finest concentration of kick-ass, big-vertical skiing between Valdez and Verbier." And for a handful of years, the resort operated a duly touted (and now sorely missed) backcountry ski operation, serving up three hot meals a day, warm beds, and thousands of acres of cross-country and alpine touring. Unfortunately, between the vicissitudes of big avalanches on the Tioga Road and a generally unsupportive county bureaucracy, wintertime operations are now on indefinite hold. The resort was also hard-hit in the massive winter of 2016–17 which caved-in roofs and flattened structures. Those accommodations that remain tend to be booked up tight throughout the summer season. Make reservations online well in advance.

Tuolumne Meadows Lodge (CA 120, Tuolumne Meadows; 888-413-8869; www.travelyosemite.com; moderate; Elevation: 8,575 feet; Open: Approximately June–September; Innkeeper: Aramark; Pets: No; Wheelchair Access: Limited Internet Access: No). Tuolumne Meadows Lodge was first opened by the Desmond Park Company in 1916 to provide lodging for travelers on the newly acquired government road. The only truly significant changes since those early days have been the paving of the road in and the parking lot, and the electrification of the kitchen and dining room. The word *lodge* may seem a bit grandiose, unless you've been out wandering in the wilderness for a forgotten period of time. *Camp* might be more appropriate. As such, it is the stopover of choice for those heading farther afield (i.e., to the High Sierra Camps), the perfect place to begin acclimation to the altitude, and a good base for day trips and other romps across the meadows. Accommodations are canvas tent-cabins with metal-frame camp beds, wool blankets, and synthetic comforters. Bring your own sleeping bag, flashlight, and thermal clothing. The ancient woodstoves, with their accompanying ration of logs, newspaper, matches, and candles, give a hint of warmth on the front and back ends of a cold High Sierra night. Tents by the river provide the best atmosphere for sleeping—especially if your neighbors haven't hiked as hard or driven as far as you have. Dining available (see "Dining").

White Wolf Lodge (Off CA 120; 888-413-8869; www.travelyosemite.com; inexpensive to moderate; Elevation: 8,000 feet; Open: Approximately late June–September; Innkeeper: Aramark; Pets: No; Wheelchair Access: Limited; Internet Access: No). Set in a small meadow along the Middle Fork of the Tuolumne, White Wolf was first used by ranchers for summer pasture, then by surveyors of the original wagon road. By 1930, according to a Park Service land survey, the property consisted of a small resort with twelve tents, two tourist cabins, a diminutive main lodge and dining room, a power plant, and a gas station. Today there are twice as many tents and no gas station. The quaint, cottage-style cabins and lodge appear exactly as in photographs from the 1930s. The main road has since moved several miles uphill to the south, giving the place an air of remoteness, but the old diesel generator still thunders away in the early evenings. One day maybe the concessionaire will find itself motivated to go solar. Tent accommodations are the same as at Tuolumne Meadows, but more reasonably priced. The cabins, with porches and Adirondack chairs looking across the road to the meadow, are the best bet. Dining available by reservation (see "Dining").

○ **Yosemite High Sierra Camps** (Five locations in Yosemite backcountry; 888-413-8869; www.travelyosemite.com; very expensive (includes two meals); Elevation: 7,150–10,300 feet; Open: Approximately late June–September; Innkeeper: Aramark; Pets: No; Wheelchair Access: No; Internet Access: No). The first of a series of backcountry camps was built at Merced Lake in 1916 at the behest of the Park Service's first director, Stephen Mather. Facilities included a row of canvas dormitory tents—for hikers and travelers on horseback—and a mess tent/lounge staffed by a manager, a cook, and a fisherman. Basic supplies were hauled in by mule. The idea took hold in the 1920s and '30s as one of the most popular ways to experience the more remote parts of the Yosemite high country. Today there are five such camps, each 5 to 10 miles apart along a rough loop, each offering the same basic luxuries as seven or eight decades ago: camp beds, mattresses, wool blankets, good society, and copious hot meals. Spend one night out or make an extended loop of all five. **Merced Lake** (7,150 feet), the lowest in elevation, closest to the valley and farthest from the Tioga Road, accommodates the most visitors and is most likely to have availability; **Vogelsang** (10,300 feet) is the highest, coldest, and most reminiscent of an overnight in the high

WHITE WOLF LODGE

Alps. **May Lake** (9,270 feet) is the easiest to access (1 mile from the parking lot) and thus best for families and children. **Glen Aulin** (7,800 feet), the smallest camp, has a waterfall and views down the Grand Canyon of the Tuolumne, and feels on some levels like it might be the most remote of the camps. **Sunrise** (9,400 feet) is the newest camp (built in 1961) and, with its open meadow vistas, it is perhaps, to the extent such can be measured, the most beautifully situated. Reservations are highly coveted and not easy to secure, made by a confounding process of mail-in lottery prior to November 30 for the following season. Call for an application or download one from the website. Canceled reservations are filled by telephone on a first-come, first-served basis. Chances for last-minute availability increase dramatically after Labor Day. Wool blankets are provided, and sleep sacks are available for purchase at each camp. Bring your own ultra-lightweight down bag if you prefer.

Also bring your own camp pillow, pack towel, toothbrush, lunch money, flashlight, whatever you require for a day on the trail between camps, and something to spike your lemonade with at trail's end. Contact the High Sierra Desk (209-372-8095) for information on how to smuggle luxury items—beer, wine, fresh oysters, down comforters, ice cream, chaise longues (at $5 per pound)—to the camps by mule. Saddle service and naturalist-guided trips also available.

YOSEMITE VALLEY

✪ **The Majestic Yosemite (aka Ahwahnee) Hotel** (Ahwahnee Road, east of Yosemite Village; 888.413.8869; www .travelyosemite.com; very expensive; Elevation: 4,000 feet; Open: Year-round; Innkeeper: Aramark; Pets: No; Wheelchair Access: Yes; Internet Access: Wireless). "A large first-class hotel is very much needed," Muir wrote in 1912. Whether there is truth to the legend that

SUNRISE HIGH SIERRA CAMP

Viscountess Nancy Astor, in the early 1920s, took one look at the old Sentinel Hotel, got back in the car, and headed straight back to London, the fact was this: The quality of the accommodations had failed to rise even partway to the grandeur of the surroundings. And so funds were raised, a prominent architect hired, and construction begun on what would become one of the most extraordinary lodges in North America—a grand, 99-room, rustic-deco-gothic-Craftsman palace made of steel, concrete, and granite—a place, as Park Service director Stephen Mather put it days before its opening in 1927, "for people who know the delights of luxury living, and to whom the artistic and material comforts of their environment is important." The lobby and lounges downstairs, open as they are to the gawking of the public, feel more crowded and democratic than at other outrageously priced properties elsewhere on the continent, but the rooms upstairs—the best have private, awning-shaded porches overlooking the valley—fit the bill quite nicely for those occasions when you simply must have the best there is (in Yosemite). A variety of suites and junior suites is available, including the one chosen for Queen Elizabeth II on her 1983 visit, and private cottages in the woods. Small pool, tennis, afternoon tea, room service.

MAJESTIC YOSEMITE (AKA AHWAHNEE) HOTEL AND ROYAL ARCHES BURKE GRIGGS

Yosemite Valley Lodge (Northside Drive, across from Yosemite Falls; 888-413-8869; www.travelyosemite.com; expensive; Elevation: 4,000 feet; Open: Year-round; Innkeeper: Aramark; Pets: No; Wheelchair Access: Yes; Internet Access: Wireless in lobby only). The U.S. Cavalry established a barrack and command post here in 1915, not far from where J. M. Hutchings had built his earliest homestead and hotel, at the base of Yosemite Falls—where young John Muir worked the sawmill. Hutchings's hotel is said to have been notoriously spartan, with curtains strung between bunks for privacy. The lodge, a collection of matching, stand-alone, two-story structures constructed in high midcentury-motor-lodge style in 1956—with louvered windows and doors, and ceiling fans in lieu of air conditioning—is still a few years away from garnering any significant architectural acclaim. Thoroughly updated by the former concessionaire in 2003 and '04, with waffle-weave shower curtains, 20-inch TVs, mini-fridges, irons, hair dryers, new carpets, and simple pine furnishings, the lodge provides the best balance between comfort and practicality. If not the most peaceful retreat in the Sierra, it is, at the very least, a giant step up from the tent cabins at Half Dome (aka Curry) Village. Private porches offer views of the falls, in season, or of the woods and meadows opposite. Convenient access to bike path and hiking trails. A short stroll to Yosemite Village. Dining, shopping, bicycle rentals, evening programs, pool.

✳ Where to Eat

"Considering the 65 miles and more of mountainous road over which all supplies must be carried for the use of the hotels, and the difficulty in getting and retaining proper help," early Kodak-slinger Samuel Douglass Dodge wrote in 1890, "no one, as he sits down to a fairly good meal at either hotel or pays his seemingly large bill will be disposed to grumble, for he will consider that there is but one Yosemite, and that it is a long way from the beaten track." These days, of course, the track is fairly beaten (and paved) all the way to the far side of the valley. The main dining rooms at the **Big Trees (aka Wawona) Lodge**, the **Yosemite Valley Lodge** (formerly the Lodge at Yosemite Falls), and the **Majestic Yosemite (aka Ahwahnee) Hotel**, leaning on the vast infrastructure of one of the world's largest facilities-services conglomerates, serve up relatively complex fare, surprisingly fresh and sometimes well prepared (especially given the volume served during the busy season), and at prices no more extravagant than one might expect, given the location. Outside the park are several excellent restaurants, at least one along each of the four routes, to remind a person what is good and desirable in civilization.

THE WAWONA ROAD (CA 41)

✪ **Erna's Elderberry House** (48688 Victoria Ln., Oakhurst; 559-683-6800; www.elderberryhouse.com; very expensive). For fans of Monty Python, the word *elderberry* (*sureau* in French) may conjure scenes somewhat inappropriate to one of the world's top-ranked restaurants. In this case it refers to a native California shrub, protected by the federal government as home to the delicate larvae of a certain threatened species of beetle. Vienna-born restaurateur Erna Kubin-Clanin made her way here via Los Angeles and then the tiny hamlet of Wawona, where, before the Park Service declined to renew her lease, the first incarnation of the Elderberry House had already garnered international acclaim. "All I had was my reputation," she says. Today that reputation includes the classification of her latest labor of love, as one of only a handful of officially designated *Relais Gourmands* in the western U.S. Multiple-course meals are served prix fixe in a dining room furnished with French antiques, tapestries, and oil paintings. The inscription above the door reads: IN HONOR OF THE GREAT AUGUSTE ESCOFFIER. Consider wearing different attire from what you've been wearing all day on the trail or in the car.

Sierra Restaurant (at the Tenaya Lodge; 1-888-514-2167; www.tenayalodge.com; expensive). Menu selections include burgers and sandwiches, pasta, seafood, filet mignon, salads, and grilled vegetables, sourced for the most part from right down the road in the Central Valley. New World wine list, full bar, leather chairs, fireplace. The chipotle chocolate pudding has proved a dangerous revelation. (For less-expensive pub fare, head instead to Jackalope's; for more expensive and fancier stuff—quail, scallops, fruit gazpacho, elk loin with vanilla essence and the like—try the Embers Restaurant.) Morning brings either the "Total Breakfast Buffet" or a standard breakfast menu, along with a view of the pool.

Big Trees (aka Wawona) Dining Room (at the Big Trees (aka Wawona) Hotel; 209-375-1425; expensive). Seating is first-come, first served, leaving plenty of time on busy summer evenings to cozy up to a string of old Depression-era standards on the piano by Tom Bopp, to peruse the lobby's historic photograph collection (printed guide available at the front desk), or to lounge on the veranda with a cool gin and tonic. The menu has expanded a bit since the days when Ah You and Ah Louie ran the kitchen, back when all the food was raised, caught,

DINING AND DRINKING HIGHLIGHTS

or shot within a few miles of the hotel. Tourist fashions have changed too, but the general atmosphere—Big Tree-motif lampshades, high mullioned windows and wainscoting—remains much the same. Gone are the linen tablecloths and the high-back oak chars. The pot roast, a standard for at least 30 years, abides. An excellent breakfast buffet is included in the price of a room. Lunch served daily. Western-style barbecue on the lawn Saturday evenings; Sunday brunch Easter through Thanksgiving and during the Christmas holidays.

GROCERIES, ETC. **Oakhurst Fruit Stand** (40842 CA 41; 559-692-2777) Last stop for farm fresh produce. Open every day.

Old Corral Grocery & Tackle Shop (41872 Road 222, Oakhurst; 559-683-7414). Basic supplies, hamburger meat, beer, ice, tackle, fishing licenses. Open daily 8 AM–8 PM.

Raley's Superstore (40041 CA 49, Oakhurst; 559-683-8300). The local full-service chain, founded in Placerville in 1935. Meat, produce, pharmacy, deli counter, bakery, Peet's Coffee bar, Wi-Fi hot spot. Open every day.

Vons (40044 CA 49, Oakhurst; 559-642-4250). The other chain. Deli, bakery, pharmacy, Starbucks, liquor, produce, and gasoline. Open every day.

EL PORTAL ROAD (CA 140)

For the last real taco-cart-style Mexican food this side of the Sierra Crest, try **Sal's Taco Truck** in Mariposa (Mariposa Rest Area between the Mariposa Museum and the post office; daily, except for every other Thursday when the truck goes to El Portal), or the newer, younger competition from **Tacos Sonora** (on the other side of the Museum parking lot). The **Happy Burger Diner** (5120 CA 140; 209-966-2719; www.happyburgerdiner.com, inexpensive), boasting without exaggeration the most voluminous menu in the Sierra, is internationally renowned for its fries, charbroiled items, and milk shakes. Oh and there's a salad bar. Plus free Wi-Fi and a vast collection of old LP covers pasted across the walls for your browsing pleasure while you wait for your order.

If you feel the need to sit down for something more substantial, try the shrimp skewers, bacon-wrapped dates, and contempo-jazz art-gallery-style atmosphere at **Savoury's** (5034 CA 140; 209-966-7677; savouryrestaurant.com; moderate to expensive); the seafood mac or the venison leg at **1850 Brewing Company** (5114 CA 140; www.1850restaurant.com; 209-966-2229); or the more traditional Western-themed surf-and-turf at the **Charles Street Dinner House** (5043 CA 140; 209-966-2366; www.charlesstreetdinnerhouse.com; expensive). For a classic American diner-style breakfast, try the Sugar Pine Café (5083 CA 140; 209-742-7793; www.sugarpinecafe.com). Otherwise, press on. It's only 7 miles to the Bug.

✪ **Café at the Bug** (6979 CA 140, Midpines; 209-966-6666; moderate). Order at the counter; eat beneath wagon-wheel chandeliers, snowboards, and a wild boar's head—or outdoors on the porch; bus your own table. No reservations, no dress code. One recent evening's menu boasted marinated grilled tri-tip, pan-fried lemon-tahini trout, and a veggie stir-fry with coconut curry over udon noodles. All good, all hearty, all excellent

HALF DOME AND CLOUDS REST FROM GLACIER POINT PHOTO BY S.C. WALKER, FROM J. M. HUTCHINGS, *IN THE HEART OF THE SIERRAS*, 1886

dry-stack retaining walls. Live music or karaoke four nights a week. Wine and beer only.

COFFEE, SANDWICHES, ETC. **Pony Expresso** (5182 CA 49, Mariposa; 209-966-5053). Coffee, smoothies, juices, icees, sandwiches, and bagels.

Mariposa Coffee Company (2045 CA 49 South, Mariposa; 209-742-7339; www.mariposacoffeecompany.com). Visit the source. Stop in for a tasting, demonstration, tour, or a pound or two of beans to go. Family-owned. Open most days all day; Sunday after noon.

Short Stop Sandwiches (5110 Jessie St., Mariposa; 209-966-7447). Real sandwiches, meat or vegetarian. Try the spicy tuna wrap or the Hawaiian. Charming shaded garden for eating in, or take 'em to go.

GROCERIES **49er Market** (CA 140 and CA 49 North, 49er Shopping Center, Mariposa; 209-9662040). Full-service market, deli. Open daily.

High Country Health Foods and Café (5186 CA 49 North, Mariposa; 209-966-5111; www.highcountryhealthfoods.com). Bulk food, trail mix, herbs, juices, vitamins, snacks, sandwiches, salads, coffee, holistic camping supplies. Open daily.

Pioneer Market (5034 Coakley Circle, at CA 140, Mariposa; 209-742-6100; www.pioneersupermarket.com). Locally owned full-service grocery. Bakery, deli, meat counter, produce, wine, and liquor. Open daily.

HERBS **Country Kitchen Herb Farm** (4959 Sierra Pines Dr., Mariposa; 209-742-6363). Pick your own organic herbs; self-conducted tours; theme gardens, pygmy goats, and sheep. Open every day but Sunday, spring through fall. Call ahead to make sure someone's there.

BIG OAK FLAT ROAD (CA 120)

The Victorian Room Restaurant (at the Groveland Hotel; 209-962-4000; www

value. Cold draft beers and a variety of quality wines. After dinner, guests of all ages and from all over the world gather around laptops, play poker, or read guidebooks by the fire. Heaping breakfasts from 7 AM. Lunch made to eat there or to take out on the trail.

TAVERNS, SALOONS, AND ROADHOUSES **The Alley** (5027-C CA 140, Mariposa; 209-742-4848; www.thealleylounge.com). Sixteen rotating craft beers and hard ciders, wine lounge, back garden, industrial fixtures.

Hideout Saloon (5031 CA 140 #F, Mariposa; 209-966-6565) Historic basement drinking establishment carved into the hillside and shored up with 150-year-old

DERRICK DODD'S TOUGH [HEN] STORY

(From J. M. Hutchings's In the Heart of the Sierras, 1886)

As a part of the usual programme, we experimented as to the time taken by different objects in reaching the bottom of the cliff. An ordinary stone tossed over remained in sight an incredibly long time, but finally vanished somewhere about the middle distance. A handkerchief with a stone tied in the corner was visible perhaps a thousand feet deeper; but even an empty box, watched by a field-glass, could not be traced to its concussion with the Valley floor. Finally, the landlord appeared on the scene, carrying an antique hen under his arm. This, in spite of the terrified ejaculations and entreaties of the ladies, he deliberately threw over the cliff's edge. A rooster might have gone thus to his doom in stoic silence, but the sex of this unfortunate bird asserted itself the moment it started on its awful journey into space. With an ear-piercing cackle, that gradually grew fainter as it fell, the poor creature shot downward; now beating the air with ineffectual wings, and now frantically clawing at the very wind, that slanted her first this way and then that; thus the hapless fowl shot down, down, until it became a mere fluff of feathers no larger than a quail. Then it dwindled to a wren's size, disappeared, then again dotted the sight a moment as a pin's point, and then—it was gone!

After drawing a long breath all round, the women folks pitched into the hen's owner with redoubled zest. But the genial McCauley shook his head knowingly, and replied:

"Don't be alarmed about that chicken, ladies. She's used to it. She goes over that cliff every day during the season."

And, sure enough, on our road back we met the old hen about half up the trail, calmly picking her way home!

.groveland.com; expensive). Bacon-wrapped scallops, warm spinach salad, a mixed-grill option featuring venison, quail, and duck-and-foie-gras sausage. Award-winning wine list. This is where Her Majesty the Crown Princess of Thailand had dinner on her trip to Yosemite in 2007. Eat outdoors on warm summer evenings or in the intimate 150-year-old formal dining room. Reservations recommended. Ask about picnic-basket lunches to go.

Evergreen Lodge Restaurant (at the Evergreen Lodge; 209-379-2606; www.evergreenlodge.com; moderate to expensive). Free-range chicken wings, French onion soup, wild boar ribs, and buffalo burgers. Start with a martini at a picnic table in the courtyard, or something from the well-considered wine list; eat outdoors, or in the tavern, or in the original dining room from 1921; finish with a chocolate Maker's Mark bread pudding and a glass of tawny port by a fire beneath the stars while the kids play pool in the game room. Open daily for breakfast, lunch, and dinner. Hours vary seasonally.

The Restaurant at Rush Creek (at the Rush Creek Lodge; 209-379-2373; www.rushcreeklodge.com). Quality steak-and-burger standards, locally-sourced veggies and salads, and a good range of innovative seasonal options served in a casual, lofty dining hall. Wild boar bolognese for crisp fall evenings; bibb salad and chilled burrata for hot summer nights. Same menu also available in the Tavern (see below). Breakfast, lunch and dinner daily.

TAVERNS, SALOONS, AND ROAD-HOUSES ✪ **Iron Door Saloon** (Main Street, Groveland; 209-962-6244; www.iron-door-saloon.com). Serving prospectors, tourists, stagecoach drivers, dam builders, and weekend motorcycle gangs since "sometime before 1852."

The grill next door serves breakfast and basic pub food. The original iron doors, still in place, made their way here from England by way of Cape Horn and a team of mules. The stone walls are locally quarried schist. Unique collection of historic artifacts, photos, natural history displays, and bullet holes, all of it available daily for public perusal. Children welcome. Quality live music most weekends. The sort of place you might hear a grunge version of "Whiskey River," where the bartender might be induced to get on stage and sing a round of "Mustang Sally," where a pause for a quick draft along the road might just turn into an overnight at the hotel next door.

Rush Creek Tavern (at the Rush Creek Lodge; 209-379-2373; www .rushcreeklodge.com). Well-curated selection of wines, craft beers, and cocktails. Big-screen sports if you need an antidote to all the twinkling stars and fresh air. Live music and karaoke some nights.

✪ **Tavern at the Green** (Evergreen Lodge; 209-379-2606; www .evergreenlodge.com). What the Iron Door is to the 19th-century Western saloon, the Tavern at the Green is to the classic pine-paneled roadhouse of the 1920s and '30s. Ten beers on tap, an impressive selection of single-malt scotches, a winning cocktail menu for the kids. Pool table, excellent live music all year long, and a world famous, four-day Halloween party. The shame of it, from this author's point of view, is that the two best bars in the Southern Sierra, each within half an hour of the other, are both shut off from the east side of the range for six months of the year—except by a two-day trek on fast skis.

GROCERIES **Main Street Market** (19000 Main St., Groveland; 209-962-7452). The last stop for fresh produce. Basic groceries, meat counter, beer, liquor, wine. Recently expanded.

TIOGA ROAD AND TUOLUMNE MEADOWS (CA 120)

✪ **Tioga Pass Resort** (CA 120, 1 mile outside the park; no phone; www .tiogapassresort.com; inexpensive to moderate). Better food, better service, better value than in the park. One of three finalists for Best Pie in the Southern Sierra.

Tuolumne Meadows Lodge (CA 120; moderate). Staffed as it is by people who'd generally rather be in the backcountry (or otherwise kicking back with beers after a long day of jamming their fists into split granite), the lodge's quality of food and service is highly variable. And likely to feel overpriced. Safest bets are the simplest and cheapest: burgers, chicken, and such. The atmosphere—the real draw—is spirited and congenial, conversations tending to the high adventures of people who have traveled much, read not a little, and appreciate a good walk. Reservations are required. Box lunches available. For happy hour try the mini-fridge by the front desk, where a cold Sierra Nevada is several dollars cheaper than in the adjacent dining room.

✪ **High Sierra Camps** (888-413-8869; expensive). The menu rotates in such a way that hikers on the loop will not have to eat the same meal two nights in a row. Halibut, pork, chicken, and more; vegetarian alternatives; pancakes, eggs, soufflés, and such for breakfast. Meals prepared in each case according to the inventive whimsy of the folks in the kitchen—generally to most excellent effect. There is no better, warmer, more copious fare to be had in the wide-open backcountry. BYOB. Meals sometimes available, especially with advance reservations, for those not staying in camp but schlepping their own accommodations.

White Wolf (209-372-8416; moderate). Essentially the same menu as at the High Sierra Camps, without the added flavor of distance from pavement—but with the benefit of red tablecloths,

THE DINING TENT AT THE MERCED LAKE HIGH SIERRA CAMP

candlelight, and a fire in a fireplace. On weekend nights, opt for the first seating if possible. Be patient. Have a beer or a glass of wine. Enjoy the front porch and the fading light. When you finally get to sit down, family-style, there's sure to be more grub on the table than you can possibly pack away—no matter what you've been up to—and all manner of rousing stories from the trail. Recent fare included a communal bowl of roasted pepper and corn bisque, a communal bowl of mixed greens with jalapeño-cantaloupe vinaigrette, and chicken fajitas. Prix fixe. Reservations required. Come as you are.

BURGERS AND SUCH **Tuolumne Meadows Grill** (Tuolumne Meadows; 209-372-8426). Basic fast food: burgers, dogs, sandwiches, fries, ice cream. Breakfast is the best bet. Closed in winter.

YOSEMITE VALLEY

In Yosemite Valley, there is food to get you over the hump to the next activity, and there is (occasionally) food worth lingering over. All of it, for better or worse—every microwave burrito, every pan-seared diver scallop—is brought to you by Philadelphia-based Aramark (ARMK), a multibillion-dollar custodial, facilities, and food-services corporation, the folks who feed and put uniforms on both the U.S. Military and the majority of the U.S. prison population, and, since 2016, the sole concessionaire charged with putting chow into as many as 25,000 mouths a day in the Yosemite Valley alone. Food services are provided in four locations: at **Half Dome (aka Curry) Village**, **Yosemite Village** (see "Food Purveyors"), the **Majestic Yosemite Hotel (aka the Ahwahnee)**, and the **Yosemite Valley Lodge**. By the quality of stuff provided at the various snack bars, ice cream stands, short-order grills, convenience stores, buffets, pizza counters, and delis, it will come as little surprise that the company was founded in 1936 by a fellow selling peanuts in Los Angeles out of the back of an old car.

Half Dome (aka Curry) Village Pavilion (inexpensive). Respectable breakfast and dinner buffets. Open daily during the summer; weekends and holidays only from December to mid-March. The ski buffet, offered some Saturday nights in winter, features food, live entertainment, and dancing. Beer and wine available.

✪ **Majestic Hotel Dining Room** (at the Majestic Yosemite (aka Ahwahnee) Hotel; 209-372-1489; expensive). With its trestle-beamed cathedral ceilings, wrought-iron chandeliers, floor-to-ceiling linen drapes, and divided-light windows, the dining room is one of the grandest halls in the American West. Dinner is elegant, if not quite formal: linen, silver, wrought-iron candelabras, the original china service from 1927, collared shirts, trousers, skirts, and dresses. The food, though plated with award-winning artistry, may not always achieve the highest standard it proclaims for itself. But as the building modestly tips its hat to the great half-cleaved cliffs from which it was hewn, so does the meal leave the greater glory to the circumstances in which it is served. Reservations suggested. By daylight, the best breakfast buffet in the valley, with overstuffed, made-to-order omelets; thick-slab French toast; local fruit; and fresh-squeezed orange juice. Outrageous Sunday brunch with nine buffet stations. For a light but civilized lunch, try the trout amandine and boysenberry pie.

Food Court at the Lodge (Yosemite Valley Lodge; 209-372-1265; inexpensive). Buffet-style: grilled items, pizza, pasta, premade salads, and desserts. Best baguette sandwiches ready-wrapped for picnics in meadows. Beer and wine available. Open daily year-round.

Mountain Room Restaurant (Yosemite Valley Lodge; 209-372-1281; www.yosemite park.com; moderate to expensive). No matter how well framed the view of the falls—and well framed it is—this is not the place to be when the sun is setting in Yosemite. Afterward, however, when the alpenglow lifts and darkness spreads across the rocks and trails and meadows, and the air takes on the scent of a thousand cookstoves grilling meat, a small army of servers in polyester waistcoats and corporate name tags awaits your pleasure in the Mountain Room. Remarkably, given the size of the hall, the distance from the kitchen to the table, and the number of meals served on a busy summer evening, the food arrives with manifest care and skill, worth hiking out of the wilderness for. The Chef's Prix Fixe is a good bet. One recent lineup featured a generous pile of organic, Madera-raised arugula and radicchio with smoked duck breast, pears, and almonds; a solicitous shank of lamb; and a pear cobbler to help ease the impending transition out of the valley. Beer, fine wine, cocktails. Open for dinner daily year-round. No reservations, except for parties of eight or more.

TAVERNS, SALOONS, AND ROADHOUSES **Majestic Yosemite Bar** (at the Majestic Yosemite [aka Ahwahnee] Hotel; 209-372-1289). Live music from the Steinway most Fridays and Saturdays. Vintage cocktails, fine cheeses, smoked salmon, and chili served among the intrepid squirrels either indoors or at tables beside the lawn. Seating first-come, first-served. Open daily.

Half Dome Village Bar (at Half Dome (aka Curry) Village Pavilion). A handful of stools at the service bar off the Pizza Deck, generally occupied by employees, resident bouldering aficionados, or big-wall climbers on shore leave. Draft beers by the pint, premixed margaritas.

Mountain Room Lounge (Yosemite Valley Lodge; 209-372-1035). The only place in the world where you can sip on a basil gimlet, catch a ball game on TV, roast marshmallows indoors, and watch the moonglow on Yosemite Falls. Appetizers and limited bar food available.

COFFEE, ETC. **Ice Cream and Coffee Corner** (Half Dome (aka Curry) Village Pavilion). Coffee, espresso, pastries, hand-dipped ice cream. The earliest coffee available each morning at Half Dome (aka Curry) Village. Open seasonally.

Degnan's Kitchen (Yosemite Village, in the A-frame between the village store

both died in the 1940s. The bread is no longer fresh, nor is it baked anywhere near Yosemite, but the sandwiches are reasonably priced and made to order. An array of convenience-style items and beverages are available to round out your picnic. Open year-round. Family-style pizza restaurant upstairs in the Loft (209-372-8245), with better pizza than at Half Dome (aka Curry) Village. Open spring through fall.

SHORT ORDER Village Grill (Yosemite Village, next to Village Store). Beef, veggie, and salmon burgers; grilled chicken sandwiches; fries; milk shakes. Open spring to fall.

SNACKS AND SWEETS Majestic Yosemite Sweet Shop (at the Majestic Yosemite (aka Ahwahnee) Hotel; 209-372-1271). Candy, cigars, wine, soft drinks, magazines, newspapers, and postcards. Open year-round.

and the post office; 209-372-8245). Coffee drinks, tea, smoothies; bread and other items baked once upon a time somewhere else. Computer terminals for public Internet browsing. Open year-round.

PIZZA Pizza Deck (Half Dome (aka Curry) Village; 209-372-8315). No-frills pies and chili dogs slung to the waiting throngs through a service window, to be eaten alfresco with the squirrels and acorns. Cold beer available next door. Tacos and nachos around the corner, depending on staff availability. The whole affair is closed early fall through late spring.

SANDWICHES AND SUCH Degnan's Kitchen (Yosemite Village, in the A-frame between the village store and the post office; 209-372-8245). Named for John Degnan, the Irishman who, with the help of his wife, baked fresh bread for everyone in the park from 1884 until they

✸ Books, Maps, and Information

THE WAWONA ROAD (CA 41)

Yosemite Sierra Visitors Bureau (41969 CA 41, Oakhurst; 559-683-4636; www.yosemitethisyear.com). Tourist and lodging information, mini store, animal books, postcards. Open every day.

    Hill's Studio and Information Center (adjacent to the Big Trees (aka Wawona) Hotel; 209-375-9531). Built in 1886. Books, maps, quality souvenirs, wilderness permits, bear canister rental. Run by the Yosemite Conservancy. Open only in summer.

EL PORTAL ROAD (CA 140)

Mariposa County Visitor Center (5158 CA 140, Mariposa; 209-966-7081 or 1-866-HALFDOME; www.homeofyosemite.com). Books, maps, brochures, and general tourism information. Open daily.

Mariposa Museum and History Center (5119 Jessie St., Mariposa; 209-966-2924; www.mariposamuseum.com). Historical bookstore and gift shop. Self-guided tour map of Mariposa. Open daily; weekends only in January.

Yosemite Bug Store (6979 CA 140, Midpines; 209-966-6666). Fine-tuned selection of relevant books and maps. Best source on CA 140 for beta on local recreation, trails, and transportation.

BIG OAK FLAT ROAD (CA 120)

Groveland Yosemite Gateway Museum (18990 CA 120, Groveland; 209-962-0300; www.grovelandmuseum.org). A variety of simple displays, including artifacts from old Priest's Station, fishing gear from the 1930s, old bottles, baskets, and animal pelts. Selection of regional books and gifts. Open daily except holidays.

TIOGA ROAD AND TUOLUMNE MEADOWS (CA 120)

✪ **Tuolumne Meadows Visitor Center** (Tuolumne Meadows; 209-372-0263). Books, maps, and more by the Yosemite Conservancy; photos; a handful of classy vintage displays illustrating aspects of glaciation, bears, butterflies, and wildflowers. Friendly rangers dispensing helpful information. Closed in winter.

YOSEMITE VALLEY

✪ **Happy Isles Nature Center** (east of Half Dome (aka Curry) Village). Kids' books, games, toys, displays, and ranger-led activities.

✪ **Valley Visitor Center** (Yosemite Village; 209-372-0299). Recently renovated series of displays and exhibits, organized in timeline fashion from the geological beginnings of the Sierra through its more recent natural and social history. Staff of friendly rangers

on hand to provide information. Video and live programs in West Auditorium Theater. Bookstore adjacent.

✪ **Yosemite Conservancy Bookstore** (Yosemite Village, next to Valley Visitors Center; 209-379-2648; www.yosemitestore.com). The park's most complete selection.

Wilderness Center (Yosemite Village, next to Ansel Adams Gallery; 209-372-0740). Specialized collection of backcountry guidebooks and maps. Interpretive displays. Wilderness permits and bear-canister rentals. Closed in winter.

THE TUOLUMNE MEADOWS VISITORS CENTER, BUILT IN 1934, ORIGINALLY AS A MESS HALL FOR A CCC CAMP

✳ Shopping

THE WAWONA ROAD (CA 41)

SPORTING GEAR AND EQUIPMENT **Big 5 Sporting Goods** (40072 CA 49, Oakhurst; 559-642-6083; www.big5sportinggoods.com). Chain retailer of basic sporting and camping equipment and apparel. Good place to buy a cooler, a stove, and camp chairs.

Yosemite Bicycle and Sport (40680 CA 41, Oakhurst, behind McDonald's; 559-641-2453; www.yosemitebicycle.com). The only full-service bike shop within semi-reasonable biking distance of the park (14 miles). In fact, the only real bike shop between Fresno and Mammoth Lakes. Guide and shuttle service; rentals available. Good local beta.

Big Trees (aka Wawona) Golf Shop (Big Trees Hotel Annex; 209-372-6572). Clubs, balls, rentals, clothing, swimwear. Open spring through fall.

Yosemite Ski and Snowboard Area (aka Badger Pass) Sport Shop (209-372-8433). Winter clothing and accessories, goggles, snow tubing (209-372-8444), sunblock, snacks. Open only in winter.

GENERAL STORES **Pioneer Gift & Grocery** (Wawona, adjacent Pioneer Village; 209-375-6574). Basic last-minute groceries, camping and fishing supplies. Sundries, souvenirs, pioneer-themed gifts, and books next door. Open all year.

EL PORTAL ROAD (CA 140)

Sporting Goods and Equipment **Blue Heron Sports & Tactical Equipment** (5081 CA 140, Mariposa; 209-742-2300). Fishing supplies, camping gear, clothing, police and fire stuff. Fly-fishing guide service available.

SUNDRIES AND SOUVENIRS **Yosemite Gifts** (5023 CA 140, Mariposa; 209-966-4343; www.yosemite-gifts.com). Classic, old-school curios shop, housed in the old Capital Saloon (established in 1867). Totem poles, rocks and minerals, fossils, jewelry, trinkets, vintage books and signs.

BIG OAK FLAT ROAD (CA 120)

SUNDRIES AND SOUVENIRS **Groveland Mercantile** (18743 Main St., Groveland; 209-962-4438). Gifts, cards, pet supplies.

GENERAL STORES ✪ **Mountain Sage** (18653 CA 120, Groveland; 209-962-4686). Just the sort of organic roadside stopover you might expect to come upon in Vermont or the Adirondacks, or in Sonoma—set in a lovingly reclaimed Victorian farmhouse with a nursery out back, fruit trees blooming in their pots, medicinal herbs, hammocks, and organic fair-trade coffee, breakfast burritos, and baked items. A tasteful selection of books, music, Nepalese woolens, and backpacking necessities, and a gallery featuring a selection of local landscape and wildlife photography. Stop by the farmers' market Saturday mornings in summer for baked goods, juices, bluegrass, and locally grown organic produce. Check the schedule at www.mountainsagemusic.org for frequent concerts and readings.

Evergreen General Store & Gift Shop (at the Evergreen Lodge; 209-379-2606). Espresso bar, soda fountain, sandwiches and quiche, convenience store, camping and fishing supplies, souvenirs, books. Open daily; hours vary according to season.

Crane Flat Store (Crane Flat, junction of CA 120 West and CA 120 East; 209-379-2742). Gas and convenience store.

TIOGA ROAD AND TUOLUMNE MEADOWS (CA 120)

GENERAL STORES **Tuolumne Meadows Store** (CA 120, Tuolumne Meadows). Souvenirs, basic convenience items, camping and fishing supplies, licenses, bear canister rental. Closed in winter.

YOSEMITE VALLEY

GALLERIES ✪ **Ansel Adams Gallery** (Yosemite Village; 650-692-3285; www .anseladams.com). Housed in the handsome "new" Best's Studio, built in the 1920s on the occasion of the Park Service–ordered abandonment of the old village. This is where Ansel Adams and Virginia Best were married in 1928. Fine-art prints, books, calendars, and posters by Adams and a rotating selection of contemporary nature photographers. Ask about upcoming photography workshops. Open year-round.

SPORTING GEAR AND EQUIPMENT ✪ **Mountain Shop** (Half Dome (aka Curry) Village; 209-372-8396). The best selection of backpacking, camping, climbing, and mountaineering gear between Mammoth Lakes and Fresno.

Clothing, footwear, Go Climb a Rock memorabilia, books, maps, and general information. Interesting display of vintage climbing hardware. Winter equipment rentals when weather warrants. Open year-round.

SUNDRIES AND SOUVENIRS **Majestic Yosemite Gift Shop** (at the Majestic Yosemite (aka Ahwahnee) Hotel; 209-372-1409). Quality themed gifts and souvenirs: bathrobes, polo shirts, sweaters, china, vintner's accessories, books, journals, and holiday ornaments. Open year-round.

GENERAL STORES **Village Store** (Yosemite Village; 209-372-1253). The biggest grocery store in the valley, with a decent stock of gourmet backpacking and picnic items, cheeses, pâtés, olives, organic chocolate, canned and dehydrated goods, basic produce, beer, wine, ice, books, maps, magazines, clothing, gifts, and souvenirs. Open daily year-round.

Yosemite Valley Lodge Store (Yosemite Valley Lodge; 209-372-1297). Basic convenience items, cold beer, books, maps, curios, stuffed-bear toys, and souvenirs. Open daily year-round.

Half Dome (aka Curry) Village Gift & Grocery (209-372-8391). Familiar array of convenience items, beer, shrink-wrapped sandwiches and microwave food, souvenirs, postcards, and batteries.

✱ Special Events

January: **Taste of Yosemite (formerly Chefs' Holidays)** (at the Majestic Yosemite (aka Ahwahnee) Hotel; 801-559-4884; www.travelyosemite.com). Cooking demonstrations by award-winning chefs, kitchen tour, gala reception and dinner, lodging packages.

February: **Camp Mather lottery** (San Francisco Recreation and Parks Department; 415-831-5500; sfrecpark .org/destination/camp-mather/). **High Sierra Camps lottery results announced. Yosemite Nordic Holiday** (Yosemite Ski and Snowboard Area [aka Yosemite Ski and Snowboard Area (aka Badger Pass)] to Glacier Point; www.travelyosemite .com). Costumes, cross-country ski, and telemark races. **Horsetail Falls Sunset "Firefall."**

March: **Southern Yosemite Automotive Film Festival** (Oakhurst; www .southernyosemite.com). Classic movies, cars, and guest appearances. **Spring Fest** (Yosemite Ski and Snowboard Area (aka Badger Pass); www.travelyosemite.com; farwestnordic.org). Sun, slush, and general closing-day craziness.

April: **Space-available reservations at High Sierra Camps** (888-413-8869; www .travelyosemite.com). **Earth Day Celebration** (park-wide; www.travelyosemite .com). Crafts, film festival, hikes, walks, talks, children's activities. **Frazil ice in Yosemite Valley waterfalls. Yosemite Conservancy Spring Gathering** (www .yosemiteconservancy.org).

JIM HERSON FLASHING THE NOSE ON EL CAPITAN PATITUCCIPHOTO

PUSHING HOT COALS OFF GLACIER POINT FOR EVENING FIREFALL SHOW, CA. 1930s COURTESY NPS, YNP

May: **Average Tioga Pass opening**
(209-372-0200; www.nps.gov/yose/
planyourvisit/conditions.htm). **Average
peak waterfall flow**.

June: **Average peak wildflower
bloom. Yosemite Indian Big Time**
(Yosemite Museum and Indian Village).
Crafts, cultural activities, games, and
dancing.

July: **Fireworks** (Mariposa County
Fairgrounds; 209-966-2432).

August: **Tuolumne Meadows Poetry
Festival** (Parsons Lodge). **Mariposa
County Fair** (Mariposa; 209-966-2432).

September: **'49er Festival
& Chili Cook-Off** (Groveland;
49erfestival.blogspot.com). Parades,
costumes, kids' activities, chili
cook-off, gold panning, gunfights,
live music. **Mountain Heritage Days**
(Oakhurst; 559-683-6570; www
.fresnoflatsmuseum.org). **Mariposa
County Farms and Ranches Tours** (www
.mariposafarmsandranches.com). Harvest weekend in the country. Wineries,

YOSEMITE NATIONAL PARK

CAMP CURRY

328   THE FIRE FALL, GLACIER POINT   92660

gardens, organic coffee roastery, bakery, olive orchard, pumpkin patch. Workshops, demonstrations, activities. **High Sierra Camps lottery opens** (888-413-8869; www.travelyosemite.com). **Wawona Celebrity Golf Tournament.**

October: **Yosemite Conservancy Fall Gathering at Wawona. Average peak fall colors. Oakhurst Fall Festival** (Oakhurst; 559-683-7766; www.oakhurstchamber .com). **Annual Las Tortugas Dance of the Dead Halloween Celebration** (Evergreen Lodge; 209-379-2606). Four days of top-notch live music, revelry, and masquerade. Book early. **High Sierra Elderberry Harvest and Dinner** (Erna's Elderberry House; 559-683-6800; www .elderberryhouse.com). Hike, harvest, and dinner.

November: **The Grand Grape Celebration (formerly Vintners' Holidays)** (at the Majestic Yosemite (aka Ahwahnee) Hotel; 801-559-4884; www .travelyosemite.com). See October. **Ostrander Ski Hut lottery** (209-379-5161;

www.yosemiteconservancy.org/ facilities-reservation). **High Sierra Camps lottery closes** (801-559-4909; www.travelyosemite.com). **Thanksgiving at the Evergreen** (Evergreen Lodge; 209-379-2606; www.evergreenlodge .com/thanksgiving.html). In the woods, pilgrim-style, only with better food and good beer. Book early. **Tioga Pass closes** (209-372-0200; www.nps.gov/yose/ planyourvisit/conditions.htm).

December: **Yosemite Ski and Snowboard Area (aka Badger Pass) opens** (209-372-8433; www.travelyosemite .com). **Yosemite National Park Annual Christmas Bird Count. Bracebridge Dinner** (at the Majestic Yosemite (aka Ahwahnee) Hotel; 801-559-4884; www.travelyosemite.com). The ultimate Christmas pageant, since 1927. Lodging packages available. Reserve early. **Space-available reservations at Ostrander Ski Hut** (209-379-5161; www.yosemiteconservancy.org/ ostrander-ski-hut).

FURTHER READING

✳ Primary Histories and Narratives

Bade, William Frederic. *The Life and Letters of John Muir* (Boston: Houghton Mifflin, 1924).

Brewer, William Henry. *Up and Down California in 1860–1864: The Journal of William H. Brewer*. 4th ed. Edited by Francis P. Farquhar (Berkeley, CA.: University of California Press, 2003).

Bunnell, Lafayette H. *Discovery of the Yosemite (& the Indian War of 1851 Which Led to That Event)* (El Portal, CA: Yosemite Association, 1991).

Greeley, Horace. *An Overland Journey from New York to San Francisco in the Summer of 1859* (Lincoln, NE: University of Nebraska Press, 1999).

Grey, Zane. *Tales of Lonely Trails* (New York: Harper & Brothers, 1922.)

Grooks, George R., ed. *The Southwest Expedition of Jedediah S. Smith* (Glendale, OK: Arthur H. Clark, 1977).

Gunsky, Frederick, R., ed. *South of Yosemite: Selected Writings of John Muir* (Berkeley, CA: Wilderness Press, 1988).

King, Clarence. *Mountaineering in the High Sierra* (El Portal, CA: Yosemite Association, 1997).

LeConte, Joseph. *A Journal of Ramblings Through the High Sierras of California* (El Portal, CA: Yosemite Association, 1994).

Olmsted, Frederick Law. *Yosemite and the Mariposa Grove: A Preliminary Report, 1865* (El Portal, CA: Yosemite Association, 1995).

Roper, Steve, ed. *Ordeal by Piton: Writings from the Golden Age of Yosemite Climbing* (Palo Alto, CA: Stanford University Press, 2003).

Steele, Carol MacRobert. *Pictorial History of Mono Hot Springs, California* (Privately printed, 2003). Available at Mono Hot Springs General Store.

Thompson, Hunter S. *Hell's Angels: A Strange and Terrible Saga* (New York: Random House, 1966).

Wright, James W. A. *The Lost Cement Mine.* Edited by Genny Smith (Mammoth Lakes, CA: Genny Smith Books, 1984).

✳ Secondary Histories and General Interest

Beesley, David. *Crow's Range: An Environmental History of the Sierra Nevada* (Reno, NV: University of Nevada Press, 2004).

Brinkley, Douglas. *The Wilderness Warrior: Theodore Roosevelt and the Crusade for America* (New York: Harper Collins, 2010).

Caldwell, Gary. *Mammoth Gold* (Mammoth Lakes, CA: Genny Smith Books, 1990).

Carle, David. *Introduction to Water in California* (Berkeley, CA: University of California Press, 2004).

Chalfant, W. A. *Death Valley: The Facts* (Palo Alto, CA: Stanford University Press, 1930).

——. *Gold, Guns & Ghost Towns* (Palo Alto, CA: Stanford University Press, 1947).

——. *The Story of Inyo*. Revised ed. (Bishop, CA: Chalfant Press, 1980).

Clifford, Hal. *Downhill Slide: Why the Corporate Ski Industry Is Bad for Skiing, Ski Towns, and the Environment* (San Francisco: Sierra Club Books, 2003).

Despain, Joel. *Hidden Beneath the Mountains: Caves of Sequoia and Kings Canyon National Parks* (Dayton, OH: Cave Books, 2003).

Dilsaver, Lary M., and William C. Tweed. *Challenge of the Big Trees: A Resource History of Sequoia and Kings Canyon National Parks* (Three Rivers, CA: Sequoia Parks Conservancy, 1990).

Farquhar, Francis P. *History of the Sierra Nevada* (Berkeley, CA: University of California Press, 1965).

Forstenzer, Martin. *Mammoth: The Sierra Legend* (Boulder, CO: Mountain Sports Press, 2002).

Ghiglieri, Michael P., and Charles R. "Butch" Farabee Jr. *Off the Wall: Death in Yosemite* (Flagstaff, AZ: Puma Press, 2007).

Hart, John. *Storm Over Mono: The Mono Lake Battle and the California Water Future* (Berkeley, CA: University of California Press, 1996).

Hartesveldt, Richard J., H. Thomas Harvey, Howard S. Shellhammer, and Ronald E. Stecker. *The Giant Sequoia of the Sierra Nevada* (Washington, DC: U.S. Department of the Interior, National Park Service, 1975).

Hartesveldt, Richard J. *Yosemite Valley Place Names*. N.p.: (Yosemite Natural History Association, 1955).

Hundley, Norris Jr. *The Great Thirst: Californians and Water, A History* (Berkeley, CA: University of California Press, 2001).

Huth, Hans. "Yosemite: The Story of an Idea." *Sierra Club Bulletin,* 33 (March, 1948), 47–78.

Kroeber, A. L. *Handbook of the Indians of California*. Bulletin 78 of the Bureau of American Ethnology of the Smithsonian Institution, 1919.

Lingenfelter, Richard E. *Death Valley and the Amargosa: A Land of Illusion* (Berkeley, CA: University of California Press, 1988).

McPhee, John. *Annals of the Former World* (New York: Farrar, Straus & Giroux, 1981).

Morgan, Dale L. *Jedediah Smith and the Opening of the West* (Lincoln, NE: University of Nebraska Press, 1953).

O'Neill, Elizabeth Stone. *Meadow in the Sky: A History of Yosemite's Tuolumne Meadows Region* (Groveland, CA: Albicaulis Press, 1984).

Paden, Irene D., and Margaret E. Schlichtmann. *The Big Oak Flat Road* (San Francisco: Emil Schlichtmann, 1955).

Randl, Chad. *A-frame* (New York: Princeton Architectural Press, 2004).

Reisner, Marc. *Cadillac Desert: The American West and Its Disappearing Water.* Revised Edition (New York: Penguin, 1993).

Russell, Carl Parcher. *100 Years in Yosemite: The Story of a Great Park and Its Friends* (Berkeley, CA: University of California Press, 1947).

Smith, Genny, ed. *Sierra East: Edge of the Great Basin* (Berkeley, CA: University of California Press, 2000).

——. *Mammoth Lakes Sierra: A Handbook for Roadside and Trail* (Mammoth Lakes, CA: Genny Smith Books, 1993).

Snyder, Susan. *Past Tents: The Way We Camped* (Berkeley, CA: Heyday Books, 2006).

Snyder, Susan, ed. *Bear in Mind: The California Grizzly* (Berkeley, CA: Heyday Books, 2003).

Storer, Tracy I., and Lloyd P. Tevis Jr. *California Grizzly* (Berkeley, CA: University of California Press, 1955).

Trexler, Keith A. *The Tioga Road, A History: 1883–1961*. Revised ed. (N.p.: Yosemite Natural History Association, 1980).

Tweed, William C., Laura E. Souliere, and Henry G. Law. *Rustic Architecture: 1916-1942* (Washington, DC: National Park Service, 1977).

Worster, Donald. *A Passion for Nature: The Life of John Muir* (New York: Oxford University Press, USA, 2008).

✳ Literary

Austin, Mary. *Land of Little Rain* (Boston and New York: Houghton Mifflin, 1903).

Hicks, Jack, James D. Houston, Maxine Hong Kingston, and Al Young, eds. *The Literature of California* (Berkeley, CA: University of California Press, 2000).

Houston, Jeanne Wakatsuki and James D. Houston. *Farewell to Manzanar: A True Story of Japanese American Experience During and After the World War II Internment* (New York: Bantam Books, 1983).

Kerouac, Jack. *Dharma Bums* (New York: Harcourt Brace, 1958).

Twain, Mark. *Roughing It* (Berkeley, CA: University of California Press, 1995).

✳ Art and Photography

Adams, Ansel. *Yosemite and the High Sierra*. Edited by Andrea G. Stillman (New York: Little, Brown & Co., 1994).

Clevenger, Vern. *Sierra Sojourns*. Edited by Jane Freeburg (Bozeman, MT: Companion Press, 2008).

Clevenger, Vern, and Wynne Benti. *Close Ups of the High Sierra* (Bishop, CA: Spotted Dog Press, 1998).

Curtis, Edward S. *The North American Indian*. Vol. 14 (Norwood, MA: Plimpton Press, 1924). Digital version online at: curtis.library.northwestern.edu/curtis.

Denny, Glenn. *Yosemite in the Sixties* (N.p.: Patagonia and T. Adler Books, 2007).

Dittli, John, and Mark A. Schlenz. *Walk the Sky: Following the John Muir Trail* (Bozeman, MT: Companion Press, 2008).

Irwin, Sue. *California's Eastern Sierra: A Visitor's Guide* (Los Olivos, CA: Cachuma Press, 1992).

Morning, Robin. *Tracks of Passion* (Mammoth Lakes, CA: Mammoth Ski Museum, 2008). Muir, John, and Galen Rowell (photographer).

The Yosemite (El Portal, CA: The Yosemite Association, 2001).

Rowell, Galen. *High & Wild: Essays and Photographs on Wilderness Adventure* (Bishop, CA: Spotted Dog Press, 2002).

———. *Galen Rowell's Sierra Nevada* (San Francisco: Sierra Club Books, 2010).

Rose, Gene. *Magic Yosemite Winters: A Century of Winter Sports* (Truckee, CA: Coldstream Press, 1999).

Scott, Amy. *Yosemite: Art of an American Icon* (Berkeley, CA: University of California Press, 2006).

Weamer, Howard. *The Perfect Art: The Ostrander Hut and Ski Touring in Yosemite* (Marceline, MO: Walsworth Publishing Co., 1995).

✳ Vintage Guidebooks

Adams, Ansel E., and Virginia Adams. *Illustrated Guide to Yosemite* (San Francisco: H. S. Crocker, 1940).

Chase, J. Smeaton. *Yosemite Trails. Camp and Pack Train in the Yosemite Region of the Sierra Nevada* (Boston: Houghton Mifflin, 1911).

Hall, Ansel F. *Handbook of Yosemite National Park* (New York: G. P. Putnam's Sons, 1921).

———. *Guide to Sequoia & General Grant National Parks* (Berkeley, CA: National Parks Publishing House, 1930).

Hutchings, James Mason. *In the Heart of the Sierras: Yosemite, Big Trees, Etc.* (Oakland, CA: Pacific Press Publishing House, 1886).

Muir, John. *The Yosemite* (New York: The Century Co., 1912).

———. *Our National Parks* (Boston: Houghton, Mifflin, 1901).

Putman, Jeff, and Genny Smith. *Deepest Valley: Guide To Owens Valley, Its Roadsides and Mountain Trails* (Reno, NV: University of Nevada Press, 1969).

Whitney, Josiah D. *The Yosemite Book* (Oakland, CA: Octavo Editions, 2003).

Works Progress Administration, Federal Writers' Project. *California: A Guide to the Golden State* (New York: Hastings House, 1939).

✳ Contemporary Guidebooks

Digonnet, Michel. *Hiking Death Valley: A Guide to Its Natural Wonders and Mining Past* (Birmingham, AL: Wilderness Press, 2004).

Flint, Wendell. *To Find the Biggest Trees* (Three Rivers, CA: Sequoia Parks Conservancy, 2002).

Gudde, Erwin C. *California Place Names: The Origin and Etymology of Current Geographical Names.* 4th ed. Revised and enlarged by William Bright (Berkeley, CA: University of California Press, 1998). Also available in a pocket edition: *1500 California Place Names.*

Hill, Mary. *Geology of the Sierra Nevada* (Berkeley, CA: University of California Press, 2006).

Horowitz, Aaron. *CA 167, Mono Lake.*

Holland, Dave. *On Location in Lone Pine: A Pictorial Guide to One of Hollywood's Favorite Movie Locations for 85 Years!* (Santa Clarita, CA: The Holland House, 1990).

Kaiser, Harvey H. *An Architectural Guidebook to the National Parks (California, Oregon, Washington)* (Salt Lake City, UT: Gibbs-Smith, 2002).

Laws, John Muir. *The Laws Field Guide to the Sierra Nevada* (Berkeley, CA: Heyday Books, California Academy of Sciences, 2007). Covers more than 1,700 species in 368 pages and 2,710 beautiful watercolor illustrations.

———. *Sierra Birds: A Hiker's Guide* (Berkeley, CA: Heyday Books, California Academy of Sciences, 2004).

Medley, Stephen D. *The Complete Guidebook to Yosemite National Park.* 6th ed. (Berkeley, CA: Heyday Books/Yosemite Association, 2008).

Mingori, Dan, and Nate Greenberg. *Backcountry Skiing California's Eastern Sierra* (Silt, CO: Wolverine, 2009).

Roney, Bob. *The Road Guide to Yosemite* (El Portal, CA: Yosemite Conservancy, 2013). Information on points of interest throughout the park, keyed to roadside markers.

Roper, Steve. *The Climber's Guide to the High Sierra* (San Francisco: Sierra Club Books, 1995). Handy, sturdy, tote-book size.

Sharp, Robert P., and Allen F. Glazner. *Geology Underfoot in Death Valley and Owens Valley* (Missoula, MT: Mountain Press Publishing Co., 1997).

Stienstra, Tom. *California Camping: The Complete Guide to More Than 1,400 Tent and RV Campgrounds* (Moon Outdoors) (Berkeley, CA: Avalon Travel, 2009).

Stienstra, Tom, and Ann Marie Brown. *Yosemite and Mammoth Lakes Camping and Hiking* (Moon Spotlight) (Berkeley, CA: Avalon Travel, 2009).

———. *Sequoia & Kings Canyon Camping and Hiking* (Moon Spotlight) (Berkeley, CA: Avalon Travel, 2009).

———. *California Deserts Camping and Hiking* (Moon Spotlight) (Berkeley, CA: Avalon Travel, 2009).

Storer, Tracy I., Robert L. Usinger, and David Lukas. *Sierra Nevada Natural History.* Revised ed. (Berkeley, CA: University of California Press, 2004).

Sunderland, Bill. *Fly Fishing the Sierra Nevada. Revised and expanded edition with photography by Rick E. Martin* (Grass Valley, CA: Mosca Loca Books, 2008).

Swedo, Suzanne. *Hiking Yosemite National Park.* 2nd ed. (Guilford, CT: Falcon Publishing, 2005).

CONTRIBUTING PHOTOGRAPHERS

Peter Amend, www.amendphoto.com. Peter is a bike mechanic and photographer based in Visalia. His work has been featured in *Men's Journal* and various local publications.

Bill Becher, www.becher.com. Bill's work has appeared in *The New York Times*, *The Los Angeles Times*, *Outside*, *National Geographic Adventure*, and other publications.

Jim Bold. Jim is a physician's assistant at Mammoth Hospital and serves on the Mono County Sheriff's Search and Rescue Team.

Cat Connor, www.catseyephotography.biz. Cat is a long-time graphic artist who moved to the Eastern Sierra eight years ago. Her images have appeared in many local publications.

Burke Griggs. Burke uses medium- and large-format cameras, black and white film, and traditional processing and printing techniques. He made many of the photographs for this volume during an epic, weeklong, rental-car circumnavigation of the vast country described herein.

Aaron Horowitz. www.bluebirdimaging.com. Aaron studied commercial and industrial photography at the Brooks Institute of Photography in Santa Barbara. He lives in Mammoth Lakes.

Dan and Janine Patitucci, www.patitucciphoto.com. Dan and Janine split their time between the Italian Dolomites and California's Eastern Sierra. Their work has appeared in countless magazines and ad campaigns for the likes of *National Geographic*, The North Face, REI, Patagonia, Clif Bar, Gore-Tex, Smartwool, and Mountain Hardware.

Rondal Partridge, www.rondalpartridge.com. Son of renowned photographer Imogen Cunningham, Rondal once served as Dorothea Lange's apprentice, and in 1937-38 worked with Ansel Adams in Yosemite. He has been a professional photographer for seven decades. He lives in Berkeley.

Christian Pondella, www.christianpondella.com. Christian is a senior photographer for *Powder* magazine and head photographer for Red Bull USA. His images have appeared in *Outside*, *Men's Journal*, *Sports Illustrated*, *ESPN The Magazine*, *GQ*, and a variety of other publications worldwide. He is based in Mammoth Lakes.

Osceola Refetoff, www.ospix.com. Osceola's editorial photography has been featured in *Artillery*, *Hemispheres*, and *WhiteHot* magazines, among others; and his fine art photography is widely exhibited including at the San Diego Art Institute, the Palm Springs Art Museum, The Main Museum, Photo LA, and Porch Gallery - Ojai. *High & Dry*, his long-term collaboration with writer/historian Christopher Langley, is syndicated on KCET's Emmy-winning program *Artbound*.

Joel St. Marie, joelstmarie.wordpress.com. An accomplished portrait photographer in his own right, Joel has worked with such luminary landscape photographers as Jim Stimson, Londie Padelsky, Vern Clevenger, and the late Galen Rowell.

Laura Alice Watt, www.lauraalicewatt.com. Laura mostly shoots on film, using a Hasselblad, various Polaroid and toy/plastic cameras, her grandfather's Rolleiflex, and her great-grandfather's Brownie. She teaches environmental history and policy at Sonoma State University.

Vern Clevenger, www.vernclevenger.com. Vern is a pioneering rock climber who still hauls 4x5 cameras all over the High Sierra. His work is featured in *Sierra Sojourns* (Companion Press), *Close Ups of the High Sierra* (Spotted Dog), and in the Mammoth Gallery.

INDEX